Happy Landings!
Patti Bender

HAPPY
LANDINGS

HAPPY
LANDINGS

Emilie Loring's
Life, Writing, and Wisdom

Patti Bender

City Point Press

www.citypointpress.com

Hardcover ISBN 978-1-947951-62-4
eBook ISBN 978-1-947951-63-1

Cover and book design by Barbara Aronica-Buck

Manufactured in the United States of America

Dedicated with appreciation
to the sincere strivings
of individual lives.

"Different times, different brands of courage."
—*Emilie Loring*

CONTENTS

ACKNOWLEDGMENTS

First thanks go to Emilie Loring, whose books kept me company from girlhood through adulthood, and whose certainty matched my own, that the beautiful things in life are as real as the ugly things in life, that things have a marvelous, unbelievable way of working out, and that there is always love.

Every hard task needs its believers, seers, confidantes, and sages. I have had all of these in Emilie Loring's grandchildren.

Thanks to:

Eve Loring Tarmey, who started it all with her generous response to my call out of the blue. She and her husband, Bill, have become my dear friends and Blue Hill buddies.

Selden Loring, whose curiosity, interest, and contributions drove the project forward. In his home, I enjoyed the gracious hospitality of his grandparents and the kindness of a friend. I am the sorriest that he will not see the book.

Selden's wife, Tuulikki Loring, a consummate hostess and enthusiastic explorer, with whom I shared wonderful trips to the Fruitlands Museum, Marblehead, and Blue Hill. She has shared without barriers and treated me as family.

Linda Loring Loveland and her husband, Bob, kindred spirits in inquiry, whose fascination with the Alaska trip opened a new side of Emilie for me and who share the search for Hollis Loring's origins.

Victor Loring, who shared the oldest memories of his grandmama, the dear memories of a child, and got me started on his father Selden's service in World War I and the Reserve Mallet.

Sandra Loring Fischer (Bruce), whom I knew too little but whose memories of Emilie's last days stayed with me.

Valentine Loring Titus, who championed the cause, trusted and challenged me, brought me into the family circle with her husband, Warren, and did everything she could to bring this biography to completion, short of picking up my pen herself.

Thank you all. I loved your grandmother, and now, I love her family.

Thanks to my own family:

Pat Fleming, Scott Konzem, and Sally Konzem Burns, who have lived with this project for decades and accommodated its intrusion and my absences in body and attention. You, better than anyone, have seen the real cost of this quest and encouraged me anyway. That's love. Thank you.

My sister Judy Bender-Ream, who loaned me her copy of *How Can the Heart Forget* on the train when we were kids, shared my girlhood love of Emilie Loring books, and always cheers me on.

My mom, Marion Bender, an accomplishing dynamo herself, whose example inspires and who read every draft with genuine interest.

Thanks to:

Captain Robert K. Slaven, Jr. who deserves a chapter for all he did for me, beginning with the search for a rock. In sharing their knowledge and love of Stone House, sailing, and Blue Hill's history and people, Bob and his wife, Linda, became dear and treasured friends. I miss them.

John Tellier, to whom I trusted a first reading and who let me know how much I needed to improve. A true friend will do that for you.

Ralph Crandall, whose reading of a partial draft lifted the quality of the manuscript immeasurably and gave me hope this would all turn out well.

Ron Plantz, whose encouragement has been constant, from travel to drafts to microfilm, and on whom I could count to enthuse with me about even the small discoveries.

Wayne Soini, who went into the writing trenches with me, wresting better prose and a better story, who represented me to agents and biographers, did research for me, and who has been my BIO buddy—my connection to the larger enterprise of biography.

Kate Mather, who read the final draft with care, made perceptive suggestions, and encouraged me by her interest.

Eddie Bouwer, my close friend and unfailing, positive support, who, at the beginning, gave me a special bottle of Tokaji Aszu with which to toast the completed project.

Armond Fields, author of multiple biographies of nineteenth century theater people, who, on our first and only meeting, spent half a day enthusing with me about thinking processes and sharing his insights about researching and writing biographies. Everything he said proved true, and his mentorship lit my way.

Ellen Jenken, the cheery creator of an extraordinary Emilie Loring Garden, who lifted me with her enthusiasm, sunny nature, and generosity. How I wish we could have had tea in her garden and read this book together.

Janice Prior-Crofoot, whose generous hospitality I have enjoyed on many occasions, and who secured an invitation for me to attend a delightful, afternoon tea at Arcady in Blue Hill.

Henry Becton, who hiked all over Sculpin Point with me to find the rocks and locations in Emilie's photos.

Leventhal "Lev" Alcott, on whose splendid craft, *Gandalf*, often under the captainship of Bob Slaven, I experienced Blue Hill and Blue Hill Bay so differently than on land.

Trudy and Neil Prior and Dorothy and Jim Carey, who shared *Tyn Y Coed* and the Owen sisters' scrapbooks.

Joanne Myers, the former Director of Education at the Fruitlands Museum in Harvard, Massachusetts, who also loved Emilie Loring and gave me a copy of Clara Endicott Sears' book, *The Power Within*.

Thank you to all, mentioned and not, for contributions large and small. It's been a long journey, and it's taken the whole village to accomplish it.

Happy Landings!

INTRODUCTION

Books have histories. They spring from a place and a time and a pen that mark them as uniquely as fingerprints. In 1941, after thirty years of writing, Emilie Loring's fingerprints were all over the world.

"I don't like the word 'interview,' but you may ask me any questions that you like." As she received Boston columnist Olga Owens in her elegant, Beacon Hill residence, Emilie Loring exuded the glamour of her characters. Impeccably and fashionably dressed, short hair coiffed in curls close to her head, her deep-brown eyes sparkled with life. When she spoke, a charming smile revealed both dimpled cheeks and chin.[1] But something warned that Mrs. Loring's charm should not be misconstrued. Eager and vibrant, gracious manners always in evidence, this woman had something to say, and she would say it.

Not that she hadn't. With ten best sellers in as many years and twenty books currently in the bookstores, Boston's beloved and distinguished novelist had become the "Queen of Romance."[2] In the heart of the Depression, a Boston bookstore reported that one man purchased fifty-three copies of *Lighted Windows* to send to everyone on his Christmas List.[3] In Australia, lending library patrons waited in lines for the next Emilie Loring novel.[4]

And she didn't disappoint. No sooner were final galleys off to the publisher than she set pencil to paper for the next novel. Her latest, *Where Beauty Dwells*, had been on bookstore shelves for three months, and *Stars in Your Eyes* was scheduled for release in time for Christmas.

An Emilie Loring novel made one feel bigger—more adventurous, more charming, nobler, more tinglingly alive. Beautiful places and lively dialogue, stories so "rattling good" that one burned more than one's share of the midnight oil, unable to put them down. She wrote to entertain, and she succeeded, but when the cover was closed, there remained an inspiring sense of having traveled to the best parts of oneself, a certainty that "the beautiful things in life are as real as the ugly things in life," that adventure and romance and challenge pave the path to worthwhile and vibrant living. Her readers clamored for more.

Over tea on that June afternoon, Olga Owens suggested that Emilie stop writing novels for a year and instead, write her own story.[5] Publishing and theater people, a bear and a ghost, a long voyage, a tragic fall, Boston's social and political parties, a mansion on Cape Cod, and a stone cutter's cottage in Maine. No wonder she hadn't written until her middle fifties. After seventy-five years, the real Emilie Baker Loring story was even more colorful and captivating than her best-seller plots.

I was ten years old when I read my first Emilie Loring novel. I read every one, and then I read them over again, at least once each year. Emilie's sunshiny personality became mine, too, and through more than fifty readings, her books became so familiar that my sister could read a line, and I would tell her the next from memory. But I couldn't say much about their author.

When I learned that Emilie Loring belonged to the generation of my great-grandparents and did most of her writing in her sixties and seventies, I was surprised. I had imagined her young, like her characters. Then I learned that some of her books were not her books at all, and I was troubled. I had looked through Emilie's eyes for nearly forty years, but there was so much I didn't know. Who was she? What did she do in the years before she wrote? How did the false books come to be? How much of what I believed about her was real?

Intimacy with her books guided two decades of research. Boston University's archives classified sixty-five loose, manuscript pages in the Emilie Loring collection as "miscellaneous," but on first reading, I placed every one. As facts appeared in documents, interviews with her grandchildren, and visits to Boston and Maine, I realized that Emilie had written about many of them, and five thousand pages of original research fit together as though recalled from memory.

Each phase of Emilie Loring's life had its own cast of characters, its own priorities, its own victories, and she went by a different name in each of them—one life in five acts. Hers was a richly varied life, and she lived it with intention. "After all, living is the biggest thing any of us have to do. Why not treat it as an art rather than in hit-or-miss fashion?"

Emilie responded to Olga Owens' request with a fresh novel each of the next ten years. She left within them, as she had from the start, clues to piece together the romance and adventure of her extraordinary life. These were the fingerprints she left behind, and this is the story they told.

ACT ONE:
Bessie Baker

"I am neither a super-optimist nor a Pollyanna, but behind the thickest cloud, behind the darkest situation, somehow, I sense the sun ready to break through. Why not? It has always."

—Emilie Loring

CHAPTER 1

Lee & Shepard, Publishers

Boston, 1870–1872

Emilie sat on Mr. Shepard's desk at Lee & Shepard's publishing office, her hair in long, dark curls, "swinging her patent leather boots while they talked of books." The five-year-old was an outspoken little sprite, and her ready opinions on children's books brought amused chuckles. Mr. Lee or Mr. Shepard often took her to lunch on Saturdays, and sometimes, the partners suggested that her father take a manuscript home to see how she liked it.[1]

For nearly thirty years, her father was the sole supervisor of publishing at Lee & Shepard. George Melville Baker "read personally the manuscript under consideration for publication and superintended the making up of all the books issued by the firm."[2] After a book was accepted, he designed it, planned its illustrations, its decorations, and its binding.[3]

His skill in this area was considerable at a time when book covers and bindings were just gaining recognition as "objects of design." More than a century later, George M. Baker's *Ballads of Bravery* was chosen from a collection of 2,400 nineteenth-century volumes to illustrate the cover of *The Art of Publishers' Bookbindings, 1815-1915*.[4]

Lee & Shepard succeeded Phillips, Sampson & Company, an intellectual enterprise that helped to create the *Atlantic Monthly* and sold large sets of books for mass distribution. William Lee and Charles Shepard shrewdly continued their profitable editions for adults, but when George M. Baker was hired in the fall of 1862, he added a new specialty in children's books.[5]

"Verily, there is a new era in the country in the literature for children," wrote *Putnam's Magazine*. George chose action-packed adventures with

"I hate to discourage you, but I'm afraid its literary merit doesn't count with her. She likes the color, the drama of the story, the robe, the ring, and what she calls 'the fattest calf.'"
Gay Courage

George Melville Baker

simple style and natural speech that became the new standard. By 1870, Lee & Shepard received 1200 to 1500 manuscripts annually[6] and published more children's books than any other publisher in the country. *The American Literary Gazette* called the men of Lee & Shepard the "most known and highly esteemed members" of the book trade. Firms on Boston's Washington Street used to state their location relative to the Old South Church, but that changed to, "The Old South Church is directly opposite Lee & Shepard's Bookstore."[7]

When Emilie was three, her father was responsible for the first American edition of Lewis Carroll's *Alice's Adventures in Wonderland*.[8] It was a small volume, with a green, cloth cover, gilt edging, and a small, gilt sketch of Alice on the front cover. With thirty-two illustrations by John Tenniel, the popular illustrator from *Punch*, Lee & Shepard's edition became the standard against which all later editions were compared.[9]

Emilie loved *Alice*. She read it countless times, to herself and to others, until the words were as familiar to her as her own thoughts.

Through the Looking-glass and What Alice Saw There debuted in England in November of 1871 and appeared in Lee & Shepard's American edition the following February 1872. Many editions of Carroll's most famous works followed, but the original, Lee & Shepard editions, which sold for $1.50, were the first in America, and George Baker was responsible.

Emilie loved her father's office. One time, children from Bangor, Maine sent an "appreciation" in the form of a black bear cub to Oliver Optic, the firm's most popular author. "Bruin" was kept in a cage right in the basement of the Lee & Shepard offices where excited visitors could see him. The bear's stay became problematic, however, and the owners resolved to set him up in a "bear house" on the Boston Common. During the transfer, "Bruin insisted on brewing trouble, and, as a sad warning to all who do likewise, he had to bear the penalty alone." The bear broke from his chain and bit both the escort and the wagon driver, whereupon the escort was handed a hatchet. "He executed the savage mandate, and poor Bruin is no more in the flesh, though he is in the bone, at the hall of the Boston Society of Natural History."[11]

Thrilling as the bear had been, it paled in comparison to the books upstairs in Lee & Shepard's great salesroom. Emilie recalled, "We always had books and books ... My father might have refused us a toy we asked for, but he would never have thought of denying us a book we wanted."[12] And what a collection! The Crusoe Library contained six volumes: *Robinson Crusoe, Arabian Nights' Entertainments, The Prairie Crusoe, or Life in the Far West; The Arctic Crusoe, or The Sea of Ice; Willis the Pilot: A Sequel to*

With Betty's soft gold curls against her shoulder Nancy read aloud from the story of *Alice in Wonderland*. She had read it so many times that her tongue glibly followed the printed lines ...
Gay Courage

"My small income will provide bread, but I would like jam with it. I had jam yesterday, I may have jam tomorrow, but I want jam today."
"Know your Alice in Wonderland, don't you? I like that."
Uncharted Seas

"I promised that I would bring Gretchen a live Teddy-bear if I could find one."
A Certain Crossroad

Books, no end of them, covered two sides of the room from ceiling to floor.
Gay Courage

Swiss Family Robinson, and *The Young Crusoe*. The Frontier Series offered *Twelve Nights in the Hunters' Camp*, *A Thousand Miles' Walk Across South America*, *Planting the Wilderness*, *The Cabin on the Prairie*, and *The Young Pioneers of the Northwest*.

Large sections of Lee & Shepard's showroom were devoted to Oliver Optic, Lee & Shepard's flagship author. From the beginning of the firm to its end, his books were mainstays, as popular with boys as baseball.[13] Oliver Optic was actually William Taylor Adams (1822–1897), a schoolteacher from Dorchester, who took his pseudonym from a burlesque character named "Dr. Optic" and added the first name Oliver for the alliteration. He wrote the Boat Club series, the Riverdale Story Books, the Soldier Boy series, and so on, until he had written nearly one thousand stories, each packed with excitement and action for adventure-hungry boys.[14]

Optic's books sold briskly but were criticized for their exciting prose and lack of moral tone. Thomas Wentworth Higginson felt differently. When he reviewed children's books for *The North American Review* in January of 1866, he praised boys' books as "those precious books that throve under shelter of school desks . . . a type of literature in itself innocuous of moral guilt—unless enormous lying was held an offense—yet which had the flavor of sin because it was read surreptitiously." Higginson's own childhood, like Oliver Optic's, had been spiced with the "little dingy volumes" of *Baron Trenck* and *Rinaldo Rinaldini*, *The Three Spaniards*, and *The Devil on Two Sticks*, and it was clear that he had not forgotten the lure, for a boy, of adventures secretly read.[15]

Girls liked adventure, too, and another large section of the showroom displayed the books of Sophie May (Rebecca Sophia Clarke). Her Little Prudy books were some of the first in which characters spoke like children and acted like children, instead of little adults. *The Literary World* called them "Pickwick Papers for children,"[16] and, again, Higginson affirmed:

Genius comes in with Little Prudy. Compared with her, all other book-children are cold creations of literature only; she alone is

---

Sidenotes:

She smiled as she recognized an old, tried and true friend, *The Swiss Family Robinson*. She must have thrilled over it an hundred times.
Swift Water

"He is one of the Oliver Optic-Trowbridge heroes come to life—from newsboy to multi-millionaire type."
The Solitary Horseman

Christopher crushed back a laugh. That phrase, "Yonder orgy" might have been lifted bodily from one of the dime novels he had read surreptitiously when a boy.
Swift Water

the real thing. All the quaintness of childhood, its originality, its tenderness and its teasing,—its infinite, unconscious drollery, the serious earnestness of its fun, the fun of its seriousness, the natural religion of its plays, and the delicious oddity of its prayers—all these waited for dear Little Prudy to embody them.[17]

Who would not be attracted to the mischief and disobedience of the Parlin children? It was hard to suppress a smile at their childish earnestness, as when Prudy reported, "I begun to be dead."[18]

Despite healthy sales and critical success, Sophie May grew tired of her book series. She wrote to George Baker of "a delicious sense of relief that I have got that everlasting Parlin family tucked away . . . What more to do with them passes the power of my imagination."[19] But the Prudy books were nearly as successful as Oliver Optic's, and George Baker wanted her to write more.

By accident or design, Emilie and Sophie May became acquainted, and Emilie served as the inspiration for Fly Thistledown, the newest Parlin relative. The dedication to *Prudy Keeping House* (1870) was the first appearance of her name in print: "To my young friend, Bessie Baker," and her character was introduced as "one of the kind that's never safe, except in bed, with the door locked, and the key in your pocket." Fly gets into all sorts of mischief—although, of course, she does it virtuously. "I solomon promised I would't go ou'doors, athout somebody lets me," she says, just before she accepts the invitation of a street vendor to wander freely through the streets of Boston.

Two years later, Sophie May's preface for *The Fairy Book* described a young girl swollen with mosquito bites. "The very next person that ever dies, I wish they'd ask God to please stop sending these awful skeeters," she complains. Photographs of Emilie—her childish face grumpy in its frame of long, dark curls—served as a model for the book's illustrations, and the dedication read, "This book of fairy tales is dedicated to little Bessie."

"Hmp! Angel!" snorted Billy. "I'm bigger'n she is an' if she's an angel I guess I'm God."
Today is Yours

"Betty, come here." The child obeyed promptly but avoided her aunt's eyes. A sure sign of guilt with her. What had she been doing?
Gay Courage

"Phyll-us says she's 'scouraged 'bout me bein' good . . . Don't be 'scouraged like Phyl-us. Try harder, God. Try harder. Amen!"
Gay Courage

Little Bessie, aka Fly Thistledown

Why "Bessie"? She was christened Maria Emily, but her family and
friends called her, alternatively, Bess, Bessie, or Betty, and the names
stuck throughout her life. Emilie's grandmother, Rachel Elizabeth Boles,
was already the namesake of Emilie's sister, who was called "Lizzie," and
"Bessie" was another variation of her name. There was a popular song, a
play, and even an actress with the name "Betsy Baker," but perhaps Emilie's
nickname came from none of these. The little girl in her novel *Gay Courage*

(1928) explains, "Gran calls me Betty Blueskin, 'cause I al-us wear blue clothes, I guess."[20] She doesn't understand her grandmother's teasing reference to Daniel Defoe's character, an inveterate pickpocket who loves a notorious robber.[21]

Like the character Betty, Emilie absorbed the familiar elements of her life but could not fully appreciate the contexts from which they had been drawn. So much had happened before her birth. She had an older sister and a younger brother now, but there used to be two more siblings. Furthermore, her father's publishing reputation and local celebrity had not always existed but had been woven together from the threads of many efforts and events, their pattern guided by a family philosophy, years before her birth.

CHAPTER 2

Albert Baker, Printer

Portland, Maine; 1832–1842

"I can't see that the expression of a lover's eyes, or the caressing inflection of his voice, is an iota more casual than when I was young. The way of depicting it in print may have changed, but the way of a man with a maid hasn't."
There Is Always Love

Emilie's grandparents were married when Albert Baker was twenty-one, and his bride, Mary Ann Shaw Remick, was nineteen. The ceremony took place on Sunday evening, April eighth,[1] and on July second—a scant, two months and twenty-four days later—George Melville was born.[2] Their daughter Louisa was born three years later, but she died when she was only ten months old.[3]

Little is known about Albert's education. His father, John Baker III, was a sail maker, and Albert might have become one, too, but his father died before Albert reached the age of apprenticeship. Then, instead of joining his older brother in the mercantile business, Albert learned a different trade. When he took his family to live on South Street, and later Brown, the Portland directory listed him as "Albert Baker, Printer."[4]

A printer in those days was a highly skilled craftsman, both technician and artist. He designed the entire page, which might be a newspaper, folio, notice, card, or stationery, each with its own requirements. He selected styles and sizes of letters, placed each one (backwards so that it would read properly when applied to the paper), controlled spacing, and inserted engraved illustrations, some which he had made himself. He had to know inks and apply them properly to the flat bed metal press, which he had to adjust, operate, and repair as needed. He had to know the different qualities of paper, how they absorbed ink, and how fast they dried. When one side had been printed, the whole process was repeated for the opposite side before embossing, trimming, folding, and packaging the final product, as needed.[5]

Albert's family grew to six, but on his birthday, October 21, 1841, baby Julia came down with scarlet fever and died a month later.[6] The same strep infection lodged in two-year-old John's lungs, and two weeks after his sister, he died of pneumonia.[7] Three Baker children were now dead, buried alongside their grandfather in Portland's Eastern Cemetery.[8] Only George and Albert Jr. remained.

One day short of Albert Sr.'s birthday the following year, a fire started in George Clark's cabinet shop on Congress Street, just west of Brown where the Bakers lived. "Scarcely ever has there been a conflagration in the city more threatening or one attended with more disaster." A strong, northwest wind drove the fire down Congress, burning through a tavern, a stable, and a lumberyard before it reached the north corner of Brown Street. To the west, a mass of wooden homes on Free Street burned, igniting the west side of Brown, which was soon entirely engulfed by flames coming from both directions. Firemen backed out and left the east side to burn as well. Families saved some of their furniture, but their homes and the trees that once sheltered them were entirely lost.[9] It was too much. Albert and Mary Ann Baker packed what they could salvage and took ten-year-old George and five-year-old Albert Jr. to start afresh in Boston.

Boston, 1842–1849

Their move was a coming home of sorts. There had been Bakers in the Boston area since 1635, when English-born Richard Baker emigrated from Kent to settle in Dorchester. Albert's grandfather, John Baker I, was born and raised in Boston before he married Susanna Brackett and moved to the Bracketts' settlement in Portland's Back Cove around 1740. (Albert descended from his grandfather's second wife, Abigail.) John's brother James remained in Dorchester and founded Baker's Cocoa Company, which his grandson Walter now managed. Albert's other uncles, aunts, and cousins spread from Charlestown to Milton.[10]

Albert and his family arrived from Portland during the flood stage of foreign immigration. Hundreds landed daily from ships, and still more were brought in by rail. Newspapers fostered a sense of community, and

"I suspect I'm a dyed-in-the-wool New Englander at heart, my father's people were Massachusetts settlers back in colonial days."
As Long as I Live

Albert Baker, Printer.

all classes of society could read them now, since the new, cylinder press and wood-pulp paper reduced their cost to only one penny a copy.[11]

New papers sprang up to fill the demand, and Albert found himself in the right place at the right time. In Portland, he had printed the *Portland Transcript*, a small, literary newspaper "of uncommon merit."[12] Now, he hired on as a compositor for the most successful of the penny papers, the *Boston Daily Times*, at 3 State Street.[13]

Two years later, Albert Baker and six more practical printers started their own newspaper, the *Daily American Eagle*, advertised in a prospectus issued November 30, 1844, as the production of "Baker, French, Harmon & Co."[14] Its aims were political, to support the Native American Party, but as support for its causes died, circulation withered.

Albert Baker knew what to do. The *Portland Transcript* began as a small, local paper, but it had since become "a first class, literary weekly" with unrivaled circulation in Maine.[15] This was achieved by keeping it "full of variety on all subjects (excepting politics)."[16] Taking that lesson to heart, he and his partners started an evening newspaper that was independent in politics and more entertaining than it was provocative. The *Boston Herald* debuted on August 31, 1846, and both papers were produced from the same office on Devonshire Street and Dock Square.[17] The *American Eagle* soon closed down, and within three years, the *Boston Herald* was the most widely circulated newspaper "in Boston or elsewhere."[18]

In the spring of 1849, just when the newspaper was hitting its stride, Albert Jr. died suddenly of an "inflammation of the brain" (encephalitis).[19] He was buried near Friends' Ground in Boston, but his parents also placed a marker near his siblings' graves in Portland's Eastern Cemetery.[20]

Of the four Baker children born in Portland, only George remained. Born in Boston, his sisters, Mary Ellen Leavitt and Sarah Francis Shaw, had never known Julia and John, the Portland house that burned, or what it was like to arrive in Boston and begin again. George had felt these losses but undertook his career with a resilient optimism that would shape the next generation of Bakers.

"...unless our native Americans in whose veins should flow the instinct of patriotism jump into the ring soon, we shall have imported leaders, possibly alien leaders. Wouldn't that be an immeasurable disgrace?"
Here Comes the Sun!

"I'm an omnivorous newspaper reader. I read everything from ads to long reports on conferences."
It's a Great World!

CHAPTER 3

George Melville Baker: Purpose and Entertainment

Boston, 1848–1865

George Melville Baker graduated from the Otis School in Boston's North End in 1848. His was a classical education of reading, spelling, grammar, history, geography, arithmetic, and writing.[1] The grammar school was fully coeducational and rewarded its best scholars with "City Medals" for the top three girls and "Franklin Medals" for the top three boys, including George.[2]

Unlike his quiet father, George had a flair for the dramatic, and he quickly joined a group of amateur dramatists who gave performances in a hired room on Cornhill. Most of the boys were about George's age, sixteen, and at first, they performed only for close friends.[3] George wrote plays for the troupe, and his first was a comedy, *Wanted: A Male Cook*. The one-act farce had only four parts, all male, each with a different accent: Boston, Maine, Irish, and French.[4]

The group's original name was "M. Y. O. B." for "Mind Your Own Business," but when they began public performances, they changed their name to the "Aurora Dramatic Club."[5] The boys tried out stage names for themselves, too. Robert F. McClannin went by "C. F. Lowell" for "Chap from Lowell," and George appeared on playbills as "G. B. Melville," reversing his middle and last names.[6]

Amateur troupes came and went, but eleven of the Aurorans became professional actors, and several, including Robert F. McClannin, William J. LeMoyne, and Dan Setchell, became bona fide stage stars.[7] Mark Twain once wrote of Setchell, "As a comedian, this man is the best the coast has seen, and is above criticism."[8]

On Saturday night, May 8, 1852, the Aurora Dramatic Club had the distinction of being the final performers ever to play in Old Drury, a Charles Bullfinch theater on the corner of Federal and Franklin[9] that first opened in 1794. Their offerings that night were "Speed the Plough" and a two-act farce, "A Nabob for an Hour," but few came to see, and the doors closed quietly.[10]

George performed by night and clerked by day. He worked first for Charles Tappan and Benjamin Whittemore, publishers of educational books, church music, and biographies. Charles Tappan's older brother was Lewis Tappan, the abolitionist lawyer who formed the anti-slavery society in 1833 and earned fame for his role in the *Amistad* case.[11]

George was at the firm in 1852 when it published *The White Slave; or, Memoirs of a Fugitive*, an extension of Richard Hildreth's 1836 novel, *The Slave*. The original was the first novel written for the express purpose of denouncing slavery, and it unsettled many with complexly portrayed enslaved characters and wrenching scenes of enslaved life. Its illustrated sequel further incensed the reading public[12] which was, by then, brooding over *Uncle Tom's Cabin*.

It was also at Tappan & Whittemore that George met Matthew Mayhew. "Matt" was the son of Dr. Julius Stewart Mayhew of New Bedford, Massachusetts, one of a long line of physicians in the Mayhew family and another vocal opponent of slavery. George and Matt became fast friends.

George lived at home, where he now had five younger siblings. In addition to Mary Ellen and Sarah, Walter Henderson was born in 1851, and then came twins: Charles Tappan and Annie Cora.

On Sundays, George attended the Second Universalist Church on School Street, a church of reformers passionately committed to both abolition and temperance.[13] Its first pastor, the Reverend Hosea Ballou, set a Baker-like example of serious purpose paired with a ready sense of humor. An esteemed lady once asked him if he preached the New Testament as the Savior had preached it. "I try to," was the reply. "Do you preach, 'Woe unto you, Scribes, Pharisees, hypocrites'?"—"Ah, no!" said he. "Those

"Besides being a publisher, [Father] was a playwright for amateurs..."
With Banners

Jean resented [the minister's] tone, resented his direct gaze which stripped off her complacency . . .
Swift Water

"Your mother! The first time my eyes met hers I said to myself: 'As Long as I Live, I'll love you,' and I will." "As Long as I Live." Her father's impassioned declaration dropped into Joan's heart and glowed like an imprisoned star.
As Long as I Live

people do not attend my meeting."[14] After Ballou's death in 1852, Alonzo Ames "A. A." Miner took over the lead job and remained the Bakers' pastor for decades. Like Ballou, Miner was intelligent and willing to say what he thought, but he managed more directly. "He was candid and outspoken and had no sympathy with a skulking coward."[15]

George Baker had at least one purpose in addition to religion when he attended Sunday services. Within the congregation was a brown-eyed brunette with long curls, named Emily Frances Boles. Her father was Jerome Boles, a housewright who sold sashes and blinds at 34 Friend Street, and her grandfather, John Gaylord Boles, was both a distinguished carpenter and a representative to the Massachusetts legislature. As luck would have it, the pretty seventeen-year-old's house on Poplar[16] was only a short walk from the Baker home on Minot Street.

Like George, Emily Boles was much older than her next younger sibling. The Boles family had lost Jerome Jr. as an infant in 1836 and four-year-old Frederick Warren in 1845. Emily was the eldest of their remaining children and the only girl, followed by Frank Gaylord, who was seven, and Albert Goodwin, who was two. George courted Emily, and when Mrs. Boles gave birth to another son in September of 1854, he was given George's middle name: Edward Melville Boles.[17]

George left Tappan and Whittemore for a position of more responsibility with Benjamin B. Mussey, a fellow congregant at Second Church and the publisher of *The Universalist* magazine. Mussey published anti-slavery books and signed a bond, along with Wendell Phillips, Samuel Sewall and others, to secure the release of Antony Burns, the "fugitive slave."[18] Soon thereafter, Mussey retired, and George worked for his successors at 29 Cornhill, Sanborn, Carter & Bazin.[19]

The firm's presses, bindery, and stock occupied the upper floors of the Gerrish Market, which burned to the ground on April 12, 1856. Flames spread to nearby buildings, including Jerome Boles' blind and sash business on Friend Street. He lost everything. The building was insured for two thousand dollars, but an equal value in stock on hand was uninsured.[20]

Similarly, Sanborn, Carter & Bazin were insured for some, but not all, of their losses.[21] In one day, George and his future father-in-law went from stable work to financial uncertainty.

George and Emily were married by the Reverend A. A. Miner at the Second Church on November 3,1856 and lived with the Boles family at 47 Poplar.[22] The combined, Baker-and-Boles family now included the bridal couple, the bride's parents, and her three little brothers.

George's good friend Matthew Mayhew was also recently married, and the young men created their own firm, "Mayhew and Baker," purvey-ors of "books, stationery and fancy goods." Their office at 208 Washington Street stocked French and American paper, stationery, and cards. They engraved wedding invitations, printed visiting cards, and soon, published their own books.[23]

George knew from his father's newspaper experience that the public's interest changed rapidly, and entertaining reading sold better than quar-relsome politics. His own experience on stage showed that comedy filled the seats. The earnestness of current issues was not lost upon him, but there was more than one way to deliver a message, and his determination was sunnier than it was grim. Mayhew and Baker sought the front wave of entertainment in the publishing business, beginning with books for youth.

George was a father now, and the usual, moral tales, devoid of humor, would not do for little Rachel Elizabeth, who was born in March 1858. Instead, Mayhew & Baker published the *Fire-side Picture Alphabet of Humor and Droll Moral Tales, or Words & Their Meanings, Illustrated* (1858). The frontispiece announced, "Laugh and Learn," and the poetical preface encouraged,

> With learning may laughter be found;
> 'Tis good to be merry and wise;
> To gayly get over the ground,
> As higher and higher we rise.

Do not expect the children to think and act as you do; if they did they wouldn't be children. Heaven preserve them from having the ambitions and sense of respon-sibility we grown-ups have.
The Mother in the Home

They introduced the letter "D" with the word "Delightful," its definition "Pleasant, Charming," and its illustration a drawing of two boys swimming. The verse read:

These boys are bathing in the stream
When they should be at school;
The master's coming round to see
Who disregards his rule

It may have been the first time that delinquency had been linked with "delightful" in a children's book, and the young men didn't stop there.

They produced pasteboard models to build "Wheelbarrows, Sledges, Windmills, Railway Cars, Carriages, &c." They created board games, "Tournament" and "Knighthood," that were printed in colors, two games on one board, as well as "Gipsey [sic] Fortune Teller," "School in an Uproar," "Yankee Land," and "Young Peddlers, or Learning to Count."[24]

More significant to posterity, the partners published *The Base Ball Player's Pocket Companion* in 1859. It was the first book entirely devoted to baseball, and it described the rules of both the New York and Massachusetts versions of the games.[25]

The Bakers' second child was a son whom they named Matthew Mayhew Baker, in honor of George's partner. "Matt" returned the courtesy a few years later when he named his first child, a daughter, "Georgie."

The two friends worked in the publishing office by day and joined a broad assemblage of merchants and other businessmen at meetings of the Mercantile Library Association at night. The "MLA" gave monthly entertainments for their own enjoyment, "real, original and simon-pure," and some of its members became famous. Dan Setchell played there before joining the professional theater, and Henry Clay Barnabee (later of the Bostonians) recalled his years at the amateur MLA as "important" but "financially unproductive."[26]

George Melville Baker, Amateur Dramatist

Barnabee was short in stature, with a round head, a large, pointed nose, and eyes too close together. One newspaper commented, "To look at him is to laugh. Barnabee is a comedian because he can't help it."[27]

George Baker wrote a short sketch called "Too Late for the Train" that he and Barnabee performed across New England for several years, with Howard M. Dow at the piano. The pair's "mirth provoking" performances brought sellout crowds to at least a dozen cities in as many weeks, and ticket buyers were warned, "all who don't want a good laugh had better stay away."[28]

They got themselves onto the playbill at P. T. Barnum's American Museum in New York, but it was not a good time to fall in with Barnum. Bankrupt again after bragging publicly about his fraudulent dealings, he attempted a revival, but the press predicted, ". . . we do not think the proposed revival will meet with the same success that attended his previous efforts."[29]

When Baker and Barnabee performed on July 10, 1858, they shared the bill with an exhibit of "that most astonishing phenomenon of nature," the stickleback fish; Wyman the wizard, and a melodrama, *The Forest of Bondy*.[30] Barnum was not in the audience. Deep in debt after squandering one-half million dollars in earnings, he had sailed for Europe,[31] and the press scorned, "Why didn't he take the double-headed girl with him? He could see his way clear with her, surely."[32]

One of George Baker's next works became Barnabee's signature show, *A Patchwork of Song and Story*.[33] Among the skits was a one-person performance of an old classic, "The Cork Leg," about an artificial leg that refused to be controlled, even after the wearer's death. Barnabee portrayed the possessed leg with hilarious contortions that delighted his audiences. When he needed an encore, George wrote "The Patent Arm" to fit the bill.[34]

Inside this arm of rare design
Was hid a dollar steam engine,
Which speed and safety both combine
And got red hot on spirits of wine . . .
He turned the screw; with an awful whack
Round came the arm, on another tack,
And flew in his face, till alas! alack!
It laid him out flat on his back.[35]

"The Cork Leg" and "The Patent Arm" were popular, comedic hits, and they remained linked with Barnabee's name long after he became a fixture at the Boston Museum.[36]

Mayhew and Baker dissolved their partnership in 1860, and each opened a shop under his own name.[37] At 23 Cornhill, George sold gifts for children—"books, games, blocks, paper dolls, soldiers, &c."—and for the adults, "writing desks, cases and portfolios, chessmen, backgammon boards, dominoes, &c." Like his father, George did job printing, offering "a complete assortment of nice English, French, and American Stationery, which I can stamp without charge with initials, whole or part name."[38]

Meanwhile, George's father traded his printer's trays for the editor's desk at the *Dedham Gazette*. Albert Baker was "a quiet man, rarely speaking," but as his wife told her children, "Your father always wrote so beautifully."[39] His tenure at the *Gazette* was short, however, and when Albert returned to compositing duties at the *Boston Herald*, George wrote a comedy about his father's experience called "Freedom of the Press."[40]

As the action begins, a frustrated editor switches places with a farmer who thinks it will be "just as easy as digging taters" to be the editor of a newspaper. "Just think of the freedom of the press! You can kick, thump, pommel, and chaw up the whole human species; and who dares to kick, thump, or pommel back? Human nater! I wish I was an editor!"[41]

George's father-in-law, Jerome Boles, changed occupations, also. He sold his interest in the beleaguered sash and blind business to his stepbrother, A. W. Hastings, and opened a saloon and billiard parlor at 2 Bowdoin Square. This made Jerome Boles one of the nearly three hundred fifty dealers in "liquors, wines, &c." listed in the 1860 city directory. By comparison, in powerfully literate Boston, there were approximately half as many printers in business that same year.[42] And there was George, temperance advocate and father of two, living under the same roof with his father-in-law, a saloon owner.

On April 12, 1861, Confederate forces fired on Fort Sumter. On that day, wrote Thomas Wentworth Higginson, "the storm burst and the whole community awakened."[43] George's shop advertised: "In Union (Glue) there is strength. George M. Baker, 23 Cornhill, has just issued the UNION GLUE, which is 'bound to stick.'"[44] That wasn't certain, however, and the Baker and Boles families, like the entire population of the United States, waited to understand what civil war would mean for them.

Baker and Boles Families

Albert Baker &
Mary Ann Shaw Remick

    George Melville Baker - - - - - - - - -
    Louisa (d. 1836, 10 mos.)
    Albert Jr. (d. 1849, 12 years)
    John E. (d. 1841, 2 years)
    Julia R. (d. 1841, 10 mos.)
    Mary Ellen
    Sarah Frances
    Walter Henderson
    Charles Tappan (twin)
    Anna Cora (twin, d. 1861, 8 years)

George Melville Baker &
Emily Frances Boles

Rachel Elizabeth "Lizzie"
  Matthew Mayhew "Mattie"
    (d. 1862, 2 years)
  Mary Annie (d. 1861, 1 month)
Maria Emily "Bessie"
Robert Melville "Bobby"

Jerome Boles &
Rachel Elizabeth Hazelton

    Jerome Jr. (d. 1836, infant)
    Emily Frances Boles - - - - - - - - -
    Frederick Warren (d. 1845, 4 years)
    Frank Gaylord
    Albert Goodwin
    Edward Melville

It was a horrible year. In May, one of the twins, George's eight-year-old sister Annie, died of scarlet fever and congestion of the brain. Four months later, George and Emily had a baby girl named Mary Annie for George's mother and his little sister Annie. But the baby's birth was premature, and her heart was not strong enough; she died on November first. Four months later, two-year-old Matthew died of diarrhea and "disease of the brain." His father wrote:

Our darling boy, Mattie; March 28, 1862
A vacant place in our household,
One less in the home of our love,
But a gladsome song, from angel throng
As they bear our child above,
Where little feet
In the Golden Street
Shall patter a welcome, our coming to greet.[45]

George closed his stationery shop and went to work for his neighbor
Charles Shepard who had recently opened Lee & Shepard Publishers in
the Old Chelsea Dye House at 155 Washington Street. Had they only
known, it was a "'til death do us part" agreement, for the men remained in
business together for the rest of their lives.

George Baker's optimistic muse could not be quieted. He wrote plays
at night, and although set in contemporary wartime, their themes were
cheerful. In *Thirty Minutes for Refreshments*, a rock-ribbed bachelor falls in
love, and in *Sylvia's Soldier*, a resistant coquette learns that succumbing to
love has its rewards.[46]

He wrote the most patriotic of his wartime plays, *Stand by the Flag*,
for the Ballou Literary Association as a benefit for the Massachusetts
Volunteers, and George appeared himself in the costume of Uncle Sam.[47]
Two brothers, torn by sympathies for opposite sides, are urged by their
father to stand together behind the flag, and the northern brother expresses
"the freeman's sympathy for the slave; the desire to extend to every one
upon the face of the continent the blessings we enjoy."[48]

The men of Lee & Shepard posted photographs of the abolitionist
Charles Sumner on their office walls[49] and published the essays of their
good friend, "The Reverend Petroleum Vesuvius Nasby," who was really
Daniel R. Locke from Toledo, Ohio.[50] Nasby belonged to a growing collection of humorists whose satires unrelentingly scrutinized the events of
war, but his special skill was the same as George Baker's—that he made

his point with kindly humor. The practice was as American as Benjamin Franklin. On the left side of his statue on School Street, Franklin bore a philosophical expression; on the right, a comical one.

James Redpath, a newspaper writer and staunch abolitionist, observed that Nasby was a "pure humorist."

> A wit laughs at you and makes others laugh at you, if he directs his wit at you. He means to wound you, and wit is the feather in his arrow. A humorist, however, makes you laugh with him and others—he never wounds you. Wit is hailstones; humor, sunbeams.[51]

"It is a comedy, but even a comedy has to be built on life, hasn't it, and aren't there tragic undertones in life?"
With Banners

Charles Sumner said it was impossible to measure the value of Nasby's letters, as they so effectively motivated the sentiments of the public against slavery. He told the story of Abraham Lincoln keeping Nasby's writings in his desk to "refresh" himself, and more than once, when he called his cabinet together for serious discussion, Lincoln began the meeting by quoting from Nasby. The President was reported to have said, "For the genius to write these things I would gladly give up my office."[52]

Lincoln defended the practice of telling amusing stories to make a point with a statement that might just as easily have come from anyone on the Lee & Shepard staff.

> I am accused of telling a great many stories. They say that it lowers the dignity of the presidential office, but I have found that plain people, *plain people*, take them as you find them, are more easily influenced by a broad and humorous illustration than in any other way, and what the hypercritical few may think, I don't care.[53]

With the support of no less than the president and Charles Sumner, Nasby might well have been smugly content, but he made fun of that, too. Like Baker and Shepard, Nasby had not enlisted in the war. When a man was drafted, he could go to war, hire a substitute, or pay a fee to the government as a conscientious objector. After the war, Nasby said he was organizing a group to be called "Survivors of the Men who sent Substitutes to the Late War." "Our motto is and was, 'Money,' not 'Blood.' We fought nobly—by proxy."[54] He wasn't fooling. Redpath estimated Nasby's wealth at well over $200,000 and observed that, like the other humorists, he was "constantly making money in every way."[55]

"Ought I not to look up the record of my $1100 substitute?" the story went. "Perhaps he was wounded, and I am entitled to a pension." "You had better not hunt down his record too closely," remarked a friend; "it might turn out that he was a deserter, and that you'll have to be shot."[56]

Another of George Baker's friends was the humorist Josh Billings. His real name was Henry Wheeler Shaw, and he was the son of the Honorable Henry Shaw whom Albert Baker and the *American Eagle* had once supported for governor. As Billings, he hit upon the idea of making intentional spelling and grammatical errors to underscore his folksy wisdom. He became famous for one-liners such as, "Natur never makes enny blunders; when she makes a phool, she means it"[57] and "The rarest thing a man ever duz is the best he can."[58]

For their time, perhaps Abraham Lincoln met Billings' standard better than most. On yet another April day, the third of the month in 1865, word came that Union forces had taken Richmond.[59] On April ninth, the secretary of war ordered the firing of a 200-gun salute "at the headquarters of every army, post and arsenal in the United States, and at the Military Academy at West Point, on the day of the receipt of this order, in commemoration of the surrender of General R. E. Lee and the Army of Northern Virginia to Lieutenant-General Grant and the army under his command."[60]

Five days later, a single gun claimed the life of the sixteenth president.[61] The nation mourned, and President Johnson asked for a day of fasting to "sorrow for the sudden and violent end" of President Lincoln. Boston's observance included a procession through town and a memorial service in Music Hall at which Charles Sumner delivered the eulogy.[62]

There was an unfortunate connection between Jerome Boles and the assassination. In 1863, Boles had moved his saloon from Bowdoin Square to 2 ½ Chapman Place, across from the Parker House Hotel. He shared the building with Floyd & Edwards' basement bowling alley and shooting range. John Wilkes Booth was often observed there in the days leading up to the assassination. Four days before he shot the president, Booth "practiced with a pistol, firing with the weapon under his leg, behind his neck, and in other strange positions . . . From this city, he must have gone almost directly to Washington, to have arrived in time to complete his preparations for his fearful crime."[63]

The observation appeared in the newspapers right away, and it took little imagination to conjecture that Booth visited Jerome Boles' saloon, too. Was that the last straw? Perhaps. Boles closed the saloon and went fishing. "We understand that he secured fifty-four beauties one day this week. He will probably remain at the Beach as long as the fish are off there."[64]

For his friends at the Mercantile Library Association, George Baker penned a poem about the past year. The soldier, traveler and seaman return from their trials to friendship's comfort and "affection's haven," until "How wakes the soul!" they venture out once more, and the soldier "plants victory's banner on the topmost height."

Prosper our ship! and may the next crew strive
To beat the famous cruise of '65![65]

These were the events that Emilie did not experience, the history that shaped her father's character and reputation, her family's resilience and optimism. The course at Lee & Shepard was clear: to pursue a brand of literature with broad appeal and universal, wholesome values, reflective of the times but always encouraging. Their books, chosen and designed by George M. Baker, were adventurous, hopeful, earnest, and expansive in playfulness and good humor.

CHAPTER 4

Born to Stage and Print

Boston, 1866–1870

Soon after the war, the Bakers moved to 5 Chardon Street near Bowdoin Square. Their home was tucked behind the Baptist Church, across from the Revere House and around the corner from the Mayhew School on Hawkins Street,[1] which George had attended as a boy. There were no fewer than five livery stables on the block, and the air was filled with the smells and sounds of a central distribution point of the horse railroads—sweat, manure, the incessant clopping of hooves, snorts of horses, calls of hostlers, the creaking of carriages, and the bells of horse cars.

Within this home, at a noisy thoroughfare in the heart of Boston, Maria Emily Baker ("Emilie") was born. She arrived on September 5, 1866, to the attentions of her parents, her eight-year-old sister Rachel, her Boles grandparents, and her three Boles uncles—more like cousins or brothers, at eleven, fourteen and eighteen. Her brother, Robert Melville Baker, was born two years later.[2]

Emilie was born into an environment whose goal was to please both children and their book-buying parents. Hers was an unconventional world of enthusiasm and imagination, filled with the scenes of which fiction stories are made, all entirely real.

From earliest childhood, Emilie knew the players of the original "Bostonians" who performed on the Boston Museum stage. Henry Clay Barnabee was their leader, and the troupe included many of George Baker's longtime friends: fellow Auroran Robert F. McClannin, leading lady Annie Clarke, and Mrs. J. R. (Mary Ann) Vincent, an elderly woman of substance, with shrewd eyes and old-fashioned curls. She was one of the

A white milk-wagon passed. The clap-clap of the horses' hoofs made a staccato accompaniment to the ring of his quick footsteps which echoed through the early-morning quiet of the dozing city. *Across the Years*

"Can't be for my birthday, that isn't due until September." *As Long as I Live*

"I was reared under the iron rule of a boy cousin. He was a relentless task-master. I smolder with indignation, I flame with wrath when I think of the training he put me through." *A Certain Crossroad*

Rachel, Mrs. Baker, and Emilie

most popular actresses of the time, the "dear old lady!" and the "favorite of favorites."[3]

With Emilie's father, sister, and uncles, the performers put on plays in the Baker home for friends and charity. Barnabee performed "The Cork Leg" for the children, Mrs. Vincent brought them homemade bread,[4] and the recently widowed Robert McClannin brought his daughter, Beth, who was near Emilie in age and a favorite playmate.

A constant stream of books also flowed into the Baker home. George Baker's favorites were Dickens, Scott, Milton, Pope, and Byron, which he quoted at will, and which appeared, not surprisingly, in Lee & Shepard editions. There were also the many books published originally by the firm, the very best of children's and popular books, often accompanied by their accomplished and popular authors.

The public's undisputed, favorite author was Charles Dickens, so there was great anticipation in 1867 when he returned to Boston on a reading tour. In the twenty-five years since Dickens' last visit, he had become more than a household name. His books were read and re-read by nearly everyone, and the prospect of hearing Charles Dickens himself read their favorite passages was "an irresistible combination."[5] Lee & Shepard immediately published a bound edition of the readings, condensed by the author himself and managed, as were all of the Lee & Shepard books, by George Baker.

It happened, however, that good friends of George's irritated Dickens a great deal during "Dickens Days." The Boston Museum decided to capitalize on Dickens' presence in town by presenting his newly published play, *No Thoroughfare*. Dickens protested, but the Museum's manager, R. M. Field, went ahead, and adding insult to injury, kept Dickens from sharing in the profits of the night. George's old friends Robert F. McClannin, Annie Clarke, and Mrs. J. R. Vincent were all in the cast. Not surprisingly, Dickens declared their performance "wretched,"[6] although one might wonder how he knew.

When Emilie was three years old, a humorist in James Redpath's lyceum made his debut in Boston's Music Hall. Mark Twain wrote to his sister, "Tonight I appear for the first time before a Boston audience—4,000 critics."[7] Twain spent several days "smoking and talking shop" with George Baker's friends Nasby and Billings in Redpath's office on School Street. The three also went to George's office at Lee & Shepard, where they "wrought havoc with business order and discipline by their merry quips and jests."[8] George managed to get the three to sit still together for a deadpan photograph that he published with the caption, "The American Humorists."[9]

What a flowery comparison. It sounded like one of Sir Walter Scott's heroes. *The Solitary Horseman*

She voted for Charles Dickens as a satisfying hardy perennial and declared that by some trick of manner, or striking oddity of feature, he made even the most unimportant characters unforgettable. *As Long as I Live*

The American Humorists. Josh Billings, Mark Twain, and Petroleum V. Nasby. Photo by George M. Baker

Twain had yet to publish *Innocents Abroad*, his first real success, and Redpath thought the young performer deserved a friendly little initiation. He told Twain that he was sitting his brother in the front row of the Music Hall and that Twain should especially exert himself to make the brother laugh. Twain tried every one-liner and gag that he had, but to no avail. At the end of the performance, Redpath told the bewildered Twain, "Mr. Clemens, I entirely forgot to tell you that he is stone deaf!"[10]

Of the three humorists that George photographed that day, only Twain's popularity lasted. In their time, Twain was sometimes considered the most successful,[11] but Lincoln's view of Nasby refuted that view. Of Twain and Nasby, Twain gained the greater literary fame, but Nasby influenced the outcome of the Civil War. Perhaps Nasby and Billings were more distinctly tied to their times and their settings in ways that did not translate to later generations of readers. Or, more likely, their broken vocabulary and grammar simply lost their entertainment value with an increasingly sophisticated public.

The Boston Lyceum advertised "Wisdom, Wit, Humor, Music," and its 1869 "Course" underscored George M. Baker's popular connections: Wendell Phillips, Josiah Phillips Quincy, Shirley Shakers, Josh Billings, the poet John G. Saxe (author of "The Blind Men and the Elephant"), Mark Twain, Irish orator William Parsons, humorist A. Miner Griswold, reformer Mrs. Mary A. Livermore, Henry Clay Barnabee, composer and organist T. P. Ryder, and George M. Baker.[12] On closing night in December, George performed an entertainment called "Bon Bons" which also included the soon-to-be-famous soprano Julia Gaylord and Lee & Shepard's William Lee. The *Boston Journal* wrote that Baker's reputation guaranteed "cheerful and charming humor, free from every alloy of vulgarity, and vitalized by a high moral purpose."[13]

But the lecture circuit was only a sidelight among George's many ventures. In addition to book publishing and amateur drama, he and his good friend Oliver Optic tried out a new idea at Lee & Shepard—a youth's magazine for "all the girls and boys under twenty." With Oliver Optic as its editor, and George Baker managing nearly everything else, the first issue of *Our Boys and Girls* came out on January 5, 1867, devoted to light-hearted fun with consistent character and purpose. Optic promised to write for "no other juvenile publication" and to supply at least four complete, serial stories each year. For the initial subscription price of two dollars per year, the magazine delivered Optic's stories, plus two others in each issue, and provided games, poems, plays, and original dialogues for home performance.[14]

"You and I will cultivate and seed the soil in which her character takes root until it sends forth lusty plants of goodness, honor, sweetness, and gaiety."
Gay Courage

"Bessie" Baker and her mother, Emily F. Baker

Willy Small! What
did his presence
here mean?
*Here Comes
the Sun!*

The magazine grew as Emilie and her brother did. Regular contributors included Optic, Sophie May, boys' author Elijah Kellogg, translator Willard Small, George Baker, and many more Lee & Shepard authors who found their way to its pages and then into the Baker home.

Increasingly, however, the Bakers' physical and social setting on Chardon Street was less ideal than their intellectual one. The horse railroad had always brought locals and visitors to Bowdoin Square in an exciting, busy, connection point, a hub of commerce and travel with two hotels at its center. But the nature of their "connection" was ever more disturbing for a family with young children.

When the Bakers first arrived in Boston during the 1840s, more than one thousand shops sold liquor in the city.[15] Sailors came up from the wharves, and the Boston peninsula seemed overrun by inebriated and rowdy crowds. In the aftermath of the Civil War, saloons and shows concentrated especially around Bowdoin Square. The Revere House hotel, which formerly housed visiting dignitaries and hosted Daniel Webster's orations, now looked over Bowdoin Square's new velocipede (bicycle) rink that showcased girls riding the new contraptions, dressed in bloomers.[16]

One evening, Emilie's grandparents, Albert and Mary Ann Baker, were asleep upstairs when robbers entered their Poplar Street home and stole "fourteen silver teaspoons, two dessert spoons, and half a dozen forks."[17] This time, a robbery. What next? They moved to the Boston Highlands, an elegant neighborhood within reach of downtown.

George took his family, as well as Mrs. Boles and her sons, and moved all the way out to 207 West Springfield Street in the new Back Bay. The next year, according to the 1870 census, a Miss Frank Howard and some of her associates occupied their old address. Next to their census entry, as for several more along the street, was penciled the notation, "ill fame."[18]

There was yet one more chapter to be written in the family's temperance lessons. That summer, 1870, the following notice appeared in the *Lowell Daily Citizen and News*: "Vermont. Jerome Boles, a well-known citizen of Boston, temporarily stopping with a friend in Danby, while in a fit of insanity early Tuesday morning, July 19, mysteriously disappeared, and at last accounts no trace of his whereabouts could be found."[19]

Telegraph inquiries were sent to Boston, and notices were put in the papers. On Saturday, a search party found Boles' badly decomposed body halfway between Danby and the community of South Wallingford. The nature of his "fit of insanity" was identified as "mania a potu,"[20] defined at that time as "mania following prolonged alcoholic excess; more violent than delirium tremens."[21] Rumors about his disappearance and discovery

"I've always been a teetotaler for myself, you know that. I hate cheapness, and if you could see and more particularly hear yourself—you've made my face burn like fire—when you are in what you call an 'incandescent glow,' you'd know what I mean by cheap."
Give Me One Summer

circulated for weeks before an eyewitness settled the matter with a full narrative in the newspaper.

Jerome Boles arrived in Danby on July fourteenth to go trout fishing with his friend and fellow lumber dealer, William R. Carnes. For the next three days, though, he remained in his hotel room, complaining of fever and chills. The night of the seventeenth, he and Mr. Carnes visited friends, and one of them observed "that he was a man of culture and ability and appeared 'all right.'"

On the morning of the eighteenth, Mr. Boles dressed, walked into a complete stranger's home, and asked for a gin cocktail. Receiving none, he asked for directions to Boston and headed out, walking, along the railroad track. Observers said later that they assumed they would hear from him when he reached Boston, one hundred sixty miles away.

Instead, a search dog found his body on a rock under the shade of a tree. A local man built a large, pine box, "for Mr. Boles was a large man and the body was very much swelled," and buried him near the railroad, "that the earth might extract the scent from the body." A second box was made to hold the first and the remains were shipped to Boston. A family member met the train at Rutland and escorted Mr. Boles' remains the rest of the way.[22]

Thus, one of the first family gatherings in the new house on West Springfield Street was Jerome Boles' funeral at "4½ o'clock p.m." on Thursday, July 28, 1870. Emilie was not quite four, but her uncles Frank, Albert, and Edward were young men when their father died—twenty-three, eighteen, and sixteen. It may have been to them that George had written the verse, "And now, young men, an old man's prayer: Leave the bright wine in your glasses there."[23]

In time, churches fled to the Back Bay and South End as their congregations had done. The Second Universalist Church, with the Reverend A. A. Miner, built a new sanctuary on Columbus Avenue and Clarendon, and the familiar, old chapel and Sunday school on School Street were closed. George was ten when he first stepped into the old building and heard the

Margin notes:

"Once upon a time, generations ago, a black sheep in Mother's family drank himself to poverty and death. She was brought up on the 'lips that touch liquor shall never touch mine,' code."
With Banners

Back to the girl's mind stole her childhood idea of the Father, of a benign, flowing-bearded giant sitting on a gold throne.
A Certain Crossroad

sermons of Reverend Hosea Ballou. His children, including Emilie, had known no other. The poem he wrote to mark the occasion, however, was celebratory;[24] endings brought beginnings, and their future was in the Back Bay.

CHAPTER 5

Resilience and Optimism

Back Bay, 1872–1873

Emilie was six, and the holiday season was approaching, when fire swept through Boston on November ninth and tenth, 1872. The Bakers' house on West Springfield Street was far from danger, but the fire burned right through Newspaper Row where Emilie's grandfather worked, and forty-eight hours of conflagration left a gaping, black hole in what used to be the busiest part of the city.

> Sixty acres of the finest warehouses in the world were swept away in a few hours by the hungry flames, and this portion of our city is now a blackened waste of dreary ruins. Hundreds of merchants and others have been suddenly reduced from affluence to penury, and hundreds more have been crippled in their resources.[1]

At first, there was relief at Lee & Shepard. Although an explosion across the street shattered its windows, the building was spared, and valuable stock was removed to safety. But then, their warehouse on Milk Street was totally destroyed, and with it, their entire stock of books ready for sale. Three of the printing houses that did Lee & Shepard's production work also burned, destroying large stocks of paper and melting the metal plates of many of Oliver Optic's books and almost all forty sets of Sophie May's books into unrecognizable globs. Ten days later, a new fire at Rand & Avery burned additional paper and plates, although the December issue of *Our Boys and Girls*, next door in Abbott's bindery, was spared.

A quarter million dollars' worth of property was lost to the company, and only half was covered by insurance. The remaining $125,000 would have to be made up, somehow. The prospect was daunting. If the twenty thousand subscribers of *Our Boys and Girls* would promptly pay their new year's $2.50 subscription fee, there would be $50,000 on hand to address the firm's immediate expenses, and the call went out in the January magazine. George Baker wrote a poem for that issue, "Ashes of Roses," which was illustrated by the magazine's dedicated artist, Miss. L. B. Humphreys.[2] The poem related real incidents and the palpable grief of those days of destruction:

> . . . Ashes of Roses! Beauty lies crushed;
> Into our garden the whirlwind has rushed,
> Blasting the garners of riches and pride,
> Breaking the strength that misfortune defied,
> Rending warm life from the hopeful and brave,
> Shrouding our joys with the gloom of the grave.

But George ended with typical, Baker optimism:

> . . . To-morrow may bring hope's cheery beam,
> And out of the darkness warm light stream;
> For all is not lost while honor survives,
> And success oft journeys with him who strives.
> To-morrow beauty from ashes shall spring,
> And labor's hammer right merrily ring,
> And the fiery whirlwind, fierce and vast,
> Hurried away in the mouldering past.[3]

George was ten when his home in Portland was destroyed by fire. Now, at age forty, he had lost four siblings, two of his own children, and much of what he had worked to create at Lee & Shepard. But he had seen other ventures fail and witnessed four years when the entire country was convulsed with loss. Each time, the fallen had picked themselves up and forged on anew. It wasn't blind hope that gave George his conviction that

She would try to remember the next time she was worried, that there was a gate in every wall, that nothing hurts forever, that problems have a marvelous, unbelievable way of straightening out. *Lighted Windows*

"What quality is it in some persons which keeps them hanging on in a desperate situation until somehow, in some miraculous way, they get out of it? What is that something which won't let them give up? That nine times out of ten pulls them through?" *There Is Always Love*

better days were ahead. It was his lived experience as well as his character and commitment. Better days were ahead; he would see to it.

Lee & Shepard's new, six-story, granite building stood at the corner of Franklin and Hawley. The shop and offices occupied the first floor, and the storage basement was so large that it stretched underneath the sidewalks on both sides of the building.[4]

It was a pretty building inside. Plate glass windows lit the first-floor offices with sunshine, and enormous stacks of books along the left wall were reached by dual, curving stairways leading to lofts above. A low railing on the right separated the subscription and magazine business from the sales floor, and there was even a satellite office provided for Harper and Brothers, who sold their *Bazar* (the second 'a' was added later), *Weekly*, and *Magazine* there.[5]

Mr. Lee had his own, immaculate office in the back, and the "auburn bearded" Mr. Shepard shared his office with Oliver Optic. A wooden slide in front of Optic's desk could be pulled up to allow conversation with Emilie's father. Otherwise, George Baker sat apart and observed the ground floor offices through a wire screen "to protect visitors from the dazzling brilliancy of his deep dark, eye." So intently was his genius admired that Optic cautioned their magazine readers, "Hush! Don't call him a man, or otherwise speak irreverently of him."[6]

Oliver Optic and George Baker were natural friends. Prolific, creative, youthful in spirit, and adventurous in the extreme, their mutual enjoyment of each other's company was evident. Adams wrote of Baker, "He is as good-natured as he is talented"[7] and claimed that George did "more for our readers every month than they can ever know."[8]

In the fall of 1872, the men took a tour to Camden, Maine, together with their families. They stayed at the Bay View Hotel, took rides in the countryside, fished, and sang songs "till the woods and the rocks [rang] around us." In the evenings, they danced to piano music and played games. "But perhaps the most enjoyable feature of our impromptu evening entertainment was the recitations of Mr. Baker, who is even greater in rendering a composition with his voice than with his pen. The ladies were delighted, and always begged for more."[9]

Circulation of *Our Boys and Girls* steadily increased, and Lee & Shepard declared it "the most popular household Monthly in the country."[10] The publishers invited comparison "not only with the juvenile, but with the literary and family magazines of the country."[11] Their pride was well earned. Optic and Baker set out to include the best writing and illustrations that they could find. Always, these included works by Lee & Shepard's best-selling authors, and sometimes, they were accompanied by timely articles from public figures that encouraged children to be brave, speak honestly, and optimistically address the problems of the day.

The Honorable Horace Maynard of Tennessee wrote "The Immigrant and the Negro," which likened the withholding of the vote from Black men to the arguments of the Native American Party to limit the vote of immigrants in the last generation.

> Let not our faith in men desert us in this our time. We are told that these poor, ignorant black men won't vote right; that they will cast the wrong ticket. That's very likely. I should be surprised if they did not. Were they not to do so, they would put you and me to the blush . . . Do not let us judge them too harshly. Let us give them time to try it over again, like ourselves, and see if they will not do it better. But we have in their case some little assurance that we have not always had in the case of our white friends.[12]

The Honorable Charles Sumner contributed an essay on "Peace":

> The true state of nature is not war, but peace. Not only every war, but every recognition of war as the mode of determining international differences, is evidence that we are yet barbarians; and so also is every ambition for empire founded on force, and not on the consent of the people.[13]

"As a prescription for fair living nothing has as yet been suggested better than the Golden Rule offered by a Certain Man almost two thousand years ago."
It's a Great World!

"I honestly believe that as a means of settling international difficulties war is on the way out and that it becomes more and more the duty of the United States to preserve peace..."
Across the Years

Horace Greeley contributed to the magazine during his 1872 campaign for president. He wrote in "Labor," "I hold that no man ever really loved work and was content to live by it, who was not essentially honest and upright." It was one of the last things he published. Caricatured mercilessly in the press, exhausted by his loss to Grant in the election, and distraught by the sudden death of his wife, he went insane and died only one month later.[14]

Despite the occasional, instructive article, however, Baker and Optic assured that *Our Boys and Girls* remained dedicated, wholeheartedly, to children's amusement. The men claimed, "We are not so old, after all! We feel boyish, and always expect to."[15] They kept their readers on "a tiptoe of expectation"[16] with their busy pens, answering critics with confidence.

> The idea is, that the boy or girl who has studied six or eight hours in the high or grammar school, shall amuse himself by reading an interesting work on the spectroscope, or an essay on light and heat. Recreation is as necessary for the mind as for the body; and the story is the amusement of the former, as rowing, sailing, base ball [sic], walking, or reclining are of the latter.[17]

When seeking light reading, Optic advised,

> Do not look for science, for history, for biography, as a general rule; do not seek to cover up a pill of knowledge with a sugar-coating of entertainment; but let the child really enjoy himself, without even a dim suspicion of solid information concealed.[18]

Christmas Eve in the Baker home was as happily indulgent as their reading lives. Mrs. Baker read the nativity story to Emilie and Robert and then sent them upstairs. From their cozy beds, they saw the white snow drifting down outside their windows. Emilie recalled:

"I haven't forgotten the stunts Mac Donovan and I used to get away with. I must have been a young savage." "A young pirate. Great Scott, how you as Captain Kidd, Donovan as your understudy, and your buccaneers used to swarm up and down the river on rafts! I can hear you now storming Nora's kitchen and shouting; "S'death woman! Hand over the cookies or you'll walk the plank.'"
Gay Courage

... I remembered how later I was awakened by clatter and a bump, bump, bump on the stairs, and how I tiptoed to the hall and heard a voice reproach, "George, you've dropped the sled!" "Great Scott, don't I know it, Kitty?" A ripple of laughter followed the gruff whisper, mother had a lovely laugh. Father's voice again, "Sssh! You'll wake the children." And I thought of the following dawn when my brother and I, in slippers and nighties, stole down the stairs, and of my shivery excitement as I cautiously opened the living room door and sniffed the spicy scent of balsam, the smokey smell of cannel coal smoldering among its bright red embers in the open grate, and saw the grotesquely bulging stockings hanging from a mantel festooned with strings of pop-corn and cranberries and the odd-shaped packages on the floor in the weird, ruddy firelight.[19]

George Baker wrote a Christmas play each year for *Our Boys and Girls* which Emilie and her siblings performed at home on Christmas Day. One year, it was an adaptation of Dickens' *A Christmas Carol*. Another year, it was an original play called *Santa Claus Frolics*, in which the children try to wait up to catch Santa in the act of delivering presents but fall asleep after all, and their presents are delivered in secret. Yet another year, it was the story of *The Merry Christmas of the Old Woman Who Lived in a Shoe*.

Mrs. Baker bore cheerfully the emptying of her house to create an eighteen-by-fifteen-foot stage or to build a ten-foot-long wooden shoe. When preparations were completed, performances at the Baker home often ran for seven nights. The scenery was painted on canvas, and a row of candles served as footlights. After the performance, there were congratulations for the performers, followed by chicken salad, "feather light Parker House rolls," coffee, and "huge quantities of vanilla ice cream" for the children. At evening's end, the guests called "Good night! Happy New Year!" over the sound of sleigh bells, and the children were sent upstairs.[20]

"Christmas, you have a pretty laugh, Kit, it's like music."
Beyond the Sound of Guns

"Poor mother. She was a heroine; she would see her treasures trucked off to set a stage without one protest. Now that I have a house of my own, I know how it must have hurt."
With Banners

"Those two weren't just lovers, they were companions, friends, wonderful friends. "
As Long as I Live

"Her mother's dark hair was dressed to show the lovely shape of her head. The brilliancy of her brown eyes and the satin texture of her magnolia tinted skin were accentuated by a green frock . . . she was still vividly beautiful.
As Long as I Live

"It's late. Scamper to bed, youngsters," father said. And I remember that as I reached the top of the stairs, I turned and saw my father and mother looking up. She was wearing a dark green silk dress, a coral brooch fastened her round lace collar, and coral dangled from her ears. One of us had stuck a sprig of holly from the Christmas pudding in her brown hair. Father's arm was around her waist, her head against his shoulder. I remember wondering why suddenly my eyes pricked as if filled with sand and my throat was so tight I couldn't swallow, and I remember how those queer feelings melted into warmth and glow and how I felt as if tender, protecting arms had closed around me as mother called softly, "I'll be up to tuck you in, dear." How secure and safe I felt, and how sorry for the children who didn't act in a play on Christmas.[21]

Emily Frances Baker

Boston, 1873–1878

In those years after the fire, the publishers worked diligently to repair their finances, a task made more difficult by the financial "Panic of 1873" that actually lasted until 1879. The essence of Lee & Shepard was to publish for the masses, to reach the widest public possible with the best of written entertainments and ideas. If they were to survive financial calamity, it would be a large public that would assure it.

Toward that end, George redoubled his personal efforts as both editor and author. His collections of plays, *The Social Stage*, *The Mimic Stage*, and *Amateur Dramas* were already popular. In 1873, he brought out two more collections, *The Drawing Room Stage* and *The Temperance Drama*. *The Drawing Room Stage* contained George's fiftieth published drama, and he took a moment in the preface to speak to the public:

> It would be a poor satisfaction to the author for his efforts, should not a few grains of truth and thought be found in his acres of caricature and burlesque. . . . For the many favorable notices by the press of his previous works, the author returns thanks; to his unfavorable critics, he can only say, that as dramatic composition with him is but a pastime, and not an occupation, perfection should not be expected.[22]

His statement was inspired by modesty more than fact, or perhaps he was not yet aware of the position he was earning as the "Shakespeare of the vestry" in amateur drama.[23]

It is difficult to find any adverse criticisms of these collections. They are always called well-written, well-constructed, natural, simple, talented, enjoyable, successful. . . . As one person remarked: "It is rather appalling to think what he might do should he make writing his business!"[24]

She couldn't remember a time during the last few years, when Monday morning hadn't found her mother figuring bills and her father shaking his white head over them.
As Long as I Live

George M. Baker. "His eyes were darkly luminous, the eyes of a dreamer; his white hair curled in soft rings over his head . . ." The Trail of Conflict

As he worked to right the firm's financial ship, Emilie's father worked nearly as hard for charities. On Wednesday evening, February 25, 1874, carpets in the parlor of Mrs. Rufus Norris' home at 40 Concord Square were rolled back for a performance to benefit the North End Mission Fair, which was raising money to care for "fallen women and neglected children." The audience sat in chairs before a makeshift stage. A row of gas lights under shades of green glass served as footlights, and programs were printed by friends T. R. Marvin & Son.

The play was George Baker's *Among the Breakers*, on its way to becoming the best-selling amateur drama of all time, topping *Uncle Tom's Cabin* with more than a million copies sold by 1935.[25] It was a tale of "revenge, remorse, repentance, and forgiveness," and the cast that night was a

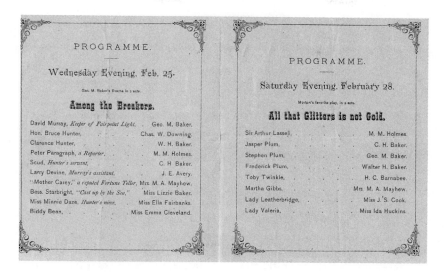

Amateur Theatricals, February 1874

veritable Who's Who of Baker family and friends. George played the part of the lighthouse keeper. His brother Walter was Clarence; Rachel "Lizzie" Baker, a month from her sixteenth birthday, played the part of young Bess Starbright; George's niece Miss Emma Cleveland played the role of Biddy Bean, and Julia Mayhew (Matthew's second wife) was a fortuneteller. The remaining parts went to friends and associates from church, the Mercantile Library Association, and the Masonic Lodge.[26]

Amateur theatricals were staged on meager budgets. A canvas backdrop might be painted, and props were fashioned from readily available household items. A table, chairs, stool and bench were all that graced the "stage" as the play began at Mrs. Norris', and a barrel was added for the second act.[27]

Costumes were also simple, devised from collections of pieces that could be adapted to many occasions, including wigs and artificial beards. George's part as lighthouse keeper David Murray required a "full black beard, iron-gray wig, dark pants, red or blue sailor's shirt, with black necktie, pea-jacket, and tarpaulin hat." Rachel's Bess Starbright wore a "short red dress, muslin waist, neat polka jacket" and a "jaunty sailor hat."[28]

To the playwrights and players, past and present, of my family. *With Banners*, Dedication

"I told her that I would loan her great-great grandmother Hilliard's gown which she wore to the reception given to Lafayette when he returned here after the revolution. I wore it once and had a white wig made to go with it . . . Everything is there except the slippers. You'll have to wear your own. Feet were smaller in great-great grand-mother's day."
Gay Courage

Special effects required ingenuity. Off-stage assistants made thunder by shaking a large sheet of iron by one corner. They used pea shooters to blow resin through candleflames to mimic flashes of lightning. Dried peas rattled from end to end in a box fitted with wooden pegs and occasional pieces of tin to make the sound of rain.[29]

Expectations for amateur dramas were distinct. When friends gathered for their relatives and neighbors to entertain them on stage, they craved surprising plot lines, meaty parts that required actors to declaim dramatically, swoon pathetically, and thieve with dastardly cunning. The action had to be wholesome enough for a family audience and to appease players who did not want to hug their older sisters or the neighborhood shopkeeper on stage. But after that, wild improbability was far more entertaining than subtlety, and the more lurid, the better!

Among the Breakers was the quintessential, improbable story, with a kidnapping, no fewer than five false identities, a fortune-teller, a stabbing, and a love story. Disinherited by his wealthy father, Paul Hunter kidnapped his usurper's daughter, threw her into the sea to drown, and created a new life for himself as lighthouse keeper David Murray. As the play opens, the usurper Bruce Hunter (really Bruce Carter) seeks shelter at the lighthouse in a storm (shaking iron, falling peas, flashing explosions!), bringing his son Clarence Hunter with him (really the lighthouse keeper's son but brought up by Hunter/Carter as his own). Clarence instantly falls in love with Bess Starbright, the beautiful orphan girl who pulled them from the sea. She is really the missing daughter of Bruce Carter, saved from drowning by the lighthouse keeper's wife, who disguised herself as fortuneteller Mother Carey and watched over her husband and Bess during the intervening years. The lighthouse keeper doesn't know that the girl he has watched grow up is the same that he tried to drown, but he does recognize his old foe Bruce and decides to stab him in his sleep, mistakenly making the attempt on his own son Clarence instead. The true identities are revealed with Mother Carey's assistance, and Paul Hunter's desire for revenge melts when he realizes that he has a chance at a new life with both his wife and his son—who will now inherit from Bruce the wealth which Paul was denied. Bruce (Carter) Hunter forgives Paul for his treachery when he learns that his daughter lives in the person of Bess Starbright, and the reconciliation of all is assured when Clarence proposes to Bess and is accepted.

With her curly, dark hair and black eyes, Rachel's portrayal of Bess was vibrant, lively, and confident. Older than Emilie and Robert by nearly a decade, Rachel performed in plays at home, at church, and with a small group composed of her Boles uncles and other youngsters. By age eighteen, when she stepped alone onto Union Hall's stage on Boylston Street for her first solo, professional reading, she was a veteran performer, only "slightly nervous" as she read Tennyson's "Dora" in a voice that rang true—"a remarkably clear, sweet-toned voice."[30]

The amateur stage served as a bridge to the professional stage. Far more amateur plays were performed in a year, and they whetted the public's interest for the professional version. Professional players fed the transition by appearing in private homes, lending distinction to the evening and serving as their own, best advertisements.

George acknowledged the fraternity among stage and amateur performers in his dedication to *The Social Stage* (1871): "To an old friend and fellow traveler, Henry C. Barnabee, Esq., never 'Too Late for the Train' when his valuable assistance is needed in a good cause, this book is fraternally inscribed." True to form, three nights later, the stage was set again in Mrs. Norris' parlor, this time featuring Henry Clay Barnabee's first stage success, *All That Glitters Is Not Gold*, with Barney himself in his stage role of Toby Twinkle.

Two new faces joined the cast that night—Miss Emma Cleveland and Miss Ida Huckins, whose father ran the dry goods store where Emilie's uncle Edward Boles worked. Within the year, Walter Baker married Emma Cleveland, and two years later, Edward Boles married Ida Huckins—proof, were it needed, that all romance was not on the stage. Nor were all of the plot twists. Emma Cleveland was the daughter of Henry Jones Cleveland,

[Her sister] waited for the greeting of applause to quiet before, without a trace of nervousness, she spoke her first line.
With Banners

Joan was thinking how really lovely her sister was, with her dark hair, her brilliant eyes that had just enough of an Oriental slant to make them fascinating, her perfect nose, her red lips curved like a cupid's bow.
As Long as I Live

"You know what dramatics do to people. What sudden friendships, what swift intimacies develop between men and girls, which, under ordinary circumstances, wouldn't form at all."
With Banners

a printer from Nantucket, who was widowed in 1868. Two years later, he married Walter and George's sister, Mary Ellen Baker,[31] which meant that Emma was Mary Ellen's stepdaughter, and therefore, Walter's new bride was also his step-niece.

Emilie, her brother, mother, and the Mayhews were audience regulars. George Baker acknowledged his old friend in the dedication of *The Mimic Stage* (1871): "To Matt A. Mayhew, Esq., proprietor of the 'Hands' and 'Laugh' which have so often given assurance of success."

On-stage comedy contrasted with sad losses in the Baker family. In the space of seven months, both of Emilie's paternal great-grandmothers died: Dorcas Shaw Remick and Sarah Hodgkins Baker Chase. Furthermore, her grandfather, Albert Baker, had tuberculosis. He stayed at work until the first of July, but on Friday, August 14, 1874, three months after his mother, he died, too. He was sixty-three.

They held the funeral in Albert's home at 31 Ball Street, which was filled with friends and relatives. His pall bearers were members of the Boston Typographical Society and Boston Printers Union—Amos Clapp, Henry W. Gill, Henry A. McGlenen, C. W. G. Mansfield, Samuel Jordan, and Hiram Pierce. Enclosed in a rosewood casket, he was buried in a newly purchased family plot on "Spruce Path" at the beautiful Forest Hills cemetery.[32] His stone symbolized his life's journey, with seaweed on top for the native of Portland, and on the back, the one line that he claimed for himself throughout his adulthood: "Albert Baker, Printer." A small stone for his daughter Annie was placed at his side.

After Emilie's birthday in September, Mrs. Baker and the children ("bag and baggage," as their father jokingly referred to them) accompanied George Baker and the Oliver Optic family on a two-week vacation to the Clifford House in Plymouth, Massachusetts. Optic praised it as "a magnificent loafing-place," high on a bluff overlooking Plymouth Beach, surrounded by a veranda richly supplied with rocking chairs and cooling breezes.[33]

Since the mid-1860s, George Baker had sold his own plays as "George M. Baker & Co." He added the inventory of the William H. Spencer company (which had already absorbed the old Herbert Sweet Company) and renamed his company "Baker's Plays"—a company that still operates today.

George charged no royalties for performances, which allowed home players to afford them, but he still earned enough, with his plays, his books, and his job, to live in the fashionable Back Bay, employ a live-in maid, and summer comfortably along the coast. Now, Walter took over management of Baker's Plays, and George kept his finger in the dike of Lee & Shepard's solvency by scouting new manuscripts and writing more himself.

His latest effort was a novel. *Running to Waste* (1874) was about a sixteen-year-old tomboy, Becky Sleeper, who "could climb a tree with the activity of a squirrel, ride a horse without saddle or bridle . . . and was considered a valuable acquisition to either side in a game of football." Becky and her brother Teddy steal apples and melons "without leave or license,"[34] but, when the local paper mill burns, Becky rushes into the burning building to save a life, her tomboy years paying off in both fitness and courage. The book's reception was warm enough, and the critics appreciated George's dramatic style; "after reading it, one is haunted by a feeling that one has beheld all its scenes not in real life but on the stage and performed by very good actors."[35]

Emilie and her friend Georgie Mayhew did their own fundraising the next spring (1875), when they organized a carnival at the Bakers' house to benefit "a poor woman." With the help of nine more eight-year-old girls, they set up a miniature bazaar with tables for flowers, dolls, clothing, art, and confections. "The little table tenders were bewitching in their unique caps and dainty aprons," while the little boys, including Emilie's six-year-old brother, "kept a sharp eye on the grabs." The day was a grand success and yielded a profit of nearly two hundred twenty-five dollars.[36]

On August 28, 1875, Lee & Shepard made a public announcement. Direct losses from the fire and the continued financial panic had proved too great to overcome, and bankruptcy was at hand.[37] The men were so popular, and their reputations so solid, however, that many investors

"My sakes, but you were a tomboy, your clothes always torn an'—"
"Soft-pedal my sinful past, Sal."
Beckoning Trails

"If you would deal wisely with your child teach him to understand the use of money; encourage him to be generous— but justly so; saving, but never penurious; acquisitive, but, never at the expense of others."
The Mother in the Home

stepped forward to help, accepting only twenty cents on the dollar and without interest.[38]

For a moment, it appeared they would be saved, but J. R. Osgood was of a different mind; he sued for his full share and forced the bankruptcy. Little did it profit him, however, as his own firm declared bankruptcy four years later.[39]

To protest Osgood's actions and to assist his friends, Thomas Wentworth Higginson brought all of the works that Osgood had previously published for him and gave them to Lee & Shepard. John Townsend Trowbridge did likewise with his novels and juveniles. *Our Boys and Girls* had to be discontinued, but Sophie May created a new, *Flaxie Frizzle* series of books, and Oliver Optic steadfastly produced adventure after thrilling adventure for Lee & Shepard's exclusive publication.

Higginson dug in deeper. Against the advice of his good friend James T. Fields (of the publisher Ticknor & Fields), he wrote a children's history of the United States for which the financially strapped publishers had paid an advance of only $1000. He labored three years in its completion, and the *Young Folks' History of the United States* (1875) proved the most successful of all of Higginson's writings as well as one of the most successful, single books in Lee & Shepard's history. The book was unique, because it spoke to children in an engaging manner and brought history alive in a way that had not been attempted before.

Colonel Higginson enjoyed a significant, literary reputation, and attaching his name to the volume was undoubtedly responsible for much of its early success: "For the first time a man of genius has undertaken to tell the story of our country's growth."[40] Higginson remarked in his diary, "It will be pleasant to think, in any case, that I have done something to make American history clear and attractive."[41]

He did more than that. Within weeks, six thousand copies were sold, and Lee & Shepard rushed to prepare thousands more. *The Boston Transcript* said, "One hundred years may come and go ere there is such a demand for another book as there is for Colonel Higginson's *Young Folks'*

History just now."[42] Mr. Shepard estimated the year's sales at forty thousand and prepared translations in French, German, and Italian. Eventually, the book was used by all Boston public schools, and Thomas Wentworth Higginson's reputation as a writer of history was sealed. He and Lee & Shepard had pushed the frontiers of popular publishing and hit upon an engaging way of writing history that produced a new standard.[43]

Lee & Shepard continued their profitable series by Oliver Optic, Sophie May, and Elijah Kellogg and also created new specialties. They offered more edited works, pioneered handsome, small-format gift volumes, and created longer books for avid readers—anything to keep their publishing ship afloat. Women's humor, for example, was newly popular, and *That Husband of Mine* (1877) by Mary Andrews (Mary A. Denison, 1826–1911) sold over one hundred thousand copies in its first three weeks in print.[44]

By the end of 1877, Lee & Shepard stood on solid, financial ground. From then until the end of the firm, their success came from "feeling the public's pulse," sensing the average reader's taste,[45] and always staying just one step in front of it. The crisis was over, and Emilie's sister and mother went to England in the spring.[46] There were no more panic seasons.

The next summer, the Bakers stayed at Leavitt's Hampton Beach Hotel in New Hampshire, "a quiet spot with no style but plenty of attractions." Situated at the less popular—and less pretentious—North Beach, its view of the ocean was stupendous, its beach "broad, smooth and level as a ball-room floor," and "every sound of the sea, from the gentle swish of the summer wavelet to the thunder of the storm-beaten surf, [could] be heard in every room."[47]

George and Rachel gave readings wherever they stayed, and the Bakers returned so often to New Hampshire that Amherst's newspaper, *The Farmer's Cabinet*, claimed them as residents: "We notice that George M. Baker, Esq., of—this town we were going to say, but suppose we must say Boston, although we should lay claim to his family as residents—has been invited to read the Declaration of Independence at the City celebration of the approaching Fourth."[48]

She crossed to the window which faced the ocean. How she loved it, loved its ever-changing values. Some days there were only blues, all tints and shades; sometimes just green with nothing else but sparkle; and sometimes it was a study in gray, sullen and menacing with not a suggestion of color. *With Banners*

He had a marvelous voice, rich and mellow with a hint of vibrato when he was deeply moved. *There Is Always Love*

Emilie's father especially appreciated a good reading. Of the entertainments, he said, readings were the most accessible.

> Where one person is really interested in music, twenty are pleased by good reading. Where one person is capable of becoming a skilful [sic] musician, twenty may become good readers. Where there is one occasion suitable for the exercise of musical talent, there are twenty for that of good reading.[49]

George Baker gave frequent readings at schools, libraries, town halls, and public meetings. He was the natural choice.

> His appearance is fine, graceful and intellectual; his voice is clear and flexible; his facial play and gesture are the spontaneous results of a bright intelligence governing emotions that are well understood; and his sense of humor is uncommonly acute. While rendering some of his selections, at times pent-up mirth could no longer be restrained, and waves of laughter and applause would drown the speaker's words.[50]

Overlooking no opportunity to provide sales for Lee & Shepard, George Baker brought out a series of *Reading Club and Handy Speakers* that included old favorites as well as new pieces of his own composition. Once started, a new edition of readings came out every year, and they sold briskly. "To read only the mail orders or watch the customers as they thronged the main office would have made one believe that he had produced about all that were ever needed."[51]

On Christmas Eve, 1877, a small stage was fashioned at one end of the vestry room at the Columbus Avenue church, which was already decorated in holiday greenery. "To the delight of the audience," the young people presented a program of skits, songs, duets, and readings, including "Christmas Morning" by Rachel Baker. The little ones received presents from a large

"'The iron tongue of midnight hath told twelve,'" she quoted under her breath in her father's most dramatic manner. Her father! The thought of him was like a potent, soothing balm on the turmoil of her spirit. She could hear his rich voice saying; "'I have set watchmen upon thy walls, O Jerusalem.'"
Gay Courage

box that Santa had apparently left for them, and everyone had Christmas treats to celebrate the evening.[52]

Emilie's first, remembered, acting role came the following spring, when she played Prince Charming in *The Fairy of the Fountain, or Diamonds and Toads*, written by M. T. Caldor and published in *Our Boys and Girls* as *Diamonds and Toads*.[53] The children's performance on Saturday, March 2, 1878, concluded a full week of amateur theatricals presented in the Baker home to benefit the Ladies' Charitable Society. Tickets were twenty-five cents, and Henry Clay Barnabee was on hand to sing afterward.

Rachel brushed her sister's dark curls, and Emilie donned the costume of the prince—a velvet coat trimmed with gold lace and beads, a pointed lace collar fastened with a brilliant jewel, a gold dagger and belt, high boots with fringe, and a cap with a long feather in it. Harry Bicknell, the well-known etcher, painted the scenery, to which family members added gaudy, green and brown leaves as they had the time.[54]

The play was about two girls—Rose, who was kind to a beggar and had a fortune in diamonds and pearls drop from her mouth, and Fanny, who was unkind to the beggar and had frogs and toads fall from her lips. Prince Charming (Emilie) is sent to Rose, and "he" instantly understands that she is the one girl for him.

> O, how gladsome is this meeting!
> Fate, propitious, means us well.
> 'Tis magical spell, O, fairy dear,
> 'Tis magic of thy spell.[55]

It was a spell that would hold. Emilie believed in true love, propitious beginnings, and happy endings. And why not? In her world, heroes triumphed over adversity, fathers worked to make children happy, and when plays were given in the parlor, there was ice cream afterwards. Belief in the best came naturally, and optimism was ready each time it was needed.

"I remembered a newspaper story of an English woman who for years had passed herself off as a man, remembered that because of the husky note in my voice I had taken men's parts in dramatics."
Lighted Windows

"Leaves! Those daubs of paint look like an explosion of green worms, and it's lucky Field put a red roof on that brown cabin or it might have been shot for a deer. However, it will all go great when the foots are on."
With Banners

"Do you believe in love at first sight—in fiction—of course?" "I do, in fiction and in real life."
Give Me One Summer

CHAPTER 6

Winds of Change

Boston, 1881–1883

One by one, the familiar comforts of Emilie's childhood passed away. Her maternal grandmother, Rachel Elizabeth Boles, had lived with the Bakers for Emilie's whole life. George Baker declared his affection for her in the dedication of *Running to Waste*:

To Mrs. Rachel E. Boles, a patient invalid, who would have me believe that a few of her weary hours have been lightened by the reading of "The Story of a Tomboy," I dedicate this book, in remembrance of a long friendship, and in gratitude for many kind acts.

Grandmother Boles fell at the house in the spring of 1881 and hurt her hip. An abscess developed, and she passed away on March thirteenth. Her husband, Jerome Boles, had been buried with his family in Mount Auburn Cemetery, but she was laid to rest in the Baker plot at Forest Hills, a testament to the schism that had existed between them.

About the same time, Lee & Shepard gave up their familiar, corner store and moved the publishing offices upstairs, with a new entrance at 27 Franklin Street. They planned to concentrate on publishing rather than retail sales, so the dear old showroom with its boxes of books was dismantled and left behind.[1] What a time Emilie had enjoyed there, sitting atop the broad desks, sliding the door on her father's peep-window, going up and down the double staircase, and selecting any book she liked from the stacks. First, her grandmother had died, and now her father's dear, old office was gone.

In the fall of 1881, Emilie departed for Dean Academy, a coeducational, preparatory school in Franklin, Massachusetts.[2] At that time, primary and grammar school were expected, and a minority of girls attended some form of "high" school. Emilie could go to a normal school to become a teacher, a Latin/classical school to prepare for college, a vocational school to prepare for a trade, or simply extend her education at an academy, as she chose to do.

Emilie arrived at Dean Academy on her fifteenth birthday, enrolled in the one-year English Preparatory course.[3] The following day was "Yellow Tuesday," September 6, 1881, when all of New England was shrouded in an eerie, amber twilight. Grass appeared blue, and yellow flowers seemed white. Speculation as to the cause ranged from smoke in the atmosphere, to a sulfurous cloud, to the end of days.[4] The strange phenomenon was followed by days of extreme heat, more conducive to stupor than to study.

The preparatory curriculum continued subjects she had studied in the public school: reading, writing, and arithmetic, augmented by geography, painting, and drawing, and both instrumental and vocal music. In addition, Dean Academy emphasized composition and required French, German and attendance at the church of her choice.[5]

That single year at Dean's was the completion of Emilie's formal education. By contrast, her sister Rachel attended the Classical School for Girls in New York City and then graduated from the two-year elocution class at Boston University. Her brother Robert would attend Boston Latin School and matriculate directly to Harvard.

Rev. Dr. A. A. Miner congratulated the Dean Academy scholars and "urged the necessity of continuous study if they would have the attainments acquired in school enhanced. Education, said he, does not end with school."[6]

All three Baker children received more formal education than their father, who took his first job as a clerk right after he graduated from the Otis grammar school. There was no one, certainly none of his children, who would have regarded him as lacking in education. Like her father's, Emilie's habits of insatiable reading provided a liberal education, and through him, she had a constant stream of new publications close at hand.

One by one, the Boles brothers had married and moved away from the Baker home. The last was Albert in November 1883. He married Annie

"I can converse in three languages, I have been brought up on the classics, housework and the Ladies' Aid ..."
Here Comes the Sun

She had adopted a program of systematic reading of American history and tuned in on her boudoir radio on subjects in which she was deeply interested. To a slight degree she was carrying on her education, as the president of her college had begged the members of the graduating class to do.
Today Is Yours

Her father and she had been boon companions ... She could hear his deep voice encourage: "You can do anything you want to do, Lindy. I hope you'll want to be a grand wife and mother, but whatever it is never forget that your Dad believes you can be tops."
There Is Always Love

Emilie "Bessie" Baker. "It was a picture in color of a starry-eyed, dark-haired girl in white organza with a string of lustrous pearls about her lovely throat." Beckoning Trails

That Chief was Mac Donovan . . . He was my most loyal, bloodthirsty understudy when he was a wicked buccaneer and I was a pirate chief . . . His family moved away from Sunnyfield. *Gay Courage*

Donovan, a young, Irish woman with five older brothers, and they moved to Sunnyside Street in Boston. When their first son was born a year later, they named him "Melville Jerome," the middle name after Albert's father and the first name for the man who had been like a father to him, George Melville Baker. Their first daughter was named "Maria Emily," underscoring the closeness of Albert to his younger niece, even though he was closer in age to Rachel.

Social Seasons, 1884–1888

The closest that Emilie came to an official introduction to society came at seventeen, in the form of a February "Leap Year Party" hosted by Mrs. O. Morse and the Ladies Club.[7] Debutante customs had loosened, but girls approaching marriageable age were still given new gowns—from Paris, if they could afford them—new hats, and invitations to teas and balls in hopes of their securing husbands. Emilie's sister, Rachel, had already completed her turn: three social seasons and a trip abroad. Emilie seemed more suited to the process, the type of girl the *Boston Herald* described as, "neither belle nor wallflower . . . a pretty, good-natured, easy-going creature, popular with everybody."[8]

The young misses' gowns were properly elegant. Emilie's friend Maud Robinson wore white cashmere, Lena Morse, albatross with white lace trimming, and Ella Lee, white nuns veiling. Emilie's dress was white albatross with red velvet and white Spanish lace. There was supper and dancing, a party "long to be remembered."[9]

Emilie's eighteenth year was fully social. On an afternoon in March 1885, she took center stage at the Park Theater on Washington Street in the first of several fundraisers to benefit a home for the soldiers and sailors of the Civil War. George M. Baker's play, *Rebecca's Triumph*, was the night's entertainment, and the theater was "filled to overflowing," including the governor, the mayor, and their wives.[10] The audience hushed, and the first on stage was Emilie, leading a "broom drill."[11]

Dressed alike in black, white, and red, the girls moved through military-like maneuvers, brandishing brooms instead of rifles. As captain, Emilie brandished a feather duster. "Present arms!" "Aim!" "Attack!" "Triumph!" The girls shouldered their brooms, and Emilie marched them off the stage, so the play could begin.[12]

Twenty-five women and girls acted in George Baker's play, *Rebecca's Triumph*, including Rachel, Emilie, Georgie Mayhew, Mrs. Mayhew, Martha Pollard, Edith Stevens, Frankie and Susie Bowker, and both

"What is a Martharine? First cousin to a Worth or a Doucet?"
"Now I know where your women friends get their clothes."
Here Comes the Sun!

She was voted the gayest, most amusing, most sympathetically understanding, most popular girl in the class.
Bright Skies

Hattie and Mary Ulman. Nearly all were members of the Young People's Fraternity at Dr. Miner's Columbia Street Church—or their mothers.[13]

The play was about an orphan girl named Rebecca who is teaching a group of girls to bake a cake that she calls "Rebecca's Triumph." Unbeknownst to Rebecca, her mother, Clara, has moved back to town, but Clara's family has disowned her, and no one realizes that Rebecca is her long-lost child. Rebecca's necklace is the clue, and when it falls out of the girls' cake, the two are reunited: "I knew it would all come right at last."[14]

A few weeks later, a "Great Carnival" honored the soldiers and sailors of the Union, twenty years after the conclusion of the Civil War, and raised money to build a Solders' Home for their continued care. The Reverend E. A. Horton spoke, "We are now twenty years away from the war, and how many of these men now present will be in need of charity twenty-five years hence?" Speeches followed, and then a service of remembrance, military drills, and horse exhibitions.[15]

Emilie tended the confectionary table with her good friends of more than a decade: Martha Pollard, Katie and Helen Newell, the Ulman sisters, Grace Temple, and all three Bowker sisters.[16] None of the other girls had parents in theater or publishing, although Mr. Ulman was a bookbinder before he went into the wine and liquor business. Mr. Pollard and Mr. Newell were in the grocery business, Mr. Temple was a broker,[17] and Mr. Bowker manufactured soda fountain drinks.[18]

Two blocks from the fair was the Bakers' new, pudding-stone house at 44 Gloucester to which they moved in May 1885. Its three stories hid an iron balcony and small garden at the rear, and the spacious living areas looked east through bay windows, toward the morning sun. The sixteen-thousand-dollar home[19] was more fashionable than West Springfield Street and closer to Back Bay social life.

When summer arrived, they rented a cottage at Hingham's Downer Landing. Thousands of people flocked to the fashionable resort every week, in addition to those who rented cottages or hotel rooms for the season.[20]

Downer's chief attractions were Melville Gardens and the Rose

"It will all come right. Things have a marvelous unbelievable way of coming right."
The Trail of Conflict

What fun she and a little girl named Grace Temple had had playing with the big dollhouse in the corner.
To Love and To Honor

Standish House. The Melville Gardens' twenty acres encompassed gardens and groves for picnics, a café that seated six hundred, a music hall, and a famous, clam-bake pavilion. Away from the crowds were observation points, ponds, a rocky island, pavilions and arbors for private assignations, bath houses, boats, bowling alleys, shooting galleries, croquet lawns, billiards, swings, and a monkey cage. *King's Handbook of Boston Harbor* said, "There is probably more fun to the acre in Melville Garden than in any other piece of Massachusetts ground."[21]

The Rose Standish House at Downer Landing was a first-class hotel with steam heat and one-hundred-fifty "homelike" rooms in three stories.[22] On the rise beyond the resort, was the cottage of "noble views," where the Bakers stayed, a place "where the foot of the amateur casual rarely intrudes, and the basket of the picnic-party is not seen."[23]

Sea views were everywhere, and yachts from Hull and Nantasket were constants. Protected from waves by the broad reach of the Nantasket peninsula, the water was calm and beach-going pleasant.[24]

It is hard to exaggerate Downer Landing's popularity. Casual visitors arrived by yacht, steamer, and rail. The Rose Standish House was entirely full for the season, and nine hundred attended the famous clam bake on a single Saturday.[25] Between visiting clubs, church groups, lodges, and societies, the Melville Gardens counted over nine thousand visitors in a single week.[26]

Summer passed quickly. On the Fourth of July, buoys marked a racecourse near the landing for a double-scull contest. Robert Baker and Willie Ulman took on Harry Ulman and Harry Gustin and won by two boat lengths.[27] The Rose Standish House hosted regular hops that brought "well-known society people" from Boston to "trip the light fantastic."[28]

In mid-August, three hundred people from Hingham, Hull, Nantasket, and Downer Landing danced by lantern-light at the Rose Standish House and strolled through the Melville Gardens, lit by electric lights until the last boat left for Boston at 9:30 p.m. Emilie's costume was "among those noticed" at the dance. She wore ecru silk with pink roses, her sister, Rachel, wore white lace, and Hattie Ulman wore blue cashmere with red, jacque-minot roses.[29]

Melville Gardens and the Rose Standish House ended their seasons in mid-September,[30] and the Bakers returned to the Back Bay and the social activities of the Columbus Avenue Unitarian Church, "Dr. Miner's Church." Emilie and Rachel belonged to its Young People's Fraternity, volunteered at the Miner Charitable Society, and acted in the amateur theatricals and musical performances that funded its works.

That November (1885), they presented *Longfellow's Dream* with a cast of one hundred, including many Baker friends and relatives: Edward and Ida Boles with their daughter Madeline; all of the Mayhews, including Emilie's friend, Georgie; Mr. and Mrs. Rufus Norris; Drs. Fred and Edwin Jack of the Massachusetts Eye and Ear Infirmary with their parents, Sally (Shaw) and Lafayette Jack; and two of the Bowker sisters, Hattie and Susie. So many acted in the play that it was a wonder there could be an audience, but the performance was well attended and a pronounced success.[31]

In the spring of 1886, Rachel and Emilie embarked together on a trip to Washington, D.C., one of the luxury tours hosted by the Raymond & Whitcomb agency. Thirty-six years in the building, the Washington Monument's final capstone and aluminum tip had finally been placed in December.[32] The edifice was now dedicated and open to the public, and there was talk of creating a Lincoln Memorial, also.[33]

Four hundred people, mainly Bostonians, left Sunday, April fourth, and arrived in drenching rain. Fortunately, there was an indoor lecture planned, a presentation by photographer John L. Stoddard on the "Passion Play at Ober-Ammergau." The location was the recently constructed Albaugh's Grand Opera House on the corner of Fifteenth Street and East Street Northwest, in sight of both the White House and the Washington Monument.[34]

Rain continued Monday, which didn't matter when they attended a White House reception and shook hands with President Cleveland.[35] The skies cleared for the remainder of the week, and Emilie and Rachel toured

The mirror above the fireplace reflected Sally Shaw's short white hair, her charming, youthful face with its saucy turned-up nose, her silver-gray costume and the dog collar of lustrous pearls at her throat. *Bright Skies*

They had passed the White House. The light from its many windows warmed even the shadows under the trees. They had watched the play of light and shade on Washington Monument, had seen the aluminum cap gleam like silver as the moon dodged from behind clouds. *It's a Great World!*

Mount Vernon and "every point of interest" in Washington before return-ing to Boston on Friday.[36]

The Bakers planned to return to Downer Landing the next summer, and this time they made reservations early to stay in the center of activity, the Rose Standish Hotel.[37] They arrived on opening day, June 15, 1886, and remained through August.

Downer Landing was even busier than the year before. Over four thousand tickets were taken at Melville Gardens on July fifth for the boat races and the evening's "grand entertainment."[38] The day began with a thirty-eight-gun salute for the thirty-eight states in the Union and was followed by a morning concert and races of many kinds: bicycle, potato, tub, and boat. In the double-scull race, Robert Baker and Willie Ulman challenged a new team this year and won yet again.

August's grand, full-dress hop was moved outdoors due to hot weather and held in a pavilion instead of the Rose Standish dining room.[39] Under electric lights, it was the "most brilliant one ever given." Clam bakes and fireworks, symphony concerts, musicales, and dances continued all season. By the end of August, more than sixty-seven thousand people had vis-ited Downer Landing that summer, fifteen thousand more than the year before.[40]

The Bakers delayed their summer plans the following year, due to the death of Emilie's little cousin, Melville Jerome Boles, in the spring. Albert, Annie, and their son stayed with the Bakers one night in the house on Gloucester. All were there—Emilie, her parents, and both Rachel and Robert. Melville had been well during the day, but the toddler came down with a rasping cough and died during the night.[41] The loss was so sudden, so sad, and it brought a mourning period that kept them near home.

Emilie's three-month mourning ended the first week of July.[42] On the ninth, she had her portrait taken in Haverhill, wearing the tall, brimmed hat-of-the-season. The next week, she and her mother attended a "bril-liant occasion" at Nantasket Beach, across the bay from Downer Landing. Thirty Cadets from the camp at Hingham joined guests from all around the

"This is my first White House Reception and I'm all tingle, tingle." ... When she was presented, she was aware of a deep voice repeating her name, of a woman beside the President in a brilliant green frock which sparkled ... *Across the Years*

Bessie Baker, 1887. "The hair visible below the brim of her
moss-green felt had a satin-sheen." There is Always Love

bay, Hingham to Hull, for an evening hop. The women wore that season's
favorite white, and the men provided "the usual profusion of clawhammer
coats, swell shirt fronts and immaculate ties."[43] It was the one, purely social
event of her summer.

The Bakers and a cadre of Lee & Shepard Associates met in Camden
for the remainder of the season. Oliver Optic once described Camden
as the preferred place for "a large majority of the sensible people, who do
not care for show and fashion."[44] Emilie, Rachel, and Robert stayed at the
Allens' boarding house on High Street with their uncle, Walter H. Baker,
of Baker's Plays. Charles Dillingham, the New York publisher for Lee
& Shepard, came to Camden, along with William Lee's daughter, Alice,

Charles Shepard's daughter, May, and the artist Irene Jerome, who planned to sketch scenery for a new, Lee & Shepard gift book. Dr. Henry Shaw and his wife, longtime family friends, were at Mountain View lodge, and Walter and Frank Badger, more friends, stayed at the Seward House.[45]

The Bakers came to entertain. On the twelfth, they performed *Comrades* in a public hall to benefit St. Thomas Church. "The audience was large, the drama an interesting one, finely presented and warmly appreciated."[46] The next week, Mrs. Waldson of High Street gave a "Hickory Dickory Dock" party for which Rachel, Emilie, and Robert sang and performed "charming and amusing" recitations."[47]

Emilie and her brother Robert were always close, both in age and relationship. Robert was handsome, five feet nine inches tall, with curly, dark-brown hair and lively, blue eyes. The older he got, the more handsome he became. The family called him "Inky" for his constant use of the pen, and his writing showed the same humorous streak as his father's. His graduation declamation at the Boston Latin School in 1888 began with a cheeky greeting, "Mr. Chairman, Ladies and Gentlemen, Fellow Members of the Society for the Prevention of Knowledge . . ." and included a new parody in a familiar cadence:

> To have it out, or not to have it out, that is the question.
> Whether 'tis better for the jaws to suffer
> The pangs and torments of an aching tooth,
> Or to take steel against a host of troubles
> And, by extracting, end them.[48]

Robert entered Harvard that fall as a "Dickey"—a member of that exclusive fraternity of students (Delta Kappa Epsilon) "distinctly fortunate in their social standing" who paid a substantial fee for their initiation.[49] He joined the Hasty Pudding Club with its amateur theatricals and hoped to be on the baseball team, too, but serious "eye problems" forced him to leave school in January.[50] His illness included "fainting spells" reminiscent

How versatile she was! She played with verve, crispness, sparkle, exuberance, and warm sentiment.
Hilltops Clear

How good looking he was! He radiated a sort of mischievous gusto, as if life were an amusing show in which he was cast for the part of comedian.
Fair Tomorrow

"Inky, aren't they? I despair of ever domesticating a fountainpen. Just as I think I have one well-trained it leaks."
Fair Tomorrow

David looked so frail, so weary, as if too strong a wind might blow him away. She shut her teeth hard in her lips. It was her job to see that a strong wind didn't touch him. Could she prevent it? Could she! She had better cut out self doubt and cut it out quick. "Must prevent" were the words she wanted. One didn't stop to question when the most precious person in one's life was in danger; one did things. *Hilltops Clear*

"Do you get the scent of flowers from shore? Reminds me of the fragrance that drifted toward us from Flores, an island miles away, when my father and I were sailing past the Azores." *Give Me One Summer*

of his Aunt Ellen's epilepsy, but the family put its hopes on a fresh-air cure. Emilie and Robert got tickets aboard the triple-masted bark *Sarah* and set sail for the Azores.

Voyage to Europe, 1889

Their journey began inauspiciously. The seas were rough, and the crew was rougher. The *Sarah* was a cargo vessel that also took passengers, and this time its cargo was petroleum and matches, which added significantly to the perilous possibilities. At one point, the voyage grew so treacherous that a rough old salt and crew member named Jeremiah Bumpus declared

Emilie, "The feel of Paris"

to all who would listen, "Me and the sea is done." Prolonging their discomfort, the voyage that was expected to be twenty days in length took more than a week longer—nineteen days to reach Fayal and nine days more to arrive in Ponta Delgada.[51]

After nearly four months in the Azores, Emilie and Robert returned to Boston via London and Paris, Emilie's one trip to Europe.[52] They arrived in Paris during the Exposition Universelle de Paris, the Paris World's Fair. Exposition attendance exceeded all expectations, and the attractions were "far beyond the most vivid conceptions of the visitors." Most striking was the brand-new Eiffel Tower, the tallest structure in the world at the time.[53]

They returned to Boston on the vessel *La Gascogne*. Traveling with them was James Lawson Karrick,[54] a young man a few years older than Emilie—five-foot-ten, with brown hair and gray eyes. At the time, he was a stationer, as her father and Matthew Mayhew had been, and a fellow congregant at Dr. Miner's church.

Robert did not re-enroll at Harvard when they returned to Boston. Their father's longtime associate Charles A. B. Shepard had died in January following a long illness,[55] and now George Baker was ill, too. Despite rest, George remained fatigued and weakened, and in July of 1889, he made the decision to leave Lee & Shepard. The house on Gloucester Street was closed, and the family left for the fresh, salt air of the Cape.

Scene: Barnstable, 1889–1891

The Bakers arrived in time for Barnstable County's horse races and fair. Prized animals, crafts, handiwork, and cooking filled the fairgrounds, and evenings brought socials and concerts and balls.

They stayed in a hotel until they found the William H. Odiorne mansion, high on a hill at the end of Jail Street. The furnished home had twelve large rooms, and a 150-foot piazza wrapped around three sides. Its substantial grounds had burned in a destructive fire the previous year[56] but still included a garden, "extensive" hen houses, and a barn.[57] With its airy

"Did you travel up from the Cape with a wardrobe trunk concealed about your person?" "'The feel of Paris.' Like them?" *Fair Tomorrow*

The afterglow tinted the roofs of the sedate old houses which bordered the main street, gilded the black bands on their white chimneys, transformed windows into molten sheets of brass and copper. *Fair Tomorrow*

rooms and fine views, the Sisters of Charity had once considered using the home as a sanitarium.[58] Now, it could serve that function for George Baker.

Unsure how long they might remain in Barnstable, the Bakers sought to rent, but the property was for sale instead. In stepped James Karrick, who bought the property and promptly leased it to the Bakers.[59] Freshly painted, it presented a "showy" appearance for their many visitors.[60]

A railway stop at the end of their road made trips back to Boston convenient. On one such trip, Mrs. Baker discovered that their house on Gloucester had been robbed. Missing were a diamond bar pin and a gold, hunting-case watch, set with diamonds, together worth over two-hundred-fifty dollars.[61] That was the trouble with leaving town; one's home was vulnerable to burglars.

Emilie's first Cape Cod friend was Louise Hallet from Yarmouth, a young woman born to wealth and social position. Her grandfather was President of the Providence National Bank and a Director of the Providence and Worcester Railroad Corporation. Her father earned his fortune early, married Ellen Sears, of the venerable, Cape Cod Sears family, and retired when Louise was still a toddler. Louise was Emilie's age, twenty-two. Her younger siblings were Henry, who was Robert's age, and then Frances, Alice, and Lizzie. Like Emilie, Louise understood the strain of family illness. Her older brother died when he was seventeen, and her father had recently developed symptoms of the disease that would eventually kill him.

What a change it was, from the bustle of Boston to the quiet of the Cape. Oliver Optic came out for a visit, but as the days grew yet shorter, summer visitors returned to their homes, and Barnstable echoed with their passing.

Sometimes, their Boston social life beckoned, as on the first of October for Georgie Mayhew's marriage to the wealthy investor Oliver Chapman.[62] He was the widowed son of a founder of the Union Pacific Railroad,[63] and if a girl's goal was to marry well to ensure her financial security, then Georgie more than succeeded.

To Louise Gordon Hallet whose friendship has glowed with a lovely light down through the years since we met on Cape Cod
Fair Tomorrow,
dedication

A lovely village, a village to return to, not one in which to spend one's youth.
Fair Tomorrow

In 1881, Oliver Chapman and Loring Chase bought and developed a tract of land in Florida that they named "Winter Park." It swiftly became an elegant resort for wealthy northerners who came for its warm weather and abundant, fresh oranges and grapefruit.[64] Chapman sold his interest in the resort years before his marriage to Georgie, but they kept his cottage there, which was considered the first home built in Winter Park, as well as a home south of Boston, in Sharon, Massachusetts.

Emilie's Grandmother Baker still lived with her son Walter at the old Baker residence on Alpine Street in Boston. On October twentieth, one day short of what would have been her husband Albert's seventy-ninth birthday, she died. It was the same date as the fire in Portland that had prompted their move to Boston so many years ago, the same time of year that had taken the lives of two of her children.

Mary Ann Shaw Remick Baker—a lady of dignity, proud of her Shaw heritage—lived to age seventy-seven. In the end, she outlived her husband, all of her siblings, and five of her children. They buried her next to Albert in the Baker plot at Forest Hills.

In the space of one year, illness had forced Robert to leave school and George to retire, the whole family had left Boston behind and moved to the Cape, and now, the elder Mrs. Baker had died. Grief was no match for Baker resilience, though, and as the days grew shorter and darker, Robert ordered a new horse and a double-seated carriage. They rented a piano for home entertainments and welcomed Albert and Annie Boles' newborn son, named for Emilie's brother, Robert Melville.

Spring arrived, and George Baker started a new play. The younger Bakers recruited locals and began rehearsals for amateur theatricals to be presented in the Masonic Hall. Robert and Rachel took acting roles, but Emilie did not. By the time the family moved to the Cape, Rachel had already made her solo reading debut, acted in the Young People's Fraternity of their church, and wrote her own plays. Outgoing, funny, and expressive, Robert, too, both acted and wrote.

Emilie was the reader and appreciative audience. She took part in

"I suppose you are fanning yourself in the shade of a palm in one of the garden spots of the world, while I am looking out on a driving snow-storm and at the town plow piling up unscal-able mountains of white at the sides of the road." *With Banners*

After all, there was nothing like an absorbing interest to make one vitally alive from head to feet. If anyone knew the truth of that, he did. *Hilltops Clear*

"You're not bad yourself, Brooke. Why didn't you take to acting?" "I ought to be good. We children were raised on dramatics and quotations." *With Banners*

family theatricals and acted on small stages, but her forte was critique. From her youngest days in the Lee & Shepard publishing house, she was the girl who read and observed and provided feedback. In fact, she claimed that she never attempted to write when she was young, because she was always too busy reading whatever was put before her—and in a family like the Bakers, that was a lot.

All that summer of 1890, longtime and well-connected friends visited the younger Bakers. Emilie's childhood friend Beth McClannin came from New York where her father acted with Maggie Mitchell's company.[65] Friends Herbert Gale and Clara E. Bond both came from Haverhill. Herbert owned his own shoe factory, and Clara, who graduated from Dean Academy the same year as Emilie, now taught school, but she also came from a Haverhill shoe manufacturing family.[66] James Karrick, who had demonstrated his friendship most sincerely during the past year, came several times,[67] as did George Badger, the youngest of the Boston Badger brothers.

The Badgers belonged to both the Eastern and Boston Yacht Clubs, and it may have been through them that the Bakers met Louis M. Clark, who came to the Cape for the Eastern Yacht Club race. Clark belonged to the Eastern, Hull, and Massachusetts Yacht Clubs,[68] was a founding member of the New England Yachting Association, and served as associate editor for the weekly newspaper *The Yachtsman*.[69] The Bakers didn't own a yacht, but they had sailed with Oliver Optic and summered at yachting destinations nearly every summer. In August, when Robert and Rachel acted in Morton's one act farce, *To Oblige Benson*, and the comedy *My Uncle's Will*, Louis Clark and Arthur Badger joined the "full and delighted" audience in Masonic Hall.[70]

George Baker felt well enough to seek treatment in Saratoga, New York that summer. His diagnosis was pernicious anemia, an illness that prevents the body from absorbing vitamin B-12 and causes deficiencies that lead, ultimately, to death. In modern days, vitamin supplements might have helped him, but these insights were unavailable then. Instead, he pinned his hopes on the "curative" waters of Saratoga,

"Everything is in place except the books. I didn't dare start unpacking those for fear one might open and I would stop to read a page or two. I'm a book addict."
Hilltops Clear

"After Dad was confined to the house, I spent hours working with him, mounting and sorting stamps. He had a lot of cronies with whom he traded, and he and I would tingle with excitement when he acquired an item we had needed."
There Is Always Love

and his condition worsened. He returned from Saratoga and never again left his bed.[71]

During the past winter, James Karrick had sold the Odiorne mansion, with the stipulation that the Bakers' one-year lease must be observed, but the lease ended while George was in New York, and the younger Bakers had to make other arrangements. Robert sold the chickens, and he, Emilie, Rachel, and Beth McClannin took rooms at the well-heeled Cotocheset for the month of August.[72]

In September, the Bakers moved to the summer home of Mrs. Austin Flint, which was in the village on Bow Street. Mrs. Flint was the widow of a famous physician who had been President of the American Medical Association, tended the wealthiest families of New York, and started two medical colleges, including Bellevue, where his son now practiced. He was also the first to describe the etiology of George's disease, pernicious anemia, and pioneered many early advances in cardiology.[73] That season, Mrs. Flint took her grandson Grover to Europe and leased her home, with its famous, tropical lilies, to the Bakers.[74]

Once again, the Cape emptied itself of visitors. In early October, the local paper observed, "Barnstable begins to have a lonesome look, so many dwellings are closed." One week later, on the evening of Sunday, October nineteenth, George Melville Baker died.

Maybe the family felt it coming. It was that same time of the year again, near his father's birthday on the twenty-first, when his little sister and brother had contracted their fatal illness, the Portland house had burned, and his mother had died. They took George's body on the morning train to Boston and planned his funeral for Wednesday morning, October twenty-second, at Dr. Horton's Second Church on Copley Square.

Boston, October 1890

The pallbearers represented every stage of George Baker's life and career. There was Matthew Mayhew, his longtime friend and partner;

"The poultry is my brother's enterprise, Mrs. Carr. I wouldn't go so far as to say that he runs it. At present it is running him—ragged."
Fair Tomorrow

Her father had said the last day they had been together: "Remember, Sandy, that the future holds nothing that your unconquerable soul, your faith, your trust cannot meet." Had she an unconquerable soul? Time alone would tell.
Uncharted Seas

Where had he gone? What was death? Were spirit and personality the same? Did they burn on forever like the light before the Cenotaph, or did they go out like a spark when there was no breath of wind to blow it into living flame?
We Ride the Gale!

T. R. (Theophilus) Marvin, the printer and fellow Mason; Charles J. Peters, the longtime stereotyper from Washington Street; John S. Lockwood, a stationer and book buyer; George Andrew, the engraver; and Henry W. Daniell, George's old friend from the Mercantile Library Association.

The pulpit was literally covered with flowers—wreaths, mounds of chrysanthemums, a star, pillows, and many loose roses. An ivy-trimmed pillow from Lee & Shepard employees bore a closed book and the word, "Rest." The Columbian Masonic Lodge sent a square wreath, and Walter, Sarah, and Charles Baker placed a large mound of ivy and white flowers with "Our Brother" written in violets before the rest.

The mourners were a testament to the esteem in which George was held. William Lee sat beside Oliver Optic. Next were Dana Estes of Estes and Lauriat, who sold books for Lee & Shepard in its early years, Benjamin Ticknor of Ticknor & Fields, salesman Emory Cleaves, publishers E. J. Williamson, F. M. Goss, and John Lander, and William R. Beatty, a bookkeeper at Lee & Shepard.[75] Mrs. Baker's cousin Angie attended with her husband, John Quincy Adams Brackett, the recently elected governor of Massachusetts, as did Henry A. McGlenen, the popular business agent of the Boston Theater who had been a pall bearer for George's father.[76]

The Temple quartet played, and when the service was over, George was buried at Forest Hills, next to his parents. A large, rugged stone was placed above him, "George M. Baker, 1832–1890," and the remembrances began.

He was a resplendent example of the working out of his own precept, his daughter thought. He was the busiest man she knew yet he always had an abundance of time for pleasure.
The Trail of Conflict

Reader Baker dead. Although well known in Boston through his connection with the publishing business, it is as a dramatist that Mr. Baker has won his greatest reputation, as his position as writer to the amateur stage, in which he has no genuine competitor, is one that cannot easily be filled.[77]

Twenty-eight years ago, Mr. Baker entered the publishing house of Lee & Shepard, and there remained until a year ago last June. He was regarded by the firm as its most valuable assistant, its right-hand literary man, and one in whom it could and did place implicit confidence as well as high personal esteem.[78]

But his final performance was not yet over. Ever busy, even in his illness, George Baker left behind a partially finished manuscript, *After Taps*, which Rachel completed for him. The Cotuit Dramatic Club performed the three-act drama on Barnstable's Masonic Hall stage on May 19, 1891. It was seven months to the day after George's death, a final tribute in his own words[79] and a love note to his wife:

> Those were good times in Oldtown. Do you remember them? . . .
> When I thought you were the purtiest girl in town; when the sight
> of you in your best bib and tucker made me feel as though there
> were an ice-cream factory in full operation on one side, and a hot
> air furnace on the other.[80]

The Bakers left Barnstable the following week, and the *Barnstable Patriot* expressed appreciation: "They are all most pleasant people and their departure from our village will be regretted by all who have the honor of their acquaintance."

With George gone, Robert's illness took priority. His eye problems were no better, and local doctors had done all they could. Robert and Rachel boarded a ship to Europe on May twenty-seventh for one last hope, a famous oculist in Switzerland.[81]

Emilie and her mother took a train to Brattleboro, Vermont, and a carriage to the Bliss farm, three miles out of town. Rudyard Kipling would write *The Jungle Book* a year later while staying in the small, Bliss cottage next door, but the Bakers stayed in the big, white house with its fabulous view. From high on a hill, they gazed across the green lawn to a panoramic view of the forested valley and distant hills.

George's death had ended more than his life. Mrs. Baker, his companion and helpmate, was now a widow. She could visit in her children's homes

"[We] started out with the conviction that marriage is a high adventure, not an obstacle race. We haven't changed our belief, though we've had some tough, grueling experiences along an often times rough and rocky road . . . Your mother and I were lavishly endowed with a sense of humor, and while love may make the world go round, it is a sense of humor that keeps the engine oiled."
As Long as I Live

Her eyes lingered on her mother perched on the arm of a couch. She did young things like that.
With Banners

On a night like this under the stars her father seemed very near. Sandra's throat tightened. Where was he? They had been gay and understanding comrades for years.
Uncharted Seas

and might have one of her own, but the shared memories of thirty-five years were now hers alone to keep. This had not been in the plan. She was still a comparatively young woman at fifty-three; her furniture could remain in place from now on, but would she?

Emilie, her father's cheery reflection, wondered how it was possible that he was really gone. His convictions had set the family compass; his positive regard had held them together in merry camaraderie. Now, she must read to have his words and remember to have his affection. George Baker had carried the family on the wave of his indefatigable creativity and optimism. Now they must take their turn at the tiller and decide whether to maintain his heading or take another tack.

ACT TWO:
Mrs. Victor J. Loring

"Women friends were all right, but it really took a man to
make things interesting."

—Emilie Loring

ANNOUNCEMENT

Boston, Fall 1891

The entrance to the Hotel Huntington was on the narrowest part of the wedge-shaped, brownstone building at the southwest corner of the Back Bay's Copley Square. Recently opened that summer of 1891, the hotel's glass doors and black walnut vestibule led to an entrance hall carpeted in a light, terra cotta floral that complemented frescoed leaves on the high, tinted ceiling. The office of Damon & Damon, proprietors, with its imposing and reassuring safe, was on the right, while the parlor and men's smoking room were to the left. American and European dining rooms were yet further back along the hallway, and above, there were 125 brand-new, luxury apartments. The Baker family engaged one of the last remaining suites in September.

Outside, no fewer than three churches bordered Copley Square—Trinity Church, Second Church, and the New Old South. The Museum of Fine Arts bordered the south side of the square, and the Art Club headquarters were to the northwest, at the corner of Dartmouth and Newbury. Centers of learning stretched down Boylston Street, from Harvard's Medical School at Exeter to the new Boston Public Library under construction at Dartmouth, past the Chauncy-Hall private school, to the Institute of Technology campus further east between Clarendon and Berkeley. Men exercised at the Boston Athletic Club on Exeter, and women had their own Ladies' Gymnasium further west. In their midst stood elegant—even palatial—hotels: the Hotel Vendome, Hotel Brunswick, Copley Square Hotel, and the Victoria, Ludlow, and Huntington.

The Bakers' apartment at the Huntington was just a few blocks southeast of their still-shuttered home on Gloucester and only a few blocks north of their longtime home on West Springfield. It felt good to be back in Boston after two years on the Cape.

"B. Damon. He's the man you want, isn't he? He's the senior member of the firm." ... What would this friend of her father's be like, Sandra had just time to wonder before she opened a door in response to a gruff, "Come in!" *Uncharted Seas*

She loved living in the city, loved this time of day and this time of year when the shops glittered with lights, when the smell of roasting chestnuts seeped from glowing braziers on corners, when the streets were jammed with traffic and every person in the crowd hurried as if he or she had somewhere to go and were on the way. *With Banners*

"I belong to a generation which believed in [romance], which shivered a little when a man's eyes looked deep into ours, when a man's lips set hard, when his face whitened— it really happened— when he asked a girl to marry him."
We Ride the Gale!

"For you must know that this great Knight was the crowning glory of his house and name. He was the most noble of spirit, the most beautiful, the bravest of heart, the greatest knight in all the country round."
A Certain Crossroad

"I'm not that much older than you." "You're just seven years older, Mister."
When Hearts Are Light Again

On October fifteenth, an announcement appeared in the *Boston Courier*: "The wedding of Miss Bessie Baker, of the Huntington, and Mr. Victor J. Loring, of Brookline, is announced to take place Dec. 9."[1]

Who was Victor J. Loring, and when did this romance begin? To Emilie, he was the Knight in Sir Walter Scott's *The Talisman*:

And sometimes the sky was like unto a great turquoise for blueness, and sometimes it was like a gray pall, and sometimes the highway wound through level radiant fields, and sometimes the rough road plunged down a steep declivity of rocks to grope blindly through dark and evil forests, and sometimes the yellow moon made mysterious twilight in the shadows. But always the Knight kept the lady's hand close in his and always he stepped forward firmly, shining eyes straight ahead, for even in the gloom all was sharp-cut and clear to his vision.[2]

(Dedication of *A Certain Crossroad*, "To V. J. L.")

To his family and acquaintances, Victor was an earnest young attorney in partnership with his brothers in Boston, the thirty-two-year-old descendant of a long line of prominent Lorings from Marlborough, Massachusetts. And to the Bakers, he was the man-of-the-moment who would soon make Emilie his bride, the first of the Baker siblings to marry.

CHAPTER 7

Victor Joseph Loring

Marlborough, MA; 1775–1872

The Loring family was distinguished by patriotism and public service. Victor's great-grandfather, William Loring, left his field on the morning of April 19, 1775, to join his brothers in the Marlborough militia. Together, they marched to join Colonel Artemas Ward's regiment to hold out against the British at Cambridge. Later, William Loring fought under Colonel Rice to subdue Shay's Rebellion,[1] and his son, Victor's grandfather Hollis C. Loring, served in the War of 1812.[2]

Victor's maternal grandfather, Winchester Hitchcock, was at West Point when Arnold attempted to surrender to the British.[3] On his record, Victor's brother Selden obtained founding membership in the newly formed Sons of the American Revolution.[4]

As a boy, Victor saw runaway slaves harbored in the basement of his Marlborough home. His father was Hollis Loring, a staunch abolitionist who operated their home as a stop on the Underground Railroad.[5] Hollis knew leading abolitionists as friends—including George Sewell Boutwell,[6] Henry Wilson,[7] and William Lloyd Garrison—and he served as chairman of the committee that drafted the first, personal liberty bill in the state (1855).[8]

In October 1861, Charles Sumner gave a speech to the Republican Convention in Worcester in which he defied President Lincoln and declared that the entire purpose of the Civil War was to eliminate slavery. The remarks divided Republicans, with Hollis Loring in full support of the speaker:

"...but right then and there I learned the difference between mere money and money with family behind it."
The Trail of Conflict

Marlboro, October 4, 1861

Hon. Ch. Sumner

Dear Sir,

Some of our public journals seem disposed to criticize your speech at Worcester on Tuesday as not reflecting the sentiments of your state. For one I will say that I listened to your speech with much pleasure. I believe you take the only correct view of the subject, and I know you reflect the sentiment of a large majority of the people in this town. Even some of the most pro-slavery Democrats of the past are fully up to your promise today. And I sometimes think that after all we may yet have to rely upon the Democratic Party to prosecute this war to a successful result [some words obliterated] some of its moves seem to lack courage, such as the crisis demands. If you are ahead of public sentiment in your views, it is certainly refreshing to see a Statesman leading public opinion rather than being led by it, as has been to [sic] often the case. But be assured, if the public is not now fully up to your standard it soon will be, for the stern logic of events will soon [overcome] all time-serving calculations.

Yours most respectfully,

Hollis Loring[9]

Mr. Loring admired the man so much that he named his fourth child "Sumner." For his part, Mr. Sumner wrote to Hollis Loring's son Edward, "I remember your father well, respected him much."

Victor, too, was named for a prominent abolitionist. The family Bible recorded him as "Joseph Story Loring," named for Joseph Story, the Supreme Court Justice and Hollis Loring's legislative colleague who denounced slavery in the Massachusetts legislature and in the 1841 case of *U.S. vs. The Amistad*. In handwriting that resembled Victor's, the entry was amended later to "Victor Joseph," which agreed with his legal birth record.[11]

(left) Hollis Loring.
(right) Charles Sumner to Edward Loring, May 3, 1872. "I remember your father well, respected him much."

Apple orchards and shoemaking were the defining elements of Marlborough, and Hollis Loring made his living as a merchant, teacher, postmaster, and Justice of the Peace. He was elected to the legislature in his thirties,[12] and from then on, the Lorings stayed keenly aware of current events and their responsibility to influence them.

When the Civil War began, Victor's eldest brother, eighteen-year-old Selden Hollis, promptly volunteered. Their father protested at first, but he realized it would not do to support abolition and refuse to have his own son go to war for the cause.[13] It had been Hollis Loring, after all, who had chaired Marlborough's Committee of Ten and had written the preamble

As far as she could see in all directions were rows and rows of trees laden with fruit of crimson and gold. She parodied aloud: "Apples to right of her, Apples to left of her, Apples in front of her reddened and ripened."
The Solitary Horseman

to the declaration by Marlborough citizens in 1861, "setting forth in patriotic language the treasonable conduct of the Southern secessionists, and a resolution to support the Government with their lives and fortunes." He had also served on committees to secure uniforms and rifles for the local volunteers and provided a hall free of charge at the Exchange Building for their training.[14] The father relented.

Selden enlisted with the Thirtieth Massachusetts Volunteer Regiment in December 1861 and mustered in on January 3, 1862, for a three-year tour of duty. He was promoted in June from Sergeant Major to Second Lieutenant and served under the command of N. A. M. Dudley at New

Lt. Selden Hollis Loring. On the reverse: "I give this to Mother. Selden"

Orleans, Vicksburg, and Baton Rouge. (This was the same Dudley who fought Native tribes in the New Mexico and Arizona territories after the war. Buffalo Bill Cody served as his chief scout, and Dudley knew Sitting Bull well enough to discuss General Custer's death with him.)

Hollis Loring recommended Dudley for promotion to General in a letter to Charles Sumner: "My son has been under his command for more than a year and has ever spoken of him in his letters in the highest terms, both as a *man* and a *soldier*."[15] Dudley got the promotion, and Selden remained under his command until his disability discharge on August 3, 1864.

Hollis Loring did not go to war himself, but still, he did not survive it. Victor was six when his father suffered a stroke (one report said it was an epileptic fit) and died three days later, on February 20, 1865.[16] Victor's little brother "Willis" (William Lawrence) contracted encephalitis at nearly the same time and died one month later.[17]

Hollis Loring was only forty-seven at death, and the local paper extolled:

> Possessing a clear mind, energy, and good business talents, he raised himself by his own individual exertions to a place among the first men of the town, and his loss in the community will be deeply felt.[18]

It was the repetition of an old, family story. Victor's grandfather, Hollis Clark Loring, never knew his own father, and no story of his parentage survives. He was adopted by William Loring and his wife, Sarah, who named him and raised him in Marlborough. Similarly, Victor's father, Hollis Loring, lost his mother when he was only three months old, his father when he was nine, and he never knew his sister, who died young. He grew to adulthood under the guardianship of his stepmother, Catherine Wilkins Loring, who became the namesake of his own daughter and was a constant in the Loring home until she died on July 30, 1864, seven months before her ward, Hollis.[19]

"Grandfather lived until I came back from the war, then his heart stopped."
Here Comes the Sun!

"The fewer ancestors one has behind one the better ancestor one must make of oneself."
The Trail of Conflict

After his discharge, Victor's brother Selden married Sarah H. Albee, the daughter of Obadiah W. Albee, an educator and another of Hollis Loring's political colleagues.[20] It fell to Selden, as the eldest, to be the head of the family, but he had experienced a lot in the three years he had been away from home, maybe too much to settle down quietly in Marlborough again. Selden left for distant posts, and the next-elder brother, nineteen-year-old Edward, became the guardian of their sister Kate and the younger brothers: Charles, George, Frederick, and Victor.[21]

As a practical matter, six-year-old Victor was now in the care of his mother, Laura, and her older sisters, Louisa and Senia. Louisa Hitchcock never married and always made her home with the Lorings. Senia Hitchcock Howe lived next door between long marriages to two widowed shoemakers, but after the second died, she, too, moved in with the family and remained.

Hollis Loring had organized the Marlborough fire department, and his sons took that mission to heart. With the help of other neighborhood boys, they organized a hook and ladder company and created a machine for fighting fires. One time, they were the first to a fire and managed to put it out. A Mister Curtis of Marlborough wanted to reward them with leather belts embossed with their company's name on them, but he protested their preferred moniker of "Tough Nuts." The boys changed to the "Tigers" and got patent leather belts lettered in red with the name.[22]

Life in Marlborough contrasted sharply with the romance and adventure of Victor's absent brother. When Victor was eleven, Selden accepted a Colonel's commission in the Franco-Prussian war. Next, he was named to a series of consular posts in Hong Kong, China from 1873 to 1878—first, deputy consul, then vice consul, and finally, consul. He was at this post when a sweeping typhoon and its following tidal wave killed nearly 20,000 people in November 1874 and closed all business in the colony with devastating loss of property.[23]

The following March, he investigated a tragic fire aboard the Pacific Mail steamship *Japan* that foundered between Yokohama and Hong Kong.

His aunts had kept pace with the changes in the room. Their gowns were silvery grey with a suggestion of modishness. Sally's was much shorter than her sister's. She must be at least ten years older than his father. In his boyhood he had felt nearer to her in spirit than to her sterner sister.
Gay Courage

He determined that insufficient help had been rendered to the passengers for their escape, and great loss of life ensued due to fear, darkness of night, the fury of the seas, and the weight of the fleeing passengers' money belts.[24]

When they left Hong Kong, Selden and his wife, Sarah, (nicknamed, inexplicably, "Pete") finished a journey around the world, and Selden wrote detailed letters home.[25] Japan, Singapore, India, the Red Sea, Cairo, Alexandria, and Italy all came to life in sensitive description. Of the Taj Majal, he wrote,

> Did you ever build a castle in the air? Here is one brought down to earth and fixed for the wonder of the ages . . . whoever can behold the Taj without feeling a thrill that sends moisture to his eyes, has no sense of beauty in his soul.

And of the Sphinx:

> The great face was so sad. So longing, so patient. It was stone, but if ever image of stone thought, it was thinking. It was looking over and beyond everything of the present and far into the past. . . . All has passed away and left the stony dreamer solitary in the midst of a stranger new age and uncomprehended scenes.

While Selden Loring remained in Hong Kong, Edward Loring managed business at home. First, he enrolled at Yale,[26] finished his legal studies, and established himself at 12 Maverick Court in East Boston. He married Ella Harris in October 1871[27] with a child already on the way. William Hollis, named for Victor's father and grandfather, was born in February but died of a strep infection in April.[28]

Edward had the Loring estate appraised, purchased it from his mother, and then invested the proceeds to give her a steady income. Their home in Marlborough and an additional property in Hudson with four dwellings on it were valued at $13,000, and personal effects added an additional

Yet the treasures which he had picked up on his travels were there. Rugs from Arabian bazaars glowed like dusky jewels on the floor. There was a brass-bound chest from China, ivory carvings of unbelievable delicacy, a cabinet full. A mandarin coat of green, heavy with gold embroidery was flung over the back of a deep couch.
Gay Courage

$1000. Secure in her finances, Laura Loring moved the family to 70 East Newton Street in Boston.

Almost immediately, in August 1872, the one girl in the family, "Kate," married Barron Clinton Moulton, a lawyer from New Hampshire. Moulton was nearly twenty years older than Kate and only six years younger than her mother, but it was the first marriage for both, and the couple made their home with the Lorings. With aunts Louisa Hitchcock and Senia Howe, there was a full household of Lorings, Moultons, and Hitchcocks in the house on East Newton.

EIGHT GENERATIONS OF LORINGS

1. Thomas – England to Hingham, MA, 1634
2. John
3. Israel – minister
4. Jonathan – lawyer
5. William – American Revolution, farmer
6. Hollis Clark (adopted) – War of 1812, trader, legislator, Justice of the Peace
7. Hollis – abolitionist, merchant, legislator
8. Selden Hollis – Civil War, consul, lawyer

   Edward Day – lawyer

   Catherine Wilkins – married Moulton

   Sumner Winchester – died young

   Charles Frances – lawyer, politician, yachtsman

   George Albert – salesman

   Frederick Lester – clerk

   Victor Joseph – lawyer, politician, churchman

   William Lawrence – died young

Boston, 1872–1886

Charles Francis was the next Loring to undertake the law. He worked in Edward's office and moved in with him at the Maverick House. The Maverick was an eighty-room hotel on Noddle Island, a popular stop for travelers on the Cunard line, and a short ferry trip from Boston.

In May 1874, Charles attended the founding meeting of the East Boston Yacht Club, an organization for gentlemen owning yachts greater than twenty-five feet in length.[29] (His was a sloop, *Napoleon*.[30]) In a few years, he was named their Commodore and remained active in yachting thereafter. Victor was a rower and belonged to the Union Boat Club, but his brother Charles brought him into the world of yachts and yachtsmen.

As a youth, Victor attended the Boston Latin School. This was the school of Benjamin Franklin and Ralph Waldo Emerson, the school which, from Boston's earliest days, developed young men for attendance at Harvard. Victor commanded the schoolboy battalion and graduated in 1878,[31] but instead of continuing to Harvard with his classmates, he entered the newly opened Boston University Law School. He graduated with honors in 1881,[32] the same year that Emilie completed grammar school.

Victor was admitted to the Suffolk County Bar and replaced his brother Edward in the firm of Loring & Loring. As "C. F. Loring & V. J. Loring," they took offices at 20 Court Street, and Edward moved his practice to Waltham. When their sister's husband, Barron Clinton Moulton, joined the firm as senior partner in January 1883,[33] they became "Moulton, Loring & Loring," with offices at 17 Pemberton Square.

By then, Selden had returned from Hong Kong, graduated from Boston University's law school as Victor had, and set up his own practice and home in Somerville. The Loring brothers were four lawyers (Selden, Edward, Charles, and Victor), a clothing salesman (George), and a jewelry clerk (Fred).

Victor Joseph Loring, ca. 1881

"I'm too busy to fall in love, Senator. When I'm tied up in a legal case, and I mean tied, I think of nothing else. Women won't stand for that. Besides, I've never met one whom I've been sure I'd like to face across the breakfast table each morning for the rest of my life" "Some day, though, you'll meet a girl and suddenly it will be all over with you. You'll have to have her. You're that type." *Across the Years*

Victor specialized in corporation, life, and fire insurance law,[34] but he took common cases as well. Once, he represented a defendant whose horse had bitten the plaintiff as he was walking down Brattle Street. The judge ruled in favor of the defendant.[35] In another, his client sued to recover ten thousand dollars for injuries caused by being "hit by a bale of hay" in the Lowell railroad sheds, and he won again.[36] In addition to law, Victor served on policy committees for the Republican party and worked on several campaigns before running for office himself.

CHAPTER 8

Emilie and Victor

Boston and Vicinity, 1885–1891

Emilie Loring wrote thirty novels about couples meeting and falling in love. It was a feature of every book. It is maddening, therefore, not to know how her own romance with Victor began, although she left clues about that, as she did with the other events of her life.

In "Limousine Ladies," a 1918 short story, she wrote:

> He had loved her always, but she had been surrounded by a bevy of adorers and he was eight years older than she. Her father had known of his love but had counseled patience.[1]

The girl in that story was named "Betty," Emilie's nickname, and it was true that Victor was about eight years older than Emilie.[2] When did they meet?

From her first social season in 1885, Victor and Emilie crossed paths. The Bakers moved to Gloucester Street that year, and although the Lorings had already moved to Allston, they kept their house on the corner of Marlborough and Gloucester, one block from the Bakers. Emilie and Victor could have met on the street, at an amateur theatrical, or at any local event, and what came next might have been the start of their friendship and romance.

When the Bakers summered at Downer Landing in '85 and '86, Victor and his brother Charles were at Hull and Hyannis. The Lorings followed the boat races—yachts for Charles, sculls for Victor, who belonged to the Union Boat Club. If he was among the thousands who came to see the Downer Landing scull races, then he saw Emilie's brother, Robert, win

"I visited her home in college days. Her brother was my best friend."
Lighted Windows

Would he become a politician? He would be an ideal candidate for any office. Fearless, unshakable in his principles but— what would become of his law practice?
Fair Tomorrow

She had loved Neil from the moment she had seen him. She had loved his strength, his steel-like resistance to her the first two weeks of his visit. Later he had told her that he had decided that women should play no part in his life until he had made his professional reputation—then, then he had met her . . .
A Certain Crossroad, dedicated to V. J. L.

each time. When Robert gave his humorous declamation at the Boston Latin School in 1888, Victor was among the judges.[3]

Politics certainly played a role in their acquaintance. Angeline Peck, a first cousin to Emilie's mother, had married John Quincy Adams Brackett of Arlington. In the summer of 1887, the Bracketts and the Pecks attended a grand banquet in the Hotel Vendome, four blocks from the Bakers' home on Gloucester Street. The Royal Arcanum hosted the event, and Victor's brother, Charles F. Loring, presided over the evening, offering toasts and inviting notable guests to respond. Victor attended as the Republican candidate for senator from the eighth Suffolk district, a race that he eventually lost by a small margin in a hard-fought campaign.[4] His mother and the other Loring siblings also attended.[5]

For nearly two years, Brackett campaigned for governor on the Republican Party ticket, and Victor served as chairman of the Republican Committee of Ward 25 that worked to nominate (1889) and then elect (1890) him. Victor was a candidate for state senator, and political activities often placed the men in the same place at the same time. Throughout this period, the Bracketts and Bakers kept close ties. They attended each other's family celebrations and visited in one another's homes.

Social events may have brought Emilie and Victor together. Emilie attended a masquerade ball and supper that December 1887 in Berkeley Hall, at the corner of Tremont and Berkeley,[6] and both Emilie and Victor's sister, Kate Moulton, were "among those noticed" at the Boston and Maine ball in January.[7] The ball raised funds for the railroad relief association, and Victor was both a frequent representative of the railroad's legal interests and a staunch supporter of charitable works.

Victor followed his brother to prominence in the Royal Arcanum, a fraternal benefit society that sponsored public entertainments to benefit widows and orphans—a purpose the Bakers shared. They held dances, concerts, musicals, and dinners, and "every performance was crowded." In June 1888, Henry Clay Barnabee's Boston Opera Company presented a musical comedy under their auspices, for which Victor gave the welcome. Dancing followed, then a light meal, well into the wee hours of the morning.[8]

Business affairs may also have played a role. In 1889, when Emilie and Robert were on their voyage, Victor became president of a new stock company that took over the Saccarappa Leather Mill in Portland, Maine[9] and sold it the next year.[10] Did his apparently sudden interest in the leatherboard used to make book covers have anything to do with George Baker?

The entire period in Barnstable was echoed in elements of Emilie Loring's 1931 novel, *Fair Tomorrow*—a sick father, a lawyer from Boston, a legal case that focused their attention, and an experiment to test the evidence. From October to December 1889, Victor came often to Barnstable County in connection with a divorce case. His law firm represented Zoeth Higgins, from Truro,[11] against his wife, Fanny. Each accused the other of infidelity, and their sensational testimony filled the courtroom with onlookers and the newspapers with stories.

Mr. Higgins and three witnesses testified that they used a sledgehammer to break down the door when they discovered a Mr. Hurney in bed with Mrs. Higgins, "in costumes of a rather unconventional character." Mr. Hurney denied the charges, but Victor's cross-examination soon had him "completely at sea" about the details. The opposing counsel, Marcellus Coggan, presented two witnesses for Mrs. Higgins who testified they had seen Mr. Higgins "in a very compromising position" in a buggy with a seventeen-year-old girl.

Much to-do was made of whether the hall lighting was sufficient for the eyewitnesses' testimonies about what was going on inside the house to be true. Victor set up an experiment to test them that involved lights and curtains and people watching from various positions.[12] The final decision, in favor of Mr. Zoeth, was handed down in December—a much-publicized victory for Victor, who was still in the middle of a political campaign.

While the spotlight was on Victor, the *Boston Journal* ran a long, biographical article about him, extolling his oratorical ability, his "large business" as a lawyer, his staunch defense of fraternal and benevolent causes, and

No wonder he was a successful advocate, he had fire and personality plus. No editor would blue-pencil that story, Pamela thought as he answered the question.
Fair Tomorrow

"I object to this melodrama, your Honor. It is irrelevant to this case. I move that it be struck off the record."
Fair Tomorrow

Don't think I am not
thrilled by your legal
victory, I am. Read
of it in the paper just
before you came
. . . Congratulations—
Governor Mallory!"
Color stole under his
bronzed skin. "Now I
know what paper
you read."
Fair Tomorrow

his advocacy on behalf of all labor movements and institutions. "He will receive the votes of all good citizens in his district irrespective of party."[13]

Victor didn't receive their votes, and he lost the election. But J. Q. A. Brackett won for a one-year term, and in April 1890, "Miss Baker" from Barnstable visited Governor and Mrs. Brackett in Arlington. During her visit, the Governor attended a military ball in Cambridgeport,[14] where many "public men of note" joined more than one hundred dancing couples.

Two bachelors visited the Bakers in Barnstable that same month— James Karrick, whom Victor knew from the Puritan Club, and Louis Clark, the politician and yachtsman.[15] Newspaper locals were famously incomplete; did Victor visit along with them? Did either of them belong to Emilie's "bevy of admirers"?

Victor and Emilie were *both* at Beach Bluff's Hotel Preston in Swampscott in July 1891. (Swampscott is at the base of the North Shore "thumb" that includes Clifton and Marblehead.) Victor and Arthur Dakin, an attorney at Moulton, Loring & Loring[16] (and soon to be Victor's best man), arrived in time for the Fourth of July.[17] Emilie and her mother returned from Brattleboro and checked in at the Hotel Preston later that month.[18] They were fortunate to have a reservation; by then, every hotel room and cottage at Beach Bluff was occupied for the season. Martha Pollard (soon to be Emilie's maid of honor) hosted tennis parties and socials at nearby Clifton, where Emilie's Aunt and Uncle Spooner and Emilie's Bowker friends from church were also staying.[19]

True to the name "Beach Bluff," the newly renovated Hotel Preston sat high on a bluff overlooking a "magnificent beach."[20] Guests "went driving" in carriages, played tennis, and attended amateur theatricals. Every Thursday, the Eastern Yacht Club hosted a concert at its club house at Marblehead, which was attended by summer visitors all along the shore. "The broad piazzas were crowded in the evening with ladies from Clifton, Swampscott, Beach Bluff, Hotel Preston and Peaches Point."[21]

Marblehead's Nanepashemet Hotel hosted its first hop of the season on July thirty-first. "The spacious dining room was converted into a ballroom and was handsomely decorated with flowers and wild ferns, and the broad piazzas of the hotel were decorated with varied colored lanterns. A large number of cottagers from Beach Bluff, the Clifton House, Hotel Preston and Clifton Heights were present, and the toilets of the ladies were elegant and beautiful."[22] The guests danced from eight until midnight to music by the Salem Cadet Orchestra.[23]

Did Victor offer Emilie his coat on an unseasonably cool evening? Did he propose on a carriage ride, on the piazza during a dance at either the Hotel Preston or the Nanepashemet?

Emilie and her mother moved to the Hotel Huntington in September, and Rachel and Robert returned from Switzerland soon thereafter. Their visit to the Swiss oculist gave them hope for Robert's eyes, although "the cure was most tedious and uncertain."[24] The three siblings—Rachel, Emilie, and Robert—returned to Barnstable, their home for the past two years, and took some time together at the Globe Hotel.

So much had changed. Emilie would soon marry, and Robert had taken a job with the Edison Electrical Illuminating Company in Boston, where he would remain five years.[25] Rachel had written three more plays and been elected chairman of the Boston Amateur Dramatic Association.[26] Their days in Barnstable had ended. A new pattern of life awaited in Boston.

Emilie and Victor announced their engagement in the Boston and Barnstable newspapers,[27] and a few days later, Martha Pollard and Herbert Gale announced their engagement, too.[28] According to prevailing custom, newspaper announcements followed receipt of personal notes by family and friends. The best guess is that Victor asked Emilie to marry him at Marblehead, as subsequent events reinforce.

Their announcement came during Charles Francis Loring's campaign for one of nine positions on the Governor's Council. Victor's reputation as an attorney was well established, but his brother Charles was more prominent. He was a judge, a Mason, and a founding member of the Royal Arcanum, a fraternal life insurance organization which he served as

Supreme Regent.[29] Rallies, speeches, and meetings kept his name on the front page through his victory on November third.[30]

Ten days later, newspapers reported that Charles was fighting for his life, stricken with paralysis and heart failure.[31] Victor sent a signed, public correction that very afternoon: His brother had contracted rheumatism during the campaign, he said, and it had settled in his leg, "but his condition otherwise need cause no alarm.—Victor Loring."[32]

The situation was soon clarified. A clot in Charles' right leg had cut off circulation below the knee, and amputation of that portion seemed likely. Despite "great pain," he remained conscious, "quite cheerful and hopeful."[33]

A team of three doctors, including the Chief Surgeon at Massachusetts General Hospital, removed the leg on November sixteenth at the Loring home in Melrose.[34] Charles was "in comfortable condition,[35] and by the end of the month, his family expressed confidence in his speedy recovery.[36] With this good prognosis, Victor and Emilie's wedding would take place on Wednesday, December ninth, in the Second Unitarian Church at the northeast corner of Copley Square.[37]

Second Church, Boston; December 9, 1891

What a night! The half moon hung in the sky like a broken silver plaque against an indigo velvet canopy sprinkled with gilt stars above shadowy ridges of hills. The earth was lightly clothed in bridal white. We Ride the Gale!

The sun had already set, and a half moon was aloft[38] when guests entered the sanctuary on Boylston Street, sweeping the fair, evening breeze with them into the cozy brownstone. Festoons of yellow chrysanthemums spiced the air and brightened stately rows of black walnut pews. Palms and ferns made a lush backdrop for the glow of sunny blossoms at the chancel rail. The ushers were Herbert Gale, James Karrick, Henry Babcock, and three physicians: Henry Dwight, and the brothers Edwin and Frederick Jack from Dr. Miner's church and the Boston Latin School.[39]

George Baker's old friend Mr. Howard M. Dow was at the organ, playing bright, theatrical pieces. He had known Emilie from her birth, those early days when he accompanied George Baker and Henry Clay Barnabee on the stage. In the intervening years, Dow had become an accompanist of renown and played regularly for the Bostonians as well as Adelina Patti, the famous opera star.[40]

Among the selections he played that evening was the overture from *Martha*. Flotow's perennially popular opera was scheduled to open the next night at the Boston Theatre,[41] which made it a timely choice; and it was the name of Emilie's maid of honor, which made it a fitting choice; but it was also a sentimental choice. *Martha* had played at Music Hall when Emilie was a teen and her father's good friend George Frothingham acted the role of the sheriff.[42] More than that, it was the sort of music that represented George's theatrical taste and the same that would characterize Emilie's later writing. A tale of mistaken identities, romance, and humor, *Martha* was vivacious, charming, and fresh.[43]

At six-thirty, Victor and his best man, Arthur Dakin, appeared at the foot of the chancel. Emilie's maid of honor, Martha Pollard, stepped forward in a soft pink and amethyst gown of embroidered mousseline de soie, her bouquet a cluster of white roses. The opening strains of Lachner's "Marche Celebre"[44] signaled the congregation to stand, and Emilie, on the arm of her brother Robert, started up the aisle.

Emilie wore a white crepe gown with demi-train, gathered to the waist in a V-shaped sash of pearls. The neckline was also trimmed with pearls and cut slightly décolleté to display Victor's wedding gift to best advantage: an enameled, pansy pendant set with diamonds. She wore a fingertip veil of tulle gathered with white orange blossoms and carried a simple bouquet of white, Cornelia Cook tea roses.[45]

It was like walking through Victor's and her histories. There, on the left, were her father's publishing and literary friends: Matthew and Julia Mayhew, of course; and William C. Ulman, the retired bookbinder and his wife from the Mercantile Library Association days. Another familiar face belonged to Mrs. Norris, who had hosted the Bakers' amateur theatricals in her parlor, and still further on were Emilie's longtime chums: Lizzie and George Hallet from the Cape, childhood playmate Beth McClannin, and the sisters Hattie and Susie Bowker from church in the Back Bay.

"She is a picture in her pearl-beaded white frock. Was there ever a lovelier bride, I wonder?"
Here Comes the Sun

(left) Victor J. Loring; (right) Emilie Baker Loring. December 9, 1891

Distinguished, public figures lined both sides of the aisle. The Bakers' cousin-in-law, the Honorable John Quincy Adams Brackett, was in attendance with his wife Angie and son John. Across the aisle sat attorney, legislator and yachtsman Louis M. Clark, physician Dr. Henry Barnes who had operated on Victor's brother, William Baldwin of the Boston Young Men's Christian Union, and numerous professional friends.

Near the front of the church awaited the members of four generations of both families. Of the oldest generation, only Great Aunt Ursula Remick, the widow of Grandmother Mary Ann Baker's brother John, was able to attend. Then came Uncle Walter, Emma, and their children, Uncle Charles Tappan Baker and his family, and Aunt Sarah (Baker) Hull. The Boles family was led by Uncle Albert and his wife Annie, who brought their five-year-old daughter Mary Emily. Uncle Edward and his wife, Ida, made a large group with their daughter Madeline, Ida's sister Pauline (Mrs. Daniel Webster Spooner) and Ida's mother, Fanny (Mrs. J. H. W. Huckins).[46]

Finally, in the front row, stood Emilie's sister Rachel and their mother, Emily Baker. In her second year of mourning, Emilie's mother wore a gown of black silk and carried a nosegay of violets in remembrance of her husband George. Rachel wore "an exquisite French creation" of pearl-gray crepe and also carried violets.[47]

The Lorings made an impressive group on the right side of the aisle: Selden, the former consul and present attorney with his wife, Sarah; George, now an architect, and Edward an attorney; then Catherine and her husband, Victor's partner Barron Moulton. Of the siblings, only Charles Francis was missing, as he was too ill to leave his bed. At the head of the family, as she had remained for more than twenty-five years, sat Victor's mother, Madam (Laura) Loring.[48]

The Reverend Edward A. Horton officiated, as he had for George Baker's funeral one year before, assisted by the Reverend Sherrod Soule of the Congregational Church in Beverly.[49] The couple exchanged their vows, and, no one forbidding the banns, the marriage of Miss Maria Emily Baker to Mr. Victor Joseph Loring was declared. Out into the evening air they poured, across Copley Square to the Hotel Huntington where a lively reception awaited.

The Huntington's parlors were filled with palms and ferns in profusion. Yellow chrysanthemums covered the dark mantels and gleaming tables. Upstairs, a large room in the family apartment filled with gifts, including a Bible from Victor's mother, inscribed "To Victor and M. Emily." The couple received their guests in the large drawing room and then proceeded to a small parlor for an "elaborate supper" overseen by the Huntington's able steward, Mr. Kendall Damon.[50] Toasts were offered, best wishes and congratulations were roundly proclaimed, and Miss Bessie Baker was now Mrs. Victor J. Loring.

After that nothing seemed real to her, nothing but Michael's firm clasp of her hand, his voice saying, "I do," the feel of a ring on her finger, a sonorously rich voice intoning solemnly: "Those whom God hath joined together let no man put asunder." The feeling of unreality persisted as she poured tea for the wedding party in the library.
We Ride the Gale!

Boston and Newton, 1892

"Any nurseryman
will tell you that
young trees grow
more sturdy by being
transplanted. It was a
wrench to tear away
from old ties and
old customs, but I've
never been sorry.
The break made me
world-minded."
Lighted Windows

It was more than a change of name. It was a change of society. The Boston of Emilie's girlhood was the richly creative, expressive world of publishing and theater. It was a world in which the finest actors performed afternoon matinees in a friend's parlor, and prominent authors wrote pieces for little children. Now, she stepped into the parallel world of politics and public service, a world of sophistication, with position and customs properly observed. From now on, she would meet the most important members of government and society and rub elbows with actors on the public stage instead of the theater stage.

Victor and Emilie planned to leave on their wedding tour and return for an "at home" on Thursday, February fourth.[51] But that plan had to change.

Charles Loring's leg had recovered, but his heart had not.[52] Despite a brief rally, and after much suffering, his heart finally gave out on Tuesday, January 26, 1892.[53] When the representatives at the State House received the news, they read a resolution in his honor: "Hon. Charles F. Loring, councillor-elect [sic] of the Commonwealth . . . a valued citizen, beloved and respected for his noble personal traits and unspotted integrity of character, and one who gave promise of distinguished service to the Commonwealth." A committee of seven was appointed to represent the House at his funeral, and then the entire body adjourned and left the chambers "out of respect for his memory."[54] The *Boston Courier* announced that Victor and Emilie would not receive guests the following week as planned.

Four days later, the family gathered for a short, private service at Charles' house in Melrose. The Reverend J. G. Taylor of the Melrose Highlands Congregational Church read prayers and scriptures, and all then proceeded to the Melrose Congregational Church for a public service at two o'clock. "Business in the town was suspended, flags on public buildings were at half-mast, and the bells were tolled."[55]

The church was entirely filled with friends, family, and large delegations from the many civic organizations of which Charles had been a part.

His casket was covered first in broadcloth and then with flowers so numerous that they overflowed to the surrounding area. The Reverend George A. Gordon of the Old South church in Boston conducted the services and was assisted by Reverend A. G. Bale of the Melrose Congregational Church as well as by the Reverend Taylor. Reverend Gordon's eulogy extolled "the honorable and upright life the deceased had led," and "his manly qualities and gentle and loving disposition."

One final time, friends and family passed by the casket and gazed upon Charles' face. Last came his brothers with their wives. His mother did not attend. Emilie walked between Edward and Selden, while Victor waited to the last and escorted Charles' wife and daughters—five-year-old Grace and two-year-old Katherine. Three members of the Royal Arcanum, and one representative each of the Home Circle, Governor's Council, and Masonic Lodge then bore the casket from the church. It was conveyed to Wyoming Cemetery where the Regent and chaplain of the Royal Arcanum read that organization's funeral ritual.[56]

As he stood with the others at Charles' funeral, how well did Victor's older brother Selden comprehend his own health problems? Struggling with the symptoms of Bright's disease, a severe inflammation of the kidneys, Selden Hollis Loring succumbed on February twenty-eighth, three days after what would have been his brother Charles' thirty-ninth birthday.

This had happened before. Their father had died, and four weeks later, so did their brother Willis. Now, four weeks after his brother Charles' death, Selden was gone, too. He was only forty-eight years old—a year older than his father, Hollis Loring, had been when he died.

It would be hard to say which of the Loring brothers, Charles or Selden, was better known. While Charles was especially prominent in Massachusetts political circles, Selden's accomplishments were in the Army, Navy, and diplomatic service. Charles was the competitive yachtsman, Selden the reflective adventurer.

The Military Order of the Loyal Legion took charge of Selden's funeral, which commenced at the New Old South Church on the corner

"Who but a dreamer like you expects anything but shadows after death? We begin life with a cell, we will end when life goes out of it," interrupted the Contessa bitterly. Christopher Wynne shook his head. "I can't believe that. You wouldn't had you seen life go out as many times as I have. You would be convinced that unused vitality and strength and experience won by valiant living was of use somewhere. There is no waste in nature."
Swift Water

He spoke tenderly of his brother, of what his loss had meant to him. He told of some of their pranks and chuckled at the memory.
As Long as I Live

of Dartmouth and Boylston at noon on Tuesday, March first. His coffin was preceded by two drummers and bugler, the drums rolling until the coffin came to rest at the chancel. Uniformed soldiers followed with state and national colors, coming to rest on either side of the presented casket. At the conclusion of the service, a cornetist played "Lost Chord," and the casket returned down the aisle, stopping halfway for "Taps."[57]

The pallbearers were an illustrious group representing Selden's history of wartime service. His former commander, Brigadier General Nathan A. M. Dudley, served with two other companions of the Loyal Legion, two members of the Grand Army of the Republic (GAR), two members of the Royal Arcanum, and one member of the Sons of the American Revolution, of which Selden was a founding member.[58]

Five of the nine Loring children survived, from Edward at forty-five to Victor, whose January birthday had brought him to thirty-three. Their father died at forty-seven, their grandfather at thirty-five, and now Charles and Selden, the most distinguished of the brothers, had died so young and so close together.

Selden gave his estate on Ivaloo Street in Somerville to his mother until her death with provision that it would then be transferred to his wife, "Pete"—Sarah Howard Loring. The remainder of the estate was left immediately in Sarah's possession, and Victor signed the appraisal papers as Justice of the Peace.

Emilie's family was next to grieve. In Newton, Edward Melville Boles lay paralyzed. Three months into their marriage, Emilie and Victor sought quarters nearby for themselves and the Bakers. The Reverend Lemuel Barnes of Newton Centre left for a trip to Palestine,[59] and the couple arranged to rent his furnished home during the absence. The house was at the corner of Cypress and Parker, just south of Beacon Street and a twenty-five-minute ride by train or carriage from Boston. The family moved in on March tenth,[60] and Emilie and Rachel announced that they would receive visitors on Thursday afternoons, but that was not to be.

Edward passed away the next day, only thirty-seven years old. He was buried at Forest Hills Cemetery.[61]

Within the space of forty-seven days, Victor and Emilie had buried three close family members. Instead of beginning their married life with congratulatory receptions, they attended bedsides and funerals.

As if to balance the ledger, a season of celebrations followed. James Karrick and Supreme Court Justice Brewer's daughter, Henrietta Louise, announced their engagement on Valentine's Day and scheduled the wedding for the day after Easter, in Washington, D.C. Victor and Emilie traveled to the Capitol and checked into the original Shoreham Hotel at 15th and H Streets, immediately northwest of the White House.[62]

The wedding took place in St. John's Episcopal Church, opposite the White House, with a commensurately formal ceremony. The exclusive reception afterward placed the Lorings among the couple's most intimate friends and important guests, including all but one of the Supreme Court Justices and a large representation of President Cleveland's cabinet.[63] The bride and groom left on an extended wedding journey to Europe and spent much of the ensuing summer aboard Karrick's yacht, *The Enigma*.

Victor and Emilie returned to Newton Centre[64] in time to celebrate the May birth of Albert and Annie's fourth child, a daughter named Rachel Elizabeth Boles. They now had a full complement of children named for the Baker siblings—Mary Emily, Robert Melville, and Rachel Elizabeth.

Marblehead, 1892–1893

Martha Pollard and Herbert Gale were wed at the Pollards' summer home at Clifton, on the Marblehead peninsula.[65] Clifton in late September was a happy mix of elegant surroundings and a lingering, vacation atmosphere. Uncle Edward's wife Ida was already at the Clifton House with her daughter Madeline and her sister Pauline (Mrs. Daniel Webster Spooner),

"Marriage means . . . love. Love which is a flame, which burns and hurts. Which makes one radiantly happy and unbearably miserable. Which carries one over a sea of trouble as if one were riding a surf-board through breakers. It means companionship and sharing joy and sorrow and responsibilities and—and having children and growing old together. Husband and wife against the world."
We Ride the Gale!

"I was winding up some business so that I could take a vacation for the first time in years, had interested Tod Kent in the location as a summer port for his cruiser, The Sphinx . . ."
Give Me One Summer

as were a selection of Bracketts, Moultons, Lorings, Bowkers, and Pratts from Boston.

As the owner of New England's "largest and most enterprising" whole-sale liquor business,[66] Marshall Pollard had numerous friends and associates, and John Gale, a prominent, shoe manufacturer and bank president, had no fewer. Six special railcars delivered more than five hundred guests to the front lawn of the mansion where a profusion of spruces, tropical shrubs, and palms provided a living backdrop for the red-carpet entrance and white marquee. A twenty-five-piece, military band played "Hail to the Chief" at the arrival of Governor William Russell and continued to entertain as Joseph Jefferson, the famous actor of "Rip Van Winkle" fame,[67] and many other notables took their seats. Following the nuptials, breakfast was served on the lawn, and guests enjoyed their panoramic view of the ocean.[68]

Emilie was clearly in the upper crust of society now, and these early years of marriage allowed her to enjoy it thoroughly. She and Victor rented Mr. Everett's house on Parker Street in Newton Centre again[69] but returned to Boston for the winter season. The Congregational Club held a huge gathering at Music Hall on Pilgrim's Day with Senator Henry Cabot Lodge as the speaker. Henry J. Byron's long-running comedy, *Our Boys* was at the Boston Museum, and, after a year in New York, the Bostonians had returned to the Tremont Theater for a limited, two- week engagement of *Robin Hood*.[70] Tickets sold fast, with Henry Clay Barnabee on the bill in his popular role as the Sheriff of Nottingham and George Frothingham as Friar Tuck.[71]

Even after the holidays, the Lorings returned often to Boston. Victor was a member of the Boston Art Club, an organization of men whose appreciations for good art and good food were equally well expressed. The club sponsored multiple exhibitions throughout the year in their gallery at Dartmouth and Newbury, each beginning with a reception for club members and followed by public display.

In June, the Boston Society of Architects displayed a selection of proposals for the aesthetic improvement of Copley Square. The public was

The girls would be in exciting wraps and adorable high-heeled slippers, the black dress clothes of the men foils for their satin and cloth of gold frocks. Scent of gardenias . . . Masculine hands lingering as they drew fur collars about bare shoulders; masculine eyes disturbingly dark and demanding across small candle-lighted tables; masculine heads bent to uplifted faces as two bodies, almost one, drifted and swayed to the smooth, mellow lure of horns, the singing of strings which set blood racing and pulses throbbing.

Hilltops Clear

encouraged to stop by, view the proposals, and vote for a favorite. The winner was a circular park with a fountain at its center and a walkway surrounding the whole,[72] but the architects imposed their own preferences in the end, and the new park was planned as today's Copley Square.

During summer months, Boston expected to be sweltering in oppressive heat. It was an annual phenomenon that triggered society's universal exodus from the city. Coastal hotels usually opened during the first, hot weeks of June and remained filled during even hotter July and muggy, sticky August. It wasn't until September that they reluctantly released their guests to return to their homes and businesses.

Victor and Emilie returned to Marblehead for their vacation and stayed with Mrs. Baker, Rachel, and Robert at the filled-to-brimming, Nanepashemet Hotel. Martha and Herbert Gale occupied one of the Pollard cottages, close by at Clifton, to make it a summer reunion of newlyweds.[73]

Regarded as the principal hotel on the Marblehead Neck, the Nanepashemet commanded expansive views of the sea. The name came from an Indian chieftain of the region, and it was joked that "but one man ever tried to pronounce it, and he died the day after, of a broken jaw."[74] An uncharacteristically cool June delayed some arrivals to the "Neck," but hot weather and the Victor Lorings appeared just in time for the yacht races.

Maybe only in heritage-conscious Boston would the connection have been recognized, but among Victor's many Loring cousins were William Caleb and Augustus Peabody Loring. Like Victor, they represented the eighth generation of Lorings in America, beginning with Thomas in 1634. The cousins diverged at the third generation with Victor's branch moving westward to Sudbury and Marlborough and the other branch remaining at Hull and Beverly. Somehow, though, their paths mirrored one another.

Victor was born in 1859, Augustus in 1857. Both graduated from law school and were admitted to the Suffolk Bar in the same year, 1881. Their older brothers, William Caleb and Charles Francis, were admitted to the Suffolk Bar within a year of one another, in 1873 and 1874. The Lorings' offices were in Pemberton Square, Augustus in number eleven and Victor

"Somewhere I read that the hotter the day the hotter the tea should be for refreshment." *I Hear Adventure Calling*

initially occupying the former office of Augustus' father, Supreme Court Justice Caleb William Loring, at number seventeen. Both had homes on Marlborough Street, Victor at 364 and Augustus at 277. Augustus wrote *A Trustee's Handbook* and advised the railroads on land acquisitions and routes. Victor took many legal trust cases and represented the Boston and Maine Railroad in several disputes. Victor ran for state senate, and Augustus was elected to the state senate from his district. Victor was an officer in the Boston Art Club at the same time that Augustus' grandfather, Charles Greely Loring, was the director of Boston's Museum of Fine Arts.

Charles Francis, William, and Augustus all belonged to the Eastern Yacht Club, and all attended an 1887 testimonial given in honor of Charles J. Paine and Edward Burgess for successfully defending the America's cup for three years in a row. Augustus, who lived at Beverly, purchased and remodeled racing yachts, including the famous, 63-foot schooner yacht *Barbara*[75] and the first Q-Class boat *Orestes*,[76] designed by Burgess' son Starling (who was also Augustus' ward) at Marblehead.[77]

The relationship between Victor and his Beverly cousins is unclear. Victor's friend Louis M. Clark was president of the Massachusetts Yacht Racing Association, belonged to the Eastern club, and judged many yachting contests. When Victor and Emilie married, they not only chose a minister from Beverly but also came to Marblehead each season, in time for the yacht races.

Beyond yachting, Marblehead offered the same activities they had enjoyed one year before at Swampscott: croquet, tennis, ball games, and weekly band concerts. Theatrical entertainments brought vacationers indoors after driving, fishing, and "surf bathing." In the evenings, there were card parties and dances for young and old alike.[78] The Bakers checked in at the quieter Hood Hotel at Nahant for a spell in July and gave Emilie and Victor some time to themselves.

In August, an early return of blustery, cold weather brought out topcoats, even during daylight hours, and the crowds began to thin.

Treacherous surf ended boating, fishing, and yachting contests, and the annual, outdoor hop was cancelled. At Nahant, inventive vacationers made the best of it, holding camera parties to take snapshots of the tossing surf,[79] but it was clear that the season was over.

Boston, 1893–1894

The Lorings and Bakers returned to Boston this time, instead of Newton Centre, and Mrs. Baker re-opened the Bakers' three-story house at 44 Gloucester. Like a theater curtain, the home had closed with George Baker at the head of the family before its move to the Cape, and now it reopened, two years later, with Emilie, Mrs. Baker, Rachel, and Robert all in place but Victor at the head instead of George. The cast had changed, but the action was familiar.

Emilie's sister Rachel was the family's resident playwright. Their Uncle Walter published her third and fourth plays, *A King's Daughter* and *Mr. Bob*, which Uncle Walter Baker published from Baker's Plays at 2 Winter Street. Robert and The Proscenium Club of Roxbury gave the first perfor-mance of *Mr. Bob* on April 27, 1894, unaware that it would become the second-best-selling amateur drama of all time, exceeded only by George M. Baker's *Among the Breakers*.[80]

Following her father's formula, Rachel's *Mr. Bob* was a story of confused identities in which a female visitor with the nickname of Bob is confused first as a suitor for the niece of the house and then with a clerk whose business at the home is unknown to all. Before they are through, each character has been mistaken for another, and even a valise believed to hold business briefs is filled with cats instead. The butt of the jokes is a lawyer like Victor who appreciates fine cigars and spends entirely too much time at yacht racing, although he wins the heart of the girl in the end. "We hasn't had so much fun in this house for weeks," says the maid. "It is as good as the theater."[81]

Springtime revealed that Emilie was pregnant, and the family began to consider new living arrangements. Victor and Emilie wanted a place in

Brooke couldn't see her mother's face. Was she remem-bering the evenings they had sat about the fire like this when her husband had been the sun about which all their lives revolved?
With Banners

the country, Mrs. Baker wanted to remain close to her children, and it was time for Robert, at twenty-seven, to have a place of his own.

By Emilie's birthday in September, they had found the answer to all: a three-acre lot on Florence Avenue in Wellesley Hills. There was room for two houses, one for the Lorings and another for the Bakers, with a stable and gardens between. The land was purchased, and construction began.

Meanwhile, law and politics filled Victor's schedule. Between cases at Moulton, Loring & Loring, he had helped the Republican Committee to elect Frederick T. Greenhalge to a first term as governor in 1893 and then watched as the governor's tenure encountered difficulty. More than five thousand demonstrators marched on the State House in February, demanding unemployment subsidies. The mob was quieted by the governor's personal reassurances, and the crowd dispersed.

It was in relief and jubilation, then, that Victor joined more than one hundred well-known Republicans of "that stalwart old republican organization," the Middlesex Club, at the Parker House to celebrate a resounding victory in Governor Greenhalge's election to a second term in November 1894. After a particularly nasty campaign, the Democratic political machine, Tammany Hall, was set back by the election of a Republican majority to Congress, and ex-Governor and Middlesex Club President Brackett rejoiced, "In the next congress there will be but a solitary democrat from New England, and he will be entirely harmless." The jubilation continued in remarks by Senator Henry Cabot Lodge and several congressmen, the final speaker concluding that, "the American people are entitled to diplomas for a thorough understanding of democratic promises and fulfillment."[82]

A few weeks later, Thanksgiving Day, November twenty-ninth, Emilie gave birth to Robert Melville Loring in their home at 44 Gloucester Street.[83] He was the third Robert Melville in the family, following Emilie's brother, Robert Melville Baker, and her five-year-old cousin, Robert Melville Boles. The baby was light-haired and healthy, and his birth brought the beginning of a cherished role for Emilie. Now, she would be known not only as Bessie, Betty, or Mrs. Loring, but also as "Mother."

"The papers are full of stories of bribery an' corruption in politics. If you could git the young men growin' up to think it more manly to be straight than to be lawbreakers an' to set to an' take hold of things, mark-my-words, 'twould be the dawn of a new day . . ."
Here Comes the Sun!

A mother's love and pride in a child was born with the child, wasn't it?
Today is Yours

Emilie and Her Son, Robert Melville Loring

ACT THREE:
"Mother"

"I married a lawyer, forgot about the making of plays and books and became absorbed in keeping my family well, happy and efficient."

—Emilie Loring

Emilie with Robert and Selden, 1899

CHAPTER 9

Homemaking and Motherhood

Wellesley Hills, 1895–1899

The Lorings' new home at Wellesley Hills was two stops west of Newton on the Boston & Albany Railroad, a suburb by location only, not at heart: "Wellesley is Boston. The relation of this town to the capital is of the same nature as the arm to the body. It is a part of it."[1]

By carriage, the trip took a little less than an hour, and by train, just twenty minutes.[2] North of the tracks were The Hundreds, an expanse of dense woods that marked the transition from city to country. Numerous brooks flowed through the woods and fed into Morse's Pond and Lake Waban, where the campus of Wellesley College was located.[3]

Wellesley included the Hills, Fells, Fens, Falls, and Village, with large plots of land at lower prices than in Boston. With easy access to the city's cultural and social opportunities, Wellesley provided the principal amenities within its own borders: good roads, schools, electricity, water, sidewalks, churches, clubs, a library, and efficient, municipal government. Within twenty years, the population would double to nearly five thousand, and land values would quadruple. It was, in short, "a harmonious, pleasant community, small enough to escape cliques and large enough to allow all the advantages which numbers and wealth admit."[4]

The Lorings' new house was on the last lot at the southwest end of Florence Avenue. Designed by architect Lewis H. Bacon and built by E. B. Newhall, the home was a 55-by-33-foot Dutch Colonial with a gambrel roof, bay windows and dormers, a side porch, and six wide steps leading to the porch and front door. One step inside revealed a broad entrance hall with stairs ahead and openings to either side. Through the left opening was the drawing room with two walls of built-in bookcases, a fireplace straight ahead, and a door leading outside to the side porch. Diamonds

"Of course, there is heartache, and suffering, and even wickedness, I suppose, but one doesn't run into it at every turn as one does in the city . . ."
With Banners

And every family needed a house in which to spread out, and blazing logs around which to gather and exchange confidences, her thoughts ran on. People slipped aside their masks in a room lighted only by the flames on the hearth.
With Banners

"To me home is not merely a convenience, a sentiment; it is a ruling passion."
With Banners

of leaded glass ornamented the curved, bay window on the left wall, and a window seat ran its full length. The firebox was made of brick, but the large mantel and chimney were painted creamy white to match the woodwork throughout the house. A small clock, an iron lion, and family photos rested atop the mantel, and hung above was the wintry portrait of a couple sitting close together in a sleigh. Area rugs warmed the wooden floors, and woven curtains at the doorway stopped cold drafts from entering when the front door was opened.

To the right of the front entry was, first, a small study whose leaded-glass windows with fleur-de-lis beheld the arrival of guests, and beyond that was the dining room with its own, cozy fireplace. Down a short hallway was a veritable routing center, with a powder room, stairs to the second-floor nursery and third-floor servants' quarters, a door leading to the kitchen, and one opening into a laundry at the rear of the house. Ornate wallpaper in the entry hall continued up the broad, curved stairway that had small windows and built-in bookshelves at its turn. At the top of the stairs, a hallway ran the full length of the house, and doors

Loring Home in Wellesley Hills, Massachusetts

Wellesley Hills Entry and Parlor

"Your brother said to me just before we left the apartment, 'I'm not afraid for Prue. She'll make a home wherever she is. She's like her mother.'" She almost smiled. "'Especially,' he said, 'if she can find rooms to re-paper.'"
Hilltops Clear

opened to five bedrooms and three baths. Some rooms had window seats, and two had a fireplace, but most had built-in bookcases, and one had a special detail: secret drawers hidden behind its volumes.[5]

The front windows looked south over fruit trees and a grassy slope of lawn, while the back windows faced the gardens, pine trees, a gambrel-roofed stable with quarters to house the stable boys, and "Burr Croft," the newly built Baker home next door.

"It isn't the garden and plants and bookshelves in themselves, it's what they stand for: safety, stability."
Across the Years

Now a father, Victor wrote a new will. He left everything to Emilie, who would also be his executrix, and expressly excluded his son and all future children—and their heirs—from any claim on the estate. He gave Emilie the unrestrained "possession and enjoyment" of his property, then concluded, "I nevertheless desire her to comply with my wishes expressed in a certain paper which I have already drawn up and which will be found among my papers at the time of my decease." This request was not, however, "in any sense legally obligatory."[6]

"They were all 'his babies'; that is what his patients call themselves when they grow up. He is a child specialist. Their mothers consulted him about them, probably until they were ten or twelve years old. They never forget him."
We Ride the Gale!

"She is fascinating, so modern, so gay. I had wondered why she is unmarried."
"It's the old story ... His wife has been a hopeless invalid for years, mentally gone. Now he is one of the biggest men in his line ..."
We Ride the Gale!

By the fall of 1896, Emilie's friend Beth McClannin was married, Rachel and Robert were both engaged, and Emilie was pregnant again. Beth had married Dr. Charles Gilmore Kerley of New York, a renowned pediatrician and child psychologist who was ten years her senior. As Emilie had done, Beth transitioned from the life of the theater, where her father, Robert F. McClannin, still performed, and entered her husband's life of social and philanthropic activities.

Rachel's romance was less conventional. John Elbridge Gale was the middle-aged father of Herbert Gale, who had ushered at Emilie's wedding and subsequently married Martha Pollard, Emilie's maid of honor. The Bakers and Lorings were well-to-do, but the scale of John Gale's fortune was on a different level altogether.

John began with no resources of his own. At fourteen, he went by himself to Portsmouth, New Hampshire, put himself through high school, and clerked at night. Five years later, he started the Gale Shoe Manufacturing Company, and before he was thirty, his personal wealth was estimated at more than eighty thousand dollars. He sold one of his homes to his younger brother for ten thousand dollars—a house so large that, with renovations, it was made into a hospital.[7]

Sales at the shoe company exceeded one million dollars in 1884 and grew so much that he expanded to a second factory, the Exeter Boot and Shoe Company, which his brother Stephen ran in Exeter, New Hampshire, and then a third, which was supervised by his son Herbert. When John left behind the day-to-day shoe business, he helped to start the Second National Bank of Haverhill, which he served the rest of his life as both president and director. Three shoe factories, a bank presidency, and a reputation for integrity, deep kindness, and long-valued friendships made him wealthy in every respect, "a patrician gentleman of the Old School,"[8] a marriage prospect of the highest sort.

There were barriers, to be sure. Rachel was nearer Herbert's age than his father's, and besides, John Gale was still married to Herbert's mother.

Mary Gale, mother to all three Gale children, was a long-term resident of the McLean Insane Asylum in Somerville. Although the children were grown, and John lived a widower's life, he was not free to court a new bride until early in January 1895 when Mary died of heart valve disease.

John left a month later, on one of Raymond and Whitcomb's rail journeys for travelers "of means and refinement." Traveling in an elegant, Pullman palace car, he stopped first in New Orleans for Mardi Gras and continued on a several-month tour of the southern cities of Mexico.[9] One year after his return, in July 1896, he and Rachel announced their engagement.

In the days prior to their wedding, the bark *Sarah*, which Emilie and Robert had taken to the Azores, met with great storms on a voyage to France and sank.[10] The immediate significance to Rachel and John was that their honeymoon trip was scheduled to depart across the same, turbulent waters in just a few days' time. On the other hand, their tickets were for the *Normannia*, a major ocean liner that was carrying over three million dollars in gold for the gold reserve of the United States treasury. If it was sturdy enough to deliver that cargo safely, they could be confident about their voyage.[11]

Rachel and John were married at noon on Tuesday, September 29, 1896, at Burr Croft, Mrs. Baker's estate next door to Emilie and Victor. The midday sun shone through the bay window of the drawing room, festooned with palms and ferns, and a small orchestra played.[12]

The "intimate" gathering of forty included only family and close friends. Among them were ex-governor Brackett, both of John Gale's sons (Herbert and Ernest), John's distinguished brother General Stephen Gale, and leaders of the leather and financial industries. Robert Baker's newly betrothed, Mary Pratt of Quincy, attended with her brother Edwin, who was also a leather dealer, and Louise Hallet[13] came in from the Cape. Their wedding gifts were sophisticated and bountiful, including "silver and cut glass without limit."[14]

Rachel wore ivory satin, her bouquet the simple green and petite white of lilies of the valley. The Reverend Edward A. Horton from Second

"Nothing old about the way he's looking at her. It's still being done that way by the youngsters."
We Ride the Gale!

Church in Boston recited the marriage ceremony, and John's son Herbert stood up with him as best man, with no bridesmaid for Rachel.[15]

Afterward, the wedding guests walked the short distance from Burr Croft to Emilie and Victor's house next door. East winds brought dark clouds, but rain and storms were not expected until well after dark. Seven months pregnant, Emilie supervised the "wedding breakfast" and then sped the newlyweds on to New York and the *Normannia*.[16]

The new Mr. and Mrs. Gale departed Thursday amid reports of hurricane-force winds wreaking havoc in Washington and Pennsylvania. Storm signals were posted all along the New England coast, and ahead awaited immense gales and high seas. When it reached the English Channel, the storm sank a schooner, swept crews overboard, set a lightship adrift,

John and Rachel Baker Gale

and tore one hundred feet of stone seawall from the coast at Ilfracombe.[17] Amidst sixty-foot seas and on-shore flooding, the sturdy *Normannia* arrived safely at Plymouth and proceeded on time to Cherbourg, France and Hamburg, Germany.[18]

Rachel and John remained in Europe nearly two months. They returned, uneventfully, via Naples, Italy at the end of November[19] and settled into their home at 36 Summer Street in Haverhill.

November also brought William McKinley's election to the presidency, and joyful Republicans celebrated with "jollification parades." In Wellesley Hills, the parade wound around town and came down Washington Street and then Worcester, right past the Loring home, with a great production of steam whistles and cheering.[20]

Emilie and Victor had a more personal reason to celebrate: the birth of their second son on November sixteenth. Again, they chose the middle name Melville, but this boy's first name honored Victor's brother: Selden Melville Loring.[21]

The choice of names said something about Victor. Edward had been his guardian and law partner, and Charles Francis had taken him yachting and introduced him to clubs, politics, and philanthropic organizations. But Selden was not only the eldest but also the most dynamic of Victor's brothers. He boldly enlisted in war when it came, served in Hong Kong, and traveled around the world. He was the appreciative observer and sensitive writer, the most romantic and adventurous of the brothers from Marlborough.

In appearance and occupation, Victor was deliberate and discerning, but he valued brave action and poetic reflection. In Emilie, he found a similar spirit of adventure and romance, to which she added both sympathetic understanding and never-fail positivity. Now, they had two sons named for their liveliest and most cherished brothers, Robert and Selden.

Robert Baker's turn at the altar came in April with his marriage to "Minnie" Pratt. Her father was Edwin Pratt, a man not unlike John Gale in his modest disposition and business acumen. He, too, started his own

> She laid her soft cheek against his. "Isn't—isn't he the dearest!" she crooned as she felt the sweet warm thrill of his satin-soft skin against her face.
> *The Trail of Conflict*

Three Melvilles: Robert Melville Baker with Selden Melville and Robert Melville Loring

leather business, made a fortune, and became a banker. However, by the time Robert courted Minnie, her father had been deceased more than a year. Her mother died when Minnie was eighteen, and five siblings had also died young. That left Minnie, her brother Edwin Jr., who ran their father's business, and her sister Bessie.[22]

Robert and Minnie's green-and-white wedding was held in Quincy's First Unitarian Church, the "Church of the Presidents" where John Adams and John Quincy Adams had attended and were now interred. The young heiress walked down the aisle on her brother's arm, her sister as maid of honor, and Victor as Robert's best man.[23] After their honeymoon, Robert and Minnie returned to Burr Croft, where they lived with Mrs. Baker. In the summer, they all went out to the coast again, the Gales at Swampscott's Lincoln House and the Lorings once more at Marblehead.

They were settled. Victor's career took him to Boston each day, and the Boston Social Register listed their address as "Melville House, Wellesley Hills."[24] It certainly made sense to call it that, with Robert Melville and

Selden Melville Loring living there, Robert Melville Baker living next door, and Robert Melville Boles a frequent visitor. While Victor worked at the law, Emilie threw herself headlong into motherhood and the job of keeping her family "well, happy and efficient."[25]

The word "efficient" was deliberately chosen. Steps were streamlined, and supplies were chosen with analytical precision. Emilie drew up the day's menus for the cook, who did the shopping and preparing. Suggesting that trays could reduce the number of steps required between the kitchen and dining room, Emilie drily observed, "The usefulness of the trays depends on the intelligence of the woman behind them." But brisk efficiency did not quell her Baker humor: "This recipe makes a dozen muffins. If they are a success, there will be none too many; if they are not, you will have just twelve more than you need."[26]

It was more than efficiency that motivated her. "After all, living is the biggest thing any of us have to do. Why not treat it as an art rather than in hit-or-miss fashion?"[27] She raised her boys with the thoughtful composition of an artist, carefully selecting the elements that make childhood rich: companionship, courtesy, adventure, learning, humor, and confidence in their own abilities.

Emilie felt a deep affection for dogs, and her boys got a black and white spaniel that slept in their room and accompanied them in their exploits. Behind the house was the stable of horses, which they kept both for riding and driving. To complete the menagerie, Emilie experimented with raising chickens and collected their eggs for the kitchen.

Emilie's parenting, like her credo for living, was based on fundamental respect. "There is a courtesy due from parents as well as children."[28] The boys were expected to do their chores and their studies, to appear properly in public and mind their manners. But apart from these basics, they were allowed to be boys, to play and run and be rough and experiment, as boys will do, without constant censure or guidance. "Don't stick pins! That is what constant suggestion and interference amounts to after a while, just sticking pins."[29]

[Homemaking] takes everything, economics, business and government laws, a communal viewpoint, and comradeship, courage, sacrifice, and last, but not least, a sense of humor. It calls for a sporting instinct if anything does.
Give Me One Summer

"After honor, good manners are the greatest asset a young person can have, young or old for that matter."
Where Beauty Dwells

"A boy without a dog and a dog without a boy aren't getting the fun out of life to which young things are entitled."
We Ride the Gale!

. . . living close together was sufficient strain on dispositions without having every move commented upon.
With Banners

She picked up Edward Lear's *Nonsense Verses* from a low stand. "What shall it be tonight, Dicky?" She knew his answer even as she asked the question. "T'Owl an' the Pussy-Cat first, an' then—" *We Ride the Gale!*

"Do is a shorter word than don't and not half as irritating. Why not use it more?" *The Mother in the Home*

"Sonia won't let me say, 'Did you bwing me a pwesent, Cousin Mike.' So you must say, 'What do you fink I bwought you, Dicky?'" "I ought to be the stern disciplinarian; instead, I can't help seeing the funny side of it." *We Ride the Gale!*

Emilie didn't care much for games, but she was a Baker, and she read for hours to her children. Between her collection and her mother's next door, she had a full library of options. One favorite was *Coquo and the King's Children*,[30] about a court jester, Coquo, who understands the speech of insects and birds, and who runs away with the king's children, in search of adventure. Years later, she told her granddaughter, Linda: "They loved it. So did I."[31]

Raised in a home of boys, Emilie understood her sons' need for adventure and expected that their exploits would land them in uncomfortable predicaments from time to time. "Love them! Laugh at them gently and with comradely understanding—often time an ounce of ridicule will accomplish more than a pound of entreaty—don't nag them, and be judiciously blind at times." When their misadventures led to mud, soakings, cuts, or torn clothing, their Swedish nurse, Freda, made sure that all was cleaned, mended, and set aright.

Robby and Selden. "I can't help seeing the funny side of it." We Ride the Gale!

Both Robby and Selden had blonde, curly hair when they were small, which darkened to brown as they grew. Their cherubic faces inherited their mother's dimples, Robby's in his chin and Selden's in his cheeks. It would be the hard mother, indeed, who would not be swayed by their entreaties, but Emilie took that philosophically:

> Put the very best of yourself into your children and remember that all crudities will pass away if you are patient and wise . . . Above all things, believe in your children![32]

The adults of Emilie's childhood took children's lives and children's thoughts seriously, and so did she. Raising her boys to be active participants in the high purpose and high spirits to which they were heirs was her first and most important work. Like everything else she attempted, she took joy in doing it as well as she could.

Home was a verb for Emilie, an active exercise of intellect, optimism, and creativity. A constant stream of authors, actors, lecturers, and abolitionists visited her childhood home, and in his "free time," her father wrote eighty-nine amateur plays, most of which the family performed, also at home. George Baker had been gone nearly a decade, but good humor, worthy ideas and events of the world still set the pace to which the Baker and Loring households kept time. All were actively involved in issues of the day, all were avid readers and conversationalists, and they were each other's first and best sounding boards, perhaps, in part, because their pursuits were so different.

More than fifteen years into his law practice, Victor and Emilie could not have differed more in their participation in the social whirl of clubs, committees, and cards. Emilie had enough to do when the boys were small. "I felt that the mother of a family should have nothing which she must do outside her home while the young people were growing up. Homemaking requires poise, and poise comes from unhurried, unhysterical [sic] judgment."[33]

"*. . . it seems to me that there is no more important, no more up-to-the-minute need, no higher career for a woman than that of wifehood and home-maker, to answer 'Here!' when a child comes home and calls, 'Where's Mother?'*"
Give Me One Summer

"*'Woman, don't you realize that the most important person in this house to be kept well is you, you, you? Aren't you wife, mother, nurse, housekeeper, teacher, mistress of the exchequer and all the other things which contribute to the making of the home? You're the dynamo. Greater still, the sunshine in whose light all the living things in a home grow and flourish.*"
The Mother in the Home

Victor, on the other hand, presided over the Royal Arcanum, as his brother Charles had done, and held continuous membership in the Union Boat Club, Republican State Central Committee, YMCA, Boston Art Club, Boston City Club, Puritan Publicity Club, Braeburne and Economic Clubs, and the American, Massachusetts, Suffolk, and Norfolk County bar associations.[34]

His reputation as an orator suggested that he, too, had the gift of expression.

> Mr. Loring is a lawyer, looks like William M. Evarts and talks like Demosthenes. His address was eloquent, filled with beautiful similes and high in tone. Seldom has such oratory been heard in North Adams. He was frequently interrupted with applause and at the close he was compelled to rise and bow his acknowledgements before the applause ceased.[35]

A Loring to the core, Victor's was the world of public service, and his connections kept him in touch with civic and political currents. The Exchange Club of Boston was an example. Limited to one thousand of Boston's "best" businessmen, the Club provided an alternate workplace away from the office—a neutral setting where business was conducted confidentially, over a meal or in the privacy of a conference room. Victor could meet clients at his office in the Old South Building, but at the Club, he might discuss current issues with any of the six hundred members who used the facility on a given day. Then, when he went home in the evening, he had the balance wheel of Emilie and the Bakers—high purpose, high spirits, and high jinks.

The Bakers and Lorings handled their differences with large doses of good humor. Rachel's play, *Mr. Bob*, poked fun at Victor's preferences for yachting and cigars. Now, *Bachelor Hall* took straight aim at the Loring-Baker juxtaposition of seriousness and irrepressible humor. The protagonist is a young attorney running for office (as Victor did twice, for state

---

"He had a marvelous voice, rich and mellow with a hint of vibrato when he was deeply moved. I've been told that lawyers would gather in court when he was about to charge a jury."
There Is Always Love

"I want to do something to help my country."
"Then keep out of politics yourself and make a home for some embryo politician which will keep his ideas and ideals up to the mark. You've got the biggest chance in the world right there."
Here Comes the Sun!

Maugus Hall Dramatics

She had the saving grace of humor. If women could only learn the persuasive value of a laugh as against tears or sulks how many marriages would be saved from the scrap-heap.
The Trail of Conflict

senate) who finds himself in a pickle. His conservative constituents will arrive to visit about solemn matters on the very evening that an amateur drama is to be staged in his home. Misdirection and prevarications are not enough, and in the end, he must own up to all.[36]

Bachelor Hall didn't spare the Bakers, as playwrights and actors took a ribbing throughout: "I think playwrights are the worst cranks I ever saw; they're so touchy!" "He has only one line . . . . Any one of average intelligence ought to grasp that within an hour." Emilie's alter ego in the play pokes fun at her romanticism: "I positively refuse to go on with my love scene without a rustic gate . . . No gate, no inspiration." But the final tease was saved for Victor. The Emilie character (thinly disguised as "Betty") places a wreath on the beleaguered politician's head and declares, "This laurel wreath we place upon thy brow. A politician once, an actor now!"[37]

When the play was performed in Wellesley Hills on October 25, 1897, it was, characteristically, a family effort. Victor's Maugus Club provided the stage, Rachel and Robert wrote the play, Robert recruited the actors of the Proscenium Club and acted the part of detective Cliverton

Sam broke off with a grimace at his sister. "Humorous, aren't you, kiddo?"
With Banners

Newcombe, and Emilie's Wellesley Hills Woman's Club sponsored the event. Musicians on guitar and banjo entertained the full clubhouse theater until the curtain rose, after which the on-stage comedy excited continual applause.[38]

That summer, the Gales and Lorings exchanged elegance for rusticity and vacationed inland, at the Bald Mountain Camps of the Rangeley Lakes of Maine. The fifty-mile chain of six lakes was called "the Switzerland of Maine" and boasted excellent salmon and trout fishing.[39] Ten hours by train from Boston to Portland to Bemis, and then a short steamer ride after that, allowed them to leave home in the morning and eat supper overlooking Lake Mooselookmeguntic.[40]

Lodgings were six "camps" (cabins) linked together by a wooden promenade and outfitted with bunks, fireplaces and little else. It was a gentile rusticity, however. The Lorings brought along Freda Nilsson, their children's Swedish nurse, and the well-staffed lodge provided hot meals and

> A row of log cabins with brand-new tin water-pails glittering like family plate on their porches rimmed the lake at a conservative distance from its pebbly shore.
> *A Certain Crossroad*

> This camping experience had poured new spirit through her veins. Never had she known life as she had lived it in the past forty-eight hours. Two nights she had slept on balsam boughs with the fragrance of pines and the smell of a woodfire stealing into the window to drug her to dreamless sleep. In the early morning she had plunged into the icy water of the lake. The cold had set her teeth chattering, her eyes shining, the blood leaping and glowing through her veins.
> *A Certain Crossroad*

Bald Mountain Camps

Victor and Emilie at the Rangeley Lakes

Robert, Selden and Spaniel: "A boy without a dog and a dog without a boy aren't getting the fun out of life to which young things are entitled." We Ride the Gale!

Rachel and Emilie

On Lake Mooselookmeguntic

Victor and Maine Guides. Seated is famed guide Herb Welch.

Fishing at Haines Landing

experienced guides. The scenery was rustic, but dinners were fine, courtesies were observed, and service was attentive.

Bakers had lived in Maine for one hundred two years (1740–1842) before returning to Boston. It was unusual to go to the forests of inland Maine rather than to the coast, but the real change in going to the Rangeley lakes was the simplified living (albeit still with service), unplanned and informal. Victor taught the boys to fish. Emilie and Victor took walks, explored the lakes in Rangeley boats, and swam in the clear, cold water.

Emilie grew up in the city and enjoyed the beaches of fine hotels and lodges along the coast, but Victor was from the more rural setting of Marlborough where boys hiked, fished, and explored forests, lakes, and streams. His brother-in-law, Barron Moulton, had fished in the Rangeley area for more than a decade,[41] and his brother, Selden, had belonged to both the Appalachian Club and the Adirondack Mountain Reserve,[42] which set aside wilderness land for sportsmen and wildlife. Of course, Robby and Selden should have their chance at this great outdoors, too.

CHAPTER 10

The New Century

Wellesley Hills, 1900–1901

As the 1890s ticked toward their end, Emilie and Victor joined Boston's Twentieth Century Club whose only requirement was that the members share, evaluate, and put ideas into practice. Unique for its time, the membership included both men and women, and perhaps more unique was its success in providing an environment "where ideas may get a sympathetic hearing, and where those holding opposite views on vital questions can meet without prejudice."[1]

The gay nineties and the Victorian age drew to a close, and one end after another closed the curtain on the last century. Three deaths marked such endings for Emilie.

The first was William Taylor Adams, "Oliver Optic," (d. 1897), whose adventure stories were on her bookshelf her entire life, her father's jovial companion and the author who carried Lee & Shepard on the strength of his sales for much of its existence. Oliver Optic's one-hundred-eight books sold more than two million copies during his lifetime.[2] How could it be true that he would be unknown to the next century when his was so daily a name in the last one?

> Alger's tales are sometimes read, out of curiosity, and Henty's are often read for pleasure and information, whereas it is highly unlikely that anyone except fanciers of nineteenth-century children's books ever reads any of Oliver Optic. *They have had their day, and the world reads something else.*[3] [Italics added]

But although the names changed, the roles remained the same, and a new writer was ready in the wings. Optic's last book, *An Undivided Union*, was finished after his death by Edward Stratemeyer, an author whose real name would never be well-known but whose many pseudonyms (and those of his ghostwriters') would be like best friends to the next two generations of the reading public: Arthur M. Winfield (The Rover Boys), Victor Appleton (Tom Swift), Carolyn Keene (Nancy Drew), and Frank Dixon (The Bobbsey Twins).[4] It is not the authors but the books of our childhoods that we love. Oliver Optic was gone, and children began to read something else.

The next death was Matthew Mayhew, George Baker's appreciative friend and his first publishing partner. Matt's laughter was an integral part of the amateur performances of Emilie's childhood, and he was the father of her friend Georgie. When the girls were in their teens, the Mayhews lived on Washington Street with Asa Morse and his family. On a visit to the home of Asa's daughter on New Year's Day of 1899, Matthew simply dropped dead of a cerebral hemorrhage.[5]

Equally abrupt was the passing of Robert F. McClannin, George Baker's friend from the Aurora Dramatic Club days and the father of Emilie's friend Beth McClannin Kerley. At age sixty-five, Robert McClannin was one of the best-known character actors on the stage, and he was set to open one night in a new play, *Rupert of Hentzau*. Instead, as he sat "joking and laughing at the supper table of the hotel where he was stopping," he suddenly was no more; he literally died laughing.[6]

With the deaths of her father's three friends, Emilie's strongest ties to George Baker's professional life were severed. He was successful too long and on too many fronts for there not to be people who remembered him still, but there were no longer the direct ties, the places where Emilie might stop by and still find the remnants of her father's surroundings, where she might still feel connected.

Besides, publishing and theater were changing. Critical acclaim in literature followed the realist and the cynic, and the fresh-faced, optimistic stories of George Baker's time were left behind as quaint but naïve. Thomas Wentworth Higginson complained that writing itself was changing.

> Things are written now to be read once, and no more; that is, they are read as often as they deserve. A book in old times took five years to write and was read five hundred times by five hundred people. Now it is written in three months and read once by five hundred thousand people. That's the proper proportion.[7]

On stage, farces and comic operas gave way to vaudeville, revue shows and the new, musical theater. Silent movies gained ground, sound was on its way, and theaters added projection screens.

It had been ten years since George Baker's death, and in those ten years, all three of the Baker children had married and moved away from Boston. Emilie and Victor lived in Wellesley Hills with their boys (ages five and three), a Swedish nurse, and an English cook. Robert, Minnie, and Mrs. Baker lived next door at Burr Croft, and Rachel and John Gale celebrated their fourth anniversary in Haverhill.

The Lorings attended the First Congregational Church of Wellesley Hills. Emilie had grown up in the Unitarian church, Victor in the Congregational, but there was little need to choose between them. From early days, the churches of Wellesley Hills maintained a spirit of cooperation that was most clearly seen in their annual, unified services on Thanksgiving. They also started a joint, monthly publication, *Our Town*, with the idea that they had more in common than they had differences. The first issue welcomed, "Enter the place of worship which most nearly meets your need and make it your home. Whatever one of these places you may choose, you will find brethren there and friendly greeting."[8]

Robert Baker published poems in the first several issues of the publication, and one marked the current state of his ambitions as a playwright:

The city. The adorable city. Resolutely she shut out the mental flash of brilliantly lighted streets; of crowds of people, laughing, frowning, pushing; of processions of automobiles, all of them going somewhere.
With Banners

... her father had presented the church with bells in memory of his mother, who far ahead of her time had believed that different creeds should, to the advantage of their souls, spiritual influence—and incidentally finances, enroll under one banner.
Swift Water

A DRAMATIC HOLD-UP

The playwright with his manuscript
  Went sadly on his way,
For near a score of managers
  Declined his play that day.
Then from a corner dark there sprang
  A robber, bold and masked,
And of the scribe with loaded gun
  His life or money asked.
"I've nothing but this play, I swear!"
  The trembling scribe replied,
"And all have said it is not worth
  The string with which it's tied."
The robber snatched the manuscript,
  And quickly sped away.
"Thank God!" the playwright said, "At last!
  A man who'll take my play!"[9]

April 1901 typified the relinquishing of the old and the welcoming of the new. In Allston, Victor's mother learned that she had the cancer that would end her life, and in Wellesley Hills, Robert and Minnie Baker welcomed their first child on April twenty-fourth. Of course, they named him "Melville"—Melville Pratt Baker.

Laura Warrener Hitchcock Loring was eighty-one years and three months old when she died on July 16, 1901,[10] and what a lot she had accomplished in that time. Widowed with seven children at the age of forty-four, she brought her family from Marlborough to Boston, saw them educated, married, and settled into successful careers and family lives, and she outlived four of them. Her will left equal sums of money to each of her surviving children, but to Victor she also left "my library, together with all books, magazines and papers which I may own at my decease."[11] The family gathered in her home for the funeral and buried her beside her husband, Hollis, in Marlborough.[12]

As for new beginnings, Melville "Mel" Baker was like a brother to Robby and Selden Loring from the very start. Emilie and her brother Robert were close, and their children, living next door to one another, were as well. Photos of the family from then on often pictured the three boys together, and the melding of Bakers and Lorings moved on to the next generation.

"No one can ever tell me, and get across with it, that a mother's influence doesn't live forever."
The Trail of Conflict

Emily F. Baker with Robby, Mel, and Selden, 1901

As the Loring boys got a little older, they began to get wise about Santa Claus. They wouldn't let Victor out of their sight, hoping to catch him in the act. A knock came at the door one Christmas Eve, and in walked the jolly "man" himself to deliver their presents! It was Rachel. Their aunt frequently spent Christmas with the boys and brought presents from her trips abroad. She was vivacious and fun, and the boys adored her.

History altered abruptly in September, one day after Emilie's thirty-fifth birthday, with the shooting of President William McKinley at the Pan American Exposition in Buffalo. As he lingered between life and death, Victor and other members of the Republican committees converged upon New York's Fifth Avenue hotels to make contingency plans.

The President died on September 14 and was laid to rest five days later. "The whole country was in mourning . . . at a given signal, the cars on electric lines and steam railroads, the steamers on the rivers, the vehicles of business paused for a few moments. Men stood with bared heads in silence . . ."[13]

For many, this was the third time in their lives that a president had been assassinated (Lincoln, Garfield, McKinley). That the motive was deemed the product of a deranged mind, the act of a single perpetrator, underscored the uncertainties of modern living, the extent to which order could be upended by unpredictable events.

Victor and Emilie packed into Town Hall with much of Wellesley for a local service of remembrance. The next month, a poem by Robert Baker appeared in *Our Town*. It might have been meant as a memorial for Victor's mother, for President McKinley, or for a Maugus Club member who was also memorialized in the issue, but it reflected trademark Baker optimism in the face of loss:

ALL'S WELL

In roll the billows with a sullen roar
  Against the rocks that guard a peaceful shore;
The spray, dashed up with a relentless force,

In its white shroud reflects the moonbeam's course.
Some lonely sails far out upon the deep,
   Like phantom shapes across the moonlight creep;
Soft o'er the molten seas sounds the ship's bell,
   Follows the sailor's cheering cry, "All's well."
On shore a life has ceased its mortal toil,
   To find a well-earned rest in hallowed soil;
That watch-cry hovers o'er the moonlit bed,
   "All's well," a benediction for the dead.[14]

Victor also printed a reaction in *Our Town*. In two months' time, he had lost his mother and mourned the loss of the president and a friend. His was the characteristic response of a Loring—to dig deeper, work harder, serve better.

For there is work for us to do besides travelling along the dusty highway of life in our daily vocation or drinking deep at the fountains of pleasure. There is a work to do for the town in which we live, something for this grand old Commonwealth of ours, God save her! Something for the Republic, for the building of which our forefathers suffered untold agony and deprivation, and for the preservation of which our fathers shed their life blood. Something for society. Something for humanity.[15]

Emilie sympathized with both points of view. Her sunshiny personality naturally gravitated to the hopeful, and her character drove her to make the most of opportunities when they came along.

Give each day its own chances. Don't load it up and hamper it with yesterday's mistakes or fears for tomorrow. Greet it hopefully. Greet it with a smile, with faith and determination to make it count in the scheme of your life and it will reflect that mood all day.[16]

"Men like you had better show up at the primaries and the polls, work to repeal the laws which you don't like and substitute something better if you object to what you get."
Here Comes the Sun!

How like her, Geoffrey thought with fervent sympathy. Always she would go forward unvanquished by life, her weapon of defense gay courage.
Gay Courage

Wellesley Hills, 1902–1906

Originals of famous cartoons hung on the walls.
Gay Courage

"Father . . . was a playwright for amateurs, but Sam is ambitious to write for the professional stage; he has one three-act comedy finished, that is, as finished as a play can be until it is put into rehearsal. That is why he is acting, that he may know all there is to know of stage technic."
With Banners

"Picture your adoring family in a box at the opening, fairly swooning with pride when the audience yells: 'Author! Auth—'"
With Banners

Emilie's brother Robert seized an opportunity of his own and drove it toward success. He had tried for some time to convince performers Joseph Hart and Carrie de Mar to let him write a play to showcase their comedic, musical talents. Hart suggested the "Foxy Grandpa" comic strip by "Bunny" Schultze as inspiration but quickly lost interest. Robert kept after it, however, and began to see how he could develop story lines around the balding, little man with glasses and a flapping coat. The finished comedy was exactly what Hart wanted, and he convinced none other than William Brady to invest in the production. The rest, as they say, is history.

Foxy Grandpa opened first in Boston, and the reception was not only enthusiastic, it was delirious. At the close of the second act, the audience shouted insistently for the writer to come on stage, a reception "such as few pieces of its kind get in conservative Boston." And it wasn't only in Boston. After two weeks in the Boston Theater, *Foxy Grandpa* played 120 performances in New York's 14th Street Theater, delighting both audiences and theater critics: "One of the cleanest, brightest, snappiest musical farces of recent years . . ." "Mr. Baker has succeeded in writing a comedy which is absolutely spotless." "Hundreds of people are being turned away at every performance of this razzle dazzle of fun, song and dance." "The demand for seats to see this amusing skit is the largest in the history of the theater." Enterprising theaters sold souvenir pillows embroidered with Foxy Grandpa's likeness, and soon there were coin banks, also. It was not just a play; it was a phenomenon.

Robert used the same device in *Foxy Grandpa* that his father, George M. Baker, had popularized forty years before: mistaken identity, witty puns, and harmless pranks to which the audience members are wise. Back in Wellesley Hills, *Our Town* rejoiced in the success of its local son:

Like his delightful English contemporary, Mr. Gilbert, Mr. Baker has shown that a man of real dramatic gifts need not descend to *risqué* situations, threatened violations of the seventh commandment, or thinly veiled salacity in order to amuse both young and old.[17]

Perhaps the world was heading toward more "sophisticated" tastes, but Robert Baker's first solo play showed that there was still an audience for simple, wholesome entertainment, and success was his for the effort.

William Brady financed a lavish production for the second Baker-Hart musical comedy, *Girls Will Be Girls*, which opened with high expectations at the beginning of the 1903 theater season. Robert delivered a constant stream of funny incidents and "mirth-provoking lines" that kept the audience engaged from beginning to end. "Laugh followed laugh, and applause followed applause, and it is very evident that success will follow last evening's performance."[18]

With the opening of their third play, *Miss Pocahontas* in 1906, Robert Baker and Joseph Hart were invited to join the Lambs, a club whose roster was—and remains—a veritable "Who's Who of American Theater." Members included the Barrymores (Maurice, Lionel, and Jack), composer Victor Herbert, producer Tony Pastor, Douglas Fairbanks, Sr., and comedians Joseph Weber and Lew Fields. Also on the list was a familiar name from home in Boston: Henry Clay Barnabee.[19]

George Baker's fellow performer Barnabee was in his eighties, but he declined the Lambs' first attempt to offer a benefit in his honor. San Francisco was in ruins after the 1906 earthquake, and he felt its citizens deserved aid more than he. In the fall, however, the benefit was held, with appreciation from one of the Lambs' newest members, the son of Barnabee's old friend George M. Baker.[20]

In the spring of 1907, Robert began a weekly column for the *Boston Daily Globe* called "Trouble's Troubles," a humorous look at the married life of one "Trouble Snow" and his new bride, Henrietta.

We had taken a flat! Two rooms and a bathinet. A bathinet is a half-portion of a bath. It's so small that you have to pull the tub

"That play is my declaration of faith that there is a big theatre public for things that matter, for something besides sordid infidelities and bawdy lines."
With Banners

"It's got everything. Humor, suspense, moving simplicity, fidelity to ideals, and unfaltering movement."
"But has it got box-office?"
"I'll gamble my last dollar on it. It's the old recipe for play-writing carried to perfection: 'Make 'em laugh; make 'em weep; make 'em wait.'"
With Banners

"A wife with neither imagination nor a sense of humor isn't a wife, she's a calamity."
A Certain Crossroad

out to get in and then pull the tub in after you. The flat was in a fancy looking place called Rotterdam Court. After we had lived in Rotterdam Court a week, we found it easier to call it by the last syllable . . . Young married couples don't care where they live the first month. Any old place is Paradise. When they wake up, they look for a real place . . .[21]

Between trips to Europe and her philanthropic and social schedules, Rachel's pen stayed busy, too. Women's changing roles in marriage and society lent themselves to the Baker humor—good fun underlain with a current of seriousness.

No Men Wanted (1903) poked fun at the "new" woman who intends to be independent of men. The young ladies in the play vow to shun men and pursue careers instead, but "It's no use—when a woman's heart begins to flutter, all de good intentions to give matrimony de other side ob de road won't hold it steady." Each acquires a secret boyfriend, talking big about independence in front of the others while secretly hoping for dates.[22]

The New Crusade (1908) addressed the relationships of women and their servants. The household mistresses need help but want to pay the least money for it, while their maids want their jobs but risk a walkout for a raise in pay. Both hold out to save face, but in the end, they all return to their places and compromise on the price.[23] Rachel knew whereof she wrote, since she and John kept a cook, a maid, and a hired man, and next door, Herbert and Martha Gale employed a live-in maid, laundress, cook, waitress and chauffeur to care for them and their two children.[24] By contrast, Emilie and Victor had a maid and nurse when the children were small but only a single, live-in servant thereafter.

While her siblings wrote plays, Emilie gave teas. "Everyone who knows Emilie Loring well smiles at her fondness for tea parties," wrote an acquaintance from Boston.[25] Polished, silver service; scones, flaky and sweet; cream, lemon, and sugar ready on the tea table; and the ritual of pouring were at its center. As important as table appointments was

"I. Independent of men. That's an absurd statement. No woman is independent of men . . . Don't get any wrong ideas about spinsterhood. It is a lonely life."
Rainbow at Dusk

"It's evident that you are not a house-keeper, Moya. If you were, you would know that Sunday is the maid's evening out," Eve explained.
It's A Great World!

David Crofton had laughed and confided to Joan in his wife's hearing: "If this house were to float down river in a flood your mother would manage a tea party on the roof."
As Long as I Live

dressing well in a lovely gown—poised, coiffed, and ready for conversation. Tea set the stage for generations to mix with one another, for friends to discharge social obligations, and to fan the potential spark of interest between new acquaintances.

Emilie served tea from four o'clock until six o'clock, whether the occasion was the usual "at home" on Thursdays, a special gathering, or just a pause in her own day at home. She kept her parties informal, so she could really enjoy her guests. Selden once commented, "I like your parties, Mother. I like the conversation."[26]

There was the occasional situation that went awry, but that was borne with as much humor and dignity as circumstances allowed. In one memorable instance, guests were enjoying a game of cards, and in walked Emilie's pet duck, Donald. It had been taught to do its "business" on paper in the house, and when the fateful moment came that a guest dropped her card, the duck did precisely as it was trained to do. A fresh deck was quickly procured.[27]

Emilie and Victor both enjoyed music, and the Maugus Club, to which Victor belonged, offered frequent invitations to musicales. One night, it was a pop concert given by a six-piece orchestra and refreshments served on a piazza lit by Japanese lanterns. Another night, they played music on the latest phonograph machine, and they danced late in their holiday best at Christmas and New Year's balls.

Throughout their lives together, Victor steadily pursued the three prongs of his public life: law, civic affairs, and the church. Late in 1903, he worked on a case with Frederick B. Greenhalge, the son of Governor Frederick T. Greenhalge who had recently—and suddenly—died in office. "Eric," as young Greenhalge was called,[28] was a Harvard graduate and the assistant attorney general for the state of Massachusetts. He soon joined Victor's law firm, which became "Moulton, Loring & Greenhalge."

They took up a new office in the Old South Building, which was constructed on an entire city block in the heart of Boston. The building was so large that it wrapped behind the Old South meetinghouse and

"How will you have your tea?" "Strong of hot water, lemon, no sugar," she answered lightly. *Across the Years*

"It looks entertaining. I'm like Alice in Wonderland. I like plenty of conversation." *There is Always Love*

"You dance like a dream," he declared after they had circled the room. "Like it, don't you?" "Love it. Always have. Always will. Those women seated against the wall with 'Too old to dance' plastered all over them give me a pain in the neck . . ." *I Hear Adventure Calling*

enveloped the former headquarters of Lee & Shepard at 10 Milk Street. It was a central and prestigious location, and Victor remained there until his retirement. At home in Wellesley Hills, there were now three family homes at the end of Florence Avenue—Emilie and Victor's home next to Mrs. Baker's, with a garden and orchard between them, and Robert and Minnie's home across the street.

Summertime in Boston always sweltered, and the Lorings usually escaped the heat by heading toward water—at the Cape,[29] Marblehead, or Maine.[30] During the summer of 1906, as Emilie's fortieth birthday approached, the Lorings did the latter. They went north to Haverhill to visit Rachel and John and continued to the familiar, Rangeley Lakes region where they stayed until late August.[31]

On the twentieth, they traveled by boat down the Maine coast to Quebec, cruised through the St. Lawrence Seaway to Montreal, and arrived in Toronto in time for the opening of Robert Baker's newest musical comedy, *Captain Careless*.[32] They traveled home over land, stopping at the most popular vacation places: Niagara, Lake Champlain, Lake George, and Saratoga.[33] They arrived home in time for Emilie's birthday in September, for which Victor remodeled and enlarged the Wellesley Hills house.[34]

In their absence, Victor's brother-in-law and law partner Barron Moulton was diagnosed with a valve disorder of his heart. On October first, he suffered a stroke, and on the fourth, he died. At fifty-six, Victor's sister was a widow, and the firm of Moulton, Loring & Greenhalge was without another of its founders.[35]

Victor's law partnerships had changed through the years from "C. F. and V. J. Loring" to "Moulton, Loring & Loring" to "Moulton, Loring & Greenhalge." With Moulton's death, Victor became the senior partner, and he could have done business as "Loring & Greenhalge," but he kept the firm's old name, "Moulton, Loring, & Greenhalge." Their reputation for "general practice in all state and federal courts" was sufficient that their references were listed as: "Old Colony Trust Company, or any bank in Boston."

CHAPTER 11

Alaska!

Summer 1907

Heat was hard to escape the next summer, 1907, when record high temperatures and humidity spread across the Northeast. The thermometer on Court Street in Boston registered 98.5, New Haven reached 100, and Portsmouth reported 95. Some died, and many more were made ill by heat indices exceeding 125 degrees. From Pennsylvania to Maine, New York to Cape Cod,[1] there was no direction one could go to get away from the discomfort—except, perhaps, west. Far west. Beyond the Great Lakes, the Dakotas, and the Rockies. All the way to Alaska!

The idea had been brewing awhile. In November, the Wellesley Hills Congregational Club hosted the Honorable John G. Brady, who went to Alaska in 1878 as a missionary and had just ended nine years as its territorial governor.[2] Alaska was about to celebrate its fortieth year as a United States Territory (1867–1907), and Brady was its ardent spokesman: "The general impression that Alaska is but a country of snow, ice, rocks, and seals was quickly dispelled as Governor Brady told of its astonishing natural resources, industrial activity, agricultural possibilities, and great mineral wealth." Mr. Brady intended to show a selection from his hundreds of lantern slides, but they did not arrive in time. Even so, his lecture was informative, and the vivid picture his descriptions painted of the Alaskan territory was persuasive.

Victor, Emilie, and the boys boarded the train in Boston on August second and rode two days to reach St. Paul, Minnesota. After a day's rest, they boarded the Canadian Pacific Railway, bound for Vancouver.

There was something for everyone on the train. The observation car had upholstered chairs for seated viewing, and for the Loring boys, at ten and twelve, an open, observation platform allowed them to stand at the

"Alaska is a big subject. It is our last American frontier. For the first time since its acquisition by the United States, there is a program in sight for utilizing great stretches of wilderness. I would advise any youngster in quest of a career to hop on the Alaskan band-wagon."
Lighted Windows

Porters wearing that air of authority and responsibility for which one might justly look in a premier or secretary of state, came and went; conductors punched tickets and answered questions more or less amiably; the wheels rattled and roared and ground ceaselessly.
The Trail of Conflict

brass railing and "brave the dust, cinders, and wind."[3] Miles sped by, revealing sights they had read about in books. But had they wanted to consult more books, there was a library car for that, and when they were hungry, snacks were available, a la carte. At four o'clock, tea and an assortment of dainty cakes appeared in the dining car atop freshly pressed, white linens. For Victor, there was a wood-paneled, leather-upholstered smoking car where twice-daily updates of news and financial markets were delivered. Finally, they reached Vancouver and checked in at the Vancouver Hotel.[4]

On August ninth, the Lorings took a local steamer to Victoria, where they would meet their boat. They visited British Columbia's Parliament building and saw the luxurious Empress Hotel which was slated to open the following January. Electric streetcars, pedestrians, bicycles, and horse drawn carriages scurried toward the city's center, but there was only time for first impressions. Toward evening, they boarded the *SS Spokane*, stowed their luggage, and toured what would be their accommodations for the next two weeks.

The *SS Spokane* was a three-deck, steel steamer, 281 feet long by 40 feet wide and 20 feet deep. It was built for the tourist trade, and all summer, it traveled the "Totem Pole Route" from Seattle and Victoria along the inside passage to Skagway. Only first-class passengers made the trip, and all accommodations were designed especially for their pleasure and comfort. It was, as Raymond & Whitcomb's brochure said, "like taking a whole floor of the Waldorf-Astoria and taking it up amongst the forest-clad islands of the Alaskan archipelago."[5]

Sleeping quarters were appointed with brass bedsteads, clothing storage, and a shared bath. They could reserve deck chairs outside their door, walk along the decks of both passenger floors or make their way to the observation deck at the stern. Games of cards helped pass the time, and convenient desks encouraged journaling and letter writing. Meals were served on the saloon deck, and the second floor's social salon was available for informal conversation.

"Visitors ashore!" a voice shouted. The ship's whistle blew a warning...The broad deck was deserted. Passengers were settling their belongings in their cabins for the long voyage. *It's A Great World!*

SS Spokane *from Totem Pole Tour Brochure*

By seven o'clock in the evening, the Lorings and 144 more passengers were underway,[6] headed for the Inside Passage. Despite the evening hour, no scenery was missed. The first of twenty thousand islands remained visible in the midnight sun until nearly twelve and appeared again at first light, between two and three in the morning.

Upstairs on the observation deck, Miss Dazie Stromstadt of Sitka introduced herself as the *Spokane*'s tour guide. She was the author of two illustrated booklets on Alaska—*Sitka, the Beautiful*[7] and *Metlakatla*[8]—and her commentary conveyed the cultural sense of the communities along their route. In her words, "Conditions in Alaska are interesting, since in many respects they are primitive; in some respects, embryonic; in all, teeming with life, energy, change, movement, progress, and intensity. Life here appeals to the man who can see opportunities and has the energy to go after them."[9]

Conditions aboard were anything but primitive. Dr. Edward Everett Hale was supposed to have said that "the good Bostonian is one who, when he is in Rome, does as the Bostonians do."[10] The truth of his observation

It was nine o'clock in the evening, but along the Alaskan coast the daylight lingers, and passengers were seated about the deck in steamer chairs, reading books and papers.
The Key to Many Doors, serial, 1915.

The possibility of adventure waiting round the corner thrilled her, not a doubt lurked in her consciousness.
Lighted Windows

"No matter what anyone says or thinks, my dear, keep on changing for evening as you would at home. It might grow easy to be careless and sloppy in this wilderness, and a sloppy woman's the meanest work of God."
Lighted Windows

"I'll acknowledge that for a moment the silence, the wildness, the terrific expanse of land, sea and sky got me by the throat. I hadn't had the slightest conception of what the word Alaska stood for, this part of it."
Lighted Windows

"I've even learned to develop films. When I return to civilization, I will be equipped to go on the lecture platform."
Lighted Windows

was borne out in five meals prepared daily by the *Spokane*'s excellent chef and served by "agile footed and attentive waiters." To maintain personal appearances, a barbershop was provided for the gentlemen and ladies' maids for their wives. Well dressed and groomed, the passengers gathered for afternoon tea and enjoyed evening musicales provided by the ship's stringed orchestra.[11]

MINA STRAITS

SS Spokane

Huge Iceberg

Floating Ice. "Water dotted with floating ice, about which mountains lifted snowy peaks gilded with sunlight . . ." Lighted Windows

"I visited the old seacoast towns of Alaska."—Emilie Loring

Gone Ashore

Davidson Glacier

Sitka Street and Volcano

Totems at Sitka

Yukon and White Pass Railway

The *Spokane* stopped briefly in Metlakatla and made a midnight pause in Ketchikan, but the first real chance to disembark was in Kasaan, which they reached in the early hours of Monday morning. After three days of travel, they were nearly six hundred miles from Seattle, and even a cold rain failed to dampen their enthusiasm as they stepped onto solid ground to explore the native settlement. Emilie photographed Victor and the boys standing between two totem poles that were more than ten times Victor's height. At the next stop, they visited Wrangell's original Chief Shake community house and snapped photos of its famous bear and orca totem poles.

On they steamed, to destinations with exotic names and intriguing histories—Petersburg, Murder Cove, Killisnoo, and Rodman. At each stop, the *Spokane* delivered the mail and picked up letters bound for other destinations. Passengers eyed the frontier Alaskans and the native

"So many on this last frontier have pasts. The mail the steamer brings is sure to jolt some one of them into activity. You only have to watch the men's eyes to know what it means."
Lighted Windows

It seemed as though the prow of the ship must collide with the wooded shores, so narrow was the course and so intricate the curves made by the vessel."
The Key to Many Doors, serial, 1915

On the horizon loomed a volcano. The front of the crater had broken away, the back rose in a jagged peak ... Far off, sportive whales sent sparkling jets of water high in the air.
Lighted Windows

Tlinglits, who, in turn, eyed the well-heeled visitors. The Gold Rush was waning, with winners and losers already decided. Pier welcoming parties included both the successful and the down-on-their-luck, some awaiting visitors, others awaiting passage to take them far away from the bleak and unyielding wilderness.

The route to Sitka passed through a mile-wide strait laid out between numerous islands formed by tectonic uplift and the deposits of ancient eruptions. To the west loomed Mount Edgecomb, a dormant volcano with the too-perfect symmetry and crowning crater that a child might draw. Its proportions were multiplied in the Pyramid Peaks between the slopes of Mt. Verstovia and Gavin Hill. Together, they created a perfectly framed, sawtooth backdrop behind Crescent Harbor and the town of Sitka. Smaller peaks scattered thickly in every direction—tree-covered for the most part, and with daily temperatures in Sitka hovering in the fifties, only the highest of them had a dusting of snow.

The Lorings explored the full length of Lincoln Street, from one end of the harbor to the other—the Russian Bishop's house, the market in front of the post office where native Tlingits sold baskets and jewelry, and the remarkable St. Michael's Orthodox Cathedral with its crowning minaret. Inside, the church's sanctuary was all white and gold, adorned with silk banners and a wealth of silver icons, candlesticks, vessels, and ornaments. Beyond St. Michael's, the Lorings toured a Tlingit village and surveyed the remnants of Russian military occupation—a blockhouse and the old, Russian cemetery—and then turned to the eastern end of Lincoln Street and Governor's Walk.

Sitka was the capital of the Alaskan territory until 1906, the home and headquarters of Governor Brady, their onetime Wellesley Hills guest. Untiring in his promotion of the region, the governor collected seventy totem poles from all over Alaska—including one named for himself—and exhibited them at the 1904 World's Fair in St. Louis and again at the 1905 Lewis & Clark Exposition in Portland before returning them to Baranov Island. In another year, their final display along the shore at Sitka was named a national monument, and the surrounding area became the Tongass National Forest. As he intended, tourism increased, and excursions such as "The Totem Pole Route" would forever after include Sitka on their itineraries.

The *Spokane* departed Sitka and sailed north to the icy blue and green wilderness of Glacier Bay. Sky and sea shimmered in every shade of silver and sapphire as the steamer pushed aside thousands of small, frozen chunks and skirted huge, floating islands of ice as tall as seventy-five feet. They failed to skirt one, however, which bent the *Spokane*'s "plates" and caused a leak, but the damage wasn't "immediately serious."[12]

Ahead was the glacier recently named for John Muir, already measurably receding, and producing, by some accounts, a new iceberg every ten minutes. It was still massive beyond belief, steep and forbidding. The only approach to it was a stone-strewn beach reached by a small rowboat lowered over the side of the steamer. It is unclear if Lorings made the landing, but later accounts by both Emilie and her sons agreed that the wooden boat was nearly swamped in the surge of water created by a new berg. Pyramid Harbor was less wild, and many went ashore to walk across a portion of Davidson Glacier.

Next came Skagway, the starting point of the Yukon and White Pass Railway, gateway to the Klondike gold fields. The Lorings' open-sided observation car retraced the journey of the Gold Rush prospectors along a steep and rugged route. It cut into the sides of mountains, passed through a single tunnel and crossed an almost impossible cantilever bridge, 215 feet above a frothy gorge. Two-and-one-half hours and twenty miles later, they reached the summit, 3,000 feet above their starting point.[13] They ate lunch before they returned the way they had come, back to the deck of the *Spokane*. At their next stops, they explored the large gold mining operation at Treadwell and walked the rustic streets of Juneau, the busy, harbor town that had become the new capital of the Alaskan territory. Before the *Spokane* headed south toward Seattle, it stopped once more, at the Taku Glacier. Years later, Emilie reflected:

Water dotted with floating ice, about which mountains lifted snowy peaks gilded with sunlight, patched with purple shadows from the drifting clouds. Dead ahead a glacier sloped back for miles. *Lighted Windows*

A railroad, looking in the vast stretch of world like a toy abandoned by a boy called away from play, twisted and turned like a glittering serpent, sometimes by caverns which were abandoned gold mines on gold-producing creeks . . . Far below, ethereal as a spider's web, unreal in that wilderness as a castle in the air, a trestle spanned a frothing river. *Lighted Windows*

She barely breathed as she met the mirrored eyes. Who was that girl really? What was she? Did she herself know what lay deep in her mind? What profundities of passion and sorrow, love and hate smoldered within her visible body? She had come north in quest of a different self, a fearless self. Had she found it? At least she had exposed her mind to new ideas, to a drastic reversal of her mode of luxurious living. Where was it taking her?
Lighted Windows

I visited the old seacoast towns of Alaska—Sitka, Juneau, Skagway and others. Eventually, a small steamer took me through straits and narrows, dotted with a hundred wooded islands, to the ice fields.

The immensity of her experience lingered as the *Spokane* finally docked in Seattle on August twenty-first. The Lorings proceeded to their hotel, passing, on their way, the brand-new public market on Pike Place. Still in its first week, the open-air market brought thousands of shoppers every day to fill "market basket, gunny sack, and shopping bag" with fresh fruits, vegetables, and fresh salmon from the "fishman" at twenty-five cents each.[15]

The Lorings stayed at the Lincoln Hotel, a seven-story, brick and stone structure on the northwest corner of Fourth Avenue and Madison Street. Guest rooms were sunny and large, many with private baths and fireplaces. The most famous feature was the Lincoln Hotel's rooftop garden, a 120-foot-square creation of green lawn, gem-like flowerbeds, and potted shrubs. Every direction offered a view, with Elliott Bay to the west and

Emilie at Lincoln Hotel's Rooftop Garden, Seattle, 1907

Grand Canyon of the Yellowstone from Lower Falls, 1907

Lake Washington to the east, where construction proceeded on the 1909 Alaska-Yukon-Pacific Exposition. In the distance, the Cascades ran from Mount Rainier to Mount Baker.[16] Emilie found a charming vantage point from which to view the full panorama—the rooftop teahouse and open-air pergola framed in vine-covered columns and hung with flowering plants.

She marked her forty-first birthday somewhere on the northern plains, as the Lorings returned eastward on the Great Northern Railway. They crossed the Cascades, northern Rockies, and Dakotas. They made one last stop at Yellowstone before returning to New England, Boston, and finally, Wellesley Hills.

Both Victor and Emilie gave presentations on Alaska when they returned. Victor went first, with a presentation for the Wellesley

Congregational club. Emilie gave hers next, for the Woman's Aid Society at their all-day sewing meeting in the Congregational Church.[17] In November, one year before, Governor Brady had given his talk on Alaska, and by the next November, the Lorings had been to Alaska and returned to give talks of their own, with slides they had taken themselves. It was just as Miss Stromstadt had said: Alaska was a place for people who could see opportunities and have the energy to go after them.

CHAPTER 12

Creative Stirrings

Wellesley Hills, 1907–1909

That fall, the boys went back to school, and the Robert Bakers had a new baby, Eileen, born on September twenty-second.[1] With Victor in Boston every day, Robert sharing time between New York and Wellesley Hills, and Rachel and John in Europe again, Emilie found herself free to take on multiple activities at once.

Emilie and Victor agreed with Progressive tenets that the quality and dignity of life for all citizens should be increased through education, exposure to art and literature, and civic participation. Naturally, Emilie leaned more toward art and literature and Victor toward civic participation.

The Boston Society of Arts and Crafts began in 1897, the first of its type in the United States, with aims to make "the artist more of a craftsman and the craftsman more of an artist."[2] The Society's initiatives aligned with the nearly genetic predisposition of New Englanders to prefer refinement to ostentation and thrift to extravagance: simple living, artisanship over mass production, and restraint in design over Victorian excess.

The Baker family's longtime friends Julia Mayhew and Ella Fairbanks were "Craftsman" members of the Society in the craft of china painting. This meant that a jury had determined their pieces to be of sufficient quality for display and sale. (Associate membership was for beginners and interested supporters, while "Master craftsman" was a distinction reserved for precisely that.)[3] Moreover, their works traveled to Paris for the first foreign exhibition of the Boston Society of Arts and Crafts in 1900.

Emilie tried her hand at china painting, but her love of color required a larger canvas. She experimented with watercolors, but when she got to metal working, she knew she had found her artistic niche. This may have been due, in part, to the influence of the Abbotts.

"He is like the old aristocrats, the best of them, who believed that privilege carried with it civic responsibility."
Uncharted Seas

Each one of the silver boxes on the tables took her back to the place where she had acquired it. She could see the very spot in an Arts and Crafts Exhibit where she had bought the oval with the red carnelian set in the cover.
I Hear Adventure Calling

Of the 748 members of the Society of Arts and Crafts in 1907, when Emilie was elected to Craftsman status,[4] only eight were from Wellesley Hills, and the first three were Abbotts. Sarah Abbott was only an enthusiast, but her brothers had attained Master status. Holker Abbott was a professional artist and a Master decorator, while Fletcher M. Abbott was a Master metalworker who was widely regarded as a true scholar of the wrought iron craft.[5]

When the Society's shop moved to Wellesley Hills for several years (1903–1906), Fletcher Abbott displayed his work locally, and the neighbors were smitten. Of the remaining five Society members from Wellesley Hills, three became Craftsman metalworkers: Emilie Loring, her neighbor Harriet Oldham, and Margaret Jones.[6] The women were at about the same stage in life. Margaret was a doctor's wife with a daughter Robert Loring's age, and Harriet was a banking agent's wife with a daughter Selden's age.

Emilie valued the tools of her trade: silver and gold, the burner, the buffer attached to a treadle for polishing, packets of gems, and jars of enamel powders ready to be transformed into glowing, colorful "jewels." She registered as a "metalworker" and made and collected silver boxes. She also made jewelry that inclined less toward restraint and more toward splash and sparkle. In one ring, glistening pink tourmalines from Maine zigzagged around lustrous pearls in a substantial, gold setting. None of her pieces are known to survive, but were one to appear, it might be identified by her artist's mark, which, for a time, at least, was "Me" for Maria Emily.

Beginning in 1907, the Society sold the works of Craftsmen and Masters in its gallery at 9 Park Street, opposite the State House.[7] An occasional exhibition was given in Copley Hall, and select pieces went on the road for public display in New York and even "out west." The price range was large, but the average member earned $160 in annual sales.[8]

One of Emilie's pieces received excellent attention in Gustav Stickley's *Craftsman* magazine of 1909. Gardner Teall's review praised,

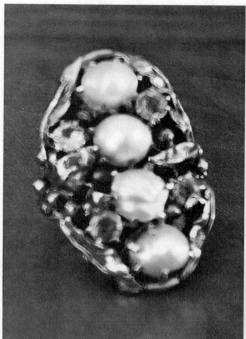

Emilie's Tourmaline and Pearl Ring

In a pendant of abalone shell and freshwater pearls, somewhat rough but very beautiful, its maker, Mrs. Victor Loring, has not only got away from the souvenir jewelry feeling that reminds one of a Niagara Falls shop, but she has created something very striking, practical, thoroughly made and within reason, so far as price is concerned. Such things are among the hopeful indications of the movement and should receive signal attention.[9]

Emilie's creative energy extended outdoors. She already had a small orchard of peach, pear, and apple trees. Now, she planted a large garden between her home and her mother's. She grew rhubarb, strawberries, raspberries, currants, gooseberries, blackberries, tomatoes, cucumbers, and grapes. Tall plumes of anchusa, spires of delphinium, and stalks

"Other girls may yearn for orchids or swoon over gardenias. It takes you to get sentimental over squashes like corpulent footballs, tomatoes gay with red paint."
My Dearest Love

Congratulations!

of lilies guarded low-growing hosta, calendula, chrysanthemums, and snapdragons.

Emilie dug and planted and watered on occasion, but daily tending and heavier work fell to the gardener, Mr. Fleming. Produce came to the kitchen to be eaten or packed into baskets for friends. Cheery bouquets brightened the table and mantel, and extras made their way to the bedsides of ill and elderly friends.

While Emilie developed her crafts and gardens, Victor's commitment to the social goals of progressivism became a passion. He served on Wellesley's school board and several years as town counsel. He joined local, ad hoc committees and donated funds for municipal projects such as the creation of Elm Park in Wellesley Hills. As a life member of the YMCA, he had frequent opportunities to support its work, and he continued in his brother's footsteps at the Royal Arcanum, the fraternal beneficiary organization.

Victor devoted himself especially to church activities. Already a member of the Wellesley Hills Congregational Club, he attended a conference in 1907 of an interdenominational "American Federation of Men's Church Organizations" whose purpose was to promote the kingdom of Christ through religious, social, and civic efforts. The Federation urged compassion and assistance to one's fellow man, not from a socialist or communist platform but from a sense of fraternal interest.[10] The organization represented more than fifteen thousand men in eastern Massachusetts, and Victor was elected their president.

The next year's Federation conference took Victor and Emilie to Boston for a month, and they stayed in the elegant Victoria Hotel on the corner of Newbury and Dartmouth.[11] It was only one block from the conference location at the Old South Church and across the street from the Boston Art Club, of which Victor was an officer. It was also nearly "home," just three blocks from the Bakers' old house on Gloucester and Victor's former home on Marlborough.

Victor earnestly desired to improve society through the individual efforts of its citizens. His address called the membership to a common vision:

> We believe in Purity, Civic Righteousness, and Fraternity. We believe in men of wholesome lives; sweet and pure family lives; neighborly lives; brotherly lives . . . We believe that the remedy for the evils of accumulation and the lawlessness of self-will which today make the Republic a subject of dire prophesy is to consider society as a unit and thereby demonstrate that the humblest member of it cannot be injured without damage to the whole body . . . For to this new crusade, self-interest urges you; patriotism inspires you; Christianity commands you.[12]

Victor traveled next to Detroit with Parris Thaxter Farwell, their minister in Wellesley Hills, who was a vice president of the Federation and edited its bimonthly publication *The Brotherhood*. Their purpose was to frame the constitution for a similar group designed specifically for Congregational men, called the "Congregational Brotherhood." The organization would bring together all of the Congregational clubs and Bible

"... but, give them a boost, and who knows but that a job, a few months in this grand country and a new deal would remake them?"
Hilltops Clear

She loved the hum and life of the city. She loved the life in a small town too, loved the neighborliness and friendliness of it.
As Long as I Live

"He is all for the beautiful and high things of life. He's firm as a rock against the bad and ugly temptations, not because he is a prude or an ascetic, but because something inside of him hates and rejects the unclean, physical, and immoral."
Lighted Windows

classes in the state and, hopefully, influence church operations. Victor and the respected journalist William Allen White, a fellow Progressive, gave keynote speeches at the meeting,[13] and when he returned to Wellesley Hills, Victor had been elected a director representing Massachusetts and a member of the new organization's executive committee of seven.[14]

During the summers of 1907 through 1909, the Lorings followed "P. T." Farwell to Cape Cod and the Sagamore Sociological Conferences, which he organized. The host was George W. Coleman, the publisher of *The Christian Endeavor World*, and the conference operated much like the Twentieth Century Club. Churchmen, businessmen and theorists came together for informal and open discussions of their divergent views of society. Each year's conference had a different focus. In 1907, it was to achieve a common understanding "of the social organism and man's social obligations." In 1908, the topic was labor.[15] Between morning and evening meetings at the Bradford Arms Hotel, Victor and Emilie socialized, swam, and walked along the nearly mile-long boardwalk of Sagamore Beach and Cape Cod Bay.

Emilie leaned toward the arts and Victor toward politics, but both believed in taking part rather than sitting on the sidelines.

"Be honest, have you ever known gloom or depression to solve a problem? Problems aren't solved that way."
Give Me One Summer

I read somewhere, "By Audacity Alone are high things accomplished." The words work like magic. If I begin to wobble, I flash them on the screen of my mind, grip determination with both hands, and shoot ahead. Of course, I make mistakes, but better to make a mistake than to huddle dejectedly on the side lines of life because one is afraid to try.[16] –Emilie Loring

CHAPTER 13

Blue Hill, Maine

Blue Hill, Summer 1909

In retrospect, the wonder wasn't that the Lorings moved to Maine the following summer but rather that they took so long to decide it. Emilie's father and Baker grandparents were Portland natives, Emilie had grown up on stories of the "down east" region, and the Lorings had returned to Maine's Rangeley Lakes, on and off, for ten years.

When she was small, her father and sister traveled to Penobscot Bay with Oliver Optic on his yacht *Violet*. Then, through the six volumes of his Yacht Club Series, Emilie's imagination sailed with Optic's characters, both boys and girls, as they went to Islesboro, Vinalhaven, Isle au Haut, Long Island's Turtle Head, between Sedgwick and Deer Isle, and through Frenchman's Bay to Mount Desert Island.

Between Penobscot Bay and Bar Harbor, solitary Blue Hill was visible to travelers by both land and sea, and Blue Hill village was easily recognized from Optic's description of his fictional "Rockhaven":

> It had two thousand tons of fishing vessels; but the granite quarries in the vicinity were the principal sources of wealth to the place. Latterly Rockhaven, which was beautifully situated on high land overlooking the waters of the lower bay, had begun to be a place of resort for summer visitors.[1]

The village of Blue Hill sits at the head of Blue Hill Bay, which carves northwest into the coast and opens roughly toward Mount Desert Island, "the Mecca of the fashionable."[2] The bay is strewn with sand bars and granite ledges that can be the devil to navigate in falling tides and nearly impassable at low tides. Even so, high tide floated the deep hulls of lumber

"There's a boat length of mud between us and water. The tide is on the run . . . We'll be stuck here for hours."
Where Beauty Dwells

Blue Hill, Maine

Evidently this was one of the stations which a paternalistic railroad organization dropped into an apparent wilderness for the use of its rich and great patrons.
Uncharted Seas

Costly summer homes, more or less architecturally fit for their surroundings, adorned or disfigured every point and curve of the inner bay which was partially separated from the outer by a disjointed peninsula of rocks and sand and glittering tide-pools.
Here Comes the Sun!

ships in the olden days, followed by granite-hauling ships as late as the early 1900s.

With the passing of the shipbuilding and quarrying trades, Blue Hill attracted a new industry: summer residents. They came when the city was too hot to bear and arrived to find clear, blue water ready for boating, swimming, fishing, and lobstering. They brought their yachts, their parties, and musical entertainments of the city. They did not arrive by automobile, as those would be forbidden in Blue Hill village for decades more. Instead, summer visitors traveled by steamer or train and then made the last of the trip by ox cart or horse and carriage. They bought up adjoining tracts of land and built summer estates to which they brought small staffs of servants.

One of the cottagers was George M. Baker's onetime agent, Miss Effie Ober. As manager of the Roberts Lyceum Bureau, Miss Ober arranged for Baker and his friend Henry Clay Barnabee to perform *Too Late for the Train* on stages throughout New England in the 1860s. When she brought Gilbert & Sullivan's *H.M.S. Pinafore* to Boston, Barnabee played the starring role of Sir Joseph. The two were indissolubly linked for the remainder of her management of the "Boston Ideals" and remained in touch long after.

Miss Ober moved to Blue Hill when Emilie was eighteen, five years before George Baker's death. She built a small cottage and named it after a comic opera, *La Mascotte*. Later, she renovated her parents' home on South Street into a veritable showplace complete with performance balconies and an oriel window overlooking the floor below. She christened it the "Ideal Lodge" (today's Barncastle Hotel) and stayed there nearly fifty summers. When her Boston colleagues, including Barnabee, transformed their former troupe into the fabulously successful Bostonians, Miss Ober wrote to them, "That my affections for those, with whom I spent so many pleasant years, has never lapsed, you who were with me, and shared my successes are fully aware."[3]

Around the time that Miss Ober returned to Blue Hill, Professor Junius Hill and a partner purchased twenty acres of land at Parker Point on the south side of Blue Hill Bay. They subdivided the property into two- to four-acre plots and sold them to arriving summer residents. Professor Hill was a professor of music at Wellesley College and sold frequently to musicians and music enthusiasts. Thanks to these sales, Miss Ober's promotional acumen, and the interpersonal chemistry of the artists, a musical colony soon thrived on Parker Point. Franz Kneisel taught chamber music at "Kneisel Hall" in the summer, music critic Henry Krehbiel was a summertime fixture, and performers included composer and organist Horatio Parker of Yale, cellist Wulf Fries, and pianist Bertha Tapper.[4]

Miss Ober's marriage to Virgil P. Kline of Cleveland brought more summer residents to Parker Point. Kline was the personal attorney for John D. Rockefeller and the legal representative for Standard Oil of Ohio for thirty years. Between them, they attracted a mixture of artists, attorneys, and wealthy friends to the summer colony.

From his bachelor days in Brookline, Victor knew Blue Hill natives who kept homes in or near the city—in particular, George A. Clough and

Julie opened the door to what in Tudor times would have been known as the minstrel gallery at Shorehaven ... Two balconies extended round three sides from which doors opened into luxurious apartments.
Here Comes the Sun!

R. G. F. Candage. George A. Clough was the first city architect of Boston. His designs included the Suffolk County Courthouse at Pemberton Square, where Victor had his first office, as well as Blue Hill's picturesque Town Hall.[5] R. G. F. Candage was a native Blue Hiller and retired ship captain who worked for the ports of Boston, served as trustee of the Boston Public Library, and, like Victor, served on local and state Republican committees. Candage published two volumes of poems about his hometown, as well as the influential *Historical Sketches of Blue Hill, Maine*.[6] Either of these men could have suggested Blue Hill as a summer residence, but no one who read a newspaper needed a special introduction.

Notices like the following appeared often in the Wellesley *Townsman*: "Quite a colony of well-known musicians are spending the summer at Bluehill . . . [actors] Richard Mansfield and Mrs. Mansfield spent a summer at Bluehill a few years ago, having a house close to the bay, where they enjoyed yachting and also driving through the beautiful country."[7]

Victor had a tangential connection to Blue Hill through the yachting community. His cousins, William Caleb and Augustus Peabody Loring, bought most of Bartlett's Island in Blue Hill Bay around the same time that the Eastern Yacht Club began its annual cruise from Marblehead to Bar Harbor. By July of 1909, "more than a score of the largest and fastest yachts of the Eastern Yacht Club" made the 250-mile trip, racing for five days and then pleasure sailing for three more days through the Casco, Penobscot and Blue Hill Bays.[8]

Locals grumbled about the arrival of summer residents, but they filled a gap in the economy, and they also brought a wealth of talent and energy to tiny Blue Hill. One of these was Marcellus Coggan, the Boston attorney who had been the opposing council in the Zoeth Higgins divorce case, all those years ago on the Cape. His home, "Seven Chimneys," was the first that visitors saw when they alighted from the steamer.

Another Blue Hill rusticator was the Lorings' neighbor on Washington Street in Wellesley Hills, Benjamin Franklin Curtis. Curtis was a partner at Curtis & Cameron, across Copley Square from the Boston Public Library.

Seven Chimneys was palatial, Sandra agreed . . . The top of the impressive porch had a lacy iron railing which enclosed the balcony from which opened a beautiful Palladian window. Moving clouds cast purple shadows on the roof; the house was of stone and clapboard, overgrown with vines, gay with window-boxes. She counted the Chimneys. Seven. *Uncharted Seas*

Curtis' lectures on the library's murals led to their first book, but their real popularity came from their "Copley prints"—duplications of famous art works in black and white, sepia, and later, color.[9]

Both Curtis and his partner, James Beaumont Noyes, were Harvard graduates and former reporters for the *Boston Herald* where Emilie's grandfather worked. Curtis was married to the former Mary Mudge, a distant cousin of long-time publisher Alfred O. Mudge who printed George Baker's first books for children.[10]

Mary Curtis and Emilie were at similar stages in life. Both belonged to the Wellesley Hills Woman's Club, loved tea parties, and had children who were close in age. Gordon Curtis was the eldest, and then came Robert Curtis who was one month older than Robert Loring, Mary Carroll who was the same age as Selden, Helen who was several years younger, and Jane Elizabeth, the Curtises' youngest, who was born in 1907 at the Curtises' summer home in Blue Hill, Maine.

While the Lorings summered at Maine's Rangeley Lakes in 1906, the Curtises purchased adjacent properties in East Blue Hill and christened their new estate "Starboard Acres." (It was to starboard when entering the bay.) They returned to Wellesley Hills that fall with a miniature pony, "about as large as a Newfoundland dog," that created quite a stir with the children.[11]

In 1907, while the Lorings traveled to Alaska, Mrs. Curtis' sister Josephine and her husband, Edward Jewett Brooks, also bought properties in East Blue Hill. Theirs were at "Friends Corner," just east of Starboard Acres. Josephine Brooks was eight years older than her sister, Mary Curtis, and the Brooks children, Elinor and Winfred, were already nineteen and twenty-two when they came to Blue Hill.

Mr. Brooks was an inventor from East Orange, New Jersey who owned more than one hundred patents. He invented "innumerable varieties of labels, seals, tags, seal presses, label racks for freight cars, window-sash locks, and lifts, lanterns and lamps, electric light carbons, baggage checks, car-door fasteners, conductors' punches, safety money packages, inking pads, post-office hand stamps and mail bags."[12] His snap seal to lock the doors of railway cars earned him a fortune when it was adopted nationwide.

The brothers-in-law each had homes upon their land, but while Curtis renovated his, Brooks brought in an architect to build something quite new for Blue Hill: a California-style bungalow with Arts and Crafts detail. Christened "Elwin Cove" (after Elinor and Winfred), the home took two years to complete, during which time the family stayed at Pendleton's hotel, near the town wharf.

The Curtises' next-door neighbors in Wellesley Hills came to Blue Hill in 1908. They were William Colburn Norcross and his wife Helen May, but they didn't buy land on the East Blue Hill side, as the others had done. Instead, they purchased their land along the Salt Pond on the other side of the bay, near Blue Hill Falls.

The falls from the Salt Pond into Blue Hill Bay were a curious phenomenon. When the tide was going out, they ran toward the sea, and the Salt Pond decreased in depth. As the tide rose again, the falls reversed and ran inland to refill the reservoir. Boaters enjoyed the challenge of riding the falls, and observers watched from a low bridge spanning the waterway.

Mill Island rested in the middle of the flow, dividing it into two streams. This was the site of first settlement at Blue Hill. The flow of the falls provided power for sawmills, and the island was an original refuge from Indians and other threats. Geography had made it so for many generations, with evidence left in the shell, bone, and pottery "heap" found on its shore. At the beginning of the 1900s, however, Mill Island was owned, almost in its entirety, by Mrs. Anne Nevin, the widow of famed composer Ethelbert Nevin. Mrs. Nevin's cottages—Wakonda, Airly Beacon, and the Tide Mill House—were filled all summer with well-connected guests who injected an extra measure of "star quality" to the summer society.

Located at the head of the bay and the foot of Blue Hill Mountain, the quiet village of Blue Hill had two churches—Congregational and Baptist—small shops along tree-shaded streets, a blacksmith, an inn, and the George Stevens Academy for high school students. Blue Hill citizens

---

"See those falls under the bridge? I have a new stunt for you. At certain tides the favorite outdoor sport here is to shoot the rapids."
Here Comes the Sun!

"This pond is eight feet above the level of the bay. The average tide here is eleven feet. In consequence the rising tide starts filling the pond an hour before flood. The outflow starts an hour after flood and increases in volume as the fall from pond to bay becomes greater."
Here Comes the Sun!

Nearer the shore nestled a village with two this-way-to-heaven sign-posts, the white spires of the churches.
Here Comes the Sun!

did the long, hard work of farmers and fishermen, lumbermen and ship builders, stonecutters and sea captains. It was no wonder they resented the abundant leisure and expensive habits of the summer residents.

It was more complex than that, of course. Miss Esther Wood (1905–2002), a lifelong resident and historian of Blue Hill, wrote that her Aunt Fan used to hide in the woods when summer residents walked by on the road, not afraid but cowed by their status. On the other hand, Esther's parents were good friends of Mr. and Mrs. Brooks, and Esther was close enough to Jane Curtis as a child that Mrs. Curtis sent Esther books every winter from the Old Corner Bookshop in Boston.[13]

Blue Hillers benefitted from the jobs that summer residents provided, at a time when the old ways of life were passing away. Young people could no longer follow their parents to the mill, shipyard or quarry. Instead, they worked as chauffeurs, private servants, cooks, and gardeners for their wealthy visitors, which meant that the groups met on uneven ground. Locals were protective of their longtime claim on the village and resentful of their dependence on the outsiders' money. For their part, the summer people wanted the status that their investment deserved and varied greatly in whether they thought of the locals as neighbors or simply a ready labor supply.

Nevertheless, Blue Hillers bragged of their acquaintance with wealthy and influential summer visitors, and in return, the summer visitors happily flaunted the rusticity of knowing lobstermen, sea captains, and farmers. In some cases, true friendships formed, with bonds of affection lasting generations. In others, the rusticators went on their way, and the locals were glad to see them go. It was a permanent, if uneasy, truce.

At the end of July in 1908, the Curtises were in Blue Hill, and the Lorings had finished at Sagamore and headed to the Rangeley Lakes. But summer didn't conclude as expected. Back in Wellesley Hills, Robert Baker's daughter, Eileen, contracted tubercular meningitis, and within two weeks, she had died. That was on August eighth, and she was cremated two days later. September twenty-second would have been her first

"But I guess your aunt wouldn't like it if she knew how friendly we was. M's. Marshall's a fine woman but she ain't no mixer."
Here Comes the Sun!

"All the young people, rustics and rusticators—that is what the natives call the summer people—played around together."
A Certain Crossroad

"You see, I've been sort of a handy man fer Brick House since I was twenty. I taught Jim to fish, to shoot, to sail a boat. He'd listen to what I said 'es though 'twas gospel. That kept me steerin' pretty straight myself."
Here Comes the Sun!

birthday, but Robert and Minnie left before then for a hotel in New York City and made plans to spend the rest of winter in the New Hampshire hills. Emilie's mother went to stay with Rachel and John in Haverhill, and that left only the Lorings at home on the family's end of Florence Avenue. It was a quiet October.

In November, Victor was elected the first president of the newly constituted Congregational Brotherhood of Massachusetts. The Reverend P. T. Farwell was elected a director at large, and Rachel's husband, John E. Gale, was elected the local director for Haverhill. It felt hollow in Wellesley Hills with the Bakers gone, and Victor had a conference to arrange in Boston, so the Lorings left Florence Avenue and headed back to the Hotel Victoria for the winter season.[14]

Victor returned to Wellesley Hills each week to teach Bible classes at the First Congregational Church. The topics were not what one might expect of religious classes, but they indicated Victor's continued, progressive drive. Under the headings of "Women in Industry" and "Wealth and Capital," separate weeks would address "What the Church Can Do," "Distribution of Wealth," and "Labor and Capital."

When spring came in 1909, the Lorings and Bakers reconvened in Wellesley Hills, everyone busy with separate projects. Emilie had metalwork projects in progress for the Society of Arts and Crafts, and Victor had several speaking engagements scheduled: in Portland for the Laymen's Christian Convention in May,[15] on the Cape for the Sagamore Sociological Conference in June, and an executive meeting of Men's Church Clubs leaders in July.[16]

Robert Baker's new play, *Beverly of Graustark*, had just opened in New York's West End theater.[17] George Barr McCutcheon's storybook romance about a European who woos an American heiress was already a smash hit as a novel, and Robert's stage version opened to enthusiastic reviews.

Rachel had just completed her play, *The New Crusade*, which she intended to produce in Wellesley the coming fall. And at fourteen, eleven, and eight, the boys of the two families—Robby, Selden, and Mel—were just eager to finish the school year and get on to summer vacation.

A sense of responsibility when there is wealth and power is the way I see life, and that's the way I intend to try to live it, live it with a man who sees it that way too.
To Love and To Honor

[They] wondered which of the plays opening that week in New York would pull the S. R. O. sign from the Success Bag, agreed that there was nothing—unless it were a book—so unpredictable.
Hilltops Clear

"Where to go?" was the question, and the Curtises provided the answer. They were going to Blue Hill in June, and they invited the Lorings to come when they were finished at the Cape. The Curtis property had woods, shoreline, and two homes upon it, and the Curtis youngsters could show the boys around.

"Starboard Acres" spread north and south of the East Blue Hill Road on old farm and quarry land. For nearly a century, trees and then stone were cut and then carried or slid down to wharves on Blue Hill Bay. There, horse-powered hoists loaded it onto ships and carried it down the New England coast to distant ports to be used in distant cities. Granite was used locally, too. It formed the foundations of Blue Hill homes, built steps and lined roadways, supported bridges, constructed wharves, and created low walls between farm fields.

"Some owners have to construct railroads; we will snake our logs down to the pond road and haul them to that old granite wharf on your shore, big lumber boats will load them—and there we are."
Hilltops Clear

Loading Granite at the Wharf

"...these State of Maine men are the dickens and all for endurance." *Here Comes the Sun!*

"Did you ever know a more typical Maine day? Here come a lot of little puffy white clouds." *Where Beauty Dwells*

The sea and the air and rocky coast set her imagination to galloping. *Here Comes the Sun!*

The windows of Stone House were faintly luminous from the afterglow. They seemed like lidless old eyes watching for home-comers. *Here Comes the Sun!*

Giants must have hoisted the huge granite blocks into place. *Here Comes the Sun!*

Some might say granite found its way into the local character, too, because the natives of Blue Hill, who came to the area in 1762, remained through the challenges of every generation, staunch, rugged, and permanent. The shore was lined with granite, swimming holes were clear above an underlayment of granite, walks in the woods led to walls and outcrops of granite, and the persistence of quarry holes was a faithful reminder of the past's recent industry.

But that wasn't what the Lorings saw first. Everywhere, there were the trademark blues and greens of Maine. Sapphire-blue water and turquoise sky, the deep black-green and spicy scent of fir and spruce, shimmering leaves along the white and gray bark of birches, ferns and sumac thick in the forest understory, moss and blueberries carpeting the ground underfoot.

The Curtis home was sprawling and relaxed. Across the road, a path led to a teahouse and swimming pool.[18] At the shore, they could swim when the tide was in and make discoveries when it receded. They found shells filled with live mussels and others left open to reveal gleaming, purple interiors. There were olive sea urchins, the telltale bubbles of clams, pebbles that crunched underfoot, and the salty-briny scent of sea air.

It was a wonderful vacation, and the Lorings didn't take long to start looking for their own place—nor to find it. Stone House sat on the south side of the East Blue Hill Road. They passed its solid, quiet exterior each time they came from town to the Curtis or Brooks homes. It was definitely "solid," for not only the foundation but also its walls were formed of huge blocks of hard, gray, Blue Hill granite. The stones were so large that only seven rows were required to achieve the structure's height and seven long slabs to span its length. A heavy version of its Cape Cod cousin, the home's rectangular base left space between the blocks for a central door and two windows on either side of it. The roof was deeply gabled.

There were also odd, mismatched parts. To the left of the door, toward East Blue Hill, was a short addition for the kitchen. Toward the village and its namesake Blue Hill, four rough-hewn wooden posts supported an

Stone House at the Beginning, 1909: With the Bay Beyond

Old Store Below

overhanging extension of the roof to create a sheltered porch across the west end of the house. Below it was a duplicate porch on the walkout basement level, supported by wooden posts and furnished, as above, with two windows and a door on the short end and three windows and a door on the back, facing Blue Hill Bay. The roof of the house was just as lop-sided: a large dormer with two windows looked out above the east side of the front entrance, and a tiny dormer with a single window peeked out above the west.

Emilie liked to quote Longfellow's poem about old houses:

All houses wherein men have lived and died
Are haunted houses. Through the open doors
The harmless phantoms on their errands glide,
With feet that make no sound upon the floors.
We meet them at the doorway, on the stairs,
Along the passages they come and go,
Impalpable impressions on the air,
A sense of something moving to and fro.[19]

... the opportunity to approach Stone House appeared heaven sent. It was more than a house; it was a personality.
Uncharted Seas

Stone House had stood through nearly a century of occupants "moving to and fro." It was like a wizened, stone grandparent with stories to tell and the sense of another time radiating from its granite walls.

If the Lorings' scholarship was correct, Stone House may have been one of the first buildings constructed in the new state of Maine when it separated from Massachusetts in 1820. No document recorded its beginning, and none took particular notice of its evolving character across the years. It was built for duty at a working quarry, pieced together from available materials, solid in performance and, like its inhabitants, not much for comment.

At the start, there were several quarries within a short walk of Stone House. One was across the road at the top of the hill, and three were located on the near side, between the house and the shore. The White

Granite Company had a high and a low quarry in operation a little to the west toward Peters Cove, but it would be fifty years before the Chase quarries were opened further east. Like Stone House, their names were casually attached—Blue Hill, Darling, Whitney, and Door Stone. These were local references, not legal titles, and like nicknames, some endured and others changed with the times.

Early on, there was a "Granite Farm" in the area, and its name was just about right for its utility. There were farms, to be sure, along the East Blue Hill Road, but farmers gave up in frustration as their plows hit hard granite shelves or turned over nothing but rock. The other side of the bay was more hospitable, with rolling loam for farmers and heavy forests to supply sawmills. Mariners made their homes on the East Blue Hill side, as did the few, doughty farmers who found bits of arable land and adequate pasture for horses. Otherwise, there was little settlement until the quarry workers came. They came for the stone, and they lived near their work. Granite Farm became the Granite Estate as temporary homes sprang up to form a worker's colony.

Stone House was the largest and most permanent building in the area for many years, and over time, it served many occupants and purposes. Its presumed builder, Jedediah Darling, used it as a home and headquarters. Later, it housed workers upstairs and the lowest floor became whatever was needed at the time—a store, a tavern, an office, or a storehouse.[20]

The main floor had three rooms for gathering, cooking, and dining, and the upstairs had two bedrooms on each end and a small room at the front which had no window, linked by a square hallway about a central staircase. There was more space than a stonecutter's family needed or could afford, so the house was shared. Initially, that happened room by room, but later, the space was allotted in east and west halves, sharing the common door but using the central stairway as a dividing point to claim bedrooms upstairs and the rooms directly beneath them.

The occupants were tenants, not owners, but when the owners decided to sell, they observed de facto possession and sold the house in halves. In

"I only stopped for a moment to look at the old house. It did something to my heart, and I lingered. I had heard so much about it."
"Of course you've heard about it; who hasn't in this part of the world?"
Uncharted Seas

1850, the house held seventeen people—the Freeman Watts family of three with three more stonecutters on the east side, and the Andrew Gavett family of eight with three more stonecutters on the west side. Darling had sold his company to a brace of Hinckleys and Holts, who operated as the "Blue Hill Granite Company," and at some point, they sold Gavett's rented half of the house to him for five hundred dollars.

Next door, the Isaac Saunders family of four lived together with four bachelor stonecutters, including Albert Whitney. Albert married Abby Saunders (thirteen years younger than he), and two daughters were born. Then, when their son Isaac was born in 1859, Hinckley, Wescott, Hinckley and Holt sold Albert one half of Stone House, dividing it "on a line with the Eastern side light of front door of Andrew Gavett's house to said Gavett's line." By then, his father-in-law, Isaac Saunders, already owned a parcel of the Granite Estate to the east of Napoleon Bonaparte Holt's, and Whitney owned a parcel to the west. For a while, the older man lived in Stone House, and the younger occupied his father-in-law's house. Later, the Gavett and Whitney families shared Stone House, with Gavett on the west and Whitney on the east, until Gavett retired and moved to Portland in 1870.[21]

Meanwhile, Eli Blagdon returned from a year of service in the Civil War, lived in the ell with his family, and operated a store in the basement. His son Charles is supposed to have carved the initials "CB" that remain on a boulder outside the ell door.[22]

That mark was more permanent than the people inside, whose history read like a George Baker play, with frequent shuffling of roles and identities. When Gavett left, he sold his western half of Stone House to Albert Whitney, who briefly owned the entire house. However, Eli Blagdon was still living in the east-side ell, so Whitney sold him Gavett's west side of the house, which Blagdon later sold to Edwin Dutton after the latter married Albert Whitney's daughter Fanny (Frances Viola). That left Whitney in the east and his son-in-law Dutton in the west of the house.

When the quarry business faltered, Dutton went to Blue Hill's newest industry, copper mining. In this, he joined the ranks of many Blue Hillers who sank their wealth and energy into mines whose treasure proved scant. R. G. F. Candage observed, in his history of Blue Hill, that "One who knew that locality before the mining craze, were he now to return to it, would witness a scene of desolation that would make him heartsick."[23] Between 1870 and 1890, the land was scalped of its forests and riddled with excavations, but the promise of copper was not fulfilled. The fortunes and hopes of much of the village were lost.

Whitney moved to Massachusetts and died there. Eli Blagdon and his wife died within a week of each other. Edwin Dutton sold off part of his holdings to Pearl Parker, and the rest was acquired by the Blue Hill Granite Company which went bankrupt and sold out to Lyman Willcutt of Boston. The Darlings, Holts, Hinckleys and Wescotts who quarried Blue Hill Granite in its heyday were all dead, as was the market for granite. Reinforced concrete made the quarrying and shipping of huge granite blocks an unnecessary expense for building. Skills of stonecutting and masonry gave way to steel and concrete. Stone House and the Granite Estate were quiet. The Willcutts looked for a buyer, and down the East Blue Hill Road came Emilie and Victor, visiting their friends, the Curtises.

"When we bought the stone house it was a curiosity," Emilie recalled.[24] The stone portion of the house was formidable, and it captured views of passersby to the north, Blue Hill to the west, and Blue Hill Bay to the south. Combining all of the associated holdings of Blue Hill Granite, the granite estate, some small properties, and Stone House, Emilie would have more than two hundred fifty acres of Maine real estate.[25]

The property started at the quarry on top of the hill and took the same path as the granite, all the way down to the old granite wharf. South of the East Blue Hill Road, it encompassed all of the former granite estate, except that portion still owned by the stonecutter Pearl Parker. Along the road, it included a former office building of the granite company and ran eastward to the Curtises' boundary, with a large tract of woods between them. At the shore, the property began west of the old granite wharf and ended beyond Sculpin Point.

"And were the jewels buried?" "Figuratively. They were sold by a black sheep who is known as the Mad Trafford in the family annals. The proceeds were used to finance a copper-mine... After a while men refused to work in the mine—there had been but a few pockets of copper there, anyway." *Here Comes the Sun!*

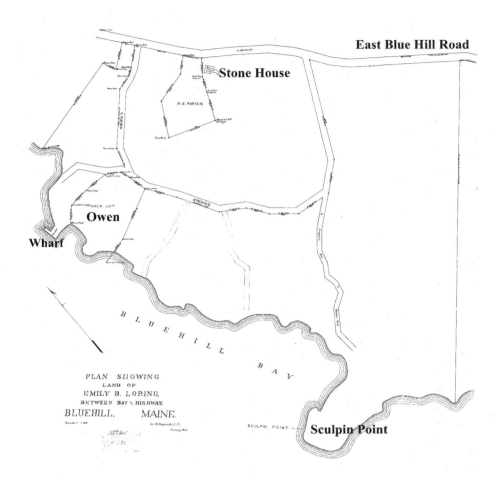

A portion of Emilie's land, south of the East Blue Hill Road

Here was the best of the Maine woods and the New England coast, put together with the conveniences of a village and the social opportunities of the city. For the next forty-two years, it would be Emilie's second home and, in many ways, her dearest.

It said something of the Lorings that they looked at the dilapidated, unbalanced, granite structure and decided to make it their home. Neither had lived in anything even remotely like it. Before marriage, Emilie had lived in a city apartment, two townhouses, two mansions, and an assortment of elegant hotels. Victor's childhood home was a temple-front, Greek revival showpiece set apart on its own lawn, tall and stately behind white columns. In Boston, his family maintained large and dignified domiciles of the type at which visiting cards were presented, and a servant ushered gloved visitors to the parlor.

The Lorings' home in Wellesley Hills was both spacious and fashionable, and one might have expected them to buy or build a summer place on stylish Parker Point. But Emilie felt something for the rough, stone shell that showed the effects of nearly one hundred years of hard winters and hard use. "The moment my glance lighted upon the deserted, down-at-the-heel mass of granite, I coveted it."[26]

No sooner had the ink dried on their purchasing documents than workers set to the task of transformation. Years of neglect and lop-sided alterations were erased. Front and rear dormers enlarged the bedrooms and brought in both fresh air and daylight. Emilie and Victor's rooms on the west looked out a bay window to Blue Hill, and the inner bay was in full view to the south.

"The element of risk is inseparable from any business enterprise, but there is such a thing as open-eyed risks. If one never embarked on a project for fear it might turn out a failure, one never would get far. Have you a plan of your land?"
Fair Tomorrow

East Blue Hill Road, Looking West from Stone House

The Lorings had a quarry of their own now, and they used their own stone to build a granite terrace supported by huge, granite arches that left the lower level open for access. "In the cellar was a well of the clearest, coolest water," but it proved inadequate as the home's sole supply. Additional spring water was piped down the hill and across the road, and flush toilets were brought in, with their reservoirs installed in the attic. Electricity was added and then a phone. They added an angled ell to the kitchen to provide small quarters for a maid.

Renovations began in September, and by April, the family moved in new furnishings for the coming season. "By the time the old house was renovated and furnished there was a hole in our bank account which tunneled underground some way into the years ahead."[27]

Stone House Renovation, Front

Stone House Renovation, Side

Stone House, Back

Wellesley Hills, Winter 1909–1910

While work proceeded on Stone House, Emilie returned to Wellesley Hills for a full season of Baker family dramatics. The Wellesley Hills Woman's Club scheduled Rachel's play *The New Crusade* for December,[28] and Emilie and Rachel hosted a tea to organize the production. Rehearsals began, described later in a poem by one of the ladies:

We remember yet—shall we ever forget?
the rehearsals in Maugus Hall,
When we tried to group our "all-star" troupe
On a stage that was twice too small.
And each of us knew the other's cue,
But nobody knew her own.[29]

There was time out for Thanksgiving and a late-November, vaudeville performance in Maugus Hall by Robert Baker. Finally, it was Gentleman's Night, and the curtain rose.

The New Crusade dealt with "the servant question." In the opening scene, the agency manager complains, "Maids and places by the score, but I cannot put them together." A comedy of complaints ensues, and one lady remarks, "This domestic problem has grown so serious. I wish that we could be independent and not have any maids for a while." That sets up a six-week experiment in which the ladies, unaccustomed to housework and cooking, give it a try:

"Only our husbands have suffered. Think of the failures the poor dears have been obliged to eat."

"When I told Mr. Brown that I would make him a pie, he said, 'My dear! Why not *buy* it!'"[30]

"After they'd walked through the first act, it was a choice between dismissing the cast or shooting them. I had a sane interval and decided not to shoot. I'm giving them tomorrow night off."
With Banners

The New Crusade highlighted tensions between classes and between the sexes. The Fourteenth Amendment to the constitution (1868) protected voting rights for all male citizens, and the Fifteenth Amendment clarified that voting rights could not be denied on the basis of race or previous servitude. But *women* still could not vote, whatever their race or condition.

Emilie's father was an early feminist. His lyceum presentation, "Xanthippe the Scold" defended Socrates' scolding wife instead of criticizing her, and he supported Julia Ward Howe's suffrage organization in an 1875 play for his magazine, *Our Boys and Girls.* "Shall Our Mothers Have the Vote?" featured a debate between boys at school. One boy argues:

"Who have governed the greatest men that ever lived? Mothers
... They spur us on to excel and guard our ways with good counsel.
Give them the ballot, and their influence will make better laws."

His opponent counters:

"Mothers govern us until we are free; once free, 'tis man's privilege
to govern them, and I am not in favor of giving up one iota of our
manly privileges, when we get them."

The women's suffrage amendment failed in the 1870s, but the issue gained new impetus with Emilie's generation. Increased educational opportunity, broadened labor roles, and the woman's club movement created a new force for women's achievement and influence across all sectors of society.

In October of 1909, Mrs. Pankhurst of England spoke to more than two thousand people in Boston's Tremont Temple. She had already spent more than fourteen weeks in prison for her confrontational tactics in Britain and was in danger of being jailed again when she returned to

"The men may like the woman—as a woman. They may admire her. But—they won't want her in office."
The Solitary Horseman

"We have talked largely about what we would do if we were given equal civic opportunity with our husbands and fathers and brothers and friends of the male persuasion. Our opportunity/ has come."
The Solitary Horseman

"If you say that woman's place is in the home, I'll throw something at you. Preferably something that squashes."
The Solitary Horseman

England, having stormed the House of Commons in June to present a petition for women's suffrage. Mrs. Pankhurst invoked the United States Bill of Rights and encouraged Massachusetts women to petition their government for the right to vote.[31]

In January of 1910, a professor from the Institute of Technology in Boston voiced the opposition. To extend suffrage to women would only increase the number of "ignorant" voters among those registered, Professor Sedgwick said. "Why burden women with the ballot when no particular good seems likely to come from such a step?"[32]

Into the fray leapt the Bakers. For a February charity event in Haverhill, Robert Baker produced Rachel's new play, *Wigs on the Green*, with Rachel acting its principal role.[33]

Now is the appointed time. It is the hour to strike for freedom! To be man's equal! Aye, his superior. At the ballot—at the polls—North or South—it does not matter which—at home— abroad—and from the Alleghanies on the East—to the Rockies on the West—we will plant our flag—emblem of the achievement of women!

But it was not yet the time. On March first, a legislative committee voted 7–4 against a suffrage bill that would have amended the Massachusetts constitution to allow women the vote. At the women's college in Wellesley, the newly constituted "Woman's Suffrage Club" was both disappointed and defiant. They had fought resistance to become a sanctioned club in the first place, and they had earned the support of their president and faculty to aid striking garment workers in New York. They were not going to give up now.

Three days later, *Wigs on the Green* was presented in Maugus Hall by the Wellesley Hills Woman's Club, to "a very large and enthusiastic audience." In typical Baker fashion, the play made its point with humor. To those who feared that giving women the vote would undermine the proper relations between men and women, an "old maids'" song was sung:

Altho' we're forty, we are quite saucy,

And we laugh at the ills of life.

Glance like this, so shy,

Gowns like this, oh, my!

We just love the good things of life.

Side-step just like this, another one like that

From fetters we are free, so we can happy be.

A knowing glance like that,

Another one like this,

We really would not miss, a tiny little kiss.

There were the trademark identity switches, with the protagonist failing utterly in her attempt to pass as a man in a fake moustache and an elaborate ruse to hide the "unseemly conduct" from two elderly aunts. The audience was left with a marching song for the cause:

We are the suffragettes

Know us by our badge of yellow.

We do not stew and fret,

Each one a jolly fellow.

No more to sew, to brew, to bake.

In other ways we'll take the cake.

We'll be the presidents of our land

And show the men we have some sand.

From the all-female cast of Rachel's play, attention shifted the next week to Victor's efforts at the all-male meeting of the American Federation of Men's Church Organizations in Boston. Once again, the goal was to break down barriers, this time denominational. Men's groups had labored individually a long while, limited in both scope and resources. Uniting under one banner, the banner of Christian men, they seized the opportunity to do Christ's work for all of society in ways that could be large in scope

Whatever the faults of the younger generation—what younger generation hasn't had them—the girls are being trained to express themselves in public. *The Solitary Horseman*

The applause was soul-satisfying. Continuous. Woman turned to woman, eyes snapping, cheeks excitement red. . . . There could be no doubt but that the female political pot was bubbling lustily. *The Solitary Horseman*

while still preserving, through democratic means, the independence and self-determination of the individual church clubs. There were representatives of the Baptist, Episcopal, Unitarian, Universalist, Congregational, Roman Catholic, Presbyterian, and Methodist churches in attendance,[34] and, again, Victor was elected their president.

A lifelong member of the Young Men's Christian Association, Victor's tenure coordinated expansion of the YMCA facilities and mission. Where there was no active YMCA, men's clubs were created wherein wholesome activities could be pursued, away from the degradations of liquor, cheapness, and vice. Men were encouraged to teach more Sunday school classes, sponsor more works of local charity, and recruit non-churchmen into their ranks.[35]

From abolition of slavery, to improved relations between the serving and the served, to women's suffrage, to unification of church denominations behind a common goal, the Bakers and Lorings spoke up. Humor was the favored tool of the Bakers; determination was the Lorings'. Emilie used both: "All of which is another way of saying 'fortune favors the brave.' 'Favors!' It gets behind and pushes."[36]

Blue Hill, Summer 1910

Blue Hill brought something new into Emilie's life. Before, summers had taken her to this hotel or that, a new camp, a different cottage, a new lodge. They were vacation places only. Stone House was a summer place, a vacation place, but it offered the stability of a fixed spot on the horizon at which to point every year.

The Baker and Loring families on Florence Avenue had drifted apart. Rachel was only fifty-two, but her husband was seventeen years older, and they stayed close to home in Haverhill, summering at nearby Swampscott. Since Eileen's death, Robert's family spent nearly half of the year in New York and summers in the New Hampshire hills. In Blue Hill, the Lorings made new friends who returned every summer, just as they did.

The summer of 1910 was the Lorings' first, full season of occupancy and required extra preparation. Furniture had been carried up and put in place in April, but unlike furnished rentals of the past, they needed to think more comprehensively for Stone House. They required their own dishes, tools, cooking implements, linens, and entertainments. They needed clothes for swimming, sailing, hiking, visiting, gardening, parties, and church. It was another household entirely, and it took the months of May and June to gather their belongings, close the Wellesley Hills house, and depart.

Emilie, Victor, Robby, and Selden took one steamer to Rockland, another to Blue Hill's steamship wharf, and then traveled the rest of the way by carriage to Stone House. The boys commandeered a room upstairs on the east, and Victor and Emilie took separate but adjoining rooms on the west, with the bay window view of Blue Hill. Their single, "maid-of-all-work" was given the small, ell room near the kitchen.

The living room, "a mammoth affair," invited summer ease with gentle color and an absence of clutter. Soft green walls, woodwork and rug complemented the deep-brown, hardwood floors. Emilie described for the Countryman's Journal:

> The casement windows, sunk into the two-foot, granite wall, are hung with cretonne, gay with the rose and crimson and green of hollyhocks. The green wicker furniture has cushions of the same material.[37]

The windows framed Blue Hill's sparkling, inner bay, sapphire blue and inviting. Inside, a gate-leg table by the hearth accommodated afternoon tea and summer reading.

> [We] built bookshelves at each end of a broad window seat from which one could look out at bay and mountain, designed to hold volumes of *Everyman's Library*. We stocked them with Dickens,

Life is much more of an adventure if a man dashes into his wife's room for her to slip in his cuff links than if he is fussing and fuming about them at his dresser in the same room."
We Ride the Gale!

Broad sofa and cushions were covered, like the wing chair, in chintz a riot of pale pink, purples, and soft greens against a white background. The desk was a Governor Winthrop reproduction.
I Hear Adventure Calling

Stone House Entry. In later years, she wrote in the "gun room" to the right.

Stone House Desk and Clock; Emilie's typewriter, with a view to the front garden and East Blue Hill Road.

Fireplace, Florals and Flowers; "A room without flowers is a room without a soul." There Is Always Love

Trollope, Jules Verne, Macaulay, Agnes Strickland in gay blue and Plato's "Republic" in sober gray, in company with many others which we hoped that our family would learn to know and enjoy. Each year I added a few volumes. Each year, alas, a few disappeared into that Never-Never Land from which no book traveler returns.[38]

The *Everyman's* volumes were color-coded by type: pale green for classical, carmine for fiction, olive for poetry and drama, blue for romance, and onward through all thirteen genres. Their endpapers and title pages were in William Morris' Arts and Crafts style and included an inspirational quotation to set the mood of each volume.[39] They were booklovers' books, and they had certainly come to the right place. As each was read, the date of completion and the reader's initials were recorded on the final page.

Along the shore, a new home was under construction. When the Lorings bought Stone House, they immediately transferred one and one-half acres to Caroline Duke Owen, and subsequent deeds brought her property's total to nearly four acres. Caroline was the youngest of the three Owen sisters from Philadelphia, daughters of Civil War general Joshua T. Owen. Owen was a Welsh immigrant-turned-lawyer who married Annie J. Sheridan, daughter of Owen Sheridan, one of the wealthiest men in Philadelphia. After serving in the War, General Owen founded a law journal, the New York *Daily Register*, but the family kept its home near the Sheridans, in a mansion at Philadelphia's Chestnut Hill.

Elizabeth Gray Owen was the eldest, born in 1860. Then came Mary Dale Owen, four years younger and closest in age to Emilie, and finally, Caroline Duke Owen, a late arrival in 1875. They were tiny women—"Bessie" five-foot-two, "Minnie" the tallest at five-foot-three, "Carrie" only four-foot-ten—and all had the blue eyes and fair skin of their Welsh heritage. Each also had a trademark color which was used in her clothing and accessories. Bessie wore green, Minnie blue, and Carrie wore purple. Esther Wood recalled, "A dress might be flowered; a coat might be trimmed with a black velvet collar, but never did a sister forget herself and use the color of another."[40]

By the time the Owen sisters began their annual visits to Blue Hill in 1906, their father and an older brother had been dead nearly twenty years

The Owen sisters: Bessie, Minnie, and Carrie

and their mother almost ten. The sisters had traveled to the British Isles, to Germany and to Italy. When they first came to Blue Hill, they lived on Parker Point at the lodge "Homestead" and three summers in the tiny cabin "Brightly."

The Owen sisters were heirs to both Sheridan and Owen money, but their principal had dwindled. Their married brother, David, took over the New York law journal after their father's death, but he eventually returned to Philadelphia with no journal, no wife, and no job. To help make ends meet, the sisters opened the Green Dragon Tea House on South Fifteenth Street in Philadelphia. They operated the tearoom during the year and vacationed at Blue Hill in the summer.

The Lorings quickly worked out a deal by which the youngest, Caroline, would purchase a prime, shoreline portion of the Stone House estate and build a summer home there. Financial circumstance notwithstanding, Caroline agreed that the home's value would be at least $1500. The resulting cottage was "Tyn-y-Coed," Welsh for "House in the Woods."[41] It might well have been christened "Ty y Clogwyn" instead, "The Cliff House," for its location directly overlooking Blue Hill Bay.

In those early years, the East Blue Hill Road hummed with projects. The Curtis' new gardens began near the house and followed a granite path to both an open-air tea house and a swimming pool. When Elwin Cove was completed, Mr. Brooks renovated two old houses on his property, one for each of his children, and then added a tennis court and miniature golf course. The Owen sisters transformed the small quarry hole near their cottage into a beautiful, sunken garden filled with ferns and lilies and spring bulbs. Stone House was already like new, but the Lorings added their own tennis court to the west of the house, and a green and white striped awning was installed above the stone terrace to provide shade for outdoor entertaining. Theirs was a society of summer friends, and the four families gathered frequently over the next two decades for clambakes, parties, teas, and conversation.

"Their father was an eminent lawyer. There was money and social position. The parents died. So did the fortune."
Where Beauty Dwells

"[I] was just deciding that I would name the tea-house, which dire necessity obliged me to start, the Blue Dragon or the Copper Flagon . . ."
The Mother in the Home

Victor J. Loring

Hands in the pockets of her cardigan, she stood in the great doorway from which she could see two fawn color and white cows grazing in a nearby pasture, the shimmering, boulder-bordered bay, the hills of Mt. Desert, a lovely amethyst against a fleece-dotted backdrop of azure sky.
Hilltops Clear

Summer residents generally arrived from May to July and remained until after the Blue Hill Fair in early September. In July, the Eastern Yacht Club made its annual, coastal tour from Marblehead to Bar Harbor, and August brought the annual baseball game between the "Visitors" and the year-round residents. Ben Curtis played piano accompaniment for Choral Society recitals, and Edward Brooks raised funds to buy firefighting equipment for the village, gaining donations from the Lorings, Slavens, and Owens on their side of the Bay.[42]

On August 17, 1910, bronze plaques were dedicated on Tenney Hill and Mill Island to commemorate the founders of Blue Hill, Joseph Wood and John Roundy. It was an important event, and Mrs. Nevin invited the more than three hundred people in attendance to her shore afterward for a picnic and clambake. Three of the four speakers at the dedication were natives of Blue Hill: R. G. F. Candage, John F. Wood, and L. Ward Peters. The fourth was Victor Loring.[43]

It was typical of Victor that he immediately involved himself with the local community and its civic affairs, but why was he, as a new arrival, chosen to speak at the dedication? There were other lawyers in Blue Hill, all with longer histories in the community. There were better known social figures with more significant fortunes. Victor had a connection to Beverly, Massachusetts, which was the hometown of the founders and the current location of President Taft's summer White House. He surely knew Captain Candage, George A. Clough, and others from Brookline. But in a town with only two churches, and one of them Congregational, it seems that Victor's prominent, national positions as the president of both the Congregational Brotherhood and the American Federation of Men's Church Organizations gave him the edge.

Living in Blue Hill was different from visiting. There was time to absorb the rhythmic change of the tides and learn to adjust one's plans to it. There was time to explore the woods and find quarry holes, wildflowers, and unexpected vistas. There was time to discover the remainders of the granite estate—logs from camps, a low fence made of stone, the occasional bit of metal or porcelain, a stream filled with old bottles.

Summer was the season of gardens and blueberries, clambakes and pleasure boating. And fog. It could come at any time, but fog was likely from May to September and particularly in July and August. Days could be turquoise blue with nary a cloud, or deep sapphire with puffs of white, and then a haze would appear in the distance that signaled fog was on its way.

"She confided in a whisper. 'I don't like little-neck clams. I always hide them in the ice.'"
"Why not leave them in their shells?"
"Why advertise my plebeian lack of taste?"
Uncharted Seas

A cold, bone-penetrating fog transformed trees into ghostly giants, houses into weird dwarfs and filled the world. Moisture dripped from twigs and branches.
Hilltops Clear

"Certain, certain, my dear. Doesn't every self-respecting property as old as this have a ghost?"
Uncharted Seas

Was it the Stone House ghost? Silly! Hadn't she pricked that spooky bubble?
Uncharted Seas

"Od's blood, woman! Did ye think to escape? You're coming with me."
Gay Courage

Locals knew that boats needed to come in or find safety. Even President Taft's yacht ran to open sea that summer when dense fog obliterated the Penobscot light. With fog horns blaring, the *Mayflower* dropped anchor outside the bay until all was clear in the morning.[44]

It was the same for those on land. Once the fog closed in, there was no going anywhere, so all had better get to where they wanted to be. At first, the fog filled mainly the hollows and low spaces, but at its thickest, a hundred-foot spruce standing outside the window was made invisible. Everything inside became damp.

The shrouded gloom, clanging bellbuoys and moaning foghorn begged for the telling of an eerie story, like the one about Stone House's ghost. Yes, Stone House was haunted—"which interesting if not wholly alluring fact was kept discreetly in the background till the purchase money had been paid," Emilie recalled.[45]

The wraith wasn't a sea captain or stone cutter; instead, it was a mother who grieved the death of her child. A female guest at the house in the mid-1800s reported that the apparition led her to the cellar. It pointed to the well and said, "They have buried my baby there." An excavation was undertaken, and no baby was found, but that didn't stop the haunting. Some saw her through the windows, others in the hall. Local lore held that, in life, the ghost had lost both her seafaring husband and her infant at the same time. After going nearly mad from sorrow, she carried her grief to the next world. More pragmatic explanations were the usual—wind, imagination, the creaking of old boards in an old house, the wail of porcupines in the forest—but the stories of ghosts kept coming.[46]

As did tales of pirates. The Maine coast teemed with accounts of Captains Kidd and Bellamy, Dixey Bull, and scores more, who were rumored to have hidden their treasure on one small island or another. Seventeenth-century French coins were once found on an island near Blue Hill,[47] and there just had to be more loot left behind. Or maybe a skull. In 1875, Samuel Drake wrote, "There is scarcely a headland or an island from Montauk to Grand Menan which according to local tradition does not contain some portion of [Kidd's] spoil."[48] Enough ships had wrecked on the shoals and islands of Blue Hill and Penobscot Bay through the years that there were always bits of timber, shards of glass, and small trinkets to excite the imagination.

Sunny days prompted hikes to the top of Blue Hill itself. The 950-foot mountain[49] appeared "blue" from a distance, but it also appeared blue up close. Its base was composed of a deep, mariner-blue granite with white veins of quartz that yielded to weathered gray at the summit. An old, bumpy trail wound across and around the hill, ever upward, to the top. It was not an easy hike. Pine and spruce roots crisscrossed the steep path, which was already studded by submerged rocks and littered with loose gravel. Alongside in the forest, smaller boulders wore jackets of moss, and old granite outcrops were covered with ferns that escaped the forest floor to live on a top-dressing of decayed, fallen leaves.

At each turn, the view behind grew increasingly wide and distant, and on a clear day, the view from the summit was spectacular. Forest green masses divided the azure blue of bays and inlets. Specks of white were sails. Bits of gray were summer cottages. Straight down, the spires of the Baptist and Congregational churches stood out from the cluster of buildings that was the village, and across the inner bay, a patch of clear green marked the new golf links near Parker Point. Directly south, Third Pond stood out, with its floating island and three smaller satellite ponds. Far beyond, the reflective shimmer interrupted by hazy, silhouetted forms was Penobscot Bay. Blue Hill's summit was bare, gray granite, except for the blueberries that grew wild in its crevices, and those were numerous. If it was a pleasant day, they enjoyed a picnic and basked in sunshine before heading back down the mountain.

No doubt but what the sinister figure leaning against the pillar was a valiant captain, a pirate chief. *Gay Courage*

In the inner harbor boats of all types and sizes swung at their moorings. At the town wharf a schooner—picturesquely colorful in the distance—was being loaded with lumber. *Here Comes the Sun!*

CHAPTER 14

Wellesley Hills Woman's Club

Wellesley Hills, Fall 1910

"He needs the contact and competition of boys of all ages. He must be trained to be captain of his soul and body. "
It's A Great World!

"You know his grin. I thought it would split his face in two parts when the Headmaster called in a stocky lad and told him to show 'Holden' around . . . He will be a good mixer."
It's A Great World!

At the conclusion of the Blue Hill fair, the Lorings returned to Wellesley Hills and delivered Robby to his first year of prep school in western Massachusetts. The Berkshire School outside Sheffield was a non-denominational, boarding school whose headmaster was both a Harvard graduate and a Unitarian. In three years, the school had grown to seventy students and nine faculty members on its three-hundred-fifty-acre campus at the foot of Mount Everett. Boys could prepare for "any College or Scientific School,"[1] although Harvard was a strong expectation. Their curriculum was a classical education combined with "exceptional opportunity for study in simple and wholesome surroundings."

In addition to exploring the scenic Housatonic Valley and wooded Mount Everett, the Berkshire School offered an "athletic field, tennis, skating, hockey, and all outdoor sports."[2] By spring, Robert was on the club baseball team, and in subsequent years, he added football, hockey, and the rifle club.[3]

Emilie maintained that a mother's job was important enough and sufficiently demanding to be her full-time occupation, but with Robby away at school and Selden nearly twelve, her time was increasingly her own. She had been a member of the Wellesley Hills Woman's Club for many years, and this year, she began the first of two, consecutive terms as vice president. The members met twice each month, from November to May, to discuss an intentionally diverse array of topics. As vice president, Emilie arranged for speakers and hosted many of the luncheon meetings in her home.

The women of the Wellesley Hills Woman's Club belonged to what Blue Hill author Mary Ellen Chase called "the last of the many generations who will have studied the classics as a matter of course."[4] If they studied beyond grammar school, they learned languages, drawing, painting, and singing.

They were well-read women who attended the opera, symphony, theater, and art gallery. They did not yet have the right to vote, but that did not deter their claim to equal intellectual pursuit and civic interest. They followed public affairs, and their purpose when they gathered for a luncheon or program was to promote "ethical, social and educational culture in the community" by bringing "the force of knowledge to bear upon questions which have heretofore only enlisted sympathies."[5]

Emilie's first choice for a speaker in November fit the bill perfectly. Mrs. Mabel Loomis Todd had traveled to the Philippines, Fiji, Hawaii, West Africa, and twice to Japan. She had written books about solar eclipses and sunsets, and—surely a unique qualification for the time—she was considered an authority on Mars.

Mabel was the daughter of an astronomer, and she married an astronomer. Her husband's work at Amherst College introduced her to the reclusive poet Emily Dickinson and started a long-term relationship between Mabel and the Dickinson family. Curiously, she never actually set eyes upon the poet until her death, but Mabel's position with the family was such that she brought Emily Dickinson's poems and letters to their first publication.

A well-publicized lawsuit ensued later, over the ownership of some Dickinson land, but it would be many decades before it was known publicly that the true source of contention was Mabel's thirteen-year love affair with Emily Dickinson's married brother. Emily Dickinson's star rose, and so did Mabel's. She established an active travel, writing, and lecture career. She wrote poems of her own and became a charter member of the newly formed Boston Authors Club.

Mabel's presentation for the Wellesley Hills Woman's Club was "An Aerial Voyage," the account of a daring trip she took in a hot-air balloon with her husband the previous May. Ascending seven thousand feet and then balancing precariously, Mabel and David Todd observed, sketched,

"You haven't told me what New York shows you liked best last winter. I go over once or twice a month. I saw them all—perhaps you can tell me why the modern playwright has such a yen for the drab and sordid—or what music you prefer, or whether you're strong for modern art—can't see anything in it myself—or what books you read."

As Long as I Live

She propped her chin in one pink palm and looked up at the starry sky. Worlds upon worlds above her. Would the riddle of the meaning of their existence ever be solved; would rocket ships ever shoot their way through airless and heatless space to the moon or to red Mars? If only she could live to see it.
Uncharted Seas

Julie sneakingly wondered if perhaps there were such a thing as a conjunction of planets which set extraordinary events in motion.
Here Comes the Sun!

Some day you'll hear of him as being the leading authority on children in the country. He is in New York one day every week.
Where's Peter?"

photographed, and took measurements of Halley's Comet, which had returned on its seventy-five-year cycle.[6]

It was most exotic—the balloon, its height, the mystery of the night and the comet, and even a gunshot that was fired at the couple while they were aloft.[7] The Todds literally dodged the bullet and remained focused on their scientific questions. Had the comet changed in size? Was its path through the sky altered since its last appearance? Was its tail curved or straight? What other observations could be made by balloon? Could they one day go high enough to break free of earth's gravity? Could they communicate with other planets?[8]

The public waited anxiously for the earth to pass through the comet's tail twelve days later. Some feared dangerous gases and went to bed with their windows closed against potential peril. Some predicted doomsday, others sought counsel from doctors and clergymen.[9] The light-hearted set up comet-watching parties atop the highest points they could find, which were often hotel roofs. At one point, more than two hundred New Yorkers crowded onto the Waldorf-Astoria's roof to peer through a telescope.[10] By November, the event was long over, but when Mrs. Mabel Loomis Todd was invited to Emilie's home to speak of her balloon experience, the Wellesley Hills Woman's Club members came in droves.

Emilie's next choice was Dr. Charles Gilmore Kerley.[11] The husband of Emilie's dear friend Beth McClannin was renowned as a children's doctor and an author of books on childcare. His book, *Short Talks with Young Mothers on the Management of Infants and Young Children*, was published at the birth of their first daughter and updated after the birth of their second. The core of his philosophy was respect for both mother and child and the pursuit of rational reasons for care decisions. Without condescension, Dr. Kerley advocated cleanliness, fresh air, exercise, a balance of healthful foods, and a respectful consideration of problems from the child's point of view.

Dr. Kerley's December presentation on "The Conservation of Children" proposed public health initiatives to establish safeguards and assistance for children in the form of school nurses, dietary programs for poor children, a program of in-home visiting nurses, and education for young mothers. Victor capitalized on the opportunity and invited all of the local physicians in active practice to attend the luncheon as well. It was, therefore, a large and mixed audience of both women and men who attended the Wellesley Hills Woman's Club event on December seventh. The event also provided an excuse for the Kerleys to come for a weeklong visit with the Lorings on Florence Avenue.

Two weeks later, Emilie Loring and Mary Curtis together hosted a luncheon that concluded with a recital by George Harris, considered by many to have "one of the finest tenor voices in the country."[12] George's father was the President of Amherst College, and George Jr. had recently returned home after three years of vocal study in Paris. In another year, he would earn acclaim as a popular soloist in the concert halls of New York, but now, his performances were given mainly for the Congregational church, where his tenor voice was described as having "an unusual range, tuneful and clear and under almost perfect control."[13]

"There's the office telephone again. The young mothers don't give Peter a moment's peace. They call him if the baby makes a face while asleep. He's a lamb."
Where's Peter?

"All preaching isn't done in the pulpit. I've seen a singing voice accomplish what talking never could have done in years... Dio mio! Your voice would waft men straight to heaven."
Swift Water

ACT FOUR:
Josephine Story

"You have come up against them, haven't you? One of those moments upon which you look back, catch your breath and think, 'Suppose I had let the chance pass? What rich experiences, what happiness, I would have missed.'"

—Emilie Loring

CHAPTER 15

Her Box of Books

Wellesley Hills, Spring 1911

Years later, Emilie acknowledged the importance of Agnes Edwards Rothery to the beginning of her writing career. Mrs. Rothery graduated from Wellesley College and wrote for the *Ladies' Home Journal* before she took charge of the woman's page at the *Boston Herald*.

Emilie didn't write. She had never submitted anything for publication, nor had she written even a poem in hopes of doing so. But she had thought about it. She had critiqued books since she was six. She came from three generations of writers, and she read voraciously. Of course, she had thought about writing. How could she not?

Then again, how could she? She was still responsible for seeing that her family was fed and dressed, that her home ran smoothly. Social and civic activities took what was left of the winter season, and Stone House now occupied her summers. How could she add two hours of writing every day?

She evaluated her activities. "Are they worth while?" she asked. What returns did they give for the effort expended? Did they benefit her spiritually, artistically, materially?

She was only forty-five, but life gave no guarantees. Death took Edward Boles at thirty-seven, Victor's brothers in their forties, and her father at fifty-eight. What was important to accomplish—now, while she had the opportunity? What goals would she set for herself?

Victor encouraged, "You have always wanted to write. Now is your chance. Write." She recalled, "His suggestion took away my breath for a minute. With so many writers in the family to live up to, could I do it? At least I could try, I decided."[1]

> Maybe everyone had to wrench free from the pattern someone else had designed for her, maybe outside that pattern the world would be made up largely of crooked lanes and rough roads, but she had to get outside and take her chance.
> *Give Me One Summer*

> From early childhood she had ached to be a writer ...
> *Give Me One Summer*

She asked Agnes Edwards Rothery if she could write a weekly book review for the *Boston Herald*. Her brother had written two successful columns for the *Boston Globe*; why not try it?

On the other hand, reading wasn't writing, and she was an untried author; what if it didn't go as well as she hoped? Would she disappoint herself or her family? She decided to write under the pseudonym "Josephine Story," a feminization of Victor's middle names.

The column was conceived as a set of letters written to a friend, "Constance," suggesting books for different purposes. The seven-letter series, "Her Box of Books" ran from March through May 1911, and each article considered a different selection of books from the box. The first introduced the series, "In which one telleth of her adventures, in the realm of fiction, while in search of books for her friend in the wilderness. Likewise, it is recounted in what ways the books seem worthy."[2]

These book reviews were the first opportunity to see her thinking—her intellect, interest, and judgment—in print. For the first letter, Constance wanted "a box of books" for a family to take on a long journey, and "Josephine" suggested a book to appeal to each family member, personalizing the selections for their sensibilities and interests.

For the eighteen-year-old daughter, she chose *The Justice of the King* by Hamilton Drummond, a novel of love and jealousy, set in the time of Louis XI: "for as girls of her age will read novels the historical setting sometimes stimulates their interest in history." She chose *Two on a Trail* by Hulbert Fultner for the mother, a romance-adventure set vividly in the Northwest. "I am ready to wager that after she has seen 'The End' mother will not once wonder if the water was turned off from the house at home before they left, and then she won't care."

The Broad Highway by Jeffrey Farnol went to the father, with "just enough drawing of knives and brandishing of pistols" to keep him "on the edge of his chair." Moreover, "The book is charmingly written, and I can see each member of the little party absorbed in it in turn." She was right about the book's appeal; it became the year's best-seller.

The second letter[3] began with an exuberant, descriptive passage. It was mid-April, and the florists' shops "look as though the long threatened yellow peril was upon us, so ablaze are they with jonquils . . ." At the milliner's:

> My dear, you should see the hats. There are great hats, small hats, high hats and fluffy hats, white hats, purple hats, hats with roses, hats with feathers, hats for mothers, sisters, cousins, they make one want them by the dozens—with humble apologies to the Pied Piper!

This time, Constance needed suggestions to fill the shelves of a new library at her home. Josephine chose current events. "With the newspapers printing in great headlines, '20,000 Men Off to the Texan Border,' 'The President Insists That There Will Be No War with Mexico,' I am filling your box this week with books on Mexico."

Each book in the box represented a different style. She suggested *The Fair God* for sixteenth-century background on Mexico, and Creelman's biography, *Diaz, Master of Mexico*, to show "how conditions for a democracy there differ from conditions for a democracy here in the United States." For contrast, she chose "romance piled upon romance" in *The Missourian* and ended with *The Patrician* by John Galsworthy. "The style is masterly, and the language fairly glows with light and color."

Again, her judgment proved prescient; Galsworthy's *The Forsyte Saga* earned him the 1932 Nobel Prize for Literature. Her father would have been proud.

Her third letter[4] looked forward to the gardening season. "Constance, Dear: The wind is shrieking around the corners, and the flames from the open fire go roaring up the chimney. Who would think this the balmy month of April?"

Her box of garden books allowed a thorough study of the undertaking. She started with a garden primer with a calendar to show when to plant what. She recommended all of Mrs. Ely's books for their colored

illustrations and helpful tips, and then *The Garden Month by Month* by
Mabel C. Sedgwick, a go-to reference for filling real or fictional gardens:

> To the credit of each month is set down the flowers that blossom
> in it, with their colors, height and length of bloom. Two hundred
> illustrations help tremendously one's imagination while at work
> on the construction of a garden.

For "delight," she suggested all of the books by "Barbara" (Mabel
Osgood Wright). "You will laugh all the way through . . . and all through
the stories like a serene river runs the garden and the garden lore." Finally,
she added "a lot of seed catalogues, for as reading matter on a cold, bleak
night they are not to be ignored. They are always so encouraging and so
inspiring."

> Now, you, too, are to join the ranks of the garden miners who
> dig and delve and think themselves well paid when they gather a
> handful of color rivalling any gems.

She evaluated current best-sellers for the fourth letter[5] in early May,
noting with pleasure the first-place position of *The Broad Highway* and
dismissing *Brazenhead the Great* as too much of "the society of the morally
or physically untubbed." She liked *The Golden Silence* for its "series of really
wonderful word pictures and dramatic events," and predicted that *A Grain
of Dust* would not "suit the 'popular taste.'" She recommended it, nevertheless, "as under an immense amount of bespangled clap-trap there is much
more than a grain of worth." Her reasoning was notable for this time in her
life: "for to me it is a strong plea for a return of the woman of wealth and
social ambition to the life of the family and home."

"Her Box of Books" for mid-May's fifth letter[6] had a back-to-the-
country theme: "Woman Wanders Afield Searching Occupation; Finds
It Near at Hand." She wrote to Constance of their friend Suzanne who

needed a way to make money at home. They decided that Suzanne could raise mushrooms, raspberries, and bees, with guidance from the *Good Housekeeping Magazine* and free bulletins from the United States Department of Agriculture. "It made me quite homesick for my farm, for you know my pet project was poultry and perennials."

Letter six[7] took on women's issues, beginning with *Labor and Woman*, which she called "a wonderful book, vividly interesting, vitally important at just this time." The themes were civic engagement and mental equality with men "for the welfare of the race," and "Not once on the pages does the expression Votes for Women appear." The next was *What 8,000,000 Women Want*, which argued for equal suffrage, "but its real strength lies in the summing up of the good things accomplished by organized groups of women."

> Perhaps the book did not impress me, as I know of a large group of that same 8,000,000 club women who not only do not want equal suffrage but take rather strenuous methods to prevent it . . .

To balance the argument, she reviewed *The Ladies' Battle*, which argued that women would vote differently from men because of their "Socialist tendency." "The book has decided charm and you won't have a dull moment while reading it, even if you can't agree with the position it takes." She ended without taking a stand:

> Perhaps I have read too much, but I must quote "Alice" to illustrate my present state of mind. Alice never could make out, in thinking it over afterward, how it was they began; all she could remember was that they were running hand in hand and the queen went so fast that it was all she could do to keep up with her, and still the queen kept crying, "Faster! Faster!" And they went so fast that at last they seemed to skim through the air, till suddenly just as Alice was getting quite exhausted, they stopped. The queen propped

her up against a tree and said kindly, "You may rest a little now."
Alice looked around her in great surprise, "Why I do believe we've
been under this tree the whole time! Everything's just as it was!"
And now good night. I will away with my puzzles and my problems to the land of dreams.

> Perplexedly yours, Josephine Story

A woman's place was in the home, and women's suffrage was a question
mark. Of the Baker siblings, Emilie's early life was the most conventional,
her roles the most traditional. The next decade would amend her thinking,
but these were her first, published works, and she wrote of what she knew.

The final letter[8] in Emilie's "Her Box of Books" series was a travelogue
to Italy, "In Which She Tells About a Summer Tour at Home."

> After much consideration, I have decided to send you to Italy, so
> have shipped to you by express one Gloucester hammock and a
> great big box of books . . . You are to place the hammock under
> the group of pines . . . take from the box the book by Henry James
> Forman, *The Ideal Italian Tour*, and begin your travels . . . Just pre-
> tend that your hammock is a gondola and the sound of the wind
> in the pines the water lapping against the sides.

She suggested books for atmosphere, including *Last Days of Pompeii*
("Of couse you have read it, but you are touring Italy now, and the story
will take on new significance"), Elliot's *Romola*, Mrs. Browning's *Casa
Guidi Windows*, and Lytton's *Rienzi*: "if you do not feel nice and shivery
when you come to its last paragraph, you have no temperament." This
last was, consciously or unconsciously, an echo of Victor's brother Selden
when he viewed the Taj Majal: "Whoever can behold the Taj without
feeling a thrill that sends moisture to his eyes, has no sense of beauty in
his soul."

Now, good luck to you on your imaginary journey, and bring home an imaginary string of just the right soft shade of pink coral beads to your devoted but stay-at-home Josephine Story.

Blue Hill, Summer 1911

When they arrived at Blue Hill in July, Emilie posed for photos at Stone House. Now forty-five, her hair was brown, her waist still slim. From that high perch, she could look across Blue Hill Bay to Parker Point. Ahead to her left was Sculpin Point and the opening to the outer bay. Behind her were the village and Blue Hill Mountain. It was the view that had sold her on Stone House, but another attraction had recently been added.

Emilie Perched on the Stone House Parapet, July 1911

Emilie at the Front of Stone House, July 1911

This year, the Lorings had a boat. The open, cruising launch had side benches and two rows of seats at the stern. With as many as a dozen passengers aboard, they picnicked on nearby islands, visited friends at Parker Point, and viewed Blue Hill from an entirely different perspective.

The *Sally Blanchard* was named for Emilie's great aunt in North Yarmouth who had died the past November. Aunt Sally lived the life that her sail-making father, John Baker III, might have wished for her. She married Captain Paul Greeley Blanchard, who came from a long line of seamen and worked his way up from the forecastle to the bridge. In his twenty-one years at sea, he crossed the Atlantic sixty times and earned regard as "an able and trustworthy sea master." He was already successful when he retired to build ships with his brothers, and their subsequent reputation for building the best merchant craft under sail made him the richest man in the area.

After her husband's death, Sally Blanchard lived many comfortable years in the home her husband had built for her, esteemed as "a lady of refined tastes and pleasing manners." She died of old age, the last of her generation of Bakers, and there was no better namesake for the Lorings' new boat.[9]

The Sally Blanchard

Victor and Sons on the Sally Blanchard

A boat made a big difference. Cottagers often arrived at Blue Hill on the steamer from Rockland, but unless they had a boat, that was the last time they enjoyed the same view until it was time to depart in the fall. Benjamin Curtis was satisfied with that. His home had a nautical name, "Starboard Acres," but that was the first and last thing nautical about Ben Curtis. "I prefer to keep my feet on terra firma," he said,[10] and followed his words with action. Otherwise, the further out one lived on the East Blue Hill Road, the larger the boat. The Owen sisters kept a small rowboat, the Lorings had their open launch, and the next was Ned Brooks' cabin cruiser at Elwin Cove.

Eastward, beyond the Brooks home, the scale of boat changed entirely. Ralph Slaven's mahogany launch *Tartar* measured sixty feet long and was clocked at a fast thirty-eight miles per hour. The Slavens' yacht, *Alfredine IV*, was 99 feet long, and Seth Milliken's yawl, *Thistle*, measured a full 103 feet. These were possible because of the granite wharves that accommodated large craft and the possession of fortunes that could afford them.

The Slavens owned Darling Island and nearly all of the Woods Point shoreline. They built the expansive "Borderland" estate with stone from the new Chase quarry and then cleared away one hundred feet of rock at the water's edge to give it a large and luxurious sand beach.[11] The Millikens and Boardmans together purchased a swath of land that fronted Morgan Bay and faced away from Blue Hill, toward the long peninsula of Newbury Neck.

Like Mary Curtis and Josephine Brooks, the Milliken and Boardman wives were sisters. Alida Leese was married to Seth M. Milliken Jr., whose father owned textile manufacturing firms in ten states and served on the boards of three banks and two life insurance companies. Seth Jr. became a surgeon despite—or perhaps because of—the paralysis of his left leg following a childhood attack of polio.

The Millikens arrived in Blue Hill in 1908, the first summer after their marriage and at about the same time as the Curtis, Brooks, and Loring families. Their daughter was born the next winter and liked to boast that she had spent every summer of her life—including one *in utero*—at Blue Hill. The other Leese sister, Dorcas, married Richard Boardman, who practiced law across Newark Bay from the Brooks home in East Orange.[12]

During the winter, the Millikens lived on New York City's exclusive Madison Avenue, the Brookses and Boardmans were in New Jersey, the Owen sisters operated their tea house in Philadelphia, and the Lorings and Curtises returned to Wellesley Hills. But every summer, they were neighbors again, as they converged upon Blue Hill, opened their summer cottages, launched their boats, and joined in the summer activities.

Navigating on Blue Hill Bay. Robert, Emilie, and Victor, 1913

CHAPTER 16

Ambition

Wellesley Hills, 1911–1912

That fall, Agnes Edwards Rothery wrote the article that Emilie credited for setting her fully on the path to authorship. Until then, at home and for the newspaper, Emilie had reviewed the work of others. "The Woman Who Wants to Write" nudged a different ambition.

> If you honestly want to write and think that you can, stop dreaming about it and go to work. Write two hours a day, and read two hours a day and do it every single solitary day for three years, and then you will have made a start . . . If you know any women who think they can write and do, perhaps, occasionally inscribe a few lines and send them on a timid quest of publication, tell them that the same laws that hold good in all the arts and all the professions, and in all businesses and trades hold good here. Maybe they can write. Probably they can, but no one will ever believe it until they do.[1]

She did want to write, and Agnes knew it.

> Suppose you try something and fail. What of it? The world will not come to an end. You will be wiser—that is all . . . Don't be afraid. Have courage. If you are asked to write a paper and want to, say you will and do your best . . . One of the most pitiful sights in the world is the woman who is afraid. And one of the most splendid is the woman who says: "I may not succeed. But I'll try."[2]

Emilie's version of this impulse was "Try It Out," an unpublished article with the same theme and a glimpse of the resistance she expected—or
received—to her new idea.

If you have an idea, a flash of intuition about something which you
might accomplish, don't let it vanish into the limbo of I-might-
have-done—try it out. No matter whether you are slim and seventeen; fat, fair, and forty; serene and seventy—if you feel an idea
for accomplishment pricking at your consciousness don't be afraid
of it. Let it out into the sunlight. Tend it. Coax it. At first it may
only creep; if it gets that far it is rather sure to walk alone; and if
it walks why not encourage it to fly?

But if in your eager enthusiasm over the child of your imagination you confide your vision, your rosy hopes of achievement to
a friend or member of the family, refuse to be wet-blanketed. Pay
no attention to such dampening remarks as "How foolish!""That's
a wild scheme!""Why, Mother! At your age!"

Suppose your gem of an idea does turn out to be paste instead
of a diamond of the first water? It isn't a tragedy. Clear for action
and try out the next one. If you acquire the habit of developing
them, inspirational ideas will be more difficult to ignore than an
alarm-clock rampant at your bedside . . .

Someday when you are decidedly out of love with yourself
and what you are accomplishing, devote a quiet hour to contem-
plating the achievements of your acquaintances who are tingling
with the zest of life, who are vivid and merry and eager over the
worthwhile things they are getting across. Trace these results back
to their beginnings. They came from mere seeds of ideas; you'll
acknowledge that . . . The trouble with most of us could-have-
dones is that because of lethargy or lack of faith in ourselves and
our idea we let that precious spark flicker and die out . . .

The next time you have an idea for achievement put your whole personality behind it, audaciously snap your fingers at failure, count the chances of success and try it out.[3]

Victor needed no such exhortation. His achievements in social issues expanded from local to regional and national levels. In October, he spoke briefly on honesty in advertising at the Publicity Club at Springfield, Massachusetts. In November, he urged the American Federation of Men's Church Organizations, of which he was president, to eliminate working conditions that promoted gambling and intemperance.

Victor also met with the social service committee of the "Men and Religion Forward Movement." Nationally, the movement included Jane Addams of Hull House in Chicago, the Russell Sage Foundation of New York, and Robert A. Woods of Boston's South End House. Representatives came from four Boston organizations with which Victor was connected: the Pilgrim Publicity Association, the YMCA, Congregational Churches, and the Boston City Club.

The committee supported organized labor, which "has already accomplished and is seeking to accomplish many reforms essential to a truly Christian civilization . . ."[4]

Emilie's siblings were well established in their careers. Rachel was in Europe again, but when she returned, she had performances planned and new plays at various stages of completion.

The Lambs Club performed Robert Baker's *Bought and Never Paid For* at their spring Gambol, and he wrote for the Harvard class book in the spring of 1912:

I have pursued the profession of a dramatologist and am still pursuing it with odds on the drama. Two of my plays have met with success, "Beverly of Graustark," a dramatization of George Barr McCutcheon's novel, and "The Trail of the Lonesome Pine," a play founded on the story by John Fox, Jr. I also have perpetrated a

Tea Party in the Orchard: Minnie and Robert Baker, Spaniel "Rusty," Rachel Gale, Mrs. Baker, Victor Loring, John Gale, Emilie Loring, Selden, and the Hound, "Phil"

crime, entitled, "Play Ball," but the game was called on account of small box-office receipts.

There was no worry about box-office receipts for *Beverly of Graustark.* The play earned him tens of thousands of dollars well into the next decade.[5]

Emilie had been "home base" for them all, but writing for the newspaper had proved an elixir of satisfaction. She wanted more.

When Selden joined his brother at the Berkshire School in September 1912, Emilie approached the *Boston Herald* about writing another set of book reviews. John Macy was the *Herald's* new editor, and he allowed her to write a set of short reviews for the paper, without a by-line.

"When the Young Folks Read" came first. Lee & Shepard's brand of wholesome adventure laced with derring-do had been the staple of her

"I'm perched on the lookout spying for goodwill ships and treasure islands, and priceless friends, and lovely summer seas with just enough squalls to make me appreciate fair weather."
Uncharted Seas

childhood and her sons'. She reviewed twice as many adventurous, boys' books as she did books for girls, and she praised the most captivating. "Just imagine the creepy sensation that must play at hide and seek along the spinal cord of a real boy when he is detailed to be scout of the Hyena Patrol."[6]

The next, "Books for the Home Maker," indulged her recent interests: *Mother and Baby*, *Successful Houses and How to Build Them*, *The Family in its Sociological Aspects*, and *Soyer's Standard Cookery*. Even without a by-line, her friends could have recognized her sensible attitude: "But no matter how pretentious or how humble one's house may be, the dwellers within it cannot exist in comfort without an intelligent study of cookbook literature."[7]

The next reviews were signed "J. S." for Josephine Story. The light touch of her criticism was characteristic. Any Baker knew that humor could make a point as easily and often more effectively, especially with authors.

It is a pity that a book so fine and well worthwhile as "The Soddy" should be thrown overboard into the sea of publicity with the weight of such an unilluminating title tied to its neck.

The almost ridiculous extravagance of the story is tempered by a few good bits of description . . . and the sentiment—well, if you like that kind you will have the kind that you like.[8]

She gave peeks into her philosophy and small scenes from her life.

Real, intimate, human books about children are rare—very rare . . . If the interest of boys for whom a book is written may serve as a test, this book ought to be one of the best juveniles of the fall. The reviewer was unable to get it away from a pair of boys who slept with it under their pillow at night.[9]

Emilie considered. What if she wrote articles and stories instead of reviews? She had spent a lifetime in conversation with interesting people of theater, publishing, politics, and the arts. Intelligent study of her duties as homemaker and mother, plus a lifetime of engaged reading and social interaction had developed her powers of observation. She knew the requirements of good writing, and she had spent a lifetime understanding popular taste. Maybe it was time for this Baker to get her own ideas into print.

Emilie remembered her next conversation with Agnes Edwards Rothery as the most important lesson of her writing career. They were discussing articles on homemaking.

> I observed vaingloriously, "I could write those." "She writes them," the editor reminded. That lesson was burned deep in my mind. That author didn't say she could write them. She wrote the articles. Talking of ideas doesn't get one anywhere. No matter how brilliant or useful they may be, until they are formulated on paper they don't count as creative writing. There is a little word of four letters W O R K work which does the trick.[10]

That was the story that was told and re-told about the beginning of Emilie's writing career. What wasn't told was that Victor also took a shot at writing that fall. His story, "Her Trial by Fire," appeared in the November 1912 issue of *Snappy Stories*, a pulp magazine for men that promised good fiction wrapped in a racy cover and a veil of suggestion. Was Emilie envious? Did Victor want a writing career, or did he write the story to challenge her? They didn't say. But Emilie got started, and Victor published no more stories.

What would she write? For twenty-two years, she had cared for her family and household without compromising either her good sense or her good humor. Her Baker creativity bridged the gap between the gracious but laborious customs of the nineteenth century and the modern efficiencies of

"No one has to tell me that no matter how one's mind sparks with ideas, unless one writes, nothing gets written. I've learned that still living truth." *Give Me One Summer*

"Middle life is a time of individual freedom, individual expression, individual development, individual thought. A time when you can express what life has taught you." *The Fountain of Youth*

the twentieth. An entire generation faced the same transition; she would write about homemaking.

Blue Hill, Summer 1913

"Mary the Temperamental had departed. In spite of the fact that she had a spirit which would have dared the devil; that her cooking was well-meant but depressing; such are the subtleties and complexities of modern homemaking that there was a stinging sensation beneath my eyelids as I saw her go." *For the Comfort of the Family: A Vacation Experiment*

It was a piece of luck that Marion Lynch, the Lorings' maid-of-all-work, resigned just before the family left for Blue Hill the next summer. It was a poor time to train a new servant, and after all, how much did they really need a maid during their summer vacation? If the family would pitch in, Emilie could implement her ideas for household effectiveness and write about them for publication.

They certainly could have decided otherwise. Victor had just earned twenty-thousand-dollars for administering the estates of two Moulton cousins (1913).[11] The Lorings paid off their mortgages at Blue Hill and Wellesley Hills and then purchased an additional lot at the foot of Florence Avenue.[12] The fees could have supported a middle-class family for more than a decade or an entire staff of servants, had they wanted, but they did not. Victor's aunts and mother had kept house on their own, and the Bakers had employed only a single maid when the children outgrew their nurse. Victor and Emilie did the same; they only ever had one live-in servant, and that summer, they chose to go without.

In Blue Hill, also, they lived less grandly than their means would have allowed. Stone House was unique and had a hundred-year history, but it was pleasant and livable, not a showplace. By contrast, the Slavens' massive Borderland estate was at least three times as large as Stone House and included Darling's Island to boot. Across the Bay, there were many beautiful cottages with stunning views, and an estate was built that summer that easily eclipsed them all in elegance and grandeur.

Anne Paul Nevin was the widow of renowned composer Ethelbert Nevin. What better place for her to come than to Blue Hill's lively music colony where her husband's prominence, and her own by extension, would be known and appreciated? By 1913, Mrs. Nevin already owned most of

Tide Mill Island and the three cottages upon it. But as stately, summer cottages accumulated along the Bay, she developed a grander vision.

She purchased a broad expanse of land on the prominent hill beyond the reversing falls and built a masterpiece to look down upon them all. "Arcady," named for one of her husband's songs, was styled after the Italian villas she had enjoyed with him in Florence and Venice. Its architecture proclaimed, "This is the life I have known. I have lived among the best."

Visitors who arrived by boat ascended a meticulously landscaped hillside, replete with gardens and columnar evergreens. The first flight of the grand staircase led to a marble statue of Mercury. At the top of the second, a bronze boy blew his horn, and peacocks and guests paraded about the terrace with equal satisfaction.

On their own side of the Bay, the Lorings boated, picnicked, read, and gardened. They stopped for tea in the afternoon and dressed for dinner on all but Sundays, but there was no need to make a show otherwise—and particularly not that summer when they had no maid.

"From the little I could see I know that your Arcady— I love the name—is a heavenly spot." *Love Came Laughing By*

Paths in a velvety green lawn led to the central point, an old-fashioned pool in the center of which a bronze boy blew a horn from which liquid diamonds rose high in the air to tinkle back with the sound of broken glass into water where goldfish flashed like living flames. *I Hear Adventure Calling*

Blue Hill Picnic: (standing) Selden and Robert Loring, (seated) Mel Baker, Minnie Baker, Rachel and John Gale, Emilie Loring, Robert Baker, Victor Loring

Linen doilies were the first casualty of Emilie's summer experiment,[13] replaced with paper versions by the hundred. "As mine would have been the task of laundering the linen doilies, think what an amount of time, strength and energy I saved by substituting paper." A quick whisking away to the morning fire, and the day was free to enjoy.

Mealtimes relied upon informality and a sense of humor. The slow cooker was set to work early, sandwiches substituted for full-course meals, and leftovers became new dishes for the table as well as the subjects of new articles. "I rack my brain for a variety of ways to serve them, sometimes making a distinct hit with my experiments—at others, well, the failures will not be recorded here."

"Country girl or not, I adore cooking. I believe it's as much of an art as interior decorating."
There Is Always Love

For unexpected guests, Emilie brought out the mainstays of her "emergency cupboard"—anchovy paste, Major Grey chutney, and a few cans of Russian caviar. Even a summer cottage had its standards, and these aristocratic condiments turned simple sandwiches into interesting and appealing canapés. The bright colors of hard-cooked eggs and pimiento at luncheon gave "the touch of a whip to a flagging appetite."

Emilie's friends contributed their own recipes to her summer experiment. Josephine Brooks supplied her favorite, sour cream cookies, and Mary Curtis gave the recipe for her chocolate brownies with nuts. The Owen sisters contributed appealing hors d'oeuvres and entrees from their Green Dragon Tea Room as well as recipes they prepared at home.

Craving appreciation, I called the Judge, our black and white hound, and crumpled a few fragments of the alleged cake into his dish.
For the Comfort of the Family

To mushrooms that Selden brought them from the pasture, the sisters added butter, cream, flour, and a bit of egg to produce a dainty entrée for their youngest sister, Carrie, who was ill and frail. Emilie wrote, ". . . having been cooking for weeks for a hungry horde, I felt as I read the amount of the ingredients that I had a prescription for bird feed."

All summer, the Loring, Owen, Curtis, and Brooks families gathered for dinners, picnics, and occasional costume parties. Esther Wood, a Blue Hill native and Janie Curtis' playmate, recalled a costume party to which Emilie wore a lampshade as a hat. When Emilie wrote about it, she assumed the character of "Aunt Jo" (from her pseudonym, Josephine

Story) who helped the local youth create costumes. These included a pirate, a scarecrow, a fortune teller, and a "Lady of Fashion," dressed in a lampshade hat.[14]

The last event of the season was always the Blue Hill Fair. Last year, Emilie had planted window boxes of nasturtiums which won first place in the fair's flower competition.[15] She tried again this year and again brought home the blue ribbon.[16]

CHAPTER 17

The Long Road to Authorship

Cambridge, MA: Fall 1913

Robert and Selden returned to school in the Berkshires that fall, and Victor and Emilie headed to Boston instead of Wellesley Hills. Summer's housekeeping experiment was over, and the antidote was full relief from domestic cares. They found it at the Riverbank Court Hotel, on the Cambridge side of the Harvard Bridge. Views across the Charles River were lovely, and the new subway line to Park Street took Victor to work in only twenty minutes. With no chores, no menus, and no household to manage, Emilie was free to polish her summer stories.

She knew before she started that writing was hard work and actively sought critiques to make hers better. When she was little, she and her siblings had acted out their father's plays at home before he finalized them. Now, she joined Robert and Rachel in giving her writing "the acid test of the family." Robert described the process: "They assemble for the operation, each armed with a hammer or a searchlight. If the play looks healthy after passing through this ordeal, I feel it has a chance with a manager."[1]

She submitted "The Woman Who Stayed at Home," to the *Saturday Evening Post* and *Atlantic Monthly*.[2] "My cheeks burned at my audacity." Its theme was the importance of a woman staying at home to take care of her family, as Emilie herself had done. Rejection followed rejection with the explanation that the theme was unpopular with the modern reader. Finally, *The Mother's Magazine* paid forty dollars for the story. They renamed it, "Converting Phyllis," and Katharine Sturges Dodge illustrated the published story.

While that story was going the rounds, Emilie submitted "The Arrogance of Youth." It was only four hundred nineteen words, but "upon reading it over, it sounded so good that I started it out on the road." That was

"No planning of meals, No cooking. No housework for three whole days. Result, happiness, to borrow from Mr. Micawber."
When Hearts Are Light Again

November 10, 1913. On November twentieth, the manuscript returned from *The People's Home Journal* with a rejection notice. She submitted it again that same afternoon, this time to *Woman's Magazine*, and waited. On Thursday, January twenty-second, she received her second notice. The magazine had accepted her story for five dollars. Success in only two tries!

Two days later, the *New York Tribune* introduced "Mrs. Victor J. Loring of Cambridge, Mass., a new writer on home economics." The name was Loring, but the message was purely Baker: "Find drama in your housework! . . . If you are faced with all kinds of complications in the household, you are the heroine of a play full of plot, but destined to be triumphant in the end, and you go at your tasks in that spirit."[3]

Emilie wanted to write for magazines, and she undertook an intelligent study of the process. How could she give her articles and stories their best chance of acceptance? The Wellesley Hills Woman's Club invited MacGregor Jenkins of the *Atlantic Monthly* to their next meeting and asked him to speak on precisely that topic.

Three weeks later, the Star Company accepted her summer articles for syndication as a series, "How I Kept House Without a Servant." Emilie's home photos illustrated place settings for a cheery breakfast, paper bag cookery, gift baskets of fresh apples, and jars of homemade jams and jellies. By the end of March, newspaper readers from San Antonio to Salt Lake City knew Josephine Story's tips for modern household efficiencies, including her best advice for dishwashing: "Do it as quickly as possible and get it over with."[4]

Emilie progressed from household articles to fiction with a very short story, "First Aid to the One-Room Housekeeper,"[5] for the *Boston Daily Globe* about a girl on her own who saves time and money by preparing meals in the forerunner of the modern crockpot. "Behold my magic health restorer, money saver, fun bestower, the fireless cooker!" She gave recipes for cornmeal mush, stewed prunes, and homemade applesauce that could be made ahead of time on the budget of a working girl. The foods were healthful and economical, but the best incentive was having enough money

She lived over the ecstatic moment when she had drawn a pink cheque from an envelope. Three dollars! It had seemed a fortune. She had sold something! Nothing much but someone had wanted it enough to pay money for it. That was the acid test.
Give Me One Summer

left over for theater tickets, flowers, and occasional shopping splurges.

This wasn't homemaking to please a husband or children; this was homemaking to please the homemaker. "Say what you like, there is no tonic equal to a legitimate good time. It clears mists from the mind, lifts burdens from the heart and gives one the courage to begin the old dry-as-dust monotonies of life with fresh enthusiasm."[6] Oliver Optic had believed it, her father had lived it, and Emilie would share their philosophy with the next generation.

Emilie's housekeeping articles fanned out like little emissaries in newspapers and magazines across the nation. At the same time, she sent the entire collection to New York's George H. Doran Company which gave her no advance but agreed to print them as a book—*For the Comfort of the Family: A Vacation Experiment*—and pay her ten percent of sales. Her first book deal!

Why not try a novelette next? She thought back across the last decade. Seven years ago, she traveled to the iceberg-strewn waters of Alaska. She had not yet discovered Stone House and Blue Hill. She was a metal worker and a photographer, but she was not yet a writer. Life took twists and turns, and one never knew what lay beyond the next bend.

With pencil and paper, she imagined a jilted fiancé and an heiress who must marry or lose her fortune, landed them in the frozen north of Alaska, and let them work it out. By the time she left for Blue Hill in the summer of 1914, her draft of "The Key to Many Doors" was ready for *Munsey's Magazine*, and she put her own name on a story for the first time: Emilie Baker Loring.

But *Munsey's* didn't want it. Neither did *Ainslee's*, *Lippincott's*, *Pictorial Review* or *Young's Magazine*. After five rejection slips in three months, she sought help. The Editor Literary Bureau advertised, "Most of the novel manuscripts revised in accordance with the definite, suggestive criticisms of The Editor Literary Bureau are sold quickly, to advantage, to leading publishers."[7] At the end of the summer, Emilie sent them her ten-thousand-word manuscript and a four-dollar fee and waited for their reply.

She also awaited letters from her Cape Cod friends Louise and Lizzie Hallet who were in Europe. After the sudden death of their brother in March, they had taken their mother to Switzerland and planned an extended stay in the south of France to aid Mrs. Hallet's chronic respiratory condition. But Austria-Hungary's Archduke Ferdinand was assassinated in June, and in August, Germany began its march across Belgium to invade France. Switzerland was too close for comfort, and France was out of the question, so the Hallets made their way instead to Italy and Rome's Palace Hotel for the fall—or until it was safe to travel again.

In the States, autumn was still pleasantly normal. Robby moved into the freshman dorm at Harvard and contacted Coach Duffy about going out for the next spring's baseball team. At the Berkshire School, Selden captained his hockey team and competed on the rifle and football teams. Emilie was home in late October when H. Doran and Company announced publication of *For the Comfort of the Family: A Vacation Experiment* by Josephine Story and sent her an advance copy.[8] At forty-eight, Emilie held her first book in her hands. What a feeling; there was nothing like it.

Her success unfolded against the backdrop of dangerous conditions developing in Europe, but so far, local interests still dominated in the press. The *Evening World* wrote four columns to promote *For the Comfort of the Family* when it was released in October but printed less than half that about the war. Alongside Emilie's suggestion that the entire family pitch in with household chores were two short articles, "Cruiser Karlsruhe Sinks 13 British Vessels in the Atlantic Ocean" and "King of Belgians leads army under guns of Germany." Emilie suggested, "Why leave the kitchen with one's nose shining and gleaming like a beacon light when a few simple toilet accessories make for comfort and presentability?" Below that tip was a report from London that the French and British had killed nearly thirty thousand Germans on the Belgian coast.[9] The juxtaposition was revealing; war in Europe was not yet America's problem. Although deplored in conversation, nearly two million casualties in Europe did not shake the United States' declared neutrality or the public's sense of detachment.

How peaceful. It was hard to believe that across the ocean General Trouble was marshalling his dangerous forces and stalking like a war lord from country to country, his heavy tread shaking the hearts of people everywhere."
As Long as I Live

For the Comfort of the Family: A Vacation Experiment

"Supper confections are quickly and easily made."
Selden posed, and Emilie arranged and photographed the illustrations.

Both Robert and Rachel had productions scheduled for December. Robert's was his first venture into the new medium of film. His play, *The Conspiracy*, had enjoyed such a long run in the theaters that he rewrote it into a novel in 1913 and then as a screenplay for Charles Frohman and Paramount Pictures in 1914. His protagonist was a mystery novelist who stumbled into thrilling, real-life crimes. Los Angeles critics praised, "It teems with baffling mystery and weird deduction, thrilling situations and romantic love making." "The play has an elementally dynamic theme that raises it far above the average dramatic plot." Robert's talent was unstoppable: amateur theatricals, vaudeville, musical comedy, and now, silent film.

Rachel caught Golden State fever, too. Her protagonist in *Rebellious Jane* was a young heiress who hides on a California ranch to evade a conventional marriage: "What does all this social whirl amount to? I want to do something worthwhile." An elder matron encourages, "If the women of today would only do something worthwhile, there would be fewer unhappy marriages. Look at me. No blighted hopes here."[10]

Emilie received word from The Editor Literary Bureau that "The Key to Many Doors" was "practically perfect technically," but its plot line needed work. She took a month to revise the story's action and sent a new, fourteen-thousand-word version to the McClure publication syndicate in January. Publication in a national magazine might reach 500,000 readers, but a newspaper syndicate put an author's name before five million readers for weeks in succession.

In five days, she had her answer from *McClure's*—sorry, no. The next day, she sent the manuscript to *The Delineator* which kept it a month before sending a rejection notice, and *Ladies' World* did the same. She accepted the process like a veteran; rejection did not stop her. She revised as necessary, typed a new copy if the old one was at all smudged, and then sent the manuscript on its way again.

Submission to *The People's Home Journal* finally did the trick. On May 5, 1915, she received an acceptance check for seventy dollars. She had done well. The Editor Literary Bureau had advised accepting no less

Another much traveled manuscript had been in an editorial office six weeks; up to this one its flights had been in the non-stop class.
Give Me One Summer

"Already I know that you are a writer." "Intend to be a writer. They tell me it's a long slow road, that only about nine percent of those who start out carry through the first year. Even after that winnowing, the fatalities are staggering." "Remember the old proverb, 'Leg over leg the dog went to Dover.' You'll arrive if you keep everlastingly at it."
Give Me One Summer

than a penny per word, and she had nearly that. Even established authors expected to submit a serial novel an average of eight times before acceptance, and this first effort of Emilie's was accepted in nine.

As the Lorings prepared to go to Blue Hill that summer, Mrs. Baker closed her house in Wellesley Hills and moved in with Rachel and John in Haverhill. John grieved the death of his son Arthur the previous spring, and now his own health was failing. Mrs. Baker knew the grief of losing both a child and a husband; Rachel needed her.

Besides, at seventy-eight, she didn't want the care of Burr Croft anymore. In fact, she didn't want the care of any of the properties that she owned—the house on Gloucester Street, parcels on Beacon Hill and Union Park, or the house in Wellesley Hills. She sold them to her children, went to live with Rachel, and used the income for herself.

Blue Hill, Summer 1915

In Blue Hill that summer, the Lorings basked in success. Fanny Parker was proud of her neighbor's published book and the serial novel that would be out in the fall. Down the East Blue Hill Road, Fanny's niece Esther Wood even took turns playing "Mrs. Emilie Loring, the author" with her friend Janey Curtis.[11] On the athletic front, Robby Loring now stood six feet tall and played baseball for Harvard. At Blue Hill's Fourth of July races, he made a clean sweep of his entries, beating Roy Grindle in the 100-yard dash, Paul Nevin in the 220, and E. Robertson in the 880.[12]

But their closest neighbors had troubles. The Owen sisters' finances were dwindling and so was Carrie Owen's health. They needed help, and they needed it soon. Mary and Elizabeth Owen fastened on the idea of running a tea shop in Blue Hill like their Green Dragon Tea Room in Philadelphia and attaching an art studio in which Carrie could produce and sell her artworks.

An old quarry office on the Lorings' land suited the purpose. It was at the juncture of the East Blue Hill Road and the small lane that led to *Tyn*

"I shall feel that I may use a little of the money your father left me. I want—I want to be in the heart of things. I'll have an experienced maid, I'll have the right clothes, and—and I'll go places, I'm dying to go places."
With Banners

Y Coed. If they fixed up the downstairs for business and stayed upstairs themselves, the Owens could rent *Tyn Y Coed* for additional income. Victor and Emilie had already sold them quarry land for a sunken garden, and now they sold them the old quarry office, as well.

Carrie designed the tearoom with a counter to sell small gifts and tables to serve luncheons and tea. Adjoining was a studio where she would display art and meet with home decorating clients. Some of the neighbors thought the outside paint looked pink, but it was intended to be lavender, Carrie's favorite color. The sisters christened it "Larkspur Lodge" and opened for business, with Carrie's "Wayside Studio" alongside.

On August twelfth, the Owens hosted a "Sylvan dramatic and musical recital" in the Lorings' old quarry, which Carrie Owen had converted to a garden.

> This is really a hall of stone, an abandoned quarry of granite having been transformed into an attractive audience room. There were tables of stone on which were blossoming plants; trailing moss and vines and evergreen trees bordered the walls. Nature smiled on the scene with sun and gentle breeze; sweet bird notes occasionally blended with the voice of the reader or singer, and always in attune.[13]

An English actress, Edith Wynne Matthison, gave several dramatic selections, Josephine Preston Peabody of Wellesley Hills and the Boston Authors Club read some of her poems, and a selection of Blue Hill musicians—Gaston Dethier, Elinor Brooks, and Carroll Curtis—performed as well. Tickets sold for $2 and $2.50, with proceeds to benefit the war relief fund, and the Owen sisters provided refreshments for sale at intermission.[14] The effort brought a large crowd and deftly advertised the Owens' new tea house on the corner.

The Curtis' strained finances forced them to sell a portion of their property between the East Blue Hill Road and the shore. They had already

"Of course you can earn money at home. Think up something different for people to eat and your fortune's made . . ."
Fair Tomorrow

Assembled for the Quarry Concert, August 12, 1915

"'From thence to a rock with a V cut in it at the southeast corner.' There isn't such a rock, Larry. I've spent the greater portion of my waking life hunting for it and most of my sleeping life dreaming of it, since the Major assured me when he called to negotiate a peace pact a week ago that it marked the boundary of the land his wife could legally claim."
Where Beauty Dwells

mortgaged property on the north side of the road, near their house. Now they mortgaged further property on the south side and offered to sell a lot to Mary Curtis' cousin, Alfred Landon Baker (no relative of Emilie), a Chicago banker and Stock Exchange mogul who had recently hired their son Robert Curtis. This last lot adjoined the Lorings' property at its eastern edge, so the Curtises hired the county surveyor to mark the boundaries before the sale.

It didn't have to be a problem, and it might not have been, had the surveyor been as careful as he needed to be. The description of the shared boundary read, "to a stake at the shore of Bluehill Bay,"[15] and all agreed on that, but the surveyor's drawing showed the spot falling west of a point jutting into the Bay when the Lorings were sure it should be on the east side of the point.

Victor's ire was roused. He disputed the survey and was loath to have his property sold by the Curtises to their cousin. Besides, if the Curtises wanted to sell, why didn't they sell to him instead?

Ben Curtis' ire was roused, also. He had hired the surveyor for just this reason, and the survey said that he was correct. He was embarrassed enough in his finances without the implication that he would steal his neighbor's land. He may also have been sore that the Lorings gave up property so willingly to the Owen sisters and then took such a hard position on this boundary line. He deeded the property to Alfred Baker as per the survey, and the neighbors parted at the end of the summer with the difference still between them.

Cambridge, MA; Fall 1915

Victor and Emilie returned to Cambridge again in the fall. Selden entered his last year at the Berkshire School, still playing hockey and baseball but also the editor of the school newspaper and art editor of his class book. Robert and Minnie Baker were in New York for the season, and Mrs. Baker remained with Rachel and John in Haverhill, so there was no point in being the only ones on the end of Florence Avenue.

Emilie submitted "An Investment in Adventure" at the end of August and again in September. While it was making the rounds, "The Key to Many Doors" was published in the *People's Home Journal*, and Emilie finished a new, 36,000-word novelette, *The Best is Yet to Be*. Like her first serial, she started this story with a jilted suitor, Anthony Vance, who needs to find a fill-in bride quickly. Lovely Hope Damon agrees to the plan, and the action is underway.

Emilie wove threads of her own experience into the story. Instead of Alaska, this story began in Central Park, which Emilie saw each time she visited the Kerleys, who lived less than a block from it. Hope Damon's physical description matched Rachel Baker's: "wavy, almost blue-black hair, with eyes which held the velvety softness of black pansies."

Robert's wife, Minnie, was a good sport, if she ignored the plot device of the main character living with a brother and his difficult wife. "He has one little boy and a wife who resents what he does for me . . . Poor old Jim, what a lot to be linked to such a woman!" Adding insult to injury, Emilie killed off the difficult wife and married the brother to a younger, sweeter girl.

She also gave a nod, sympathetic this time, to the Owen sisters and Blue Hill. After a hurried marriage to Anthony, Hope hides out for a year in a tea house in Maine, which is located, like the Owens' to the east of a solitary, blue mountain and in sight of a glittering bay. The tea house is so successful that "People drop in at all hours of the day," and the proprietor "is a veritable gold mine of expedients to keep them coming."

Vance's mother was modeled after Victor's. "He had not yet become accustomed to his aching sense of loss whenever he thought of his mother . . . How they all adored Anthony Vance's mother! Could she ever win such affection?"

This was the first story in which Emilie quoted *Alice in Wonderland*— later a trademark of hers—a nod to her father and to the book's childhood meaning for her. She also tucked a message of inspiration into her titles. "The Key to Many Doors" referred to the many ways that marriage could be realized. "The Best is Yet to Be" referenced Robert Browning's poem, "Grow old along with me, the best is yet to be." "That line is my inspiration! It turns dangers into molehills and difficulties into high adventure; it takes the sting out of disillusionment, makes the future rosy and encourages me to hope." The title and the sentiment suited John and Rachel, but by the time it was published, John was dead. He died at home on February 1, 1916, and the household in Haverhill prepared for its second funeral in a year.

Snow clouds hid the sun on the following day and many days thereafter, as spring came in like a lion.[16] From February eleventh to the thirteenth, seventeen inches of snow fell in Boston, the heaviest snowfall in twenty-four years.[17] It kept coming, through February and through March, until over seventy-five inches had fallen. Even that was nothing compared to Selden's school in the Berkshires where the winter's total was 134 inches. The latest storm there left five feet on the level, and drifts over twenty feet high stopped railway traffic.[18]

CHRISTMAS VACATION 1915

Wellesley Hills, Winter 1915–16

Snowed in, Emilie had time to review her professional earnings. A statement of royalties from her first book, *For the Comfort of the Family*, listed three free copies, two hundred twenty-three on hand, and domestic sales of only eighteen copies. At ten cents per copy, she had earned one dollar and eighty cents from the effort. By comparison, recipes she sent to the *People's Home Journal* brought a dollar twenty-five. Her non-fiction articles had earned $124.41 altogether, but there had been so many of them. By contrast, her first short story sold for five dollars, her first serial for seventy dollars, and her second serial, *The Best is Yet to Be*, garnered three hundred fifty. Fiction clearly paid better.

Emilie did not begin to write because she needed money, and she did not continue to write because she needed money but earning money from her efforts was rewarding. Knowing that people read her stories in newspapers and magazines was gratifying, and so was recognition as an author. There was no satisfaction in rejection notices, but there was considerable

She wanted to write fiction, in spite of the fact that an editor had warned her to think well before she started on the rough and rocky road to authorship, that the woods, to say nothing of the park benches, were full of would-be writers.
Give Me One Summer

reward when determination and smart revision turned rejections to acceptance checks. Emilie's family liked to tease her about a dream she had which they believed was particularly symbolic of her. In the dream, Emilie overheard the comment of someone who came to pay respects after her death, "She died, but she did it!"[19]

Her father called writing his "pastime," but Emilie treated hers as a profession and recorded each story's progress on a six-by-eight-inch author card. There was space at the top for the title and story number, word count, and required postage. Below were lined columns for date, publisher's name and address, outcome (returned, accepted, published, paid, amount), and remarks. After ten entries, she turned the card over and wrote on the back. Occasionally, she forgot an entry and had to put it lower in the list, but she was generally as disciplined in her record keeping as she was in her writing.

Sometimes, she complied with a reviewer's suggestions for revision. At other times, she stuck to her guns and simply submitted her story elsewhere. This was the case in the winter of 1915–16 with her short stories "An Investment in Adventure," "The Feeling of Home," and "The Evening and the Morning."

"Will you let it go for four subscriptions to their dinky magazine? Will you let them change the ending?" "No, to that last question."
Give Me One Summer

The editor at *Pictorial Review* offended Emilie by calling "The Evening and the Morning" "almost good." She revised the story, but instead of returning it, she sent her new version to *Cosmopolitan*, which rejected it also. She tried *Ainslee's*, *Smart Set*, *Everybody's*, *Munsey's*, *Woman's Home Companion*, *Metropolitan*, and *Blue Book*. In May, she finally mailed the revised story back to *Pictorial Review* with a new title, "Destiny & Mrs. Deland." It was returned in four days, barely time for the postal delivery to New York and back. The next day, it was in the mail again, this time addressed to *The Editor* whom she trusted for criticism. She set the story aside, but she did not give up; she would find a publisher.

By then, Emilie had two distinct writing personalities—Josephine Story who gave advice and Emilie Loring who told stories. All that winter, papers and magazines discussed the European war and the United States' response to it, but Josephine Story left current events to others and focused instead on the eternal role of motherhood. There was no person in a better position to influence the future than a mother. From her, children learned to manage themselves responsibly and deal courteously with others. As they faced the hurdles of childhood with her guidance, they developed strength of character, values, and a sense of purpose. In the dedication, Emilie quoted Daniel Webster, "They work, not upon the canvas that shall perish, or the marble that shall crumble into dust, but upon the mind, upon spirit which is to last forever and which is to bear, for good or evil, throughout its duration the impress of a mother's plastic hand."

Emilie adapted Charles Kerley's "On the Conservation of Children" to "The Conservation of Mothers." If a woman's place was in the home, she should thrive—not merely survive—there.

> Never mind if the house isn't dusted or the socks go undarned that day. The family will soon adjust itself to your holiday and your "day out" will become a matter of course . . .
> Think matters out clearly and constructively, then, whatever you start to do, keep at it until you have accomplished it, or you have demonstrated to your entire satisfaction that you were mistaken in your first conclusion.[20]

Later articles addressed common topics of mothers—how to get children to pick up after themselves, manage their money, be considerate of others, and develop social graces. Whatever the issue, she advised respect. Lead children to learn lessons for themselves without preaching or scolding. Treat them kindly and fairly, allow them the phases of childhood, but require respect in return. "Consider the happiness and comfort of every member of the family; then, with inflexible decision, insist that each member consider yours."

Emilie followed her own advice: "Decide on your goals, then start for them, determinedly, sanely, and with a joyous certainty of success."[21] Over a two-year period, twenty Josephine Story articles appeared in *Mother's*

"That's because in a secluded corner of your children's twentieth century hearts you early planted and cultivated a garden of nineteenth century ideals," Nancy acknowledged tenderly.
Gay Courage

Magazine, American Motherhood, Woman's Magazine, Holland's Magazine, The Sunday American and *St. Nicholas*, and Emilie commenced her third serial story.

As tenacious as Emilie, Victor still hadn't let go of the boundary issue in Blue Hill. During the spring of 1916, he hired Ira Hagan, the same surveyor that Ben Curtis had used, and had him survey the property again. This time, the drawing was in the Lorings' favor. Alfred Baker owned the parcel along their border, but that border was now clearly established on the east side of the "V." Victor was triumphant.

Meanwhile, Ben Curtis headed to London to shore up his finances with an arrangement for Curtis & Cameron to serve as the American branch of the Medici Society.[22] The Society produced replica art works in England with a reputation for reliable quality that equaled Curtis & Cameron's. Ben took considerable, personal risk in going. Since the sinking of the *Lusitania*, no ship was safe from German U-boats, and Curtis' ship left port during an especially protracted sea battle between Britain and Germany. Even on land, occasional bombs rained down on London from German dirigibles, but Ben Curtis was there with a purpose.

He returned from London[23] flush with success, a signed agreement in hand and a beautiful gown for his wife Mary. She wore it to Emilie's grand party that August. All of their East Blue Hill Road friends attended, as well as friends from the city, village, and Parker Point. There were so many guests that Emilie pressed her grandmother's old, porcelain teacups into service.

As bad luck would have it, Mary lifted a dainty cup by its handle, which broke, and hot tea spilled onto her new gown. Esther Wood worked as Emilie's housemaid that summer,[24] and she overheard the altercation between Victor and Mr. Curtis.

Said the mortified host, "I'll buy Mary a new gown." Snapped back the angry Curtis, "You will do no such thing. I can well afford to buy gowns for Mary. But in the future, I shall see to it that my wife does not frequent homes where guests are given cracked cups."[25]

The problem was pride, not teacups. It was hard enough that Ben had been rebuked during the land deal, but to be treated to what he viewed as condescension by a neighbor at the very moment when he hoped to have his praises sung was beyond toleration. Emilie and Mary remained friendly, but the teacup incident marked the end, not only of the summer but also of their husbands' friendship.

They were contentious times. Events overseas had people feeling uneasy, sometimes defensive, occasionally combative. In the spring, Robert Baker's silent film, *The Flying Torpedo*, was released in Los Angeles. It was called "well done," "interesting," and "great fun," but it had a serious side and a sober back story.

The premise was a future attack on the United States and the offer of a reward to anyone who could come up with a sure defense. The play's hero designs a radio-controlled device that sends torpedoes through the air to their targets—guided missiles, although they would not be invented for several more decades. On the surface, it was humorous science fiction, but its deeper message was anti-war. If one remembered their purpose, a future of flying torpedoes was not funny at all.

The film's director, D. W. Griffiths, benefited from Robert Baker's humorous approach to the story. A pioneer of cinema, Griffiths' most famous and controversial work, *The Birth of a Nation* (1915) was simultaneously lauded for its cinematic technique and vilified for its racist portrayals.

This was a lesson that the Bakers knew well, learned first by Albert Baker at the *American Eagle* and developed through years of George Baker's amateur dramas. Serious messages provoked serious responses. An earnest message could be slipped into a humorous vehicle and reach its target without backlash. Robert Baker wrote the screenplay for *The Flying*

Torpedo with trademark Baker humor, and the anti-war message was delivered with a smile.

Griffiths' Triangle Pictures distributed Robert's next two films, also—people-pleasers with big star power. *Reggie Mixes In* (June 1916) starred the highest paid actor of the time, Douglas Fairbanks, Sr., as a prosperous gentleman who runs afoul of gangsters. In *Flirting with Fate* (July 1916), Fairbanks played a despairing artist who hires a hit man to murder him but then inherits a million dollars, and many comedic situations unfold before the artist and the hitman work out a new deal.

Robert Baker was in Hollywood with the biggest producer, the biggest stars, and the biggest issues of the day. He responded with another musical comedy, *Arms and the Girl,* "an amusing little romance that unfolds during the first hours of the invasion of Belgium." The *New York Times* called it "light, bright, and amusing," although *Theater Magazine* complained, "I am tempted to suggest as topics having equally amusing possibilities the epidemic of poliomyelitis and the massacres in Armenia."[26] Another problem was narrowly skirted, too.

Burton E. Stevenson claimed that the play infringed on the copyright of his book *Little Comrade* and took Robert to court, but the judge denied the motion. Taken together, he ruled, the two stories had many similar elements and "enough spys to have discovered all the secrets of Europe," but Baker's play was allowed to "proceed on its way . . . free from fear of a court order and concerned only with the net result after the box office receipts shall have been counted."[27]

Accidentally bumping into another's creative territory was easy to do, either by parallel creation or subconscious assimilation. Indeed, prolific writers had trouble not copying themselves. Boy gets girl, boy loses girl, boy gets girl again. The details might change, but the territory was familiar, and at what point did similar stories get too close to one another? The judge answered, "Of necessity, certain kinds of incidents must be found in many books and plays, and originality, when dealing with incidents familiar in life or fiction, lies in the association and grouping of those incidents

Emilie Loring at Atlantic City, January 24, 1917

in such a manner that the work under consideration presents a new conception or a novel arrangement of events."[28]

On Saturday, December ninth, Emilie and Victor celebrated their
twenty-fifth wedding anniversary. They entertained friends and family at
their home in Wellesley Hills and received "many pieces of silverware."[29]
When they married, Emilie was twenty-five; now, she was fifty, the mother
of two adult sons, and a published author.

Emilie attended the opening of *Arms and the Girl* in Atlantic City
and posed for her fiftieth-year portrait on the boardwalk on January 24,
1917—a little fuller of figure, carriage proud, her dark, Baker eyes directed
upward, as in thought. When she returned home, she sent "The Key to
Many Doors" to Griffiths' Fine Arts Film Company. The story's mixture of
romance, hasty marriage, and plot twists was suited to the silver screen, and
her brother's association with Griffiths might be helpful. She also sent her
motherhood articles to the Pilgrim Press of the Congregational Society,
of which Victor was currently president. Nothing came of the film script,
and she set that aside for the time being, but her articles were accepted for
publication as Josephine Story's second book, *The Mother in the Home*.

She ended that book with a story called, "The Compensating Years," a
"this, too, shall pass" encouragement. She had reached the compensating
years herself and gloried in them. Separately, she published "How Women
Should Prepare for Life's Best Part,"[30] which praised the harried, young
mother for the "big, thrilling, vital job" of being a homemaker, but advised
her to "take—seize—steal the time" for herself and take heart from the
example of women whose children are grown.

They have time for the activities they love, perhaps for a coveted
avocation. They are eager and alert and conversant with the affairs
of the great world; they have opportunities to enjoy little journeys
with their husbands in true honeymoon fashion.

CHAPTER 18

World War I: Her Father's Daughter

Boston, Spring 1917

President Wilson was reelected in October of 1916 with the slogan, "He kept us out of war," but that did not last. Over a million lives had been lost in the trenches of France without appreciable change in territory. Germany recruited Mexico as a second-flank ally and sank one hundred sixty-seven vessels in December, nearly half of them from neutral countries.[1]

It was said that Blue Hill's Ben Curtis did not care for politics, but he could not have been ignorant of them when he traveled to England in late January 1917. His son Robert stood guard at the Mexican border, and while Ben was in London, the Germans announced an all-out submarine campaign from which no nation's vessels were safe. The day that he boarded the *New York* to return home, the United States cut its diplomatic ties with Germany. U.S. merchant ships positioned weapons on deck, and patrols monitored the New England coast for German periscopes. When Curtis arrived home that time, he stayed home.

For the time being, the Lorings lived in Cambridge. Victor and Emilie had their apartment at the Riverbank Court Hotel, and their sons boarded in the dormitories at Harvard. After pitching a year on the freshman baseball team and another on the "seconds," Robby earned a spot on the Varsity. This was a big deal. Last year's team had beaten Babe Ruth and the World Series Champion Red Sox, 1-0. Eyes were on the Crimson and now on Robby, who would take the mound.[2]

Emilie wrote steadily. The first installment of her serial "The Best is Yet to Be" appeared in February's issue of *The People's Home Journal*, and she submitted two new stories in March, "The Yellow Hat" and "The Girl

"Don't you realize what this country is up against? Don't you care that a U-boat campaign is being waged with success within a few miles, almost within gunshot of our shores?"
Rainbow At Dusk

Who Lacked Class." The first gave as good a description of Emilie's burgeoning writing career as she had yet offered: "Then, all at once, in a flash, I woke to the consciousness that I was an individual; not old, not tied to this house; a person with life tingling through my veins, with a love of beauty and clothes, with a desire to write and express my views . . ."[3]

But that desire was postponed; Emilie put down her writing and did not return to it for months as the European conflict finally hit home. German ambitions were clear, and they stopped at no border. Russia's Bolshevik revolution weakened Europe's eastern front. Trenches on the western front filled with corpses but did not move forward—or backward—even a little. The seas were unsafe, and unless something happened to change the balance, the allies faced exhaustion and defeat.

That something was the United States. President Wilson had hoped a "league of nations" would bring peace without involving American troops, but when German submarines sent three American ships to the bottom of the cold Atlantic, neutrality came to an end. President Wilson asked Congress to declare war, and on April 6, 1917, the declaration was made.[4] Two days later, Victor Loring spoke to a meeting of the Boston Art Club and "congratulated Americans on the fact that in this crisis they were not only a United States, but a united people."[5]

Four days before their starting game against the Braves, the Harvard Crimson's season was cancelled, and Robby's baseball career was over. The Selective Draft Act authorized the conscription of 500,000 civilian males in a first round of drafts and an additional 500,000 should they be needed.[6] There was no possibility of a substitute for this war. Every able-bodied male from twenty-one to thirty was called to serve in the armed forces, including Robby, who was twenty-two.

Professors gave final exams early to accommodate the nearly forty percent of Harvard's student body that would depart. All who had completed twelve of their required sixteen credits were forgiven the final four and granted "war degrees." Instead of a college junior and varsity pitcher, Robby was suddenly a college graduate and a soldier.

The fourth and final installment of "The Best is Yet to Be" arrived to a changed world. In February, the United States was yet at peace, Emilie wrote in Cambridge, and her boys attended Harvard. Four months later, the country was at war, Victor and Emilie had returned to Wellesley Hills, and their sons faced uncertain futures.

From June through August, Robby trained as a cadet corporal in Company K of Harvard's Reserve Officers Training Corps (ROTC).[7] Then he entered Plattsburg's new officers training camp on the shore of Lake Champlain. Citizens' military camps on the Plattsburg model had already trained more than sixteen thousand officers, and when war came, the government adopted the model in its entirety. Conscription supplied the National Army's soldiers, and Plattsburg camps would supply its officers.[8]

Robby entered the second class of 1917, Company 1 of the 17th Provisional Training Regiment. From August through November, he practiced with rifles, pistols, bayonets, hand grenades, and machine guns. He drew maps, dug trenches, wore a gas mask, and learned to recognize gas delivered on the wind or in small explosions. By his birthday in November, he was commissioned a First Lieutenant in the 78th Division Infantry and awaited orders.[9]

In 1898, Robert Baker had hoisted young Robby and Selden above his head in a victory pose for the camera, American flag in hand. The framed photo was titled, "Our Boys." Now, nineteen years later, the boys posed with their uncle for another "Our Boys" photograph, Robert Baker holding an American flag and held aloft this time by Robby and Selden, all smiling broadly.

Selden's twenty-first birthday was not until November, but like his namesake, he volunteered. While Robby trained in Cambridge, Selden boarded the Cunard steamship *Aurania* with forty-four other volunteers for the American Ambulance Field Service and more than two hundred nurses headed for base hospitals in France. They arrived in Liverpool on July twenty-second, took the train to Southampton, crossed the English Channel to LeHavre, and assembled at the AFS headquarters at 21 Rue Raynouard in Paris.[10]

"If you were needed you and every man who talks like you would be the first to answer the call to the colors. I know you. You jumped in at the first sign of trouble. You'd do it again."
The Trail of Conflict

"Our Boys"

"Our Boys," Nineteen Years Later

Blue Hill, Summer 1917

The Owens arrived in Blue Hill at their usual time in early June. Carrie's forty-second birthday was on the fourteenth, but she fell deeply ill almost as soon as she arrived and died three weeks later, on June twenty-seventh. The doctor said she died of organic heart disease brought on by several years of "intestinal poisoning." Frail Carrie, with her love of beauty and her sweet, artistic ways, was gone. Bessie and Mary Owen had cared for their little sister for so long that they could not bear to be parted from her now. As she had asked, Carrie's tiny body was buried in the sunken garden among the ferns and the lilies that had so often delighted her.[11]

It was the beginning of a Blue Hill summer unlike those of recent memory. Red, white, and blue cards appeared on front doors, "A Man from This House is Fighting in France,"[12] and the *Ellsworth American* announced more young men every week who were "called to service"—perhaps death. It was the unspoken but constant fear of their families. The death toll in Europe from gunfire, explosion, poison gas, and disease had been staggering for years, and now their own sons and brothers were going across.

There was no distinction between cottagers and native Blue Hillers now. Gordon Curtis trained at Plattsburg and was assigned to the 76th Division's 302nd Field Artillery; Blue Hill's John Parker went to the 303rd. Paul Nevin was stationed on a naval transport; Fred Emerton was on the *USS Fulton*. Doris Nevin went to France with the Red Cross; Blue Hill's Flora Hinckley went with the Army Nurse Corps. In 1915, Anne Paul Nevin helped create the American Fund for French Wounded (AFFW) that shipped hospital supplies overseas. With America in the war, she served as chairman of AFFW headquarters in New York and oversaw delivery of thousands of cases of hospital articles and surgical dressings to more than three hundred hospitals in the war zone.[13]

At home, the very qualities that made the Maine coast attractive became vulnerabilities. Numerous inlets and islands could hide enemy craft, and busy ports were hard to monitor. Blue Hillers watched from

Rodney Gerard parted the ferns and crimson gladioli which almost obscured a bronze tablet set in a moss-grown boulder. She read the inscription. Whispered: "How lovely! What profound silence! It sinks into one's soul."
Hilltops Clear

land for the periscopes of German submarines, and at sea, Robert Curtis commanded a Navy submarine chaser whose job was to destroy enemy periscopes and force their vessels to the surface.

Since the declaration of war, the entire Atlantic coastline was considered a war zone. The steamer *Boothbay*, whose familiar horn had meant the arrival of cottagers to Blue Hill, became the *USS Boothbay* and delivered personnel and equipment from Naval headquarters at Washington D.C. to docks in Virginia and Maryland. The Slavens' yacht *Alfredine IV* was recommissioned the *USS Edithia*[14] and patrolled the Long Island Sound where the perceived threat from German submarines was so great that troops bound for Europe left under cover of the strictest darkness. Not even a cigarette was lit on deck as the carriers steamed into the black Atlantic, tense and alert.[15]

If the Germans slipped past the United States Navy and onto American soil, Americans would be ready. Men too young or old for the draft undertook military-style training at home. In New York, five hundred women of the Woman's League for Self Defense learned to handle rifles, operate wireless radios, and drive ambulances.[16] Men and women signed on as Red Cross ambulance drivers in donated vehicles, while others cooked and served food at canteens for departing and returning servicemen.

United States troops abroad needed both clothing and food, but after three years of war, Europe had little of either. Newspapers published patterns, and American women knitted vests, mufflers, mittens, wristlets, and even "helmets" of gray wool to send overseas.[17] Women students at Wellesley were so dedicated to these projects that the administration admonished them to refrain from knitting during lectures.

Families economized on meals, served rice, corn and potatoes instead of bread, and grew their own vegetable gardens to send more of the nation's food supply to the troops. "Food will win the war, and the nation whose food resources are best conserved will be the victor,"[18] promoted the government. To set an example in Blue Hill, Ned Brooks planted a four-foot-square by five-foot-tall potato hill in his front yard and invited villagers to

"Hooverizing on colors was a measure of economy with us Lorraines so I dyed all the girls' white hand-me-downs violet to match my eyes when they are not blue."
Here Comes the Sun!

pay a quarter to guess how many potatoes it would produce. The prizewinner received ten dollars, and the rest went to the Red Cross.[19]

Restaurants, and soon the public, observed one meatless day and one wheatless day per week. Casseroles and meat loaf became popular, and homemakers made strategic substitutions—potatoes for eggs and flour, corn starch for eggs; eggs, cheese, nuts and beans for meat. The new conservation was called "Hooverizing" (after U. S. Food Administrator Herbert Hoover),[20] and the goal was to conserve carefully at home to send more to France. "Waste in your kitchen means starvation in some other kitchen across the sea."[21]

France, Fall 1917

Selden arrived in France at a strategic juncture. April's French offensive at the Chemin des Dames had failed miserably.[22] If the French were going to beat back the Germans, they needed to deliver more ammunition and supplies to their soldiers on the front, but they were short seven thousand drivers, and the French army sent no reinforcements. After three years of killing, there were few conscripts left, and many of them were old. To meet the need, American Ambulance Field Service volunteers joined the transport corps. Instead of driving ambulances under the semi-protection of a Red Cross emblem, they became strategic—and explosive—targets.

Following six weeks of training at Chavigny Farm, Selden reported to Soissons and Motor Transport Unit, T.M. 397 of the Réserve Mallet, commanded by the French Army.

"T.M." stood for "Transport Materiel" and therein we have an explanation of the work performed. It was to carry any kind of material needed in the war, at any time, to any place.[23]

The drivers lived in trailers hidden under elm trees along the south bank of the Aisne River. The area had once been a beautiful park, but that was laid to ruin in the 1914 Battle of the Marne that stopped the Germans on their march toward Paris.[24]

By his mother's birthday on September fifth, Selden had begun the urgent task of hauling ammunition to the front at the Chemin des Dames ridge. Two months would pass before the United States Army lost the first soldier under its command in France, but the transport division lost men regularly. At a memorial for two fallen Americans that month, a French officer praised, "[They] were both students and nothing obliged them to leave their home and join our army to go into danger . . . they offered to our country their youth, their heart, and their blood."[25]

As United States troops mobilized in France during the fall of 1917, AFS drivers enlisted in the U.S. National Army, and most took the chance to leave for other American installations. Selden was among three hundred who chose to remain with the Reservé Mallet. "The transport service was considered more of a man's job, more arduous, difficult, and dangerous, and certainly of much use to the French government."[26] They had accepted a sacred charge, and they would not abandon it. Their new name was the "Motor Transport Division of the U. S. Quartermaster Corps," but their work was the same as before, and the French were still in command.

Orders came during the day, but the trucks drove only under cover of darkness, "with no lights, keeping on the road by sheer force of habit— nothing else."[27] Loaded with many times their weight, they followed nose-to-tail, engine noise camouflaged by the rumbles, bursts, and explosions of German guns, their movements disguised by burlap-draped barbed wire left behind by the Germans. Their heavy trucks carried heavy loads on roads slick with mud and pocked with holes. They passed villages turned to rubble and crossed waterways clogged with the rusted remnants of exploded vehicles.

Some nights, rain clouds blacked out the stars, and the darkness was so intense that men's eyes gave no guidance. They sniffed the air for changes in the wind and for the odor of lethal gas. Hearing and touch sharpened at changes in reverberation and vibration. Muscles tense, they drove ready to

"We were buddies in World War I, drove camions filled with ammunition to the front, evacuated Hill 67 together. We both left college in our freshman year to join the Field Service, later became second looeys in the U. S. Army."
Keepers of the Faith

"What you called the other day, 'Gay courage,' the phrase has stuck in my mind. That's life, isn't it? We can't sulk. We can't run—and be soldiers. We've got to go straight on."
Gay Courage

stop or swerve, sometimes ducking instinctively. The closer they came to the front lines, the nearer the shells landed and the greater the chance that a sudden flash would reveal their position.

Miles took hours. They hauled each other out of the mud with ropes and chains and inched forward to the drop-off point, only half a mile from the front-line trenches. Weary, mud-soaked, and often under fire, they unloaded the trucks and turned them around for the ragged drive back to camp, only to find "the roads just as slippery, the holes just as big, and the night just as dark."[28]

Twenty-hour days followed twenty-hour days with rest scarce and sleep scarcer. Along the road, they saw soldiers brought from the trenches for brief respite—gray men covered with gray dust, their eyes dull and hollow from all they had seen, their ears deafened by constant blasts. Nothing had prepared any of them for the bleak horror of the trenches. Nothing would stop the drivers from supplying them with the ammunition to survive, to fight back, and to finally triumph.

Days blurred into weeks and months. The transport corps hauled barbed wire, I-beams, sheet iron, trench sides, cross-braces, logs, posts, lathes, roofing, lime, cement, sandbags, rifles, machine guns, revolvers, cannon, powder, fuses, grenades, signal rockets, bombs, and mines. They carried camouflage, gasoline, picks, shovels, sand, rock, nails, tools, hardware, shells, and cases. They also carried food and wine. When they could get it, French *poilus* ate two meals a day, accompanied by a steadying allotment of wine. Otherwise, they received hardtack and tinned beef and made them last.

Selden's unit hauled more than 3200 pieces of artillery and more than a million shells to the Chemin des Dames, and when the French finally attacked on October 23, all seemed to fire at once. "[The] air was overflowing with sound."[29] At the height of battle, 75 mm field artillery guns fired 2330 explosive shells per minute, accompanied by the 95-pound explosive, gas, and shrapnel shells of the 155 mm howitzer and the man-killing spray of machine guns. In three days, the French reached the top of the ridge, and the Germans retreated.[30] Fellow camion driver David Darrah wrote afterward, "That was worth coming to France for."

"Remember how shoulder to shoulder they pressed steadily forward through the forest? Snipers. Machine-guns. Traps. Comrades falling in horrible, huddled heaps. Yet on they marched, caution reconnoitering in their eyes, smiles curving their lips."
Gay Courage

Selden Melville Loring

French Helmet and Gas Mask Used at Verdun, France

On November first, Selden was promoted to Quartermaster Sergeant for his company and fitted everyone for uniforms—"which is some job as the size tags on some are a delusion and a snare—also crazy," he wrote home. When snow came, battlefield action slowed, and the outfit got weeks of respite from deliveries. Some drivers were given liberty to go to Paris or Nice, and where they were able, American units enjoyed approximations of Thanksgiving

In early December, Selden and thirty other ambulance and camion drivers were sent to the French Army Officers Training School at Meaux to learn how to service and repair their Pierce-Arrow transports and Ford ambulances. They took apart trucks, drew the shape of every piece from multiple angles, and then put them back together. The process was repeated until they knew every inch of the chassis, engine, and drive train. The next time a camion broke down in the dark and mud, they would have a chance to get it rolling again. A second benefit of the training was that Selden spent both Christmas and New Year's at Meaux, twenty-six miles east of Paris and forty miles further from the front.

The Home Front, Fall 1917–Spring 1918

Letters took weeks, so by the time they arrived, they were old news. In January, Robby received a letter from his brother that jauntily detailed experiences of eating in Soissons at the Lion Rouge, "where one can be dined, wined, pied, and pirated all at once," and the Hotel Crois d'Or, which served a croquette with vegetables, "a la mowed, as Inky [Robert Baker] would say." Humorous descriptions of food, showers, and decor yielded at last to reflection:

> By the way, speaking of guns, I wish Inky could hear a big shell when they are strafing a town. He could use it in a war sketch or play and get great suspense. They come starting way off with a high whistle and toning down to a swish with a little pause and complete silence before the crash. You can't tell whether it's going to hit near at hand or quite a way off. The little pause before the explosion is the most nerve-wracking time imaginable.
>
> Well, a merry Christmas to everybody if it's not too late. Merry Christmas is right—also Sherman. Love to all, Sel.[31]

"Sherman Was Right" was popular shorthand for Civil War General Sherman's assertion: "There is many a boy here today who looks on war as all glory, but, boys, it is all hell." "Sherman Was Right" became the title of a farce comedy and a silent film. It captioned postcards and appeared in many soldiers' letters home. Much could not be expressed and get past the censors; "War is hell" became "Sherman was right."

Emilie's book on motherhood came out when both of her sons were away, and the advice she gave about worry was timely. "I can't afford to worry. I need every ounce of strength, thought and courage I possess to solve my problems." When worries intruded, she got outdoors and put her imagination to work.

Why, why, couldn't a way be found to stop war forever? Killing, maiming of human beings, destruction of homes and property was such a senseless way to settle a dispute. Why didn't women, billions strong, do something about the wholesale slaughter of children they had brought into the world?
Beyond the Sound of Guns

"War is just what Sherman said it was—plus."
Keepers of the Faith

"Color does to me
what the touch of
the earth did to the
giant Antaeus—sends
new life, vitality,
courage, initiative
surging through me.
Sometime the
scientists will dis-
cover that color is a
renewer of life."
Hilltops Clear

"If, when they reach
'the end' they forget
to go back for their
problems and march
blithely toward the
day's work pepped
up and refreshed,
refreshed—it's a
great word, isn't it—I
shall feel that I have
achieved something."
Give Me One Summer

"I have been an
interested, keen,
fairly intelligent
observer of the
human comedy for a
great many years."
Rainbow at Dusk

As I tramped, I planned the refurnishing of this house. Neither a very spiritual nor intellectual thought-refuge but one full of light and color and hope. It required concentration also, and every time one of those malicious worry imps poked his head into my mind, I gave him a sharp slap and changed the color scheme of a room."[32] (*The Mother in the Home*)

She appreciated as never before the experience of her parents' generation. Hollis Loring watched his son Selden march off to the Civil War in a uniform that he provided, while he stayed home and waged the war of politics to decide what the sacrifice would mean in the end. The Bakers sent no one to fight on the Civil War battlefield, but two of their children died during wartime, and George did his own kind of war work. Amidst agony, fear and heartbreak, his plays provided moments of respite, inspiration to summon courage, and humor to lighten the load. If people set aside their cares awhile and received rest, if they left the theater with their shoulders straighter and their heads held higher, perhaps they might endure a little better. If their children came through the cauldron with happy hearts and valiant spirits, then there was better hope for the world.

Emilie's third serial, "An Elusive Legacy," followed her father's lead. "A gripping story of love and mystery," it opened on horseback with a broken engagement and led through murder and impersonation to love. Tests of character, flirtatious dialogue, and compelling romance played against up-to-the-minute details including a Zeppelin and a Wright brothers airplane. The characters were real, their problems believable, and their settings were so attractive that the reader was transported out of the world of war and into a better place for a while. The story ran from October through January in *Woman's Weekly*.[33]

In mid-December, Robby was sent to Camp Dix in New Jersey, the jumping-off point for troops headed to France. Fully ninety percent of Plattsburg trainees were sent overseas, but at the end of January, he was detailed instead to remain in the 153rd Depot Brigade at Camp Dix as an instructor. Army public relations described the depot brigade as a set of ready replacements, already trained and prepared to step into roles left vacant by their fallen brothers. The truth of it was that these recruits were not ready for assignments overseas. By spirit or talent or choice, they failed to meet the standards of soldiers in the field, but the next months would get them ready for duty.

Robby taught the recruits how to throw hand grenades. The delivery was overhead, like a pitch, but a grenade weighed three times as much as a baseball, and four ounces of it was high explosive. The throw had to be strong, well-timed, and accomplished accurately from any position. There were no balls and strikes in hand grenades; the consequences of a poor throw now were life and death.[34]

How it must have rankled to learn that Harvard's baseball team would play its spring season in 1918. This was supposed to be Robby's senior year, his best year on the mound. But the National Army was filled with young men like Robby who were called away from sports teams, some of them nearly professionals. Camp Dix put together two leagues of baseball at camp, and Robby was on its single, traveling team that played a schedule of games against the colleges, but the roster was constantly interrupted as players were called with their units to France.

Sports teams were only one of the army's efforts to release steam from the pressure cooker of youth and restricted quarters. Beginning with the Civil War, the military relied on the YMCA to provide for troops' rest, relief, and entertainment. During World War I, there was a YMCA hut not only in each camp but in every section of each camp in the United States.[35]

In France, more than 13,000 volunteers built and staffed 491 huts that served as home, church, theater, and club for the young Americans so far from home. They served as grocery stores and banks, provided athletic equipment and games, taught courses from basic literacy through college-level subjects, and presented an impressive range of entertainments including live concerts and plays, first-run movies, and company

"...and there he had stayed through the war training raw recruits, such raw recruits! How he had rebelled! How he had tried to get across."
The Solitary Horseman

Robert Melville Loring

Camp Dix Baseball Team, 1918

sing-alongs. During the course of the war, 1,470 professional and semi-professional entertainers performed at YMCA huts.[36]

YMCA volunteers went as close to the front lines as the commanders would allow, sometimes all the way to the trenches where they risked every danger to distribute chocolate, reading material, and comfort. When battle lines advanced and retreated in the space of a day, 1,045 tents served as portable YMCA centers that moved with each unit. They were truly tents, and there was only one for every five hundred men, but the good that they did was greater than their size.[37]

The Army considered one week's leave every four months "essential to health and morale," so the YMCA arranged hotels and cafes near the front and converted famous resorts at Aix-les-Bains, the Alps, and the French Riviera into leave areas for the troops. At Nancy, shell-shocked young men shed their filthy, war-stained clothing, soaked themselves clean in the famed thermal baths, and returned to their units in fresh, clean clothing, from their underwear to their pants, shirts, and socks.[38]

Of all the entertainments provided by the YMCA, movies were the most popular. Between April 1918 and July 1919, 157,000 screenings attracted a combined attendance of over ninety-four million at more than five thousand venues, always free to soldiers.[39] The Community Motion Picture Bureau sent thousands of films each week, which fueled a high demand for new scripts. Robert Baker's films had already gone across, and in May, Emilie submitted her story "The Best is Yet to Be" to the Lasky Studios for consideration.

William Howard Taft called entertainment "a necessity" for troop morale, and he was in a position to judge. By turns, he served as secretary of war, president of the United States, co-chairman of the National War Labor Board, and Chief Justice of the Supreme Court. While he was still on the Court, he took time to write a book about the YMCA's work during the war, including the thousands of actors, writers, and performers who contributed "indispensable" benefit, "as necessary as exchange of air in a room." His summary echoed the Bakers' philosophy:

> For the outcome of their service was not merely an hour's plea-sure. It was a new spirit and new resolve. It lifted away a heavy load of weariness and homesickness, and, dissolving anxiety in laughter, restored the natural buoyancy which, for most men, is an essential of efficiency. No time or money was more profitably spent than that which set men's feet to tapping, and let them live for a little time in a world of imagination . . .[40]

Emergency in Europe, Spring 1918

On the first day of spring, the Germans struck at the Somme, just miles from Selden's unit at Soissons. Fast evacuation was their only defense, so they loaded up quickly and towed their trailers to their old training camp at Chavigny. Six weeks later, the Germans attacked at the Aisne River, and the "bombardment was so intense" that the Reservé Mallet retreated with French soldiers hanging onto the sides of their trucks. On May 27, they hauled supplies to the makeshift, front lines, but a day later, under rapid German advance, they evacuated Chavigny also. This time, they left so quickly that dearly needed supplies were left behind. Under fire, the drivers went back to salvage parts from the one, sure source they had: their own abandoned vehicles. Without those parts, they made do with whatever they found; when tires gave out, the trucks rolled on mismatched rings of iron.[41]

The Germans attacked for ten days before they halted on the fourth of June, but the camion drivers took no rest. Every day, they hauled ammunition and supplies to the front, and if the army was repulsed and moved backward, they set up a new point of departure and began hauling again.[42]

The Germans launched five offensives, and Selden's unit was on the receiving end of four of them. The onslaught "staggered the Allied Armies and for the moment threatened irremediable disaster." Twenty French divisions poured into a sixteen-mile gap in the defensive line and held out for help to arrive. General Pershing recommended that "the entire American Army be transported to France as speedily as possible without further training and without equipment other than rifles and absolute essentials." By August, 250,000 soldiers arrived per month, a rate sustained only by expanding the draft to men between eighteen and forty-five.[43]

It was a big swing in America from isolationism to a mandatory draft that sent hundreds of thousands to the trenches of France. Some took the moral position that "God is on the side, not of America against Germany, but on the side of humanity against inhumanity, on the side of justice against injustice."[44] Others refused to serve as a matter of religious, politi-cal, or personal conscience.

Under the Espionage Act, "disloyal," antiwar statements were prohib-ited under penalty of arrest. Alongside notices of men called to service, newspapers published the names of those who were called but petitioned not to go, with their reasons and their cases' outcomes. Public shaming of dissenters was rife, and their treatment on military bases was hostile until the army came to grips with the issue.

In June 1918, Robby Loring was put in charge of the conscientious objectors at Camp Dix with orders to treat them decently and to find non-combatant duties for those who were willing to undertake them.[45] Those who refused were brought before a board of inquiry which could sentence them to imprisonment, life terms, and even death. It was alienating duty to be mistrusted by the conscientious objectors, to mistrust them in return, and to be negatively associated with them in the eyes of others.

The Camp Dix war garden provided an unexpected solution. Garden work was war work with a moral imperative: "The world is facing famine today. Every article of food raised enlarges the circle of nourished people. The bit you raise or induce others to raise pushes that famine circle back one bit more." Most of the gardeners were regular army staff, but Robby assigned conscientious objectors to work the 400-acre plot, also.[46] It was tangible work in keeping with both their pacifist principles and the war effort—a useful compromise.

The civilian war garden movement was led by women with little prior experience. A socialite observed, "My mother was a garden-lover, but I never saw her touch the earth." The Women's National Farm and Garden Association encouraged, "Even untrained, city-bred women" could garden efficiently "under supervision,"[47] and by 1918, there were more than five million war gardens in cultivation, one for every four households. The effect on food supply was drastic. A mind-boggling 1,450,000,000 quarts of food were canned that year, freeing commercial crops and transport machinery to supply Europe and the troops instead. *Woman's Journal*

"The effects of gas and shot and shell aren't in it with the intolerable sense of shame which a man, who didn't do his best to get into the war, will carry through the years."
The Trail of Conflict

"Then I shall treat you as I did the fake conscientious objectors when they refused to put on uniform. Make you get into it."
Behind the Cloud, (first draft)

praised, "The woman with a hoe is easily discernible just back of the man with the gun."[48]

Emilie already had a flower garden, but she threw herself into war gardening with characteristic dedication. She joined the Women's National Farm and Garden Association,[49] and then she got to work on the large area between her home and Burr Croft. She bought chickens and planted potatoes, vegetables, and herbs. For the time being, she produced foodstuffs instead of stories; she called them her "wartime best sellers."

Allied Offensive, July to November 1918

Emilie's next serial was "Garth the Gunmaker," about a munitions factory hunting a possible saboteur. The story ran in *Woman's Weekly* from July to September, as the Allies prepared a massive counter-offensive, and an unexpected attack proved more deadly than guns.

Within two years, influenza killed between twenty and forty million people worldwide, the deadliest epidemic in history. In America, one-fourth of the population contracted the disease, and 675,000 died—twelve times the number of American soldiers that were killed in battle overseas.

Living in close quarters, the influenza rate in military camps was higher than for civilians. "It ultimately killed more American military personnel than did enemy machine guns and artillery."[50] At Camp Dix, sixty-two died in one day, and by the end of September, there were more than six thousand active cases and nearly four hundred deaths.

The flu reached Selden's unit in France on June fifteenth, between defensive battles with the Germans at Montdidier-Noyon and Champagne-Marne, but the camions kept moving. Sick or not, their loads of ammunition, supplies, and personnel had to reach the front in time for the coordinated offensive.

The allies started shooting on July fifteenth and did not stop until victory. They pushed back through all of the territory that had been lost—Champagne-Marne, Aisne-Marne, the Somme, and the Oise-Aisne. The

"Flu. Sharp attack. Left her with a type of nervous exhaustion. She thought it was her heart when things faded out." *We Ride the Gale!*

"I have a firm convic-
tion that a person can
put through any wor-
thy thing on which he
is determined. How
else do you account
for the seeming mir-
acles men got away
with in the World
War? The test is, how
much do you want
it? I've gone on that
principle all my life,
and it's worked, I tell
you, it's worked!"
The Trail of Conflict

guns fired right up to the eleventh minute of the eleventh hour of the eleventh day of the eleventh month, and then . . . silence. After five years, seventeen million military and civilian deaths, and the widespread, physical
destruction of both France and Belgium, the Great War was over.

Selden wrote to ninety-five-year-old Walter Brackett, a renowned artist, founder of the Boston Art Club, and family friend. His letter showed
that he had inherited his family's light touch.

My lengthy stay in this country has been full of interest of course
and more or less "excitement" especially since the nasty 'Uns
staged their great Spring Opening of Fancy Driving. Having been
blessed with orchestra seats for the whole show, I have been forced
to observe at close quarters most of the methods of modern war-
fare and have been included in nearly all the offensives both Allied
and German.

Selden's unit was at the St. Quentin, La Fere front when the armistice
was signed. He concluded his letter to Mr. Brackett:

Father writes of seeing you often and I hope it will not be long
before I can enjoy the same privilege, but, in "this man's army"
the only thing to be sure of is that any rumors as to when we
get through are entirely false and worthless except as a means of
diversion and an exercise in imagination.[51]

Selden's unit began immediate deliveries to Sedan in northern France
where the railroads had been destroyed. Robert remained at Camp Dix as
active troops and conscientious objectors were returned to their homes.

There was more work to do, but the war was over. Emilie's sons were
alive, safe, and would soon be on their way home. She sharpened her pencils.

ACT FIVE:
Emilie Loring

"Writing is <u>work</u>. Imagination plays an important part, but only work, with plenty of mental steam behind it, will make that imagination a producer."

—Emilie Loring

Portrait of Emilie Loring by Henry Fitzpatrick, 1922

CHAPTER 19

Writing is W-O-R-K

Wellesley Hills, Spring 1919

In a long state of solitude after the holidays, Emilie wrote "Kismet Takes a Hand,"[1] a New York story that made no reference to war, except that the romantic lead had "a distinct trace of military distinction." The world was war weary. In an article for *The Editor*, J. S. Salls advised, "The ears of the world are straining to hear messages of hope. They need love. They need faith. They need the tonic of cheer."[2] Bruce Cameron is a virile, wholesome millionaire whose biggest problem is that his love interest, Patricia Langdon, has a chronic mistrust of the wealthy. Hiding his identity, Bruce hires her to make a jeweled collar for his cat, Kismet, which gives him an excuse to visit every day. Romantic tension finds relief in the cat's comic actions, and when Bruce's sterling character is proven, the last obstacle to their love is removed.[3]

Next came "I'll Tell the World!"—a Blue Hill story in which a thunderstorm tears down barriers of misunderstanding between a handsome war veteran and the girl who had admired him since before he went across. Familiar, Blue Hill features provided the setting: the Loring boat (renamed *Saucy Sally*), landmarks of the inner bay, guests arriving on the steamer, and a clambake on "the Neck." It was also the first appearance of Emilie's father as a character—an understanding advisor with wisdom, humor, and "that discretion which fathers with attractive daughters acquire in time."[4]

Emilie finished a five-thousand-word story every two weeks. "I'll Tell the World!" was completed on February 7, "The Grey Sheep" on February 21, and "Denise and the Dragon" on March 8. In between, she found time to pen three Josephine Story articles, "A Clean Slate," "Is Your Home in Trouble?" and "Saving to Spend." "A Clean Slate" was only 355 words in twenty sentences, but it reflected the determination she felt for her writing.

She looked up in surprise. Her work had burned up the hours. She interned the typewriter and closed her desk with a bang.
The Trail of Conflict

"What have you been doing?" "Writing every morning." "How's the old imagination working?" "Overtime. Better plots and more of them is its slogan."
Give Me One Summer

"Don't stop to make excuses. Make good. You have three hundred and sixty-five chances each year."[5]

She usually mailed a story or article on the same day it was finished. She counted the words, recorded the required postage, and then logged the manuscript's destination as she sent it off. If it came back with a rejection notice, she sent it as quickly as possible to the next publisher.

There was more work to this than the non-writer supposed. From February through April, three stories and three articles together accounted for forty-one submissions before one was accepted. She had no control over the postal service or the time that an editor would take to review her work and send a reply, but she disciplined herself to write on schedule and held onto a manuscript only as long as it took to revise, if necessary, and send it in a fresh envelope to the next publisher.

Emilie Loring on Her Wellesley Hills Porch. "She typed on and on until tired, but triumphant, she curled up in the wicker chair and read aloud what she had written." Give Me One Summer

Emilie's first housekeeping articles were syndicated in newspapers, and the articles on motherhood and her first fiction stories went to juvenile and women's magazines. She had placed two serial novels in the popular *People's Home Journal*. Now, she sought higher-circulation women's magazines that published well-known authors. Three specific goals for her fiction that season were *Woman's Home Companion, Designer,* and *Ladies' Home Journal,* in that order.

It was like directing trains in Grand Central Station to manage multiple stories and articles through multiple submissions, rejections, and re-submissions. A story might be sent to *Woman's Home Companion* and an article to *Christian Herald*. When they returned, the first was sent to *Designer* and the second to the *New York Sun*. By then, another article was finished and sent for its try at the *Christian Herald*. In this way, each manuscript kept moving to its next opportunity, and each publishing house received Emilie Loring stories or articles in succession.

Of the four stories and three articles she worked on that spring, none were accepted by any of her top three choices. Only "Kismet Takes a Hand" and "I'll Tell the World!" made it to print, in the *Chicago Tribune*, and the others were set aside. A less determined author might have quit, but a less determined author would not have succeeded as Emilie was about to do.

Before times got better, they got worse. In early April 1919, Albert Boles died, the last of Mrs. Baker's siblings in Boston. He was Emilie's closest Boles relative, more like a brother than an uncle. It was he who named his children after the Bakers—Maria Emily, now a department salesgirl; Robert Melville, a janitor; and Rachel Elizabeth, a stenographer. Albert was buried on April fifth in the Baker lot at Forest Hills, next to his mother and his first child, Melville Jerome, who was buried on the same date, thirty-two years before.[6]

When Emilie returned to her work, she followed up on neglected submissions. "The Key to Many Doors" was turned down by Griffiths' Fine Arts Film Company in 1916, so she had sent it to *The Editor* in November

1917 and asked for referral to a publisher who might take it as a small book. But there had been no answer. Upon her first inquiry this April, *The Editor* claimed no knowledge of the manuscript, so Emilie sent a quick response to clarify and waited again for a verdict. "The Best is Yet to Be" traveled in the opposite order; lengthened to 53,000 words, it went to book publishers first and then was submitted to Goldwyn Pictures in May 1918. Nearly a year later, there had been no response from Goldwyn, so Emilie mailed that inquiry, too, and waited for answers.

Her short story "NY 1300" appeared in Munsey's *Argosy and Railroad Man's Magazine* two days later, and Emilie decided to make it her third try for the silver screen. She spent a week transforming the prose into a movie synopsis and sent it out as soon as it was finished, on May 3, to the Famous Player-Laskey Corporation.

Her submissions arrived during the film industry's move from New York to Hollywood. Metro-Goldwyn-Mayer was still separate picture studios—Metro, Goldwyn, and Louis B. Mayer. Paramount was still Famous-Player-Laskey. There was no Egyptian or Chinese Theater; there were no footprints or stars in the concrete on Hollywood Boulevard. Movie people were actors, producers, and writers who had been in theater, publishing or vaudeville and then made the switch to film.

Emilie's brother, Robert Baker, made the transition easily. A movie synopsis was written like a play. Each scene had a setting, action, and dialogue, and its contribution to the film's momentum was clear. Robert was at Edison for the very beginning of film in America, and his skills had kept pace as kinetoscope was replaced by silent films, and now, the talkies.

The acquisitions editor at Goldwyn had a harder time of it. As an editor for Hearst publications, Elizabeth Jordan had discovered Zona Gale, Eleanor H. Porter, Dorothy Canfield, and Sinclair Lewis. But she did not have the same knack for judging drama, and her short tenure in moving pictures was considered her "one unsuccessful venture."[7] After a year of waiting, Emilie received a rejection letter from Miss Jordan on May eighth. She wasted no time, put her synopsis into a new envelope, and sent it out again the same day, this time to independent film producer Lewis J. Selznick.

That was the day her mother died, May 8, 1919.[8] Mrs. Baker had returned to Wellesley Hills at the start of the war, when recently widowed Rachel moved into an apartment at The Puritan in Boston. Because Robert and Minnie traveled so much for the theater and movie seasons, Mrs. Baker stayed mostly at Emilie and Victor's house.

In fact, Emilie had just written an appreciative, Josephine Story article inspired by her mother, "The Delicate Art of Being a Mother-In-Law." She observed that a mother-in-law adapts more easily to her daughter's husband than to her son's wife—another reason, perhaps, that Mrs. Baker stayed at Victor and Emilie's. In the end, it was the early training a mother gave her children that counted most. The article ended appreciatively, "If a woman has been big enough and fine enough to train daughter or son like this, she'll never be an 'in-law', she'll be just—*Mother*."

On May tenth, Mrs. Baker was buried at Forest Hills, next to her husband and near her brother Albert. Her name and dates were chiseled into the opposite side of George Melville Baker's tombstone, "Emily F. Baker, 1835–1919." Ten years later, Emilie's memory was still vivid:

Day had followed unreal day—like dull beads on a string which Time relentlessly counted off one by one—as she had sorted and disposed of her mother's intimate belongings. Letters to be read before destroying, others to be tossed unopened into the fire as though they scorched her fingers; stopping to re-live an occasion which the mere folding of a gown had conjured from a care-free past; gazing down upon a box of intricately carved gold, seeing only the shimmer of the aquamarine sea before the little shop where her mother had bought it; reading through blinding tears, "Jean's first shoe" on the sole of the bit of leather she had found in the strong box. A short dark curl was there too, a marriage certificate. The shawls had been the hardest to touch. Warm colors, all of them. Gay, embroidered, dripping with fringes, delicately fragrant with perfume. (*Swift Water*, 1929)

"I never knew what a man could be till I met the Lieutenant, Mrs. Courtlandt. I'd always thought that a rich guy was bound to be soft, but he's tested steel."
The Trail of Conflict

Neither Robert nor Selden could attend the funeral, but the day after, Robert was released from the Army to return home. Nothing had gone quite as he had expected. There was a time when he thought he would be a baseball pitcher. Instead, he joined the army. Then he imagined he might command troops abroad in the Great War. Instead, he commanded misfits and conscientious objectors in New Jersey. His commanding officer recommended him for promotion to Captain before the Armistice but then wrote, "the cessation of hostilities prevented this promotion, which he so well deserved."[9] Robert retained his entry rank, First Lieutenant, and went home with three silver service chevrons. War required many roles. He had done the duty he was assigned, and he was safely home.

In May 1919, the Boston Authors Club elected Emilie to membership in recognition of her books *For the Comfort of the Family* and *The Mother in the Home*. The "BAC" was limited to only one-hundred-fifty authors—a select group in Boston, "where every tenth person is suspected of having written a book."[10] The club was started late in 1899 by her father's colleagues and writing friends. Julia Ward Howe, who contributed articles to George Baker's *Our Boys and Girls*, was the first president, and Thomas Wentworth Higginson, who took his business to Lee & Shepard after the fire of 1872, was its second.[11] Had George Baker lived ten years more, he would have been among them.

The purpose of the Boston Authors Club was the social support of authors "in a fellowship where sympathy outgoes criticism."[12] The *New York Times* snorted at their habit of drinking tea instead of "any other cheering liquid,"[13] but the Boston club outstripped its New York counterpart by including both men and women from the beginning. Emilie's parents couldn't witness her success, but once again, she was connected to the world of books and publishing. This time, she had earned it herself. In June, Selden Loring boarded the *Espagne* in LeHavre, and nine days later, on the sixteenth of June, he arrived in New York and stepped back onto American soil. He was unchanged in appearance, with the same dimples and wavy hair, but his memory held so much that his family could only imagine. He served overseas twenty-three months and wore campaign ribbons for ten theaters of war. The Reservé Mallet's newsletter printed the camion drivers' reflections.[14] Would Selden be among "The Vanquished?"

"Welcome to this side of the Atlantic. Not a long breath have I drawn since your departure. "
"The Limousine Lady," 1918"

> Somewhere along the scarred Chemin des Dames,
> I lost my Youth.
> Something has dimmed the old ideals I sought;
> A sterner sadder Self is left instead.

Or would resilience prevail?

"They told me in the village that he wears ten bars on his Victory medal."
"Yes, for carrying ammunition to the Front of the Front in ten campaigns."
Hilltops Clear

> We disagree with David D who says he lost his youth.
> 'Tis our advice to sacrifice poetic thoughts to truth.
> Though we regret we fail to get
> Much inspiration from the war,
> Cusses like me, we seem to be
> More childish than before.

Selden had his own share of Baker blood; one might have guessed how he would respond.

These were the happy days for which Emilie had waited, and yet there was still so much to absorb: the war and its aftermath, her mother's death and Albert's, election to the Boston Authors Club, and the return of Robby and Selden. A much-needed, summer vacation stretched lazily before her: Stone House, her gardens, tea with friends, sun on the veranda, a good book in a comfy chair, and long walks in the Maine woods.

Blue Hill, Summer 1919

Victor and Emilie crossed Blue Hill Bay to join the Appalachian Club's celebration of the brand-new Lafayette National Park (now "Acadia") on Mount Desert Island. In their party was Frederick Law Olmsted, Jr., who pioneered the training of landscape architects and supervised the largest and most prestigious landscape architecture firm in the world.

Olmsted's firm had actually designed the Curtis' entryway and gardens at Starboard Acres, after which Victor had written to them about designing gardens for the Wellesley Hills house, too. Even the estimate was expensive, however, and the Lorings ultimately decided to do the work themselves.[15]

Olmsted's father was famous, but Olmsted Jr. had earned his own reputation with designs for the Columbia Exposition, Vanderbilt Estate, and the National Mall in Washington, D.C. His statement of the mission of the National Parks, written at the request of Theodore Roosevelt in 1910, remained the guiding principle for the National Park Service ever after.[16] So, when ten thousand acres of Appalachian wilderness were proclaimed the first eastern National Park, he came to advise on the design of its roads, trails, and public areas.

The party of fifty met first at the Jordan Pond House for its famous, broiled chicken dinner and popovers.[17] Then, for a full week, they "tramped" on mountain trails by day and danced or played whist by night at Seal Harbor's Seaside Inn. On the Fourth of July, they made patriotic speeches and danced to orchestra music around a huge bonfire. Another day, they took the steamer *J. T. Morse* to Bar Harbor and rode in automobiles to the home of George B. Dorr, donor of the first five thousand acres of park land and its first superintendent. From there, they hiked over Dry (now "Dorr") and Green (now "Cadillac") mountains back to Seal Harbor before crossing Blue Hill Bay to a reunion of friends along the East Blue Hill Road.

After all they had been through, summer was both comfort and respite. The Owen sisters, now without Carrie, rented out Larkspur Lodge

"I can recommend the popovers. They always pop. They never let you down. Like jam?" She said she loved it, black-currant if they had it.
There Is Always Love

for extra income and served tea on the veranda at Tyn Y Coed. Like the Lorings, the Curtises celebrated the safe return of two sons, but only after believing that one of them was dead. They might have expected the worst for Gordon Curtis who was in the Meuse-Argonne where fully half of all American battle deaths occurred in the last weeks of the war, but he came through safely. When the dreaded notification came, it was about their younger son, Robert.

The ship that Robert Curtis commanded was patrolling for submarines near the Azores when an internal explosion sank it in just thirty minutes, killing seven of his crewmen but not Robert. Badly burned, he spent a month in a Portuguese hospital, and as soon as he was able, he went to Washington to request formal discharge. There he learned, to his surprise, that he had been declared dead, and his parents and pregnant wife had already been notified. It took some doing to get through the red tape, but at last, he was declared alive and returned to his family.[18]

Emilie's wartime story, "Prue of Prosperity Farm," appeared in *Woman's Weekly* for six weeks that August and September. Set in Blue Hill, the serial incorporated familiar landmarks and her home front experiences with gardening and chicken raising. Unfortunately, the August second segment was published under the wrong name, "Emilie Loring Baker." (It was corrected for August 16th.) Around the same time, the *New York Herald Tribune* paid three dollars and fifty cents for another of her Josephine Story articles, "Is Your Home in Trouble?"

Wellesley Hills, Fall 1919

The Lorings settled into a comfortable, new pattern that fall. Granted time for war service, Selden had only two years to finish at Harvard. Each morning, he left for classes in Cambridge, and Victor went to his law office at the Old South Building. Through the Hallet sisters, Robert got a job selling wool and frequently traveled to textile manufacturers out of town. When the men were off, Emilie consulted with the cook about the day's

"When he heard over the radio that Douglas Clayton had turned up, alive and well, he insisted on coming along. Is it true?"
A Candle in Her Heart

Farming might be thrilling, but it certainly took a lot of energy and strength when one was new at it, Prudence reflected...
Hilltops Clear

She entered the
house by the rear
door, stopped to
listen . . . She didn't
want to break her
train of thought by
talking with anyone.
As Long as I Live

menus and made sure the household and accounts were shipshape. Then she had about four hours in which to write before dressing for dinner.

Persistence paid off the day after Emilie's birthday in September 1919, when "Known in Advance" was accepted at last. The title was ironic, because she clearly had not known the story's path in advance. This was the fourth iteration of "The Evening and the Morning," her "almost good" story that traveled to so many markets in 1915. The next year, Emilie shortened it from 4,850 to 4,049 words and sent it out as "Destiny and Mrs. Deland." In 1918, she shortened it by a third and submitted it to publishers all that year as "A Wartime Wooing." Finally, in 1919, she lengthened it to 3,900 words and tried more publishers.

"It isn't a dinky
magazine. It has
good backing, but
I think too much of
my ch—child—
her voice caught, "to
let it go for that."
Give Me One Summer

In later years, book jackets read, "She sold her first story on its forty-fifth submission." This wasn't her first story, and she recorded forty-three trips, not forty-five, but how many new authors had the temerity and the pure, dogged determination to persevere, to keep revising, keep submitting, keep accepting defeat and moving past it, for four years and forty-three submissions, all for ten dollars and eventual publication in the small-town newspaper *Grit*? As she opened the acceptance letter, she might well have recalled the tribute from her old dream, "She died, but she did it!"[19]

CHAPTER 20

Boston Authors Club

Boston, Fall 1919

Just before Thanksgiving 1919, the Boston Authors Club held a special meeting to honor new members from the last two years. Emilie's class of fourteen included a poet, two English professors, two novelists, and writers who focused on specific topics: children, philosophy, religion, and Emilie for homemaking. With her new member's carnation pinned to her dress, she entered the club rooms at Trinity Court.[1]

Every member was a working, published author, but beyond that, they were a varied lot. Some had careers well in hand, like Thornton W. Burgess, whose adventures of Peter Cottontail, Prickly Porky, and Jimmy Skunk were loved by children and their parents. Reminiscent of Oliver Optic, Burgess had written a new story for the *New York Herald Tribune* every day of the week since 1912, and he wrote many dozens of books besides.[2] Others were fledgling authors, and some wrote as sidelines to established careers. Everyone had an interest; every book had a story to tell.

Emilie knew this feeling. It was the same that she had as a child in the Lee & Shepard showroom. Her "Box of Books" was now a "Club of Authors," many of whom were already acquaintances. Agnes Edwards Rothery had provided the invaluable spur for her to write; her friend Mabel Loomis Todd of hot-air-balloon fame wrote a biography of Emily Dickinson and had the original idea to start a Boston authors' club; and Parris T. Farwell, the pastor of the Wellesley Hills Congregational Church organized the Sagamore Sociological Conferences she and Victor attended. Through Victor, she knew Judge Robert Grant of the Suffolk County probate court. His play, *The Little Tin Gods-on-Wheels*, satirized Bostonians of the Gilded Age: "We the young men who don't rise in the morning, wedded to style, and without occupation." Another acquaintance was George

Barr McCutcheon, whose novel *Beverly of Graustark* her brother Robert had adapted to the stage with such success.

Josephine Preston Peabody was a charter member, a renowned poet whose early publications inspired letters and sketches from an utterly smitten Kahlil Gibran. She was also Emilie's neighbor in Maine. The poet came down the East Blue Hill Road in 1914 carrying a map marked with the location of her new land and only two names—Owen and Loring.[3] Christened "Two Valleys," the Marks' land overlooked Webber Cove beyond the Millikens in East Blue Hill, and Josephine loved every bit of it.

> For it is really the most beautiful Land that anybody ever owned
> ... It has everything from cliffs to cranberries; rock pools to cedar-
> walks ... Only think of it! Blueberries everywhere, to walk on;
> bay-shrubs and wintergreen and ground-pine, and pyrola, and
> wild iris—and crowds of wild roses trying to climb on air![4]

Emilie was among kindred spirits at the Boston Authors Club, but two, in particular, struck a receptive chord. "From that time until her death, no Club meeting seemed important unless she was sitting near the front of the room with her two intimate friends, Clara Endicott Sears and Sara Ware Bassett."[5]

Sara Ware Bassett was a spark of a woman, with more energy and determination than her small frame suggested. As a girl, she dreamed of attending her first ball dressed all in pale blue. When the day arrived, she had a blue dress and blue stockings but only black slippers to wear. Undaunted, she applied a primer coat of white oil paint and then several coats of the pale blue she wanted. "They did smell of turpentine, but I had faith to believe that when thoroughly dry this odor would not be noticed."[6]

When she was fifteen, her mother and grandmother died of infections, three days apart. For the next decade, Sara Ware traveled with her father, a companionable man with a head for both business and education. Charles Bassett's Puritan ancestors brought books to America "when what

"Ever worked before?" "No." "What have you been doing?" "Traveling with my father since my mother's death."
Uncharted Seas

was needed so desperately were seeds, hoes and ploughs,"[7] so he naturally encouraged both of his daughters in their studies.

The older sister, Alice, graduated from Boston University's homeopathic medical school and completed advanced studies in Chicago and Vienna. Artistic Sara Ware earned a certificate of textile design from MIT's Lowell School of Design and received an honorable mention at the 1893 World's Columbian Exposition in Chicago. She had an offer to design silk fabrics in Manchester, New Hampshire, but moving away from home was more than her widowed father's broadmindedness could bear.

Next, she considered designing wallcoverings for a Boston firm, but he judged the work beneath her dignity and vetoed that, also. Instead, she left design behind, spent three years at the Symonds Kindergarten Training School, and then taught kindergarten at the same school in Newton that she had attended as a child. "I didn't have another plan. I determined to like kindergarten whether I did or not."[8]

Sara Ware's occupation was held to a narrow path, but her productive mind could not be. In her hours after school, she studied writing, psychology and philosophy at Radcliffe and Boston University. She wondered, could she create with words as she had done with textile fibers? In 1907, her short story "Mrs. Christy's Bridge Party" appeared in the newspapers. Two children's stories followed, both published in *St. Nicholas* magazine.[9] Yes, she answered herself, she could.

She responded to the Penn Publishing Company's advertisement for a writer of children's educational books, and her first visit with Charles Shoemaker was telling. "What do you know about lumber?" he challenged. "I know nothing about lumber," she replied, "but I will tomorrow."[10] *The Story of Lumber* was published in 1912, followed by the stories of leather, glass, sugar, silk, and porcelain.

After she joined the Boston Authors Club in 1914, Sara Ware Bassett published her first novel. *The Taming of Zenas Henry* (George Doran, 1915), took place in the fictional, Cape Cod town of "Belleport" which she described so convincingly that visitors came to the Cape seeking the town and its inhabitants. *Zenas* was her first best seller, and when her second novel, *The Wayfarers at the Angel's* (George Doran, 1917) did well, too, Penn offered to publish her third, *The Harbor Road* (1919).

For ten years, Sara Ware wrote in the evenings after work, but after her father died, she decided she was through with kindergarten. When Emilie met her at the Boston Authors Club, Sara Ware Bassett was a full-time author who was writing a series of book condensations for the *Boston Sunday Post*. Her synopses could be read in a single sitting and provided enough guidance that the curious reader might decide to read the original, while the less inclined could be satisfied with knowing enough of the story for polite conversation.

Of her original works, Little, Brown had just published *An American Poilu* for which Sara Ware had written the introduction, and she had a contract for her next novel, *The Wall Between*. This Cape Cod story involved a feud between neighbors and a girl who manages better than Sara Ware did at rebuffing familial control: "I must be the one to decide what it is right for me to do. Remember, I am not a child. I have a conscience as well as you, and I am old enough to use it." Although she and Joseph Lincoln were the two acknowledged chroniclers of Cape Cod life, she never met him or read any of his works. She didn't want to "subconsciously pick something up."[11]

Emilie's other new friend was Clara Endicott Sears, the author of three books, all histories. Clara's keen awareness of the past came naturally. She descended from colonial governors and a family tree of Boston Brahmin names—Winthrop, Peabody, Sears, Crowninshield, and Endicott. She had a fortune, an enviable figure, and constant attention in the society pages. Judge Robert Grant summered near the Searses in Nahant and wrote a poem for young Clara and her sister Mamie, calling them "The Fatal Sisters:"

> I know two maidens wonderfully fair
> Men call them Fatal Sisters and with truth
> For safe from their enchantment who shall be?[12]

Mamie was married seven years but died after the birth of her second child. A year later, the same year that Emilie's father died, Clara's father announced at the dinner table, "I cannot swallow. What does this mean?" And died. The following year, both of Clara's maternal (Peabody) grandparents died, also. Between 1890 and 1892, she lost her only sibling, her father, and the last of her grandparents.

Clara and her mother were alone—if they could be considered "alone" with an English butler, Swedish cook, four maids, and a laundress. For the next eighteen years, Clara and her mother traveled and maintained homes in the city, at the shore, and in the country. Within the bounds of her social set, she made herself useful but repressed the zeal and industry she had inherited from her ancestors. Her thirties came and went, and her forties were nearly gone when she took herself in hand and resolved upon a change. From now on, she would do something that mattered, something entirely her own.

In 1910, she purchased a small plot of land in the Nashua River Valley at Harvard, Massachusetts, west of Boston, and over the next three years, she enlarged it to more than 250 acres. For her own use, she compiled and privately printed *The Power Within*, a book of daily, inspirational quotations beginning with, "Our mental attitude today determines our success tomorrow." Then she designed "a villa with English comforts" for herself and named it the "Pergolas" for the white, marble pillars she acquired from a palace in Venice, Italy to shelter her garden. The Pergolas' view captured a distant mountain and the forested, river valley below. Its cloister was decorated with the busts of thinkers that Clara admired: Socrates, Plato, Pericles, Ralph Waldo Emerson, and Amos Bronson Alcott. She had a lovely backdrop for entertaining and an even better place to pursue the intellectual and spiritual life she craved.

The Nashua Valley echoed with the strivings of bygone days. There were the Transcendentalists who attempted to establish a utopian colony there, the Shakers who found it a refuge from persecution, and the native, Pokanoket tribe for whom the area would always be a spiritual home.

"The power within," Gail said softly and wondered where the phrase had come from. *When Hearts Are Light Again*

Clara admired their purpose and dedication and resolved to preserve their histories.

In 1914, she launched the Fruitlands Museum to preserve the record of Bronson Alcott's experiment in communal living. With assistance from his daughter, the author Louisa May Alcott, the Alcott home was preserved in its entirety, right down to the library books and bedside appointments. The two women wrote *Bronson Alcott's Fruitlands*, which Houghton Mifflin published in 1915, and Clara's invitation to the Boston Authors Club came the following year. The book opened with a quote from Longfellow, the same that Emilie liked so well: "All homes wherein people have lived are haunted houses." Clara spoke frequently of the vibrations she felt in old places, as though there remained a trace of their former inhabitants' mental and spiritual strivings. She developed a sympathetic relationship with the few remaining members of the Shaker sect nearby, and in 1917, she published *Gleanings from Old Shaker Journals*, reflections on Shaker life. The following year, she preserved a story from Shaker oral tradition in *The Bell Ringer*.[13]

Gradually, Clara shaped her professional mission, aware of another quote from *The Power Within*, "As one develops individuality, he is very sure to be misunderstood by his domestic circle." (Newcomb) She was handsome, rich, and cultured, but she left fashionable, summer homes at Nahant and Groton to create her haven of solitude in the quiet country. She had generations of famous forbears with historical accomplishments, but she chose to write about the otherwise forgotten who had largely failed to reach their goals. The key to Clara was not external acclaim but rather, the power within.

Can we not always tell when a person has found his spiritual centre? There is a tranquility, a repose, a breeziness about him. You feel that the air he breathes is more invigorating than the atmosphere in which most people live. There is a certain unlimited air about him,—an air of the open plains or mountain tops, an exhilaration which lifts you up and out of all your difficulties, and makes you know that you yourself are superior to and master of all conditions that heretofore seemed to master you. (Katharine H. Newcomb, quoted in *The Power Within*)[14]

Sara Ware Bassett and Clara Endicott Sears joined the Boston Authors Club in 1914 and 1916, respectively, and were already friends when Emilie met them. Each could trace her ancestors back to the Plymouth colony, but by Boston standards, Clara's status was superior. Sara Ware's immigrant ancestor William Bassett came to Plymouth, but Clara's fifth-great-grandfather was John Winthrop, the first Governor of Massachusetts. Sara Ware traveled to Europe with her father on several occasions; Clara was educated there from the age of seven. Sara Ware lived in a house on Beacon Hill; Clara lived in the five-story, Sears mansion on Beacon Street.

In community service, they met on more equal terms. Clara served on the boards of many charitable societies to which she also donated, while the Bassetts had an intimate connection with Fernside, the summer vacation home for working girls in Princeton, Massachusetts. Sara Ware lived with her sister, Dr. Alice H. Bassett, and Alice's partner, Geraldine Cummings. Geraldine served on Fernside's executive committee, and Alice, who practiced homeopathic medicine on Commonwealth Avenue, was its physician. Each summer, the Bassets and Miss Cummings lodged across the road from the boarding house, less than fifteen minutes from Clara at the Pergolas in Harvard.[15]

Clara and Sara Ware were also kindred spirits when it came to cultural preservation. Clara was passionate about preserving the history and stories of the Nashua Valley, and Sara Ware devoted her pen to portraying a Cape Cod life she feared might fade away forever.

With the addition of Emilie, the women were a trio of contrasts. Clara Endicott Sears was from old family and old money. From birth, her responsibility had been to dress fashionably, honor her lineage through social connections and charitable works, and maintain a "furnished mind" equal to her status. She made a striking picture, slim and implacably regal in a tailored suit, two strands of pearls, and a modish hat.

Sara Ware paid little mind to convention and even less to fashion. One observer said she looked like an English woman detective in a tweed skirt, man's shirt and sturdy walking shoes.[16] As a career woman, Sara Ware chose her own way of doing things, and she had the freedom to begin writing earlier than the others, at thirty-four.

Emilie was up-to-the-minute in both fashion and outlook, and she lived differently from the other two. Clara went home in the evening to her mother in the Sears mansion; Sara Ware returned to the career women in her row house on Cedar Street, and Emilie lived with her husband and sons on two acres in the suburbs, complete with an orchard, stable, and gardens.

Nevertheless, the three had much in common. All preferred forthright conversation and independent action. None was likely to have silly friends, but enthusiastic and straightforward ones they attracted by the score.

During the war, Clara's Nahant estate was a key observation point for the detection of enemy submarines. From her rural home in Harvard, she devised a food drying enterprise that was responsible for significant shipments of provisions overseas. Emilie served at canteen and joined the first American Legion Women's Auxiliary in Wellesley, and Sara Ware wrote the foreword to the published letters of Elmer Stetson Harden, an American soldier in France. "The war . . . has left us face to face with the true metal of a myriad of souls before whose naked purity and selflessness we bow in homage."[17]

All three had enjoyed responsive relationships with the men in their families. Emilie spent many days by her father's side at Lee & Shepard, participating in conversations and voicing her opinions. For years, Sara Ware traveled with her father, whom she described as a sympathetic companion. And although Clara's father was unfailingly courteous, it was her maternal grandfather, George Peabody, who spoke to her heart. One day, as the sun was setting, he told her, "Remember, little Clara, you will never see a sky like that again. Every sky is different. The Almighty creates every-thing new."[18]

Observation was important to writing, but so was imagination and the ability to realize it. Emilie and Sara Ware had each tried art before writing and had developed their skills to a degree that allowed exhibition—Emilie in jewelry and metalworking, Sara Ware in painting and textiles. Vivid color in any hue was an elixir to Emilie, and Sara Ware's love of blue was unremitting. She wore blue clothing, filled her garden with larkspur and other blue flowers, and had a uniform set of her books made with all-blue bindings. When the women turned to writing, descriptive passages indulged their love of color and composition. But it was more than that. The exhilarating confidence to create spilled into their writing as buoyant optimism, good-natured humor and resolute determination:

> When your imagination suggests a proposition, consider well if it be worth doing; then, if you decide in the affirmative, bring to its achievement all the conquering energy of your will. Force the project to completion. (Emilie Loring, December 1919)[19]

Clara was more serious than the other two, but behind her proper and regal bearing, she, too, had an artistic enthusiasm: the theater. As a girl, she watched in fascination from the windows of the Vendome Hotel as theater people came and went, the very opposite of Boston reserve. She kept a scrapbook in which she pasted newspaper articles about plays and players, along with photos and theater programs.[20] What an attraction, then, when Clara met Sara Ware, whose father had owned the Park Theater, and then Emilie, who had known the people of her scrapbook as family friends—Henry Clay Barnabee, Robert F. McClannin, Mrs. J. R. Vincent, William LeMoyne, Annie Clarke, George Frothingham, and so many more.

Soon after the BAC party, Emilie and Sara Ware encouraged each other to send a manuscript to Hollywood for a chance at stardom. Robert Baker's detective story, *Counterfeit*, had recently premiered as a silent film

Great bergs of green ice, surmounted by flocks of lavender and white gulls, floated oceanward. Quite near were snow-crowned mountains whose sides, striped in vivid and dull green, reminded him of the slashed sleeve of a troubadour. *Lighted Windows*

in Los Angeles, and Sara Ware Bassett's good friend Eleanor H. Porter got her story "Pollyanna" onto the silver screen through United Artists with Mary Pickford in the starring role. Sara Ware sent "The Harbor Road" to Universal Pictures, and Emilie did the same with "The Best is Yet to Be." Sara Ware's story was accepted and went into production as "Danger Ahead!" but Emilie's was rejected, and she finally acquiesced. Her much-traveled manuscript went to *The People's Home Journal* "to place," and she made no more attempts at film.[21]

Emilie now lived in three places: Wellesley Hills, Blue Hill, and Boston. Wellesley Hills was home, with all that meant—her house and gardens, neighbors, the Woman's Club, and the longtime headquarters for her family. Blue Hill beckoned with a fresh sense of freedom and fun, every year a carefree adventure with friends who had become dear. And now Boston, which held so many memories, and her new association with authors striving as she was. She wrote mainly in Wellesley Hills for the next few years, but increasingly, she returned to Boston for club meetings and author events.

CHAPTER 21

Identity: 1920–28

Boston, 1920

Introductions in Boston invariably included a reference to lineage. Emilie's husband was a Loring? Was he of the Lorings at Beverly? And her family was Baker? Were those the Bakers of Dorchester or of Philadelphia? It wasn't enough to know one's parents; it was necessary to know one's clan and immigrant ancestors.

Cleveland Amory wrote of the proper Bostonian, "So close is his identification with his ancestors that in answer to the simple question, 'How long have you been in Boston?' such a man is likely to reply, 'I've been here since 1730, or 1700—and he really thinks he has."[1] Amory further observed that, in a town that labeled the trees in its public garden with their proper family names, the people who lived there could hardly do otherwise.[2]

Clara Endicott Sears' name declared two prominent branches of her lineage, and everyone knew she was also a Winthrop. To descend from John Winthrop, the first Governor of Massachusetts, was as close to royal family as one got in Boston.

Clara was a longtime friend of Katharine P. Loring who had recently contributed to *Loring Genealogy* by Charles Henry Pope (1917). Miss Katharine P. Loring was, indeed, of the Lorings at Beverly, a sister to the attorneys Augustus Peabody and William Caleb Loring who bought Bartlett's Island in Blue Hill Bay. The Loring genealogy noted the adoption of Victor's grandfather by William Loring and politely dismissed, "He has many worthy descendants." Worthy, perhaps, but not sufficiently pedigreed to be listed in the 424-page book of bona fide Lorings.[3] A Plymouth descendant's lineage unfolded across three hundred years with the American Revolution at its midpoint. On that scale, Victor's

Great blooded Shorthorns turned ruminative eyes upon her; she had seen women with that same expression when at a society function another entered as to whose social status they were in doubt.
The Trail of Conflict

three-generation, paternal pedigree was current history, and where it began was uncertain.

Emilie grew up in the world of stage names and noms de plume in which one was identified by works more than family history: "This is Henry Clay Barnabee, lead player in the Boston Museum Company." "Meet Oliver Optic, author of the Yacht Club series." Her grandfather and father were remembered not as scions of the Baker clan, but because one founded the *Boston Herald*, and the other was the best-selling amateur dramatist of all time.

Yet, Emilie's and Victor's parents and grandparents were all gone, as were most of their parents' generation of the Baker, Boles, and Loring families. It was time to learn more before the trail turned cold. Emilie attacked the project so thoroughly that, by the time the census taker appeared at the door in January 1920, a household member reported her occupation as "historian, at home."[4]

Victor Loring belonged to the Bostonian Society, and his brother Charles Francis gained acceptance to the Sons of the American Revolution in its charter year, so they had already researched much of the Loring genealogy. All of Victor's maternal ancestors were in the colonies by 1644. The Hitchcocks settled in Springfield and Connecticut and included first-family progenitor Henry Wolcott. Wolcott appeared on the first list of freemen in Boston in 1630 and founded the colony of Connecticut in 1635. The Winchester members of Victor's ancestry were in the colonies by 1635 and settled right where Victor lived when Emilie met him—in Brookline, Massachusetts (only it was called "Muddy River" then).[5]

Victor's family was especially proud of its Hitchcock line. Victor's third-great-grandfather Luke Hitchcock fought in King Phillips' war, and the next generation's cousin, the Reverend Enos Hitchcock, appeared in the painting *General Burgoyne's Surrender at Saratoga*, which hung in the Capitol Rotunda in Washington, D.C. Closer to home, Victor's maternal grandfather Winchester Hitchcock marched from Springfield at nineteen to serve in the Revolution. Although Victor was a Loring, he installed a stained-glass window reminiscent of the Hitchcock crest—gold fleur-de-lis on an azure background—in his study at Wellesley Hills.

Emilie's family tree was as deeply rooted. Her fifth-great-grandfather Richard Baker arrived in Dorchester from Kent, England in 1635. The "Dorchester Bakers" remained largely in place until after the Revolution when John Baker went to Portland (which was still Massachusetts then). His son, Emilie's great-grandfather John Baker III, married Sarah Hodgkins, daughter of Captain Thomas Hodgkins who was quartermaster at the Battle of Bunker Hill and fought at Butts' Hill in Rhode Island. Thomas' third-great-grandfather William "Hoskins" arrived in Plymouth in 1632 and married Governor John Winthrop's first cousin Anne Winthrop.[6] Ten generations deep, Clara and Emilie were related.

Emilie's Baker grandmother Mary Ann Shaw Remick descended from one of the earliest settlers in Kittery, Maine. A distant cousin, the water-colorist Christian Remick, illustrated the Revolutionary period in Boston, and Emilie's grandfather John Remick served as Captain in the War of 1812. But John Remick and his four siblings carried the name of Remick only because their unmarried mother, Deborah Remick, kept the secret of their paternity. In consequence, Emilie's grandmother claimed greater connection with her mother's Shaw ancestry.

Nathaniel Shaw descended from five generations of Shaws in Hampton, New Hampshire, beginning with Roger who lived in Cambridge, Massachusetts in 1638 and moved to Hampton in 1648. This branch also included the Hilliards and Philbricks, longtime Maine families who all arrived by the 1630s. When British troops burned Falmouth on October 18, 1775, Nathaniel Shaw's harness shop in Portland was the first building to be set afire.[7] Nathaniel enlisted and served three years in the 15th Massachusetts Regiment which fought at Saratoga, Valley Forge, and Monmouth.[8]

Emilie's mother was a Boles and a Hazelton. Recent history's highest point on the Boles side was the marriage of first cousin Angeline Moore Peck to Governor John Quincy Adams Brackett, and its lowest point was likely the drunken death of Emilie's grandfather near the railroad tracks in Danby, Vermont. Earlier history included Emilie's second-great-grandfather, patriot Reuben Boles, who served as a minuteman under Captain Elisha Whitney, and his wife Lucy Brown, a direct descendant of "old goodman Brown" who came to Ipswich in 1642. The Hazelton branch had lately been carpenters and farmers in Maine, but before them were five generations in Haverhill, including John Hazelton who arrived in Salem from England in 1637 and was one of the first settlers of both Bradford and Haverhill, Massachusetts.

Which was more important: family wealth or ancestral pedigree? Emilie took up the question in her next serial story, "The Trail of Conflict." Stephen Courtlandt and Geraldine Glamorgan marry to satisfy a business deal between their fathers—Stephen to clear his father's debts to Glamorgan and "Jerry" to add the Courtlandt name and distinction to the Glamorgans' working-class family tree. Wounded pride threatens to ruin any chance they have of friendship until an uncle's death sends them to Wyoming under a new set of ground rules. Jerry must give up her money and live with Stephen on the ranch for an entire year in order for Stephen to inherit. Their new state of affairs sets romance in motion, and adventure follows.

When asked where her ideas came from, Emilie answered, "From everywhere!" and the truth of that was evident in this story. Her sister's play, *Rebellious Jane*, required the protagonist to live on a California ranch for six months in order to inherit it from her uncle. The Glamorgan names and background came from the Owen sisters in Blue Hill, whose father came from Glamorgan, Wales to Pennsylvania and married an heiress with a long pedigree.

Emilie subscribed to a Wyoming newspaper to glean location details of the story's setting: in the southern part of the state, near the Devil's Gap, Sweetwater River, and the Union Pacific Railroad. Into her descriptions of the train trip westward poured details she had observed on her journey to Alaska; she provided particulars of an Alexandrite ring at Tiffany's in New

"...but right then and there I learned the difference between mere money and money with family behind it."
The Trail of Conflict

York where cousin Albert Remick was a salesman; and her characterization of Stephen Courtlandt as the "Whistling Lieutenant" came from her son Robert.

As Emilie wrote, word came that her last Boles uncle, Frank, had died in Phoenix. Except for her brother and sister, the entire household of her childhood had passed away, three in the last twenty-two months. Death had been a constant intrusion, and it pervaded her writing, too. Long hours in a train and on horseback allowed her characters Stephen and Jerry to puzzle at its mystery.

"They said that Phil went out like a candle, Mother. Where did he go? Where are you? It can't be the end. If it were, I shouldn't feel as though you were with me wherever I am."

Elderly Doc Rand tells Jerry,

"I find it profoundly interesting to wonder and imagine what follows this world. For instance, look at the question in this way. At this moment I can send my mind to the Manor; in spirit I'm pacing the terrace with Sir Peter. I can see the boats chugging up and down the river, can smell the queer fragrance which the sun is baking out of the box hedge in the garden, can hear the birds twittering among the vines. If I can do all that now, what will it be when the spirit is not hampered by the body? It will be like flying, won't it?"

A cattle rustling, pretend elopement, and train hold-up lead Stephen and Jerry into each other's arms, and the plot is resolved. What matters most is neither wealth nor heritage but character—in Stephen, who remains a courteous gentleman regardless of provocation; Jerry, who keeps her word; Tommy Benson, who has the classics at his tongue; and a range runner's wife who behaves with quiet dignity and kindness despite her

Jerry liked her dignity. She showed no consciousness of the difference between her three-room shack and the luxurious ranch-house from which the visitor had come. "Thoroughbred," thought the girl as she preceded her hostess into a small but immaculately clean room.
The Trail of Conflict

"I don't care who Peggy marries if he is clean and upstanding, with self-respect and love for my girl."
The Trail of Conflict

The war had side-tracked his plan, but as soon as he received his discharge, he had gone into a mill to learn wool.
"With Intent to Sell"

"Remember also, when you go out with intent to sell, you may take your opinions along, but you're to can your prejudices. We don't want salesmen who make enemies; we want salesmen who make good."
"With Intent to Sell"

humble surroundings. Furthermore, whatever the tangle, "Things have a marvelous, unbelievable way of coming right." This was the lesson of her childhood, and it became the subtext of all her writing.

Spring 1921

As usual, Emilie kept multiple stories in motion. In March 1921, she earned two hundred dollars for "You Never Know," which was changed to "Behind the Cloud" for *Woman's Weekly*. James Montgomery Flagg, who created the iconic "Uncle Sam Wants You" poster, illustrated her short story "A Box from Nixon's" that appeared in *Woman's Home Companion*.

"With Intent to Sell," published in *Leslie's Weekly*, took her son Robert to task. The main character, like Robert, is a wool salesman known for his whistling, but that is the end of his character strengths. Instead of developing relationships with his clients, he mocks and antagonizes them and stands to lose both his business and his girl, if he doesn't change his ways. But, with the help of a checkered coat and a glowering bovine, he does change his ways, and the story ends happily.

Several special events occurred that summer. In June, Selden graduated from Harvard with his art degree and began work as a commercial artist. Selden had drawn since he was a child. In high school, he illustrated his school's yearbook. In France, he sketched pictures of life in the Army and American Field Service and designed an Indian head that he painted on the doors of each of the unit's transport vehicles. When he returned to college, he was art editor of *Harvard Magazine*[9] and illustrated many stories and articles with his own work. Now, with a bachelor's degree tucked under his arm, he began work as a commercial artist for the advertisers Fitzpatrick & Murphy of Boston.

Also in June, more than one hundred Boston Authors filled "touring motorcars" and rode to Clara Endicott Sears' estate in Harvard, Massachusetts for the final club tea of the season. The Pergolas' impeccable gardens and long view across the Nashua Valley provided the backdrop for conversations over tea, sandwiches, and cakes. Approaching on the calendar was Sara Ware Bassett's full-length film *Danger Ahead!*, which was set to open in July at the Park Theater. Otherwise, the club members headed off to their summer cottages and would not meet again until fall.[10]

Wellesley Hills, 1921-1922

The next events aligned fortuitously for Emilie's writing career. *Munsey's Magazine* accepted *The Trail of Conflict* for serial publication while its longtime editor Bob Davis was out on his own as an independent, literary editor. Davis had a seemingly unlimited capacity for reviewing literary submissions. At one time, he read for all of the Munsey publications, including *Munsey's Magazine*, *All-Story Magazine*, *Scrap Book*, *Railroad Man's Magazine*, *Woman*, *The Ocean*, *The Live Wire*, and *The Cavalier*.

Weary editors complained that there were only a limited number of plots, to which Davis responded, "Rot! There are only eight notes in music, but whoever said there are only eight tunes?" The working out was what separated the excellent from the ordinary in authors, and he had identified enough literary stars to prove his point. His successes included short story master O. Henry, mystery writer Mary Roberts Rinehart, and Montague Glass, who wrote the fabulously popular "Potash and Perlmutter" stories for the *New York Evening Post*.[11]

The Trail of Conflict began in the first issue of *Munsey's Magazine* after Davis' return, December 1921, and ran through April 1922. Davis passed the story along to Carl Milligan, who took over Davis' Literary Bureau as the "Service for Authors, Inc." Milligan showed the story to Charles Shoemaker of the Penn Publishing Company of Philadelphia, and on February 7, 1922, Emilie signed and Victor witnessed her first contract for a full-length, hard-cover novel.[12]

The book's publication was scheduled for fall 1922, and she would receive ten free copies. Her advance was two-hundred-fifty dollars against ten percent of the first five thousand copies, twelve and a half percent of the next five thousand, and fifteen percent thereafter. At a cover price of one dollar and seventy-five cents, she would earn seventeen to twenty-six cents per book, and Penn needed to sell just under 1500 books to cover her advance.

Penn claimed exclusive, foreign and domestic rights for the story in book form. After one year, a "popular edition" could be arranged with a guaranteed royalty of no less than five cents per copy, so fast sales gave a distinct advantage. The original contract called for the same five-cent royalty for foreign editions, but Victor negotiated for one-half of the royalties instead.

Looking to the future, the contract gave Penn the first option to publish the novel she had submitted to Milligan a week before, *The Princess and the Pilgrim*, as well as each of her next two novels, not yet started. If accepted, *The Princess and the Pilgrim* would have the same terms and come out by the fall of 1923, but terms of the later novels would be negotiated later. Emilie, Victor, and Charles Shoemaker signed the contract, and the deal was made. After ten years of writing, she had an agent and a publisher, and her first hard-cover story was on its way. At fifty-five, Emilie Loring was a novelist.

The Boston Authors Club's invited speaker in January was Helen Sard Hughes, an English professor at Bryn Mawr. Professor Hughes had gray hair, gray eyes, and a grim attitude. She found fault with children reading *Treasure Island*, *Cinderella*, and *Robin Hood* instead of Thackeray, Eliot, and Poe. She criticized romance for "the unreasoning intoxication that comes with too ardent idealism." In her talk at the BAC, she complained that "the virgins of earlier centuries preferred the literature of delight to the literature of education not less than the flappers of today, flourishing side by side with the advocates of intellectual culture."[13]

The three friends bristled. How short-sighted, to assume that literature must be grim to have merit. These were the same complaints leveled at Lee & Shepard's authors after the Civil War, and these twentieth-century authors had the same answer. From the worst times to the best times in history, people could use an uplifting story, and if it came with a dose of humor, so much the better. Sara Ware argued,

> I am well aware that the humorous, optimistic novel is looked down upon by the more sophisticated, although just why tragedy, immorality, frustration and futility should be regarded as of greater merit I have never understood. Nothing is easier to write than tragedy. Driven into a corner the author has only to kill whoever blocks his way and presto, the way is clear![14]

What did it matter, if critics panned their work? The book-buying public saw things differently. In cheerful defiance, the three friends dubbed themselves "Flapper's Row" and got on with their writing.

Sara Ware Bassett and Clara Endicott Sears both had romance novels published that year, and how their conceptions of romance differed! The heroine of Sara Ware Bassett's *Granite and Clay*[15] is in love with the idea of romance but can't shed herself of the feeling that she is only playing a part. What she wants more than to find a man is to find herself, and that means becoming an author. Clearly autobiographical, Sara Ware's protagonist, Penelope, lives in a home nearly identical to her own on Beacon Hill, with a fan-shaped glass in the door, mahogany furniture inside, and the Misses Endicott and Sears who arrive for tea. Sara Ware described the trials of writing in a talk to the Boston Authors Club the previous December, and she dramatized them in the book:

> "She's there mornin', noon an' night. I went up yesterday to see if I could make out what was keepin' her, an' there she sat on a little stool, writin' away on the top of Uncle 'Lisha's old sea chest. When I asked her couldn't she find any better place than that to write she just told me to go away, please, an' not bother her. She had a ream of paper, I guess, all scrawled over an' scratched up."

"Optimist, aren't you?"
"I hate that word, because so many of the people who use it put a sting in it. Be honest, have you ever known gloom or depression to solve a problem? Problems aren't solved that way."
Give Me One Summer

"I'll leave the miseries, ironies, vain hopes, and frustrated dreams to more experienced writers. I want to write the kind of story—it will be just as much a part of the real world—that will cause persons who see 'Melissa Barclay' on a cover to plump down their problems—and incidentally the price—and seize the book."
Give Me One Summer

When Penelope falls in love with her publisher, he declares his love in the words she most needed to hear:

"I shall not be selfish with you, sweetheart," hurried on the man, his sentences coming swiftly. "I do not mean to wall you up in my home, make a slave of you, and cut you off from the career that lies ahead of you. You shall live your own life—"

Penelope trembles as she leans her face against his chest, then softly pledges her affection:

With a gesture exquisite with tenderness she raised her head and placed both her hands in his: "My real life is with you," she said softly. "I do not want any other."

Sara Ware had never had a lover. Her sister had a "Boston marriage" with Gertrude, and her father's marriage to a young woman the same age as Sara Ware seemed less a romance of equals than a replacement for his career-minded daughters. Sara Ware's desire to put herself into the story was explained, "And now I've come to a new act, and something has got to happen; and as long as I'm the heroine, it's got to happen to me, don't you see?"

The closest Clara came to a real-life love affair was several years of unrequited pining after a married, older man. When she healed from that heartache, she committed her mind and heart to a higher plane.[16] The heroine of Clara's *Romance of Fiddler's Green* acknowledges, "Maybe I'm too serious-minded—folks have told me so; but I was born that way and it can't be helped. I'd want to be quiet and understand my happiness— that's the way I'd feel." Myrtle's heart is won when John plants a garden and pledges to sit there under the apple tree with her.

"The time has come to enter the garden same as we planned," he said, looking at her with love glowing in his eyes; "we'll go in hand in hand, Myrtle, and sit on the seat under the apple tree same as we said we would." Quite solemnly she put her hand in his and they went in together . . .[17]

Emilie's childhood was filled with romance, from comedic and melo-dramatic versions on stage, to countless versions in print, to her parents' real-life love affair that made her father feel like "an ice-cream factory in full operation on one side, and a hot air furnace on the other." She and Victor had been companionably married for thirty years, and their sons were now of courting age themselves. Her ideas of romance were decidedly more advanced.

From the beginning of *The Trail of Conflict*, there is sexual tension between Stephen and Jerry.

> She caught a glint of challenge in Stephen's eyes and rose. Her color was high, her breath a bit uneven as she smiled at him with bewildering charm.

They spend more time together, and his attraction to her builds,

> He took an involuntary step forward, then thrust his hands into his pockets. Lord, how impellingly beautiful she was!

Mid-novel, he loses control.

> Even his lips were white as he caught her by the shoulders. "I don't know what Greyson has been told, but he'll get it straight from me that you are mine—mine—" With sudden savage ruthlessness he caught her in his arms and kissed her shining hair, her throat,

"Never marry, Di, until the touch of a man's shoulder against your cheek catches at your breath, the look in his eyes sets you afire to feel his lips on yours, turns you weak with desire to be in his arms."
Where Beauty Dwells

her eyes. He let her go. "Now perhaps you understand it, too," he announced huskily.

She begins to realize that she has fallen in love with her husband:

She caught her breath as a vision of his face as he had held her in his arms crowded itself into her mind. She raced up the court steps to elude her clamorous thoughts.

The scales fall from their eyes, and the next observation comes in a letter written by Jerry's sister:

"They were the nearest to cold-storage newly-weds that I had ever seen. Now—ye gods!—when I look up and see Steve's eyes on Jerry my heart *stampedes*. I feel as though I had made the unpardonable break of opening a closed door without knocking. Jerry behaves a little better. She keeps her eyes to heel but her *voice*—"

Three women, three books, three visions of romance. Willie, the inventor bachelor in Sara Ware Bassett's *Flood Tide* (1921) had it right when he said, "Women may be all alike, take 'em in the main, but they're almighty different when you get 'em to the fine point, an' that's what raises the devil with makin' any general rule for managin' 'em."

Emilie studied prose techniques as she transitioned to full-length novels. Dialogue and drama came naturally, but what about plot? A novel's length required more characters and greater complexity. Willard E. Hawkins wrote short stories for the *Chicago Ledger* at the same time as Emilie and then edited his own writer's magazines, *The Student-Writer* and *The Author & Journalist*. He wrote, "The most successful recipe for a plot that I know of is: a problem and its solution."[18] He described the construction of plots as webs of connections between elements in a story.

"Know the best definition of a plot? The problem and its solution."
Fair Tomorrow

A is the main character, B another. The story follows A, but the plot is created when the lines of B, C, and D are woven across the main narrative, creating suspense and dramatic interest. When successful, the reader was captivated, like the publisher in Sara Ware Bassett's *Granite and Clay*:

> But the first line had caught his attention, the second had held it and by the time he had reached the third, he was as powerless to lay aside the story as a child is to part from Goldilocks and the Three Bears.

The first draft of Emilie's next novel, *The Princess and the Pilgrim*, did not meet this standard. She recorded on its card, "Had such adverse criticism (except from Milligan) called it in & sent to Hawkins for criticism, Mar. 22, 1922."

The story took place in the familiar environs of Boston, and this time, she had a mission. Guns were stilled in France, but the war continued for victims of gas and shell shock. As a member of the American Legion Women's Auxiliary in Wellesley Hills, Emilie recruited community members to take shell-shocked veterans on two-hour drives in the country to relieve their mental burdens. "Do you care?" she asked in the Wellesley *Townsman* newspaper.

> For two years, men suffering from shell-shock and gas have come and gone at the West Roxbury Hospital situated within twenty minutes run by automobile from Wellesley . . . There is an insidious suggestion creeping over the country, it even steals through the keyholes and under the doors of the hospital, that people "Don't Care." You do? Then say it with automobiles.[19]

It was difficult to write an engaging and entertaining tale that also tackled the personal costs of war—mental illness, physical disability, broken relationships, and lackluster job opportunities. The story's happy ending

"In our English course at college we made diagrams of plots. Mr. A starts for B at the other end of a straight line. Half way he meets C. That contact sidetracks him to D . . . Let's make a plot diagram for today, Terry. We will call the advertiser who is coming, A, and his friend, B. C is their objective, the house to which they return from here. Perhaps I'll get a story germ."
Fair Tomorrow

left thoughts uncomfortably churning. Do you care? Then do something to make a difference.

Willard Hawkins returned *The Princess and the Pilgrim*, and Emilie noted, "Returned Apr 20, 1922; favorable criticism but with suggestions which set me to rewriting." She sat down the same day and began revisions, but nearly three months passed before she had the revised manuscript ready for her agent.

Robert Baker's son, Mel, graduated from Harvard in June 1922. True to family tradition, Mel had been president of the school's magazine, *The Harvard Crimson*, and belonged to the Hasty Pudding (theater) and Signet (Arts) clubs. Still in the family footsteps, he took a job as a play reader for Daniel Frohman in New York. This was the same Frohman whose Famous Players Film Co. had produced Robert Baker's movie, *The Conspiracy*, before the war. Of the Baker descendants—Robert, Selden, and Mel—he seemed most likely to carry the writing business into the next generation.

Wellesley Hills, 1922–1923

The Trail of Conflict was copyrighted on October second and "at all bookstores" within the week. Newspaper ads called the novel "a stirring love affair of the west," "thrilling and dramatic." *The Harvard Crimson* said that she "told the story originally and with effect . . . avoiding the conventionalities of most novels of the west." The public version was a green, hardcover book, but Charles Shoemaker gave her a commemorative, leather-bound copy, inscribed: "To the Author from the publisher with the hope that this first copy may be followed by another hundred thousand. C.C. Shoemaker, 30 August 1922."[20]

Emilie presented a copy to the Boston Authors Club for its library. Inside the cover, she attached a photograph of herself feeding her chickens, alongside a drawing by Selden of a French cathedral and cannon. She inscribed it: "Introducing the author and her war-time best-sellers. Cordially Yours, Emilie Loring."[21]

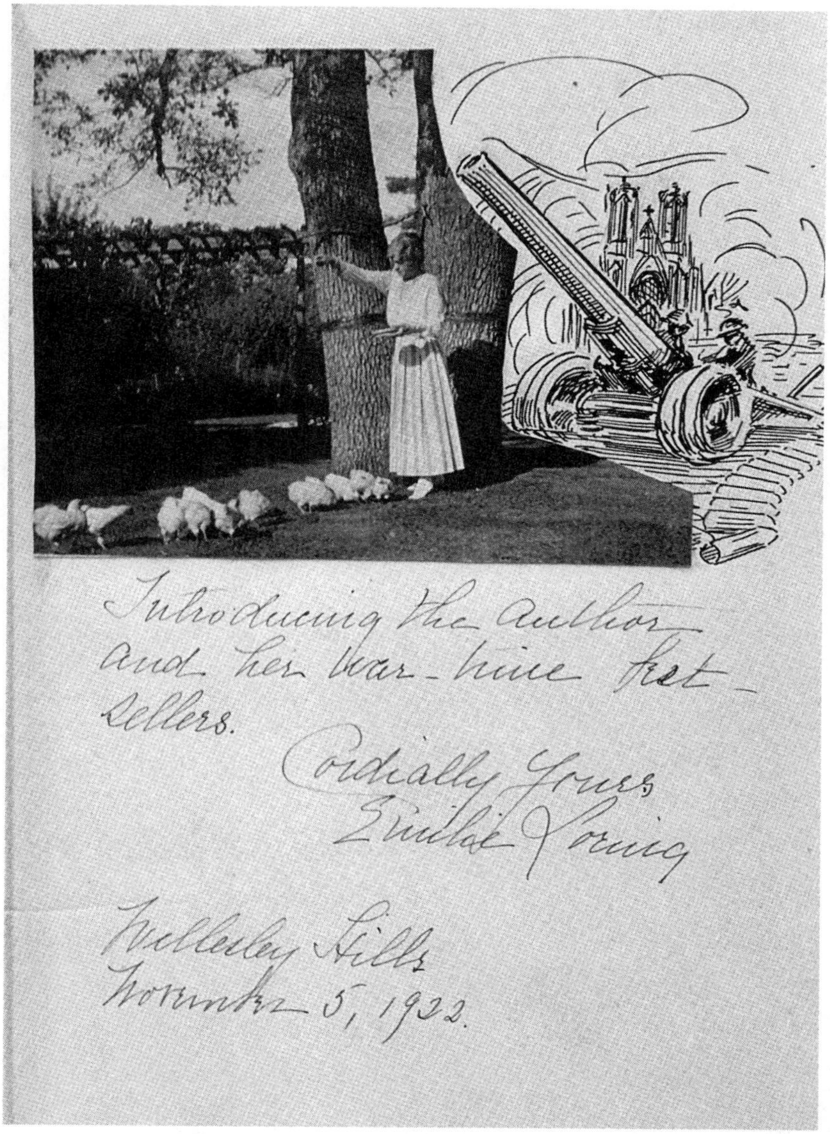

Introducing the Author and Her War-Time Best-Sellers

An old friend from Emilie's Cape Cod days presented a copy of *The Trail of Conflict* to the Sturgis Library at Barnstable. It had been thirty years since the Bakers had lived in Barnstable, but the local paper praised, "Mrs. Loring will be remembered for her charm and beauty which still win for her many friends. The story in itself is . . . a human, searching study of character development under change of environment seasoned with action and told in a forceful, stirring style. When this is coupled with a pleasant acquaintance with the author its interest cannot be measured."[22]

Milligan declined his option for *The Princess and the Pilgrim*, and no other publishers seemed interested, so she started a new story on October thirtieth. *The Dragon Slayer* featured a mill owner in a Maine village who sticks firmly to the high road in his campaign for senator against a mud-slinging opponent.

The details she required were fresh in her memory. Only weeks ago, she had waded, swum, and picnicked at Blue Hill. From the family's favorite spot on the rocks at Sculpin Point, she could see the outer bay and Mount Desert to the east, the inner bay and Blue Hill Mountain to the west. Emilie used Blue Hill village for the fictional "Clearwater," Effie Kline's Ideal Lodge (today's Barncastle Hotel) for her character's home "Shorehaven," the reversing falls and inner and outer bays as themselves, and rum-running for a touch of crime. Blue Hill was her vacation place, and this story had the same feeling—relaxed, happy, and above all, entertaining.

That wasn't to everyone's taste. The Great War had unleashed horrors on a scale that left nerves bare and challenged former boundaries of literary expression. Sunshiny stories were criticized as unrealistic, but extreme realism was disheartening and risked censorship. Authors lined up on both sides. This was the year of *Siddhartha* (Hermann Hesse), *The Wasteland* (T. S. Eliot), and *Babbitt* (Sinclair Lewis). It was also the year of *The Velveteen Rabbit* (Margery Williams), *Etiquette* (Emily Post), and *The Enchanted April* (Elizabeth von Arnim).

For Emilie, it was less a matter of avoiding the negative and more that she was committed to the positive. Life brought hard times to every generation, and the Bakers had a time-tested response. It took courage to look straight at what the world had just been through and tell that story. It took even more to look squarely at the destruction and then set a steady course

. . . the curve of the inner bay which was partially separated from the outer by a disjointed peninsula of rocks and sand and glittering tide pools. Here Comes the Sun!

past disillusionment, beyond apathy, toward the better ideals and better times of which man was capable.

Her new story began with "The New Day" by Richard Watson Gilder:

More bright the East became, the ocean turned
Dark and more dark against the brightening sky—
Sharper against the sky the long sea line.
The hollows of the breakers on the shore
Were green like leaves whereon no sun doth shine,
Though sunlight make the outer branches hoar.
From rose to red the level heaven burned;
Then sudden, as if a sword fell from on high,
A blade of gold flashed on the ocean's rim.

James Trafford's *Mayflower* ancestor landed in the new world with only a shilling and the portrait of a Duchess. "A regal creature with sapphires in her fair hair, sapphires at her ears, a great sapphire on her finger, sapphires fastening her blue and gold bodice and a King Charles spaniel under one arm . . . And that was when the first part of the prophecy came true." The portrait, Blue Hill's abandoned copper mines, and a near-accident at the Reversing Falls propel the characters through a bitter political campaign and several, romantic miscues before they bring the mystery, election, and romance to successful resolutions.

James Trafford and Julie Lorraine begin as equal partners with a pragmatic disregard for convention. When they seek shelter in an abandoned cabin, Julie lights the fire while Jim forages for food. Her dress is wet, so she dons a bathrobe without embarrassment, and he reassures, "Life is bigger than conventions, Goldilocks." Jim is chivalrous, Julie spirited, and it takes acts of integrity on both of their parts to bring their problems to successful resolutions.

"I've seen men plunge into glittering dissipation, I've been caught in what seemed like blind-alleys of temptation but something has strengthened my power of resistance. Perhaps it was the hand of some God-fearing, ideal-worshiping Trafford on my shoulder."
Here Comes the Sun!

BLUEHILL FALLS

Reversing Falls: "Before it reached the bay the water churned into white falls and tumbled under a low bridge across which the road lazed." Here Comes the Sun!

Emilie completed *The Dragon Slayer* in May 1923. *The Trail of Conflict* was in its third printing, but the rejection of *The Princess and the Pilgrim* remained sharp in memory. She sent the new story to *Munsey's*, as she had done with *The Trail of Conflict*, but it came back a week later. She sought the advice of the literary agency Brandt & Kirkpatrick, which represented Joseph Conrad and Edna St. Vincent Millay.

Emilie started one story and polished another over the summer, but her focus was elsewhere, as the family enclave at the end of Longfellow Road finally broke up for good. Mrs. Baker's home had already been sold, and now Robert sold his house, too. Robert's work for stage and screen kept him in New York and Los Angeles, and with Mel Baker's first play, *The Swan*, scheduled to open that fall in New York, the Bakers moved to Manhattan.

Charles Shoemaker responded in August that he was interested in *The Dragon Slayer*, but the revisions he suggested took Emilie two months to complete. In early November, she received a check for two-hundred-fifty dollars in advance of U.S. publication. A British firm, T. Fisher Unwin

Ltd., agreed to publish the book as *The Dragon Slayer* in London,[23] but Shoemaker thought the title was too grim and suggested *Here Comes the Sun!* for American readers. The world still clamored for good news, and *Here Comes the Sun!* promised a happy ending.

Emilie expanded on her belief in happy endings for Penn's 1924 promotional flyer, "Novels of Romance and Adventure."

I am neither a super-optimist nor a Pollyanna, but behind the thickest cloud, behind the darkest situation, somehow, I sense the sun ready to break through. Why not? It has always.[24]

Optimism couldn't heal Emilie's sister, Rachel. She was ill with a muscle-wasting disease that forced her steady decline. Initially, it was hard to control her hands to write, and then walking became difficult. Emilie and Victor stayed a long season in Wellesley, then moved to the Fritz-Carlton Hotel[25] to be near Rachel at the Puritan Hotel on Commonwealth. But Rachel contracted pneumonia on November seventh and died just two days later.[26] Rachel, the cheery dynamo, suffragist, and humorist; infused with her father's spirit, trained by him in elocution and dramatics; the amateur dramatist who sold more than a quarter-million copies of a single play; Rachel the big sister, Robby and Selden's beloved aunt, was gone.

Her funeral was held three days later in the Second Church, where Emilie and Victor were married. The Reverend E. A. Horton, who had officiated at both of the sisters' weddings, and the Reverend Thomas Van Ness from the Second Unitarian Society in Brookline officiated. Rachel was buried next to her husband, John, and his first wife, Mary, in Haverhill.[27]

Emilie and Robert handled Rachel's considerable estate, which was valued at nearly ninety thousand dollars. Each of her nephews—Robert, Selden, and Mel—received five hundred dollars, and Rachel left jewelry to each of the women in the family. Emilie received Rachel's pearl necklace and two diamond and sapphire rings, plus half of Rachel's remaining furniture, personal property, stocks, and bonds.

A passion of fury swept Diane. Merry was so exquisite, so—so sweet—so helpless. Why—why had it had to happen to her—to Merry, of all people, Merry who was naturally as gay as her name, who had always been so unselfish, so thoughtful of everyone? She wished that her father and mother had not died . . . Perhaps it was better that way. Their hearts would be shredded to ribbons to see their adored daughter as she was now.
Where Beauty Dwells

She looked at the lovely, gleaming thing which dripped from her pink palm. Her sister's pearls!
Hilltops Clear

Spring 1924

Emilie and her brother had always been close, but now they were the last of their family, and Emilie visited New York more often. On New Year's Day, Robert's son, Mel, announced his engagement to Gladys Franklin Gould, a stockbroker's daughter who worked on the editorial staff of *McCall's Magazine*. The two were married on February fifteenth at St. Matthews and St. Timothy's Episcopal Church in Manhattan.[28]

In the meantime, Emilie finished "Glycerine Tears," a story with truth behind it. For two years, Clara Endicott Sears had remained locked in a court dispute with her erstwhile farm foreman, Cornelius Lucey. Clara dismissed the man for negligent care of her cattle, but he refused to leave, saying that his contract guaranteed a year's employment, and he could not be fired without compensation. According to Lucey, Clara then sent a gang of men who broke down his door and removed furniture, paintings, and even food from his home on the Pergolas estate. Clara's countersuits said that Lucey had allowed her cattle to get "the itch," and that he and his wife had damaged her property, likely under the influence of liquor, as evidenced by liquor bottles found in the house. Lucey claimed she had scattered the liquor bottles about to incriminate him. Both parties asked for five thousand dollars in damages.[29]

Clara was "one of the wealthiest and most beautiful society women of Boston," and Lucey's charges and the sordid details that emerged in testimony threatened her spotless reputation. Then she lost. The jury awarded Lucey eighteen hundred dollars for back pay and property damage but gave nothing to Miss Sears. The public rebuke stung even more when the Luceys shook hands with jury members afterward.

The story "Glycerine Tears" was relevant anywhere, but a Bostonian could not fail to make the connection between the details of the story and Clara Endicott Sears' current troubles. "The injustice of it! Hadn't witnesses proved that Brown had neglected the cattle? Hadn't one sworn that he had poured pail after pail of milk into the brook to the accompaniment of uproarious drunken laughter?"

Emilie finished the story at the end of January, but this time, she didn't submit it herself. She acquired a New York agent, J. Jefferson Jones, who was, like Robert Baker, a member of the New York Players Club. Before establishing himself as an independent, literary agent, Jones had worked for George H. Doran (who published Emilie's first book, *For the Comfort of the Family: A Vacation Experiment*) and managed the London publishing house of John Lane & Co.[30] She gave "Glycerine Tears" to Jones, and he submitted it twice before placing it with *Delineator* in May. She wrote "The Game" in February, sent it to Jones in March, and saw it published by *Munsey's* as "Goal" in November. Jones charged a ten percent commission on the four hundred paid by *Delineator* and the eighty paid by *Munsey's*.[31]

Here Comes the Sun! was released on the ninth of February 1924 and sold out only ten days later. The *New York Herald-Sun* praised, "This opens like the popping of a bunch of firecrackers and sparkles along through the whole plot. An excellently entertaining story."[32] Emilie had hit the sweet spot with her lively mix of adventure, optimism, and romance. She was right to follow her sunshiny nature and Bob Davis' advice: "The public, not the editors, decide whether or not the author shall survive."[33] In this case, the public earned her a royalty check of over five hundred dollars for American sales, and its British version, *The Dragon Slayer*, earned her additional royalties in England.

Emilie described her path to authorship in a March article for *The Editor*, "Avoiding Rhetorical Bypaths in the Novel." She described her childhood in the worlds of publishing and drama and then said, "Aside from my inheritance I have taught myself what I know of writing. It has not been easy." She credited *The Editor* for early guidance and reflected that she used to read it for instruction, and now, she was writing an article for other authors to read. It seemed to her "the very button on the cap of Fortune." "Today as I write this letter in response to the request of the

"Come in to dinner and I'll let each of you feel this $500 check."
The Yellow Hat

editor of *The Editor*, I, like the old woman in Mother Goose, am wondering if I be really I."[34]

She also credited Clayton Hamilton's *A Manual of the Art of Fiction* which she "read and re-read and read again." "The truest characters of fiction," Hamilton wrote, "are so real that even their creator has no power to make them do what they will not." Set them amidst well-chosen elements, arranged logically, and a gripping tale was the result.[35]

"Write what you know" was old advice but good to remember. Emilie's first novel, *The Trail of Conflict*, began in a drawing room, the details of which Emilie knew well, and then left for a ranch in Wyoming where the setting was acquired second-hand. The vividness of her characters won her an appreciative audience, but she improved with her second book. *Here Comes the Sun!* incorporated details from Blue Hill that Emilie knew intimately. Combined with the "true" characters she created so well, the result was, as Hamilton described it, a reading both "absorbing and voluptuous"—but not too voluptuous.

> My besetting temptation when at work upon a story is to hike along rhetorical bypaths. As a reminder that every sentence should move a story on, I have thumb-tacked above my typewriter that admonition of Stevenson's:
>
> "From all its chapters, from all its sentences, the well-written novel echoes and re-echoes its one creative and controlling thought: to this must every incident and character contribute; the style must have been pitched in unison with this; and if there is anywhere a word that looks another way, the book would be stronger, clearer, and (I had almost said) fuller without it.[36]

All of Flapper's Row had new books that spring. Clara Endicott Sears' *Days of Delusion* was called "immeasurably her best work so far" and "an authoritative work of real historic importance." Clara collected reminiscences of the period in 1843–44 when William Miller predicted that the world would end. The Transcendentalist preacher Theodore Parker deadpanned, "It does not concern me, for I live in Boston," but many others were persuaded. "Hundreds, and in some places thousands, of people fell under the spell of it . . . watching for the heavens to open and for the appearance of the Saviour in clouds of glory."[37] Clara attributed the period to a "compelling agitation" that takes hold of the world from time to time and leads some to great thought and others to preposterous notions.

Sara Ware Bassett's latest was *Carl and the Cotton Gin*. Carl's mother tells him, "That is what progress is. We learn continually to cast aside outgrown notions and adopt wiser and better ones . . . Men are going to say: *'Think of those poor, stupid old things back in nineteen hundred and twenty-three who believed so-and-so! How could they have done it?'*"

Emilie had written no new material since Rachel's death, except her article in *The Editor* in which she acknowledged, "I am a home-maker before I am an author and often my literary self has been submerged by a domestic wave. Each time I have fairly forced my head above water, gasping to be sure, but determined to cling to my avocation which has enriched my life immeasurably."[38] In the time left before summer, she kept herself afloat by dusting off several manuscripts she had on hand and giving them to J. Jefferson Jones to place.

"The Yellow Hat" was last submitted in November 1922. The heartening story brought Emilie back to herself, reminded her of the lift she got from a new piece of fashion, her realization that she wanted to write, and her pride in having money she had earned herself. Yellow hats were in vogue that season. Their cheery, hopeful color was just the inspiration to set one back on the path to achievement. She sent "The Yellow Hat" to *Our Young People* at the end of June and received a twelve-dollar payment three weeks later. Before she went to Blue Hill, Emilie shipped off two more articles she had on hand, "Why Talk About It?" and "A Clean Slate." She had clearly taken her own advice:

"A short time ago you started dolling yourself up like a fashion ad—now you appear to be a talented young authoress."
The Yellow Hat

Suppose when you waken in the morning instead of wrinkling your brow and worrying over lurking perplexities you vigorously slam the door of your mind against them and turn your thoughts towards the good things coming your way. Count them, count every possibility of good and when you have exhausted the possibilities begin on the probabilities you have culled from them. That setting-up exercise of the imagination is magical in its effect. Your troubled mind will become more serene, your outlook more happy, that Any-thing-is-possible elixir will steal through your veins until you are filled with a sense of strength with which to level and dispatch your mountains of problems. ("A Clean Slate," 1924)

Blue Hill, Summer 1924

When Emilie returned to Maine in the summer, she was ready to write again. The jagged coast that harbored pirates in earlier times now hid Prohibition-busting rum runners. Fleets of boats laden with liquor stayed safely outside the twenty-one-mile "rum line" and sent their cargo ashore via small boats to rocky inlets too numerous to patrol. Liquor was hidden in lobster traps and sardine crates, then delivered on the sly. Pillars of the community railed against the dangers of alcohol in public but kept private stashes in their homes.[39] Emilie sharpened her pencils and began: "From directly overhead the late July sun blazed down upon a bold stretch of New England coast . . ."

A Certain Crossroad was the story of heiress Judith Halliday who runs away from an impulsive marriage to Doctor Neil Peyton only to run into him again in a small, Maine village. Against a backdrop of liquor smuggled in blueberry cans, Judith tries to make amends. Before, she had thought only of her own happiness, and she had lost both the man she loved and her self-respect. "Now she craved time to think, to recollect herself—she had seen that phrase somewhere lately and liked it. Recollect oneself. It meant so much."

Emilie and Victor looked out over the sapphire water of Blue Hill Bay. Emilie was writing again, encouraged by her best companion and friend. She was happy. She posed for a photograph on the parapet of their veranda, hands clasped, smiling the smile that follows a laugh, eyes alight with pleasure. Across the years, it remained her favorite. She made it into an ink stamp and a postage-sized stamp. She used it in newspaper advertisements and on her book jackets. None of her formal portraits smiled; this was more like her.

Emilie on the Stone House Parapet, August 1924

Blue Hill staged an amateur drama in August. The driving force came from Seth Milliken. A member of both the Eastern and New York Yacht Clubs, Milliken lived and breathed yachting. He traded his 103-foot yacht *Thistle* for the 117-foot schooner *Shawna*, which he sailed in regattas from Maine to Bermuda. In the spirit of a true enthusiast, he would not rest until he had drawn friends and family into the activity.

In 1920, when the eldest of his five children, Alida and Seth, were twelve and eleven, he gave each of them a stable, starter-boat called a "Brutal Beast." Brutal Beasts were a brand-new style of sailboat, designed by Starling Burgess only a year before as training boats for the Eastern Yacht Club.[40]

Ten more Blue Hill families ordered boats for their children, enough for a little "yacht club." The children met and sailed from the Millikens' boathouse in East Blue Hill. The yacht club adopted a "burgee" (club flag) of blue, green, and white. Mrs. Milliken suggested the name, "Kollegewidgwok Yacht Club." Kollegewidgwok was Abenaki for "where the mountain meets the sea," connected to Blue Hill in R. G. F. Candage's 1901 poem, "Kolligwigwauk." The name had the virtue of being unique, if not easily spelled.

All summer long, the "KYC" boats sailed from the Millikens' granite wharf in the outer bay, past the Slaven, Brooks, and Curtis cottages, around Sculpin Point to enter the inner bay, and then along the Loring shore to the Lorings' granite wharf. But this summer, Seth Milliken devised a special plan to keep his children occupied. The idea, of course, included a boat.

He decided to put on Gilbert & Sullivan's *H.M.S. Pinafore*, the jaunty musical which Blue Hill's Effie Ober Kline had cast in Boston nearly fifty years before, with Henry Clay Barnabee in the lead.[41] Seth had just come into an inheritance, and the production was done as a man with four million new dollars might conceive of it. Staging called for rigging and brasses to suggest the quarterdeck of a boat, but Milliken went those one better with the real thing, his schooner *Shawna*. He persuaded the directors of Blue Hill's Kneisel Hall, which brought some of the best chamber music instructors and students to the village every summer, to place its musicians and their valuable instruments on a raft anchored alongside to provide accompaniment. The Milliken dinghy delivered actors to the "stage," and lights from friends' automobiles lit the scene. The Milliken, Boardman, Patterson, and Sullivan families provided cast members, and for staging advice, Robert Baker and Emilie Loring had put on enough plays between them to have done it in their sleep.[42]

Rehearsals led to a dry run and the premier performance in August. Summer people from both sides of the bay gathered on the lawn and faced the water in anticipation. Car lights flicked on, and the music began. So did the wind and rain. Choppy waves rose ever higher, making the transfer of actors from dinghy to deck a perilous prospect. But that was the fun of it. The excitement of amateur drama was the unexpected, and this was Maine, after all. Writing and drama: Emilie was in her element. An "anything-is-possible" elixir surged through her veins.

Wellesley Hills, Fall 1924

Emilie in the Wellesley Hills Garden, 1924

Emilie with the Grapes from Her Garden

Emilie invited the Boston Authors Club to open its fall season with a tea party at the Lorings' house in Wellesley Hills.[43] It was her opportunity to exercise an old dream. "I had dreamt of giving a tea with a girl playing a flute under an apple tree." The men of her household teased, "A girl! A flute! Funny!" But she persevered. If a pianist and strings could play from a raft, surely a flute player could play in her orchard. Emilie seated the flute player beneath an apple tree with her flute held inside her coat to protect it from the fall air. The guests arrived, the flute player played, and "even my scoffing men folks were impressed!" Her fellow Boston Authors Club member Nixon Waterman penned a tribute:

> In Emilie Loring's orchard,
> How fine it is and good
> To meet with mind magicians—
> The penfolks' brotherhood.
> Here in this restful haven
> Where Emilie Loring, she
> Picks plots for clever stories
> Like apples from the tree.
> In Emilie Loring's orchard,
> We all can fancy why
> She is, to Victor Loring
> The apple of his eye.
> But we should like to ask her,
> Here in this happy shade,
> Which are the real hard apples,
> Of which hard cider's made?[44]

Nixon Waterman was one of the Boston Authors Club's five directors, along with Clara Endicott Sears, Sara Ware Bassett, novelist Abbie Farwell Brown, and theologian Abraham Rihbany. So far, Emilie had served on the Prose Committee and twice on the Club-Room Committee, for which she was now chair. Club-room duty was essentially hostessing, her forte, and many were the meetings in the club's rooms at 8 Newbury Street to which Emilie, Clara, and Sara Ware brought cakes and pies.

Emilie and Victor stayed at the Fritz-Carlton in Boston again that winter while she completed *A Certain Crossroad*. She also gave more on-hand stories to her agent to place.

"Dan Kicks a Goal" was the story of an estranged, married couple that rediscovers love at the annual Harvard vs. Yale football game. The victory of the Crimson over the Bulldogs was a little present for Harvard fans, who had lost the most recent contest.[45]

Thrift was the theme of "Result: Happiness," a moral tale in which a mother lives on half of her income to teach her children fiscal and fil- ial responsibility. Selden illustrated the story, and the female character was perhaps the most interesting thing about that publication. The sleek portrait bore a striking resemblance to the girl Selden was dating, Mary Valentine. Robby had dated her first and then introduced them. A cynic might have said that he brought them together in spite, as the physician's daughter from Lexington could be a little "difficult," but Selden's illustra- tion showed only her smooth, sleek, good looks.

Emilie wrote "Gold Chains" that fall for *Harper's Magazine*'s 1924–25 Short Story Contest. Fellow BAC member and Athenaeum writer Alice Brown won the $1250 first prize in the first of four rounds in the contest.[46] The prize money was quite an inducement; the most Emilie had earned yet from a short story was four hundred dollars. She completed "Gold Chains" on December twentieth, in time for the last round. Over ten thousand stories were submitted in the four rounds,[47] and hers was not a winner.[48]

She sent the story to her agent, J. Jefferson Jones, but he returned it with his apologies. Like Bob Davis, Jones had decided the job of an agent was less satisfying than that of an editor. J. P. Lippincott publishers made him their vice president and editor, and he remained there for the rest of his career.[49]

Boston, Spring 1925

The new year began with a "brilliant gathering" at the Vendome to honor the twenty-fifth anniversary of the Boston Authors Club. Emilie Loring, Clara Endicott Sears, and Sara Ware Bassett were all in attendance. *The Christian Science Monitor* reported, "Every man and woman invited to this evening's dinner has contributed to the literary history of this country."[50]

Shortly thereafter, Clara sent a photograph of herself with a large collie, and Emilie wrote to her from the Hotel Carlton,

My dear Girl! Do you call that lovely thing a snap-shot? I am overwhelmed. The photograph has everything; spirit, truth, atmosphere . . . As for the dog—bless him! He has set my convictions to rocking madly on their foundations. My sons have been clamoring for a dog. I have protested: "Never again!" I love them

Clara Endicott Sears and her dog.

too hard. "When you have homes of your own, etc. etc." But I *don't* know—what a touch to add to an author's photograph![51]

Living in a hotel for a season left their empty home vulnerable, and thieves broke in while the Lorings were away. They took cash, including a stack of Confederate money that Victor had saved, but no furnishings or jewelry. The local paper scoffed that a professional would have looked, instead, for items that could be sold.[52]

If only the thieves had known, a final account of Rachel's will had just been made in the Norfolk County Court. Emilie and Robert received identical halves of everything, which meant a payment of over thirty-thousand dollars each. Rachel's pearl necklace and the two sapphire and diamond necklaces that Emilie received were valued together at four thousand dollars (over sixty-five thousand today).[53]

Emilie signed a contract for *A Certain Crossroad* on January thirteenth and dedicated the book to her husband with the same quotation from Sir Walter Scott that she used for her main character, Neil Peyton: "But always the Knight kept the Lady's hand close in his and always he stepped forward firmly, shining eyes straight ahead, for even in the gloom all was sharp-cut and clear to his vision."

A Certain Crossroad went on sale in March, and Emilie's friend Mrs. Francis Young donated a copy, as usual, to the Sturgis Library in Barnstable. The advertising copy read "Mystery—Love—Thrills—Adventure," and the heroine's description could have been Emilie's: a girl who "knows how to handle a boat, a man, and herself." The last week of April, *A Certain Crossroad* was a "best-seller of the week."[54]

"It is a pity that the word, 'lady-like,' has acquired a belittling, even derisory connotation," wrote *The Saturday Review*. "It would exactly describe such novels as this, if it could be used with no derogatory sense. This is ladylike romance and a very good specimen of its kind: a pleasing tale, conceived and told entirely from a woman's point of view . . ."[55]

Judith Halliday, was "the gallant girl type, headstrong, intelligent, a bit inclined to be selfish, but capable of outgrowing that: a really engaging young woman displayed with much skill in character drawing." The hero was "noble, but not too noble," and the villain would "at least retain a semblance of good manners." The plot was compared to mystery writer Mary Roberts Rinehart's, "cleverly tangled up until the disclosure is quite due and then the puzzle is neatly unraveled."[56]

At the season-ending Boston Authors Club meeting in May, Emilie Loring was elected one of the club's five directors, along with Clara Endicott Sears, Arthur Stanwood Pier, John Clair Minot, and Abraham Rihbany. As they prepared for the summer break, the BAC newsletter cautioned, "this will be the time in our year when new thoughts will come dancing into us, and out, unless we catch one of them now and then and tie it to our clumsy coach wheel."[57]

Summer 1925

Emilie and Victor "gained a daughter" on July sixteenth when Selden married Mary Valentine in a private ceremony in her parents' garden. Mary wore her mother's dress and carried a small bouquet of lilies of the valley. There were no attendants, and the reception was held at the Valentine home, also.[58]

Mary's father was a respected Lexington physician, but her mother was a Sherburne, the daughter of a millionaire whose imposing Lexington home was on the historic register, and Mary identified with the Sherburne social status. She graduated from the Dana Hall School for Girls in Wellesley and belonged to Lexington's venerable Old Belfry Club whose membership roll had a long waiting list. In the short of it, Mary was snooty and kept to those in her own social standing. But she was lovely and well-educated, and if she lacked empathy or humor, quiet, good-natured Selden had enough for both of them.

Their wedding in the Valentine garden underscored "a certain crossroad" for the whole family. Since the deaths of Mrs. Baker and Rachel and the Bakers' move to New York, it was as though a magnet under the Boston Common drew the Lorings back to the Hub.

South of the Common, on Boylston, was Selden's advertising office. To the east was Victor's law office at Old South on Washington Street, the Congregational Church offices on Beacon, and Robby's wool office at 233 Summer Street. Emilie belonged to the Women's City Club which met at 40 Beacon, the Women's Republican Club at 46 Beacon, and the Boston Authors Club which met on Newbury, west of the Common and Public Garden.

It was not easy to leave her home of thirty-two years, where her sons grew from infants to men, the last place where the Bakers and Lorings were all together. Evenings spent discussing the day's events, reading and critiquing each other's works, Robby and Selden putting on plays of their own, Mrs. Baker rocking and smiling, the regular rhythms of their family enclave in the country . . . All were gone.

But Boston. The Protean spring of creativity that had inspired generations of Emilie's family. This was where her grandfather started anew and founded the *Boston Herald*. It was where her father had forged one career in publishing and another in amateur drama. Boston was the creative hub of her childhood, the revitalizing center of her adulthood.

This was the place to write. It was not easy to leave Wellesley Hills behind, but Boston's call was stronger.

Beacon Hill, Fall 1925

Chestnut Street used to be called "Horsechestnut Street" for the livery stables that still occupied its western end, across from the Charles River Embankment. The Union Boat Club, to which Victor belonged, kept headquarters there, and the renovated swimming hole at the end of the street was the first public swimming pool in the country, where John Quincy Adams had taken lessons. East of the shops on Charles Street,

Chestnut was strictly residential. The street was said, in fact, to represent "more of the old Boston flavor than the other streets of 'The Hill.'"[59]

In recent times, Beacon Hill had swelled with working class immigrants who overflowed from Boston's North End, but old-timers remembered when it was the most esteemed neighborhood in the city, home to literary salons and influential, Boston families. As jobs opened up in the Back Bay and outer suburbs, the workers followed, and Beacon Hill's cachet returned, aided by the writings of Allen Chamberlain.

From 1923 to 1925, Chamberlain wrote articles for the *Transcript* that he published as a book in 1925.[60] He detailed the pedigrees of Beacon Hills homes and reminded Bostonians of their historical desirability. These were homes backed by centuries of tradition, brick streets still lit by gaslight, stables still operating, private gardens still inviting below original, violet-paned windows.

Twenty-five Chestnut was built in 1809, a brick and stone six-story with a Federal-style portico and entrance. An uphill walk led to Joy Street, the State House, and downtown Boston. The other direction went to West Cedar, Charles Street, and the Charles River. A quick cut-through at Spruce or Walnut led straight to the Boston Common.

In the late 1800s, Twenty-five Chestnut was the address of "Miss Hersey's School for Girls." Arts and Crafts jeweler Elsa Schroeder lived there at the turn of the century, and then a series of temporary tenants followed until, by 1925, it was essentially a boarding house for tradespeople. The property's revival came when Arts and Crafts architect J. Lovell Little purchased it from Miss Hersey and added kitchenettes to outfit five apartments.[61]

Victor, Emilie, and Robby moved into one apartment. Another went to Guy Murchie, formerly one of Teddy Roosevelt's Rough Riders, now a lawyer and summer resident of Bar Harbor whose wife sold antiques in the Back Bay. The next apartment went to Mrs. Woolsey Hopkins, a physician's widow who served on the Boston State Hospital's Board of Trustees.

And another served as the Boston quarters for Seth F. Low, a resident of Salem. His family's jewelry company, Daniel Low & Co., started the tradition of souvenir spoons and also popularized "Parisian Ivory," a faux ivory used in ladies' vanity sets. There was a connection there, because Emilie's cousin Albert Remick had been a jeweler at Low's before he went to work for Tiffany's in New York.

On writing days, Sara Ware Bassett arrived at the Boston Athenaeum first, at nine o'clock, from her home on West Cedar. Then came Clara Endicott Sears from Beacon Street and Alice Brown from Pinckney. Emilie joined them from Chestnut Street, and the authors retreated to separate alcoves on the Athenaeum's fifth floor. Each alcove had a writing table and its own window. Emilie's looked over the Granary Burying Ground.

The Boston Athenaeum was an exclusive, members-only library, so self-possessed that it bore only its address on the door, "10½," and no sign. The Athenaeum's historian Walter Whitehill explained this as "the general Boston assumption that anyone with serious business knows where things are; those who do not should inform themselves by other means than gaping at signs."[62]

Emilie owned no shares in the library, but she gained admittance on Mrs. Charles Pelham Greenough's ticket. Mrs. Greenough's husband had died a year before, but the Greenoughs had known Victor and had lived for a time in Arthur Dakin's home (Victor Loring's best man) on Marlborough Street.

Each day, Emilie sat down with her emerging draft, fresh paper, and two-dozen, sharpened pencils to begin. There was no small talk, nor talk of any kind, until two o'clock. The fifth floor's inviolable rule was complete silence. An indrawn breath, the scratch of pencil across paper, were easily heard across the room and felt like infractions.

They wrote for four hours before they put away their materials and assembled on the third floor. Over five-cent tea and crackers, they discussed the day's progress.

It was all so familiar—the company of writers, the rhythms of creation and revision and collaboration. Emilie missed the good-humored, incisive critique between Rachel, Robert, and herself, but she had a new group of writing friends now.

Sara Ware Bassett worked that fall on her latest tale of fictional Belleport, which produced an endless supply of taciturn, curmudgeonly, lovable characters. Her current creation was Asaph Holmes, a shy man with no thought for matrimony, who "could do as he pleased without running the risk of being nagged, prodded or reformed."

Clara Endicott Sears disciplined herself to write, although her mother had recently been diagnosed with cancer, and Clara had a growth on her own back which she "kept in check" with iodine. After two years of treatment, Clara weighed only one-hundred-ten pounds,[63] but she kept writing. Transparently, her next story was about a girl in her own village of Harvard, whose prospects for marriage are limited, because she must care for an ailing mother.

Alice Brown had written longer than any of them. A past-president of the Boston Authors Club, her home at 11 Pinckney was considered "the center of literary activities not only for the Club but for the city."[64] Like Sara Ware, Alice had taught school first and hated it. She wrote successful, "local-color" New England books in the 1880s and '90s and was said to have "genius and the craftsman's skilled combined."[65] But standards had changed from the last generation to this. *The Saturday Review* called her most recent book, *The Mysteries of Ann*, "good, light reading,"[66] and *The Outlook* said it was "preposterous to literal-minded readers but excellent fun all the same."

After the upheaval of moving, Emilie suddenly had plenty of time to write and a supportive atmosphere in which to do it. Her next novel, *The Solitary Horseman*, took place in a town like Victor's hometown of Marlborough, filled with apple orchards. The "solitary horseman" was Tony Hamilton, who worked ten years for the Grahame family to atone for an early wrong. Rose Grahame is like a sister to him, and although he allows her to do bookkeeping at the family orchard, he has reservations when she decides to run for public office. "I am afraid that public life will fascinate you. That you won't want to marry."

In later years, Emilie Loring called *The Solitary Horseman* one of her favorites, "because it is a mother and sons story. I have two sons." Tony is "A in everything" and stands for the best. Like Emilie's son Selden, he becomes engaged to a girl that his brother used to date, and his mother vents her concern, "But always I have thought of Tony as smashing crashing into love. This affair isn't even lukewarm."

Tony Hamilton's brother, Mark, like Robby Loring, is still single and playing the field. "Doubtless the two brothers started with the same mental and physical equipment but looking at Mark is like looking at a blurred duplicate of Anthony." This was the second time she had taken a shot at Robby in a story; how did he take it?

Rose's political campaign runs headlong into prejudices against newly enfranchised women and their roles in the community. She argues,

> "Most of us women have to consider the dollar. We are trained to that much more than are men. There is criticism of the few women who are filling political offices in the country. Is there any reason why the woman whom we propose couldn't make good? Let's elect her and see that she does make good."

The sexual tension between Rose and Tony is like George Baker's description of "an ice-cream factory in full operation on one side, and a hot air furnace on the other:"[67]

> Flame under snow. Lightning slashing a cool sky. Volcanic warning within a green hill.

> What would happen if he kissed her smotheringly, possessively till—the thought set his heart to pounding deafeningly.

"The men may like the woman—as a woman. They may admire her. But— they won't want her in office."
The Solitary Horseman

Writing in Boston went so well that Emilie was able to work on both the new novel and a series of short stories that season. She started "Winds of the World" shortly after her birthday in September, finished it in a week, and sent it to Hawkins for criticism. He suggested revisions. She finished "Cecily Ann Floats" in October and sent it for criticism, too, with the same result. This was the hard sledding of authorship; she knew it well. She launched into rewriting.

In early November, she sent a revised manuscript of "Winds of the World" to *Good Housekeeping*, *Scribner*, and *Women's Home Journal* with no success. The new "Cecily Ann Floats" went to *Delineator* and *Women's Home Journal*. No success there, either. She revised again and sent the twice-improved "Cecily Ann Floats" to *American Magazine* and *Fawcett*. Still no. "Free Food," which she finished a year before, had its own series of submissions. It, too, remained "on hand."

The Boston Authors Club moved to more convenient headquarters that fall, from its old rooms on Arlington Street to 3 Joy Street on Beacon Hill. Emilie had only to walk up Chestnut Street and turn right, onto Joy Street, and she was there.

Meetings were on the upper floor, above the Twentieth Century Club. West windows framed a view of the Back Bay, and the east looked toward the State House and Boston Athenaeum. Members "hung the crane" in the new club room and gave themselves a housewarming party.

Weekly club meetings were on Fridays, and Emilie attended executive committee meetings on Wednesdays. Most meetings were social, but starting that year, an invited speaker gave a "shop talk" at the first meeting of every month.

That was the Lorings' first Christmas on Beacon Hill, a celebration rich with tradition. On Christmas Eve, the residents of Louisburg Square pulled their curtains aside to reveal the old-fashioned interiors behind them. Hundreds of carolers and bell ringers went door to door and stopped at open houses for hot drinks and sweet treats. Fresh greens hung on gaslights, candles glowed in violet-paned windows, and open doors at the Twentieth Century and Boston Authors Clubs offered free, hot coffee and doughnuts.

Robert Baker's play, *The Conspiracy*, came to Boston for the first time that season, and Mel Baker had two plays on stage, *Carnival* and *The Swan*. Mel's translations of the French originals were classic Baker, their timing and humor scaled for American taste. *The Swan* proved so popular that it was made into a silent film with Frances Howard as Princess Alexandra and Adolphe Menjou as the prince. Decades later, it would be adapted to sound film with Grace Kelly and Alec Guinness.

Spring 1926

Emilie read her short story "Gold Chains" on stage that February in a rare, "performed magazine" for the Wellesley Hills Woman's Club.[68] Authors read their works aloud, and members posed in carefully designed sets as "advertisements." Hers was billed as "A tale of rebellion against slavery by a woman who knew what she wanted."

A new member of the Boston Authors Club joined the Athenaeum group in February. John P. Marquand was a journalist the age of Emilie's sons who had served in the AEF during World War I. He was elected to the Club for his well-received biography *Lord Timothy Dexter of Newburyport, Massachusetts* and his novel *The Black Cargo*, both published in 1925. A native of Newburyport, where Alice Brown also summered, he worked as an advertising copy editor before he married the daughter of a magazine publisher. From then, he wrote full-time, including nearly twenty short stories for *The Saturday Evening Post*.

Emilie admired Marquand's knack for making characters memorable. That wasn't hard to do with Lord Timothy Dexter; the eighteenth-century businessman called his wife a ghost—although she lived—and caned her for not crying enough at his fake funeral. When Dexter wrote his autobiography, *A Pickle for the Knowing Ones*, he used no punctuation but provided a separate page with punctuation marks on it and instructions to distribute them throughout the text. Marquand's treatment of the eccentric was called "a rollicking chronicle,"[69] "a tapestry . . . with one leaping, exotic figure."[70]

Also new to the Boston Authors Club was Dorothea Lawrance Mann. Dorothea's father was elected to the BAC for his biography of singing abolitionists, the Hutchinson Family, and also served as the club's corresponding secretary. Dorothea earned her place with a poetry volume, *An Acreage of Lyric*, but her real forte was biography, with her fellow authors as her subjects. She understood their writing lives:

> There is something about the sight of a person seated at a typewriter, or engaged in the composition of a sentence, which seems to invite interruption . . . A closed door means nothing, a locked door may be pounded upon, a telephone is no respecter of composition.
>
> Moreover, one of the strangest hallucinations of the ordinary individual is that though you may be busy when they hear the typewriter going, the moment the noise ceases, they feel free to talk to you. Yet as a matter of fact, as anyone remotely concerned with writing will tell, it is when the typewriter stops that you are planning the next sentence or developing the next idea, and it is the very time of all times when you do not want to be interrupted on any matter, urgent or not![71]

That was the benefit of the Boston Athenaeum. Come what may, the fifth floor remained resolutely silent.

In March, Emilie wrote a story about disciplining a four-year-old boy, "In the 19th Century Manner," and sent it out. *Delineator*, *Women's Home Companion*, *Ladies Home Journal*, and *Good Housekeeping* all returned it. Even *Children* refused the story.

In April, she wrote "Blue Smocks" and sent it to *The Saturday Evening Post*, where John P. Marquand had published nearly twenty stories. She had no better luck there. She submitted the story to *McClure's* and *Women's*

Home Companion, and at the same time, she mailed her much traveled, "By Audacity Alone," to the Dell Publishing Company.

By the first week of May, all of her short story submissions had been rejected, but she didn't give up. There must have been some level of encouragement in the refusals by *McClure's*, because she rewrote "Blue Smocks" and sent it back to them for another try. When that didn't work, she kept the story moving to *Red Book* and *Liberty*.

The Boston Authors Club's annual President's Day Dinner was held on April thirtieth, downstairs in the larger rooms of the Twentieth Century Club. Sixty authors and their guests attended, including all of "Flappers' Row"—Emilie, Clara, and Sara Ware.[72]

Soon after, they were all writing in the Athenaeum when Sara Ware passed out, cold. In following days, she lost the ability to use a typewriter and had no memory of her current novel, *The Green Dolphin*. Robert Grant called it a "break down" and cautioned her not to work so hard. Her physician advised complete rest. She retreated to her home in Princeton and didn't return for nearly two years.[73]

May eighteenth was Boston's second annual Dickens Dinner,[74] organized by the Dickens Fellowship, an international organization of Dickens enthusiasts. The evening reproduced, as exactly as possible, the dinner given for Charles Dickens when he first visited Boston in 1842. The height to which Dickens' star had risen was hard to overestimate. Bostonians could quote Shakespeare, Dickens, Scott, and Thackeray, but Boston was Dickens' favorite American city, and Dickens remained Boston's favorite author.

Emilie and Victor signed a contract for her new novel, *The Solitary Horseman* before they left for summer at Stone House. The story was fleshed out with contemporary details, like a rare series of earthquakes that hit New England in February and March: "Months before, an earthquake had set the room to swaying." And there were shades of her father's puns: "Now R. E. Morse is all right in moderation but being a gob of gloom don't do anyone good." The Chinese Coromandel screen had a real-life counterpart in Blue Hill, three folding, opaque panels on little legs, its design in gold.

Her glance fell on the Chinese Coromandel screen of vivid red lacquer which stood at the entrance of the garden room. She prickled with imagination. Always it had that effect upon her. Always it seemed to whisper mysteriously: "Dare you to look behind me! Dare you!" And always she had forced herself to look before she dashed away as though a legion of imps were at her heels. Of course, she had outgrown that foolishness now, but—that bit of Oriental color still exuded an aura of sinister mystery.

Nearing her sixtieth birthday, Emilie spoke through Mrs. Grahame. When asked by her daughter if she still cares about being attractive, she responds, "Care! Of course I care. Do you think that I don't care for lovely frocks? That I don't care when a man's eyes flash into interest when he looks at me? When I cease to care the real me will be gone though this body of mine lives on."

He did not judge a woman by her age but by her intellect and attractiveness. He was as charming and attentive to her mother as he was to her.
The Solitary Horseman

Blue Hill, Summer 1926

On their way to Blue Hill in July, Emilie and Victor stopped off in Bucksport and signed a mortgage for twenty-thousand dollars.[75] This paid off an earlier mortgage and perpetuated the loan to a future date. Their purpose was to build a new house on the lot between their home at Wellesley Hills and her mother's. They didn't plan to live in it; they wanted to develop the bare half-acre to sell, and Robert would be both contractor and realtor for the project.

When they arrived at Blue Hill, Emilie set up her study in the "gun room," to the left of the front entrance. She turned her desk away from the door to prevent distraction, but she could look out the window to her left onto the small garden along the kitchen ell. Practiced at writing in her Athenaeum cubicle, she needed only the bare essentials to begin—paper, pencils, and a pencil sharpener.

Dorothea Lawrance Mann reviewed another Blue Hill author in June. She was Mary Ellen Chase, whose widowed mother lived on Union Street. After several years in Wisconsin and Minnesota, Mary Ellen had just accepted a professorship at Smith College to support her mother, brother, and herself. Mary Ellen Chase was to build her reputation on regional stories about her beloved Maine and the rugged people who inhabited it. *Mary Christmas* was her third book, and after two westerns, this was the first about Maine. Dorothea Lawrance Mann observed, "A wistful charm of personality and a mellow appreciation of living combine to make her little chronicle unusual."[76]

Emilie turned sixty on September fifth, while they were still in Blue Hill, and what a decade it marked. When she was fifty, her mother, sister, and brother had still lived nearby at the end of their road in Wellesley Hills. Emilie had published her cookbook and was writing articles on motherhood. Her sons had yet to go off to war, and Mel Baker was only a teenager. Ten years later, her mother and Rachel had died, Mel and his bride lived in New York near Robert and Minnie, and the Lorings lived on Beacon Hill in Boston. Blue Hill was the new gathering place, and this year, Selden brought his bride.

Fall 1926

When the Lorings returned to Beacon Hill at the end of September, the club season had begun. From the venerable Somerset and St. Botolph clubs to their political, literary, athletic, and dining cousins, club membership meant inclusion in the city's conversations. In fact, the Boston City Club, to which Victor belonged, had exactly that in mind when it promised to:

bring together in friendly association as many men as we can, of as many creeds as we can, and thus create new conditions of good fellowship and good citizenship for the service of the city, and also to destroy the class, religious, and racial prejudices which exist when men don't know each other, and which are used by grafters and selfish men to further their schemes to the great harm of the City, the State, and the nation.

Membership increased beyond five thousand members, and its distaff equivalent, the Women's City Club of Boston, to which Emilie belonged, signed more than four thousand.

Emilie and Victor both volunteered time to the Women's Educational and Industrial Union (WEIU) of Boston that worked to reduce barriers between women of the lowest and highest economic status, to improve the lives of all women, and to protect women's interests in education, law, and families. The club sponsored job training, so that women could acquire self-supporting work, investigated unsafe working conditions, and lobbied for legal protections of both women and children in industry.

Emilie served tea at an afternoon meeting of the WEIU in 1914 that proposed serving healthy lunches in the high schools. By 1926, they were serving lunches to more than thirteen thousand students in Boston's high and technical schools. Funds came from benefits and fund-raisers. Cooks prepared fresh bread, cake, soup, and sandwiches each morning, and volunteers delivered them in wicker baskets to twenty-two Boston schools.[77]

From its founding in 1868 by Julia Ward Howe and others, the New England Women's Club had three prongs: art and literature, "work," and business. Over the years, the club cooperated with other women's organizations to improve the working and living conditions of women and promote their greater representation and consideration in political and civic affairs. Their club rooms at 585 Boylston Street had once been home to the Women's Suffrage Association and the *Woman's Journal*. Now, the New England Women's Club met on Mondays and loaned the space to other

"I am trying to teach you to cook food properly that you may keep your families well and efficient, so that your children will grow up sound and strong." *Rainbow at Dusk*

women's civic groups during the week, such as the League of Nursing and the Jewish Children's Aid Society.[78] At one of its literary meetings in late November, Emilie read from her works; Agnes L. Dodge, a granddaughter of Blue Hill's John Peters, talked about her recent, African cruise; and a lecturer from MIT gave "A Portrait of a Modern Novelist."[79]

Spring 1927

The Solitary Horseman came out on February sixth, dedicated "To my sons." The *Boston Transcript* wrote a special, feature review with a portrait of Emilie that the Boston Authors Club newsletter called "a wonderful likeness of a beautiful woman."

John Clair Minot praised the book on his radio show, "Monday Evening Book Talk," and wrote an enthusiastic article for The *Boston Herald*:

> This is Mrs. Loring's fourth novel, and it is her strongest and most satisfying. There is real vitality in the characterization, a sureness of touch in the plot development, and a human understanding which gives the story its most attractive quality . . . The story has mystery and adventure as well as clean romance, and if it provides thrills, they are not beyond the possibilities of the New England communities that you know. There is no lapse or lagging in the movement of the story and no failure in the author's fine sense of human values. Altogether, "The Solitary Horseman" is a story worthy of warm commendation.[80]

By the end of March, the book was in its second printing, and her publicity portrait appeared again, this time in the *Sunday Herald*'s "Rotogravure Section." She sat in an open posture, confident and feminine, a single strand of matched pearls about her neck. Ironically, given the purpose of the photo and the book's feminist issues, the caption gave her husband's credentials before hers: "Emilie Loring of 25 Chestnut Street,

"A wonderful likeness of a beautiful woman."

Boston and Wellesley Hills, wife of a prominent Boston lawyer and author of 'The Solitary Horseman,' a romance of present-day New England."[81]

Selden and Mary's first baby was due before summer. Emilie's cousin Angie Brackett wrote from Arlington, Massachusetts:

I am glad for you indeed that a dear little grandchild is coming into the family. You are looking forward—I know—to much comfort and happiness as every grandmother must.[82]

"Grandmother." That would be something new!

Emilie and Victor sold the new, Colonial home they built between their house and Burr Croft in Wellesley Hills and committed themselves to Boston. Boys had always been Emilie's favorite, and when her grandson arrived on May eleventh, she was delighted. He was named for his grandfather—Victor Joseph Loring, II.[83]

When she became "Grandmama," Emilie Loring's writing career was at its highest point, to date. A *New York Times* ad read, "Emilie Loring's *The Solitary Horseman* rides fast and far from coast to coast." In recognition, the Boston Authors Club again elected Emilie to their Board as well as to the membership committee that invited new authors. No longer was she striving to get a foothold; she had arrived.

Blue Hill, Summer 1927

Baby Victor's birth made it clear that the family needed more room in Blue Hill. They started the process when Selden married, taking out a four-thousand-dollar mortgage to define a three-acre lot across the road. This year, they took out an additional, six-thousand-dollar loan to pay for construction and began to plan in earnest.

By this time, Emilie had built two houses and renovated another. In the decades since her time-and-motion analysis of housekeeping, she had observed a lot about the effect of design on everyday living, which she shared now in a story for *Youth* called "Open for Inspection."

"See that ventilator? Carries off the odor of cooking so it can't penetrate to the living room and hall. Been done in big houses but not much in small ones where it's needed more. Here's the built-in ironing board with electric plug and here is the breakfast nook. See that peach of a window? Morning sun. Man of the house eats breakfast here and starts off all lighted up with courage."

The color scheme was the same that she used in Stone House.

"I can just see this with table and seats painted a soul-satisfying green—not apple, not sea—woodwork in the kitchen the same, cream walls, gray and white tiled linoleum on the floor and a gray and white shade on the hanging light in the nook. It would be adorable . . . Your house is marvelous. Something human about it. Looks as though it were saying: 'Hurry up and finish me! I want a family!'"

Sam grinned.

"That isn't what it says to me. It yells: 'Get a hustle on! Finish me! If you don't old Fee Fi Fo Fum Construction Loan will gobble me.'"

Emilie gardened all summer and began to imagine her next character as a garden-maker. What luxury, to enjoy bountiful gardens at the touch of a pen:

Above the fence nodded a welter of bloom sparkling with brilliants left by the shower. Marigolds, a gold mine of them. An occasional tall spike of larkspur lingering long beyond its time as though loath to give way to its rival, purple monkshood, giant masses of it. There were patches of deepest orange. Tall pink lilies. Drifts of white cosmos, nuances of pale rose against dark greens. Gladioli in gorgeous profusion. Cloudy mists of gypsophila. Brilliant color massed in the middle of the border shaded down to cool tints at the ends. (*Gay Courage*)

Gardening at Blue Hill. "Against the gray stone walls of the house, perennials put on a flower show of gorgeous color . . ." To Love and to Honor

Again, she designed with the owner's experience in mind:

"I've been making a little, spring garden-spot for the woman who does our laundry. She spends most of her time over washtubs but she's pathetically eager for a flower. She'll be able to see this from the shed where she scrubs."

Garden images spilled onto the page. Nancy Caswell's bedroom was "cool with orchid and yellow tints," dancers wore "pumpkin yellow," and "a few late perennials were nodding encouragement to Betty Caswell as she dug in the garden." She even described music with plants:

> The air was spicy with the scent of spruce and balsam, it tickled,
> and sparkled and boomed with the rhythm of brasses and strings.

This was the first time that Emilie wrote her father into a story, and the affection between Noah Caswell and his daughter, Nancy, was palpable.

> How wonderful Noah Caswell was with his imperishable belief that humanity is capable of dwelling on the mountaintops of high thinking, noble, unselfish living. Erect. Lean. His features were those of a Greek god. But no Greek god's face radiated such spiritual beauty, no Greek god's head ever was crowned with soft waves of silver hair, no Greek god would wear that shabby velveteen coat, nor a broad tie with one end dangling.
>
> A lovely light warmed the girl's eyes. "That's Dad. He orates on all occasions, especially when he's shaving. Sometime I expect to find him with an ear hanging by a thread."

Emilie infused the story with George Baker's amused wisdom. Nancy admits to her father that Geoffrey Hilliard's photograph has "a sort of hypnotic attraction" for her and then learns of his plans.

> Nancy experienced the sensation of being dropped several floors in a lift. Here to stay! Was she responsible? . . .
>
> [Geoffrey] commented curtly;
>
> "You look frightened. Because I'm staying? Little girls shouldn't set sparks to fuses unless they're game to watch them go off. Good-night!"

He departed as suddenly as he had appeared. A too emphatically closed door shook the firearms. Noah Caswell regarded his daughter quizzically . . . His lips twitched as he observed irrelevantly,

"Strangely potent this thing we call, for want of a better name, 'attraction,' isn't it?"

Boston, Fall 1927

The *Boston Herald* reported:

Charles C. Shoemaker of Philadelphia, president of the Penn Publishing Company, is in Boston for a few days and at a dinner party at the Union Club last evening entertained two of his best-known authors, Temple Bailey of East Orange, N. J., who has been in New England this summer, and Emilie Loring of Wellesley Hills and Chestnut Street, Boston, who is just back from her summer home at Blue Hill, Me.[84]

Emilie returned to the Boston Athenaeum to write. After a year on Mrs. Greenough's ticket, she now had permission to use Anita Saltonstall Ward's membership. "Anita" was Anna Saltonstall Ward—of the Boston Brahmin Saltonstalls. Anita and her sister Caroline had co-owned one library share since 1891, but Caroline died, and Anita invited Emilie to use her privilege.

It truly was a privilege, described in the Athenaeum bulletin: "Here remains a retreat for those who would enjoy the humanity of books." A membership share at the Athenaeum cost about $850, and there were fewer than a thousand shares in use. Members provided admission cards to non-proprietors, as Anita did for Emilie, to the effect that slightly more non-proprietors used the library than members. An endowment provided fresh flowers for the desks, and the third-floor tearoom offered a four-o'clock cup of tea and a cracker for just a few cents.

Afternoon tea was quiet that fall, as Emilie wrote in relative solitude. Clara Endicott Sears' mother had grown so ill that her extended family was summoned. She recovered, but Clara stayed home to care for her and manage her own health. She confided: "When I came here, I was so tired that I was frightened, because you see I have to carry my responsibilities alone. It would never do for me to get down and out."[85]

Judge Grant retreated in grief to his law office on State Street after the presumed suicide of his son Patrick in late October. A wealthy banker and stockbroker, Patrick Grant entered his fifth-floor office one Friday morning and fell from the open window, still wearing his overcoat.[86]

"The loss is indeed a crushing one for us," Judge Grant wrote to Sara Ware Bassett, "as my dear son Pat had a radiant, loving personality & had lately shown marked ability. But we shall have to bear our sorrow bravely, as so many others do, & take some comfort from our memories and the affection of our friends."[87]

Holed up in her house at Princeton, Sara Ware Bassett was under orders not to write or otherwise exert herself. She truly could not manage to work on a book but sent condolences to Judge Grant, who chided:

It was very sweet of you, but wrong I fear even by permission of the doctor, to write me at such length in your own hand . . . So full of cheer, patience and humor, although you are still facing a very long (for you) sentence of mental inactivity . . . But I feel confident—and hope with all my heart that the complete rest prescribed will presently bring back your strength and enable you in the end to get on even keel again.[88]

Clara Endicott Sears counseled:

You were going it too hard & your body resented it. And perhaps
it did you a good turn for I can hardly believe that a book written
by force of will could equal one that evolves from a rested mind.

Charles Lindbergh had just made the first successful, nonstop solo
flight across the Atlantic, and Clara encouraged,

And what a Godsend that young man is to this blasé, sophisticated, pessimistic, old world! He has inoculated its veins with
romance & hero-worship & has quickened a craving for what is
sincere & straight. My cousin, Mrs. Carnegie, met him in London when he visited Westminster Abbey. She says he has a very
remarkable personality—quiet, reserved & singularly poised, &
that London simply went wild & lost its head over him!
Well now, dear Miss Bassett, is not that good to hear? After all,
life is a grand adventure & right prevails![89]

Emilie's friends faced grief, illness, and burdensome duty with such
pluck and good will. That would be her book's theme and title: *Gay Courage.*

"What you called the other day, 'Gay courage,' the phrase has stuck
in my mind. That's life, isn't it? We can't sulk. We can't run—and
be soldiers. We've got to go straight on."

Circumstances couldn't have been more different for Emilie and her
family, who worked happily on new projects that fall. Late in November,
the Penn Publishing Company advertised last notice for its Second Prize
Play Contest.

The plays must be at least three acts, comedies, melodramas or serious plays. The costuming and setting should be simple; the plots clearly defined; the plays free from objectionable features. Contest closes December 31st, 1927. Prize winners to be announced March 15th. In the event of a tie for any of the prizes, a prize of the amount offered will be awarded to each of the tying contestants.[90]

First prize was one thousand dollars, equal to the royalties for a first run of ten thousand books. Why not try?

Emilie's story came together quickly. Peter Maxwell takes over the practice of longtime pediatrician Jim Kellogg, and his new secretary, Cynthia Brooks, is a mystery. Could she be the missing fiancé of Multan Khan, Crown Prince of Hokipoka? Or is she Jim Kellogg's missing assistant who disappeared with important documents?

Emilie's father was already on her mind from writing *Gay Courage*. Now, she remembered how he wrote his plays at night and tried them out with the family, the familiar elements of his farces, his methods of working out costumes and staging. Copying his method, she made a stick puppet for each character and worked out stage directions on a small platform.[91]

The play came alive as her father's had done: Jim discovers that Cynthia is really Jim Kellogg's long-lost daughter, sent to live with another family after her mother died in childbirth. Widow Belle Steele works her wiles, but Cynthia captures Peter's heart and is reunited with her father. Emilie polished the dialogue and mailed *Where's Peter?* to Penn's office in Philadelphia.

Emilie's brother and son also wrote a play that fall, perhaps for the same contest. In school, Selden won a short story prize, and he had more recently written and illustrated articles for the *Harvard Crimson*. Now, he and his uncle, "Inky," wrote "Reluctant Romeo," a three-act play about a confirmed womanhater who is "educated in romance" by a quartette of girls.

Selden was clearly more Baker than his brother, Robert, and the differences between them widened. Selden had a wife and son and social position boosted by his wealthy in-laws. In the fall, he won a doubles tennis tournament at the Old Belfry Club in Lexington, the toney club to which the Valentines belonged, while Robert still lived with his parents on Beacon Hill. He worked for them, too, as he left wool-selling and became the contractor for their building projects.

Boston, Spring 1928

In so many ways, this was the nicest stretch Emilie had enjoyed in a long while. She signed the contract for *Gay Courage* in January, and in March, she learned that her play, *Where's Peter?* had won fifth prize in the Penn Prize Play contest. The reward was only fifty dollars, but she would split the performance royalties evenly with the publisher (ten dollars plus fifty cents per book). That was enough, as she later wrote, "to pay for theatre tickets several times when the girl friend and I celebrate."[92]

Her nephew, Mel Baker, added to his credits in Hollywood. His first film, *High Hat*, was a Robert T. Kane production, filmed at Hearst's Cosmopolitan Studio in New York. Now, Lasky Studios announced that Gary Cooper and Fay Wray would star in *The Circus Kid*, co-written by Mel and James Ashmore Creelman.

The situation for others was more complicated. Her brother, Robert, contributed to the *Secretary's Report on Harvard's Class of 1892*:

I think I could play football as well as I used to—for a minute. I use the same philosophy, to take what's coming to me and stand the gaff. I believe I have reached years of discretion in that I don't try nature's patience too far. I am still married—to the SAME wife which, in these days, is worthy of mention . . . My son speaks of me as "a swell guy"; that may or may not mean that I have proved a success as a parent.[93]

But thirty years of treatments had produced no cure for his failing eyesight, and he struggled to write more than part-time. *Beverly of Graustark* came to the silver screen, but "they left out all of the play," and his latest play was rejected, because "it had plenty of heart interest but lacked tart interest."[94]

As his eyesight failed further, Robert changed his priorities and left for the South Seas, "Object—the pursuit of sunshine AND moonshine." On the *SS Aorangi*, a beyond-luxurious ocean-liner, he traveled from Auckland, New Zealand to Fiji and on to Honolulu. His wife, Minnie, met him there, and they stayed a full month at Hale Kukui, above Honolulu. They returned together on the *SS President Jackson* to San Francisco and by train to New York.

Back in Boston, Sara Ware's long illness now included appendicitis. She underwent an appendectomy in February and required months of absolute rest before she could return to the Athenaeum. She wrote to Judge Robert Grant that her head "lagged behind" her body, so that she could not read, sew, or write, but she remained optimistic that time outdoors in her garden would effect a full cure.[95]

Clara Endicott Sears felt better, herself, but as her mother's cancer neared the latter stages, she left writing altogether and stayed close to home. It was not like her to remain inactive, though, so when farm hands discovered arrowheads in her Harvard orchards, she quickly devised a plan to create an Indian Museum on the grounds. She pored through books on Indian history and wrote nationwide to purchase significant artifacts. Her "Native American Museum" opened to the public in June, and the Boston Authors Club visited for their last meeting of the season.[96]

The last club *Bulletin* for the season reported, "If all Mrs. Emilie Loring's books come out in Braille, I shall be happy," was the earnest exclamation last week of a blind worker among the blind of Boston, who did not know that her words could ever reach the author. *Here Comes the Sun*, she added, "is the best love story I ever read. My pupils all say the same."[97]

Blue Hill, Summer 1928

The Lorings named their new cottage "The Ledges," because it sat on a stone ledge, over thirty feet above the East Blue Hill Road. A home movie taken that summer of 1928 showed Emilie and Victor descending its steep, stone staircase—Emilie's step dainty, Victor's firm.

The cottage had nearly the same floor plan as Stone House, flipped one-hundred-eighty degrees to put the fireplace on the left of the entrance and the dining room and kitchen on the right. It had built-in bookshelves for summer reading, and above the fireplace was a stone chimney that depicted a sailboat with full rudder and keel. That was a creation of architects Kilham, Hopkins & Greeley, who used the same, stone sailboat idea years later, in their 1941 design for Boston's Community Sailing boat house on the Charles River.

> "An artist in stone must have built that chimney."
> *Hilltops Clear*

Like the fictional parsonage in *Gay Courage*, The Ledges had painted shutters with "little rabbits with upstanding ears" cut into them. Later Lorings remember it as "Calendula Cottage," which may have been an earlier—or later—name. In addition, The Ledges had its own blueberry field and naturalized drifts of daffodils and narcissus.[98]

Minnie, Bessie, and David Owen returned to Tyn Y Coed from Philadelphia, but the Curtis' *Starboard Acres* remained empty. Mary Curtis had died in March, and her husband, Ben, sold most of their property to his brother-in-law, Ned Brooks. Their shore property went to Blossom Alcott, and their Mudge cousin Alfred completed the family exodus by selling Ned Brooks the parcel of land along the Loring's property line that had once caused such consternation.

There was no Blue Hill Troupe performance at the Millikens that summer, either. The group had moved to New York City, where the Millikens lived during the winter season. Seth and Alida Milliken concentrated on the Kollegewidgwok Yacht Club. All summer long, children raced from the Millikens' playhouse in Morgan Bay to the Lorings' granite pier in Blue Hill's Inner Bay.

"The Ledges"

Inside "The Ledges." Note the stone sailboat above the mantel and the wall of books

Descending Steps at "The Ledges," 1928

Rabbit Shutters. "There were little rabbits with upstanding ears cut in the yellow shutters." Gay
Courage

Robert and Minnie Baker came to Blue Hill directly after their one-month cruise to Hawaii. Emilie and Victor came next, and then Selden, Mary, and one-year-old Victor. Selden's new movie camera captured little Victor on his scooter and Emilie visiting with Mary, while "Grandpapa," Victor, puffed on his cigar and filled the kitchen with smoke.

By then, Baker's Plays had published Robert and Selden's *Reluctant Romeo* for amateur use. One review called it "cleverly written" with "plenty of amusing situations, witty dialogue, and 'wise cracks.'"[99] Pleased with the success of her play, *Where's Peter?*, Emilie re-worked one of her novels for the stage: *The Solitary Horseman: A Romantic Comedy in Three Acts by Emilie Loring*. The setting was wistfully nostalgic:

Just before the guns shook Europe
While we still dressed for dinner

She was reminded in the process of a limitation in plays that novels didn't have. The original had a dog in it, but she found it was too hard to control the animal on stage and took him out.

Emilie craved a writer's retreat with no interruptions, and Emilie's sons decided to build her one. They found a level area in the forest between Stone House and the water, where stonecutters' camps once stood. They cut logs, notched their corners, and fitted them together to define a room that would be big enough for a desk and chair, with a future door on one side and a future window looking through the forest to the water beyond. Pure quiet and complete solitude . . . eventually.

Louise and Lizzy Hallet spent that summer in Bar Harbor and visits went back and forth between Stone House and Mount Desert. The Hallets had lived in Europe with their mother since 1914, first in Rome and then more than a decade at Menton, on the French Riviera. It had been a year since their mother's death in Paris, and now that her body was safely interred in the Hallet's West Yarmouth plot, that familial duty was over.

"My cabin, isn't it? I had no idea it was so—so luxurious . . . Rather nice. I came here the other day with Jim Armstrong, but we didn't come in. What huge logs in the walls!"
Hilltops Clear

Writer's Cabin in the Stone House Woods (1929). "Was she just seeing things or was it—it was a log cabin!" Hilltops Clear

Their visits were heartwarming and fun, with "giggling sessions" between the "girls" and storytelling from shared memories.[100] The Hallets remembered Emilie's father, mother, and sister, Rachel. In return, Emilie and Robert remembered the Hallets' family, too, their house in West Yarmouth, and the many activities their families shared in those two years on the Cape. Their connection proved more important than they could know.

Books and plays, generations of family gathered together with old friends and new, the spicy scents of spruce and pine on salt-sea air, popovers and lobster at Mount Desert's Jordan Pond House, and the hectic and lazy activities of summer merged into one, happy vacation. They would remember that summer forever.

Boston, Fall 1928

Gay Courage came out in late October, a full nine months after the finished manuscript was delivered to Penn. "It has the charm that entertains," said *The Atlanta Constitution*.

In recognition of her mounting book sales and reputation, Boston Authors Club member Dorothea Lawrance Mann wrote a tribute to Emilie Loring. Miss Mann had already written "Ellen Glasgow: Citizen of the World" and "Dorothy Canfield Fisher: The Little Vermonter." They were short biographical sketches, intended to frame what would one day be called their authors' "brands."

From her earliest years, Emilie's father and his publishing friends had listened to her. She enjoyed a companionship of equals with her husband, Victor. She didn't need to fight for influence, respect, or equal treatment within the family; she had those. Miss Mann might have written, "Emilie Loring: Living the Future for Women." Instead, she focused on the romance of Emilie's childhood: *Emilie Loring: A Twentieth Century Romanticist*.[101]

Emilie Loring is a romantic, living in an age of realism. That is now and always the source of her real charm.

Emilie grew up among creative people, learned from the earliest age to act in plays, and had books of all kinds at her fingertips.

Small wonder that Emilie Loring, daughter of a playwright, play publisher and an amateur actor of note, should secure as the publisher of her novels and plays, The Penn Publishing Company, another firm noted for its amateur plays as well as its long list of books.

Miss Mann had a personal reason for feeling sentimental about Emilie Loring's childhood. As editor of the *BAC Bulletin*, she acknowledged some years later, "The first books ever presented to the editor of the Bulletin by a publisher were a gift to her from the firm of Lee & Shepard when she was seven years old."[102] Her father, Charles Edward Mann, compiled and edited *Story of the Hutchinsons*, with a foreword by Frederick Douglass, which was published by Lee & Shepard in 1896. An officer of the New England Historical and Genealogical Society, and the author of numerous biographical sketches himself, it was easy to see how Miss Mann developed her interest in biography.

CHAPTER 22

Crisis: 1929

Spring 1929

Emilie's uncle, Walter H. Baker, the longtime manager of Baker's Plays, died at his home in Boston in early January, and the loss was keenly felt. He had been a fixture in the family, closely allied with Emilie's father in both publishing and amateur drama.

The sole remaining Baker from her father's generation was Charles Tappan Baker who lived in Wollaston, Massachusetts. Like his brothers, he was a publisher—a bookbinder by trade and president of Lothrop, Lee & Shepard for two decades.[1] He was the Baker family historian whose work helped Emilie to complete her application to the National Society of the Daughters of the American Revolution. It was new to think of that part of the Baker family as "history" instead of the present.

The BAC *Bulletin* announced Dorothea Lawrance Mann's tribute, "Emilie Loring: A Twentieth Century Romanticist," on March 5, 1929: "a delightful 'Appreciation' of Emilie Loring, incidentally sketching the novelist's life, which is in itself a fine romance."

Did Emilie mind Mann's characterization, which focused on the romance of her stories and bypassed their adventure and calls to character? For whatever reason, Emilie Loring's next novel, *Swift Water*, was a distinct departure from those that came before or after. This time, her heroine was less likable than the hero and had a deeper set of internal conflicts. Jean Randolph has a "Terrible Twin"—that part of herself that thumbs her nose at authority and flies in the face of good judgment.

—the closet! A surge of anger, rebellion, swept her. How many times had her naughty double, "The Terrible Twin" been incarcerated there, in "the Dungeon" till "good little Jean" should come out? She would hate to count up.

Jean speeds into trouble on her first day in town and meets Christopher Wynne, the virtuous but disturbingly compelling minister of her hometown. The characters question virtue, conscience, faith—and love—as the town is flooded, and they must fight for their neighbors' lives and their own.

The story kernel from which *Swift Water* grew seems to have been an article from the *New York Times* one year before: "Dam Threat Causes Panic Near Rutland: Thousands Below It Fled Until Structure Was Strengthened—City Still Flood-Bound."

> They suddenly found themselves in deep and *swift water*. [emphasis added] Kennedy and Allwell escaped. Cebola clung for a time to a fence but could not swim and was finally washed away and drowned.[2]

In this story of opposites, Jean Randolph's better self struggles with her "Terrible Twin," and each of her parents represents a different side of her character—the father who is wise and caring, the mother who is remote and selfish. Expectations turn upside-down when a dark closet becomes a modern powder-room, liveried servants are compared to robots, and a minister is the town's heartthrob.

Emilie signed the contract for *Swift Water* in March and dedicated it to her publisher at Penn, Charles C. Shoemaker, "to whose sympathy and encouragement I owe much of my progress along the rocky road of authorship." Clara Endicott Sears accused Shoemaker of driving Sara Ware Bassett too hard, but Emilie thrived under deadlines and pressure.

She wrote her own entry for a book of author biographies that Penn published in May and concluded:

"Opposition sends you plunging ahead. You think defiance spells courage. It doesn't. Nine times out of ten it spells lack of intelligence. Some day when you're caught in swift water whirled and tossed and submerged you will remember this."
Swift Water

Sometimes, I am convinced that the domestic career and the literary career are hereditary enemies. But I cling tight to both; the combination is, to quote Dulcy, "won-derful!"[3]

She started right away on her next novel. From her idea file, she pulled a newspaper clipping:

Found: Sunday night. between Kenmore . . . and corner of Dartmouth and New . . . black satin slipper with buckle.
L. P. Dodge. 208 Beacon St. city.

She described later in *The Editor*, "Curious, I thought, that only one slipper had been lost. I wonder why—and the story had started."[4]

While she worked on the new book, Robert and Minnie Baker traveled to Bermuda with the Millikens and Gordon and Katherine Curtis from Blue Hill. They stayed at the pink, luxury hotel, the Hamilton Princess, while the Millikens and their yacht, *Shawna*, competed in local races.

They talked about the new summer school of drama and theater that was coming to Surry. Since the departure of the Blue Hill Troupe to New York, the Blue Hill peninsula had no local theater group. Mrs. Ethelbert (Anne) Nevin proposed a summer school of drama and theater to operate in nearby Surry. It would be a Wellesley-New York collaboration. Leighton Rollins, who pioneered the "dinner theater" concept with the Try Out Theater in Wellesley, would direct the school, and Eva McAdoo of New York would teach its theatrical workshop.

Miss McAdoo taught theater and lived with her parents on Park Avenue in New York City. Her father, William McAdoo, was the well-known Chief City Magistrate of New York who had served President Cleveland as Assistant Secretary of the Navy. McAdoo was an incorruptible and fair-minded judge, unafraid to risk his career to root out corruption. Constance Purdy, also of Wellesley, offered her Surry estate for the performance space, and English Professor Grace Hazard

Conkling of Smith College planned to teach creative writing the following season.

The Bakers returned to New York on April tenth. When he came alone, Robert sometimes stayed at The Lambs Club on 44th Street, but he and Minnie checked in at the new, Westbury Hotel at 69th Street and Madison Avenue, only blocks from the Millikens at 951 Madison Avenue. The hotel's headliners included newly married Fanny Brice and Billy Rose.

Emilie was surrounded by "literary headliners" when the Boston Branch of the League of American Pen Women held their annual "Celebrity Breakfast" that same month.[5] There were so many notable novelists, poets, composers, painters and sculptors in attendance that the "head table" had to circle the room.

The day's speaker, Professor Dallas Lore Sharp, recommended that the writers in the group keep a daily journal. When one wrote down everything that happened in a twenty-four-hour period, he said, there was a rich "library" of ideas from which to draw. No journal recorded the events of May 6, 1929, but over the next few weeks, Emilie pieced together the details.

While Minnie Baker was out shopping, Robert had a health crisis. The illness he had struggled with all of his life had never let go. Early on, he called it an "eye problem," but it seemed like more. His current doctor, internist Maximilian D. Touart, said Robert had gone nearly blind and was subject to both nervous disorders and fainting spells. This time, he struggled even to breathe.

He called down to the front desk, "I'm fainting! I'm choking—send help." A steward rushed to his door but found it locked and went for a passkey. Inside, Robert gasped for air and went to the window.

Minutes later, the steward turned the key in the lock, opened the door, and saw only the open window. He looked down. Robert lay on the concrete, twelve floors below.

Minnie returned at nearly the same time and found a crowd gathered outside the Westbury. The observers parted, and there lay her husband, his head laid open on impact.

"Fractured skull, lacerated brain, hemorrhagic shock, fell or jumped from hotel window 12 floors down to sidewalk below" read the coroner's report.[6] "Playwright Dies in 12-story Fall" announced the *New York Times*:

> The police record said "fell or jumped," but detectives said the evidence indicated that he had tumbled from the window during a fainting spell . . . Detectives said they found marks on the windowsill that seemed to indicate that he had rushed there to get a breath of air, fallen and, as he fell, tried to grasp the sill to hold himself.

Robert died on May 6, 1929, ten years after his mother's death on May 10, 1919. Was he distraught? Was it suicide? Or was it a sad, horrible accident? The *Marysville Tribune* of Ohio reported:

> Leaps to Death
>
> Haunted by dread of blindness to which his doctor told him he was doomed, Robert M. Baker, 55, playwright, of Boston late yesterday was instantly killed in a fall or jump from a window in his rooms on the twelfth floor of the Hotel Westbury.

Emilie was in Boston when she got the news. She and Robert had been close from their days in nightgowns when they put on plays in the parlor. They took the treacherous *Sarah* voyage together, built their homes together, raised their children together, mourned their mother and sister together. Robert was the last member of her childhood family, the last person who shared her memories of home.

Emilie was optimistic, forthright, and tender when needed. She had a fine sense of humor . . . but she wasn't funny. She didn't make a whole room laugh with her songs, antics, and silly stories. Emilie had always been more like her mother, Robert more like their father. It was Robert who provided the ready quip, the instant laugh. Maybe that was why she had been so close to her father and such good pals with her brother.

Victor and Robert had been such friends that Robert had chosen Victor to be his best man. Like Emilie, Victor had a ready sense of humor, but his strengths lay in the force of his convictions and his steady, forthright actions. Robert had been the light-hearted raconteur who filled the emotional gap left behind by Victor's brother Selden. How would they light that space again, fill the void he left behind?

There were practical details to settle. Robert's body was cremated and brought back to Boston in an elaborate, Art Deco urn. After a private service, they placed the urn alongside his daughter Eileen's in the mausoleum vault at Forest Hills.

Robert's estate was valued between fifty- and one-hundred-thousand dollars. Like Rachel, he gave five-hundred dollars each to "his boys," Robert

"Our Boys," One Last Time. Robert Melville Baker with Robert and Selden Loring

and Selden. His own son, Mel, received five thousand dollars plus Robert's copyrights, manuscripts, and royalties. Minnie Baker received the rest—all of their household and personal effects, bank accounts, and investments. If there were residuals, they would pass to Mel upon her death.[7]

Mel didn't need his father's material. Robert's talent had been undeniable, but Mel's career in Hollywood was going places.

> If Melville Baker, the young New York playwright, continues at the pace he set in his first, screen adaptation for Paramount, he will soon be known for his speedy continuities. It was just five weeks ago that Baker was first assigned the job of writing the adaptation and the dialogue for "The Concert," Adolphe Menjou's current starring vehicle, and now the picture is almost completed.[8]

Mel's adaptation became Paramount's *Fashions in Love*, the first talking picture for Adolphe Menjou. His dialogues were called "lilting," "sophisticated," and "deft."

The Boston Authors Club screened *Fashions in Love* when they met in late June to end their season. Clara Endicott Sears hosted 125 guests—authors and their spouses—who traveled out to Harvard in buses and private motorcars to watch the preview showing, a full week before it was released in Hollywood.

Mel's next project was another adaptation, this time Sir Phillip Gibbs' *Darkened Rooms*. Paramount signed him to adapt the tale "of mystery and intrigue, built around the machinations of a fake spiritualistic medium and his efforts to possess Ross Jaffray." Gary Cooper was supposed to star in the lead role, but when he pulled out, Neil Hamilton stepped in. Hamilton, like Cooper, was a handsome, leading man but would be remembered most for his role as Police Commissioner Gordon in the 1960s series, *Batman*.

Summer 1929

By the time the Lorings arrived at Blue Hill in mid-July, the rest of their friends were already there: the Owen sisters, Luella Coggan, Josephine and Ned Brooks, Gladys (Mrs. Henry H.) Rousseau, Ellen Slaven, and Emilie's former maid, now back from Radcliffe, Esther Wood.

The Owen sisters re-opened their tearoom, Larkspur Lodge, and across the road, Judge William McAdoo and his family had rented The Ledges for the duration of the Surry Playhouse's premiere season. In fact, the premiere performance had just taken place. Governor Gardiner pulled the first curtain, a packed house cheered a performance of *March Hares*, and the refurbished barn was hailed as "one of the loveliest and most complete small theatres in America."[9]

The Lorings were still in Blue Hill when Clara Endicott Sears' mother passed away at the Pergolas on August twenty-eighth. At ninety-three, Mrs. Sears' death was expected, but she had hung on for years, through cancer, surgery, and worsening health. Her death was hard. Clara wrote, "It was terrible, morphine had no effect. I did not know anything could be so terrible." Clara and her mother had been each other's sole living companion for nearly forty years. Like Emilie, she was now the lone survivor of her childhood family. It became a bond between them.

The Lorings stayed in Blue Hill through Emilie's birthday and the Blue Hill Fair in September and then departed. Judge McAdoo and his family left at the same time with plans to return the following summer.

Stock Market Crash, Fall 1929

What people seldom remember about that fall, when the stock market crashed, is that the market had been volatile a long while. In the past, big drops in stock prices had been followed by at least a modest recovery, but this time, none was in sight. On October first, a man jumped to his death from the eleventh floor of a New York hotel. His suicide note read,

"Last April I was worth $100,000. Today, I am $24,000 in the red." Three days later, the *New York Times* reported, "Year's Worst Break Hits Stock Market."[10]

So many orders came in for *Swift Water* when it was announced on October fifth that a second edition was printed before the first was even released.[11] The theme of *Swift Water* was death, danger, and a crisis of the soul. The public could relate.

On Black Thursday, stock prices plummeted and triggered a panicked sell-off. On October 29, the stock market completely collapsed, and banks called in their loans. Thirty billion dollars in stock disappeared by mid-November.

Laurence Paine Dodge—the "L. P. Dodge" who found a black slipper and placed the newspaper ad that would inspire *Lighted Windows*—lost everything. The details were forever murky, but the forty-four-year-old stockbroker was apparently unlicensed, lost his fortune and other people's, too, and never worked again.[12]

The Lorings managed fine. Their real property held its value, Victor continued to work, and the royalties from Emilie's books were considerable. The bigger struggle that year was emotional, not financial. It was lonesome to be the last remaining member of her original family. Emilie's memories and family knowledge stretched back nearly seven decades, but who would share those memories now?

Clara Endicott Sears felt it, too. She was born wealthy and remained so after the crash. She owned her estate and museums at Harvard, and she lived comfortably on the proceeds of her father's estate. While others were losing their fortunes, she inherited the lion's share of her mother's estate. Valued at over six million dollars then, the principal was the equivalent in economic prestige of nearly one hundred million today (2022). This included the Sears estates at both Nahant and 132 Beacon in Boston, "furnishings, plate, jewelry, clothing, horses and autos," and one-thousand dollars in cash.[13] But she, too, was alone at the top of her family, and she began to think of the legacy she would leave behind.

As the days passed, her sense of aloneness grew rather than diminished. Sometimes when she woke in the night and couldn't sleep, she would get panicky, thinking distorted thoughts of what illness would mean; it seemed as if she could hear the hours hurrying along. It made one curiously shivery to realize that one was the last of one's family. The dogs and Irish Bridie were her only confidantes, but she could not say to them: "Do you remember when . . ."
Uncharted Seas

CHAPTER 23

Resilience: 1930–34

Emilie said in later years that she used writing to give herself something that she wanted terribly. Her example was a red hat she had seen in a shop window, but the themes of her books worked the same way, across the years. As her characters worked out their problems, Emilie felt the benefit, too.

Her first novels dealt with identity. What kind of person would she be? What was her duty to others? What would she stand for, fight for? Geraldine Glamorgan defied her father to define her marriage for herself (*The Trail of Conflict*); Julie Lorraine defied her matchmaking aunt and "Julie will do it" expectations (*Here Comes the Sun!*); Judith Halliday revised what it took for her to feel loved (*A Certain Crossroad*); Rose Grahame fought to be taken seriously as an adult and as a woman (*The Solitary Horseman*); and Nancy Caswell had to overcome her own biases before she could find happiness (*Gay Courage*).

Then came the deep, personal challenge that she wrote about in *Swift Water* the year that her brother died. When tested, would she rise or fall? The public faced the same crisis as the Depression deepened and showed no signs of lifting. What would become of their values, hopes, and dreams? Emilie Loring's next novels had themes of resilience.

Lighted Windows reframed "uncertainty" as "adventure." Disguised as a boy, Janice Trent eludes her rich, unfaithful fiancé in New York and heads for the clean, fresh expanse of Alaska. Determined to conquer her fears, she goes to a new place for a new job and entirely new acquaintances. Emilie knew firsthand the difference that a trip to Alaska could make, and memory brought back the feeling.

Why was it, when one couldn't sleep, one thought of all the pesky little misfortunes which might occur, instead of radiant possibilities? . . . She had come north in quest of a different self, a fearless self.
Lighted Windows

There were no dark places in her soul this morning. Gone was the sense of monotony. The possibility of adventure waiting round the corner thrilled her, not a doubt lurked in her consciousness. Something might happen on this expedition, something big, the atmosphere tingled with possibilities. She had been wise to follow her hunch. Transplanting had broken up the old design of her life. It had developed a determination to make an art of living, to conquer her fear complex, to meet problems and disappointments with gay courage. It had set her mind pulsing with new ideas, new ambitions, new plans.

Janice's brother never appears in the story. Although he is alive, his furniture is shrouded, his apartment closed. Her one anchor to the past is her brother's best friend, Bruce Harcourt. Victor fit this description. He was Robert's best man, and their two families lived next door to one another for nearly three decades. He shared the changes in Emilie's life and understood their importance.

They talked of her family, the loss of her mother and father, of Billy, of the enormous growth of the city, of the changes in it, in the fashion of plays, of books, of clothes since he was last in New York.

Emilie wrote through the Christmas season, when Beacon Hill glowed with old-fashioned Christmas spirit. It literally glowed, with traditional, gas lanterns on the streets and newly lit candles in residents' windows. She wrote that feeling into her story. Far from all she had known, Janice felt the comfort of "home."

Stars, like a million lighted windows. They gave a sense of home glowing through the darkness, sent her courage soaring like a captive balloon let loose. All her life lighted windows had fascinated her. In the city at twilight she would pass them slowly, imagining what was going on behind them. Always to her they suggested home-coming men, someone calling, "Is that you, dear?" That had been her mother's gay, tender greeting to her menfolk. Mother. She seemed very near out here under the stars.

Boston, January 1930

Late in January, the Lorings' first granddaughter was born. They named her "Valentine," which was her mother's maiden name. Selden, Mary, little Victor, and Valentine lived at 6 Hancock Avenue in a rather new, Dutch Colonial Revival house which was valued at ten-thousand dollars, even after the crash.

"Now don't you worry. Remember there's a gate in every wall."
Lighted Windows

What a time they had all come through—fear and fortitude, death and birth, the end of one family and the beginnings of another. When tested, Emilie lived up to the historical motto of the Baker family: *dum spiro spero*, While I breathe, I hope. At the end of February, she signed a contract with Penn for *Lighted Windows*, and dedicated it:

> To the readers of my stories who, by spoken or written word, have recognized beneath the magic glamour of romance and adventure the clear flame of my belief that the beautiful things of life are as real as the ugly things of life, that gay courage may turn threatened defeat into victory, that hitching one's wagon to the star of achievement will lift one high above the quicksands of discouragement.

By then, ten thousand copies of *Swift Water* had already sold, and the novel went into its third printing. Mr. Shoemaker and Penn Publishing took first option on her next two titles and urged her to get started right away.

Her next idea came from Louise and Lizzy Hallet. At the moment, they were in Europe, living in London's Goring Hotel, but last summer, they had reminisced with Emilie and Robert about their years together in Barnstable. Her new story was nostalgic. From an old, model-ship collection to black bands on village chimneys and her mother's menu for Thanksgiving, *Fair Tomorrow* exuded old times on the Cape.

As the novel opens, Pamela Leigh's mother is dead, and her father is married to a fortune-hunter who took off when the family lost its fortune in the financial crash. Aided by her brother Terry, Pamela opens the Silver Moon Chowder House in a home filled with antiques that she inherited from her grandmother. Her father lives upstairs, ill and irascible, and debt collectors are at the door.

> How life tore at one's heart. Was it ever simple? For her there seemed always some crippling complication. Would she go on for years fighting herself? Fighting in a circle?

Duty keeps her there, but Pamela has dreams for herself. She has written newspaper features and hopes to write novels someday.

> "I haven't touched my typewriter for months. Looking back from the 1950s I may sparkle on the pages of Who's Who, but at present my name is not one to be used on a magazine cover to lure subscribers."

Her brother encourages:

> "Brace up, Pam. We'll get out of the woods yet. Remember that poem of Holman Day's I came across the other day about the two frogs in the pail of milk? One gave up and was drowned. The other kicked till he churned an island of butter and hopped out." He patted her shoulder. "Kick, frog, kick! Don't you worry about me . . ."

Pamela laughed. Not too steadily, not too convincingly, but it passed.

"Managing the Silver Moon is just one disillusioning experience after another, isn't it?"
Fair Tomorrow

Attorney Scott Mallory comes to the Silver Moon looking for an old-fashioned Thanksgiving dinner. By the end of the evening, he is engaged to help the Leighs with their legal and financial concerns and is smitten with the spirited Pamela Leigh.

So much of the story mirrored Emilie's years in Barnstable: isolation in an old-fashioned setting, a sick father who collected stamps,[1] a brother who had to leave school, and falling in love with a Boston lawyer. The relief she felt at returning to Boston is evident: "The city! The adorable city! She had been starved for it."

The parts about writing were autobiographical, too. Pamela sees the events in her life as elements for future stories.

> "Let's make a plot diagram for today, Terry. We will call the adver-
> tiser who is coming, A, and his friend, B. C is their objective, the
> house to which they return from here. Perhaps I'll get a story germ."

Emilie said that her characters were composites of people she had known, and the story's father was a good example. His interest in stamps came from George Baker, who was listed as a collector in *The American Philatelist*. The character's reclusive and defensive personality, however, came from Louise Hallet's father who suffered from syphilis during those years at the Cape and withdrew from all around him.

This novel also incorporated one of her earlier short stories. Stephen Mallory's counsel came from her 1930 story, "By Audacity Alone Are High Things Accomplished."[2]

> "The element of risk is inseparable from any business enterprise,
> but there is such a thing as open-eyed risks. If one never embarked
> on a project for fear it might turn out a failure, one never would
> get far."

There had been two times in her life when Emilie had felt alone. The first was after her father's death, when it was impossible to imagine that the sun of their family orbit was gone. This was the other time. No one she knew had grown up in a family like hers. Now, even Robert was gone, the last person who understood.

The road proved not so straight as she remembered. Was it because she was alone? Now that the tumult and the shouting within her had died down she would better check-up emotionally, her life seemed all loose ends. Where was she going?

Robert's son, Mel, struggled, too, though on the surface, he appeared to thrive. *One Romantic Night*, the film version of his play, *The Swan*, debuted in May with Lillian Gish in her talkie debut. In off hours, he played cards with screenwriters Frances Goodrich and Albert Hackett (*The Thin Man*, *The Diary of Anne Frank*), sometimes with F. Scott Fitzgerald and Ogden Nash, who described Mel as "greener than ever."[3]

His lifestyle and coping with his father's gruesome death took a toll on Mel's marriage. Gladys filed for divorce in April, and their divorce was finalized in May. For a time, he boarded with a movie studio art director, but his inheritance soon paid for a brand-new home in Bel Air.

Blue Hill, Summer 1930

Losses continued through the summer. Before they left for Blue Hill, the Lorings learned that Ned Brooks of Elwin Cove had died at his New Jersey home.[4] Ned's wife and daughter came to Blue Hill in July, and so did David, Minnie, and Bessie Owen. But Blossom Alcott now lived in the Curtis' cottage beyond Sculpin Point, and the Lorings' cottage across the road remained empty. Judge William McAdoo had rented it again for the summer, but he died suddenly, in New York.[5]

Perhaps the hardest Blue Hill loss came next. Elizabeth Gray "Bessie" Owen came down with what everyone thought was a minor illness, but she died on August ninth.

> Friends of Miss Elizabeth G. Owen were shocked to hear of her sudden death last Saturday evening, after a brief illness. Miss Owen was a native of Philadelphia and had been a summer resident of Bluehill for over twenty years. She was one of the most popular members of the summer colony and was admired and respected by all who knew her.[6]

Bessie wasn't buried in Tyn Y Coed's garden with her sister Carrie. Instead, she was buried at Seaside Cemetery, near the plot where Anne Nevin had moved her husband, Paul. Her epitaph read, "The dawn of a glad morning." Eventually, Carrie would be moved to Seaside, but as long as there were Owens at Tyn Y Coed, her grave remained in the sunken garden; it was too dear a shrine.

Mary Curtis, two of the Owen sisters, Ned Brooks . . . The deaths of so many friends near Emilie's age were enough to make anyone feel vulnerable. The East Blue Hill Road would have been lonesome but for the comfort and company of family. Robert, Selden, and Mary came for weeks at a time, and now they brought grandchildren, too.

With renters across the road and small children to manage, the Lorings realized the need for better routes through their property and down to the shore. Loring Road made a neat loop down to Tyn Y Coed, past several small quarry holes, and back up to the East Blue Hill Road, but the only way to get to Sculpin Point was still on a footpath through thick woods. They laid out the road and got started, but this project was going to take much time and effort.

A storm blew down trees onto the log cabin in the woods.[7] The well-intended start on Emilie's writer's retreat would never be completed, except in fiction. Instead, Emilie adopted the "gun room," immediately to

Tea on the Stone House Veranda, 1930

the left when entering the front door. She placed her writing desk so that she could look out over the kitchen ell's flower garden and hung Manning de V. Lee's oil painting for *Gay Courage* above it. She sharpened her pencils and sat down to write.

> Nothing now between her and her chosen work. Life, liberty, and the pursuit of plot germs! At present her mind was empty of ideas for stories and articles as a squeezed orange was of juice; but once she touched her typewriter they would come trooping along, she knew from experience.

> Victor, her husband of almost forty years, was imperturbable. His stalwart presence was reassuring.

> Fair tomorrow! Terrifying and disillusioning much of the year behind her; but fair tomorrow and all the tomorrows so long as she and Scott were together, Pamela told herself passionately . . .

Gay Courage *Writing Desk*

After all, it was Scott, who, since the day he had stepped into the green and white kitchen had been unfailingly tender; Scott, who loved her, with whom she was crossing this strange threshold. Her radiant eyes confirmed the lilt in her voice as she answered: "Happy? Top of the world!"

Emilie's *Lighted Windows* came out in late August 1930, but after nearly a decade of submissions, Clara Endicott Sears' novel, *Nephew Dave*, had still not found a publisher. Like their fellow Boston Athenaeum writer, Alice Brown, she seemed to have written "what nobody wants."[8]

That was never going to stop Clara. For sixty-four years, her mother had been the mistress of their family home on Beacon Street. After her death, Clara had taken charge with an energy that was not only resilient but forceful.

She moved the entrance from the narrow side facing Beacon Street to create a broad, impressive façade on Berkeley. She removed dormers,

From the long window she looked out at the Basin. It was the time of day she loved. Blue sky turning pink and violet beyond the Technology Buildings . . .
Keepers of the Faith

added windows, even moved floors and ceilings, so that every space inside was truly new. The third floor was especially grand, with soaring ceilings and an outside balcony overlooking the Charles River.

From her multi-million-dollar collection, she donated the full-size portrait of her sister, Mary, to Boston's Museum of Fine Arts but kept the pair of French vases that had belonged to Napoleon's wife, the Empress Josephine. Her own youthful portrait, painted in France, stayed, and she commissioned a new likeness of herself, wearing her favorite hat and pearls.

Ever the preserver of someone else's history, Clara yearned to leave a lasting mark of her own. She had no children, no best-selling books. Her most personal mark was the design of her homes, but she must have known, even then, that those would not last.

Her biggest writing success, so far, was her recent poem, "Hymn to America." Set to music by Mrs. M. H. Gulesian, the song was endorsed by the Massachusetts State Board of Education and sent to all of the schools in the state. Twelve-thousand Girl Scouts sang it in May, and a choir of four hundred public school children sang it for a patriotic celebration in Symphony Hall.[9]

But Clara was determined to get her second novel into print. She changed the title to *Whispering Pines: A Romance on a New England Hillside* and contracted with the Enterprise Press in Falmouth, Massachusetts (Cape Cod) to print one-thousand copies. Her preface expressed some of the nostalgia that Emilie felt, too:

> The world changes. Times change. People change. Habits change. Standards change. Life in the country villages has changed.
>
> Types of character are as historically interesting and revealing as events. I write of those recorded in this story with affection, for I have known most of them. Before the memory of them is gone I want to preserve them. They belong to the old, picturesque days before the World War.

She put down carefully the one she had been examining, a lovely thing of mother-of-pearl with an exquisite miniature of the Empress Josephine. "Did this really belong to Napoleon?"
Forsaking All Others

Mrs. Gulesian was a summer resident of Falmouth. Straight away, she went to work, "composing theme songs for 'Whispering Pines' in anticipation of its appearance in the movies."[10] Emilie enthused:

My dear—Whispering Pines arrived yesterday. Isn't it grand! This is just to let you know that I have it. Have not had a chance to read it. Victor claims first chance at the story.[11]

Then, when she got her chance:

I started the story, sat on the edge of my chair through the horse race, then put the book aside for a few days. I was writing something myself and I found myself so enveloped in Harvard atmosphere that I was afraid that it might creep into my story. You have done a most artistic, convincing piece of work in your setting. Your characters are alive. I will ask you a question which is so often asked me: How did you, in your environment, ever conceive such a deep-dyed villain as Buck Cragin? I liked David and I had a sneaking fondness for his uncle. You have added a vivid book to your literary family. I appreciate my autographed copy. Hope that it will run into several editions. It should.[12]

Whispering Pines' two editions totaled only two thousand copies. There would be no movie.

Boston, Fall 1930

Emilie signed the contract for *Fair Tomorrow* on her birthday, September 5, 1930, and dedicated the story "To Louise Gordon Hallet, whose friendship has glowed with a lovely light down through the years since we met on Cape Cod." Due to the uncertainties of the Depression,

Mr. Shoemaker took a forty-five-day option on her next book only, and not her next two, as had been his custom.

She had kept up a fast schedule and turned in two finished manuscripts in one year. Work kept her from fretting, but it also kept her from coming to peace in her mind. She missed Robert, she missed her old life, she missed her friends.

Victor, Robert, and all of Selden's family drove off in the Lorings' new motor car and left Emilie in Blue Hill for a week by herself.[13] At last, she had space to think, and as she had done so often before, she worked out her ideas in a story. Grief for her brother poured out in the thoughts of her next character, Sandra Duval.

She had thought that during the months since her father's death she had plumbed the depths of loneliness, but never had she known loneliness of the spirit like this. There was desolation in it and heartache unbelievable.

Now he was gone, and she was like thousands of others in these United States, a girl on her own.

It made one curiously shivery to realize that one was the last of one's family. The dogs and Irish Bridie were her only confidantes, but she could not say to them: "Do you remember when . . . ?"

Her father had said the last day they had been together: "Remember, Sandy, that the future holds nothing that your unconquerable soul, your faith, your trust cannot meet." Had she an unconquerable soul? Time alone would tell.

Sandra Duval is a girl on her own. At the advice of her father's old friend, she takes a position as social secretary to horsewoman Pat Newsome at her country estate, Seven Chimneys. Nicholas Hoyt arranges to pick her

As the days passed, her sense of aloneness grew rather than diminished. Sometimes when she woke in the night and couldn't sleep, she would get panicky, thinking distorted thoughts of what illness would mean; it seemed as if she could hear the hours hurrying along.
Uncharted Seas

Curious things, doors, one never knew what lay behind them, she thought, as she had thought once before that day, and pressed the bell.
Uncharted Seas

Seven Chimneys

up at the station, pretending he is a down-on-his-luck horse trainer instead of a crack-a-jack horseman and the owner of neighboring Stone House.

The setting is clearly Blue Hill, with both Stone House and Seven Chimneys used by name. At the time when Emilie wrote, Mrs. Linus Coggan still lived there, daughter-in-law to Victor's former colleague, Marcellus Coggan.[14] Later remodeling removed the chimneys, but the Coggans' home survived atop its promontory in Blue Hill's inner bay.

"Nicholas Hoyt" was another local detail, a nod to Blue Hill's first town moderator, Nicholas Holt. Holt's grandson, Thomas Jefferson Napoleon Bonaparte Holt, married Clarissa Peters and was an original owner of the Lorings' Stone House.

Along comes Philippe Rousseau (another Blue Hill name), a claimant to Nick's property and the owner of Iron Man, which will compete with Nick's horse, Fortune. Sandy is torn between Philippe, whom she met in Europe, and Nick, who keeps intruding into her thoughts.

If this were love—and it was, she admitted it—it was the most distracting experience of her life.
Uncharted Seas

. . . she had a curious presentiment that after today she never would be quite the same person again, that the old pattern would be torn to shreds and a new pattern substituted. It was a curious sensation.

Emilie gave the story a good start and then returned to Boston. By then, Selden and Mary had moved from Hancock Street to 55 Bloomfield Street in Lexington. The attractive two-story would remain in Selden's family more than eighty years.

Little Victor was about three years old at the time. In later years, he recounted that he was taking a nap in the afternoon, and when he woke up, his "Grandmama" began combing his hair. "We have a surprise for you," she said. "Grandpapa" had a black and white dog in his lap. "This is Mr. Bingo," Emilie said. Little Victor went up to the dog, whose head was on its paws. When he reached out to pet Mr. Bingo, the dog snapped at him, but they kept the pup anyway.[15]

Writing on the Athenaeum's fifth floor, Emilie set the characters of *Uncharted Seas* in motion again. Life at Seven Chimneys is so complicated that Sandra has little time to think of her own problems. The maid is sneaky, her employer is bitter, and the rest are either trying to "fix" the horse race, steal someone else's property, or find out who is.

> She had the end of a thread to a mystery in her fingers. If she kept pulling and following it must get her somewhere.
> *Uncharted Seas*

. . . She hated to hurt anyone. Life took care of that. It kept such a lot of heartaches up its sleeve which it dealt out impartially like cards from a pack, making sure each human got a few in his hand to make of them what he could.

It was going to be a lean Christmas for many that year, and Emilie wrote "Christmas Ships" for the magazine *Youth* with a way to give gifts that wouldn't cost money. She suggested writing letters with themes and filled with information.

She looked for color, drama, beauty. She searched for "human variety" and sent them out as "Christmas Ships." Freighted with love and her best work, they would set sail from her room . . .

Tough economic times fueled a nationwide crime spree. Four times, burglars used fake keys to enter Victor Loring's office on Street and tried—but failed—to open the safe.[16] Holdups and robberies increased. From gems, payrolls and cars to purses and pocket change, crime was rampant. Gangsters stole with impunity, but so did schoolboys. For the first time, the Boston police provided security for Beacon Hill's Christmas carolers.

Despite the economy, sales for *Lighted Windows* soared. One Boston bookstore vouched that a man bought *fifty-three* copies for Christmas gifts.[17] Again, Emilie had sensed the public's need—and hers, also—"that gay courage may turn threatened defeat into victory."

The popularity of *Swift Water* and *Lighted Windows* put a spotlight on Emilie. *The Editor* asked her to write an article about how she had come up with the idea for *Lighted Windows* and published her essay in December.

So many years ago that the paper on which it was printed has yellowed, I clipped from a newspaper the following:

LOST: Sunday night, black satin slipper with buckle.

I dropped the advertisement into my notebook, sure that sometime it would make a story. Occasionally I would come across it, say to myself, "It's good," and put it back. One day it struck a spark in my imagination. I decided to use it. Problems arose at once. How? Why? Where?

I sat down at my typewriter and stuck the clipping in front of me. I gazed unseeingly at the black letters and numerals on the keyboard of the machine. Then, as clearly as you see the print you are reading, I saw:

Fifth Avenue. In that quiet hour before dawn when for a trifling interval the city dozes, it never sleeps. The gleaming asphalt, blanched to silvery whiteness by arc lights, stretched ahead illimitably between looming skyscrapers, phantoms of concrete and steel, brick and glass, shadowy and unreal as the backdrop in a pantomime. In the middle of its polished sur- face, like a dark isle in a glistening ribbon of river, rested a slipper. Black, satin, buckled with brilliants which caught the light and threw it back transmuted into a thousand colorful sparks. A slipper of parts, unquestionably.

So far so good. I had planted the slipper. Now what? Almost before I could answer the question:

Bruce Harcourt stopped short in his long stride to regard it incredulously. How had it come there? He looked up and down the broad deserted avenue before he salvaged it. A spot of red light was dimming eastward.

It was not all so easy as that. I spent almost a year writing the story. Enthusiastic readers of "Lighted Windows" (Penn Publish- ing Company) write me that they sit up all night to finish it. That is the result for which I worked. When I commence to tell a story, like the Ancient Mariner who held the Bridegroom with his skiny [sic] hand and glittering eye, I say to my reader:

"Now listen. Don't move till I get through."

Even then, when a person says to me, "I couldn't put the book down until I had finished it," the remark is like fingers at my throat, I am so touched and thrilled."[18]

Boston, Spring 1931

Economics delayed publication of *Fair Tomorrow*, but *Lighted Windows* went into a third edition in May. At the price of two dollars apiece, Emilie earned fifteen percent, or thirty cents, per copy. With ten thousand copies per printing, she had earned nine thousand dollars since August ($143,000 in 2023 dollars).

Publishers sought "fewer and better books," and it was a compliment to be published at all. Little, Brown, for example, published ninety-three new books in 1930 and only sixty-seven in 1931.[19] That made it harder to judge an author's readership. The public bought fewer books and relied on libraries instead. Fewer copies were sold, but each book had more readers; privately owned, it might be read several times, but in a library, hundreds might read it.

Sara Ware Bassett was also among the favored. Finally returned to good health, she wrote her seventh novel, *Bayberry Lane*. Like Joseph Lincoln's, her upbeat Cape Cod stories had a ready audience. Mr. Shoemaker scheduled that book for summer release, and she started on her next, *Twin Lights*. She wrote steadily thereafter, "groping my way toward the goal my heart is set upon and which I well know I shall never reach."[20]

Clara Endicott Sears' accomplishment for the spring was the installation of a sculpture of Pumunangwet, *He Who Shoots the Stars*, at her American Indian Museum. Victor and Emilie joined a large gathering to witness the unveiling and dedication. Clara treated the assemblage to luncheon and appearances by a representative from the Sioux tribe in impressive ceremonial dress, Boy and Girl Scouts bearing banners and flags, and an orchestra. A bugler sounded *reveille*, David Buffalo Bear called the statue to awaken, and the blankets shrouding the bronze were pulled away.[21]

Emilie finished *Uncharted Seas* before she left for Blue Hill. Philippe Rousseau proves false in every way, and before the finish line of a race, Nick's jockey, Mrs. Newsome's husband, is killed in a fall.

"Life itself isn't cruel, Pat." No ice in his voice now; it was protectingly gentle. There are cruel hours, perhaps days, sometimes months, but there are radiant spots in between—otherwise we couldn't bear it."
Uncharted Seas

She gripped Nicholas Hoyt's arm. "Nick—Nick—Curt's fall was an accident, wasn't it?"

"Sure, Pat. Something—something broke and—and he pitched over Fortune's head."

Mrs. Newsome's drooping mouth trembled; tragic skepticism

hardened her eyes. She shrugged her heavy shoulders.

"Something broke in equipment belonging to you? That's a joke. Trying to let me down easy. I get you. Curt's heart broke."

The details of her brother's death still played in her mind—Robert gasping for air at the open window, failing to see the sill, and falling to the sidewalk below. Her character's fall over the head of his racehorse suggested that she considered the possibility that Robert's fall was intentional. "Trying to let me down easy; I get you."

But she had turned the corner on grief, and despite every loss of the past years, *Uncharted Seas* was a call to dream again:

Dreams are the source of much of the new thinking, new convictions, new power in the world. They send the adventurous out on uncharted seas, dangerous seas, and it is danger, not security, which develops strength in mind and spirit. (Dedication)

This was the first story in which she used "happy landings," a fixture in her books from then on. A 1930 musical about aviation, *Flying High*, featured a chorus called "Happy Landing," and the phrase had been a popular send-off in aviation since the 1920s. "You blazed the way for others to follow," read a congratulatory telegram to Charles Lindbergh on the first anniversary of his New York to Paris flight. "Many happy landings."[22]

After *Swift Water's* theme of loss and *Fair Tomorrow's* faith that better times were ahead, "uncharted seas" combined with "happy landings" was Emilie Loring's buoyant optimism coming through. In *Uncharted Seas*, Sandra Duval is literally carried by a Happy Landing—it's the name of her horse—and when she is thrown, she exclaims, laughingly, "A happy landing. See it? Speed but no control." The phrase could be used humorously, ironically, or sincerely, but like a talisman, Emilie Loring used "happy landings" in every book thereafter.

Boston, 1931–1932

Emilie's sixty-fifth birthday found its way into *Uncharted Seas*: "I'm not so juvenile as to consider sixty-five old." A manuscript she had on hand expanded on her thoughts:

Keep in the vanguard of progress and eager, enthusiastic living, forgetful, except as they enrich life, that the years are passing. Enthusiasm, absorbing interests, have a marvelous, unbelievable way of keeping one mentally and physically fit and tinglingly alive. The years bestow great gifts. A sense of values. The inestimable power to see things in their right proportions, the small things small and the large things large, the opportunity to translate the bright and shining dreams and visions of youth into gorgeous reality.

Forget age. Take hold of life vividly.[23]

Emilie's birthday presents were the August return of the Hallet sisters from Europe and the publishing of Selden Loring's original play, *Little Sherlock,* in September. Selden's story followed the family formula: a case of mistaken identity, a mysterious butler, and much confusion before who's who becomes clear.

Later in the month, one year after its contract, *Fair Tomorrow* finally debuted in bookstores. The *Boston Globe*'s review probed the reason for her success, "a quality in certain writers of fiction:"

Thackeray has it, and DuMaurier and Barrie. They love their characters, and they love their incident. It isn't that they "circus" their stories, but they tell them with a certain enthusiasm that will make tame plots fascinating, and people, who probably wouldn't be much noticed in a crowd, terribly important. Also, this quality makes their tales live and beloved. Emilie Loring has this quality.

Emilie turned the article she had written for *The Editor*, about the beginnings of *Lighted Windows*, into a "shop talk" that she gave to the members of the Boston Authors Club in October. She called it "A Writer in the Making,"[24] and the focus was less on the book than on the many steps she had taken along the road to authorship. Her talk was a hit, and she repeated it for library clubs across Massachusetts.

Nationwide, unemployment neared twenty-five percent, and farmers abandoned drought-stricken farms. Major publishers, for the first time, showed no profit. They printed only half as many books that year as they had in 1929.[25] No-cost entertainment flourished, and in March, more than five hundred women attended a play presented by the Women's Professional Club at the Hotel Statler.[26] A week later, Clara Endicott Sears hosted the Boston Pen Women at her renovated home on Beacon Street, where Emilie presented "A Writer in the Making," and a soprano sang three poems of Miss Sears' that were set to music by Mrs. Grace Warner Gulesian.[27]

The next day, Emilie was an honored guest—along with three military men, two Broadway actresses, a sculptor, and a bandleader—at yet another performance hosted by the Women's Professional Club. A quartet from the Boston Symphony played several pieces, but the focus of the night was actor Conrad Nagle (who had recently starred in Mel Baker's *One Romantic Night*), who spoke in support of the motion picture industry and against censorship.

The 1930 Motion Picture Production Code remained controversial, and its censorship guidelines were unevenly enforced. The Boston Authors Club maintained that "censorship is what should be censored" and recalled Dr. Johnson's answer to the question, "Sir, don't you think the Venus de Medici is indecent?" "Sir, I think the question is."[28]

Emilie Loring was not a boundary-pusher, but neither was she a prude or ignorant of contemporary society. Her books had already broken with three stipulations of the censorship code.

According to the guidelines, all crime had to be punished, and the criminal could not be portrayed sympathetically, but Millicent Hale

(*Lighted Windows*) kills her husband, and the authorities agree it is only a tragic mistake. Authority had to be treated with respect, and clergy could not be made to look ridiculous or villainous, but Luther Calvin was portrayed as both in *Swift Water*. Scenes with real or suggested nudity were prohibited, but Julie Lorraine (*Here Comes the Sun!*) removes her wet dress and sits companionably with Jim Trafford, wearing only a borrowed robe and slippers, just minutes after first setting eyes on him. Now, *Uncharted Seas* touched on the banned topic of suicide.

Emilie Loring was the only author who was recognized at the meeting; her sales were soaring. The Boston Authors Club newsletter reported that the second edition of *Fair Tomorrow* sold out so fast that Plimpton Press scrambled to get a third edition out in four days' time, "a rush order which probably has seldom if ever been equaled."[29]

Blue Hill, Summer 1932

Emilie signed the contract for *Uncharted Seas* on June tenth, before she left for Blue Hill, and Penn Publishers had it in bookstores on August twenty-sixth.[30] No more twelve-month delays for an Emilie Loring book; the public would buy them as fast as they were written. Penn's advertising copy read, "In this adventure romance of a New England countryside, with a background of the turf world, this popular author is in her happiest mood."

Uncharted Seas was Emilie Loring's first, bona-fide best-seller. "In fact, it is one romance so nicely diversified in its interests and incidents that there is not a tedious page in it. And it is all written in a manner that so holds your interest, you fairly live through some of the incidents yourself."[31]

Sara Ware Bassett's *Twin Lights* came out at the same time ("an old-fashioned, quaintly sweet and sentimental tale"), and Temple Bailey's *Little Girl Lost* ahead of them in July ("another of her Cinderella tales in modern dress"). Emilie's sales numbers were ahead of Sara Ware Bassett's and far behind Temple Bailey's, but they had different audiences. The heroines of Bailey's and Bassett's novels had the spunk of real women, but their ideas of romance were no more developed than their authors had lived themselves. Temple still lived with her mother and Sara Ware with her older sister.

The *Boston Herald*'s literary editor, John Clair Minot, wrote a full-column review that summarized Emilie Loring's status:

> The novels of Mrs. Loring are getting close to half a score—good romances all of them, glowing with life and swinging along with vigorous action. Each one in turn has revealed a surer touch, a more confident mastery of the craft of building an engaging and convincing story. Early in the series the last trace of the beginner vanished . . .

He ended, "And it is a relief that Mrs. Loring speaks of 'the late depression.'"[32]

The Lorings crossed Blue Hill Bay and paid visits to their friends in Bar Harbor that summer. Lizzie and Louise Hallet, along with their spats-wearing chauffeur, Peter Hamill, registered at the Belmont Hotel in late July to stay through August. Dr. Frederick Jack, one of the ushers at Emilie and Victor's wedding, joined them for several weeks. The resort community hosted lectures, tea parties, boating, live theater, concerts, and dancing. This year, there was a new road to the top of Cadillac Mountain, a fireworks show, the annual flower show, and the Bar Harbor Relief Association's annual concert and ball.[33] As usual, though, the season ended after Emilie's birthday and the Blue Hill Fair.

Boston, 1932–1933

When the Lorings returned to Boston, the presidential race dominated the headlines. Emilie was a lifelong Republican and a member of the Women's Republican Club, but her tenth story echoed Democrat Franklin D. Roosevelt's October campaign speech. He argued for living within one's means, farm relief, and responsible management of the nation's timber resources. *Hilltops Clear* was about a girl who makes her own way on a small farm by selling some of the lumber on her forest land.

Prudence Schuyler has multiple loads to bear—the treachery of an affair between her sister's husband and brother's wife, her sister's sudden death, and her brother's debilitating illness. She is on her own; she must succeed on her own.

Emilie Loring's theme, "hilltops clear," came from a Congregational hymn:

> We praise thee for the journey's end
> The inn, all warmth and light and cheer,
> But more for lengthening roads that wend
> Through dust and heat to hilltops clear.[34]

Authentic Blue Hill details set the scene. Forest, shoreline, fog, and the Owens' sunken garden all contributed atmosphere.

> A cold, bone-penetrating fog transformed trees into ghostly giants, houses into weird dwarfs and filled the world. Moisture dripped from twigs and branches . . .
>
> The last of September, with flames in the maples, asters, and goldenrod outside the garden fence . . . A mother-of-pearl sail on the horizon, frills on the cobalt blue sea, a white ribbon in the wake of a speedboat. A fish-hawk sailing swift and strong in the infinite turquoise of the sky.

Emilie made no attempt to hide the similarity of Prudence Schuyler's brother, David, to her brother, Robert. She dedicated the book, "To the memory of my brother, Robert M. Baker," and many of the story's details recalled his illness, his humor, and his indefatigable spirit.

Once she had expected life to hand her the crystal ball of Happiness. Now she would consider herself lucky if she found enough shining pieces as she went along to enable her to visualize the perfect sphere.
Hilltops Clear

He was tall and pathetically thin, but he held his head, with its thick, dark hair, with royal dignity.

"Bloody but unbowed." The words flashed into Prue's mind as she looked up at him. His deep-set eyes, his perfect nose, his sensitive lips blurred for an instant. As if he read her thoughts, his hand tightened on her shoulder.

"Everything's going to be all right now, Prue. Already I feel stronger."

Prue raises chickens and engages Rodney Gerard to help her harvest trees from her forest. Before her back-to-the-land venture, Prue was a metal worker, as Emilie had been. Now, she supplements her income with orders for jewelry and metal boxes.

She opened a packet. With pincers she laid a large emerald in the center of a ring design on white paper, placed small diamonds. She indicated spaces.

"I want studding baguette diamonds there and there and a platinum setting. When I've made my fortune on the farm, I'll make this ring for myself."

Hilltops Clear was Emilie's most personal story, so far, and it marked a transition. The tide had turned, in the economy and in her own life. Roosevelt's campaign song might have been hers: "Happy Days Are Here Again!"

To survive was no longer enough; now she would thrive. Her stories changed from themes of resilience to "making good."

"I told you that I had put my yesterdays behind me. When I opened my eyes this morning, it seemed as if I emerged from a smothering fog into light and life—full, vigorous, courageous

Prudence laughed. "I discontented!" Somebody once said, 'Tragedy is chic but discontent is dowdy.' Now, I ask you, can you think of me as being dowdy?" *Hilltops Clear*

life—with a renewed assurance of the indestructibility of the human soul. Through the corridors of my mind echoed the fragment of a verse I haven't thought of for years:

"'Lengthening roads that wind through dust and heat to hilltops clear.' Hilltops clear! I awoke on one this morning."

Throughout the 1930s, Emilie Loring was as popular in lending libraries as she was in bookstores. The Boston Authors Club *Bulletin* lauded:

It was a pleasant bit of information we culled from a bookseller in a nearby suburb who told us that the only author whose books equaled Emilie Loring's in popularity among the lending library readers was Kathleen Norris. We were also told that a reader of one of Mrs. Loring's books could almost certainly be relied upon to come back for others of her books.[35]

She received a letter from a librarian in Melbourne, Australia:

We love your books here, and as a librarian, I am able to state that they are amongst the most popular on our bookshelves. [Ours] is one of the largest libraries in this city, and we have to buy heavily of each of your titles as they come along. For beautiful, wholesome writing we think your books are without equal.[36]

Emilie signed the contract for *Hilltops Clear* on March fourteenth. In a sign of the uncertain times, Mr. Shoemaker omitted the 45-day option on her next novel. He used to take an option on her next two, then her next one, and now, no option at all for her next novels.

That didn't matter. Advance orders on *Hilltops Clear* exceeded those for *Uncharted Seas*. Two quick printings were required to meet even the initial demand in June.

The *Daily Boston Globe* called *Hilltops Clear* "a well-written and a thoroughly pleasing romance." The *Atlanta Constitution* declared it "so full of human interest that it will appeal to every class of readers."[37]

Mr. Shoemaker pressed Emilie to "push the new story," which would become *We Ride the Gale!* Still in Boston, she wrote to Clara Endicott Sears, "It is going like a breeze and I hate to stop work to get ready to go away. Would like to have it in shape to finish before I go. If this weather will remain cool, we will not mind staying in town."[38]

Blue Hill, Summer 1933

The Lorings left Boston at 2:30 in the afternoon on July fifteenth and pulled into the Stone House driveway at 11:30 p.m., a nine-hour drive that Emilie called "a perfect trip down." Their beds were ready, and they went straight to sleep. After that, as she wrote to Clara, "Have been planting since I came and have a thousand muscles I didn't know I had!"

Vic and Val at Blue Hill, 1933

Clearing Loring Road, 1933

Selden, Mary, and their two children, Victor and Valentine, came for ten days in late August. Both families stayed in Stone House, as there was a tenant across the road, and Victor and Emilie enjoyed the little ones. "They are nice children."

Soon after they arrived, though, the cook got sick. "We got along with just the waitress for four days thinking that the cook would return. She didn't." It turned out that the young high school teacher who had been driving for them could cook. Problem solved.

The several-year project to clear Loring Road continued. The narrow roadway looped around the Stone House property, past Tyn Y Coed, to a "wood road" that led the rest of the way to Sculpin Point. With many of the trees cleared, they now used their car, a chain, and their combined muscle to move granite boulders that remained in their way.

Emilie worked on her new story but planned to write more when Victor and Robert returned to Boston for a week.

I can get a lot of work done if I stay, I hope. Victor is at this moment—there is a driving rain outside—reading the manuscript of the new story. He didn't move as he read the last half of it last evening and once, he laughed aloud, so I hope that it has its points.

We Ride the Gale's plot develops around Sonia Carson who wants Guy Farr to acknowledge her deceased sister Ruby's son as his own. Sonia and the boy come to live at Kingscourt, the home of Guy's brother Michael, who is as principled and responsible as his brother is not. To manage local gossip, Aunt Serena Farr concocts a story that Sonia and Ruby were long-lost cousins. This was a massaged family detail: Emilie's cousin Frank Boles had a daughter named Ruby who died young.

The central plot was like one of Victor Loring's legal cases in the 1920s. A young boy had remained with his aunt since his mother's death, and although he'd had no part in his son's life, the father refused to give up custody.

The personality difference between the Farr brothers, Michael and Guy, also had a basis in truth. Emilie's elder son, Robert, remained unmarried, a bit of a playboy, and more cynical in nature than her younger son, Selden.

"No woman will ever slip the ball-and-chain on me ..."

[Guy] hadn't liked the shifting of his brother's eyes when he had declared that his life was an open book. The present leaf might be clean, but the preceding pages would make snappy reading, or he would miss his guess.

As she chose the theme for this story, Emilie considered the troubles and challenges of the recent past—Minnie Baker, who went out shopping and came back a widow:

One moment her husband had been with her, laughing, singing, babbling that he was "b-boilin' hot," and in a second he had flashed out of life with the speed of the meteor she had watched.

She thought of her own loneliness:

It was a strange and lonely feeling to be the last grown-up of one's family.

And she thought about the millions who lost so much during the Crash, for so many reasons:

"I have lost my job. I have a hundred dollars in a bank. What does a bank account amount to these days?"

"Let me see, the Carsons were swept off in the flu epidemic— *the* flu epidemic—that sets them far enough back so there will not be embarrassing questions."

For many reasons, life could change drastically in just an instant.

"Bret Harte said that the only sure thing about luck is that it will change. Remember that? Of course you don't. Who reads Bret Harte now?

"A terrifying moment. A moment at the crossroads. A moment patched with the grim shadows of possible mistakes and the glitter of traps for her hesitant feet. Everything was bound to change and never be the same again.

But loss wasn't her message now. Perseverance was.

The story had come down through the generations that once when menaced by the fury of a storm, with his ship tossing like a chip in foaming seas, with wind roaring, spray hissing, the rigging rattling, moaning, creaking, splitting, he had clung to a mast, had shaken his fist at the mountainous waves, had shouted above the tumult:

"Damn you! We ride the gale!"

His defiance had been handed from father to son as the Farr challenge to difficulties and defeat: "We ride the gale!"

There was a reason to ride out the storm. Survivors got to their destinations. They made good on their dreams and promises.

Sonia, an architect, designs a row of cottages:

"This is my chance. The chance for which I have been waiting for years. I couldn't turn it down. I've got to try out my ideas."

There it was! Her house! The house she had planned with such thrilled conviction that it would be a gem. The windows seemed like friendly eyes beaming a welcome.

And Michael Farr makes good in local politics.

"I don't expect to prove a miracle-man and make over the world, but I do expect to take a crack at crime prevention and make a dent at least."

For twenty minutes they listened. When he had finished, an ovation shook the roof.

Boston, Fall 1933

Victor and Emilie returned to Boston after her birthday in September and began the social rounds. They dined at the Hotel Lincolnshire on Charles Street and motored out to Harvard to have tea with Clara Endicott Sears at her Fruitlands Tea Room. "The Late Christopher Bean" with Pauline Lord was playing at New York's Majestic Theater, and Emilie offered to get tickets, if Clara wanted to go.[39] She sent a note afterward,

> As always, when I turn and wave to you standing in the doorway, the bottom drops out of things for a minute, I so hate to go and leave you alone. And then I think that if you didn't want to be alone, you wouldn't be, and I feel a little better.[40]

She wrote another letter to Clara in November, after she signed the contract for *We Ride the Gale!*

> My dear,
> Because of its timeliness and because world conditions change so fast that a book should be published as it comes hot from the typewriter—stories like mine, I mean—my publishers have decided to bring out my new book, *We Ride the Gale!* about the first of February.
>
> If you have no objection, I would like to use the enclosed dedication. When you consider it just realize that your name will be used thousands of times and, if this book sells as have my others, will go on through the years. If you have the slightest feeling against having it so used, don't hesitate to say so. I shall quite understand and remain, as always,
>
> Devotedly yours,
Emilie Loring[41]

Clara agreed. The dedication read, "To Clara Endicott Sears, whose stirring poems and buoyant spirit have helped many a storm-tossed mariner Ride the Gale!"[42]

Emilie's reference to "stories like mine, I mean" was a courtesy to Clara, whose latest, *The Great Powwow*, was accepted by Houghton Mifflin but faced a publication lag of nearly a year. Their relative positions had changed. Clara Endicott Sears remained above her in social status, but as an author, Emilie's success easily outstripped Clara's. She was right; if *We Ride the Gale!* sold "as have my others," it would continue through many editions.

Pragmatically, Clara gave up on novels to concentrate on history and poetry, which were nearer her nature and better suited to her talents. Sara Ware Bassett and Emilie Loring, however, started new novels. Sara Ware's was *Turning Tide*. Emilie's was *With Banners*.

CHAPTER 24
Make Good: 1934-39

With Banners began, as her writing did, at Thanksgiving. Brooke Reyburn has just inherited a home and income that will allow her to live comfortably on her own. Her new house is divided down the middle, and attorney Mark Trent lives in the other half.

Mark thinks Brooke's inheritance is invalid and that the entire house should be his. Where is the will he signed? He moves in next door to search. Meanwhile, Brooke's brother decides to stage a community play, and Brooke's household staff are up to no good.

Emilie often used writing to give herself something she wanted badly. This time, it was her family. Brooke's mother, Mrs. Reyburn, is Mrs. Baker; Lucette is Emilie's sister, Rachel; and Sam is her brother, Robert. Brooke's father, like Emilie's, had died years before.

Brooke's throat contracted as her glance rested on the large, flat-topped mahogany desk. That, as well as the books had been her father's. There had been no room for them in the apartment. If only he could have lived to share her good fortune. He had been such a wonderful father.

Brooke's mother spoke for Emilie, who was nearing seventy:

"I'm getting used, though not resigned, to picking up the paper and seeing that someone with whom I had played cards, perhaps the day before, had been paged, had been touched on the shoulder with that mysterious summons: 'Wanted on long distance, madam.'"

Mrs. Reyburn smiled and nodded. She would make her home-coming children think she had had a nice day, if the heavens had fallen. She was like that.
With Banners

That steels her determination to get more out of life.

"I love life! I wouldn't give up my place in this problem-logged world for all the starry halos and golden harps you could offer."

Brooke's family supports her acceptance of the inheritance, but they have their own dreams to pursue.

Mother Reyburn: "I want—I want to be in the heart of things. I'll have an experienced maid, I'll have the right clothes, and—and I'll go places, I'm dying to go places."

Brother Sam: "That play is my declaration of faith that there is a big theatre public for things that matter, for something besides sordid infidelities and bawdy lines."

Sister Lucette: "I'm going to work as Brooke worked till I get her job and hit the airlanes."

Brooke feels challenged but confident.

As she waited for the telephone call to go through, she told herself that she had learned one inestimable lesson: she had learned that for every person the gateway to success was in himself; that achievement was a matter of keeping on keeping on, of giving one's best and trying, everlastingly trying to make that best better.

That statement summed up where Emilie was, personally and professionally—"a matter of keeping on keeping on, of giving one's best and trying, everlastingly trying to make that best better."

"Sam is ambitious to write for the professional stage; he has one three-act comedy finished—that is, as finished as a play can be until it is put into rehearsal. That is why he is acting, that he may know all there is to know of stage technic."
With Banners

Boston, Spring 1934

We Ride the Gale! debuted in mid-February 1934, "a stormy romance with amusing and thrilling adventures."[1] Penn's advertising called it "As up-to-date as Blue Eagles," referring to the insignia of President Roosevelt's National Recovery Act. The *Philadelphia Inquirer* acknowledged "the increasing popularity of Emilie Loring."[2]

John Clair Minot praised in the *Boston Herald*, "It is her strongest novel yet. It tells a good story well, which is the real test of a novel, after all, and it leads the reader through a plot that does not seem artificial to a satisfactory ending without clogging up the vigorous action with too much sugary substance." Further, "we have followed Mrs. Loring's work through a dozen volumes of increasing sureness of touch, from those beginnings when she was merely a writer of first-class romantic tales until **she has won an undisputed place among our novelists of importance.**"[3] [emphasis added]

She autographed books at the Jordan Marsh Department Store, "one of the most successful personal appearances in the long list of authors who have been seen in Boston bookstores."

She also gave the first shop talk of the spring season at the Boston Authors Club.[4] Again, she spoke about "A Writer in the Making," but this time she added the way that she selected her titles, including her latest.

During the late, if not lamented, bank holiday, depositors were notified that on a certain day the munificent sum of ten dollars might be drawn from each account. When I entered the bank, I was amazed by the atmosphere of cheer. The crowded room seemed like an afternoon tea running on eight cylinders. Everyone was gay, everyone was laughing and chatting. I thought: "This is a flame of the spirit which dared the wilderness, which sent descendants of the pioneers across the prairies in covered wagons, which urged them on to the adventure on unknown rivers and seas, the spirit on which American character was built." Into my mind flashed, "We Ride the Gale!" "There's the title for the novel I'm writing now," I told myself, and sure enough it was.[5]

Hilltops Clear had been out less than a year, but the Western Newspaper Union had already released it nationwide in newspapers. "You'd pay $2 for the book in any bookstore," the advertisement read. "The same novel, printed *complete* in special form as pictured above is yours, FREE, with tomorrow's *Sunday Free Press.*"

"Special form" included illustrations which the printed books did not have, but their claim that it was "the same novel" was false. Side stories were eliminated, dialogues truncated, and descriptions drastically shortened. The Puffers' black and white English setter was nowhere to be found—no dog, although she had said she always had a dog in her stories, because she loved them.

> ~~She snuggled her face against one floppy black ear.~~ "What do you think of that? ~~When you licked my hand, the fog seemed to thin, I felt almost happy. Happy. A name for you. I'll call you Happy. Happy! Like it, old dear?" The setter whacked his tail rapturously.~~

Rodney Gerard lost his mustache, and conversations lost much of their personability.

> "Oh, how tempting! ~~That array of pickles and condiments would make the original 57 Varieties hide their heads in shame.~~ Come, Macky, aren't you starved? Mrs. Puffer, won't you sit with us and serve? It will seem more homey to have you here . . ."
>
> "Dearie, I'll do just that. ~~When you smile and that deep dimple pricks through at the corner of your mouth, I feel's if I could die for you—though I guess I can be more use to you living," she added practically.~~

Key parts of Prue's and Rod's personalities were eliminated, as was verbal sparring that established the tension of their attraction to each other.

"If that invitation was meant for me, I can't go. I'm busy."
~~"You look it."~~

~~"Just because I'm sitting here with my hands in my pockets doesn't mean that I'm not working. I'm thinking.~~ The hens are approaching the season of diminishing returns—to put it conservatively, 'High yields and large profits' must be my battle-cry. Ever heard of an economic graph? Mr. Si and I have been tracing one."
~~"Come and think in the roadster. I promise not to talk."~~
~~"Don't wheedle. I can't."~~
~~"Won't, you mean."~~
~~"Won't, then, if you like that better.~~ You seem to forget that I am a woman of affairs. I can't waste time playing with idle little boys like you."

The result was a tighter narrative, but it had less of Emilie Loring in it. The story was less heartwarming.

"Macky, think of having a whole house in which to spread out after years in an apartment! We'll make it a dream. We will warm it with color till it makes hearts glow just to come into it."
~~A faint pink crept under the woman's skin. Her washed-out eyes shone with a lovely light.~~
~~"You'll make hearts glow all right, Miss Prue. Your brother said to me just before we left the apartment, 'I'm not afraid for Prue. She'll make a home wherever she is. She's like her mother.' She almost smiled. "Especially,' he said, 'if she can find rooms to re-paper.' Guess he was right; that was what you meant when you said, 'warm it with color,' wasn't it?"~~

~~"Did David say that, Macky? He must be feeling better, he always teased me about my re-papering complex."~~

~~She~~ **Prue** slipped her hand within the crook of the woman's thin arm and for an instant pressed her cheek against her hard shoulder.

It's hard to imagine Emilie Loring making these changes herself. Someone trimmed the word count to meet space requirements, and the public was none the wiser.

Emilie's son Selden emerged as a short story writer for youth publications that spring. After his one play, *Little Sherlock,* his first published short story was "Homicide in Blue" in the June 1933 issue of *The Underworld Magazine. Boys' Life* accepted three more stories to run in its spring 1934 issues: "The Suicide Sled" (March), "Dynamite for Señor McGonigle" (April), and "Six Shells for Señor Swanson" (June). "Rope for a Spy" appeared in May's issue of *The Open Road for Boys.*

Two of Selden's short stories, "Dynamite for Señor McGonigle" and "Six Shells for Señor Swanson" took place in South America against revolutionary rebels. South America was the new, popular darling of foreign destinations. Cruises took honeymooning couples to Buenos Aires, sports teams held competitions there, and *Flying Down to Rio* was the first film in which Fred Astaire and Ginger Rogers appeared together.

By April, *We Ride the Gale!* was in its second edition, which included copies in braille. John Clair Minot's column, "Books of the Year and their Authors," began with a tribute to Emilie Loring and the sales of her latest best-seller. He noted that her style of writing was the current trend: romantic novels "with a lift at the end . . . in contrast with the extreme products of realistic fiction with which we had been overfed in past years."[6] In a letter to Clara Endicott Sears, Emilie remarked:

Victor and I dined with Mr. Shoemaker last evening. He feels that conditions in the book business are improving. He reports that every day brings orders for *We Ride the Gale!* Not large ones but a steady sale.

She cheered the *Boston Herald*'s review of *The Great Powwow*:

Isn't it wonderful? Not only that but it is so well deserved. I have pasted it into my copy of the book.[7]

Emilie signed the contract for *With Banners* before she left for Blue Hill and dedicated the story "to the playwrights and players, past and present, of my family." Six times in the book, she used the lines:

"Don't apologize."
"I'm not apologizing. I'm just explaining."

The lines had also appeared once in *The Trail of Conflict* and twice in *Uncharted Seas*. Six times in one book was no accident. These were familiar, family lines, from an old play by the same name. Their repetition brought back the sense of her childhood home when the whole family was in on the lighthearted fun.

Then, in a neat turning of the page, she declared through the silver-haired Mrs. Gregory, "I haven't time to look back; I'm going forward, 'with banners,' to borrow Brooke's favorite phrase."

Emilie put away her paper and pens for the summer and headed to Blue Hill. Selden's family came for a week, and Emilie motored down to Wiscasset for a meeting of the Pen Women, where she gave "A Writer in the Making" to yet another audience.

Boston, 1934-1935

The Lorings returned to Boston in September and met Louise and Lizzy Hallet when they returned from England. This was becoming the Hallets' new pattern—May to September in Europe, winter season in the United States. In Boston, they stayed at the Puritan Hotel, but their winter apartment this year was at the Hay-Adams luxury hotel in Washington, D.C. Inspired by the new locale, Emilie set her next story in Washington, D.C. and gave her heroine an apartment of her own.

"Think of it! A place all my own, and I'm earning it! Can you imagine anything more perfect?"

Eve nestled deeper into the chair. At last she was on her own. My party! My apartment! My maid! My fire, she exulted

Eve Travis is an orphaned heiress—no immediate family, no reminiscing about the past. Instead, she has Jeff Kilburn, whom she has known since childhood, and her Uncle Jock, a senator in the nation's capital. Eve thinks Jeff is despondent because the girl he loved, Moya, has just married another man. In truth, Jeff is upset because he has just learned that Eve's fortune was squandered away by her guardian.

Motivated by their misconceptions, Eve proposes marriage to save Jeff from either killing himself or marrying a "man-eating widow," and he goes through with the marriage to save her from being alone and penniless. Moya's husband dies in a plane crash, Eve learns that her money is gone, and their whole plan falls apart. Uncle Jock convinces them to keep their marriage quiet while Jeff is on top-secret business in South America, but they will have to get past misunderstandings and hurt pride to solve an international conspiracy.

As she worked on the new manuscript, *With Banners* was published in mid-October. Radio station WABI in Bangor, Maine called it "a crisp, swift-moving story of love and complications, with a quality of glamour that is irresistible, and always pleases."[8] The book moved swiftly off the shelves and went into a second printing within the month.

Out in Hollywood, Emilie's nephew, Melville Baker, already had eleven films to his credit, with ever-rising, star-power casts.[9] In Boston, Sara Ware Bassett was amused that two of her books had made it into the movies at all. Her first was *Danger Ahead* (1921) from her novel *The Harbor Road*. This year, her 1915 best-seller, *The Taming of Zenas Henry*, became RKO's movie *Captain Hurricane*, and the publicity began in February. John Potter's interview of her for the Boston papers displayed Sara Ware's favorite photograph of herself, which was the opposite of a Hollywood portrait. In fact, it was not a portrait at all, but a photo of her standing by a wooden dory on Cape Cod.

Sara Ware rarely went to the "pictures" and liked stage performances better. "The very speed of the camera ruins the leisurely atmosphere of such a book." During filming, RKO couldn't find a hymn that was in her novel. She received a telegram, "Spare us oh Lord not found in Hollywood."

Sara Ware Bassett, Cape Cod

"Well, I was not surprised that Hollywood could not find the anthem," she wrote in her autobiography. "It wasn't exactly their sort."[10]

Unlike Sara Ware, Emilie made a conscious effort to keep her stories up-to-the-minute. Prohibition was repealed a year before, and although her current protagonist, Eve Travis, chooses sparkling juice for herself, deciding what someone else should choose was distinctly démodé. Senator Holden complains to his wife,

> "You won't have wine served in the house because you don't approve of it. Who are you to decide what another person shall drink?"

The theme of Emilie's current novel was, "It's a great world to the valiant!" Those who strove when things got tough, who relied on their own resources to accomplish what was needed, found the world an exciting, fulfilling place.

> "If you think in terms of defeat you will be defeated. Pin on your red badge of courage. It's a great world to the valiant. Hold your head high and believe in your star and in the man you love."

> "Unstampedable. It's a great quality, isn't it?"

Jeff and Eve begin as friends, marry as friends, and then discover that their love is something more. They play at cross-purposes, each unaware of the other's feelings, until the final scene, when Eve shows up on the boat Jeff is taking to South America.

> "Happy landings!" he shouted to the men who already were fading into the dusk . . .

Emilie signed the contract for *It's a Great World!* on April first, but at signing, the title was *To the Valiant*. Again, Mr. Shoemaker chose a cheerier version. There was no dedication this time, only the complete sentence, "It's a great world to the valiant"—without the cover's exclamation point.

Emilie had an important publicity portrait taken that May 1935. This wasn't her first Bachrach photo, but Emilie's last had been more severe: plain V-neck dress, direct gaze, no smile. Her new portrait was luminous. She wore a lace dress with a deep, square neckline and faced rightward, light illuminating her profile. Her eyes and her lips were turned, inspirationally, upward.

Emilie Loring's new photo debuted in a full-page article on the front page of *The Boston Evening Transcript*'s book section on June twenty-second. "Emilie Loring Says It's a Great World: Her Latest Novel Takes Her Readers into the Whirlpool of Washington Social and Political Life."[11] Dorothea Lawrance Mann wrote the article and borrowed liberally from her tribute six years before. She described generations of Baker writers and added Selden's recent forays into short-story writing.

New in her article were sales figures of Emilie Loring's books for the past year—seventy-seven-thousand copies. At her royalty rate, that meant about thirteen-thousand dollars—over one and a half million in today's dollars.[12]

Miss Mann described *It's a Great World*'s Eve Travis: "She is in open and hot rebellion at the beginning of the story. She wants freedom and an opportunity to do things in the world, and she wants a chance to be herself." The relationship between Eve and Jeff is "the story of two star-crossed lovers who have started out in the wrong way, who are separated again and again by misunderstandings, and who have in the end to discover how much they love each other." Miss Mann concluded, "It is an interesting thing to have watched a career like that of Emilie Loring with its ever-widening circles of success."[13]

Blue Hill, Summer 1935

Louise and Lizzy Hallet didn't go to Europe that summer. With Victor Loring's help, they sold off some inherited parcels of land on the

> "Why tag a woman like you with the number of her years who earns more with her brain per annum than the salary of the President of the United States?"
> *Beckoning Trails*

Emilie Loring, Bachrach Photo, 1935

Cape. Then, when the Lorings went to Blue Hill, the Hallet sisters also traveled downeast and secured rooms at the Malvern Hotel, one of the most exclusive hotels in Bar Harbor.

Two important events occurred on July third. In Blue Hill, David Sheridan Owen, older brother to the Owen sisters of Tyn Y Coed, passed away. Minnie, the last surviving sibling, made arrangements for David to be buried in Seaside Cemetery next to Elizabeth ("Bessie"). She then made the difficult decision to move their sister Carrie at last from the sunken garden to join the others. When Minnie died, there would be no one left to care for her grave and watch over her; the Owen family needed to be together.

At least, that is probably what happened. It is sure that Minnie ordered a matching stone for Carrie and placed it next to David's and Bessie's. She made arrangements for herself to be buried in Seaside Cemetery, too, when the time would come. It is unclear whether Carrie's remains were moved or not; no record was ever made.

The second important event, on July third, was the marriage of the Lorings' son Robert to Irma Inman Tassinari. At nearly forty, Robert had played the field long enough. Irma was ten years younger than he, her father an Italian immigrant, and her mother from a longtime Cape Cod family, the Lothrops. It was whispered that Irma might have had a "wild" past, but the woman Robert brought home made a pleasant impression.[14] "You will like my new daughter," Emilie wrote to Clara Endicott Sears.[15]

Ten days later, Irma and Robert drove up to Blue Hill with a second-hand car to replace Victor and Emilie's old one, which "showed every indication of folding up on the road." Robert drove the "new" car, and Irma drove Robert's, arriving at Stone House at two o'clock in the morning. "That seems to me to be about as unselfish a proceeding as I have heard of in a long time," Emilie continued.

Robert reported that Selden's wife, Mary, "was wonderful at his wedding, doing everything that she could to help." Everyone remembered that Mary had dated Robert first. Now, Emilie concluded, "I feel that I am rich in daughters. I hope that I may be able to help them as much as I know they will help me."[16]

A month later, Emilie wrote to Clara again:

Now that The Thundering Herd, as Robby calls Selden's family, has departed I take my typewriter in hand to answer the question in your letter of August 11th. No, nothing was troubling me—

more than my usual problems—except the effort to provide three meals a day for a family of eight and weekends ten people. You know it is quite a stunt.

Her usual problems? Help her as much as she helps them? Emilie was sixty-eight, and Victor was seventy-six. Had one of them been ill?

However, Selden's family was here three weeks, and we had a most harmonious, happy time. The children were wonderful. I had only to express a wish that they do a thing, and it was done.

Both families brought dogs, which Emilie loved, although Selden's got into a fight with her tenant's dog across the street and nearly lost an eye.

Sel's dog has returned to his winter home and Robby's dog will depart next week-end, then I hope to begin my real vacation. Don't think from that that I have not loved having my family with me. I have, dogs and all although at times life has seemed strenuous and I am a total loss when it comes to planning desserts.

Robert and Irma continued to drive down each weekend.

I had thought that perhaps she would rebel after one or two long trips, but she seems to enjoy the place more each time ... We like Irma more and more and think her well suited to Robert. She is very quiet BUT she gets there.

For the first time, other than school or the service, Robert moved out of his parents' home. He and Irma found an apartment at 69 Revere Street in Boston. Robby and Irma painted the woodwork and hired a professional to do the ceilings and wallpaper. "He is quite excited that it has window boxes at the front windows. It sounds most attractive."

Victor and Emilie passed an unusually hot, Blue Hill summer reading. Emilie expressed hope to Clara that Sara Ware's latest, *Hidden Shoals*, would do well, but she confided that she thought it outmoded:

> I can't believe that Cape Cod women of this day—and it is a story
> of today—would use the language her women who belong to a
> Woman's Club use. I may be wrong.

Her letters to Clara showed what equal partners she and Victor were when it came to book matters. They agreed that *Those Elder Rebels* by Helen Abbott Beals began well and then fizzled out.

> I read it with greatest interest, chuckled over the first half,
> thought, "Now, here's a writer!" when suddenly the story went to
> pieces . . . I said nothing to Victor of my reactions and enjoyed
> his chuckles, but when he closed the book he said, "What the
> dickens happened to that story which started out so well?"

She reported that Mr. Shoemaker let her know that *It's a Great World!* had fallen off the best seller list for a week, "but last week it came in strong again. I so hope it will go and sell and sell and sell." She signed her letter, "Devotedly yours, Betty Loring."[17]

Before returning to Boston, Emilie started her next novel, *Give Me One Summer*. She liked a photograph she saw of a girl in a motorboat and started her story there. In later remarks for radio, she described:

> As if to encourage me in my rash adventure, a benign provi-
> dence—the newspapers said it was the Outboard Motorboat Rac-
> ing Association—staged a race on Charles River Basin. During
> that race one man was spilled overboard, his boat went crazy and
> whizzed round and round till it smashed into the Embankment.
> Do you wonder I believe that Providence had me by the hand?

Would one ask for a more dramatic take-off for a story than that?
I unhooded my typewriter and started.

She listed story elements and why she included them—a Maine harbor, because she knew Maine harbors; a dog, "because what is home or a story without a dog?" She included rented cottages, "because I've had tenants myself"; and an island with a lighthouse, because the government was just then selling one.

The story began in June and progressed for one summer, through September and the county fair. One summer . . . *Give Me One Summer.* "From the beginning I had a grand time writing that story . . ."[18]

What she didn't say in her remarks was that the fledgling writer, Melissa Barclay, was modeled on herself. She hid a clue in the writer's initials, M. B.—Melissa Barclay, Maria Baker. But the content wasn't hidden; Emilie spoke directly through Melissa about her writing. The details were the same as she had presented so often in "A Writer in the Making."

She lived over the ecstatic moment when she had drawn a pink cheque from an envelope. Three dollars! It had seemed a fortune. She had sold something! Nothing much but someone had wanted it enough to pay money for it. That was the acid test. Another much traveled manuscript had been in an editorial office six weeks; up to this one its flights had been in the non-stop class. She had had a nervous chill every time she opened the mailbag for fear she would find it. Other stories had gone out and had done the homing-pigeon act, but not that one. If she did receive a cheque for it, she would deposit it in a travel fund.

She declined hastily. "Can't. I've got to work. No one has to tell me that no matter how one's mind sparks with ideas, unless one writes, nothing gets written. I've learned that still living truth. I'm writing a novel. Don't laugh."

Long ago she had discovered that the power to close the door on problems was one of the perquisites of creative writing. One dwelt in another world when one was at work on a story.

"Writers who get there don't have hysterics. I've always claimed that success in writing—provided of course one had what it takes to make a writer—is like success in marriage, largely a question of good sportsmanship, of keeping on keeping on, of giving one's best and trying, everlastingly trying to make that best, better."

"I've been doing some village visiting and each family suggested a story. I love people. They're my assets. They are interesting to me even when they're shallow and inconsequential."

Boston, Fall 1935

Emilie presented "A Writer in the Making" again in October, this time at Boston's R. H. White department store on Washington Street. Hers was the second in a series of free, author's lectures provided on the third floor for the shopping public.

Lloyd C. Douglas spoke first in the series. He had yet to write his most famous work, *The Robe*, but *The Magnificent Obsession* and *The Green Light* were already out, and both became movies. Later speakers were book designer and author William Dana Orcutt; Ben Ames Williams, who wrote outdoors novels in Searsmont, Maine; Phoebe A. Taylor, author of the Asey Mayo Cape Cod mysteries; and Miriam Skirball, author of *Ibsen in England*.

Emilie spoke yet again in December for the "Authors Day" program of the Women's Republican Club. She presented "A Writer in the Making," and Clara Endicott Sears read some of her poems, but neither was as exotic as Mrs. Larz Anderson's account of a recent trip to the Galapagos Islands, soon to be featured in her new book, *Zigzagging the South Seas*.

Over the years, Emilie Loring and Mrs. Anderson appeared often at the same functions and occasionally served tea together at Pen Women luncheons. The wealthy heiress and her diplomat husband traveled the world, collected art works, and entertained lavishly at their home and museum, "Weld," in Brookline. Mrs. Anderson wrote thirty books about their adventures with enticing titles like *The Spell of Japan*, *The Spell of Belgium*, and *Polly the Pagan*.[19]

Boston, Spring 1936

Emilie signed the contract for *Give Me One Summer* on April sixth, and the novel was on bookstore shelves by late June. Dedicated to her new daughter-in-law, Irma Inman Loring, her "new and sparkling romance" promised "a summer of enchantment for Lex Carson and Lissa Barclay, mixed with doubts and heartaches."

The Sunday *New York Times* condescended, "The book is superficial, lightly amusing, warm weather fiction." The *Daily Boston Globe* credited the atmosphere but not the plot: "... a setting that makes the reader want to pack up and start immediately for the rock-bound coast of Maine. If you're not too critical and like a pretty smooth-flowing love story, 'Give Me One Summer' will provide entertainment for an hour or two."[20]

That was okay with Emilie. What the reviewers criticized was precisely what she wanted to achieve. Her character Melissa Barclay spoke for her:

"I'll never write masterpieces. I'll leave the miseries, ironies, vain hopes, and frustrated dreams to more experienced writers. I want to write the kind of story—it will be just as much a part of the real world—that will cause persons who see 'Melissa Barclay' on a cover to plump down their problems—and incidentally the price—and seize the book. If, when they reach 'the end' they forget to go back for their problems and march blithely toward the day's work pepped up and refreshed, refreshed—it's a great word, isn't it—I shall feel that I have achieved something."

Dorothea Lawrance Mann highlighted Emilie's skill in crafting a mystery and creating vivid characters in her newspaper column:

> We feel and hear and see the Maine coast as we read the story. The scene where the blinding, frightening Maine fog comes in and makes even the most familiar roads strange and terrifying is perhaps the best episode in the entire book . . .
> It is a more complicated mystery, and it is handled with a good deal of skill, making us feel that *Give Me One Summer* may mark a transition in Mrs. Loring's writing . . .
>
> Marty only appears a few times, yet we have an exceedingly vivid impression of her. Whenever she appears Marty is remarkably real.

The public agreed. During the first month after its release, *Give Me One Summer* was number four among the top-ten, best-selling books in America. *Gone With the Wind* by Margaret Mitchell took first place, followed by Vincent Sheean's historical novel *San Felice* and Alice Grant Rosman's *Mother of the Bride*.

Emilie Loring's sales during that period exceeded those of mystery writer Mary Roberts Rinehart (*The Doctor*) and romance author Grace Livingston Hill (*Mystery Flowers*). Her balance of romance and mystery was a winning combination. She had a nationwide best-seller.

Miss Mann made one criticism of *Give Me One Summer*'s characters: "It is easier to like people when you are not always expected to admire them. Even the fine people in life are likely to have their failings, and Lex and Lissa are singularly without faults."

Emilie listened and made adjustments in her next story, *As Long as I Live*. The protagonist, Joan Crofton, submits her artwork to an ad agency like that where Selden Loring worked as a commercial artist. At their first meeting, Craig Lamont accuses Joan of using another artist's work, and at their second, Joan hits him in the face with a pan of hot scones. So much for faultless.

Another critic observed that there were few living mothers in her stories. Emilie hadn't intended that, but a quick look confirmed that it was true. Of her fourteen novels, only four had mothers living (*Here Comes the Sun! The Solitary Horseman, Swift Water, and With Banners*). Of these, only Claire Grahame (*The Solitary Horseman*) and Celia Reyburn (*With Banners*) were active in the story. She made sure *As Long as I Live* had a mother who was front and center at times.

Patty Crofton's description came straight from the oil painting of Emilie's mother, Emily Boles Baker, that hung on the wall:

> Her mother's dark hair was dressed to show the lovely shape of her head. The brilliancy of her brown eyes and the satin texture of her magnolia tinted skin were accentuated by a green frock. She had been the belle of her county when dashing young David Crofton had snatched her from a dozen adorers, she was still vividly beautiful.
>
> "Your mother! The first time my eyes met hers I said to myself: 'As Long as I Live, I'll love you,' and I will."

Moreover, the Croftons are long-time lovers and companions, the best examples of marriage done right.

> "Patty and I started out with the conviction that marriage is a high adventure, not an obstacle race. We haven't changed our belief, though we've had some tough, grueling experiences along an often times rough and rocky road. However, we've pulled through. We still think this is a great old world and look forward to the future with a tingling sense of more adventure to come."

"My mind is like a magnet," Emilie said. "Ideas for stories leap from the printed page, from a chance meeting, and hang there like bits of steel until I use them or from disuse drop into my subconscious to surge to the top of my mind when I least expect it." She had tea at The Pergolas in Harvard, Massachusetts and looked out over the Nashaway Valley and the dark mountain beyond. "I caught the glint of glass on its top. Straightaway my plot nerves began to tingle. 'I can use that mountain,' I told myself. The service road they drive on resembled the service road that led up Blue Hill mountain, and Harvard fit the description of the "imaginary village" in which she set the story, "about thirty miles from the city, a place of stately homes and beautiful gardens."[21]

Philip Bard takes Joan to lunch at "T-Wharf," which existed then as a "T" extension of Long Wharf. The Blue Ship Tea Room Restaurant was their destination, on the third floor of the last building on the wharf, with a broad view of the harbor. Emilie described the setting with authentic details.

> Joan's eyes glowed like stars as she seated herself in a bright blue chair at a chrome yellow table in the low-ceilinged crowded room which was redolent of frying fish and coffee. Through the haze from an incredible number of cigarettes, she saw a dull-toned old map of Clipper Ship Days in Boston Harbor, another of Colonial Boston. Dusty murals presented ships and sail boats going in different directions under billowing sail, presumably in the same wind, against impossible blue sky and luridly green water.

Blue Hill, Summer 1936

The Loring grandchildren came to Stone House for a week in the summer. Victor and Val, nine and six, took art classes at Adelaide Pearson's "Rowantrees Pottery." Victor remembered, "We made hideous ashtrays, and Grandmama was delighted."

Their father had another short story published that summer in *The Open Road for Boys*, "The Durham Wildcat," and their Grandmama, who loved their ugly ashtrays, made the *New York Times* best-seller list.

She wrote to Sara Ware Bassett, "Hope that Eternal Deeps is breaking all records and that you are having a grand summer." Her postcard showed Stone House with window boxes at all the upper and lower windows, trellises at either side of the door, and big rocks along the street with gardens both inside them and to their sides. The card was postmarked, "Blue Hill, Aug 26, 1936," and she added, "Stone House Bluehill Maine," using the town's older spelling.

Boston, Fall 1936

In early November, Emilie was the first guest of radio station WEEI's nationwide "Meet the Author" series. She prepared her fifteen minutes of remarks ahead of time, typing them in long form and correcting the copy by hand. They were a direct and personal glimpse into her writing process.

Thank you, Miss Peck. An introduction like that is a springboard. It gives a speaker a grand start. So here I go through the air to you who are listening.

Asked where she got her story ideas, she replied, "The air is full of them. They prick at one's imagination. They clamor to be written." The origins of both *Lighted Windows* and *Fair Tomorrow* were found in the want-ads and *Give Me One Summer* was the product of a front-page article and a photo.

Perhaps a year ago I came across a photograph of a lovely, laughing girl in an outboard motorboat. Story! Story! Prodded the sprite who perches on the lookout of my imagination.

Curiosity propelled her imagination from there.

I'll confess that a subject of which I know little lures me, that a subject of which I know nothing proves irresistible, one learns so much as one follows it up.

"'The gods provide the thread once the web is started.'" That favorite axiom of her father's slipped into Sandra's thoughts as she dressed for the ball. *Uncharted Seas*

Sometimes, a story started, not with an idea but with the *need* for an idea. Emilie had said there was hardly anything that couldn't provide a story. Put something interesting out where she could see it, and the combination of curiosity and imagination would do the rest. The lost-and-found ad for a "black satin slipper with rhinestone buckle" that inspired *Lighted Windows* sat in her file for years.

Each time I saw it in my file I would think there's a story in there. One day I needed an idea for a novel and stuck the clipping where I could see it. Curious, I thought, that only one slipper had been lost. I wonder why—and the story had started.

Emilie corrected her remarks for the radio program as she would a story, with active verbs and a personal perspective. "From that moment things began to happen" became "I lived that story:"

Salt spray whipped my face and stung like needles. I breathed deep of the pine and balsam-scented air; was lost in a dense dripping fog through which hollow voices drifted like the voices of disembodied spirits. Dashed for the lighthouse through a torrential downpour and the crack and crash and flash of the thunderstorm of the ages, watched the coloring of garden borders change from the pastel pinks and blues and tender yellows of June to the warmer tints of midsummer and then deepen to the crimson, scarlet, rusty browns and golden orange shades of September; tingled with the excitement and choked with the dust of the midway in a County Fair, while through it all my vital characters worked out their problems and laughed and loved, thought and felt, and fought their way to victory or defeat.

She corrected an exaggeration: she wrote only five days per week, not six.

Inspiration is a tricky undependable jade. ~~Six~~ Five days in the week I work approximately five hours a day. If when I sit down at my desk the story refuses to get under way, I go back several chapters and read until I reach the page where I stopped the day before. By that time, I am so thrilled and excited that the characters pick up the thread of the story and carry on. That is, nine times out of ten they do, but the tenth time they may balk as one did not so long ago.

Slowly, she fed out details, building rapport with the reader and heightening suspense all the way.

The chapter setting was an up-to-the-minute apartment house. Our hero had sprinted up three flights of stairs in pursuit of a clue—yes, there was an elevator, but, if ever you have hot-footed after a mystery clue, you can understand that he didn't want to be seen by the operator. To return to the stairs; at the top step he stopped. So did the story. You know the rigidity of a run-down mechanical toy? The aforementioned toy had nothing on our hero. Apparently, he had reverted to the Stone Age. I tried everything short of chopping down the stairs to get him to move. He wouldn't.

Followed a bad attack of jitters. I thought, "Has my imagination dried up?" *Have I gone stale?* Commonsense nudged my elbow. "Don't be foolish, *gal.* ~~"Think!" it commanded.~~ You've gone lazy. You've had it too easy. Think!"

I shut my eyes and pondered. What ~~can~~ could I do to vitalize that rigid figure? ~~I asked myself.~~ Thought-flash! Suppose our hero had gone downstairs instead of up, had gone to the street? Suppose he knew where to find that clue better than I did? Tingling with hope I jerked him round and started him down. Click! He took the steps three at a leap and hurtled out the front door The story was off at such a pace that I was breathless trying to keep up with it. Now, on the wall above my desk is thumbtacked the sage advice:

WHEN STUCK REVERSE YOUR ENGINE

She advised would-be writers to make their work as good as possible, then determinedly seek a publisher. Handwritten corrections to this section of her remarks show that she followed her own advice to constantly revise.

I wish I knew an ~~infallible~~ formula for writing a short story or a novel that would ~~prove~~ *make the creation* irresistible to an editor—I could use one myself—but, alas, I don't. I have taught myself to write by the trial and error method, going over and over a story, adding here, deleting there, strengthening a character, shading a situation, pacing it by discarding pages, the contents of which I liked very much indeed . . .

Later that month, Emilie's publisher wrote with a flattering request.

November 28, 1936

We wish to submit to the committee that selects the books for the Pulitzer Prize your "Give Me One Summer," but in order to do so we must have the date of your birth. If you do not care to disclose this to your publisher, we would suggest that you put it on a card and place it in a sealed envelope and then we will send it along with the book.

Your prompt attention will be appreciated because the committee is at work and I happen to know that one of them is very favorably disposed toward our books.

Yours very truly,
CC Shoemaker[22]

Charles Shoemaker's delicacy regarding age was both quaint and serious. Emilie Loring's characters were principally young women in their twenties, and her writing persona was vibrant and youthful in spirit. Keeping her age a secret—even from her publisher—preserved her public image. "I won't have photographs show an old-fashioned hair-do," she insisted, "It is no use having smart heroines if their creator is dowdy."[23]

At seventy, she was to be nominated for a Pulitzer Prize! What a compliment! And perhaps not a prize too impossible to contemplate. The 1935 winner was a first-time author, H. L. Davis for *Honey in the Horn*, and Emilie already had fourteen novels to her credit. She had entered and placed in several writing contests already, and since publication, *Give Me One Summer* had remained among the top best-sellers of the year.

On the other hand, the Pulitzer's interest had always been journalistic. Two members of the committee worked in Columbia University's School of Journalism, and the other twelve were newspapermen. Journalism shaped their standards for excellence, in both style ("terseness" was recommended) and purpose. The focus of the Pulitzer was writing that accomplished a "public good commanding public attention and respect." The focus was societal, the perspective was decidedly male,[24] and the winners tended to be cerebral, if not depressing. No woman sat on the Pulitzer Prize Board until 1980,[25] and a humorous novel wouldn't win until 2018.[26] Still, it was worth a try.

Boston, Spring 1937

Record-breaking crowds greeted the New Year in Boston. The Great Depression was over and Social Security begun. Nationwide, there had been unprecedented floods, heat, and dust storms. The Boulder Dam was completed, Jesse Owens had earned four gold medals at the Olympic games, and there was deepening instability in Europe and the Far East.

As Long as I Live was published by Penn on February nineteenth, and Emilie presented copies to her sons, as was her custom. Below her inscription, she pasted a postage-sized "stamp" with her likeness from the 1924 parapet photo.

Emilie Loring Stamp, February 1937

The *Boston Globe* called her novel "stimulating and refreshing, an irresistible story ending on a high note of romance."[27] Emilie appeared on Ruth Moss' broadcast for The Yankee Network and received a note of thanks: "*As Long as I Live* is a grand story, and I am happy to have the chance to read it and find your personality reflected in its chapters."[28]

The Jordan Marsh Company advertised, "Emilie Loring, Boston-born author whose romantic novels have won her nation-wide popularity, will appear at Jordan Marsh Company's book department tomorrow at 2:30 p.m. to autograph copies of her latest book, 'As Long as I Live.'" Mail and telephone orders were accepted. The Boston Athenaeum amended the title page of its copy with traditional delicacy: "*Mrs.* Emilie Loring." Readers rushed to the stores, and Emilie Loring had another best-seller.

Two weeks later, Emilie and Victor attended Little, Brown's one-hundredth anniversary dinner at the Copley Plaza Hotel. It was the pulisher's most successful year since 1930,[29] and the same could be said for Emilie Loring. The Depression had forced her to use more avenues to reach her readers, and in the process, she became a celebrity author. She sold foreign rights to her books in Canada and the United Kingdom, and she signed on with the syndicates to publish her previous novels nation-wide in the newspapers. The WNU ran them as serials, and the *Detroit Free Press* offered "A Complete Novel Every Week."[30]

Between them, Emilie Loring's books maintained a national presence. For example, in February, the "Story Book Lady" of WHBL in Sheboygan, Wisconsin, read *Fair Tomorrow* (1931) aloud in thirty-minute segments.[31] And in May, the *Frontenac Press* of Kansas ran the serial *With Banners* (1934). Series of reprints brought new copies of her older books back to the market.

Emilie Loring still wrote the occasional short story. "Once in a Hundred Years" appeared in the Canadian magazine *National Home Monthly* in February (1937). The premise had book potential: June Darcy is to marry Dick Marshall, but a woman protests during the ceremony, and she is left at the altar. Neil Trevor, whom she'd met only two days before, offers marriage, and June agrees. Neil sails for South America, Dick returns to get her back, and June has some deciding to do.

On February 25, 1937, Selden Loring's third child, Selden Melville Loring, II was born. Selden, Sr. still worked as a commercial artist, but like his grandfather before him, he wrote in his evening hours. His first book came out in April—*Mighty Magic*, published by Holiday House, Inc., a relatively new publisher that specialized in children's literature. Reviews of the "almost true story of pirates and Indians" were mixed. Perhaps his writing needed polishing, but there was "no doubt at all that the story fulfills its purpose, that of entertaining and amusing young readers."[32]

Meanwhile, his mother was at work on the manuscript for her sixteenth novel, due to her publisher in September. Her sons were both married now, and the theme of *Today Is Yours* was making good in marriage:

> You can do it if you'll forget the yesterdays and remember that today is yours, and the miracle is, it is always today.

If her readers expected the typical, happily-ever-after love story, they were in for a surprise. When the story opens, Brian and Gay Romney have already been married two years—one "love is heaven" year and a year of separation on the way to divorce. Gay's time alone has been hard—and good—for her. She had to learn "to shape her own plans, keep her own counsel" and "provide jam for her bread and butter."

Brian's uncle, William Romney, asks Gay and Brian to live with him and put up "a happily married front to the world" while they address serious problems at the Romney Manufacturing Company. The kernel for this aspect of the story may have come from her uncle, Charles Tappan Baker, whose place of work, the Colonial Publishing Company in Quincy, had just endured a strike.

The happily married front faces challenges from the beginning. Gay declares that she is in love with Jim Seaverns and intends to marry him, and Brian tries to make her jealous by playing around with the devious widow, Bee Ware. Joining forces to help "Major Willum" breaks down the barriers between them, and they reassess, not only their relationship but themselves.

> She had changed. She no longer felt bewildered. She felt grown-
> up, competent to meet life as it came with head erect and a sense
> of marching forward to the rhythm and beat of far-off music.

Emilie stuck to her practice of not using family names in her books, but the children in the story, William Romney II and his sister, Rose, were named for their grandparents, as Victor II and Valentine were.

May's announcement that the Pulitzer Prize had been awarded to Margaret Mitchell's *Gone with the Wind* was expected, even though she was the first woman to receive the prestigious award. Mitchell's first and only novel was a phenomenon that would quickly outsell the entire careers of more prolific authors.[33]

Emilie Loring's nomination for the Pulitzer was but a final act of respect and encouragement from her longtime publisher, Charles Shoemaker. In February, he had checked into the hospital for prostate surgery but suffered a coronary occlusion from which he never recovered. He died on May twenty-second.[34]

Mr. Shoemaker's support through the years had been like a sturdy stake to a young sapling. In her early years, she could write without having to sell each book to an agent, because he had already taken the option. His push for quicker manuscripts propped up his own finances during the Depression, but it also propelled Emilie Loring to the front of the reading public's attention alongside Penn's other flagship author, Temple Bailey.

Emilie signed on with Little, Brown, a longtime publishing house whose first office was in the same building as Tappan & Whittemore, where her father's career began. Their diverse author list included some of the most prolific authors and popular works of all time: Louisa May Alcott, Emily Dickinson, *The Fannie Farmer Cook Book*, and fellow BAC authors, John P. Marquand and Thornton Burgess (whose sales already exceeded four million books).[35] She was firmly in the big league now.

Blue Hill, Summer 1937

Before they went to Blue Hill for the summer, Emilie and Victor took care of some land business. First, Robert and Irma moved into the Wellesley Hills house. Years had passed since the Lorings had tried to sell it, but two sales had failed during Depression years, and a day before Halloween, 1934, the property bounced back, due to foreclosure. The main house, the carriage house, and the triangular portion of the lot toward Worcester Avenue were theirs once more. Selden and Mary already had their home in Lexington, so Robert and Irma accepted the opportunity to move into the house on Longfellow Road.

Next, Emilie sold a portion of their property in Blue Hill to Fisher and Josephine Boyd of Bryn Mawr, Pennsylvania. The Boyds had two daughters, Mary and Sidney, and their lot was next door to the Owen property, Tyn Y Coed. It's unclear why the Lorings sold at that time, except that their land, with its half-mile of shoreline was more extensive than they needed in their seventies and eighties.

Emilie signed the contract for *Today Is Yours* on August twenty-fifth and dedicated it to her author son: "To Selden Melville Loring, From One to Another." Republishing was limited to serials only, with profits split, fifty-fifty, with Little Brown. She promised to deliver the final manuscript by mid-September, and Little, Brown took the option on the next two.[36]

New in this agreement was a two-thousand-dollar advertising budget for the first ten thousand copies and twenty cents per copy for as long as five hundred copies were sold per month. An advertising budget! This *was* a different environment.

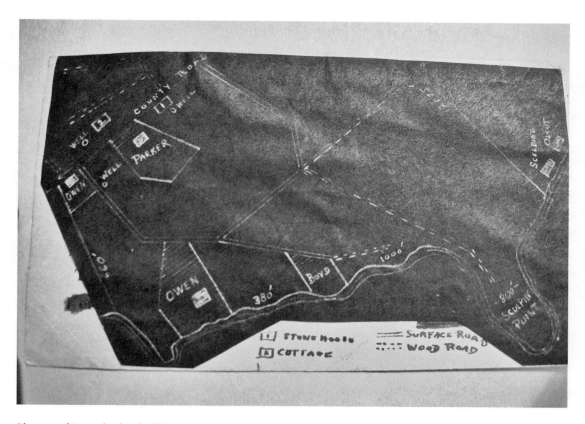

Blueprint of Loring land and sold lots, showing Stone House (1), The Ledges (2), Owen, Parker and Boyd properties, the surface Loring Road, and the wood road to Sculpin Point.

Boston, Fall 1937

The Hallets were absent from Boston all summer and fall. They were in London and witnessed part of the biggest story of the year: King Edward's romance with the American Wallis Simpson, his subsequent abdication, and King George VI's ascension to the English throne.[37] They stayed at The Goring, the closest hotel to Buckingham Palace, and joined the throngs on May twelfth to cheer the coronation of King George VI at Westminster Abbey.

More than Amelia Earhart's last flight or the crash of the Hindenburg, the royals' story of love, power, and loyalty captured and held the world's attention. When the Duke reunited with Mrs. Simpson in France, news articles romanticized every detail:

> Breathless and radiant, Wallis Simpson met the Duke on the doorstep of the rambling chateau . . . The Duke leaped from the car. He dashed to the threshold. There he took the wide-eyed Wallis tenderly in his arms.[38]

Pride in birth and family had been bred into these people for generations. She glanced at her grandfather beside her and felt a sudden overwhelming surge of that same pride.
High of Heart

Like so many Bostonians, Emilie cherished her English ancestry and enjoyed English customs. Bostonians may have dumped tea in the harbor, but they drank plenty of it later. In their pearls and sensible shoes, they paid close attention to events unfolding in their ancestral homeland.

Back in Boston, Emilie chose England for the setting of her next novel, *High of Heart* and recounted for a radio interview with Charles Lee, the *Boston Herald*'s literary editor:

> I wanted terribly to go to England. I couldn't go, so I used it as a setting for a novel. While at work I read the *London Times*, English *Country Life* regularly, and innumerable books. In short, steeped myself in English atmosphere till I became so British that I caught myself saying "lift," "cinema" and "will you please pass the sugar basin?" I loved that winter in England.[39]

The Times of London ran a series of stories about manor home ghosts that had scared prospective buyers away. *Country Life* magazine also had a ghost story. While photographing Raynham Hall in Norfolk, England, they captured on film what they believed was a ghost that had haunted the home for a hundred years. The idea was irresistible; *High of Heart* acquired a ghost.

> "Didn't your father tell you, my lady? Didn't he tell you of the ghost of a woman in gauzy silver draperies who appears at that

long window with our coat of arms enameled in colors on the glass, when the waning moon is visible from this room?"

In the new story, Constance Trent has lived with the Coreys since childhood, but her grandfather intends that she will inherit his English manor home and remain. Constance rejects her grandfather's invitation, but the Coreys persuade her to at least meet her grandfather and hear him out. Soon, the whole family is off to Trentmere Towers, where Constance feels the affectionate tug of her father's old home and falls in love with her stiff but kindly grandfather and her father's warm-hearted nanny.

The theme of this book was loyalty. Would Constance renounce her American citizenship, become an English subject, and claim her inheritance? Would Peter Corey, like King Edward, give up his responsibilities and life in the land of his birth to pursue his love for Constance?

The answer was "no" to both. Loyalty to the Corey family and to the United States won out over the romance of inheritance overseas.

Emilie dedicated the book "to my friend Beth Kerley whose middle name is loyalty." There was more to this, left unexplained. Beth was an indefatigable churchwoman, elected to serve a second term as diocesan president, when "it was made clear that her primary obligation lay elsewhere, and her fine sense of values would not permit her to give any other effort but her best."[40]

His grandmother was right, she was sweet and sound to the core and loyalty was her middle name.
High of Heart

Spring 1938

Novelist Loring Retains Public Minus Publicity.
Her "Today is Yours" Sells without Need for Bally-hoo[41]

Twelve thousand orders for *Today Is Yours* poured in from around the country as soon as the book was announced. Before publication, publicity, or reviews, the book was committed to a second printing.

Today Is Yours Book Signing. All of her books remained in print throughout her lifetime.

In their first week of new releases, Emilie Loring outsold both Faith Baldwin (*Enchanted Oasis*) and Agatha Christie (*Death on the Nile*).[42] That wasn't to say that she was more popular overall. Faith Baldwin sold hundreds of thousands of books each year, and Agatha Christie was well on her way to becoming the best-selling author of all time. But Emilie ranked ahead of Dora Aydelotte and Mary Borden, who flashed briefly on the best-seller list but would not endure the decades, and Kenneth Roberts (*Northwest Passage*) and Robert Nathan (*The Bishop's Wife*), whose reputations each rested on a one-time success.

It was heady stuff to be on the national best-seller lists with Pearl Buck, Sinclair Lewis, Faith Baldwin, and Agatha Christie. No wonder Little, Brown had secured first-option publishing rights for her next two novels, whatever they might be, and *Today Is Yours'* Gay Romney spoke so confidently of doing as well as possible in anything she undertook. That was Emilie's credo, also, but how did she stack up?

Emilie Loring enjoyed name recognition and celebrity status. New authors were compared to her, her name was used to draw customers to events, and she sat at the head and honored-guest tables of community groups from the Professional Women's Club to the Women's Republican Club and the Boston League of American Pen Women. Still, like A. J. Cronin, Emilie Loring "delighted readers all over the world but induced only lukewarm receptions from critics."[43] John Clair Minot had declared her an "important" author, but she wrote in a disappearing genre. Were her novels good literature or only good sellers?

In 1928, she won fifth prize in a play contest run by her own publisher. How would she do in an impersonal, national contest? She submitted *Today Is Yours* to the annual contest sponsored by the National League of American Pen Women. Now, she would see.

The League awarded prizes in April at its biennial conference in Washington, D. C. When Eleanor Roosevelt opened the authors' breakfast at the Willard Hotel on Pennsylvania Avenue, she spoke of the "heavy responsibility of spreading the thoughts of women around the world."

This was a charge with which Emilie Loring could identify. The women in Emilie Loring's stories tackled grief, disillusionment, loneliness, ambition, and prejudice. Her way of writing took the reader directly into her characters' thoughts, and their intelligent—occasionally emotional—approach to challenges was both up-to-date and relatable.

There were readings, more speeches, the book fair, and finally, author awards. The first prize for fiction went to *The Lost Queen of Egypt* by Lucile P. Morrison. Second prize was *Wild Peach* by Claire Cave, and the third prize went to *Today is Yours* by Emilie Loring. The first prize winner received ten dollars as her prize. Emilie received a book.[44]

The Boston chapter of the NLAPW celebrated Emilie's award when she returned. Her books were not the *best* sellers, but they were best-sellers.

Through sixteen novels, Emilie Loring had carved out a niche for herself with absorbing stories that reset one's aspirational compass and gave heart for the road ahead. Her books had the qualities of good friends: intelligent, interesting, and inspiring, with good taste, charming manners, and light-hearted humor.

Emilie Loring's books stayed a middle ground: neither prudish nor prurient, as mindful of a man's point of view as a woman's, considerate of each age from young to old, and sympathetic to characters from varied social and cultural backgrounds. An Emilie Loring book was like a cardigan sweater—classic, comfortable, never too much or too little. Not a trend-setter, but somehow, always just right.

Summer 1938

The well-to-do characters in Emilie Loring's stories were based on her friends, her family, and her neighbors, who were neither the highest nor the lowest of society. Their homes were her settings, their exploits her characters' actions. She didn't criticize, mock, or chastise them; she was one of them.

Melville Baker's latest film, *The First 100 Years*, was constructed along similar lines. Virginia Bruce played a successful Hollywood agent who is ordered in divorce proceedings to pay alimony to her yacht-designer husband, played by Robert Montgomery. The *New York Times* observed, "Everything takes place pleasantly and, so to speak, hygienically, within the upper-income brackets.[45]

Like his aunt, Mel Baker had simply written about the life he knew. A year after his divorce from Gladys Gould, he married Humphrey Bogart's agent, Mary Huntoon. The petite brunette engineered lucrative actor-writer-director deals for Humphrey Bogart and Ronald Coleman, among others.

Mel Baker built a home in Bel Air, and his mother, Minnie Baker, moved into Bel Air's glamorous Château Élysée with a Who's Who of

"Last week I moved to this hotel—note the impressive letterhead—because I learned that many of the movies live here—that's what the actors and actresses are called out here—what you see on the screen is a picture. Each time I go up or down in the lift I see one or two. It's thrilling."
As Long as I Live

Hollywood: Bette Davis, Errol Flynn, Edward G. Robinson, Carole Lombard, Humphrey Bogart, Clark Gable, Ginger Rogers, Ed Sullivan, Gracie Allen and George Burns, Lillian Gish, Katharine Hepburn, George Gershwin, and Cary Grant.

Mel spoke several languages, moved with ease in the Hollywood scene, and competed with a city full of talent to turn out movies at the same rate as his aunt wrote her novels. His early movies included the mystery *Darkened Rooms*, *His Woman* with Gary Cooper and Claudette Colbert, and *Next Time We Love*, starring newcomer Jimmy Stewart. Since 1933, he had been on the executive board of the Screen Actors Guild, which his friend Humphrey Bogart also supported.

The Bakers' social circle included the headliners of Hollywood. Mel played cards with F. Scott Fitzgerald and Ogden Nash, attended benefits with Mary Pickford, Fred Astaire, Mae West, Bette Davis, Charlie Chaplin, and Louis B. Mayer.

In August, when Humphrey Bogart married his third wife, the actress Jane Methot, the wedding was held at the Bakers' Bel Air home. Mel was "Bogie's" best man.[46]

Washington, D. C., Fall 1938

A visit to her friend Louise Hallet in the nation's capital inspired Emilie's next novel, *Across the Years*. The Hallet sisters kept an apartment at The Puritan in Boston, but as they had in Europe, they hotel-hopped from one luxury hotel to another, with the seasons. After summer at Bar Harbor's Malvern Hotel, they rented an apartment in Washington D. C.'s Mayflower Hotel for the winter season.

Four blocks from the White House, the Mayflower Hotel was the "Grand Dame of Washington, D.C." with more 24K gold leaf decoration than any building except the Library of Congress. The Mayflower's newsletter claimed that its daily register of guests "has always reflected the national and international scene."[47] Franklin D. Roosevelt stayed at

---

"I have the most curious feeling I've seen him, the tilt of his hat, before."
He laughed.
"Sure you have. In the movies. That is bad boy Humphrey Bogart's tilt to the fraction of an inch."
To Love and to Honor

...she had returned to the United States after eight years in Europe... What lay ahead? Whatever it was she could take it, she was tingling to meet it.
Across the Years

"Tell him the Senator's orders changed my plans, that I must attend a tea at the Mayflower."
Across the Years

the Mayflower the night before his inauguration in 1933 and wrote his famous first inaugural there: "the only thing we have to fear is fear itself." Its Grand Ballroom had hosted every inaugural ball since Coolidge, and when Charles Lindbergh flew around the world, his 1000-guest, celebration breakfast was held at the Mayflower.

In Emilie's next story, Faith Jarvis comes to Washington to work as social secretary to Senator Teele's sister. Both her brother, Ben, and his best friend, Duke Tremaine, work for the senator, and both are also engaged in hush-hush, anti-spy activities. It isn't long before Faith is involved in mystery, counterespionage, and romance against a backdrop of pre–World-War-II politics.

The Lincoln Memorial, Smithsonian, White House and National Mall provided the story's realistic backdrop. A scene about being presented to the president came from her visit to Washington in 1886 with her sister, Rachel. Duke Tremaine's Argyle House, which "makes even the most blasé cave-dweller sigh with envy," was real. So, too, were Emilie's forty silver boxes that she mentions not once, not twice, but ten times in the story.

Emilie culled details of the Washington, D.C. atmosphere from the "Mayflower Log" newsletter. In one fanciful scene, the Teeles' duck, Jemima, escapes the house and runs around Dupont Circle.

> What was that white thing ahead? It couldn't be! It was! Jemima waddling toward her in the middle of the sidewalk . . . "Jemima. Nice Jemima!" she cajoled . . . She was angrily aware that she was making a spectacle of herself as the duck squatted, flew, pranced on tiptoes and she raced, clutched, raced and clutched with no success to the accompaniment of chuckles, cheers, guffaws, shouts of good-natured derision from persons passing. Duke had said that the world needed laughter. Thanks to the act that silly duck was putting on, it was getting it this morning—plus.

She filled two weekend cases, one with silver boxes, they were the darlings of her heart.
Across the Years

The real duck's name was Osgood, and it lived at 1826 Massachusetts Avenue, the pet of a Mr. Thomas Henson. In the heaviest of traffic, the duck would waddle out and splash in puddles, amazing passers-by and disrupting traffic until it waddled away again.[48]

The theme of this story was the importance of character in the nation's capital:

"The surface is stimulating, shining, mirroring high ideals, brilliant plans, honest thinking and endeavor, but underneath, the current of temptation runs strong and deep to sweep men from their feet, the temptation to use power and prestige and the trust of fellow workers for self-gain."

CHAPTER 25

Favorite American Novelist

Spring 1939

The last year of the 1930s opened with Victor's eightieth birthday on January eleventh and the birth of Selden and Mary's daughter Linda on February eleventh. Her birth completed their family of six: Selden, Mary, Victor, Valentine, Selden, and now, baby Linda. Selden still wrote in his leisure hours, and his "Ghost Guards Gold" appeared in *The Open Road for Boys* that month.

Emilie had written a short story, too, but gone were the days when she recorded submissions and returns on cards. She wrote to Ann Elmo of the AFG Literary Agency in New York City:

Dear Miss Elmo—

I have had the title of the accompanying short story in my mind for several years, chuckling each time I thought of it and hardly daring to think of it for fear it might get on the air before I had a chance to develop a story from it. Recently, I submitted it to a literary expert whose opinion I value, and he wrote,

"I agree with you. It's a darned fine title."

This isn't written to influence your judgment. Just as a sort of pat on my own shoulder.

If you like the story will you try to place it. No pulps, syndicate or Canadian markets, please. If it is worth anything, it is worth good money.

In case it helps; 61,642 copies of my novels were sold during 1938.

Sincerely yours, Emilie Loring[1]

At fifteen percent of the two-dollar purchase price, Emilie had received over eighteen-thousand dollars in royalties during the past year. By comparison, an experienced lawyer earned an annual salary of about seven thousand dollars; a physician, eight thousand; and an experienced public-school teacher earned less than three thousand dollars in the same year.[2] Twice as much as a doctor or lawyer wasn't bad.

The same day that Emilie wrote to Miss Elmo, she received a request from the publicity director at Little, Brown to write a greeting to the Wellesley Hills Woman's Club for its April luncheon. This was her home club, and Olga Owens, an assistant book editor at the *Boston Transcript*, was in charge of the luncheon. She responded:

To the Wellesley Hills Woman's Club:
Greetings from a one-time member.

When I was asked to send a word of remembrance to you, my thoughts flew back to the days when I was actively interested in this Club. My term as one of its vice-presidents proved stimulating and inspiring. It was my first experience with Club work and almost my last as other interests absorbed my time and attention. That year Congressman Robert Luce was one of the speakers. Agnes Repplier was another and I still remember my thrilled excitement as I consulted the CENTURY DICTIONARY for the proper pronunciation of her name. It seemed an event of great importance to have a woman of national and international reputation come to speak to us.

My interest in your Club and its activities is as keen as if I had left it only yesterday. When my eyes catch the words WELLESLEY HILLS WOMAN'S CLUB in the newspapers, immediately upon the silver screen of memory is projected a close-up of Maugus Hall, row upon row of eager, interested faces, a poised dignified figure on the platform, and I hear a voice saying:

"Madam President, members and guests of the Club."

Sometime, I hope to hear it again, though I shall miss, even as I remember with warm affection, many of those eager faces. Meanwhile, my best wishes for the achievement of your high ideals and aims for your Club.[3]

A few weeks later, Margaret Ford wrote a full-page story for the *Boston Herald* about the "eminently successful group of Boston Authors" who wrote in the "rarefied atmosphere" of the Boston Athenaeum.[4] With Emilie Loring on the list were John P. Marquand, Sara Ware Bassett, Alice Brown, Clara Endicott Sears, Henry Boston, and Judge Robert Grant.

Every morning, Miss Ford described, the authors "step out of a noisy city into the incredible tranquility of the Athenaeum." They write in tiny, sunlit alcoves on the preciously quiet fifth floor where even the pigeons "seem to coo with a peculiarly inoffensive coo."

Except in the case of an emergency, no one is disturbed while writing. This is an inviolate rule . . . broken only once—when a family of squirrels scampered in from the balcony and went on a rampage which sent them up and down the room, over tables and chairs, then out to the grill and balcony again.

So shocking was the interruption, so unheard of the cause of it, that things have been more or less dated by it ever since. "I think I finished my last chapter before the squirrels came in that day," a lady author will say to a friend. Or, "wasn't it a few days after the squirrels came that he addressed the Authors Club."

. . . The only noises are the rustle of paper and the scratch of pen or pencil. The mere idea of a typewriter is enough to send any of the authors into a dead faint.

She reported that Mrs. Loring began the day "with two dozen finely pointed pencils before her, picks up the thread of a novel on which she had been working the previous morning . . ."

They write until it's time for tea and then repair to the third floor where they pay five cents to "sip tea and nibble crackers" before returning to their homes.

What did the authors think about as they wrote? Where did they get their inspiration, and what were their lives like away from writing?

Charles Lee, the literary editor of the *Boston Herald*, asked these questions in his "Meet the Author" series on the radio. The authors were all "leading literary personalities" who told "chatty stories of their private and professional lives."[5]

WEEI broadcasted Emilie's "Meet the Author" interview at four o'clock on May third. First, Charles Lee commented on New England's most popular, current books. John Marquand's *Wickford Point* led the way, followed by John Steinbeck's *The Grapes of Wrath* and Van Wyck Mason's *Three Harbors*. Rachel Field's *All This and Heaven Too* and Dorothy Canfield's *Seasoned Timber* rounded out the field.

Mr. Lee then introduced Emilie Loring, "a favorite American novelist." That was it. He had found the right descriptor. She wasn't the best-selling or the most critically acclaimed, not a political or social activist or trend-setter, but she was most definitely a favorite, and remaining a perennial favorite took work.[6]

She advised aspiring authors:

A writer who is determined to make good should cut the word discouragement from her vocabulary.

I have always believed that writing is a full-time job, that it is not a profession for those who want their rewards to come easily. . . Writing is work. Imagination plays an important part, but

Hadn't she figured that making good as a writer wasn't such a different proposition from making good in matrimony? Both professions were a matter of sportsmanship, of keeping on keeping on in the face of discouragement, of continually giving one's best, and trying, everlastingly trying, to make it better.
Fair Tomorrow

Emilie Loring, Favorite American Novelist

only work, with plenty of mental steam behind it, will make that imagination a producer. Any engine needs fuel. And imagination needs work.

Mr. Lee asked what she did to relax and break up her routine.

I like to meet people. Have you ever thought that a writer's characters are like a writer's friends? That the more time she spends with them, the more she knows what they really are? I like housekeeping and my garden in summer, games, some of them, collecting silver boxes and historical novels, love the theatre, enjoy the "cinema," and would rather read a good book than eat. I adore fashion shows. You can understand they play a most important part in my work. They help me keep the costumes of my heroines up-to-the-minute.

"I suppose," he began, like most successful authors, you are constantly asked whether you have a formula."

A formula, Mr. Lee, is like a unicorn. There isn't any such animal for me. Sometimes I wish I knew one when the going gets rough, but would there be as much of a thrill, would little chills feather through my veins, when one of my characters gets in a jam which astounds me, if I did? They have their problems, their ideals, to work out. Life, our chaotic, fascinating, ordinary human life, doesn't run itself according to formula.

"And you've enjoyed every minute of it?" he asked.

Every minute. I loved it. Whether the writing came hard or easy, it gave me, and does still, a thrilled sense of satisfaction, of achievement.[7]

Emilie sent the manuscript for *Across the Years* to Little, Brown before she left for Maine. When she started it in December, international tensions were building toward war in Europe. She finished the story in April with hope that the worst could still be averted:

I honestly believe that as a means of settling international difficulties war is on the way out and that it becomes more and more the duty of the United States to preserve peace, to insure the right of every man to life, liberty and the pursuit of happiness on this Western Hemisphere.

"Clothes go to my head like laughing gas."
Keepers of the Faith

Fall 1939

Across the Years was published on October fourth. By then, Germany had invaded Poland, and on September 3, 1939, Britain and France declared war on Germany. Russia invaded Poland from the east, and by the end of the month, Warsaw had surrendered. Americans hoped against hope that war would be kept from their shores. Again, Emilie felt the public's pulse:

> "Rousseau said: 'There never was a time when civilization was in need of spiritual awakening that it did not arrive.' We're in need of it right now, and it will come, just watch it." *Across the Years*

Her next novel took place in New York, with the contrast of war in Europe and peace at home.

> Mid-September in New York with bulletins of air raids, bombed ships, cities reduced to shambles broadcast constantly from one radio station or another; with theaters opening, with enchanting places to dance to music caressingly sweet, or blatantly saxophonic, and not a man to ask her to step out with him.

For the first time, Emilie used the name of a family member, newly born granddaughter Linda, for a character. Linda Bourne and her friend Ruth take an apartment inspired by Beth Kerley's apartment on East 81st Street, less than a block from Central Park and the Metropolitan Museum of Art.

> There was light enough to see the swaying trees in the Park below. Beyond the Park tall towers pierced by tier upon tier of lighted windows drew an irregular line against a sweep of star-sprinkled sky . . . "I never tire of our view at night, Ruth. It's blazingly,

unbelievably beautiful. It twinkles and sparkles and glows like a fabulous city."

Change drove the plot:

"There is only one common-sense move when you don't like your life. Do something about it. Get out. Go somewhere. Follow a rainbow. Who knows, you may find the legendary pot of gold at the end of it."

Linda Bourne is fed up with her mother's favoritism for her sister and the "bed of nettles" at her job. Her best friend, Ruth, is tired of her old-fashioned life in their backwater town. The two women set themselves up in a swanky, New York apartment to find "New friends. New surroundings. New problems, harder ones perhaps, but new."

Was there someone in the city who was even now moving toward her? Someone to whom she would say one day, "I knew you were coming. I waited for you"? Perhaps he would come from one of those buildings which loomed tall and great against the skyline.

But he doesn't. Greg Merton is a New Yorker, but he met "Lindy" back in her own hometown. He is the man her mother wants her sister Hester to marry. He is also competing with Linda's boss to sell Madam Steele's fabulous estate.

From experience, Emilie appreciated the change that transplanting oneself can bring, and Linda Bourne feels that way about her move to New York.

The experience was doing a lot for her. She felt a growing confidence and courage. It was as if her blood flowed more warmly and redly through her veins and gave a rosy cast to life. She met

people more easily and by their response knew that she gave out
something of the glow within her and—she glanced at herself in
the mirror—she was acquiring that intangible patina which, for
want of a better word, is called style.

In early November, Emilie Loring accepted an invitation to promote a
Chinese jewelry sale to benefit Madam Chiang-Kai-Shek's War Orphans
Fund. The collection came from Mrs. Theodore Roosevelt's New York gal-
lery, and she recruited celebrities to showcase the items. Carmen Miranda,
Helen Hayes, Judy Garland, and Tallulah Bankhead had all participated in
New York. The Boston event featured Emilie Loring, Broadway star Mary
Martin, and another novelist, Dorothy Walker.[8]

New York events framed her story's setting. Chapter seventeen's
"parade of horses" was the National Horse Show at Madison Square
Garden. The Philharmonic's performance of Debussy's *Berceuse Héroïque*
on Armistice Day really happened. Emilie described it as "a mournful
commentary on wars and their consequences." "Solemnly impressive," said
the *New York Times*.[9]

The "Fair," including the Brazilian exhibit and World of Tomorrow,
was New York's 1939–40 World's Fair. Exhibits included an "electric stairway" (escalator), a robot, nylon fabric, and the first View-Master. NBC
began regular television broadcasting at the Fair and displayed televisions
in transparent cases to prove they weren't just tricks.

The story was nearing completion but still without a title when she
signed its contract on December eighth. She promised to deliver the finished manuscript by the New Year and pressed on.

The *Boston Globe*'s Christmas book list focused on American books
with American themes, "not because it represents any tub-thumping
nationalism, but because it seems to indicate a steady growth of our belief
in ourselves as a cultural entity." Along those lines, John P. Marquand's
Wickford Point was "still a good present," and Emilie Loring's *Across the
Years* "is just beginning to enjoy the sale it deserves."[10]

The United States remained officially neutral, but no one who had lived through World War I underestimated the gravity and threat of the war abroad. Russia attacked Finland as Germany prepared to invade the rest of Europe. First bombs fell in Scotland, Canadian troops arrived in Britain, and Indian troops reinforced France. Eyes were on Washington, D.C., and Emilie spoke at an American Pen Women's meeting[11] about "The Washington Scene as a Plot Influence."

"The very name," she said, "suggests dozens of plots. The beautiful tradition packed city, even though only a name to the majority of Americans, is woven into the very fabric of their lives. To me it has suggested always romance and adventure . . . I turned the spotlight of imagination on different facets of Washington life 'til they flashed and sparkled in my mind."

At seventy-three, Emilie Loring believed, more than ever, in the importance of love and love stories when the world went awry.

> "Empires may rise
> and fall, yet there
> is always love."
> *There Is Always Love*

They are based on an invincible truth. The world may be convulsed with war and hate; the earth may tremble from the onward march of army tanks and heavy guns; our economic cauldron may boil violently; empires may rise and fall, yet there is always love. Love between husband and wife, between parent and child, between friends, between boy and girl, love for the Church. *There is Always Love*

With all that can go wrong between people and nations, there is always another choice. There is always love. She had her title.

Spring 1940

Emilie turned in her manuscript at the first of the new year and started right in on *Where Beauty Dwells*, a wholly Blue Hill story. She wrote from memory, and her descriptions were longingly nostalgic.

Now, as always when she entered the old house, she had the sense of stepping into a bygone world. A world of crumbling wood fires, candlelight on colonial maple and braided rugs, on portraits of men and women gone many a year, who had helped lay the foundations of a great nation while the secrets of the automobile, glands and hormones, the airplane, radio and the cosmic ray were still tightly locked away in the future.

As the story opens, Di Vernon is trout fishing, and Mac Cameron's hail from the bridge causes her to fall into the brook and hit her head. The Lorings crossed that bridge and trout stream every time they passed Peters Cove on their way to Stone House. Just beyond the bridge, the trout stream disappeared into the woods with a trail running along-side it.

Di and Mac might have been friends, but she suspects he is there to "steal" her land for his stepfather, Major Lovell. The Curtises and Brookses had died, and Emilie used the real-life incident between Victor Loring and Ben Curtis, when they argued about where the line lay between their two properties. Her sister, Rachel, inspired Diane Vernon's sister, Merry, who is wheelchair bound. She modeled the character Trudy partly on Esther Wood, the local girl who had been Janey Curtis' playmate and later, the Lorings' summer maid.

> Trout water . . . The answer to a fisherman's prayer . . . Dollars to dimes there were wily old veterans darting or lying like dusky shadows on the bottom of that dark basin between two jutting brown rocks. *Where Beauty Dwells*

She's a bright girl. Having a job and earning money has done a lot for her. But then, it does a lot for anyone. It gives a person a sense of responsibility and a sort of *What-a-big-boy—or girl—am-I satisfaction. Where Beauty Dwells*

Thoughts of war intruded—in the quiet of the Athenaeum, where she wrote, and in the minds of her characters.

"No matter what I am doing, all the time in the back of my mind
I hear the beat of drums of war. One can't ignore it in the life of
today any more than one can a minor motif in a symphony."

Emilie and Fanny Fern Andrews poured tea at the Chilton Club for
the Boston branch meeting of American Pen Women,[12] and she found,
to her pleasure, that she was in like-minded company. The women were
from the same generation, and, like Emilie, Mrs. Andrews "began to make
a serious investigation" of any goal she pursued.

Before World War I, she lobbied for an international education organization to promote peace through collaboration in education, science,
and culture. Her vision wouldn't be realized until 1946, with the creation of UNESCO, the United Nations Education, Science, and Culture
Organization. Recently, Mrs. Andrews had toured ten capitals in Europe
and recalled, "there were ominous warnings as one event followed another."

One of these occurred close-by in April, less than half a block from
the Lorings' home on Beacon Hill. The German consul raised the swastika
flag at the consulate to celebrate Hitler's fifty-first birthday. Bostonians
protested, not that the swastika had risen, but that it had not been accompanied by the Stars and Stripes, also. Tempers flared, and the police kept
vigil in case of demonstrations.

The Germans maintained that they were not required to fly both flags,
but the swastika was lowered, just the same.[13] They had already invaded
Finland and Denmark and now battled three British and French divisions
in Norway. They were not ready to provoke the United States. The event
felt personal to Emilie. Not only had it happened on her street, but 39
Chestnut, now the German consulate, had once belonged to her mother.

The Blitzkrieg was underway. Germany attacked France and occupied
Luxembourg. The Netherlands and Belgium surrendered within days.
Norway held out until June.

Against a backdrop of international tumult, a Baker family scandal
unfolded that influenced Emilie's current book and the next. It involved

her first cousin Roy Cleveland Baker, a son of her father's last surviving sibling, Charles Tappan Baker.[14]

Roy's first marriage produced two sons and a daughter but ended in divorce. His second marriage, to Marion Thomas, lasted nearly twenty years, until she filed for a Reno divorce. That's when the drama began.

Within weeks, Roy married Leah Ojanen, who was just twenty-seven years old to his fifty-two. According to his ex-wife Marion, that relationship soured, and Roy came back to her. A Boston lawyer advised that Roy and Marion's Reno divorce was not recognized in Massachusetts, and therefore, under Massachusetts law, they were still married. Roy annulled his marriage to Leah and lived again with Marion.

Five days before Christmas in 1939, Roy told Marion he was leaving on a business trip, but he actually went to Worcester, Massachusetts, got the judge to waive the five-day waiting period, and married Leah again. Marion charged Roy with bigamy, a warrant was issued for his arrest, and newspapers jumped on the story of "Baker the bigamist."

Arrested in New York, Roy returned voluntarily to Massachusetts where a Worcester judge found him guilty of the bigamy charge, ordered him to pay a one hundred dollar fine, and granted his second divorce from Marion. Roy and Leah married again, and the two left in April 1940 for a new life in Buenos Aires, Argentina.

Roy Baker's new employer, the W. M. Jackson Company, published tour books of South America. Roy's job was to set up printing plants in Argentina to expand their offerings in Spanish and Portuguese.[15] It was an interesting career choice at that time, amid the tug-of-war between Germany and the United States for South American sympathies and the risk of getting stuck on the losing side.

By the time *There Is Always Love* came out on June twelfth, Italy had joined the Axis powers and attacked southern France. Near Paris, the French had retreated to the Marne in a last-ditch effort to save their capital. Refugees fled from city to country to the country beyond. Americans abroad sought passage home on American ships which were threatened by

---

"The Missus' lawyer has served notice that the divorce is final. He ought to be hugging himself that he's free."
Stars In Your Eyes

"Change 'really married' to legally married and it makes a whale of a lot of difference. There's another word, annulment, remember."
Stars in Your Eyes

He described . . . the harbor of Rio at night, set in a rim of sparkling lights; the streamers, horns, balloons and floats of the Buenos Aires Carnival . . .
Where Beauty Dwells

I've read heaps of confessions about what it means to be an Italian or an Armenian, or Jew or Norwegian in a strange country.
Stars in Your Eyes

German submarines, and Italians in the United States lined up to declare their American citizenship.[15]

Emilie's sons were too old to be drafted, if it came to that, and her eldest grandchild, Victor, was too young. Robert still lived in the family house at Wellesley Hills and worked as an insurance agent. Selden, who lived in Lexington with his wife and four children, worked for the ad agency by day and wrote stories by night, as his grandfather had done. His story, "That Was a Horse Race," had appeared in *Atlantic Monthly* in January, and his daughter Valentine had even earned a place on the *Boston Herald's* "Poetry Honor Roll."[16]

But Selden had served overseas during the first World War. Marne, Oise, and Argonne—all were places where he had walked, driven, and slept, under fire. He understood the personal cost behind the headlines, "Nazis fight to Bridge Seine at Rouen." He had gone to France's aid before his country declared war. When was the right time to act now?

Officially, hope held that the Allies would defeat the Axis powers and keep war away from American shores. The Germans showed no signs of wearing down, however, and an attack on the United States by sea or sky seemed increasingly possible. President Roosevelt pledged "the material resources of this nation" to the Allies and, at the same time, vowed to equip and train "we ourselves in the Americas . . . to the task of any emergency and every defense."[17]

Hope for the best, prepare for the worst. For now, they would go on with life as usual, albeit cautiously.

"Although our own Government policies, our speeding-up defense preparedness and the tragedy overseas are the topics uppermost in everyone's mind, I shall endeavor to turn the thoughts of my congregation toward hope, toward glimpses, hints and promises of goodness . . ." *Where Beauty Dwells*

My Purpose is to Entertain

In June 1940, Agnes Carr wrote for the *Boston Herald*, "In her latest novel, Mrs. Loring combines love, adventure and suspense in fascinating manner, and the result is rich entertainment."[18] The *Daily Boston Globe* called *There Is Always Love* "first-rate summer reading," but damned with faint praise:

> Emilie Loring ranks high on the list of our favorite authors, not because she is a very charming Bostonian, but because she has remained impervious to various literary trends and has per-servered [sic] in turning out gay, amusing, clean romance year after year.
>
> Mrs. Loring would probably be the last to make any great literary pretensions for her books, but there must be a good deal of satis-faction in entertaining a large number of persons once or twice a year with pleasant novels about pleasant characters.

Certainly, Emilie Loring's books entertained; they were *meant* to entertain. She must have written a note about it to Olga Owens at the *Transcript*, for a few days after she autographed books at Jordan Marsh again, she received a letter from Olga:[19]

> Would you, I wonder, sometime write a letter for our Saturday Box, expressing the thoughts in this private letter to me—the need of entertainment in this troubled world of today? Coming from you, these words would carry weight, and I would appreciate the gesture more than I can say.

She followed two weeks later:[20]

My dear Mrs. Loring,

If we do not use your letter very soon, I promise to destroy it. However, it took you a lot of time, and I like it so very much that I think it can be worked in all by itself. Thank you ever so much for bothering with us.

Sincerely,

Olga

Emilie Loring's letter appeared in the July thirteenth *Boston Transcript*. At length, she described the purpose and process that produced her entertaining novels. As much as any style of writing, she described, entertaining fiction is a craft that must be carefully honed, and in the darkest times, its value shines brightest.

A Well-Beloved Author Writes to Please

To the Book Editor:

May I say, "Thank you," here for the sympathetic understanding of my novels expressed by Ida M. Parker in your Letter Box?

I hereby frankly declare that I write to entertain. It is my hope, more than ever now when the deep and bitter tragedy of this anguished world lies heavy on every heart, that when my name appears on a gay book jacket, my followers will promptly park their problems outside the cover and fare forth with me into the realm of imagination, where there is always romance, always adventure in a story, salted not too heavily I trust, with my philosophy of life. If, when those same readers reach THE END, they forget to pick up some of their problems, Victory perches on my banner.

I write of the ideals and ideas, hopes and fears, joys and sorrows, ambitions and failures, the loves and hates of persons whom I understand. The fact that they wear up-to-the-minute clothes,

"I liked the story very much indeed. The author has written to entertain, not to educate. That's what I want when I pick up a novel in the middle of a sleepless night."
Across the Years

live in charming houses, serve tea in colorful gardens, own cars and sometimes spectacular jewels, does not make them less vulnerable to mistakes and despair, says I.

RE: those same luxurious possessions. I devote from nine to ten months to a novel and during the major part of each day I exist in the world I am creating. Why spend all that time in a sordid environment? I like charming surroundings. I laugh, weep, thrill with the characters. I snap off pencil-point after pencil-point as I dig it into a sheet of yellow paper in my breathless eagerness to rescue the daring from a desperate situation.

Every little while I re-discover the thrill—and perils—of novel writing. Only yesterday the male lead in the story upon which I am at work landed his plane casually, too casually, it appears, at LaGuardia Field. Today I learned that while any "ship" may land in our own East Boston Airport, only one equipped with a two-way radio may come down in LaGuardia Field.

Ice splinters slithered through my veins as I realized the flood of criticism which would be let loose on me via U.S. Mail were I to make that break. ZOOM! I shot the plane up tail first like a moving picture in reverse. I installed a two-way radio in that "ship" with a speed which would cause a skilled mechanic to go pop-eyed with surprise, turn green with envy. Now, our hero is circling the blue like a great silver bird (heaven help us both if his fuel gives out) while I skurry [sic] round to find out what he should do next, how to use the aforementioned radio. (Aviators with a Boy Scout training, please take notice.)

So, you see, life is real, life is earnest, and the creative way is pitted with shell-holes even for the author who writes to entertain. Emilie Loring

Fall 1940

By fall, 1940, Emilie had turned in the manuscript for *Where Beauty Dwells* and started on a novel in a brand-new location: Mexico. Subversive, "fifth column" activities were in the news, and they brought attention to the country's southern neighbors.

> "I'm sorry to have to admit that the Mexicans are not completely sold on Americans; they are being harassed by propaganda. There is a foreign element here which loses no opportunity to create ill-feeling between them."

She already had background from "Her Box of Books" about Mexico. She also subscribed to a Mexican-American magazine and wrote to a Congressman for pamphlets to get information about the Consular Service that would play a part in the story.

As the story opens, Kay Chesney is on her way to live with her stepbrother, who is an American consul to Mexico. Kay is forced at gunpoint to marry Drex Hamilton, an American with a Mexican stepfamily. He admires her bravery, and she trusts him on sight, impressed by his quick thinking.

Kay learns that Drex is her stepbrother's best friend and will forfeit a large inheritance if their marriage is discovered. The stage is set for a romantic comedy in which the characters willfully misunderstand each other and work at cross-purposes, but these don't. When next they meet, their initial trust and friendliness holds.

> She had forgotten he was so tall; hadn't realized he was so darkly handsome . . . His hair was black, as was his slight mustache. His features were clear cut. His skin was a rich bronze . . . his eyes . . . a clear, dark blue . . . Well-knit compact body. Lean hips and waist. A man who would get things done.

"This country is a superbly placed vantage ground from which to strike at the United States."
Stars In Your Eyes

"What is this? A movie company on location?" . . . He bent as if to kiss her, whispered: "Name's Drex. Danger."
Stars In Your Eyes

. . . "If I'm a judge of the female of the species, and I am, your sister will be the toast of the town's caballeros." He grinned boyishly. "You'll have to agree that I'm off to a flying start with the lady, Consul."

Emilie confessed later that she fell "desperately, secretly in love" with Drex as she wrote, attracted to his sense of humor and partnership. "He shares 50-50 with Kay in her great adventure."[21]

Equality between partners mattered to Emilie. They might begin at different levels socially, financially, or strategically, but she saw to it that the field was leveled before they gave their hearts.

After all, if he didn't take the mix-up seriously, why should she? "If keeping afloat means pulling together, I'm right beside you, Skipper."

One of the bad guys in this novel is Herr Von Haas:

"Our hostess has a nice sense of humor." In such a voice and inflection Von Haas might have ordered a victim to a concentration camp.

Von Haas is involved in a scheme to use foreign vessels to reroute Mexican resources to the Third Reich, and Kay pleads:

"She made them realize that North, Central and South America are one country. "
Stars in Your Eyes

"Don't believe this man. Don't take his government's money. As for our intention to annex Mexico, it's absurd. Much as we like you, we don't want to take on your problems. Would you want to tackle ours? I bet you wouldn't. We are both working for hemisphere solidarity. One America."

The swastika-raising incident in Boston became a question about why the American flag wasn't flown above the American consulate in Mexico.

"Why aren't the Stars and Stripes floating above the consulate, Gordon?" she asked as a white-suited Indian swung the gate open. "The flag is displayed only on occasions of special ceremony."

Central and South America were in turmoil, caught in a fight between the United States and Germany for the hearts and minds of their citizens and leaders. Agents discovered a German plot to overthrow Uruguay with help from confederates in both Brazil and Argentina. Brazil's President Vargas claimed solidarity with the Americas but then defended the Germans' fascist principles. Roy Baker's presence in Argentina raised questions. Was it possible to live in Buenos Aires and remain unaffected?

Kay learns the story of the Plumed Serpent (Quetzalcoatl) of Mexico, in which stars symbolize peace and the vigilance required to protect it. The Plumed Serpent was "a wise king, a lover of peace, honored by his people. He knew about the stars and how they moved in heaven." Shamed and dishonored by Smoking Mirror, "who loved war and violence," the Plumed Serpent threw himself into the flames, and his heart rose to become the evening star. Drex voices the book's title:

Thank heaven for the stars. They looked friendly. *Stars In Your Eyes*

"Stars in your eyes, sister."
"What does that mean? You've said it before."
"When at Casa Fresco you looked up at me, I thought, 'An unconquerable soul. One with such stars of valor in her eyes will refuse to accept defeat. She has a winner's heart.'"

While Emilie wrote, her son Selden added "Quiz Master" for radio WBZ's "Ask the Children" program to his many roles. Each week, five children, aged twelve to fifteen, met before a studio audience of three hundred to compete in questions of general knowledge.

"Mr. Loring" sat at a desk and microphone opposite the children, who had microphones hanging down above their desks, also. Each evening, the announcer, "Jack" Manning, introduced the children and recited the old adage that "Children should be seen and not heard." He then asked the audience to vote on whether the rule could be relaxed for the night, and after a loud "aye," the show began.

Selden asked questions, the children answered, and points were awarded for fully- and partially correct answers. "Name three women famous in battle." "What was the first state added to the original thirteen?" "What two fruits have the same letters making up their names?" During a time-out, members of the audience were asked to step to the microphone and answer questions, too, which they did with varying degrees of success and amusement.

More questions for the children followed, and the two or three with the highest score got to return for the next week's show. Children earned ten dollars for a first appearance, fifteen for a second, twenty for a third, and twenty-five dollars for each appearance beyond that.[22]

Emilie got a chance to be on a quiz show, herself, when Charles Lee, the literary editor of the *Philadelphia Record*, invited her to be a guest "Scholar" on the "9 O'clock Scholars" show.[23]

We don't pay our guest stars, but, of course, we do pay their expenses, both railroad and hotel, and we do give them a lot of publicity in the Record and on the air, which has never yet failed to produce results for their books.

These programs are held every Wednesday at 9 o'clock on Station WIP. If you could make it for any Wednesday from December 18th on, it would be swell for us and I hope for you also. We would like to have you for dinner if you could arrange to get here by that time, but you wouldn't have to be at the radio station, which is located at 35 S. 9th St. (Gimbel Bros. Store), until 8:30."

She responded:

Your proposition that I join the 9 o'clock scholars on Wednesday, December 18th sounds very interesting . . . Now, before I decide, please let me know a little more of what is expected of me on the program. Am I to be one of the "experts to be stumped"? I can fit the date, December 18th, into my schedule. As soon as I hear from you, I will send a definite answer to your invitation.

Mr. Lee's letter had been addressed to "Miss Emilie Loring." She signed hers, tactfully:

Sincerely yours,
(Mrs.) Emilie Loring.

Mr. Lee reassured in a letter addressed, properly, to Mrs. Loring:

There are four "experts" on every week, and they submit to a cross-examination by the Masters of Ceremonies. Questions are varied, entertaining and not too hard. I know you would find the experience interesting and your part on the program easy to perform.

Her reply was crisp:[24]

Dear Mr. Lee,
This is to make the date of December 18th definite. Here's hoping that I do myself credit as a "9 O'clock Scholar". I receive a great deal of fan mail from Pennsylvania. I must make good on your program.

She reminded him of her membership in the Boston Branch of the National League of American Pen Women and that there was a large branch of the organization in Philadelphia. Mindful of the publicity he had promised, she concluded:

THERE IS ALWAYS LOVE published in June was my nineteenth novel. The galley-proofs of my twentieth have just arrived for correction. Thrilling, isn't it?

The next week, she wrote again to Mr. Lee, and emphasized current events among her many interests.[25]

In answer to your query as to my outside interests and hobbies. My family and my writing are my major interests. After them, I should list first THE WORLD TODAY. The tragic surge of events keeps one emotionally stirred and intellectually on the run in the effort not to fall too far behind the daily news.

Books, the stage, my Maine garden, and always people and their stories, what spark of an idea blazed into a successful career. It is hard to catalogue my interests when I find life so stimulating and exciting.

I will be in the lobby of the Benjamin Franklin Hotel on December 18th at 7 p.m.

Sincerely yours, Emilie Loring

Emilie stayed with friends in New York and took the train to Philadelphia on the day of the broadcast. Her performance earned the Scholars seven out of eleven points. She remembered that the Duchess of Windsor (Wallis Simpson) had lost a tooth in Miami and that Manhattan socialite Lady Decies had lost a fur coat to Hermann Goering, but she didn't know her own astrological sign (Virgo).[26]

Despite Mr. Lee's promises, Emilie did not get "a lot of publicity." She followed up—on Christmas Day—with diplomatic insistence.[27]

> It was a grand and glorious experience. I enjoyed every moment of it, liked my co-performers immensely and fervently thanked my lucky star that I knew a few of the answers.
>
> Not until I was on my way to New York did I realize that my current, well-selling novel hadn't been mentioned by name. If I had interested your 45,000 listeners, a plug for the novel might have had results. I wonder if you could or would make up for the omission at the next broadcast. Your fine Master of Ceremonies might announce:
>
> "In answer to many queries; the name of Emilie Loring's latest best-seller novel is *There Is Always Love*. It's a gay, up-to-the-minute story of romance and adventure dashed with mystery." Or words to that effect which would not consume more than a couple of seconds and might do a lot for the book.

Beloved Boston Novelist

Emilie's celebrity status made fans curious about her as a person. Book jackets touted her family's accomplishments and influence, but fans wanted to know more about *her*. What was she like? What were her interests? What was it like to be a writer?

In an interview with Priscilla Fortesque on WEEI radio,[28] Emilie welcomed, "I love my work. I love to talk about it almost as much." What was it like to be a writer?

> Writing was such an experiment at first that I depended on that tricky jade, Inspiration, to lure me to the typewriter. It didn't take long to learn that I would not become a real writer until I set apart regular hours for it.

After a long day of writing,

I'm only too glad to resume homemaking activities. Concocting a dessert, preparing a salad, even scrubbing Idaho potatoes for baking till they're clean and shining is a restful change from hours of mental concentration.

What was it like to have twenty-one books published and a twenty-second on the way? She replied,

Often when I look at the row on my bookshelves of Emilie Lorings (that's the way they are referred to by the trade) I think, where did all the characters between those covers come from? They are still living laughing, adventuring, loving persons to me.

Asked how she wrote her novels, Emilie responded with prepared remarks.

I don't know. I only know that when I sit down at my desk and pick up my yellow pencil, I slip into a different world. A technicolor world of enchantment where anything may happen and usually does with breath-snatching speed . . . The very day after the manuscript of my novel rolls off the assembly line to my publishers, I start a new story. There can be no vacation for my imagination while it is working with speed and precision.

She repeated her philosophy, the "clear flame" of her belief that

The beautiful things of life are as real as the ugly things of life; that gay courage may turn threatened defeat into victory; that hitching one's wagon to the star of achievement lifts one high above the quicksands of discouragement.

Not that I want to preach, I have a horror of that, but a story like
a life should be built upon the firm foundation of a worthwhile
belief and that happens to be mine.

Natalie Gordon featured Emilie in a *Boston Traveler* series called "Our
Gracious Ladies."[29] Miss Gordon's physical description flattered, "she is
striking in appearance, with expressive brown eyes, white hair and wide
smile."

Her white hair, preference for Charles Dickens, and the furnishings
of her Chestnut Street apartment—"antiques, chintz and old family portraits"—all fit expectations for a "gracious lady." So did her taste in art—
Rembrandt, Rubens and Titian.

The remainder of Miss Gordon's article, though, revealed how a seventy-
four-year-old could write twenty-something characters so convincingly.

Has a mania for collecting boxes (silver or shiny pasteboard, it
makes no difference); and she likes red hats, dramatic dinner
dresses, and "anything that glitters," be it diamonds or neon lights
. . . Adores white lilacs, Strauss waltzes and rainy days; and her
major irritation is an open door. . . Likes informal gatherings;
enjoys playing rummy, but shies from contract bridge . . .

Her club memberships placed her squarely in her social class on the
hill: the Boston Authors Club, Association of American Pen Women,
Women's Republican Club, and the D. A. R. More personal details were
rare for their sharing:

Has four grandchildren and is known as "Betty" to her family,
with whom she makes a point of never discussing shop.

When *Where Beauty Dwells* appeared on bookstore shelves, Agnes
Carr wrote, "A new book by Emilie Loring, Boston's much-beloved writer,

is always a joy to her legion of admirers . . . It would be unfair to reveal all the angles of the thrilling plot which is new and timely and mingles adventure with the most delightful kind of romance."[30]

Fellow Boston Authors Club members asked how she created her plots when Emilie was their guest speaker on April fourth.[31] Did she plan an entire story before writing it? She answered, "No. I expect the characters to make the plot. I start with a theme—self-sacrifice—honor—generosity—like the text of a sermon. The plot evolves from the incidents which demonstrate that theme." She also never thought about whether the story would work on stage or screen. "I am writing a novel, not a play. After I get to know the characters, I hurl them against situations for drama."

She spoke crisply and decisively. "I have heard it argued that one should keep one's public in mind. I'm afraid I don't." She mentioned a minor character she had expected to be more important to the story she was then writing (*Stars In Your Eyes*), but he "remains wooden. I suspect that in the second draft he will be handed his walking papers."

She also read aloud a new composition, "The Story the Titles Told," which used all of her book titles in order of publication. Her father had done the same with Charles Dickens' titles. Hers told the history of her career.

> Like all beginning writers I fared forth on THE TRAIL OF CONFLICT, then plodded on til suddenly I exclaimed, HERE COMES THE SUN! On I went until I reached A CERTAIN CROSSROAD. As I lingered, wondering which turn to make, up galloped THE SOLITARY HORSEMAN. He smiled and pointed. I tripped along with GAY COURAGE, crossed a bridge above SWIFT WATER and saw LIGHTED WINDOWS glowing on the shore of UNCHARTED SEAS. FAIR TOMORROW, I predicted, as HILLTOPS CLEAR loomed on the horizon, WE'LL RIDE THE GALE. We set sail WITH BANNERS flying and reached the glorious coast of Maine. IT'S A GREAT WORLD! I exclaimed; GIVE ME ONE SUMMER

here and I'll stay AS LONG AS I LIVE. But an inner voice whispered, "Don't linger, remember TODAY IS YOURS." So, HIGH OF HEART I fared on gayly until I reached a city, a beautiful city which the eyes of the whole world are watching, to which the ears of the whole world are listening. As I looked ACROSS THE YEARS I thought, no matter how the earth may tremble from the tramp of advancing armies, the rumble of murderous tanks, the shriek and crash of bombs, THERE IS ALWAYS LOVE. Love for God, for country, for mankind. Love endures forever in the human mind and heart and soul WHERE BEAUTY DWELLS.

The *Boston Traveler* and *Boston Herald* published their features on Emilie Loring in the spring. The *Boston Post* followed in June. "A Beloved Boston Novelist Talks About Work and Play"[32] was an intimate portrait of the author by the *Post*'s new book editor, Olga Owens.

Olga and Emilie had known each other quite a while. Olga was a reviewer and columnist for the *Boston Herald* when Emilie published her first novels. When Emilie signed on with Little, Brown, Olga Owens was one of their manuscript readers. Olga belonged to the Boston Authors Club by virtue of articles she wrote for *Life* and *The Saturday Evening Post*. While she was the assistant literary editor for the *Boston Evening Transcript*, she had invited Emilie to write about the importance of entertainment literature, and now, she was in the head spot at the *Boston Post*.

The women also knew each other from Wellesley Hills. Olga and her husband, Stuart Huckins, lived on Bancroft Road in Wellesley Hills. Their home nearly backed up to the Loring property on Longfellow Road. They were a generation younger, so they started their family about the same time that Emilie and Victor first considered moving to Beacon Hill. Olga still belonged to the Wellesley Hills Woman's Club and had recently read aloud Emilie's greeting to the group.

When the women met in the Lorings' apartment on Chestnut Street, their relaxed conversation wandered comfortably between personal and professional topics. The resulting article was warm with the sorts of details a friend would know. She introduced Emilie's "four adorable grandchildren" by name— "Valentine, Linda, Victor, Jr., and Denny . . . but not one of them has inherited their grandmother's big brown eyes . . ." She also knew that they called Emilie "Grand'-ma-*ma*":

"By the way, do you know any other grandmama who writes a best seller every year? We don't."

"I detest fashions for the so-called older woman—they are so apt to be old-ladyish—size sixteen styles appeal to me . . . But I still have sufficient self-discipline not to buy them."
Rainbow at Dusk

Olga acknowledged Emilie's impeccable style: "Mrs. Loring's frocks speak of Vogue, her silver is all sterling." But instead of a Bachrach portrait, the accompanying photograph showed Emilie at her desk, her side to the camera, ostensibly reading a paper she held in one hand, with her chin resting on the other.

The "candid" photo was carefully put together. She wore no glasses, although she had required them for reading since her forties and had even tied pairs of them on furniture throughout her house, so they would always be at hand. Without glasses, she wrote in large script—half-inch capitals and quarter-inch lower-case—and could not have read the document she now held in her hand.

Because I had left my spectacles upstairs, I read a recipe wrong. . .
For the Comfort of the Family

Her hair was carefully marcelled, but she wore a casual skirt and blouse, and her desk wasn't set for company.

Cubby-holes bulged with mail, presumably from her fans, and framed photos filled the space above—one of her grandfather, Albert Baker, the first of the Bakers in publishing. It was a working woman's desk for the "Queen of Romance, Emilie Loring, whose twenty popular novels have sold nearly three-quarters of a million copies."

"It is Emilie Loring's gayety that is so great a part of her charm as a person and as a writer," Olga wrote. They read a fan letter together: "Thank you for your cheery words of comfort. Your last book was written just for me." Olga went on,

Emilie Loring at Her Desk

Her Handwriting

It is this intimate feeling of gratitude that colors so many of the countless fan letters that come to this Boston woman every year . . . "You know there are wars and terrors, but you remind us, too, that 'there is always love.'"

It wasn't only that her novels were pleasant. They connected. And the reason they connected was that she stayed up-to-date and had the experience and insight to know what her readers cared about. Like Lee & Shepard before her, Emilie Loring's success came from sensing the public's taste and always staying just one step in front of it.

Emilie was already collecting ideas for a new book (*Rainbow at Dusk*) which she described as "singularly timely." Insisting upon "authenticity in every detail," she scoured newspapers and local references for helpful information and organized her notes by color: pink for character, blue for atmosphere, white for dialogue. "I collect and collect," said Mrs. Loring, "and then perhaps out of any number of notes, use only one small thing." A plot might start with one incident, and then bits and pieces came together, one by one, with a central theme to guide them.

The story was going to deal with avoiding war while simultaneously preparing for it. Civilians took Red Cross and motor corps courses that included first aid, ambulance driving, car mechanics, and lighting an airfield. "Under her gayety," Olga wrote, "there is this awareness of the opposite.'You can't hold up the action of a story to philosophize, no matter how you may want to,' [Emilie] said. Yet now and then she does let a favorite character reveal some of the depths of her personality."

Maine Author

Emilie Loring having summered in Maine for more than three decades, the Maine State Library accepted her as one of their own and requested a copy of *Where Beauty Dwells* for their Maine Author Collection. "We realize that we cannot claim you through birth. Any claim would of necessity

> "I agree with all you say about helping other countries, but first a steady, unwavering tide of determination to restore law and order at home and freedom for each citizen to work where, when and how he pleases, is what this country needs most."
> *Rainbow at Dusk*

be as toward Laura E. Richards, also born in Boston . . . and others who are not Maine natives but have lived here or written about the state."[33]

Emilie had known Laura E. Richards from childhood. Laura's mother was Julia Ward Howe, an associate of her father's, and Richards' *Julia Ward Howe Birthday Book* was one of the last books published under George Baker's auspices at Lee & Shepard. Laura E. Richards moved to Gardiner, Maine after her marriage in the 1870s and earned a Pulitzer in 1917 for the biography of her famous mother. By then, she had written what she called "an unconscionable number" of books, most of which were out of print, except *Captain January*, which remained popular long after its publication.

Mary Ellen Chase, Blue Hill's most famous author, recalled listening to Richards read *Captain January* aloud in nearby Ellsworth. Although she was only twelve at the time, she called it "one of the high-water marks of my life."[34] A year later, she met another famous Maine author, Sarah Orne Jewett, and shared her ambition to write books. "I'm sure you will," replied Jewett. "And good ones, too—all about Maine."[35]

An English professor at Smith College, Mary Ellen Chase became a best-selling author and one of the most important regional writers in America. *Windswept*, to be published in November, would prove her most commercially successful book, but she regarded her first autobiography, *A Goodly Heritage* (1932), about her childhood amongst the people of Blue Hill, as her most important work.

In addition to Emilie Loring and Mary Ellen Chase, Blue Hill enjoyed the presence that summer of A. J. Cronin, author of *The Citadel*, who had rented one of the Slaven cottages. With nine best-sellers already to his credit, *The Keys of the Kingdom* had just been published by Little, Brown in May and sold nearly three hundred thousand copies in only four days. *Keys* was written in Maine but did not qualify Cronin as a Maine author; one had to be born in Maine, write about Maine, or be a long-time summer resident of the state.

One more author lived in nearby North Brooklin. A popular essayist for the *New Yorker* and *Harper's Magazine*, E. B. "Andy" White was born in New York but summered in Blue Hill as a young man and bought his Allen Cove cottage in 1933. His given name was "Elwyn Brooks White," which was interesting, since Ned Brooks' home was named "Elwin Cove" for his daughter Elinor and son Winfield "Win" Brooks.

White would be invited to the Maine Authors Collection in another year, for *One Man's Meat* (1942). Still later, he would be recognized as perhaps the most popular of Maine authors for *Stuart Little* (1945) and *Charlotte's Web* (1950, set at the Blue Hill Fair). For now, though, Mary Ellen Chase and Emilie Loring were Blue Hill's "Maine Authors."

Emilie sent an inscribed copy of *Where Beauty Dwells* to the Maine State Library, whose secretary replied, "The charming inscription is exceptionally pleasing, and we appreciate its words. We are very glad to include WHERE BEAUTY DWELLS, with its varied characterizations, its clouds and rocks and herbs and calendulas, its gallantry and romance and should its author find a visit to the library possible, she is assured of a most cordial welcome."[36] Emilie's inscription read: "Presented to the Maine Author collection by a writer who believes that the State of Maine is a land where family dwells. Emilie Loring."[37]

Contemporary Fiction is Contemporary History

Emilie signed the contract for *Stars in Your Eyes* in September and promised another manuscript by the following June (1942). Little, Brown took the option on her next book, as well.

In late October, she sat among the guests of honor at a luncheon hosted by the Boston branch of the National League of American Pen Women. The event was held in conjunction with the annual Boston Herald Book Fair, which brought prominent authors together and allowed the public to buy autographed copies of their latest books.

Stars In Your Eyes was timed for release that week—maximum exposure for Emilie Loring's twenty-first book: "a novel of love, adventure and mystery in modern Mexico." Little, Brown posted a large ad in the major papers. No mention was made of her seventy-fifth birthday. Only: "Thank you, once again, Mrs. Loring!"

Emilie Loring has now written twenty-one novels of which 750,000 copies have been sold. Each of her books is still in print, evidence of the enduring satisfaction they give to readers old and new . . ."

"Thank you for more happy hours . . . for more of the wholesome pleasure you alone know how to give." Each time a new Emilie Loring novel is published letters with words like these come to the author from readers who feel they must express their gratitude to a writer who believes that life can be pleasant and that most people are decent.

These letters reveal the deep-rooted hunger for the kind of books Mrs. Loring writes—the almost universal longing for romance that doesn't need scandal to make it exciting . . .[38]

All of this was perfectly true. Her novels entertained, as she intended. But she didn't work so hard at the details of her stories for nothing. She accepted the praise without telling all she thought. She confided in notes for an interview:

I'll begin by confessing that the most embarrassing moment of my life is when a friend introduces me somewhat in this fashion: "Miss Blank, I want you to meet Emilie Loring. Of course, you read her work." Miss Blank goes slightly red and for an instant more than slightly tongue-tied, then rallies, "I must be honest and say that I don't. You see, I'm so busy I don't have time to read fiction." To which statement I want to reply, "Gal, contemporary fiction is contemporary history. Read it." Instead, I smile and say, "Life is so full of a number of things, isn't it?" and move on.[39]

She had read "frank" novels. Not many, she hated them. Always they produced the hotly embarrassed sense of having opened a bedroom door by mistake.
The Solitary Horseman

That was Aunt Ellen. She wore neither her loves nor her aversions on her sleeve for the public to peck at; her good manners were inviolable."
Rainbow at Dusk

CHAPTER 26

Fight for the Right: 1941–46

How long would the sense of security last?
Rainbow at Dusk

"...it's a terrifying responsibility to take on when one realizes that quick, accurate identification of hostile aircraft may depend upon a spotter's ability to recognize the sounds as well as the outlines of different types of planes."
Rainbow at Dusk

In Emilie Loring's new story, as in the real world, Europe was at war, and the United States teetered on the edge. Jessamine Ramsay, named for the yellow-flowering vine, visits her great-aunt Ellen Marshall whose North Carolina estate, Karrisbrooke, is being used by the military for war preparedness. Major Vance Trent breaks an ankle during a parachuting exercise that lands him on the Karrisbrooke lawn. Jess administers first aid, and the higher-ups keep Trent at the estate to investigate possible bootlegging and sabotage.

Emilie developed the story through September, October, and November. At first, Jessamine hopes that the United States can stay out of war; later, she feels its inevitability.

> Suddenly it was as if she saw swift and terrible thunderheads of war surging up from the glowing horizon. For an instant terror stopped her breath....

Threats at home felt real. Civilians watched for German U-boats offshore and enemy airplanes overhead. If there were an air raid, the public warning was a series of short blasts on whatever device a community had, bells, siren, or whistle. The all-clear would be signaled by two minutes of continuous sound from the same device.[1] Then came December 7, 1941:

> Vance Trent's grave voice sent a little shiver of apprehension along Jessamine's nerves. Even in the dim light she could see the whiteness of his face. "Japan has attacked Pearl Harbor. It looks like war at last."

"It's come," Ellen Marshall said. "Now we know where we stand—united—or we won't stand."

The attack on Pearl Harbor eclipsed Victor and Emilie's fiftieth wedding anniversary on December ninth. A practice air raid alarm sounded shortly after noon, and until the all-clear came nearly two hours later, people across New England cast anxious eyes skyward and hurried to designated places of safety.

The Red Cross and Massachusetts Women's Defense Corps mobilized hundreds of members "to administer first aid, feed the homeless, suffocate bombs, or evacuate the civilian population to safety."

On the radio that night, President Roosevelt acknowledged "serious defeats" in the Pacific.[2] "We are now in this war. We are all in it—all the way . . . It will not only be a long war, it will be a hard war."[3]

Spring 1942

The sneak-attack on Pearl Harbor already seemed a hundred years ago. At last she was beginning to emerge from the shock of war declared . . . Humiliating as it was to have been caught napping, the catastrophe had served to unite the citizens of the United States in a gigantic war program. (*Rainbow at Dusk*)

Emilie's careful notes kept events in order. Usually, her novels summarized events less identifiably, but she called these by name.

First the *Allen Jackson* went down in a sea of flames [18 January 1942]. The *Malay's* rudder was shot away. She foundered [19 January]. Two other ships followed her to the bottom [*Norvana*, 19 January; *Venore*, 24 January]."

"We must all do more to help, stand like an invincible army behind our fighting men. I lie awake nights thinking how I can more fully justify my reason for living in the most critical period in the history of civilization."
Rainbow at Dusk

They weren't only ships; they were people's fathers, sons, husbands, and brothers.

At the end of January, Emilie was one of a large group to sponsor a gathering of literary and women's groups at Copley Square to discuss the role of authors during wartime. The luncheon included the biggest names in social and literary circles, members of the Boston Authors Club, Professional Women's Club, the Boston branch of the League of American Pen Women, the Manuscript Club, and the New England Women's Press Association. As a Baker, Emilie recognized the clarion call: "In the midst of war and a changing world, time out for a mental uplift is important and it is to writers the world looks to build up courage and sustain morale."[4]

In March, the gold dome of the State House was painted "dull war-gray" to hide it from enemy aircraft.[5] The very thought, that a building so revered—and just down the street from her own home—should be in hiding, was sobering.

She finished her manuscript in June. The original title was *Rainbow at Night*:

Rainbow at night, sailor's delight . . . It means to the sailor that the day of storm is behind him, that he may confidently look forward to the favoring winds and sunshine of a fair tomorrow.

But dusk, the final light of twilight before night descends, was the right label for this book's time period, those final hours before war was declared. "*Rainbow at Dusk*" signaled that the storm was not yet behind, that victory could not be taken for granted. She gave vent to her consternation:

Why, why had this savage war had to happen? A war which pulled men of all ages, in all countries, up by the roots to fling them, their families, homes, businesses, creative talents, into the maelstrom of blood and destruction?

. . . The waste, the tragic waste of it.

Summer 1942

Travel was not yet specifically prohibited, but all were encouraged to set aside vacation and weekend travel to save gasoline. Last summer, the Lorings rented their cottage across the road to a performer at Blue Hill's Kneisel Hall. Povla Frijsh was a soprano from Denmark who debuted as a soloist in Paris and sang opera in Copenhagen. In 1910, Gustav Mahler chose her to sing his Second Symphony in Cologne, and she made her United States debut in 1915. Decades later, she taught at Juilliard and commanded large audiences for her annual recitals in New York.[6] Now, The Ledges was hers, and the Lorings had one fewer responsibility in Blue Hill.

Fall 1942

Rainbow at Dusk was published by Little, Brown in September 1942 with the same physical qualities as her earlier books. Grosset & Dunlap's edition was noticeably thinner, though, and it bore a wartime publishing announcement:

> This book, while produced under wartime conditions, in full compliance with government regulations for the conservation of paper and other essential materials, is COMPLETE AND UNABRIDGED.

Little, Brown's advertisement presented only the book's sunny face, "Emilie Loring's new novel of love and adventure in war-time." Her reputation was, rightly, optimistic. But the cheerful optimism that relied on stalwart character to overcome fear, danger, and uncertainty for a higher purpose was so different from simply a happy story. Better was the *Boston Herald*'s review on the front page of its book section, which called it a "timely and delightfully complicated romance," "as relevant to today as this morning's coffee."

Emilie pressed on with the third book covered by her most recent contract with Little, Brown: *When Hearts Are Light Again*. It was a happy title to accompany the birth of Robert's first child, Sandra, on September fourteenth, and fittingly, it began in mid-September.

Her theme, like that of President Roosevelt, was a call to service at home and staunch support of the country's fighting forces.

"I'll remind you of what the President said the other day. 'Victory cannot be bought with any amount of money, however large. Victory is achieved by the blood of soldiers, the sweat of working men and women and the sacrifices of all people.' I'll add, on my own, and the absolute loyalty of each worker to his or her job."

Hopes hung on news from the front. Every victory encouraged; every defeat was disheartening.

"Everyone is tense now, Aunt Jane, and will be till the time comes when hearts are light again."

"When hearts are light again. That's a thought for anxious days and wakeful nights. Just the sound of the words lifts the weight from my spirit and reminds me that the skies always clear."

Pilot Gregory Hunt wants to even the score in the Pacific where he was shot down. Instead, he is assigned to discover the source of faulty airplane parts coming out of the Clifton Works, a plant charged with turning out more and safer airplanes. Gail Trevor is his friend's kid sister and a secretary at the Works. She gave up a Washington, D.C. job to take care of her brother and his two children when their mother enlisted. Slinky Lila Tenney is Greg's social-climbing fiancé.

Writing was interrupted by the sudden death of her lifetime friend Beth Kerley in late October. The funeral was held at her home parish, St.

Thomas' Episcopal Church in New York. She was only seventy-one, five years younger than Emilie.

Just one year before, in the spring of 1941, Emilie had taken her grandchildren, Valentine and Victor, to visit Beth. They stayed a week at the Barbizon Plaza and saw both the *Queen Mary* and the *Normandie*,[7] which had been brought into New York harbor to protect them from German submarines. Now, the *Normandie* lay at the bottom of the harbor, and Beth was gone, but Emilie had no intention of "going."

> "What do you mean, 'go'? Die? I've no intention of dying for
> years and years. In times like these one stiffens and carries on.
> One doesn't weaken. There is too much to be done here on earth."
> (*Rainbow at Dusk*)

The United States Navy suffered defeats at Bataan and Corregidor. Thousands of Marines had been killed or taken captive by the Japanese. Anxious families awaited news that didn't come or was sometimes wrong. In an unusual appearance of Emilie's characters in two books, she provided news about Vance Trent and Johnny Grant from *Rainbow at Dusk*:

> "Isn't that a letter sticking from your pocket? Why not sit here
> and read it?
>
> "It's from Jess Ramsay," she explained eagerly . . . 'Vance is
> back, terribly thin, the skin of his drawn face looks like leather and
> so grim that until he caught me in his arms I wondered if he still
> loved me, but he's whole. Aunt Ellen and I flew to Washington
> to see him receive his decoration. The men he had trained came
> through so magnificently he has been detailed to head the para-
> chute instruction division at a camp here. Am I happy? I'm telling
> you. Remember Johnny? He'll not come back—ever.'"

The need for men was endless. Emilie's nephew, Melville Baker, registered for the "young men's draft" in February and enlisted in December to create films for the War Department. Her sons had both served in World War I but registered for the "old man's" draft for men up to age sixty-four—just in case.

Christmas would be limited this year, but Olga Owens pointed out in the *Boston Post* that books, at least, were not yet rationed:

> It has been difficult to find enough sales people, this year, to take care of the enormous and constant demand by the public, who realize as keenly as you and I do, that books make the most economical, long-lasting, and pleasure-giving presents in the world, with the added attraction that you can GET them.[8]
>
> No, there are no ceilings on books, and the gallant authors who help us to forget our worries and deeper troubles for a time, distill their written magic for our delight, assuring Boston, the book lovingest metropolis in America, a literate as well as delightful Christmas. Here in Boston maybe found good cheer as of old; refreshment for the mind, and strength for the spirit.

Olga's essay introduced a feature article, "Emilie Loring Remembers Her Own White Christmas,"[9] complete with her childhood photograph, captioned "Tiny Emilie." Emilie wrote as though in a letter to Olga Owens, almost immediately referencing her favorite, *Alice*.

> Dear O. O.—When you wrote, "Would you do a little piece about childhood in New England touching upon Christmas," you handed me a golden key to a door at the end of a dusky corridor of memory, a door just high enough for a little girl to enter.

She told of her mother reading the Christmas story to her and Robert on Christmas Eve, of her parents making noise downstairs as they played

Santa, of acting in "The Fairy of the Fountain" and Henry Clay Barnabee's performance afterwards.

Before Christmas, Emilie and Victor attended the funeral of Charles Tappan Baker,[10] the last of her father's siblings and a player in some of her childhood theatricals. Like the other Bakers, Charles spent his professional life in publishing, first in bookbinding and later as president of Lothrop, Lee & Shepard publishers. For the first twenty years of their sixty-six years of marriage, Charles and his wife, Jennie, acted in amateur theatricals. As the Baker family historian, he gave Emilie the supporting material for her application to the Daughters of the American Revolution, addressing his letters to "Bess" or "Betty."

When Christmas came, Emilie and Victor alternated between Robert's and Selden's families. "They really took care of us," her grandson Victor recalled. His Grandmama "would bring the damnedest things," including "huge oranges from Florida." His sister Valentine remembered the oranges, too. They would peel the fruits and slice them into little rounds that they ate with dainty forks. Selden remembered that Victor wouldn't open his presents when they were together but took them home to open in private.

Each of the grandchildren had a different image of their grandmother.[11] Victor remembered Emilie affectionately as "stately, very nice" and talkative. She "doted on males," which was nice for them. When "Denny" (Seldon Jr.) developed an interest in cars, Emilie sent him brochures of Chryslers she had received in an inquiry for a book she was writing.

When their family visited Emilie and Victor in Boston, Victor continued, they always had dinner at the Boston City Club, not at the apartment, and they had to be on their best behavior. Emilie was "very dignified" and taught the children good table manners, "but she wouldn't get annoyed at that." In Wellesley Hills, the children had room to roam and play, and expectations were relaxed.

Valentine recalled her grandmother as "not awfully tall but well turned out," neither heavy nor slender, buxom, and not particularly active. Although she was about five-foot-five, Emilie stood very tall, which "gave

> "Perfect. You remembered that I like my orange sliced and lots of cream for my coffee."
> *Keepers of the Faith*

Loring Family Picnic, Wellesley Hills

the impression of height," and "her hair was always nicely curled." To "Val," Emilie seemed cold and a little "imperious," not approachable, and her grandfather had "no grandfatherly attitude," but she acknowledged that, as a child, she had not thought herself so warm, either. She read all of her grandmother's books, but they never talked to each other about them.

The children saw their grandmother about three or four times per year—on Thanksgiving, Christmas, and perhaps one or two times in the summer. In contrast with Victor, who was quiet, Linda thought Emilie was "a livewire." Aware that her grandmother was an author, Linda gave her a story she wrote, about riding a horse. She didn't remember Emilie's response, but she was "always pleasant, always elegant," and at Christmas, she always brought hard sauce for the Christmas pudding.

Emilie Loring with Treats, Christmas 1942

Boston, Spring 1943

Emilie adjusted her manuscript to reflect changing home front conditions. President Roosevelt proposed a budget in January that was entirely focused on diverting assets and resources to the war effort. "Total war demands simplification of American life. By giving up what we do not need, all of us will be better able to get what we do need." Faced with the exodus of Petunia the maid, Gail Trevor echoes:

"Total war demands the simplification of living. I can manage with Cissie-Lou, Billy and Hilda to help."

"Pleasure driving" was strictly forbidden after January sixth; a vehicle parked at a movie theater or sporting event was clearly in violation.[12] Emilie returned to her manuscript and put her characters on bicycles and on foot. In two pages alone, she mentioned Gail's bicycle four times. Gail's date with Mark Croston was, appealingly, on foot, "walking home under a sky silver-gilt with stars."

Elements of the story mirrored the Roy Baker bigamy scandal. Roy's third wife was the secretary at the publishing company where he worked in Clinton, Massachusetts, like Gail Trevor is at the Clifton Works. Roy's first wife had an affair and left Roy with their two children; Doc's wife Rhoda enlists and leaves him with their two children.

By coincidence, Mel Baker's *Above Suspicion* also echoed the Roy Baker storyline. In 1940, Roy and Leah married and took off for South America, a hotbed of intrigue and espionage, where Roy's job was to scout sites for publishing plants. In Mel Baker's 1943 movie, a honeymooning couple is recruited by the British Secret Service to spy on the Germans, because a couple on their honeymoon would be "above suspicion."

Summer in Boston, 1943

There was no trip to Blue Hill that summer. January's prohibition against "pleasure driving" meant that Emilie would remain in Boston. Even trips to Wellesley Hills were curtailed. Robert and Irma had lived in the Wellesley Hills house for some years, and after Sandy's birth, Victor and Emilie deeded the house to him.

Emilie let her imagination do the traveling for her. She subscribed to the *Washington Post* and collected notes for a second story in the nation's capital.

When Hearts Are Light Again was released to bookstores on August nineteenth. Emilie wrote a special message to readers that appeared on the back book cover, a stern departure from the publisher's usual, romantic introduction:

A Message from EMILIE LORING to Her Readers

We are at war. At the very hour its envoys in Washington were discussing a pacific settlement of differences a nation treacherously, devastatingly struck at our defenses.

They call this a mechanistic age, but no machine has been invented that will equal the human spirit in the scope and glory of its accomplishment when it feels the fierce compulsion to right a wrong to its country. Never before in the history of civilization has it been challenged as now when the foul monsters, savagery, butchery, rape, torture and slavery have been loosed on the world.

By indifference, by procrastination, citizens of the United States can retard, even paralyze, the fight of their own country and of the United Nations to throttle the forces of evil and to bestow or restore to all the peoples of the earth the right to life, liberty, and the pursuit of happiness. Conversely, by wholehearted co-operation they can make that fight end in victory, that ideal a living, glowing reality.

If circumstances deny us the opportunity to express loyalty and patriotism by heroic acts, burning eloquence, by service on the home front, we can express it by buying our country's War Bonds and Stamps, proof that we stand heart, soul and purse behind the valiant men who are taking our place at the front and in the factories which are pouring forth materiel that will keep our forces fighting on land, in the air, on and under the sea. Heroes of Lexington and Concord. Valley Forge. Pearl Harbor. Bataan.

Corregidor. We can't let those patriots down. Buy War Bonds as they never have been bought before.

From housetops, from crossroads, from marketplaces, proclaim to the enemy that this great nation is united in its determination to exterminate forever the Powers of Evil now stalking the world. This is *your* war. Enlist in the citizens' army. March on to Victory.

Emilie Loring

Buy War Bonds and Stamps . . . a sound investment for your country and yourself

The gay comedy had left the audience refreshed and rested, its problems pushed into the background.
I Hear Adventure Calling

Her message was added to the record of War Finance in the United States Treasury archives.[13] Little, Brown included its own message on the dust jacket. Although paper rationing required their books to be smaller and lighter, what mattered, they said, was the content, "whether it provides good entertainment or sound information to the reader, whether it stimulates the mind, whether it is first class of its kind. This Company's policy of publishing 'fewer and better books' has never been more strictly followed than during this period of world crisis."

As they had during the Depression, Emilie Loring's reliably optimistic—and best-selling—novels made the cut. Her fellow authors on the Little, Brown list included John P. Marquand, Walter Lippmann, Ngaio Marsh, Ellery Queen, Ogden Nash, C. S. Forester, James Truslow Adams, Herbert Agar, Martha Albrand, James Hilton, Phyllis Bottome, William Henry Chamberlain, Allan Nevins, Henry Steele Commager, Ethel Vance, Anna Seghers, James Aldridge, Evelyn Waugh, Carey McWilliams, and Rose C. Feld.[14]

Winnifred Willard, the executive secretary of the National League of American Pen Women (NLAPW), wrote to Emilie that she was enjoying *When Hearts Are Light Again*. Moreover, "Your skill, your vision, your power with words, command my sincere admiration."

Winnifred wrote uplifting pieces called "Vitagrams" that were very much in line with Emilie's philosophy. She asked Emilie to write a short testimonial for the League bulletin, and Emilie obliged with lines about Winnifred that she might also have penned about herself:

> Always she has something to say which helps one to keep on keeping on toward the achievement of one's ideals and ambitions, that confirms one's belief that the beautiful qualities of life are real and attainable. She doesn't preach. She writes vitally, sympathetically, and with charm.[15]

Emilie gave Ruth Moss of WNAC radio an interview on Friday, August twentieth.[16] She described herself as "a working housekeeper, saving fats, tin cans, extending meat—when I can get it—making the best use of my ration coupons." That effort, she said, inspired the setting for *When Hearts Are Light Again*.

The next would be her twenty-fourth book. "My record is still one book a year. Sometimes one and a half. The morning after I turn in a manuscript to my publisher, I start another novel just so I won't forget how it is done."

By "starting," she meant research. She had a nice rhythm going: read and collect ideas all summer, write in the fall, revise in the spring, and turn in a completed manuscript before summer vacation.

She dismissed concerns about writing for her audience. "I can't imagine anything more destructive to spontaneity and inventiveness than to create with one ear of the mind turned inward to listen to the imagination and the other outward to listen to the reading public."

In prepared remarks, she described the "ideal woman" of her books:

> Loyalty to God, Country, and Family. Tenderness, sympathetic understanding, honesty, gay courage, the intuition to know when laughter will avert a ticklish domestic crisis and when it won't, the determination to do what has to be done superlatively well—it's

surprising what a tingling interest that adds to life as one grows older—and self-respect which keeps her on her toes to make herself attractive to listen to and terribly important, say I, to look at.

Miss Moss asked, "And what about the men? Did you ever find a man possessing the qualities of your very fine heroes?" Emilie replied, "Of course. Otherwise, how could I create them?"

Her attention to craft was evident:

One of the temptations to easy writing I have to guard against, is to allow things to happen off stage, to *tell* of an incident instead of showing it happening so that the reader may see it, feel the impact and be part of it.

She enthused,

This time, I have the title first—and what a title—and the theme. Now I am faring forth on vacation. When I return, just watch my yellow pencils smoke.

The following Tuesday, August twenty-fourth, she spoke with the *Boston Herald's* literary editor, Alice Dixon Bond, on her weekly program for WEEI radio, "The Book Page of the Air."[17] She related that her son visited with a neighbor who had read *When Hearts Are Light Again*. The neighbor said, "I like your mother's stories because she writes of people as they ought to be." Emilie responded, "Tell your neighbor that *I* think I write of people as they are."

She shared that writing helped her to work off a "hanker." "When I can't have a longed-for object, I put it in a story and it is mine, in a way." She had entered her "red" fashion phase and gave garnet earrings to one heroine, a gorgeous red hat to another.

My milliner tempted me. "It does a lot for you," she urged. Just as if I couldn't see that . . . I presented the hat to an older woman in a novel. Her son exclaimed, "Mother, you're stunning! Why doesn't every white-haired woman wear a red hat?" That's the genesis of my red hat wardrobe."

Boston, Fall 1943

In September, Emilie's frequent interviewer, Ruth Moss, joined the Marines. Emilie wrote to her:

We see by the papers that you are off to the wars. May good fortune attend you as you do your part to bring this terrible conflict to a close, a victorious close for the United Nations, and peace, liberty and the pursuit of happiness to the countries now involved. Your radio public will miss you but think of us all as in the cheering-stand spurring you on. Cordially yours, Emilie Loring.[18]

Emilie's daily walks to the Boston Athenaeum's quiet fifth floor resumed. Pencils sharpened, she began *Keepers of the Faith*.

Nancy Barton is fed up with her half-sister's interference and moves to Washington, D.C. to work as an interpreter at the newly completed Pentagon. She stays in a private home in Arlington where a senator's widow has taken in boarders: Suzanne Dupree, a gossip columnist with a past; Admiral Zeb Howe, a veteran of WWI; Oliver Stiles, a "radio bigwig," and Major Bill Jerrold, a decorated Marine who met Nan when he was feverish from malaria and who is now following the trail of a German spy.

Nan's brother-in-law, Sam, served in World War I with a record like Selden Loring's. His reminiscence reminded her that they had made it through World War I, and they would make it through this war, too.

"By the time this humble war is over the dependent woman will be as extinct as the prairie hen."
Keepers of the Faith

"We were buddies in World War I, drove camions filled with ammunition to the front, evacuated Hill 67 together. We both left college in our freshman year to join the Field Service, later became second looeys in the U. S. Army."
Keepers of the Faith

Having come through that hell safely, we told ourselves we could pull through anything."

Emilie's focus in this novel was the home front:

She thought of the brides, wives with young children, mothers, and fathers, who, like Amy Trask, turned rigid with fear at sight of a yellow envelope, of those whose hearts already had been pulled up by the roots by one of the messages. The women who are the keepers of the faith, as Sam had said.

"I'll just remind you that so tense and in such danger is this country today, that even happenings that seem unimportant, fragmentary, may change the course of a life, of a battle, tragically."
Keepers of the Faith

"... In here, dearie, to leave your wrap. It's called the Female Strangers' Room because, legend has it, a mysterious lady languished and died in it."
Keepers of the Faith

It would be interesting to know how much a ring like that would set one back.
Keepers of the Faith

A chance meeting with a Frenchman makes Nan suspicious. Is Francois Bouvoir really her childhood acquaintance Carl Brouner from Germany? Could he be the spy that Bill is looking for? Is he sending messages to the enemy via Oliver Stiles' radio show? How is Suzanne Dupree mixed up in it?

The setting was a veritable tour guide of wartime Washington, D.C.— the Pentagon, National Mall, Blair House, and current events. Emilie couldn't resist the legend of the Female Stranger at Gadsby's Tavern in Alexandria. The woman died in Room Eight of the Tavern in 1816, and one hundred years of conjecture and embellishment kept her mystery alive.

Bill and Nan are inextricably drawn to one another, and he remembers, as he passes a jeweler's window, her preference for "splashy" rings. Emilie repeated this preference often, and the ring was familiar, too, a near cousin to the one she described in *Hilltops Clear*, with the diamond and emeralds reversed: "An outsize square diamond was set in a narrow border of emeralds, they in turn were surrounded by baguettes of diamonds."

Necessity of the moment leads Nan and Bill to a pastor's house well after dark, and they are married. This story was like one told by Sherrod Soule, the minister who married Emilie and Victor. A knock came in the night, and the bathrobed pastor Soule conducted a hurry-up marriage ceremony in his own living room.[19]

The novel ends with King George's Christmas Day speech on the radio. His description matched her experience and Emilie's hope for the nation:

They have laid the foundations of new friendships between nations and strengthened old ones formed long ago. As a result, there is springing up in every country fresh hope that out of comradeship and sacrifice comes the power to restore and power to build anew.

Boston, Spring 1944

When Hearts Are Light Again had been published in August, and the Boston Authors Club *Bulletin* observed in January that it was still being advertised nationwide. "We did not need to ask whether the book was doing well."[20]

Indeed, the novel had gone into five printings by December. The *Boston Herald* said it was her best novel yet and explained: "Mrs. Loring always places her books in the tumultuous present but manages through the alchemy of her own spirit to make us forget misfortunes and horror and live for an all too brief moment where there is beauty and love."[21]

Emilie went back to college in the spring, this time as a lecturer. The Massachusetts Department of Education sponsored a "Recent Books" extension course on Tuesday nights in Harvard's Sever Hall.[22] The first lecture was "The Man Behind the Book" by the *Boston Herald*'s literary editor, Alice Dixon Bond. The other lecturers were an English professor and two more literary editors, so it may have been Emilie's book review column that put her on the list. Her class, for which she earned $5.50, was on March twenty-eighth, titled "Reader Response."[23]

She started with her usual career summary and admonitions to start writing and then keep a regular writing schedule. "The real writer doesn't find time. He fights for it." "Doubtless writing forbears have helped, but I have worked, how I have worked, studying, reading, writing, rewriting, doing my best and everlastingly trying to make that best, better."[24]

Once begun, the writer's craft was to create an absorbing story and making characters "real" was essential. In her preparation notes, she wrote:

> Words weave a spell for a writer of imaginative prose in which he sees, not only the character he has created but that character's background unto the third, maybe fourth generation. Of course, all that doesn't appear in the final draft of the story, but it has served to make the characters vital and real to the author. If he doesn't fall under the spell, he has presented a lot of skeletons dressed in garments through which the bones show as they would through cellophane clothing.

She concluded, "Some weeks ago, I was invited to speak at a writers' luncheon to tell all that I could about my writing in two minutes. You'll agree with me that it was quite an assignment."

On May fifth, Emilie and Victor's sixth and final grandchild, Eve, was born. Eve's parents were a little older than customary—Robert fifty and Irma forty—and although Emilie was careful not to name characters after living persons, both of Robert's daughters bore the names of characters who were already in Emilie's books—Sandra (*Uncharted Seas*) and Eve (*It's a Great World!*).

Dorothy Hillyer, the *Boston Globe*'s literary editor and one of the extension course presenters, reported from the latest Authors Luncheon at Copley Square, "Emilie Loring, long a Boston favorite, told us she was completing her 24th book, but had warned her friends and publishers, Little Brown, to hold off celebration until the 25th."[25]

The twenty-fourth was *Keepers of the Faith*, which she gave to her publisher in May. Dorothy Hillyer complimented the "pretty red roses" on Emilie's hat and observed, "There's always a red hat in a Loring book and as a symbol always a touch of red on a Loring hat." This was a recent preference, but the comment was copied by others who hadn't read her books until it was taken for granted.

Summer in Boston, 1944

On June sixth, allied troops stormed the beaches at Normandy. In August, they liberated Paris. The tide was turning in Europe but not yet in the Pacific.

Blue Hill's Ernest Carter, who went in with the "Go Devils" at Normandy, was killed in France. Franklin Wescott, a navigator in the Pacific, died taking off in a B-24 bomber in the Philippines. It was impossible to know how many more young men and their families would sacrifice all on the way to peace and recovery. In her next book, Emilie would meld Ernest Carter and Franklin Wescott together to create "Seth Carter, Jr.," a young pilot lost in the Pacific.

It was another summer without travel. Emilie was "fed up" with Boston and yearned to get out and away to wide open spaces. She subscribed to the *Wyoming State Tribune* and began to imagine.

"Not Seth, Jr. Not young Seth?"
"... He was with a plane carrier in the Pacific. Pilot. Seth senior has been wonderful." Wonderful was an understatement, Rex thought, as during dinner Seth Carter reported the gossip of the community without once referring to his own grief and loss.
Beyond the Sound of Guns

Boston, Fall 1944

Emilie wrote the first draft of *Beyond the Sound of Guns* on green, unlined paper. The story opens on a Wyoming ranch in September 1944. Kit Marlowe's brother, Dick, has lost the use of one arm in the Pacific Theater, and Colonel Rex Danton is on leave from the Combat Engineers with a leg injury. Far from the front, the clouds still have "gun-metal centers," and rain drops pelt "like machine-gun bullets."

Rehabilitation is the theme, but it won't come easy. Dick must learn to run his new cattle ranch—named "Double H" for "Health and Happiness—but he's in a "to hell with everything depression." Rex Danton is "fed up with conflict," but he stands accused of swindling Dick and stealing his fiancé, and he also has to find and capture an escaped prisoner of war. Kit is determined to lift her brother from despair and get him started in his new life.

Nine fighter planes, flying low in echelons of three, were passing overhead on their way to the airfield. Even here, beyond the sound of guns, the war was present.
Beyond the Sound of Guns

"Perhaps life was like that. Storm, tears, and despair followed by the sunshine of hope and joy and courage."

Emilie's prose encouraged readers to drop their problems awhile and feel refreshed when they were ready to take them up again. She knew it was hard to do.

"There are times when the horrors I have seen and been part of get an octopus grip on my mind . . ."
Beyond the Sound of Guns

As he slowly mounted the steps, he was aware that his stomach was putting on the sinking act it had staged when he had jumped into the water from an LST ramp on D Day and with his men behind him had slugged through the surf to the beach under a sky swept with enemy shell bursts . . .

He couldn't tell her that the outstanding nightmare for him had been obeying orders to blow in a tunnel and to bury alive a company of the enemy which had been stealing out to snipe for days, getting their man, or men, with each shot.

Kit hums Bing Crosby's "Going My Way," the Langleys waft French perfume wherever they go, and Kit considers the year's fashion forecast:

This year's gal will show lots of skin—pedal pants, neither shorts nor trousers, but something in between that tapers below the knee . . . The pretty-lady sort of evening frock . . .

Ma Snell and her Ouija board disappear, Sally tricks Dick into using his injured right arm, and the escaped prisoners of war steal Kit's pearls. Over the action hangs the constant specter of war from which they cannot escape, even beyond the sound of guns.

Why, why, couldn't a way be found to stop war forever? Killing, maiming of human beings, destruction of homes and property was such a senseless way to settle a dispute. Why didn't women, billions strong, *do* something about the wholesale slaughter of children they had brought into the world?

In October, the *Boston Herald Annual Book Fair Section* announced *Keepers of the Faith* with a three-column-wide photo of the cover art by Manning de V. Lee, in which Nan sits bemused, chin in hand, at a table set for two, as Bill Jerrold, in uniform, arrives. Jerrold is a Marine, but the uniform on the cover is Air Force. It was an odd mistake to make, unless there was a reason. Did an earlier draft of the book have Jerrold in the Air Force? Could it have been a secret nod to Mel Baker, who received a promotion that month from First Lieutenant to Captain in the Air Force? The caption read:

> Redheads and Saboteurs figure in Emilie Loring's newest roman-tic adventure story, "Keepers of the Faith," helping to make it one of the season's fastest moving novels. Little, Brown will publish this latest book of a perennially popular author tomorrow.[26]

Spring and Summer 1945

Emilie gave *Beyond the Sound of Guns* to the publisher at the start of the new year. The Germans launched a final offensive, the Battle of the Bulge, attempting to split the allies and re-take Belgium. But by January first, the Germans were in retreat.

J. Donald Abrams published a heartening book about turning tides in February, *The Shape of Books to Come*. Twenty years as editor of the *New York Times* book review gave him the perspective and qualifi-cations to reflect on the past decades of American literature and what was called for in the new. He predicted "that literature during the years immediately ahead will seek above all else to restore the dignity of the human spirit . . . there is, I believe, the first light of a new dawn of hope and will."

For nearly a quarter of a century, he said, disillusioned writers "have been expressing man's disgust with man." Faulkner, Steinbeck, Hemingway, Joyce, Eliot . . . "It seemed that all the most powerful writers . . . were bent on proving that life is a dark little pocket." His book's reviewer added, "What did the novelists say but that nothing good exists, that only the ugly is real, the perverted, the distorted."[27]

Emilie had countered that thought her entire career. Most directly, in the dedication of *Lighted Windows*, she expressed her belief "that the beautiful things of life are as real as the ugly things of life, that gay courage may turn threatened defeat into victory, that hitching one's wagon to the star of achievement will lift one high above the quicksands of discouragement." The literary pendulum was headed back her way.

Out in Hollywood, Emilie's sister-in-law, Minnie Baker, died of heart disease on April twentieth, but her son, Melville, would not be discharged until August. The next day, Mary Dale "Minnie" Owen died at the hospital in Chestnut Hill, Pennsylvania. She was the last of the Owen sisters from Tyn Y Coed; that chapter was over. Her remains were cremated and sent to Blue Hill to be buried next to her sisters in Seaside Cemetery.

The deaths of both Minnies represented the last vestiges of earlier times. Minnie Baker belonged to those years in Wellesley Hills when the Lorings and Bakers lived in a happy enclave on their end of Florence Avenue, raising their sons and reviewing each other's creative works. Minnie Owen belonged to a longer period, the decades of good friends who summered along the East Blue Hill Road.

But scarcely had the news arrived and the losses begun to sink in than bigger news came from the war in rapid succession. Adolph Hitler died by suicide on April thirtieth. One week later, Germany surrendered, and on May eighth, "VE Day," Victory in Europe, was declared.

War in the Pacific continued, and Mel Baker, still in the Air Force, had a new film assignment. *They Had to Go First* was a collaboration between "Captain Mel Baker" and one of the first pilots to fly a B-29 over Tokyo,

Captain Vince Evans. Their job was to edit nearly five hundred thousand feet of film to relate firsthand impressions of the Tokyo fire-bombings in March that killed over one hundred thousand Japanese citizens and destroyed half of the city.[28]

Before the film could be completed, the United States released atom bombs on Hiroshima (August sixth) and Nagasaki (August ninth). Strict prohibitions were placed on the publication of photographs or artworks depicting bombings or the devastation they left behind. There would be no film; Mel Baker was released from the Air Force and announced that he would work instead on MGM's next comedy in the Thin Man series.[29]

The Japanese surrendered on September 2, 1945. World War II was over.

Boston, Fall 1945

Emilie was seventy-nine years old. Born in the shadow of the Civil War, her generation had witnessed three presidents' assassinations, the flu epidemic, the Great Depression, and two World Wars. The theme of her next story would be renewal, the bright skies of hope.

Green pastures are before me
Which yet I have not seen;
Bright skies will soon be o'er me
Where darkest clouds have been[30]

On the eve of war, Cam Fulton and Patricia Carey's whirlwind romance led to a marriage proposal, but Pat reneged when Cam was ordered overseas. Now, two years later, both have returned from war service, and it's time to settle things between them.

Bright Skies is set in Hawaii, where images of Pearl Harbor seared war's reality into the collective minds and hearts of Americans. But peace and paradise have now returned. Pink and green, the colors of spring, are

"He'd probably never get out of the service alive–they were so secret about where he was, we suspected he had something to do with those terrible bombs–"
To Love and To Honor

"Pink coral towers rose from the dark green of trees and above the trees coconut palms waved featherlike topknots."
Bright Skies

everywhere, and "the rain-washed world smelled as if it had been sprayed with flower scents."

Pat came down the stairs in a soft green frock, carrying an overnight case. The gloves in her right hand were the exact shade of pink of the mammoth rose in her flower hat.

Rationing has disappeared. Fashion shows and opulent dining have returned. Even so, the scars of war remain.

"When I see those rows and rows of white crosses on the mountainside, I remember the men under them who fought and died for a better world, and I think of the mess of strife and confusion that same world is in today. I hope their spirits haunt the troublemakers."

The plot revolves around a set of troublemakers. Cam Fulton is on an intelligence mission to capture Nazi agents who were after a hoard of Nazi money seized by the Allies, and Captain Monty Dane and his wife blunder their way into the scheme.

Emilie used family names in the story and alluded to others. The name "Madam Shaw-Ruskin" sounded like her great-grandmother, Dorcas Shaw-Remick. Dorcas' sister, Sally Shaw, was a single woman who left her entire estate in Portland to Emilie's grandmother, Mary Ann Shaw (Remick) Baker, for her sole and personal use. Mary Ann had a sister Sally and a brother John (Remick, not Shaw), and Emilie's granddaughter Linda remembered playing "Sally and John Shaw" with her dolls as a child. Finally, two of the ushers in Emilie and Victor's wedding were the Jack brothers, and their mother's maiden name was Sally Shaw.

Each of Emilie Loring's novels started in a particular time of year—often September—and progressed as she wrote it, usually ending sometime

"Since my parents died ten years ago, I've made my headquarters at Silver Ledges in Honolulu with my father's sister, Sally, who married an Islander, John Shaw."
Bright Skies

between Christmas and early spring. In *Bright Skies*, however, the time was continual June, as though time had paused to allow everyone to savor the sweet blessings of peace, for everything to go back to normal.

The *Boston Herald* introduced *Beyond the Sound of Guns* in mid-November, "Emilie Loring Writes her 25th Anniversary Novel." Her "silver anniversary" story was called, "vibrant," "exciting," "the best of good fun," and, perhaps not the best association, "as modern as the atomic bomb."[31] Six months after Victory in Europe, two months after Victory in the Pacific, its message of rehabilitation was timely.[32]

That same week, Emilie Loring was a guest of honor at a "Celebrity Breakfast" hosted by the Newton Center Woman's Club. The publicity photograph showed Emilie seated in the center of the front row, flanked by Lillian Smith and her sister Esther. Lillian's book about interracial relationships, *Strange Fruit*, was banned in Boston but a best-seller, nonetheless. The other women were wives of celebrities. Mrs. George Patton, Jr. was the most notable, and there were also the wives of an author, a mayor, and a local insurance man. The men were John F. Kennedy, son of the Ambassador and a war hero, whose brother Joe's death was headline news; author Rollo Walter Brown; and Francis Dahl, a cartoonist for the *Boston Herald*.[33]

Emilie Loring was the only woman author in Little, Brown's holiday advertisement, "Give the Books You'd Like to Get." The seven men on the list were John P. Marquand, Clifford Dowdey, C. S. Forester, James Hilton, A. J. Cronin, Charles Nordhoff, and James Norman Hall. Her inclusion was notable, especially considering the women on Little, Brown's list who could have been included but weren't: mystery writers Ngaio Marsh and Martha Albrand, spy novelist Helen MacInnes, Katherine Anne Porter (*Ship of Fools*), and Margery Sharp, whose *Cluny Brown* and *The Adventurers* later became movies.

"Sometimes I wonder when real writers get the time to write, if they are besieged with temptations to do other and easier things as I am."
Bright Skies

CHAPTER 27

Individual Spirit: 1946-51

Boston, Spring 1946

Emilie's husband, Victor, reviewed and signed Emilie's publishing contracts through the years, but he now suffered from heart disease. Before his eighty-seventh birthday in 1946, he helped her to put her writing affairs in order for the future. She assigned all of her titles previously published with the Penn Publishing Company—*The Trail of Conflict* through *We Ride the Gale!*—to Little, Brown. She retained their copyright, and a provision returned all rights to her, should the books ever go out of print, which, at the moment, didn't seem likely.

Their grandson Victor had graduated from high school in 1945 and enlisted in the Army in November. During his basic training at Camp Croft in South Carolina, Emilie wrote to him faithfully. He "went everywhere by train" in those days and recalled that he would see "a prim lady of indeterminate age," and invariably, she would be reading an Emilie Loring book. In a letter to his grandmother, he wrote, "Saw a lot of your books in the Gastonia Public Library. Gee, but they were battered and dirty, so I guess they are popular."[1]

After basic training, Victor went to Germany as part of the occupying security forces that would replace the tactical, military troops. Now that the war was over, the messy job of transition began. Emilie added to her current story:

"The shooting is over, but this country needs men like you to keep up its prestige in conquered territory. We must have soldiers of peace to finish the job. We are in for a long occupation of Germany. We must not forget, we must not forget, the horrors of the war years which may be timed to become a scourge the minute we soften up."

In February, Emilie sat at the head table for the annual literary luncheon at Copley Square,[2] and in May, she read "The Tale the Titles Told" for the New England Woman's Press Association breakfast.[3] Otherwise, she lay low. Victor's health continued to decline, and she spent more time at home with him.

Blue Hill, Summer 1946

Emilie reviewed the galley proofs for *Bright Skies* at the end of summer. The book jacket's copy read, "Emilie Loring has brought to this novel all the glamour, excitement and romance of her previous books. Pat Carey, the heroine, returns from Red Cross work in Europe to find international intrigue and complex personal problems lurking beneath the bright skies of postwar Honolulu."

After her birthday in September, Emilie, Victor, and son Robert met with several members of the Kollegewidgwok Yacht Club who were interested in buying the Loring's granite wharf for their new headquarters. The account which became the accepted history of the transactions was written in hindsight twenty years later. The more complete account follows:

A real estate committee from the "KYC" came to Stone House on Friday, September thirteenth. They were Lieutenant Colonel Homer K. Heller, who had just returned in March from military service in Africa; Douglas Byers, an archaeologist from Andover, Massachusetts who had excavated and described "The Nevin Shellheap" on Blue Hill's Mill Island; and Lieutenant Alvin R. L. Dohme, recently returned from duty in the Pacific.

As Dohme recalled twenty years later, ". . . not a soul among the entire club membership had ever set eyes on [Emilie Loring] to the best of their knowledge."[4] That may have been true for him, but the KYC's Commodore

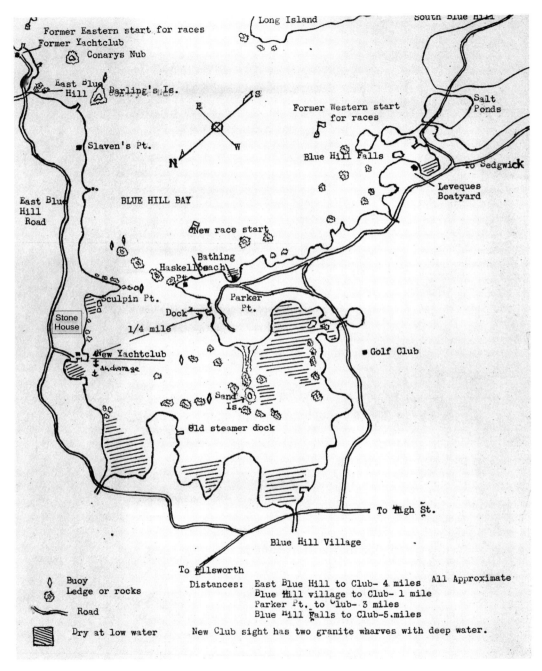

Map of Blue Hill Bay: Stone House and the new yacht club at left, Blue Hill Village at the bottom. (Note: The single line marks the shore. The middle is all water.)

had been, and remained, Seth Milliken, whom the Lorings had known nearly forty years. Furthermore, "Doug" Byers was the younger brother of Randolph "RK" Byers, who played tennis on the Lorings' court and whose 1920 passport application Victor had signed, "acting as a friend."

The real estate committee envisioned a clubhouse, sundeck and loading pier to be built at the Lorings' granite wharf. Even at low tide, the water there was six feet deep, sufficient to load granite slabs onto schooners or serve as an excellent pier for club yachts.

The idea suited Victor's lifetime interest in wholesome, youth activities, and although their sons had not participated, "Brutal Beasts" had sailed between the Milliken and Loring wharves for years. Bit by bit, the Lorings had sold off portions of their property to the Owens, Boyds, Bectons, and Madam Frijsh. With Minnie Owen's death, Tyn Y Coed would now pass to a Sheridan cousin. The Lorings' closest friends in Blue Hill were gone. That chapter had ended, and the granite wharf could find another use.

Alvin Dohme recalled Emilie, "dressed to the nines," as "a delightful person, so sympathetic to the cause that she offered the quarry property for a ridiculously modest figure . . . There and then, in her own charming living room, she was voted a lifetime honorary member of the new yacht club in the making."

Three days later, Homer Heller, writing to the Lorings as the KYC's Secretary-Treasurer, recounted the visit and made "our tentative offer of $2000 to purchase the approximately six acres of waterfront land for the future site of the Kollegewidgwok Yacht Club" and supplied "a check to the amount of $300 drawn on the Bangor Savings Bank to the order of Mrs. Emilie Loring, to accompany this offer."[5]

Fall 1946

The formal sales agreement was made on October twenty-sixth between "Emilie B. Loring of Boston, Massachusetts and the Kollegewidgwok Yacht Club of Bluehill, Maine." Their agreement stipulated that

Loring Wharf, Future Site of KYC

the yacht club would be built within two years or revert back to the Lorings with the purchase price returned. The land could only be used for a yacht club, and nothing could be done on the property that would prove a nuisance to Emilie, her heirs or assigns, or to the neighborhood—no sewage, no loud noises, no alcohol. These stipulations were made with a permanent assurance: should they be violated at any time, ownership would return to the Lorings, their heirs, or issue.

Like Emilie, Victor had a family reason to shun alcohol. With three generations of upstanding patriots behind him, his maternal great-grandfather Caleb Hitchcock proved the one disappointment. Despite "naturally greater intellectual abilities," both his ministry and a subsequent mercantile business failed because of his drinking.[6]

Finally, if the KYC ever sold the land, it must be offered first to the Lorings or their heirs or assigns "at a fair prevailing price." One thousand dollars were paid, with the remainder to come when the deed was delivered. Emilie, Victor, Seth Milliken as Commodore, and Homer K. Heller as Secretary-Treasurer all signed the agreement.

Victor's health worsened. Emilie hired professional help to care for him and started her next story. Did Victor suggest that she write herself into the book? Did she write her early drafts to entertain him?

She yearned to write a murder mystery someday and had even started one during the war. That story was a blood-thirsty affair: Aunt Anastasia Stewart's French companion, "Mamselle Reneé," stabs a judge to prevent him from marrying Mrs. Stewart, stabs another woman, Cecily Ann, who witnessed the killing, and then dies by suicide herself. Now, Emilie revised the story and kept the mystery of the judge's murder but added a story line about authorship and another for romance.[7]

The authors in Emilie's earlier stories, Pamela Leigh (*Fair Tomorrow*) and Melissa Barclay (*Give Me One Summer*), had been fledgling writers. Her new character was a successful, internationally famous, mystery author, Madam Roger Stewart, who wrote under the pseudonym "Molly Burton."

This was the second time she gave a fictional author her own initials, "MB" for Maria Baker: Melissa Barclay, Molly Burton. Those closest to Madam Stewart call her "Molly B," a nickname used before, in Rachel's play. Emilie Baker—Emilie B—Molly B.

Emilie wrote her early drafts in first person: "The looking-glass girl returned my grin." The device helped her to inhabit the thoughts of her characters as she created scenes in her imagination. Later drafts changed action to third person and retained characters' thoughts that she had already written. Characters could live better on the page when they started as thinking beings, not just as puppets moved from place to place with thoughts added later.

She had another reason. One by one, the vestiges of her earlier life were falling away, but she wasn't ready to quit. Always, her books had given her something she wanted herself, so now, when she wanted to feel again the promise of romance and adventure, she wrote in first person.

Details from her earlier books reappeared in a way that suggested they could have been drawn from real life. Mrs. Stewart reads aloud from the newspaper:

"Heavenly day, how I worked after that. Before my husband died, I was able to provide professional care for him."
Beckoning Trails

"My first novel made a slight stir." "I wouldn't call ten printings 'slight.'"
Beckoning Trails

"We have it on good authority that a certain Washington Judge, he of the red carnation, is to run for the Senate. He'll have keen competition . . . The Judge confided his senatorial ambition to me. 'Family man', my aunt repeated thoughtfully, 'I wonder if he married me, if he would come under that head?"

"Carnation Carr" was the eloquent judge in *Fair Tomorrow*, Emilie's Cape Cod story, and now, a carnation-wearing judge was repeated. Early in their acquaintance, Victor was called "Demosthenes" for his eloquence,

Victor J. Loring

argued a Cape Cod legal case, and ran for the state senate. He, too, was often called "Judge." Did *he* wear a carnation in his lapel when he argued a case?

Debby Randall aspires to write, and she learns from Molly B's example and advice:

> "She never has guests when the WOMAN AT WORK sign is out, till the manuscript is in the hands of the magazine editor or her publisher."
>
> "I agree with you that Molly B.'s technique of staggering the disclosures in her stories is the touch of a master craftsman."
>
> "My study of the motives behind actions has helped me understand the human heart—at least, my fans believe I understand it—"
>
> "I never talk of my plots or of what I am writing till the novel is in print."

Tim Grant is the love interest, a war veteran who has come to lead the local science center. He and Debby team up to solve the mysteries at Beechcroft. "From now on, so far as you and I are concerned, there is a suspect behind every bush, a clue at the end of every beckoning trail."

Beacon Hill, Spring, 1947

Emilie and Victor celebrated their fifty-fifth anniversary in December and Victor's eighty-eighth birthday on January eleventh. Victor worked sixty-eight years as an attorney and never retired. He died of heart failure on February 8, 1947.[8]

He and Emilie had been the best of companions, from Boston to Maine and Alaska. After her brother's death, Victor had been Emilie's first reader and confidant, the one with whom she shared fledgling stories on the way to completed drafts. Her appreciation inspired a passage in her present story:

> "I admired him, his money meant nothing. I was earning plenty myself, but, we enjoyed the same things, he was enormously proud of what I had accomplished. We were great companions, and Debby, in the last analysis, the good companion is what counts most in marriage."

Grandson Victor returned from Europe in time to attend the funeral. He remembered "Grandpapa" as dignified, very jolly, and quite affectionate. Valentine and Linda thought of him as "the quiet one," and grandson Selden remembered one of his favorite expressions, "If you all come down with cholera morbus, you can blame me."

Victor's ashes were placed in a cylindrical, gold-metal urn, with his signature etched into the side. The family held a private funeral, and his urn was placed next to Robert Baker's in the mausoleum at Forest Hills.

In Emilie's final draft, Madam Stewart's marriage is a sweet memory. "The Bedouin Song," which was popular when Emilie and Victor married, floats across the lake like a wraith of remembrance. She used only the first line, but the full verse was:

> From the Desert I come to thee on a stallion shod with fire;
> And the winds are left behind in the speed of my desire.
> Under thy window I stand, and the midnight hears my cry:
> I love thee, I love but thee, with a love that shall not die
> > *Till the sun grows cold,*
> > *And the stars are old,*
> > *And the leaves of the Judgment Book Unfold!*

Much of Molly B's—and Emilie's—writing career was also in the past. Emilie described as she took a last look around in the apartment at 25 Chestnut Street:

> Paintings which had been designed for the jackets of Molly Burton's books lent color—and an occasional touch of gruesomeness—to the cool, gray walls. There were full-page ads, photographs of the author along the years, framed letters from three world-famous persons who had taken time from their crowded lives to tell her they had read all night to find the solution of a mystery only to discover that they had guessed wrong as to the murderer, letters that would be as well worth stealing for the signatures as some of her jewels.

The sense of the book, however, was neither melancholy nor nostalgic. Her title set the theme: *Beckoning Trails*. Life was vitally interesting, filled with romance and mystery.

> The hint of frost in the fragrant air set her blood tingling. This morning she had awakened with the sense of expectancy, the world-is-mine buoyancy . . .

Neither she nor Molly Burton had any intention of stopping.

> "For Pete's sake, forget that age obsession. Some psychiatrist should start a movement to isolate the age bug. It does more harm than the boll weevil by the loss to the world of experienced workers."
> "I have plots for ten more novels at least before I sign off."

Emilie's number was actually three. When the book was published, she signed a copy to Mary and Selden: "This makes twenty-seven down and three to go. Emilie Loring"[9]

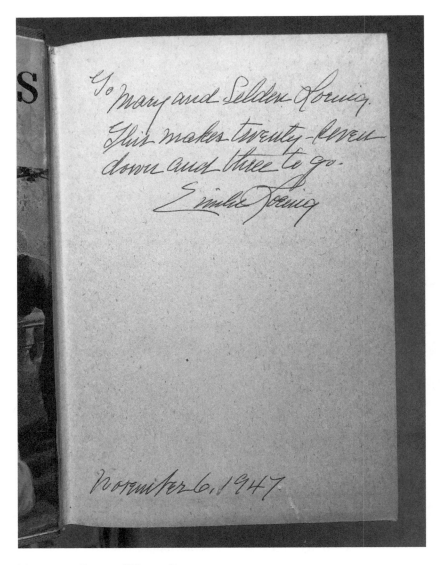

Twenty-seven Down and Three to Go

At the end of May, Louise Hallet witnessed the contract for *Beckoning Trails* in place of Victor—a sad change but a staunch support from Emilie's longtime friend. The contract included a "work to follow," but before she could begin another book, Emilie had business to finish in Blue Hill.

Ogunquit, Maine; Summer 1947

In June, she transferred the deed to the Trustees of the Kollege-widgwok Yacht Club—Seth M. Milliken, Douglas M. Byers, Alvin R. L. Dohme, Homer K. Heller, William P. Palmer, and Samuel Taylor. The beginning read, "I, Emilie Baker Loring, widow."[10]

Her parents, sister, brother, many friends, and now, her husband, had died. She was eighty years old herself; of course, she considered her age and her own mortality. But she had a longtime conviction about them.

"I've observed that the man or woman with a big interest in life never is age-conscious. They are too busy to count passing years."

She would be too sad if she stayed the summer at Stone House without Victor, but there were distinguished hotels all along the Maine coast where she might find inspiration, and who knew? Maybe some adventure, too.

She chose the Lookout Hotel at Ogunquit, Maine. It was vacation season, and the town was a paradise for vacationers who liked the sea. "They were sprinkled over boardinghouse lawns, perched on boardinghouse rails, crowded the street in every variety of sports clothing." Chief among Ogunquit's attractions was the Marginal Way, a mile-long walk along the prominent cliff between Ogunquit Beach and Perkins Cove.

Emilie walked through the hotel garden, still looking for inspiration, when another guest challenged, "What can a writer find to write about here?" Emilie replied, "Can't a writer get a story wherever there is human nature?"[11] And off she went to prove it. She even wrote the incident into her story: "Don't thrilling things happen wherever there are people?"

In the new story, Fran Phillips, like Emilie, leaves Boston for the Maine coast in search of adventure.

> "I have lived such a tight little life for the last few years that I want to get away. Besides, I hear adventure calling."

"I must take hold of life with both hands and all my intelligence."
Beckoning Trails

"I'll take a chance on Maine."
I Hear Adventure Calling

"It is only for the summer. When fall comes I will have a brand-new outlook, will have recovered my sense of direction, will know what I want to do with my life."
I Hear Adventure Calling

The work was intensely interesting, the contact with outstanding achievement stimulating. Keeping in step with this job would leave no time for fear.
I Hear Adventure Calling

Emilie attended the Ogunquit Playhouse and made mental notes for her new story. Small galleries in the art colony at Perkins Cove suggested her character's position as a sales assistant for a small gallery. With a missing painting and a handsome but unwanted guardian, her story was ready to take off.

Hotel Bellevue, Fall 1947

Emilie moved most of her belongings from Beacon Hill back to the house in Wellesley Hills where her elder son, Robert, now lived. The accumulations of a lifetime were there, from those first days when the house and her marriage were new, through every stage of her life since then— Mrs. Victor Loring, Mother, Josephine Story, and Emilie Loring, favorite American novelist. She wasn't ready to retire, but her reflective mood found its way into her twenty-eighth story.

> Things. Things. Things. Too bad her put-my-house-in-order attack hadn't started on this accumulation. She would tackle it next. She was the last of her family, there were no relatives to whom it would mean anything, but it ought to be of use to someone.
>
> I won't give away these costumes, she decided as she lifted the cover of the cedar chest. They represent too much fun and the fun one has had can't be snitched away, she philosophized . . .

She took Apartment 511 at the Hotel Bellevue, next to the State House and nearly opposite the entrance to the Boston Athenaeum. The story began in early summer. Fall's chrysanthemums in a copper bowl were replaced by a silver bowl filled with "pink peonies and snapdragon, purple iris and pale-yellow, late tulips."

Fran Phillips chafes at the appointment of Myles Jaffray as her guardian while her brother is on postwar duty, and if there was any doubt that

Fran represented Emilie in the story, it was dismissed when they shared the same birthday: "The new trustee can't hold back my income due September fifth if I sidestep meeting him, can he?"

A passage about marriage as a "great adventure" echoed Joan Crofton's parents—and Emilie's—in *As Long as I Live*:

> "If a couple goes into marriage knowing that adjustments are bound to be tough, that the going may be plenty rough in spots, yet, believing it to be the great adventure, that the rewards in companionship, in sunny stretches of road, in shared laughter, shared intimacies and interests will overbalance the hazards, such a marriage ought to result in a genuine till-death-do-us-part relationship and that is the only one I will settle for."

When the *Boston Herald* introduced *Beckoning Trails* in November, literary editor Agnes Carr predicted, "The reader will fall in love with Deborah, be intrigued by the mystery as it unravels under the author's clever fingers and close the book with a sigh of contentment." Olga Owens of the *Boston Post* agreed, "one of Emilie Loring's very best stories. No wonder all her novels become best sellers."[12]

"Patty and I started out with the conviction that marriage is a high adventure, not an obstacle race. We haven't changed our belief, though we've had some tough, grueling experiences along an often times rough and rocky road. However, we've pulled through. We still think this is a great old world and look forward to the future with a tingling sense of more adventure to come."
As Long as I Live

Flappers Row, Spring 1948

Despite the passing years, the women of "Flapper's Row" were as they had always been, albeit with changed addresses. Emilie's apartment at the Hotel Bellevue was scarcely three blocks from her twenty-five-year apartment at 25 Chestnut, still in the middle of the Boston she'd known since childhood. She could easily walk to her father's old building at 10 Milk Street or wander through the Boston Common and Public Garden with little more effort than she had done before.

Clara Endicott Sears gave up the Beacon Hill house as far too large for a woman on her own—no matter how many servants she employed.

She never married, keeping an agreement she made with her cousin Mary. The girls couldn't stand the idea of being dependent upon a man and agreed not to marry unless they found just the right kind of man[13]—and he had not appeared. She took an apartment at the Hotel Vendome on Commonwealth Avenue, where she had watched from her window for theater people when she was a girl. She could take the subway to the Boston Athenaeum on writing days, or she could enjoy the brisk walk.

Sara Ware Bassett was never going to move; she was going to stay in her home at 56 West Cedar until the end. As she aged, someone suggested that she move her bedroom from the upper floor to a lower one, so she could avoid climbing two flights of stairs every night, but she would have none of it. Her bedroom was where it was and would be for seventy years. Another time, her housekeeper offered to help her blow out the candles on her birthday cake. "Indeed not!" she snapped, "This isn't your birthday!" When all but one candle went out, she crowed, "Good! I've got another year to go!"[14]

Creatively, too, the women were indefatigable. At eighty-four, Clara busily wrote poems, lyrics, and interpretive works for her Harvard museums. Her most recent was *Highlights Among the Hudson River Artists* (1947).

Sara Ware, who was the youngest at seventy-six, had the same writing goal as Emilie, one book per year, and she remained committed to telling Cape Cod stories. Her latest was *Head Winds* (1947), and *Within the Harbor* would be out in May. "You know what to expect in these Cape Cod stories," wrote Kenneth Horan for the *Chicago Tribune*, "but somehow they are neither tiresome nor stale. The beauty of the country, the smell of the sea, and the complete independence of the people, make them always original."[15]

Now eighty-one, Emilie enjoyed her foray into mystery-writing. Her books had always had a touch of mystery, but the added intrigue and intellectual puzzling over new plots made writing days even more exciting.

In the Ogunquit story, gallery assistant Fran Phillips has access to all of the Sargent gallery's valuable collection. When a painting is stolen, suspicion falls on her, and it doesn't help that the Sargent's daughter, Gene, resented her presence in the first place. Fran had sworn to stay away from Myles Jaffray, but they join forces to figure out who is behind the thefts and to clear her name.

Lest people on the homefront forget, Emilie referenced the armed forces still in Germany, including her grandson, Victor. "We are fighting over there to make the purpose of the United States understood and appreciated, to prove that we are not in Europe for selfish gains, but to help people work together, to create conditions within which every individual may thrive without dragging down another. In short, opportunity for all."

Emilie often said that she dwelt in the atmosphere of her book while she was writing, and she missed her Maine garden, so she wrote gardens into the story. One was Anne Paul Nevin's "Arcady" garden in Blue Hill, correct to a detail:

> Pink peonies, gigantic spikes of heavenly blue anchusa, foxgloves and Canterbury bells, stately Madonna lilies and Shasta daisies for a white touch, day lilies for yellow, tall, late purple tulips, against a background of dark rhododendrons. Paths in a velvety green lawn led to the central point, an old-fashioned pool in the center of which a bronze boy blew a horn from which liquid diamonds rose high in the air to tinkle back with the sound of broken glass into water where goldfish flashed like living flames.

Another might have been her own at Wellesley Hills:

> Zinnias in pastel shades of yellow, salmon and mauve towered; giant asters were bursting into bloom; gladiolus in heavenly shades held proud heads high; regal lilies nodded pearly petals above the patchwork of gold, yellow, purple, white, light blue, dark blue, violet, reds of all shades and the green foliage of annuals.

"Ken writes that he intends to remain in Germany during this critical period as long as he is needed, which at present means indefinitely."
I Hear Adventure Calling

Hotel Bellevue, Fall 1948

I Hear Adventure Calling hit bookstore shelves in November. "Wholesome and exciting entertainment" was the advertising description, a "smooth blend of romance, mystery and adventure." "Another exciting love story from the warm, masterful pen of Emilie Loring." She signed her advance copy, "Emilie Loring. Her book. October 16, 1948."

By then, her twenty-ninth story, *Love Came Laughing By*, was well underway. She began with a quote from Herbert Shipman's poem, "No Thoroughfare."

Across the gateway of my heart, I wrote "No Thoroughfare,"
But love came laughing by, and cried, "I enter everywhere."

"Leave me at the Mayflower first, driver." Love Came Laughing By

The first scene is on a train bound for the nation's capital, a trip she had taken many times since the first with Rachel and the next with Victor. She knew the route from the train station to the Mayflower Hotel from her many visits to the Hallets.

Her foot was on the lowest step of the Pullman when she saw him striding toward the train. Instantly she abandoned her intention to buy a novel at the newsstand, turned, charged up the steps narrowly escaping collision with the colored man in dark blue who had started down.

"I told you, Porter, I was not to be disturbed."

Wendy Adair darts into a compartment at the end of the car.

Her heart stopped, broke into quickstep. The room she had thought empty had an occupant. The man in gray who was bending over an open briefcase on the table at the window already littered with official-looking papers straightened and glared at her. A surge of red deepened the brown of his stern face.

"What's this? A plant?" he demanded.

More than half of Latin American countries had changed govern-
ments by revolt in the last four years, and Vance Tyler, a second-term congressman from the Northwest, quickly comprehends Wendy's situation as
they breakfast in the dining car.

> "You fled from a city ablaze with revolution, in that same city, a
> friend—interrogation point—is attached to a U. S. Embassy. You
> suspect you were followed after leaving the plane, discounting
> your beauty and charm, I can think of only one reason for your
> evident terror. You are carrying a message. If I can help you when
> we reach Washington, Mrs. John Smith—"

Secret agents, a missing gun, a drugged dog, and a zoo's missing viper
all figure in the mystery.

> "The Case of the Sleuthing Gal. What a title for E.S.G. Perhaps
> the celebrated writer of mystery yarns will collaborate with me."

In her original draft, Emilie used Sherlock Holmes, but he was the
sleuthing standard of the previous generation. "E. S. G." was Erle Stanley
Gardner, the creator of Perry Mason.

Her writing was spare and effective:

"A shadow cautiously stole down the path between the terraces." "The
east turned pink while she tried to work out an answer."

Boston, Spring 1949

In January, Emilie gave an interview to Doris Ricker Marston for the
Boston Globe in advance of a Boston Authors Club luncheon at which she
was to be the guest of honor. *I Hear Adventure Calling* was "hot off the
press," and her previous twenty-eight had sold more than a million copies
already.[16]

"Gosh, it's a
revolution,
they are a
dime a dozen
down here."
*Love Came
Laughing By*

They met in Emilie's room at the Hotel Bellevue, personalized with photos of her grandchildren, three original paintings from her book covers, and her collection of silver boxes. She wore a silver-gray gown, "a sign of her second-year mourning for her husband, Victor." Emilie Loring was a modern woman, but she retained that Victorian custom.[17]

She described her writing routine and admitted, "I never know what is going to happen in a book until it evolves. Often, I have to go back and insert some clews [sic] to future happenings to be fair to the reader—clews that I could not insert before because I did not know myself what was going to happen."[18]

The day came for the Boston Authors Club reception.[19] Seated at the front of the ballroom were the editors of both Little, Brown and Grosset & Dunlap. The guest speakers were columnists who had written about Emilie Loring over the years: Alice Dixon Bond, Olga Owens, and Helen Abbott Beals, plus an English professor and a librarian. Representatives from the Boston Branch of American Pen Women and the New England Woman's Press Association joined the Boston authors in the audience. When tributes had been paid, Mrs. Francis J. "Fannie" Flagg introduced Emilie with Nixon Waterman's poem, "A Rose to the Living."

> A rose to the living is more
> Than sumptuous wreaths to the dead;
> In filling love's infinite store,
> A rose to the living is more,
> If graciously given before
> The hungering spirit is fled—
> A rose to the living is more
> Than sumptuous wreaths to the dead.

Then, it was Emilie's turn to speak. "Smartly gowned," she rose and smiled at the audience of family, friends, and distinguished authors.

When she spoke, her voice was soft and "a little tremulous with emotion." She recalled when Victor encouraged her, "You have always wanted to write. Now is your chance. Write." She told the story of her career, from first book reviews to the challenge that produced *I Hear Adventure Calling*. "Instantly, the idea scout who perches on a hillock in my imagination signaled, 'I hear adventure calling. There's your title.' And, sure enough, it was."[20]

She had mentioned that idea scout many times over the years. Sometimes, it counseled her to go ahead, sometimes to go slow. In *High of Heart*, she called it "that character scout who perches on the hillock of Conscience." It was a "mental observation and deduction scout" in *Across the Years*.

For all its help through the years, however, and despite her experience and skill, one hard truth remained: "writing, believe it or not, is work, with a capital 'W.'" To make a success of it, she had learned say "No" to other commitments and not interrupt her work schedule. The eighty-two-year-old counseled, "One must keep everlastingly at it."

She continued work on her latest story, and as always, she wove bits of her own life into it—now even more transparently. Wendy Adair has a children's radio program.

"Miss Adair, you were a smash hit. You sang as if you were singing to very special children you love."
"I was. Believe it or not, as I sang, I saw the Browns' two little blonde girls, Sandra and Eve, part of the time I visualized a small girl-and-boy combination, Linda and Denny, neighbors at home. I wasn't on the air, I pretended I was with them, it helped me get my music across. I love children."

Sandra and Eve, Linda and Denny, were Emilie Loring's younger grandchildren. She seldom used real names in her books, but she was

"Now they've reached the giggling stage, you should have heard them in our room this morning, whispering and giggling, with the cat spitting and meowing protest."
Love Came Laughing By

Eve and Sandy

nearly to the end of her thirty-book goal, and she made the exception. Since she had alluded to Victor and Valentine in *Today is Yours*, she had gotten all six of her grandchildren into her books.

"Run down and put on your hats and coats, kiddies. Watch for Grandmama. 'Whoo-hoo' when she comes."

Wistful lines acknowledged how much she missed Victor, who had been gone more than two years already.

Her lips twitched in sympathy with his spontaneous laugh. One could love a man for that laugh alone. Perhaps it was because for two—almost three years—she had been in an environment where there was little laughter that his meant so much to her.

"That's the Number One comfort of having a husband, Wendy, someone with whom to talk over things, things you can't speak of to anyone else."

Her spirit, however, was unshaken.

"I'm never bored. Life is too exciting. Even with all my problems, I never feel defeated."

She included her optimistic, signature phrase twice, once at the beginning and once toward the end of the story.

He had planted a hasty kiss in the region of her right ear and then, as if realizing that she was going, caught her in his arms. "Happy landings," he whispered. Was it a prophecy or only a hope, she had wondered as he dashed for the exit.

He cleared his gruff voice. "I'll wait here till you are inside the building. Happy landings."

York, Maine; Summer 1949

Doris Ricker Martin fleshed out her notes from the January interview and wrote a feature article about Emilie Loring for the *Lewiston Journal*'s June magazine section, "Emilie Loring Gets Inspiration from Maine for Many Stories."[21] New in this article was the admission that Louisa May Alcott was another of Emilie's favorite authors—although Dickens remained most important to her.

That "little voice" appeared again as she described her start in writing. "I said, 'It's silly to try it,' but a voice said, 'Here's your chance. Take it.' So I did, and it worked out surprisingly well."

She also revealed how she protected her concentration when writing. Instead of reading, which would have been a distraction, she knitted. The rhythmic, constant action formed a backdrop against which she mentally worked out the details of her stories. "I've been knitting shawls," she said. "I made one of aqua wool while thinking out my last book and sent it to an 82-year-old woman in England. She wrote me that she wears

"I know what you don't believe, that I'm eighty-two. Between you and me I don't believe it myself. I'm as full of zest and ambition as I was at forty. Must be a mistake in the birth record."
Rainbow at Dusk

it while walking in her garden."[22] She might have kept it; she, too, was eighty-two.

Emilie hoped to return to Blue Hill one day, but two years had not erased the sadness she felt at going there without Victor. Instead, on the recommendation of Louise Hallet, she went to the Marshall House in York. She wrote to her editor on July fourth:

> It is huge. Beautiful surroundings. Table excellent. Very well managed. Music twice daily. So far, the guests appear to be of the "Proper Bostonian" type, the season guests, I mean. No social hostess. Nothing planned for the entertainment of guests like card parties or tournaments—that is, nothing I have heard of to date. Friendly atmosphere. Easy walks and a glorious beach. Those are my impressions after a week here. "Liable to change" of course as time goes on.[23]

She exchanged letters with her granddaughter Linda, too. In January, she had written,

> Lindy dear, I was delighted to learn from your letter that you are getting so much pleasure from reading. Good books are companions that never fail one . . . With much love, Gran.[24]

Now, she wrote on Marshall House stationery:

> This is a huge hotel, much larger than The Lookout where you came to see me two years ago. Three big yachts came into the harbor yesterday. From the veranda we can look down at the pier where there are a lot of people fishing. Nearby is a large swimming pool, full of swimmers yesterday when the temperature went up to ninety . . . Lots of love to you and Val. Devotedly, Gran.[25]

In each letter, she encouraged the ten-year-old. "I liked the sketch." "Glad to hear that you passed the swimming test." "Try that sometime."

During a patch of sunny days, Emilie entered the hotel's putting contest and won it. When foggy weather followed, she stayed indoors and read. She enjoyed John P. Marquand's *The Late George Apley* "immensely." "He was so real I had to keep reminding myself that he was a fictional character." She found *A Wreath for Rivera* by Ngaio Marsh "hard sledding" until she got past a host of introductions at the beginning.[26]

When next she wrote to her editor, a week of fog had been replaced with "two days of gorgeous weather." She expected the galleys of *I Hear Adventure Calling* to be delivered in early August for publication in November and promised, "I will return them with my corrections at the earliest possible moment."[27]

Hotel Bellevue, 1949-1950

Emilie returned in the fall to the Hotel Bellevue and her writing alcove on the Athenaeum's fifth floor. She sharpened her pencils and let the summer's experiences flow onto the yellow-lined paper of her thirtieth story's first draft.

To Love and to Honor begins three years after Cindy Clinton's marriage to Naval officer Ken Stewart—a man she has never met—to save their fathers' oil interests during wartime. Now that the war is over, their common oil interests will be sold, and the marriage can be annulled.

Bill Damon arrives to represent Stewart's legal interests, while Hal Harding and Thomas Slade vie for Cindy's affections. Cindy and Bill meet in the gift shop, but there's a hitch: Bill is actually her husband, Ken Stewart, whom she thinks is still overseas with the Navy. She and Ken have only exchanged business letters, but sometimes, she has wondered . . .

Cindy's pride is hurt when "Bill Damon" arrives instead of her husband, but he's every bit as attractive as she'd imagined Stewart might be. Trust builds as they unmask a burglary ring, but the problem of identity

"You said that you loved to putt. I'll plan soon for you to try the green at The Castle."
To Love and to Honor

is still between them. Will Cindy love "Bill" when she finds out he is really Ken Stewart?

Blue Hill's Seth and Alida Milliken were alluded to in the characters Seth Armstrong and Alida Barclay, but in the story, Seth is an attorney instead of a surgeon, and Alida is a secret agent. "Pirate's Cove" and "The Castle" were real places at Popham Beach, and the outboard "Mighty Mo" was named for the navy battleship on which the Japanese surrendered.

Cindy receives pearls from her husband, a match for Emilie's own, except that Cindy's are a single strand, and Emilie's had four.

> "Oo-o-oh. How exquisite! How lustrous! The center pearls in the string are as big as the peas Sary served for dinner. The diamond clasp is superb. Are they—they can't be *real?*"
> "Sure, they are real. Matched Orientals."

"I've read that color and bright light kindle the flame of the human spirit . . ."
To Love and To Honor

Emilie gave full rein to her descriptive passages, from sky to ocean, from interior furnishings to an evening dinner, in vivid color.

> The horizon, against which a bridge was etched in black, was crimson; shades of red rayed upward; planes of pink melted into fields of vivid green which faded into soft yellow at the upper edge which in turn fused into violet where it met and lost itself in the blue sky.

Dinners were mouth-watering:

> She continued to hover after she served a delicately roasted squab chicken, a flaky baked potato, outsize peas of a sweet and melting tenderness, a fluffy roll, and currant jelly red as a mammoth pigeon-blood ruby . . .

Her theme became the title: *To Love and to Honor.*

Emilie Loring, Four Strands of Pearls. "*The necklace is fully insured. Wear it. Don't worry about the value.*" To Love and to Honor

"When I promise 'to love and to honor' I'll mean it with all my heart and soul and mind."

"Hold everything, Cinderella, you have it wrong. In the marriage service the words are 'to love and to cherish'—I ought to know."

His heartless chuckle increased her determination to make him understand.

"I still stick to 'to love and to honor'—accent on honor. If you honor a person, you'd be bound to cherish him or her, wouldn't you?"

Emilie's health declined as she wrote *To Love and to Honor*. Since the November after Victor's death, she had coped with an enlarged and dilated heart which caused fatigue, swelling, and shortness of breath. Then, in April 1950, she was diagnosed with rheumatoid arthritis. Her joints were stiff and painful. She tired more easily than before and developed a slight tremor.

Her enthusiasm, however, was undimmed. She augmented the standard statement about the novel and characters being fictitious with a compliment to "The Pine Tree State": "The setting is a composite of many charming villages unified by the brilliant sunlight, the ocean tang, golden beaches, rocky shores and the fragrant breath of colorful gardens generic to the glorious coast of Maine."[28]

Wellesley Hills, Summer 1950

She gave her manuscript to the publisher in June and signed a contract for her thirty-first book, to be delivered one year later, June 1951. Then she moved out of the Hotel Bellevue and back to the Wellesley Hills house for good.

Hers was the bedroom to the left at the top of the stairs, the one with hidden drawers behind the books on the built-in shelves. Her granddaughter Eve, who was nearly seven at the time, later recalled:

On the second floor were five bedrooms and three bathrooms. Nana's room was looking over the porch when she lived with us ... In her room there was a window seat with a cushion and shelves with a door on it. Behind the shelves were secret drawers where I used to hide my special things ...[29]

Her older sister, Sandy, who was eight then, remembered that Emilie's room was generally "off bounds," and their father was not forthcoming about why. Sometimes, Emilie would look with the girls at dresses in the Sears catalog. She played Patti Page records and was "very much into fashion and social events." Both girls recalled their grandmother's fancy dresses and that she enjoyed having tea in the afternoon, on nice dishes. In Sandy's words, she was "very much a lady."[30]

Wellesley Hills, Fall 1950

For All Your Life began, as did most of Emilie Loring's novels, in the fall. It was her favorite time of year, when the burnished golds and rusts and purples were at their height.

"Motorists will begin to flock to see the foliage tomorrow. The different shapes and colors of these metal leaves are guides to locate the varieties. Crimson indicates sweet gum and red maple. Purple: mountain ash. Clear yellow: American beech and willow."

It was, typically, also the end of her summer vacation, when she returned to the city and her writing routine.

Out of the blue, Anne Kendrick inherits a large estate in the White Mountains of New Hampshire. There is another claimant to the estate, and two men vie for Anne's attention—Congressman Griffith Trent and Ned Crane, a philandering ne'er do well.

Anne Kendrick's father, like Emilie's, had been an actor who gave the wise advice that suggested the story's title and matched Emilie's effort to complete this, her thirty-first novel.

"Anne, here's a rule for all your life," he had begun gravely. "When you have decided on a course of action, go to it. No matter if discouragement blocks the way, keep swinging. Each swing will inch you forward though it may seem to you that you haven't moved. Then, before you know it, you will have achieved your goal."

Despite her health challenges, *For All Your Life* had the best qualities of Emilie's previous thirty novels. There were vibrant descriptions:

Across the room a log fire leaped and blazed. It threw patterns on the light mahogany walls and set figures dancing in shadowy corners.

Her characters were approachable and real:

Griff was reminded of Anne Kendrick, with her simple, uncalculated manners, her warm unstudied graciousness, her gaiety of spirit, the eyes that met his squarely and honestly. Anne was genuine and real.

And her flair for intrigue and mystery was in full force.

Since she had entered the wood road, she had imagined she was being followed. Perhaps it wasn't imagination . . .
"Queer things have been going on at Mountain Lodge since Mrs. Williams' sudden death . . ."
Anne did not answer but she felt as though a cold hand had touched her spine. Although the room was warm, she shivered.

She didn't mention this technique when interviewed, but once again, she adopted a first-person narrative for her initial draft. One portion was a six-page letter from Anne Kendrick to Joe Bennet. The original read:

Inside a gay little fire is crackling under the mantel while your correspondent in cherry red pullover, cardigan and matching plaid skirt—worn to add cheer to the day—sits at the desk that once was Mayme Williams', wrinkling her brow and nibbling her pen between bursts of creative writing.

She changed the final copy to third person and edited the details:

Inside, a gay little fire crackled under the mantel while Anne, in cherry-red pullover, cardigan and matching plaid skirt, sat at her desk nibbling her pen.

To Love and to Honor debuted on November 3, 1950, and the *Boston Herald* announced, "A marriage by proxy, a hatred that turned to love, a thrilling jewel robbery—from these dramatic ingredients Emilie Loring spins her 30th story—one that all who want wholesome entertainment will enjoy completely."[31] Emilie remembered to send a copy to the Maine Author Collection with the inscription, "To the Maine State Library with the compliments of the author."

Next came the predictable flock of fan letters. Emilie—or her publisher—wrote a dedication for the book in progress:

From North to South, from East to West they came; the letters you wrote me when TO LOVE AND TO HONOR was published. Wonderful letters, full of commendation, affection, and good wishes. I would have liked to answer each one, but it would have taken weeks, and you all asked for another story. I couldn't do both, so I am dedicating FOR ALL YOUR LIFE to each one of you in appreciation of your generous and warm-hearted encouragement.

Spring 1951

Early in January 1951, the Women's City Club of Boston announced a talk about "Books and Authors" by Alice Dixon Bond of the *Herald-Traveler*. Authors Emilie Loring, Sara Ware Bassett, Mrs. William Pearson and Agnes C. Lyons agreed to assist with hospitality.[32]

There was an earnestness about the characters in Emilie's current novel that reflected her internal state.

"You know, Joe," Anne went on, "since my arrival I've gone about in a daze, trying to realize what has happened to me. I must take hold of life with both hands and all my intelligence."

After serving in the Army in the aftermath of World War II, Emilie's grandson, Victor Joseph, signed up with the Marines on January 15, 1951 and was sent to Parris Island for training. She wrote:

"How do they feel about your enlistment in the Marines, Joe?"

"How do any parents feel? They wouldn't have me not go, but I figure they have let-down moments. I'm their one and only . . . I'll be back on leave. And there is a U.S. mail delivered at Parris Island. Keep me posted."

Emilie wrote only a bit further than this, about one-third of the finished novel, and stopped at the end of her long letter to Joe:

What a letter. I can imagine you already nodding over it in your tent.

No news of you know what.

Warm regards. Keep me posted.

Affectionately yours,

Anne Kendrick

On March tenth, Emilie came down with a virus that caused laryngo-tracheo-bronchitis ("croup"). Within twenty-four hours, the infection became broncho-pneumonia.

Two days later, on Tuesday, March 13, 1951, Emilie Loring died at home in Wellesley Hills.[33] Dr. Robert I. Blakesley of the Wellesley Hills Congregational Church conducted an open casket funeral in the Forest Hills Cemetery Chapel, after which her remains were cremated, placed in an urn that matched Victor's (a gold-metal cylinder with her signature engraved on it), and placed in the niche next to his and her brother Robert's in the Forest Hills mausoleum. Her grandson Selden recalled her funeral as "matter-of-fact," without a lot of grieving. The younger grandchildren didn't realize she had died; one day, she was simply gone.[34]

Emilie's longtime friend, Clara Endicott Sears, eulogized with greater emotion in the Boston Authors Club *Bulletin*:

The Boston Authors Club lost a very vibrant spark of energy, talent, and decisive personality when our member, Emilie Loring, passed away. She has left a very definite impression on all who knew her. In the thirty novels she has left behind her she has contributed to thousands of readers some of her ardent joy of living. This world seemed very good to her, and she wanted to go on living in it. Strange as it seems, that was not to be, in spite of the gallant fight she made for a year to hold onto it.

We shall miss her very, very much in many different ways, and we shall remember her.[35]

Emilie Loring's obituary appeared in newspapers across the country. The Wellesley *Townsman* noted that she was "one of the early members of the Woman's Association of the First Congregational Church of Wellesley Hills and a member of the church since 1907." The *New York Times* recalled her literary family and said that "'a wholesome love story' was her success recipe." *Time* magazine called her books "drugstore-and-newsstand romantic novels," and her sons refused to ever have the magazine in their homes again.[36] The Boston Authors Club acknowledged that, from the time she joined their organization, "no Club meeting seemed important unless she was sitting near the front of the room with her two intimate friends, Clara Endicott Sears and Sara Ware Bassett."[37]

Robert Loring wrote to Clara Endicott Sears one week after his mother's death: "Your friendship was one of the shining points in her life, and I thank you from the bottom of my heart for being so wonderful to her."[38] He also wrote to Dean Academy: "I received about one hundred letters telling me what a fine author she was, but, having been with her almost constantly the past fifty-five years, I want to say that she was a fine mother, too."[39]

Emilie's will divided her estate equally between her sons, Robert and Selden, who were also her executors. She authorized them to retain, amend, or sell any of her contract rights with respect to her writings. Furthermore, she authorized them to "apply for or do anything else necessary or desirable in their judgment to obtain the extension, or to preserve or conserve the value of any copyright standing in my name." Finally, she authorized her sons to distribute her property as they deemed fair.[40]

Selden, Jr. recalled that Robert, called "Bobbo" by his nieces and nephews, gave one of Emilie's rings to each of the grandchildren. Six of the original, book jacket paintings eventually went to the grandchildren, as did some of her silver spoons, teacups, and silver boxes. Paintings, statues, books, and furniture were divided. The brothers kept what was important to them and sold the rest to antique dealers.

"To my mind, one of the most tragic aftermaths of a death is the fact that things are so apt to cause trouble in families."
There Is Always Love

Emilie had written, "Old age is merely life into which you put no enthusiasm, for enthusiasm is the fountain of youth." Until her death at age eighty-four, Emilie Loring continued to write the youthful, romantic stories for which she is so well known. She never reached old age.

"Something tells me that our internationally famous author had this finale plotted last September."
Beckoning Trails

CHAPTER 28
The Real Emilie Loring

Ghostwritten Books

Emilie Loring's partially completed novel, *For All Your Life*, would not meet its June 1951 deadline. This was her last story, a manuscript she had dedicated herself to finishing, pushing back the oppression of her illness. In 1952, her sons contracted with Elinore Denniston, a writer from New York, to complete the novel at eighty-thousand words for publication.

Elinore Denniston was an accomplished writer of moderate success. She wrote under her own name and several pseudonyms: Dennis Allan, Helen Maxwell, and Rae Foley. Her books tended to be mysteries, the best of which was the Rae Foley series about a sleuth named Hiram Potter. These were called "run-of-the-mill," her plots "unimaginative."

When Chapter XIII of *For All Your Life* begins, it is apparent that there is a new author, and her writing is not of the same caliber as Emilie Loring's.

Anyhow, as she had told Joe Bennet, she could not cry on Cosgrove's shoulder.

"Anyhow, I have been hearing a lot about you, Miss Kendrick." —

"Anyhow, Anne wouldn't marry me—or anyone—on those conditions."

"Anyhow, I want to know what Minna is really after."

Confident Anne Kendrick suddenly becomes mousey:

"I'm the career gal who only a few weeks ago was going to do big things in television. Remember? And now all I hear is a little voice saying a woman's best career is marriage."

Even Emilie's trademark russet and gold chrysanthemums lost their color: "With bowls of massed autumn flowers on the table, desk and mantel, the room was warm and bright."

Miss Denniston ignored already established story elements and introduced conflicting ones later in the narrative. In Emilie's chapters, Gaston Cosgrove knows the details of Mame Williams' attempt to get Griffith Trent to marry Anne. In Miss Denniston's chapters, he has no idea: "It seems to be a general rumor."

Emilie crafted her stories carefully and never left a page until she made it as good as she could. But now, she had a ghostwriter, and Elinore Denniston's errors, awkwardness, and tone—her writing personality—would now be attributed to Emilie Loring.

For All Your Life marked a turning point in Emilie Loring's reputation and legacy. None of the books after *To Love and to Honor* was fully hers, and the real Emilie Loring began to blur, not distinguished from the committee of writers who wrote under her name. Some of the writing was hers and connected with readers as always, while the new styles connected with some and repelled others.

Emilie died with several serial stories "on hand," and her sons hired Miss Denniston to turn those into full-length novels, also. Next, they had her cobble together several short stories at a time to produce more "Emilie Lorings." It cannot have been easy.

There was precedent for this in Emilie's writing. *The Trail of Conflict* began as a serial story, and another of her serial stories, "Behind the Cloud," began with two short stories, "There's Always a Silver Lining" and "You Never Know."

In the reverse direction, Emilie then took elements from "Behind the Cloud" and distributed them among her later stories. The name "Andy

"Will you let them change the ending?"
"No, to that last question."
Give Me One Summer

Carson" is used again in *Give Me One Summer*; the canning beets incident was used again in *Hilltops Clear*; and *Lighted Windows* borrowed the drama of an iceberg's calving.

There was even precedent in the family for finishing another author's writing after their death; Rachel had completed George Baker's play, *After Taps* following his death in 1890. With significant parts already written, Emilie's *My Dearest Love*, *I Take This Man*, and *The Shadow of Suspicion* could all be completed. But when Miss Denniston began to create novels from collections of short stories without a central theme or plot, she needed a different process.

She made a list of the incidents that occurred in Emilie Loring's novels to learn her patterns and to have ready ideas at hand. She outlined each book, chapter by chapter, incident by incident, working her additions around Emilie's text. Her process was formulaic, but no formula could produce an Emilie Loring story. Emilie never knew, herself, what was going to happen in her stories, until her characters let her know. But what else could Miss Denniston do?

The differences in their writing were everywhere, from conception to realization. Emilie wrote from a lifetime of experiences that Miss Denniston never had. The Baker legacy of optimism and courage was a real thing, taught from the cradle and honed with hard work. So was her writing craft.

When Emilie Loring sat down to write, she started with a theme and a situation that sparked her imagination. Her purpose was to entertain, not by creating a particular form or outline, but using language to create a desired effect. Miss Denniston's purpose was to copy what Emilie did as closely as she could, but she could mimic only the form, not the internal spirit and the experienced craft that produced it.

Amos R. Wells described the difference in an essay for the Boston Authors Club *Bulletin* in March 1919, "Inevitable Writing."

"It's amazing how Life straightens out problems if one sits tight and works one's head off to help, isn't it?"
"You believe in Life, don't you? Believe in the best."
"I do. Isn't it stupid not to?"
There Is Always Love

Discussions of form are interesting, but do they not indicate a lack of the writer's authentic inspiration? The prime characteristic of all worthy writing is its inevitableness . . . all writings that move men are merely the overflow of personality. Back of them is no trick or mode; back of them is fullness of life. Granted the inborn gift of expression, the one secret of a great book is a great soul.

There was no chance of copying that.

Over time, Selden and Robert Loring also took turns as ghostwriters to produce new novels from their mother's material. Selden had written and published his own stories and books; he was the more likely one to do the work now. But Robert had stepped in after his father's death to read Emilie's stories and provide feedback, and although he always seemed to be in someone else's shadow—usually his brother's—he had his own share of Baker/Loring talent.

Both men had jobs and families, but neither earned a great deal of money. Each also believed the other to be "better off" than they—Robert in the big home at Wellesley Hills and Selden in a home he had bought himself, along with a membership to the Old Belfry Club. The truth was that both families needed the income from Emilie Loring's significant royalties.

The *Christian Science Monitor* called Emilie Loring "unsinkable": "It is sometimes darkly hinted in publishing circles that Emilie Loring no longer exists, but light novels under her name continue to appear, and after 40 years, 'Emilie Loring' remains one of those names virtually unknown to readers of book reviews but tenaciously established in her market." An estimated five million copies had been sold in all editions, including braille and translations in nine languages. "Congratulations, Mrs. Loring, whoever you are."[1]

In addition to bringing out a new novel each year, the brothers re-serialized Emilie Loring's previous novels, and after updating them for the times, they published her short stories again, too. Shortly after her death, Robert wrote to the Pilgrim Press about his mother's Josephine Story books. Apparently, Emilie's original copies could not be found. The publisher didn't have them, either.

After years of working together on the books, a quarrel arose between Robert and Selden. Robert didn't want to continue the books, but Selden did. Selden died, with the quarrel still between them, in August 1970. Robert didn't attend his funeral. He did, however, publish two more "as by Emilie Loring" books after that— *Forsaking All Others* and *The Shining Years*. He could have stopped, but he didn't. Maybe theirs was a different quarrel.

Reputation and Legacy

Emilie Loring's legacy was summed up in a Little, Brown advertisement in 1945:

Some of you can look back almost a quarter of a century to the first Emilie Loring novel that you read, and the long list of those that followed it—each as delightful as the last . . . All of you know that in every Emilie Loring novel you will meet real people, people you like, people whose happiness you desire almost as strongly as your own, and people whom you want to meet again and again— by rereading your favorites.[2]

Equal parts adventure, mystery, and romance, Emilie Loring's novels portray women as they want to see themselves: confident, independent, achieving worthy goals and finding equal partners in love. Many read her books, then and now, for the first time at age ten and re-read them through their teens, twenties, careers, parenthood, and into retirement. That they connect at every age and in every decade is a testament to the books' quality and to their author's insight and skill.

Alice Dixon Bond said that a good book entertains but also presents an understanding of character and life "in words descriptive of thought and feeling."[3]

If a book tells you nothing, it is not a great book. It is a good book, if you read something which stays with you and if it uncovers something that you can take for yourself.[4]

Emilie Loring's fan mail from the 1940s met Miss Bond's criteria. The *New York Herald Tribune's* "Weekly Book Review" quoted letters received from all over the country:

"It may seem greedy, but it is too bad you cannot write as fast as we Loring lovers read." (Connecticut)

"I wonder if you realize the pleasure you are giving when you write your interesting books. I love them." (Indiana)

"Your books bring happiness and lifting of spirits where other methods have failed. Those who have never read them are missing one of the great pleasures of life." (New York)

"I own every book of yours and have enjoyed every one even more than the preceding. Each novel reflects the time in which it was written. What people were thinking, doing, wearing, singing, even eating. I feel that in my Emilie Loring collection I have a contemporary history." (Kentucky)

"Some ten years ago, I read my first Loring book and since then have been an ardent Loring fan. Thank you for the many hours of pleasure you have given me." (Tennessee)

Emilie Loring's literary "fingerprints" stretched around the world. In the 1960s, a man wrote, with some exasperation, that when he was in China, he craved an English-language novel. At the bookstore, his only option was an Emilie Loring.[5]

The *New York Times* reported in 1969 that Grace Livingston Hill still had ten books on the best-seller list. Emilie Loring had *forty-one*. Hill's books were "soupy," but "Emilie Loring is far above such inanities. Her specialty: smoothly written domestic mysteries . . . The salesmen in the field can't get enough of them."[6]

New books continued to appear into the 1970s, and her fans had no idea that she had died. Their letters sounded like those of the last generation.[7] A seventeen-year-old wrote from Silver Spring, Maryland that she wanted to be a writer and asked if Emilie Loring could give her some advice. Another wrote to Mrs. Loring about her 1940s war novels: "That was a time I never knew, and now I know."

"I read her books when I was a young girl and am now rereading them with just as much enjoyment. My married daughter is now discovering what a great author Emilie Loring is." (Texas)

"I would like to know everything or anything about her." (Arkansas)

Another fifty years after that, original readers, their daughters, and their granddaughters, are still on board.

"What a joy and surprise to find I am not alone in my love of Emilie Loring and her philosophy of optimism! I began reading Emilie Loring around the age of 10 and spent the remaining of my school years scouring used bookstores looking for 'new' stories." Vanessa

"It's been more than 50 years since I read my first Emilie Loring novel, and I still fondly remember her books . . . I give credit to Ms. Loring for turning me into an avid life-long reader." Sue

"I am now a widow and a grandma, but I still dream of "perching" on a stone wall in the moonlight with the scent of flowers wafting through the air, the faint sound of dance music and tinkling china and the strong, comforting arm of a handsome gentleman at my side!" Judy

"I fully intend to talk my two daughters into reading Emilie Loring books when they're older!" Debbie

"Re-reading *The Key to Many Doors* just confirmed my opinion of the post-1951 stories. They're nice enough, but they are not Emilie Loring." Susan

"EL will reach the next generation, if we carry the torch." Ellen Jenken

In 1969, Dorothy Van Doren wrote in the *Delaware County Times*, "Who is Emilie Loring? I ask this question not idly; I really wish I knew." She stopped by a rack of paperbacks in the five-and-dime store. "There it was, a whole bookcase, from top to bottom, full of the novels of Emilie Loring. I counted 41 titles. The book I bought . . . has gone through three hard cover editions, four printings by Grosset and Dunlap, and 15 by Bantam Books. This could easily add up to more than a million books of this one title alone; and 44 titles were given." Emilie Loring didn't need to advertise. "She has her public all tied up and more than willing. She receives thousands of letters asking for another story."[8]

She concluded, as so many of Emilie Loring's readers have done: "I still wonder about Emilie Loring. Is she a committee that turns out romances to order? Is she rich as Croesus, living in her tasteful house, taking time off once a month to dictate another story to a neatly dressed secretary? The next time I go to Woolworth's, I'll look over her books more carefully. Maybe one of them contains a biography of the author."

Emilie Loring's biography is here. Happy landings!

AFTERWORD

I never intended to write this book. I was simply curious about Emilie Loring, and as her story grew, I felt a responsibility to share it. The process had more the feeling of a quest than a research project.

First, I fell in love with Boston. Everything about it was different from what I had known before. I loved the old buildings, the Public Garden, and the Esplanade. I loved the Italian cafe on Charles Street and everything about the Boston Public Library. In my own town, I can tell you what used to be on a certain corner before it became what it is now, and I began to do that where Emilie lived.

Then I met the Lorings, who shared generously from their memories, photographs, and memorabilia. From the beginning, they encouraged me to tell Emilie's full story, without limitation. Through their hospitality and friendship over the years, I gained a sense of their grandmother that transcended her books.

I absolutely love research. I am curious and well-skilled. I love finding a tiny bit of information that connects in memory with another little bit and then doing the detective work that turns them into understanding. Days on end in a microfilm room or examining photos with a magnifying glass—heaven.

The more I discovered, the more real Emilie Loring's books became. The more I learned, the more her books guided me to new discoveries.

As a professor, I taught that "everything you learn allows you to see more." This was true with Emilie Loring. As her history fell into place, her books gave up more information. *Fair Tomorrow* is closest to telling the story of her romance with Victor. *With Banners* is about her family of dramatists, and *Hilltops Clear* an ode to her brother. *Here Comes the Sun!* is all about Blue Hill, and *Lighted Windows* marked the change, as her Alaska trip had done, from one outlook on life to another.

Blue Hill, Maine started as Emilie's and became mine, too. As in Boston, I can look at what is and see what used to be. I know the rhythm of the tides in Blue Hill Bay, the feel of the air, the scents, sounds, and tastes of summer. You may think Emilie's descriptions are long, but trust me, she held back.

Biography can be a lonely undertaking, but in "Captain Bob" Slaven, I had a partner in sleuthing and learned things I could never have discovered otherwise about old times and new on the east side of Blue Hill Bay. Plus, Bob witnessed the Stone House ghost, and a story like that is worth hearing first-hand.

Doing Biography

Telling whole lives, especially women's lives, is tricky. We write about people because of their accomplishments but ask too little about who they were apart from those. Women's lives are especially difficult, because their worth to biography is something other than home and motherhood, but the significance of home and motherhood to their lives may be equal or greater. We are all so much more than our public accomplishments.

This is especially true for a woman born in the middle of the nineteenth century, who left fewer traces than we do now. What would Emilie Loring have done with Instagram?

Fortunately, Emilie's unique childhood left traces. She also wrote about herself directly, as a daughter, sister, homemaker, mother, and author, and others did, too. Hers is a more complete picture than we usually see of a woman in her times.

I abhor the idea of finding a "central theme" of a person's life and tying everything to that. Real lives aren't lived that way. We live moment to moment, without knowing what is ahead, and we change along the way. In hindsight, we can cherry-pick the parts that led to what resulted, but a life is more interesting if we do less of that.

This project took so long—too long, to my mind, and an unintended consequence was that I experienced more of what Emilie had experienced—the death of a revered father, a cherished sister, and far too many friends. When her cheery writing took those "unexpected" turns, as I used to think of them, now I understood.

Losses have made me acutely aware of how much I would have missed, had I not begun when I did. I was lucky to stop by Stone House when Bob Slaven's parents still lived there. After the librarian who gave me directions, they were the ones who provided the thread in Blue Hill that I've pulled on ever since. They welcomed me into their home, shared their file of Stone House articles, and introduced me, right then and there, to Esther Wood, the local historian, who told me she had been Emilie Loring's teenage maid.

Finding those threads is a charming part of discovery. It takes awareness and knowledge but also depends quite often on chance and the kindness of strangers. Dave Danielson could have turned me away when I stopped in at KYC, a stranger, and asked for help finding a rock. Instead, he introduced me to Bob Slaven, and we went looking for it.

Am I sick of Emilie Loring? You'd surely think so. But I'm not. Learning about her has made her more meaningful; it's the reason I wrote this book. Her characters were models for me in my childhood, and when it was my turn to write, Emilie's advice got me through.

I like writing but wrestling this biography down has been a much bigger task than I ever imagined. The pure slug work to get to the end has been . . . well, just that.

I am sure I have made errors. When two events are known, the temptation is to assume a straight line between them, but the unknown "between" may be very different. I have discovered this error many times, and there is no way around it.

This is *my* story of Emilie Loring. I have read her books more than fifty times each, and I have spent more than twenty years researching her life with access that can never again be given. I am confident that I am the world's expert on Emilie Loring. Nevertheless, I know that mine is only one lens.

"The fact is, that no man is the same under different aspects, and never the same to those who know him best and those who know him least." (John Neal, *Portland Illustrated*, 1874)

How I See Her Now

I admire Emilie Loring. She strove with sincerity, worked hard to improve, and kept her sense of humor doing it. She had her faults and her down days, but how else could we identify with her? Behind a good book is good character, and hers are very good books.

We need books that entertain, lift spirits, and restore optimism, not only in times of crisis but for a steady wind in our sails. I wish the literary world treasured them more.

Is Emilie Loring the best author ever? Of course not. Who could claim it? But something special is afoot when two generations of women read an author's books over and over again, love them from childhood through old age, and pass them down to their daughters and granddaughters.

The passing of eras is a little sad. We read some authors from the past, but it's such a small subset of those we could. Now that Emilie Loring e-books books are available, new readers can discover her. I hope they do.

Emilie Loring had the qualities of a good friend: intelligent, inspiring, and insightful, with good taste, charming manners, and light-hearted humor. Her books are like cardigan sweaters—classic, comfortable, never too much or too little. Not trend-setters, but somehow, always just right.

—Patti Bender

APPENDIX I

Emilie Loring Publications

Books

As Josephine Story

Copyrighted by George H. Doran Co.
    1914   *For the Comfort of the Family: A Vacation Experiment*
Copyrighted by Frank M. Sheldon
    1917   *The Mother in The Home*

As Emilie Loring

Copyrighted by Emilie Loring:
1922	*The Trail of Conflict* – Jerry Glamorgan, Steve Courtlandt
1924	*Here Comes the Sun!* – Julie Lorraine, James Trafford
1925	*A Certain Crossroad* – Judith Halliday, Neil Peyton
1927	*The Solitary Horseman* – Rose Grahame, Tony Hamilton
1928	*Gay Courage* – Nancy Caswell, Geoffrey Hilliard
	Play: "Where's Peter?" – Cynthia Brooks, Peter Maxwell
1929	*Swift Water* – Jean Randolph, Christopher Wynne
1930	*Lighted Windows* – Janice Trent, Bruce Harcourt
1931	*Fair Tomorrow* – Pamela Leigh, Scott Mallory
1932	*Uncharted Seas* – Sandra Duval, Nicholas Hoyt
1933	*Hilltops Clear* – Prudence Schuyler, Rodney Gerard
1934 (Feb)	*We Ride the Gale!* – Sonia Carson, Michael Farr
1934 (Oct)	*With Banners* – Brooke Reyburn, Mark Trent
1935	*It's A Great World!* – Eve Travis, Jeffrey Kilburn
1936	*Give Me One Summer* – Melissa Barclay, Alexander Carson
1937	*As Long As I Live* – Joan Crofton, Craig Lamont
1938 (Feb)	*Today Is Yours* – Gay and Brian Romney
1938 (Nov)	*High of Heart* – Constance Trent, Peter Corey
1939	*Across the Years* – Faith Jarvis, Duke Tremaine
1940	*There Is Always Love* – Linda Bourne, Gregory Merton
1941 (Mar)	*Where Beauty Dwells* – Diane Vernon, Mackenzie Cameron

1941 (Oct)	*Stars In Your Eyes* – Kay Chesney, Drex Hamilton
1942	*Rainbow At Dusk* – Jessamine Ramsey, Vance Trent
1943	*When Hearts Are Light Again* – Gail Trevor, Gregory Hunt
1944	*Keepers of the Faith* – Nancy Barton, Bill Jerrold
1945	*Beyond the Sound of Guns* – Katharine Marlowe, Rex Danton
1946	*Bright Skies* – Patricia Carey, Cameron Fulton
1947	*Beckoning Trails* – Deborah Randall, Timothy Grant
1948	*I Hear Adventure Calling* – Fran Phillips, Myles Jaffray
1949	*Love Came Laughing By* – Wendy Adair, Vance Tyler
1950	*To Love and to Honor* – Cindy Clinton, Ken Stewart

Copyrighted by the publisher after Emilie Loring's death in 1951

1952	*For All Your Life* – Anne Kendrick, Griffith Trent
1954	*My Dearest Love* – Elizabeth Gilbert, Christopher Bradford
1954	*I Take This Man* – Penelope Sherrod, Donald Garth
1955	*The Shadow of Suspicion* – Julie Ames, Donald Bruce

Copyrighted by Seldon & Robert Loring after Emilie Loring's death

1955	*With This Ring* – Cynthia Farley, Alexander Houston
1956	*What Then Is Love* – Patricia Langston, Andrew Harcourt
1957	*Look to the Stars* – Faith Randolph, Scott Pelham
1958	*Behind the Cloud* – Dee Tremaine, Bill Mason
1960	*How Can the Heart Forget* – Ann Jerome, Myles Langdon
1961	*Throw Wide the Door* – Elinor Parks, Steve Sewall
1963	*Follow Your Heart* – Jill Bellamy, James Trevor
1964	*A Candle In Her Heart* – Leslie Blake, Douglas Clayton (Donald Shaw)
1965	*Forever and A Day* – Tony Carew, Rodney Meredith
1966	*Spring Always Comes* – Constance Wyndham, Jefferson Gray
1967	*The Key to Many Doors* – Nancy Jones, Peter Gerard
1968	*In Times Like These* – Page Wilburn, Vance Cooper
1969	*Love With Honor* – Randi Scott, Cary Hamilton
1970	*No Time For Love* – Julie Bryce, Mark Sefton
1971	*Forsaking All Others* – Jennifer Haydon, Bradley Maxwell
1972	*The Shining Years* – Sherry Winthrop, Stanley Holbrook

Short Stories and Articles

As Josephine Story

1911

"A Box of Books," column, *Boston Herald*

    Letter #1, Fiction, March 20

    Letter #2, Mexico, April 20

    Letter #3, Gardening, April 27

    Letter #4, Six Best-sellers, May 4

    Letter #5, Home Produce, May 18

    Letter #6, Women's Roles, May 25

    Letter #7, Armchair Travel, June 5

"Converting Phyllis," *The Mother's Magazine*

1914

"Find Drama in Your Housework!" *New York Tribune*, January 25, 1914

"How I Kept House Without a Servant: Gifts from the Garden," *Salt Lake Tribune*, March 22, 1914

"How I Kept House Without a Servant: Care of the Invalid," *Salt Lake Tribune*, March 29, 1914

"First Aid to the One-Room Housekeeper," *Boston Daily Globe*, July 12, 1914

"To Market, To Market," *The Designer*, August 1914

"Rush Order for Fancy Dress," *St. Nicholas*, September 1914.

"How We Became Town Mothers," *The Woman's Magazine*, October 1914, 33.

"The New Paper Jelly Cups," *Ladies' Home Journal*, June 1914.

"Why?" *The Spinning Wheel*, 1914

1915

"Maids Will Deceive," *Hair Culturist*, 1915.

"Gossip: An Endless Chain," *St. Nicholas*, 42: 508-9, April 1915.

"Why?" *The Spinning Wheel*, August 1915, 599-607.

"Dress and the Girl," *American Motherhood*, September 15, 1915.

"The Key to Many Doors," serial, *People's Home Journal*, Oct, Nov 1915.

"Do Your Christmas Planning Early," *American Motherhood*, November 1915.

"Her Christmas Ships," *Spinning Wheel*, Autumn, 1915, I (12), syndicated 1920.

1917

"The Best is Yet to Be," serial, begins March – 1917.

"How Women Should Prepare for Life's Best Part," *Des Moines Register*,
   February 11, 1917.

"For a Simple and Sane Sunday," *Table Talk*, *The National Food Magazine*,
   May 1917.

1918

"An Elusive Legacy," *Woman's Weekly*, August 3 – September 27 1917?

"Garth the Gunmaker," *Woman's Weekly*," August 3 – September 27 1918.

"The Limousine Lady," *The Oldsmobile Pacemaker*, I (5), February 1918.

"My Fifty-Cent Garden: Choosing My Flowers to Fit My Rooms," *The
   Country Gentleman*, 83 (1), 1918.

1919

"Kismet Takes a Hand," *Chicago Sunday Tribune*, April 27, 1919.

NY 1300.00X," *Argosy and Railroad Man's Magazine*, April 26, 1919.

"The Lady and the Looker," *Chicago Ledger*, May 1919.

"The Delicate Art of Being a Mother-in-law," *Woman's Home Companion*,
   46:100, June 1919.

"I'll Tell the World," *Chicago Daily Tribune*, June 8, 1919.

"Prue of Prosperity Farm," *Woman's Weekly*, July 24 – September 16.

"Known in Advance," *Grit*, Oct 1919 (final title of War Time Wooing)

1920

"White Magic," novella, February 15, 1920

"Keep Young," *The Labor Digest*, 12 (5), June 1920, 28–9.

"Try It Out!" *Pictorial Review*, October 1920, 76.

"The Seventh Day," *Pictorial Review*, October

As Emilie (Baker) Loring

1921

"Box from Nixon's," EL, *Woman's Home Companion*, 48: 9-10, May 1921.

"My First Real Vacation," *Social Progress*, May 1921, 161.

"Behind the Cloud," EL, *Woman's Weekly*, July 30 – September 17, 1921.

"The Fountain of Youth," pamphlet, ca. 1921

"With Intent to Sell," EL, *Leslie's Weekly*, May 7, 1921.

"The Trail of Conflict," EL, *Munsey's*, 83 (3), 571. December '21, January '22,
   February, March, April 1921.

1924

"Dan Kicks a Goal," *Munsey's Magazine*, December 1924.

"The Yellow Hat," *Our Young People*, September 21, 1924.

1925

"Result: Happiness," *Thrift*, January 1925.

"Glycerine Tears," *The Delineator*, March 1925.

1928

"Where's Peter?" play, Penn Publishing Co.

"Open for Inspection," *Youth*

"The Silver Tree," *The Classmate*, December 22, 1928.

1930

"By Audacity Alone," *Youth*, May 1930.

"Christmas Ships," *Youth*, December 1930.

"Lighted Windows," *The Editor*, December 27, 1930, 245.

1933

"Titles," *Village Booklet*, March

1934

"Lighted Windows," *Philadelphia Public Ledger*, January 21

1935

"Freedom for Two," *Rural Progress Magazine*, March

1937

"Once In a Hundred Years," *National Home Monthly*, February

1938

"She Didn't Like Flying," *Boston Globe Magazine*, October 30, 1938

1940

"The Story the Titles Told," includes titles through *Where Beauty Dwells*.

"We Ride the Gale!" *Grit*, December 8, 1940.

1942

"Woman's Chance," read April 17, 1942. re: Soldier Voting Act of 1942.

Posthumous, Republished and/or Partially Ghostwritten/Updated

1955

"Across the Court," *Grit*, December 4

"Hand of Fatima," *Grit*, September 25

{"She Didn't Like Flying," *Grit*, October 30

1956

{"Returning Feet," *Grit*, February 26}

"The Yellow Hat," *Grit*, June 17

{"Why," *Grit*, 8 July, previously published in *The Spinning Wheel*}

{"Open for Inspection," *Grit*, September 16}

"What Then Is Love," *Toronto Star*, September 29

{"With Intent to Sell," *Grit*, December 9}

{"The Box from Nixon's," *Grit*, December 23}

1957

"Across the Court," *Crosier*, June

1958

"Under New Management," *Crosier*, ca. August

1963

"Gold Chains," *Today's Family*, May

1980

"Lighted Windows," *The Editor*, December 27

Completed: on hand, absorbed, or unknown publishing

"A Clean Slate"

"Blue Smocks"

"Cecily Ann Floats"

"How to Begin"

"In the 19th Century Manner"

"One Day at a Time"

"That Little Matter of Age"

"The System"

"Why Apologize"

"Winds of the World" became "Returning Feet."

"Without Pain?" (dentist story)

APPENDIX II

Source material for ghostwritten novels

My Dearest Love (1954)

Published in March of 1954, three years after Emilie Loring's death, this story was based on her 1917 serial novel, "An Elusive Legacy."

I Take This Man (1954)

This was the third of four novels copyrighted by Little, Brown after Emilie Loring's death. It was based on a 1918 serial novel, "Garth the Gunmaker."

The Shadow of Suspicion (1955)

Miss Denniston completed this story from a substantial manuscript that Emilie Loring left behind. It has the same errors of tone, vocabulary, and story that characterized the later books but achieves an absorbing mystery.

With This Ring (1955)

A portion of this story was crafted from Emilie's short stories, "She Didn't Like Flying" (1938) and "Hand of Fatima." The lucky piece in "Hand of Fatima" changes from the shape of a hand with a blue stone in the center to a miniature, gold star.

What Then Is Love (1956)

The fifth Elinore Denniston novel, the story is action-packed but implausible, and the prose is not up to Emilie Loring's standards.

Look to the Stars (1957)

The contract for this book read, "as by Emilie Loring." Miss Denniston had no role. It was completed by Selden and Robert Loring from Emilie's unpublished *Princess and the Pilgrim* (1923).

Behind the Cloud (1958)

There was no Miss Denniston on this book, either. Emilie Loring's sons completed the novel from the serial novel with the same title, published in *Woman's Weekly* (1921). They had traveled to Alaska with their mother in 1907 and could appreciate and contribute setting details.

How Can the Heart Forget (1960)

This novel cobbled together Emilie Loring's short stories, "Home is the Fighter," "Most Men Like Blue," and "Tonight at 12."

Throw Wide the Door (1961)

Miss Denniston used her home city, New York, as the background for this novel. The disparaging tone at the beginning is entirely her own.

Follow Your Heart (1963)

Miss Denniston tells—not "shows"—what her characters are like. The result is persistent distance between the reader and the story.

A Candle In Her Heart (1964)

Repeated in this novel was the story of a serviceman, believed to be dead, who returns home alive, as Robert Curtis did in World War I. It is likely from material on hand, but the record does not survive.

Forever and a Day (1965)

Another New York story. Miss Denniston wove personal experience into this novel as Emilie Loring did—hers, not Emilie's.

Spring Always Comes (1966)

The blend of new and old writing in this story is obvious. Constance Wyndham vacillates between strength and helplessness, and the condescension toward women suggests a male writer.

The Key to Many Doors (1967)

The kernel for this story's plot was Emilie Loring's 1915 serial with the same title. She used elements of the serial, herself, for *Lighted Windows*, which was also set in Alaska. Despite having the same title, the earlier serial and later book are dissimilar, the second more cynical and with new plot lines. Cynthia Barbee may allude to Blue Hill's Cynthia Barber, sister to Joan Coggan Becton, who bought Emilie Loring's Sculpin Point, and a Peter Gerard owned a cottage on Parker Point. Neither appeared in the original story.

In Times Like These (1968)

Published in 1968, *In Times Like These* is a different style of ghostwritten book. The beginning is based on Emilie Loring's 1921 short story, "The Box from Nixon's," with a new and complicated plot of treason and undercover investigation. The 1921 story is more modern in outlook. In "The Box from Nixon's," Jean and Miles are on equal footing in their humorous, flirtatious sparring. Vance and Page, in the 1968 version, are the big man/little woman.

Love With Honor (1969)

Elements of this story suggest the relationship between John Gale, Herbert Gale, and Rachel Baker, but the connections are few.

No Time for Love (1970)

Publicity called Julie Bryce "independent," but her character doesn't live up to the description.

Forsaking All Others (1971)

California, Broadway, a doctor's wife, the Empress Josephine . . . Emilie Loring's reminiscences fill this book, which seems partly formed from her play, *Where's Peter?* Mrs. Maxwell was one of Miss Denniston's pseudonyms.

The Shining Years (1972)

Robert Loring wrote this book, based on "Revolt of 66," "Her Christmas Ships," and "Result Happiness." His brother, Selden, had died two years earlier, and Miss Denniston was not engaged for this, the last Emilie Loring book.

The elderly Aunt Ellen is the hero, a combination of grace and wisdom. "He found himself wishing he could have known her when she was a girl." He was also kinder to his daughter Eve's husband, Bill, than they remembered. Using their names directly, he expressed concern that Eve needed an interest in her life but acknowledged that Bill made any room brighter by just coming into it.

PHOTO CREDITS

Except for the following, all photos are from the Private Loring Collections.

From the author:

    Page 155, Emilie's Tourmaline and Pearl Ring

    Page 155, Ring, side view

    Page 224, *For the Comfort of the Family: A Vacation Experiment*

    Page 224, "Supper confections are quickly and easily made."

    Page 368, Seven Chimneys, (derived from a photo in the Prior collection)

From the Emilie Loring Collection, Boston University Libraries, Howard
Gotlieb Archival Research Center:

    Page 8, Little Bessie, aka Fly Thistledown

    Page 64, Emilie, "The feel of Paris"

    Page 73, Mrs. Victor J. Loring

    Page 94, Emilie Baker Loring

    Page 116, Three Melvilles

    Page 205, Emilie Perched on the Stone House Parapet, July 1911

    Page 206, Emilie at the Front of Stone House, July 1911

    Page 237, Emilie Loring at Atlantic City, Jan 24, 1917

    Page 399, Emilie Loring, Bachrach Photo, 1935

    Page 422 *Today Is Yours* Book Signing

    Page 432, Emilie Loring, Favorite American Novelist

    Page 457, Her Handwriting

From the Sara Ware Bassett Collection, Boston Public Library:

    Page 396, Sara Ware Bassett, Cape Cod

From the Private collection, Lorenzo Mitchell:

    Page 341, "The Ledges"

    Page 341, Inside "The Ledges." Note the stone sailboat above the mantel and
the wall of books

Page 342, Rabbit Shutters. "There were little rabbits with upstanding ears cut in the yellow shutters." Gay Courage

From the Private collection, Neil and Trudy Prior:
Page 186, The Owen Sisters: Bessie, Minnie, and Carrie

From the Private collection, Capt. Robert K. Slaven, Jr.:
Page 490, Map of Blue Hill Bay

From the Private collection, Leo Horacek:
Page 12, Albert Baker, Printer

From the Hancock County Deeds:
Page 174, A portion of Emilie's Land, South of the East Blue Hill Road

NOTES

Introduction

1. Olga Owens, "A Beloved Boston Novelist Talks About Work and Play," *Boston Sunday Post*, June 8, 1941.
2. Owens, "Beloved."
3. *Boston Authors Club (BAC), Bulletin*, February 1931. Boston Authors Club Records Collection, Boston Public Library.
4. Jeanne G. Shain to Emilie Loring, May 20, 1933, Emilie Loring Collection, Boston University Libraries, Howard Gotlieb Archival Research Center.
5. Owens, "Beloved."

Act One: Bessie Baker

Chapter 1 Lee & Shepard, Publishers

1. Dorothea Lawrance Mann, *Emilie Loring: A Twentieth Century Romanticist* (Philadelphia: Penn, 1928), 7.
2. "George M. Baker," *Boston Evening Transcript*, October 21, 1890.
3. Raymond L. Kilgour, *Lee and Shepard: Publishers for the People* (Hamden, CT: Shoe String Press, 1965), 243.
4. Ruari McLean, foreword to The Art of Publishers' Bookbindings, 1815-1915 (Los Angeles: William Dailey Rare Books, Ltd., 2000).
5. Kilgour, *Lee and Shepard*, 18, 27.
6. Kilgour, *Lee and Shepard*, 111
7. Kilgour, *Lee and Shepard*, 141
8. Kilgour, *Lee and Shepard*, 91.
9. Lewis Carroll, *Alice in Wonderland*, first edition (Boston: Lee & Shepard, 1865), G. Edward Cassady, M.D. and Margaret Elizabeth Cassady, R.N. Lewis Carroll Collection, Collection no. 0392, Special Collections, USC Libraries, University of Southern California.
10. Typescript, G. Edward Cassady, M.D. and Margaret Elizabeth Cassady, R.N. Lewis Carroll Collection, Collection no. 0392, Special Collections, USC Libraries, University of Southern California.
11. Oliver Optic, "Our Bear," *Our Boys and Girls*, February 1869, 176.

12. Mann, *Emilie Loring*, 13.

13. "Walks and Talks About Town: Personal Sketches of Boston Men, Oliver Optic," *Boston Daily Advertiser*, June 6, 1868,

14. "Has Written 125 Books: 'Oliver Optic,' a Name That Every Boy Knows," *Boston Daily Globe*, March 12, 1893.

15. Thomas Wentworth Higginson, *Cheerful Yesterdays* (United States: Houghton, Mifflin and Co., 1898).

16. Kilgour, *Lee and Shepard*, 89

17. Kilgour *Lee and Shepard*, 43.

18. Sophie May, *Little Prudy* (Boston: Lee & Shepard), 55.

19. Kilgour, *Lee and Shepard*, p. 88.

20. Emilie Loring, *Gay Courage* (Philadelphia: PA, 1928), 30.

21. Daniel Defoe and William Lee, *Daniel Defoe: His Life and Recently Discovered Writings Extending from 1716 to 1769* (London: John Camden Hotten, 1869), 389.

Chapter 2 Albert Baker, Printer

1. Maine, Marriage Records, 1705-1922, s.v. "Albert Baker" (married April 8, 1832), Ancestry.com.

2. Charles Tappan Baker to "Betty" (Emilie Loring), March 30, 1935; (George M. Baker born two months after parents' marriage, "I guess you will have to draw your own conclusions"). Private collection, Linda Loring Loveland.

3. "In this City," Eastern Argus, July 8, 1835.

4. Directory of the City of Portland (Portland, ME: Samuel Colman, 1830; Arthur Shirley, 1831–1837), s.v. "Albert Baker."

5. Anthony Burton, "My Ancestor Was a Printer," *Who Do You Think You Are*, May 22, 2015.

6. Maine, Death Records, 1761–1922, s.v. "Julia R. Baker," (died November 21, 1841, scarlet fever, age nine months); Ancestry.com.

7. Maine, Death Records, 1761–1922, s.v. "John E. Baker," (died December 4, 1841, Affection of the lungs, three years old); Ancestry.com.

8. Memorial pages for John Edward Baker (December 4, 1841) and Julia R. Baker (November 21, 1841), citing Eastern Cemetery, Portland, Cumberland County, Maine; Findagrave.com.

9. "Great Fire at Portland: Twenty Buildings Destroyed, *Bangor Daily Whig and Courier*, October 15, 1842; "Disastrous Fire at Portland, The Farmer's Cabinet," October 21, 1842; "Fire in Portland," *Trumpet and Universalist Magazine*, October 22, 1842.

10. Baker Genealogy compiled by Charles Tappan Baker. Private collection, Linda Loring Loveland.

11. Census Reports Tenth Census: The newspaper and periodical press (United States: U.S. Government Printing Office, 1884), 89-90.

12. John Neal, Portland Illustrated (Portland, ME: W.S. Jones, 1874), 78.

13. Edwin A. Perry, *The Boston Herald and Its History: How, when and where it was Founded. Its Early Struggles and Hard-won Successes . . . .* (United States: The Herald, 1878), 3.

14. *Daily American Eagle* (Boston), first issue, December 3, 1844.

15. Joseph Griffin, ed., *History of the Press of Maine* (Brunswick: J. Griffin, 1872), 58-9.

16. John Neal, *Portland Illustrated* (Portland: W. S. Jones, 1874), 78.

17. Perry, *Herald*, 3.

18. "Boston Herald," *The Bay State Monthly*, October 1884.

19. Massachusetts, U.S., Town and Vital Records, 1620–1988; Boston: Boston Deaths, 1849; s.v. "Albert Baker," (May 1849, Inflammation of brain, age twelve).

20. Burial Records 1717–1962 of the Eastern Cemetery, Portland, Maine, compiled by William B. Jordan, Jr. (United States: Heritage Books, Inc., 1987), 6.

Chapter 3 George Baker: Purpose and Entertainment

1. School Committee, *The Report of the Annual Examination of the Public Schools of the City of Boston* (United States: John H. Eastburn, city printer, 1848).

2. "Examination of the Schools," *Boston Evening Transcript*, July 25, 1848.

3. Oliver B. Stebbins, "A Famous Boston Amateur Dramatic Club" in *The Bostonian* (United States: Bostonian Publishing Company, 1895), 131; Google Books.

4. George Melville Baker, *Wanted: A Male Cook* (Boston: W. H. Baker & Company, 1894).

5. Stebbins, Bostonian, 131.

6. Stebbins, *Bostonian*, 139.

7. Stebbins, *Bostonian*, 132.

8. Mark Twain, "A Voice for Setchell," *The Californian*, May 27, 1865.

9. Edwin Monroe Bacon, *King's Dictionary of Boston* (Cambridge, MA: Moses King, 1883), 157.

10. William Warland Clapp, *A Record of the Boston Stage* (United States: J. Monroe & Co., 1853), 395-6.

11. "Second Appeal to the Public, On Behalf of the Africans Taken in the Amistad," *The Liberator*, October 23, 1840.

12. Richard Hildreth, *The White Slave; or, Memoirs of a Fugitive* (Boston: Tappan and Whittemore, 1852).

13. *The Memorial History of Boston: Including Suffolk County, Massachusetts, 1630–1880* (Boston: James R. Osgood and Co., 1881-1883), 495.

14. *Memorial History*, 496.

15. Rev. S. H. Roblin, "Hero of Heroes," *Boston Daily Globe*, June 24, 1895.

16. "Boston Streets: Mapping Directory," Digital Collections and Archives, Tufts University.

17. Loring family Bible; Private collection, Loring family.

18. "Mussey and the Fugitive Slave," *Boston Courier*, May 27, 1854.

19. "Death of George M. Baker: Well Known as Publisher, Playwright and Author," *Boston Herald*, October 21, 1890.

20. "Burning of the Gerrish Market," *Boston Daily Advertiser*, April 14,1856.

21. "Affairs About Home: The Gerrish Market Conflagration," *Boston Herald*, April 14, 1856.

22. Massachusetts, U.S., town and Vital Records, 1620–1988. s. v. "George M. Baker," (Married Emily F. Boles, November 3, 1856), Ancestry.com; The Boston Directory, s.v. "George M. Baker," (Boston: Adams, Sampson & Company, 1857).

23. "Copartnership Notice," *Boston Evening Transcript*, September 8, 1857.

24. Advertisement in: *Percy Bolingbroke St. John, The Sea of Ice, Or, The Arctic Adventurers* (Boston: Mayhew and Baker, 1859), 249.

25. Amy Whorf McGuiggan, *Take Me Out to the Ball Game: The Story of the Sensational Baseball Song* (Lincoln: University of Nebraska Press, 2009), 7.

26. Henry Clay Barnabee, *My Wanderings: Reminiscences of Henry Clay Barnabee*, 105.

27. Barnabee, *Reminiscences*, 161.

28. Scrapbook, Henry Clay Barnabee Collection, Portsmouth Public Library, Portsmouth, NH.

29. "City Summary," *New York Clipper*, June 5, 1858.

30. Broadside, July 1858, Henry Clay Barnabee Collection, Portsmouth Public Library, Portsmouth, NH.

31. "Barnum Sails Away," *New York Times*, June 10, 1858.

32. "City Summary," *New York Clipper*, June 26, 1858.

33. Barnabee, *Reminiscences*, 239.

34. Barnabee, *Reminiscences*, 190.

35. Barnabee, *Reminiscences*, 193-195.

36. "Cork Leg and Patent Arm," *Boston Daily Globe*, Nov 15, 1878.

37. Notice, Mayhew & Baker, Boston Evening Transcript May 18, 1860.

38. Advertisement, George M. Baker, Commercial Bulletin, December 14, 1861.

39. Mann, *Emilie Loring*, 6.

40. George M. Baker, "The Freedom of the Press," *Ten Plays for Boys* (United States: Walter H. Baker, 1918).

41. Baker, *Ten Plays*, 163.

42. The Boston Directory (Boston: Adams, Sampson & Company, 1860).

43. Higginson, Cheerful Yesterdays, 245.

44. Advertisement, George M. Baker, *Boston Evening Transcript*, February 9, 1861.

45. Requiem poem for Matthew Mayhew Baker, 1861. Private collection, Linda Loring Loveland.

46. George Melville Baker, *Thirty Minutes for Refreshments: A Farce in One Act* (United States: W.H. Baker, 1920); and George Melville Baker, "Sylvia's Soldier" in *The Amateur Drama* (Boston: Lee & Shepard, 1868).

47. "Local Matters: Aid for the Volunteers," *Boston Daily Advertiser*, May 15, 1861.

48. George M. Baker, "Stand by the Flag" in *The Amateur Drama* (Boston: Lee & Shepard, 1868), 13.

49. "Lee & Shepard's Publishing House," *Our Boys and Girls*, July 1874, 541-6.

50. "He was Nasby's Friend: Charles Shepard's Reminiscences of the Noted Journalist," *Boston Daily Globe*, February 16, 1888.

51. "Petroleum V. Nasby, P.M.: A Pen Picture of the Famous Western Humorist," *Boston Daily Globe*, December 30, 1879.

52. "American Humor: Some of the Humorists of the Days of the War," *Boston Globe*, November 11, 1882.

53. Chauncy M. Depew, *My Memories of Eighty Years* (New York: C. Scribner's Sons, 1924), 57.

54. "The Young Man About Town," *Boston Globe*, August 26, 1883.

55. "Petroleum V. Nasby, P.M.: A Pen Picture of the Famous Western Humorist," *Boston Globe*, December 30, 1879.

56. "Young Man About Town," *Boston Globe*.

57. Barnabee, *Reminiscences*, 258-259.

58. Barnabee, *Reminiscences*, 258-259.

59. "Local Matters: The News of the Victory, Rejoicings in the City," *Boston Daily Advertiser*, April 4, 1865.

60. "By Telegraph: Peace!" *Boston Daily Advertiser*, April 10, 1865.

61. "National Calamity: Assassination of President Lincoln! Edwin M. Stanton,

Secretary of War," *Lowell Daily Citizen and News* (Lowell, MA), April 15, 1865.

62. "The National Fast: Its Observance in Boston," *Boston Daily Advertiser*, June 3, 1865.

63. "Abraham Lincoln," *Boston Semi-weekly Advertiser*, April 19, 1865.

64. "Good Luck," *Boston Traveler*, July 14, 1866.

65. George M. Baker, "Our Twelve Months' Cruise: A Valedictory," (Boston: private distribution, 1866).

Chapter 4 Born to Stage and Print

1. Insurance Map of Boston, Volume 1 (New York: D.A. Sanborn, 1867), number 116.

2. Massachusetts, Birth Records, 1840-1915, s.v. "Maria Emily Baker" (born September 5, 1866 at 5 Chardon St., Boston, Massachusetts to George M., Clerk, and Emily F.); s.v. "Robert Melville Baker" (born October 4, 1868 at 5 Chardon St., Boston, Massachusetts to George M., Clerk, and Emily F.), Ancestry.com.

3. "Honored and Loved: Mrs. J. R. Vincent Soon Keeps the 'Golden Anniversary,'" *Boston Daily Globe*, February 22, 1885.

4. Mann, *Emilie Loring*, 10.

5. Edward F. Payne, *Dickens Days in Boston: A Record of Daily Events, Etc.* (Boston: Houghton Mifflin, 1927), 141.

6. *Dickens Days*, 215.

7. Jim Vrabel, *When in Boston: A Time Line & Almanac* (Boston: Northeastern University Press, 2004), 187.

8. "Chronicle and Comment," *The Bookman: An Illustrated Literary Journal*, III, (New York: Dodd, Mead and Company), March 1896–August 1896, 390. Google Books.

9. Vrabel, *When in Boston*, 187.

10. Barnabee, *Reminiscences*, 260.

11. "Cincinnati Commercial: Mark Twain, Josh Billings, Petroleum Nasby," *Plain Dealer* (Cleveland, OH), February 14, 1871; "Letters of Public Entertainers 50 Years Ago," *Columbus Dispatch*, February 1, 1925.

12. "Boston Lyceum Course," *Boston Journal*, Sep 29, 1869.

13. "Dramatic and Musical," *Boston Journal*, Dec 15, 1869.

14. Oliver Optic, "Editorial Chitchat," *Our Boys and Girls*, July 1873, 509.

15. Vrabel, *When in Boston*, 153.

16. "Amusements," *Boston Herald*, March 23, 1869.

17. "House Robbery," *Boston Herald*, March 27, 1869.

18. 1870 United States Census, Boston, Suffolk County, Massachusetts, s.v. "Chardon," Ancestry.com.

19. "Vermont," *Lowell Daily Citizen and News*, July 27, 1870.

20. "New England Items: Rutland County," *Vermont Chronicle*, July 30, 1870.

21. John Shaw Billings, *The National Medical Dictionary* (Philadelphia: Lea Brothers & Co., 1890), 110.

22. Letters to the Editor, *Rutland Independent*, July 30, 1870.

23. George M. Baker, *An Old Man's Prayer* (Boston: Rand & Avery, 1867). Illustrations by Hammatt Billings, engraved by S. S. Kilburn.

24. George Homer Emerson, *Life of Alonzo Ames Miner* (United States: Universalist Publishing House, 1896), 225.

Chapter 5 Resilience and Optimism

1. Oliver Optic, "Editorial Correspondence," *Our Boys and Girls*, January 1873, 78.

2. Note: Miss "L. B." is Lizbeth Bullock Humphreys, b. 1841

3. George M. Baker, "Ashes of Roses," *Our Boys and Girls*, January 1873, 128.

4. "Lee & Shepard's Publishing House," *Our Boys and Girls*, July 1874, 541-6.

5. "Publishing House," *OBG*.

6. "Publishing House," *OBG*.

7. Oliver Optic, "Editorial Chitchat," *Our Boys and Girls*, May 1873, 348.

8. Oliver Optic, "Editorial Chitchat," *Our Boys and Girls*, November 1872, 765.

9. Oliver Optic, "Editorial Correspondence," *Our Boys and Girls*, September 1872, 622-3.

10. Oliver Optic, "Editorial Chitchat," *Our Boys and Girls*, December 1873, 509.

11. Oliver Optic, "Editorial Chitchat," *Our Boys and Girls*, August 1873, 509.

12. Horace Maynard, "The Immigrant and the Negro," *Our Boys and Girls*, June 1867, 260.

13. Charles Sumner, "Peace," *Our Boys and Girls*, April 1872, 278.

14. Horace Greeley, "Labor," *Our Boys and Girls*, September 1872, 615.

15. Oliver Optic, "Dear Boys and Girls," *Our Boys and Girls*, January 1872, 78.

16. Oliver Optic, "Dear Boys and Girls," *Our Boys and Girls*, January 1872, 79.

17. Oliver Optic, "Editorial Gossip," *Our Boys and Girls*, November 1872, 766.

18. "Books for Boys and Girls," *Our Boys and Girls*, March 1872, 206.

19. "Emilie Loring Remembers Her Own White Christmas," *Boston Post*, December 6, 1942.

20. "White Christmas," *Boston Post*.

21. "White Christmas," *Boston Post*.

22. George M. Baker, *The Drawing Room Stage* (Boston: Lee and Shepard, 1873), preface.

23. Walter Grotyohann, "Oddly Enough Not All Drama Is Broadway's," *New York Times*, February 17, 1935.

24. Kilgour, *Lee and Shepard*, 135.

25. "A Successful Playwright," *Buffalo Courier*, April 6, 1890.

26. "Amateur Theatricals in Aid of the North End Mission Fair," program (Boston: T.R. Marvin & Son, 1874).

27. George M. Baker, *Among the Breakers, A drama in two acts* (Boston: Walter H. Baker & Co., 1900), 5.

28. Baker, *Breakers*, 3.

29. Baker, *Breakers*, 2.

30. "Entertainment at the Christian Union," *Boston Globe*, April 20, 1876; Boston Daily Advertiser, April 20, 1876.

31. Edmund Janes Cleveland and Horace Gillette Cleveland, "An Attempt to Trace, in Both the Male and Female Lines, the Posterity of Moses Cleveland, Who Came from Ipswich, County Suffolk, England, About 1635, Was of Woburn, Middlesex County, Massachusetts, of Alexander Cleveland, of Prince William County" (Hartford, CT: Case, Lockwood & Brainard Co., 1899), 969.

32. "Albert Baker," *Boston Traveler*, August 17, 1874; Boston Typographical Union, Illustrated Historical Souvenir, Fiftieth Anniversary, 1848-1898, Boston Typographical Union, No. 13. December 14, 1898 (Madison: Rockwell & Churchill Press, 1898.

33. Oliver Optic, "Editorial Chitchat," *Our Boys and Girls*, October 1874, 798.

34. George M. Baker, "Running to Waste," *Our Boys and Girls* (Boston: Lee and Shepard, 1874).

35. "New Literature: Running to Waste," *Boston Daily Globe*, September 18, 1874.

36. "About Town," *Boston Daily Advertiser*, April 10, 1875.

37. Kilgour, *Lee and Shepard*, 170.

38. Kilgour, *Lee and Shepard*, 169-70.

39. Kilgour, *Lee and Shepard*, 171-2.

40. Kilgour, *Lee and Shepard*, 160.

41. Kilgour, *Lee and Shepard*, 161.

42. Kilgour, *Lee and Shepard*, 162.

43. Kilgour, *Lee and Shepard*, 161.

44. Kilgour, *Lee and Shepard*, 179.

45. Kilgour, *Lee and Shepard*, 198.

46. New York, Passenger Lists, 1820–1957, s.v. "Rachel Baker," (Female, b. 1857, age 20, origin USA, departed Liverpool, England and Queenstown, Ireland; arrived May 14, 1877 at New York, New York, ship *England*; Companion Mary Baker, age 40). Ancestry.com; "About Town," *Boston Daily Advertiser*, May 17, 1877. ("Mrs. George M. Baker, Miss Rachel E. Baker and Dr. George C. Ainsworth were passengers on the steamship *England* from Europe on Monday.")

47. "New Hampshire's Coast," *Weekly Detroit Free Press*, August 28, 1886.

48. "Public Readings," *The Farmer's Cabinet*, June 25, 1878.

49. Baker, George M., "Introduction," *Elocution Simplified: With an Appendix on Lisping, Stammering, Stuttering, and Other Defects of handy speakers Speech, by Walter K. Fobes* (Boston: Lee and Shepard, 1877).

50. "Public Readings," *The Farmer's Cabinet* (Amherst, NH), May 28, 1878.

51. Kilgour, *Lee and Shepard*, 237.

52. "Merry Christmas Time. How Boston and the Suburbs Keep the Day," *Boston Daily Globe*, Dec 25, 1877.

53. M. T. Caldor, "Diamonds and Toads: An Operatissimo," *Our Boys and Girls*, June 1872, 401-6; Mann, *Emilie Loring*, 9.

54. Mann, *Emilie Loring*, 9.

55. Caldor, "Diamonds and Toads."

Chapter 6 Winds of Change

1. Kilgour, *Lee and Shepard*, 301.

2. "Emilie M. Baker, 1881-1882," Dean Academy academic record, Franklin, MA.

3. "Emilie M. Baker," Dean Academy.

4. "Yellow Tuesday: The Extent of the Phenomena," *Boston Daily Globe*, Sept 7, 1881.

5. Advertisement, *Boston Daily Globe*, September 11, 1877.

6. "Dean Academy Exercises," *Boston Journal*, June 23, 1882.

7. "Our Hub Letter," *New York Globe*, February 9, 1884.

8. "The 'Coming Out' Season: The Thrilling Experiences of the Debutante," *Sunday Boston Herald*, December 26, 1886.

9. "Our Hub Letter," *New York Globe*, February 9, 1884.

10. "In Aid of the Soldiers' Home: Dramatic Performance at the Park Theatre Yesterday, Programme of the Coming Carnival," *Boston Daily Globe*, March 20, 1885.

11. "Rebecca's Triumph: A Company of Amateurs Produce a Play at the Park

Theatre for Charitable Purposes," *Boston Post*, March 20, 1885.

12. George Bradford Bartlett, *New Games for Parlor and Lawn* (United States: Harper and brothers, 1882), 127-32.

13. "Rebecca's Triumph: A Company of Amateurs Produce a Play at the Park Theatre for Charitable Purposes," *Boston Post*, March 20, 1885.

14. George M. Baker, *Rebecca's Triumph* (Boston: Walter H. Baker & Co., 1879).

15. "Not Forgotten: Soldiers and Sailors of the Union," *Boston Globe Supplement*, April 13, 1885.

16. "Features of the Fair," *Boston Globe Supplement*, April 13, 1885.

17. 1880 United States Census, Boston, Suffolk County, Massachusetts, digital images, s.v. "William C. Ulman," "M.S.P. Pollard," "Katie Newell," "Grace Temple," Ancestry.com.

18. "Drink it! The Great Summer Drink, Dr. Bowker's Birch Beer" *Star Tribune* (Minneapolis) June 25, 1879, Newspapers.com.

19. "Real Estate," *Boston Globe*, May 17, 1885.

20. Moses Foster Sweetser, *King's Handbook of Boston Harbor* (United States: Moses King Corporation, 1888), 82-3.

21. Sweetser, *King's Handbook*, 82-3

22. "Downer Landing: Many Merry People at Picnics," *Boston Globe*, July 19, 1885.

23. Sweetser, *King's Handbook*, 82.

24. "Downer Landing: The Season Will Open Wednesday," *Boston Globe*, June 28, 1885.

25. "Downer Landing: A Daughter's Return Hailed with Greetings from Many Relatives," *Boston Globe*, August 16, 1885.

26. "Downer Landing," *Boston Globe*, July 26, 1885.

27. "Notes from Downer Landing," *Boston Globe*, July 5, 1885.

28. "Downer Landing: Social Hops at the Rose Standish House," *Boston Globe*, July 12, 1885.

29. "Downer Landing: Picnics in Abundance, Hotel Gayeties of the Week," *Boston Daily Globe*, August 23, 1885.

30. "The Week at Downer Landing," *Boston Globe*, September 6, 1885.

31. "Longfellow's Dream, As Pictured in Dr. Miner's Church Last Night," *Boston Daily Globe*, November 13, 1885.

32. "The Washington Monument: History and Culture," Online resource, nps.gov.

33. "At the Capitol Today: Proposed Monument to Lincoln," *Evening Star*, March 30, 1886.

34. "The Boston Excursionists," *Boston Herald*, April 5, 1886.

35. "The President's Reception," *Evening Star* (Washington, DC), April 5, 1886.

36. Annette Moritt Dunlap, "Stage Struck: Frances Cleveland and the Theater," Online resource, whitehousehistory.org

37. "The Rose Standish House," *Boston Herald*, June 6, 1886.

38. "Downer Landing: Arrivals, Entertainments and Society Gatherings," *Boston Globe*, July 11, 1886.

39. "Festivities at Downer's: A Largely Attended Hop at the Rose Standish House," *Boston Globe*, August 28, 1886.

40. "Downer Landing: Full Dress Hop and Musicale at Rose Standish House," *Boston Herald*, August 29, 1886.

41. Massachusetts, U.S., Town and Vital Records, 1620-1988, s.v. "Melville J. Boles," (Died April 2, 1887, 44 Gloucester, laryngismus, spasmodic croup, 1 day).

42. Eliza Bisbee Duffey, *The Ladies' and Gentlemen's Etiquette: A Complete Manual of the Manners and Dress of American Society : Containing Forms of Letters, Invitations, Acceptances and Regrets, with a Copious Index* (United States: Porter and Coates, 1877), 298.

43. "Rockland House Hop: Brilliant Occasion at Nantasket Beach," *Boston Globe*, July 15, 1887.

44. "Editorial Correspondence," *Our Boys and Girls*, September 1872, 622.

45. "Camden the Beautiful: Pleasure-Seekers in the Nook of Nature," *Boston Daily Globe*, August 8, 1887.

46. Locals, *Camden Herald*, August 12, 1887.

47. Locals, *Camden Herald*, August 19, 1887.

48. Fortieth Annual Report of the Board of Education: Together with the Fortieth Annual Report of the Secretary of the Board (Boston: Albert J. Wright, State Printer, 1877), 328.

49. "Harvard's D.K.E. Society: The Cause of Recent Strictures on the University," *New York Times*, December 27, 1891.

50. Harvard University Report, IV, 1907, s.v. "Robert M. Baker."

51. Mann, *Emilie Loring*, 11-12.

52. "Personal," *Boston Evening Transcript*, June 4, 1889.

53. Edward Turner Jeffery, *Paris Universal Exposition, 1889* (Chicago: Citizens' Executive Committee, 1889), 53, 67.

54. Passenger Lists of Vessels Arriving at New York, New York, 1820-1897, s.v. "M J L Karrick" (Arrival June 3, 1889 at New York, New York on *La Gascogne*, departed LeHavre, France; destination Boston, Massachusetts), Ancestry.com. Entries for Emilie and Robert are directly above Karrick's in the list, Emilie's partially obscured.

55. "Charles A. B. Shepard Dead: His Success as Joint partner in the Firm of Lee

& Shepard," *Boston Daily Globe*, January 26, 1889; Kilgour, *Lee and Shepard*, 242.

56. "Destructive Forest Fire!" *Barnstable Patriot*, April 3, 1888.

57. "The Summer Residence of W. H. Odiorne," *Barnstable Patriot*, June 17, 1884.

58. "'Country Week' in Barnstable," *Barnstable Patriot*, July 8, 1884.

59. Deed dated August 30, 1889, John E. Humphrey to James L. Karrick, Barnstable County Deeds, 181:532.

60. "Barnstable," *Barnstable Patriot*, December 3, 1889.

61. "Valuable Watch Stolen," *Boston Herald*, August 6, 1889.

62. "Married," *Boston Daily Advertiser*, October 3, 1889; Massachusetts, U.S., Town and Vital Records, 1620-1988, s.v. "Georgie Mayhew," (married October 1, 1889), Ancestry.com.

63. Robin Chapman, *Winter Park in Vintage Postcards* (Charleston, SC: Arcadia Publishing, 2005), 7.

64. Chapman, *Winter Park*, 17

65. "Barnstable," *Barnstable Patriot*, July 29, 1890.

66. "Dean Academy, Franklin," *Boston Journal*, June 23, 1882.

67. "Barnstable," *Barnstable Patriot*, July 29, 1890.

68. Joshua Lawrence Chamberlain, *Universities and Their Sons*, Volume 5, 449.

69. "Yachting News," *New York Times*, April 29, 1889;
League of American Wheelmen, *The Bicycling world & L.A.W. Bulletin* (Boston: Wheelman Co., 1889), 12.

70. "Barnstable," *Barnstable Patriot*, August 19, 1890.

71. "Recent Deaths: George M. Baker," *Boston Transcript*, October 20, 1890.

72. "All 'Long Shore," *Barnstable Patriot*, August 19, 1890.

73. Nirav J. Mehta, Rajal N. Mehta, and Ijaz A. Khan, "Austin Flint: Clinician, Teacher, and Visionary," *Texas Heart Institute Journal*, 27, no. 2 (2000): 386-9, https://www.ncbi.nlm.nih.gov/pmc/articles/PMC101108/.

74. "Barnstable," *Yarmouth Register*, September 20, 1890.

75. Boston City Directory, 1890 (Boston: Sampson, Murdock and Co., 1890).

76. "Drama and Concert: Mr. H. A. McGlenen's Entertainment," *Boston Daily Globe*, May 3, 1885.

77. "Reader Baker Dead," *Boston Daily Globe*, October 21, 1890.

78. "George M. Baker," *New York Clipper*, October 25, 1890.

79. "Barnstable," *Barnstable Patriot*, May 19, 1891.

80. George M. Baker and Rachel E. Baker, "*After Taps*" in The Globe Drama (Boston: Walter H. Baker & Co., 1891), 6; Gutenberg.org.

81. "Barnstable," *Barnstable Patriot*, April 28, 1891.

Act Two: Mrs. Victor J. Loring

1. "Engagement," *Boston Courier*, October 15, 1891. Also *Boston Daily Advertiser*, October 15, 1891; and *Barnstable Patriot*, October 13, 1891.

2. Emilie Loring, *A Certain Crossroad* (United States: Penn Publishing Co., 1925), dedication.

Chapter 7 Victor Joseph Loring

1. Charles Henry Pope and Katharine Peabody Loring, Loring Genealogy (Cambridge, MA: Murray and Emery Company, 1917), 93.

2. Records of the Massachusetts volunteer militia called out by the Governor of Massachusetts to suppress a threatened invasion during the war of 1812–14 (United States: Wright & Potter Print. Company, State printers, 1913), 387. Note: Hollis C Loring served in the War of 1812: Oct 16-Oct 23, 1814. Service at State Arsenal, Sgt. C Russell's Guard detached from LT Col Page's Regiment of Charlestown, under supervision of Major Jaques.

3. Frederick Clifton Pierce, *Field Genealogy* (United States: W. B. Conkey, 1901), 304.

4. U.S., Sons of the American Revolution Membership Applications, 1889-1970, s.v. "H. Selden Loring," (Number 320, Received and approved, December 8, 1890, Patriot ancestor Winchester Hitchcock), Ancestry.com.

5. Selden M. Loring, Jr., in discussion with the author, July 13, 2003; Selden M. Loring, Jr. to Valentine Loring Titus, October 3, 1965. Private collection of Selden M. Loring.

6. "Biographical Dictionary of the United States Congress," s.v. "George Sewell Boutwell," https://bioguide.congress.gov.

7. "Biographical Dictionary of the United States Congress," s.v. "Henry Wilson," https://bioguide.congress.gov.

8. Unpublished biographical summary of Victor J. Loring, Private Collection, Eve Loring Tarmey.

9. "The papers of Charles Sumner, 1811–1874" (Alexandria VA, Chadwyck-Healey, 1988), reel 23, frames 306 and 307.

10. Charles Sumner to Edward Loring; Private collection, Selden M. Loring.

11. Massachusetts, U.S., Birth Records, 1840-1915, s.v. "Victor J. Loring" (Born at Marlborough, January 11, 1859, parents Hollis and Laura).

12. Charles Hudson and Joseph Allen, History of the Town of Marlborough, Middlesex County, Massachusetts (Boston: T. R. Marvin & Son, 1862), 411.

13. Selden Melville Loring, Jr. to Valentine Loring Titus, October 3, 1965. Private collection of Selden M. Loring, Jr.

14. Ella A. Bigelow, *Historical reminiscences of the early times in Marlborough, Massachusetts, prominent events from 1860 to 1910, including brief allusions to many individuals and an account of the celebration of the two hundred and fiftieth anniversary of the incorporation of the town* (Marlboro, MA; Times Publishing Company, 1910), 312-17.

15. Hollis Loring to Charles Sumner, Marlborough, Massachusetts, June 8, 1863, Personal collection of Selden Melville Loring, Jr.

16. Massachusetts, Death Records, 1841–1915, s.v. "Hollis Loring," (died February 20, 1865, Marlborough, MA), Ancestry.com.

17. Loring family Bible, Private collection of Selden M. Loring, Jr.

18. "Death of Hollis Loring," unattributed newspaper clipping, Private collection of Selden M. Loring, Jr.

19. Loring family Bible.

20. Bigelow, *Historical reminiscences*, 280.

21. Massachusetts, U.S., Wills and Probate Records, 1635–1991, s.v. "Hollis Loring," Will Date February 17, 1865, Probate Court March 28, 1865 (Edward Loring appointed guardian of minor Loring children).

22. Handwritten narrative. Private collection, Linda Loring Loveland.

23. "The Old World: Details of the Terrible Loss of Life and Property by the September Typhoon—the Most Destructive Tempest on Record—20,000 Lives Lost, Etc., Etc.," *Boston Daily Globe*, November 9, 1874.

24. "The Loss of the Japan," *Boston Daily Globe*, March 6, 1875.

25. Selden H. Loring to his mother, Laura W. Loring, Personal collection, Selden M. Loring, Jr.

26. *The Yale Banner and Pot-pourri: The Annual Yearbook of the Students of Yale University, Volume 1, 1865-66* (New Haven: Yale College, 1866), 19. Note: Edward Day Loring in Class of '69.

27. Massachusetts, U.S., Marriage Records, 1840-1915, s.v. "Edward Day Loring," (Married Ella C. Harris, October 26, 1871 at Milford, Massachusetts), Ancestry.com.

28. Massachusetts, Death Records, 1841-1915, s.v. "William Hollis Loring," (Died April 21, 1872, age 2 mos 13 days), Ancestry.com.

29. "East Boston Yacht Club," *Boston Daily Globe*, May 9, 1874.

30. "Yachting Gossip," *Boston Herald*, June 15, 1884.

31. "The Boston Latin School," *Boston Globe*, June 8, 1878.

32. "The State Campaign," *Boston Journal*, November 4, 1889.

33. "Victor J. Loring," biographical summary. Private collection, Eve Loring Tarmey.

34. "VJL," Tarmey.

35. "Court Record," *Boston Globe*, March 15, 1890.

36. "Court Record," *Boston Globe*, March 20, 1890.

Chapter 8 Emilie and Victor

1. Emilie Loring, "Limousine Ladies," Oldsmobile Pacemaker, 1918.

2. Victor Loring's birthdate was January 11, 1859. Emilie Baker's birthdate was September 5, 1866. They were seven years, seven months, and twenty-five days apart. From Victor's birthday to Emilie's, they were "eight" years apart; from Emile's birthday until Victor's, they were "seven" years apart. Both estimates appear in her books.

3. "Prizes Awarded: Members of Boston Latin School Receive Their Honors," *Boston Daily Advertiser*, January 9, 1888.

4. "Election Echoes," *Boston Daily Advertiser*, November 10, 1887.

5. "Royal Arcanum Banquet," *Boston Daily Globe*, June 11, 1887.

6. "Masquerade Ball: Large Gathering and Unique Costumes at Berkeley Hall," *Boston Globe*, December 27, 1887.

7. "Boston & Maine Ball," *Boston Globe*, January 28, 1888.

8. "Brief Locals," *Boston Evening Transcript*, June 12, 1888.

9. "Saccarappa Leatherboard Company," *Portland Daily Press*, May 9, 1889.

10. "Business Troubles," *Boston Globe*, January 10, 1890.

11. Massachusetts, U.S., Town and Vital Records, 1620-1988, s.v. "Zoheth R. Higgins" (Zoheth R. Higgins, 35, Provision dealer born in Truro, married Fannie Fenlee, 30, of Reichford, VT, November 26, 1885).

12. "Arguments of Counsel Made: Evidence Concluded in the Trial of the Higgins Divorce Case," *Boston Herald*, October 29, 1889.

13. "The State Campaign: An Appeal to the Voters of the Eighth Suffolk District," *Boston Journal*, November 4, 1889.

14. "Diamonds Flashed," *Boston Daily Globe*, April 10, 1890.

15. "Barnstable," *Barnstable Patriot*, April 8, 1890.

16. "Arthur H. Dakin, 74, Boston Lawyer, Dies," *New York Times*, October 22, 1936.

17. "Beach Bluffs Hobby: Riding and Driving Occupy the Time of Pleasure Seekers," *Boston Sunday Globe*, July 5, 1891.

18. "At Beach Bluff: Driving and Coaching Parties at the Sea Shore," *Boston Sunday Globe*, July 26, 1891.

19. "Personal and Social Gossip," *Boston Herald*, July 18

20. "Right on the edge of the ocean," Hotel Preston advertisement, *Boston Home Journal*, 42 (Cambridge, MA: Samuel T. Cobb, 1898), 14.

21. "Pleasant Evening at Marblehead," *Boston Post*, July 7, 1891.

22. "Danced by the Ocean Side: Brilliant Hop at Hotel Nanepashemet, Marblehead Neck," *Boston Herald*, August 1, 1891.

23. "Personal and Social Gossip," *Boston Herald*, July 26, 1891.

24. "Miss Baker's New Play," Harrisburg Daily Independent (Pennsylvania), October 29, 1891.

25. Harvard College, Record of the Class of 1892 (Boston: Fort Hill Press, 1912), 187.

26. "Miss Baker's New Play."

27. "All 'Long Shore," Barnstable Patriot, October 13, 1891; "Engagement," *Boston Courier*, October 15, 1891.

28. "Table Gossip," *Boston Globe*, October 18, 1891.

29. In Memoriam.

30. "Condition Serious. Hon. Charles F. Loring Stricken with Paralysis This Morning—He is One of the New Members—Elect of the Executive Council," *Boston Journal*, November 13, 1891.

31. "Condition Serious," *Boston Journal*.

32. Councilor Loring's Illness: No Cause for Alarm—Solicitous Friends Reassured by the Family," *Boston Journal*, November 14, 1891.

33. "Hon. Charles F. Loring," *Boston Evening Transcript*, January 26, 1892.

34. "Mr. Loring's Leg Cut Off," *Boston Daily Globe*, November 17, 1891.

35. "Councillor Loring Comfortable," *Boston Daily Globe*, November 18, 1891.

36. "Personal," *Boston Journal*, November 30, 1891.

37. "Locals," *Boston Courier*, November 29, 1891; "Events in Society," *Boston Herald*, December 6, 1891.

38. "Weather," *Boston Daily Globe*, December 10, 1891; "Almanac," *Boston Herald*, December 9, 1891.

39. "Chrysanthemum Wedding," *Boston Globe*, December 10, 1891; "Baker-Loring," *Boston Daily Advertiser*, December 10, 1891; "Impressive Church Wedding," *Boston Herald*, December 10, 1891.

40. "Musician 52 Years," *Boston Daily Globe*, January 28, 1906.

41. "Opera Week," *Boston Daily Globe*, December 6, 1891.

42. "The Ideals in Martha," *Boston Daily Globe*, October 15, 1884.

43. "Martha, Synopsis: An Opera by Friedrich von Flowtow," Online resource, musicwithease.com.

44. Note: *Suite 1 in D Minor*, Opus 113, movement III, variationen and marsch; arranged for organ by Lux

45. "Town Talk," *Boston Courier*, December 13, 1891.

46. "Chrysanthemum Wedding," *Boston Globe*, December 10, 1891.

47. "Town Talk," *Courier*.

48. "Chrysanthemum Wedding."

49. "Impressive Church Wedding: Miss Emilie Baker and Mr. Victor Loring Married Last Evening," *Boston Herald*, December 10, 1891.

50. "Town Talk," *Courier*.

51. "Impressive Church Wedding: Miss Emilie Baker and Mr. Victor Loring Married Last Evening," *Boston Herald*, December 10, 1891.

52. "Not So Bad: Reports Regarding Charles F. Loring's Condition Exaggerated," *Boston Journal*, January 8, 1892.

53. "Charles F. Loring: His Death Occurs at Melrose This Morning, Leader of the Royal Arcanum in America" *Boston Journal*, January 26, 1892.

54. *Massachusetts Secretary of the Commonwealth, Acts and Resolves Passed by the General Court of Massachusetts* (Boston: Wright & Potter Printing Co., State Printers, 1892), 548.

55. *In Memoriam: An Account of the Life and Public Services, Death and Burial of Charles F. Loring, Supreme Regent of the Royal Arcanum, March 1892* (Boston: Royal Arcanum, 1892).

56. In Memoriam.

57. "Funerals of Prominent Men: Military Honors Paid to Colonel Selden H. Loring's Memory," *Boston Evening Transcript*, March 1, 1892.

58. "Funerals of Prominent Men."

59. "Newton Center," *The Newton Journal*, September 2, 1892.

60. "Mrs. G. W. Baker and family of Boston will occupy their new house in Newton Center about March 10," *The Newton Journal*, March 4, 1892; *The Newton Graphic*, March 11, 1892.

61. "Died," *Boston Herald*, March 12, 1892. (At Newtonville, March 11. Edward Melville Boles, 37 yrs 6 mos. Funeral from 435 Columbus Avenue, Boston, Sunday, March 13, at 2 o'clock.)

62. "Arrivals at the Hotels," *Washington Post*, April 6, 1892.

63. "Table Talk," *Boston Daily Globe*, April 24, 1892.

64. "Mr. and Mrs. Victor Loring have returned from their trip South." *The Newton Journal*, April 22, 1892.

65. "Pollard-Gale: A Brilliant Society Wedding Performed by Rev. G. A. Gordon at Clifton," *Boston Daily Advertiser*, September 30, 1892.

66. "A Notable New Building," *Boston Daily Globe*, January 1, 1891.

67. "The Drama," *Boston Daily Globe*, April 21, 1878.

68. "Autumn Brides: Celebration at Clifton of Gale-Pollard Nuptials," *Boston Daily Globe*, September 30, 1892.

69. "Newton," *The Newton Journal*, August 26, 1892.

70. "Opera and Concert," *Boston Daily Globe*, December 25, 1892.

71. "Saints and Sinners: Robin Hood Sung by the Bostonians," *Boston Daily Globe*, December 27, 1892.

72. "To Beautify Copley Square," *Boston Daily Globe*, July 9, 1893.

73. "Added Beauties," *Boston Daily Globe*, June 25, 1893.

74. *Moses Foster Sweetser, Here and There in New England and Canada: Illustrated* (United States: Passenger department Boston & Maine railroad, 1889), 32. Google Books.

75. "Hollis Burgess Sales." Fore 'n' Aft, Volume 2 (1), June 1906, 86.

76. Yachting, Volume 3 (6), June 1908, p. 329.

77. Note: Three generations, Edward Burgess > William Starling Burgess > Starling Burgess (aka "Tasha Tudor")

78. "Along the North Shore," *Boston Daily Globe*, July 23, 1893; "About Marblehead," *Boston Daily Globe*, June 10, 1894.

79. "Early Comers Leaving," *Boston Daily Globe*, August 27, 1893.

80. Walter Grotyohann, "Oddly Enough Not All Drama Is Broadway's," *New York Times*, February 17, 1935.

81. Rachel E. Baker, *Mr. Bob* (Boston: Walter H. Baker Company, 1894), 35.

82. "Cup is Full: Republicans Quaff From That of Happiness," *Boston Daily Globe*, November 11, 1894.

83. Massachusetts, U.S., Town and Vital Records, 1620–1988, s.v. "Robert M. Loring" (born November 29, 1894).

Act Three: "Mother"

Chapter 9 Homemaking and Motherhood

1. Joseph E. Fiske, "Wellesley as a place of residence, II" Our Town, II (7), July 1899, 3-4.

2. Fiske, "Wellesley," 3-4.

3. Fiske, "Wellesley," 5.

4. Fiske, "Wellesley," 4.

5. Eve Loring Tarmey, in conversation with the author.

6. Will of Victor J. Loring. Private collection, Eve Loring Tarmey.

7. Samuel A. Eliot, *Biographical History of Massachusetts: Biographies and*

Autobiographies of the Leading Men in the State, Volume 7 (United States: Massachusetts Biographical Society, 1917), 176-180. Online resource, FamilySearch.

8. Samuel A. Eliot, *Biographical History of Massachusetts: Biographies and Autobiographies of the Leading Men in the State*, Volume 7 (United States: Massachusetts Biographical Society, 1917), 176-180. Online resource, FamilySearch.

9. "Many come to the carnival capital," *The Daily Picayune* (New Orleans), February 26, 1895.

10. "Packet Bark Sarah Wrecked," *Boston Globe*, September 26, 1896.

11. "Gossip of the Day," *Milwaukee Journal*, September 27, 1896.

12. "Bank President Weds: Mr. John E. Gale of Haverhill Takes a Bride," *Boston Daily Globe*, September 30, 1896.

13. "Miss Louise G. Hallet attended the wedding of Miss Rachel Baker in Boston last week," *Barnstable Patriot*, October 5, 1896.

14. "The Breakfast Hour: Baker-Gale," *Boston Daily Advertiser*, September 30, 1896.

15. "Baker-Gale."

16. "Baker-Gale."

17. *Boston Daily Advertiser*, October 9,1896.

18. "Movements of Ocean Steamships," *Daily InterOcean*, October 9, 1896.

19. New York, U.S., Arriving Passenger and Crew Lists, s.v. "John E. Gale" (John E Gale, 38, and Mrs. J. E. Gale, 35, Naples to New York, arrived November 24, 1896).

20. "Crowds Were Out," *Boston Daily Globe*, November 11, 1896.

21. His initial birth certificate said, "Selden Milton Loring" but Milton was corrected to Melville: "Additions to and Corrections in the Copies of Records of Births returned to the Secretary of the Commonwealth from the Town of Wellesley for the Year 1896," Selden Melville Loring born November 16; Date of amended record, December 21, 1917.

22. "Edwin B. Pratt Dead," *Boston Daily Globe*, May 7, 1895.

23. "Baker-Pratt: A Daughter of Quincy is Wedded to a Man of Wellesley," *Boston Journal*, April 13, 1897.

24. Social Register, Boston, 1905 (New York: Social Register Association, 1904), 85.

25. Advertising, Emilie Loring, "Moments of Decision," Penn Publishing Co., 1936, Emilie Loring Collection, Boston University Libraries, Howard Gotlieb Archival Research Center.

26. *Josephine Story, For the Comfort of the Family: A Vacation Experiment* (New York: George H. Doran, 1914), 15, 63.

27. Josephine Story, *The Mother in the Home* (Boston: Pilgrim Press, 1917), 81.

28. Story, *Mother*, 47.

29. Story, *Mother*, 53.

30. Cornelia Baker, *Coquo & the King's Children* (Chicago: A. C. McClure, 1902).

31. Emilie Loring to Linda Loring, January 16, 1949. Private collection of Linda Loring Loveland.

32. Story, *Mother*, 47.

33. Story, *Mother*, 7.

34. Leonard Augustus Jones and Conrad Reno, *Biographical: Massachusetts* (United States: Century Memorial Publishing Company, 1901), 356-8.

35. "Of Pleasant Memory Is the Third Annual Banquet of Berkshire Council, Royal Arcanum; The Eloquent Victor J. Loring Thrills His Hearers with His Beautiful Word Pictures and His Oratorical Climaxes," *The North Adams Evening Transcript*, May 17, 1898.

36. Rachel Baker Gale, *Mr. Bob: A Comedy in Two Acts* (Boston: Walter H. Baker, 1924).

37. Rachel E. and Robert M. Baker, *Bachelor Hall* (Boston: Walter H. Baker, 1898).

38. "Wellesley's '400' There," *Boston Daily Globe*, October 26, 1897.

39. *Annual Report of the Bureau of Industrial and Labor Statistics for the State of Maine*, Vol. 6 (Augusta: Kennebec Journal Printers, 1898), 108.

40. Arthur L. Golden, "The Rangeley Lakes," *New England Magazine*, March 1900, 565-83.

41. "Newport," *Bangor Daily News*, June 25, 1902.

42. Craig Gilborn, *Adirondack Camps: Homes Away from Home, 1850-1950* (United States: Syracuse University Press, 2000), 146.

Chapter 10 The New Century

1. "Twentieth Century Club's Anniversary," *Boston Daily Globe*, January 11, 1914.

2. Oliver Optic, *An Undivided Union*, completed by Edward Stratemeyer (Boston: Lee & Shepard, 1899).

3. Kilgour, *Lee and Shepard*, 271

4. Kilgour, *Lee and Shepard*, 270.

5. Massachusetts, U.S., Death Records, 1841–1915, s.v. "Matthew A. Mayhew (Died January 1, 1899, cerebral hemorrhage, publisher, age 65)."

6. "An Old Boston Favorite Drops Dead, Was Joking at the Supper Table in a Hartford Hotel," *Boston Daily Globe*, September 19, 1899.

7. Thomas Wentworth Higginson, "Books Unread" in *Part of a Man's Life* (1905), 351. Quoting Lady Eastlake's comments on English literature.

8. *Our Town*, January 1898, 1.

9. "A Dramatic Hold Up," *Our Town*, May 1901, 21.

10. Loring family Bible, Private collection of Selden M. Loring, Jr.

11. Massachusetts, U.S., Wills and Probate Records, 1635-1991, s.v. "Laura W. Loring."

12. "Mme. Loring," Boston Transcript, July 16, 1901.

13. "Thursday, Sept. 19, 1901," *Our Town*, September 1901, 18.

14. Robert M. Baker, "All's Well," *Our Town*, November 1901, 4.

15. Victor J. Loring, "American Citizenship," *Our Town*, January 1902, 2-3.

16. Emilie Loring, "A Clean Slate," manuscript, Emilie Loring Collection, Boston University Libraries, Howard Gotlieb Archival Research Center.

17. "Foxy Grandpa," *Our Town*, February 1902, 2.

18. "Girls Will Be Girls," *New York Clipper*, September 3, 1904, 638.

19. "The Roster of Past and Living Lambs," Online, www.the-lambs.org.

20. "Barnabee Benefit Big Success," *New York Tribune*, December 12, 1906.

21. Robert M. Baker, "Troubles Troubles: III. The Condensed Life," *Boston Daily Globe*, May 5, 1907.

22. Rachel Baker Gale, *No Men Wanted* (Boston: W. H. Baker, 1903).

23. Rachel Baker Gale, *The New Crusade* (Boston: W. H. Baker, 1908).

24. 1910 United States Census, Haverhill, Essex County, Massachusetts, s.v. "Rachel Gale," Ancestry.com.

25. Mann, *Emilie Loring*, 15.

26. Typescript, Notes typed at Hotel Carlton, 1138 Boylston St., Boston, prepared for interview with Priscilla Fortesque. Emilie Loring Collection, Boston University Libraries, Howard Gotlieb Archival Research Center.

27. Victor J. Loring, II, in conversation with the author, 2006.

28. "Charms Without Trying: Mrs Frederick T. Greenhalge is a True Home Maker. 'Eric' is modest and a hard student, but Dick dotes on fame," *Boston Daily Globe*, November 12, 1893. Proquest Newspapers.

29. "Osterville," Boston Herald, August 2, 1903. Selden and Robert Loring with their grandmother, Emily F. Baker arrived at the Hotel Cotocheset.

30. *Boston Herald*, September 10, 1905. "Victor J. Loring and family have returned to Wellesley Hills after spending several weeks in their camp in the Maine woods."

31. "The Hills," *The Townsman*, July 20, 1906.

32. Clifton Crawford, Captain Careless, lyrics by Robert M. Baker (Detroit: J. H. Remick, 1906).

33. "The Hills," *The Townsman*, August 17, 1906.

34. "The Hills," *The Townsman*, September 7, 1906.

35. Massachusetts, U.S., Death Records, 1841-1915, s.v. "Barron C. Moulton (Died October 4, 1906 at 112 Brighton Avenue, Boston, age 78 yr 7 mos 29 days; of apoplexy, 4 days; Valve disease of the heart, with dilatation).

Chapter 11 Alaska!

1. "Three Deaths from the Heat," *Boston Daily Globe*, June 25, 1907; "Five Killed and Many are Prostrated by the Heat," *Boston Daily Globe*, July 19, 1907.

2. "Ex-Gov John G. Brady Dies. Once a New York Waif, He Was Alaska's Executive for Three Terms," *New York Times*, December 19, 1918.

3. "1905 Oriental Limited," on Ted's Great Northern Homepage, http://www.gnflyer.com/1905.

4. "Hotel Arrivals," *Vancouver World*, August 8, 1907. ("Mr. and Mrs. Victor Loring and sons, Wellesley, Mass")

5. "The Totem Pole Route," Raymond & Whitcomb brochure, 1907.

6. "The Totem Pole Route."

7. Dazie Stromstadt, *Sitka the Beautiful* (Seattle: The Homer M. Hill Publishing Co., 1906).

8. Dazie Stromstadt, *Metlakatla* (Seattle, The Homer M. Hill Publishing Co., 1907).

9. "Culture Conditions in Alaska" by Dazie M. Stromstadt, in *Education*, ed. Richard G. Boone and Frank H. Palmer, vol XXVII, Sept 1906-June 1907, (Boston: The Palmer Company).

10. Lilian Whiting, "In Arizona's Wonderland," *New York Times*, August 12, 1906.

11. "The Totem Pole Route," Raymond & Whitcomb brochure, 1907.

12. "Spokane Struck Ice," *Daily News Advertiser* (Vancouver, British Columbia, Canada), August 23, 1907.

13. "White Pass & Yukon Route Condensed Time Table," Online resource, wpyr.com/history/brochures/summerexcursions.

14. Typescript. Emilie Loring, "To my readers." Emilie Loring Collection, Boston University Libraries, Howard Gotlieb Archival Research Center.

15. "Women Patronize Public Market," *Seattle Star*, August 20, 1907.

16. *Prosperous Washington: Seattle* (Seattle: Seattle Post-Intelligencer, 1906), 146.

17. "The Hills," *The Townsman*, November 29, 1907.

Chapter 12 Creative Stirrings

1. Massachusetts, U.S., Birth Records, 1840-1915, s.v. "Eileen Baker" (Born September 22, 1907, parents Robert M. Baker and Minnie J. Pratt).
2. "It's in Sight. Society to Foster Exhibitions of Arts and Crafts, Boston Journal, April 30, 1897.
3. Allen H. Eaton, Handicrafts of New England (United States: Harper Brothers, 1949), 283-4.
4. How long she remained active is unclear. As late as 1926, "Emily B. Loring (Mrs. Victor J. Loring), Worcester St., Wellesley Hills, MA" was listed as a member of the Boston Society of Arts and Crafts.
5. "Fletcher M. Abbott Funeral Tuesday," Boston Daily Globe, August 30, 1925, A17.
6. Annual Report, Boston Society of Arts and Crafts (Boston: Society of Arts and Crafts), 2004-2006; Mrs. Gilbert (Margaret A.) Jones, metal worker, Wellesley Hills (2004); Mrs. John E. (Harriet E.) Oldham, metal worker, Wellesley Hills (1906); Mrs. Victor J. (Emilie) Loring, metal worker, Wellesley Hills (1908).
7. Frederic Allen Whiting, "The Arts and Crafts at the Louisiana Purchase Exposition," The International Studio, July-October, 1904.
8. Handcraft, 1906, p. 12
9. Gardner Teall, "The National Arts Club of New York: Its Position as a Factor in the Encouragement of the Fine Arts, and Why It is Worth While," The Craftsman, Gustav Stickley, Ed., February 1909, 604-613. This quote, p. 612.
10. "Federation of Men's Clubs," Boston Daily Globe, November 10, 1907.
11. "Wellesley Hills," Wellesley Townsman, November 27, 1908.
12. Victor J. Loring, "The Field and Mission of the Federation," The Brotherhood. (United States: Executive Committee of the American Federation of Men's Church Organizations, 1906),11. Google Books.
13. "Brotherhood Organized," Boston Daily Globe, November 20, 1908.
14. "Wellesley Congregational Club," The Townsman, May 8, 1908.
15. "The Sagamore Sociological Conference," News-Democrat, July 1, 1908; "Labor and Socialism," Boston Daily Globe, June 20, 1908.
16. Typescript, Emilie Loring, "By Audacity Alone," Emilie Loring Collection, Boston University Libraries, Howard Gotlieb Archival Research Center.

Chapter 13 Blue Hill, Maine

1. Oliver Optic, "The Coming Wave," Our Boys and Girls, January 1874, 14.

2. "Mount Desert," The Weekly Detroit Free Press, September 4, 1886, 3.

3. Effie Ober to Henry Clay Barnabee, September 1887, Henry Clay Barnabee Collection, Portsmouth Public Library, Portsmouth, NH.

4. Annie L. Clough, Head of the Bay: Sketches and Pictures of Blue Hill, Maine, 1762-1952 (Woodstock, VT: Elm Tree Press, 1953). "Blue Hill and Parker Point, Maine," Historical paper read at a meeting of the Parker Point Summer Colony by Mrs. Virgil P. Kline at the cottage of J. C. Rose, Esq. on August 31, 1908, Special Collections, Blue Hill Public Library, Blue Hill, Maine; Robin Clements, "Parker Point: The First Hundred Years (Almost)," 1983, unpublished, Blue Hill Public Library, Blue Hill, Maine.

5. Anthony Mitchell Sammarco, and James Kyprianos, Downtown Boston (United States: Arcadia Publishing, 2002), 7.

6. Rufus George Frederick Candage, Historical Sketches of Bluehill, Maine (Ellsworth, ME: Hancock County, 1905).

7. "Table Gossip," Boston Daily Globe, July 15, 1906.

8. "Taft Will Present Yachting Trophy," New York Times, August 15, 1909.

9. "Curtis & Cameron," Our Town, March 1903, 47.

10. The Copley Prints: Reproductions of Notable Paintings Publicly & Privately Owned in America; Also of the Mural Decorations in the New Library of Congress, the Boston Public Library & Other Public Buildings. (Boston: Curtis & Cameron, 1907), 7-10.

11. "Town Gossip," The Townsman, September 14, 1906

12. The National Encyclopaedia of American Biography, vol VII, (NY: James T. White & Co., 1897), p. 526.

13. Esther Wood, Saltwater Seasons: Recollections of a Country Woman (United States: Down East Books, 1980) and Esther Wood, Deep Roots: A Maine Legacy (United States: Rodale Press,1990).

14. "Wellesley Hills," Wellesley Townsman, November 27, 1908.

15. "The Laymen's Christian Convention," The Bar Harbor Record, May 12, 1909.

16. "Sagamore Conference of Brotherhood Men," The Brotherhood, June 1909, p. 96.

17. "Beverly of Graustark," New York Times, April 5, 1911.

18. Esther Wood, Deep Roots: A Maine Legacy (Camden, Maine: Yankee Books, 1990), 83.

19. Henry Wadsworth Longfellow, "Haunted Houses." Longfellow's Poems (Boston: J. R. Osgood, 1878), 214.

20. Esther Wood to Robert K. Slaven, Sr. Private collection of Robert K. Slaven, Jr.

21. Hancock County Deeds, Maine. 120:213, 155:399, 162:528, 241:508, 253:256, and 462:176.
22. Handwritten. Esther Wood, History of Stone House, Private collection, Robert K. Slaven, Jr.
23. R. G. F. Candage, Historical Sketches of Bluehill, Maine (Ellsworth, Maine: Bluehill Historical Society, 1905), 67.
24. Josephine Story, "My Fifty-cent Garden: Choosing My Flowers to Fit My Rooms," The Country Gentleman, 83(1), 1918, 51.
25. Survey recorded at Hancock County, Maine by Ira Hagan, January 1916, Hancock County Deeds, Maine.
26. Story, "Fifty-cent."
27. Story, "Fifty-Cent."
28. "Wellesley Hills," The Townsman, October 29, 1909.
29. "Mrs. Walter Hersey's Response," The Townsman, May 13, 1910.
30. Rachel Baker Gale, The New Crusade (Boston: W. H. Baker, 1908).
31. "Mrs. Pankhurst is Welcomed, Militant Suffragist Speaks at Tremont Temple," Boston Globe, October 23, 1909.
32. "Attack Woman's Suffrage," Boston Evening Transcript, January 20, 1910.
33. "Fun Found in Woman Suffrage Movement," Boston Daily Globe, February 4, 1910.
34. William B. Patterson, Modern Church Brotherhoods: A Survey of the Practical Activities of the Churchmen's Clubs and Brotherhoods (New York: Fleming H. Revell Co., 1911), 115.
35. Patterson, Church Brotherhoods, 105-6.
36. Emilie Loring, "By Audacity Alone," Youth, May 1930.
37. Story, "Fifty-Cent Garden," 51.
38. "Customers' Choice," The Publisher's Weekly, Vol 122 (New York: R. R. Bowker Co., 1933), 578-9.
39. "Collecting Everyman's Library," Online resource, everymanslibrarycollecting.com.
40. Wood, Saltwater, 53.
41. Note: The name is a contraction of "Tyn y Coed."
42. "Bluehill," Ellsworth American, September 28, 1910. "
43. "Tablet of First Settlers," Ellsworth American, August 24, 1910.
44. "Mayflower, In Fog, Anchors on Shoal," New York Times, July 26, 1910.
45. Story, "Fifty-Cent Garden," 51.
46. Captain Robert K. Slaven, Jr. in conversation with the author; Sharon Abbott, "Ghost in the Old Stone House has been Quiet Lately; Slavens Not Worried" and "The Ghost of the Stone House," unattributed clippings,

Private collection of Robert K. Slaven, Sr.; Phil Blampied, "Is it Haunted?
A Halloween Look at Several Local Houses with Ghostly Reputations,"
Compass, supplement to The Weekly Packet, October 26, 1989.

47. Mary Ellen Chase, A Goodly Heritage (New York: Henry Holt and Co.,
1932), 170.

48. Samuel Adams Drake, Nooks and Corners of the New England
Coast. (United States: Harper & brothers, 1875), 37. Google books.

49. George J. Varney, "History of Blue Hill, Maine," A Gazetteer of the State of
Maine (Boston: B. B. Russell, 1881), 121. Google books.

Chapter 14 Wellesley Hills Woman's Club

1. *Who's Who in New England*, Volume 1, Ed. Albert Nelson Marquis (Chicago:
A. N. Marquis & Co., 1909), 1081. Google books.

2. *Harper's Magazine* (New York: Harper & Brothers Publishers, 1908) November 1908, 1012.

3. Berkshire School Yearbook, 1914; s. v. "Robert M. Loring."

4. Mary Ellen Chase, *A Goodly Heritage* (New York: Henry Holt, 1932), 297.

5. Annie S. Amory, "The Wellesley Hills Woman's Club," *Our Town*, May 1898,
5-6.

6. "To View Comet from Balloon," *Boston Daily Globe*, May 5, 1910.

7. "View Comet from Balloon: Prof. David Todd, Wife, and a Friend Ascend
7,000 Feet," *Washington Post*, May 7, 1910, ProQuest Historical Newspapers.

8. "'Wake-Up, Mars!' Prof Todd is Coming Up to Wish You a Merry Christmas:
It Will Be a Sad Blow if Amherst Astronomer and Expert Balloonist fail
in their trip from Omaha, Neb to the Well-Known Planet—New Balloon,
New Idea," *Boston Daily Globe*, October 12, 1919, ProQuest Historical
Newspapers.

9. "Comet to Bounce Off Earth Today: Tough Old World Will Bore Through
Gaseous Tail and 'You Won't Know the Difference,'" *Chicago Daily Tribune*,
May 18, 1910; ProQuest Historical Newspapers.

10. "Comet Gazers See Flashes: And Then at 2:30 A.M., The Comet's Tail,
100 Degrees Long," New York Times, May 19, 1910; ProQuest Historical
Newspapers.

11. "Wellesley Hills," *Wellesley Townsman*, December 2, 1910.

12. Ibid.

13. "The Swan and the Sky-Lark Sung: Thomas' Cantata at the Fourth Church,"
The Hartford Courant, March 8, 1911.

Act Four: Josephine Story

Chapter 15 Her Box of Books

1. Emilie Loring, typescript, notes for interview with Ruth Moss, 1936, Emilie Loring Collection, Boston University Libraries, Howard Gotlieb Archival Research Center.
2. Josephine Story, "Her Box of Books," *Boston Herald*, March 20, 1911.
3. Josephine Story, "Her Box of Books," *Boston Herald*, April 20, 1911.
4. Josephine Story, "Her Box of Books," *Boston Herald*, April 27, 1911.
5. Josephine Story, "Her Box of Books," *Boston Herald*, May 4, 1911.
6. Josephine Story, "Her Box of Books," *Boston Herald*, May 18, 1911.
7. Josephine Story, "Her Box of Books," *Boston Herald*, May 25, 1911.
8. Josephine Story, "Her Box of Books," *Boston Herald*, June 5, 1911.
9. Obituary, Six Towns Times (Yarmouth, Maine), November 11, 1910; 3, 6.
10. Wood, Deep Roots, p. 97
11. Captain Robert K. Slaven, Jr. of Blue Hill, Maine, in conversation with the author.
12. "Milliken-Boardman," *New York Times*, October 6, 1907.

Chapter 16 Ambition

1. "Agnes Edwards' Morning Talk: The Woman Who Wants to Write," *Boston Herald*, November 3, 1911.
2. "Agnes Edwards' Morning Talk: Having Courage to Try," *Boston Herald*, November 1, 1911.
3. Typescript, Emilie Loring, "Try it Out," Personal collection of Eve Loring Tarmey.
4. "Indorses Union Labor Efforts," *Boston Herald*, December 17, 1911.
5. James L. W. West, *American Authors and the Literary Marketplace Since 1900* (United States: University of Pennsylvania, Incorporated, 2011), 121.
6. Josephine Story, "When the Young Folks Read," *Boston Herald*, October 26, 1912.
7. Josephine Story, "Books for the Home Maker," *Boston Herald*, November 2, 1912.
8. Josephine Story, "Between You and Me," *Boston Herald*, November 9, 1912.
9. Josephine Story, "An Excellent Juvenile Book," *Boston Herald*, November 16, 1912.
10. Typescript and handwritten, Emilie Loring, "Recent Books" lecture for Harvard University Extension course, March 28, 1944. Emilie Loring

Collection, Boston University Libraries, Howard Gotlieb Archival Research Center.

11. "Awards $20,869.79," *Boston Globe*, June 3, 1913.

12. Mortgage of October 6, 1910, on two and a half acres in Wellesley Hills (Loring home), discharged November 18, 1913.

13. Josephine Story, *For the Comfort of the Family: A Vacation Experiment* (New York: George H. Doran, 1914).

14. Josephine Story, "A Rush Order for Fancy Dress," *St. Nicholas Magazine*, September 1914; Esther Wood, *Deep Roots*, 101.

15. "Bluehill Fair," *Ellsworth American*, September 11, 1912. "1. Mrs. Victor J. Loring, nasturtiums."

16. "Bluehill Fair," *Ellsworth American*, September 10, 1913.

Chapter 17 The Long Road to Authorship

1. "Confessions of a Boston Dramatist: Robert Baker Tells How He Writes Plays," *Boston Daily Globe*, October 19, 1913.

2. Sections on submissions and their outcomes are all from: Handwritten, Emilie Loring, Emilie Loring Collection, Boston University Libraries, Howard Gotlieb Archival Research Center.

3. Josephine Story, "Find Drama in Your Housework!" *New York Tribune*, January 25, 1914.

4. Josephine Story, "How I Kept House Without a Servant," *Salt Lake Tribune*, March 1, March 22 and March 29, 1914.

5. Josephine Story, "First Aid to the One-Room Housekeeper," *Boston Daily Globe*, July 12, 1914.

6. Story, "First Aid."

7. Advertisement, *The Editor*, July 4, 1914, 547.

8. "News of Books: Interesting Plans in Fall Catalogues of Publishers," *New York Times*, 11 Oct 1914; Proquest Historical Newspapers.

9. *Evening World*, October 23, 1914, 8.

10. Rachel Baker Gale, *Rebellious Jane* (Boston: W. H. Baker, 1916).

11. Wood, *Deep Roots*, 93.

12. "The Fourth in Bluehill," *Ellsworth American*, July 14, 1915.

13. "Bluehill: Sylvan Recital and Nevin Concert Two Most Delightful Events of the Season," *Bangor Daily News*, Aug 18, 1915.

14. "Sylvan Recital," *Bangor Daily News*.

15. Hancock County Deeds, Book 516 Page 550, signed 25 Aug 1915, recorded 19 September 1915.

16. "Ground Hog Snowed In: Storm May Continue Today and the Weather Man Says That a Cold Wave Is Due Tomorrow," *Boston Daily Globe*, February 3, 1916.

17. "Heaviest Snowstorm in 24 Years Buries Boston," *Boston Daily Globe*, February 14, 1916.

18. Berkshires Buried in Snow: Total Fall This Year Has Been 134 Inches, Beating All Records—One Town Killed a Steer to Get Tallow For Candles—Houses Are Buried to the Eaves and Many Roads Are Impassable—Drifts of 20 Feet Block Trolley Traffic—October Mountain Moose Starving," *Boston Daily Globe*, March 27, 1916.

19. Mann, *Emilie Loring*, 13.

20. Josephine Story, *The Mother in the Home* (Boston: Pilgrim Press, 1917), 1-8.

21. Story, *Mother*, 33.

22. "U.S., Passport Applications, 1795-1925," #25529," s.v. "Benjamin Curtis," (sailing on ship "New York," June 10, 1916), Ancestry.com.

23. "Passenger List," s.v. "Benjamin F. Curtis" ("St. Louis," arrived July 16, 1916, left Liverpool July 8, 1916), Ancestry.com.

24. Esther Wood at her home in Blue Hill, Maine; interview by the author, July 1998.

25. Esther Wood, "Broken Friendship" in *Deep Roots: A Maine Legacy* (Camden, Maine: Yankee Books, 1990), 92-6.

26. Arthur Hornblow, "Mr. Hornblow Goes to the Play," *Theater Magazine*, November 1916, 283.

27. Carl G. Jahn, Jay Ford Laning, William John Tossell, "Decision or Fiction?" *Ohio Law Bulletin*, Vol 62, 67.

28. Jahn, et al., "Decision," 68.

29. *Wellesley Townsman*, December 15, 1916.

30. Josephine Story, "How Women Should Prepare for Life's Best Part," *Des Moines Register*, February 11, 1917.

Chapter 18 World War I: Her Father's Daughter

1. Jahn, et al., "Decision," 119-20.

2. *Harvard Graduates Magazine*, XXIV, 1915-16; "1918 Defeated Brookline High," *Harvard Crimson*, April 14, 1915. "R. M. Loring '18 pitched excellent ball, striking out nine men in eight innings." "1920 Baseball Managers Report," *The Harvard Crimson*, February 15, 1917.

3. Emilie Loring, "The Yellow Hat," Emilie Loring Collection, Boston University Libraries, Howard Gotlieb Archival Research Center.

4. "House by 373 to 50 Votes for War, German Ships in Port Siezed," *Boston Daily Globe*, April 6, 1917.

5. "Luce Declares Autocracy is on Last Legs," *Boston Herald*, April 8, 1917.

6. "Selective Draft Act, May 18, 1917," *War Reprint* (United States: McKinley Publishing Company, 1918), 5. Google books.

7. "R. O. T. C. Will Hike July 16 to August 16," *Harvard Crimson*, May 19, 1917. "Reserve Officers' Training Corps," *Harvard Crimson*, June 4, 1917. "Company K: Cadet Corporal, R. M. Loring."

8. Penelope D. Clute, "The Plattsburg Idea," New York Archives, Fall, 2005.

9. The Plattsburger (Plattsburg, New York: The Plattsburger, Inc., 1917), 15-21.

10. UK and Ireland, Incoming Passenger Lists, Aurania departed New York and arrived in Liverpool July 22, 1917, Selden Loring #57 on passenger list, Ancestry.com;

11. Maine, U.S., Death Records, 1761-1922, s.v. "Caroline Duke Owen" (Died June 26, 1917 at Blue Hill, age 42 yr 0 mo 12 d, organic heart disease, 3 weeks; intestinal poisoning, several years); Bessie Owen to Gwen Roger-Jones, Private collection of Rosina Roger-Jones, courtesy of Angela Watts.

12. Main Exhibit, National World War I Museum, Kansas City, Missouri.

13. "Santa Claus War Sufferer, Organizations Making Strenuous Efforts to Provide Cheer, Despite Lighter Contributions," *New York Times*, December 18, 1915.

14. "Civilian Ships," Naval Historical Center, Department of the Navy, online https://www.history.navy.mil/content/history/nhhc, s.v. "USS Boothbay." Re: Slaven Yacht to Edithia, Captain Robert K. Slaven, Jr., USN, in conversation with the author.

15. "First United States Troops Left Under Convoy of Many Warships: No One In the Port from Which they Sailed was Aware of Actual Departure," *Ellsworth American*, July 4, 1917.

16. "The Photographic News of the World," *People's Home Journal*, May 1917, 25.

17. "How You Can Do Your 'Bit,' With Some Knitting Directions by Margaret Kingsland," *People's Home Journal*, August 1917.

18. C. Houston Goudiss and Alberta M. Goudiss, *Foods That Will Win the War and How to Cook Them* (New York: Forecast Publishing Co., 1918), 4-5. Online resource, Project Gutenberg.

19. "County Gossip," *Ellsworth American*, September 19, 1917.

20. "Making the Most of Meat Flavor and Hooverizing Sunday Dinners," *Sunday Herald* (Boston), January 20, 1918.

21. *Win the War in the Kitchen: What to Eat and How to Cook It* (Chicago: Food Administration, 1918).

22. Frank O. Robinson, "The Reservé Mallet," *History of the American Field Service in France, Told by Its Members*, Vol III (United States: Houghton Mifflin Company, 1920), 12-20. Online resource, collections.nlm.nih.gov.

23. Robinson, *History of AFS*, 12-20.

24. David Darrah, "Camion Sections at Soissons," *History of AFS*, 62-5. Note: Darrah was in Selden Loring's unit, from Akron, Ohio; Municipal University of Akron; T.M.U. 397; three months in Field Service; subsequently a Sergeant, U.S. Motor Transport Corps (Réserve Mallet).

25. *American Field Service Bulletin*, #11, September 15, 1917

26. *Memorial Volume of the American Field Service in France*, Ed. James W. D. Seymour (Boston: American Field Service, 1921), 85.

27. *The 302nd Field Artillery, United States Army* (United States: 302nd Field Artillery Association, 1919), 60.

28. *302nd Field Artillery*, 85

29. Frederick W. Kurth, *History of the American Field Service in France, Told by Its Members*, Vol III (United States: Houghton Mifflin Company, 1920), 112.

30. Walter Hines Page and Arthur Wilson Page, *The World's Work*, vol. 36, 407.

31. Selden Loring to Robby Loring, printed in *The Townsman*, December 1918.

32. Josephine Story, "The Extravagance of Worry," *The Mother in the Home* (Boston: Pilgrim Press, 1917), 25-30.

33. Emilie Loring, "An Elusive Legacy," *Woman's Weekly*, October 1917 to January 1918.

34. James P. Cole and Oliver Schoonmaker, *Military Instructor's Manual*, (New York: Edwin N. Appleton, 1917),168-75. Google books.

35. Summary of World War I Work of the American YMCA (YMCA National War Work Council), 9-10.

36. YMCA, 26.

37. YMCA, 32

38. YMCA, 28

39. YMCA, 126.

40. William Howard Taft, *Service with Fighting Men: An Account of the Work of the American Young Men's Christian Associations in the World War* (United States: Associated Press, 1922), exchange of air, 620; feet tapping, 636.

41. *American Field Service Bulletin*, Number 84 (Paris: American Field Service, 1919), 16-17.

42. *AFS Bulletin* (84), 18-19.

43. *AFS Bulletin* (84), 8-9

44. William Eleazar Barton, *The Moral Meanings of the World War: A Sermon in the First Congregational Church of Oak Park, Illinois, Sunday, June 16, 1918* (Oak Park, IL: Men's Bible Class, First Congregational Church, 1918). Hathi Trust.

45. Harvard's Military Record in the World War, "Loring, Robert Melville, c '14-'17." . . . Detailed as instructor Division School, 78th Division, March 20; detailed to Company of Conscientious Objectors, Draft Evaders and Alien Enemies June to September as officer in command; discharged May 11, 1919."

46. "Objectors Will Work in Camp War Gardens: Patch of 400 Acres at Dix Opens Movemen—Will Use Prisoners, Too," *Philadelphia Inquirer*, June 2, 1918.

47. Women's National Farm and Garden Association Bulletin, February 1918, 7, 15.

48. Cecilia Gowdy-Wygant, *Cultivating Victory: The Women's Land Army and the Victory Garden Movement* (United States: University of Pittsburgh Press, 2013), 31, 87. "Woman with a hoe," quoted by Elaine F. Weiss, *Fruits of Victory: The Woman's Land Army of America in the Great War*, (United States: Potomac Books, 2008), 36.

49. Women's National Farm and Garden Association Bulletin, Aug-Sep, 1918, 41. Members from Wellesley Hills include Mrs. Victor J. Loring and her neighbors, Mrs. John E. Oldham, Miss Alice J. Osgood. Emilie does flower and vegetable gardening, grows small fruits and tree fruits.

50. Carol R. Byerly, "The U.S. Military and the Influenza Pandemic of 1918-1919," Public Health, 2010, vol. 125, 83.

51. Selden M. Loring to Walter Brackett, printed in *The Townsman*, December 9, 1918.

Act Five: Emilie Loring

Chapter 19 *Writing is W-O-R-K*

1. Submissions and results recorded on cards, Emilie Loring Collection, Boston University Libraries, Howard Gotlieb Archival Research Center.

2. J. S. Salls, "The World We Write For," *The Editor* (United States: Editor Council, 1920), 99-100.

3. Emilie Baker Loring, "Kismet Takes a Hand," *Chicago Sunday Tribune*, April 27, 1919.

4. Emilie Baker Loring, "I'll Tell the World," *Chicago Daily Tribune*, June 8, 1919.

5. Typescript, Emilie Loring, "A Clean Slate," Private collection of Eve Loring Tarmey.

6. List of Burials, Baker Family Plot, Spruce Lane, Forest Hills Cemetery.

7. *Notable American Women, 1607-1950: A Biographical Dictionary*, Vol 2, Ed. Edward T. James, Janet Vilson James, Paul S. Boyer (United States: Harvard University Press, 1971), s.v. "Elizabeth Garver Jordan."

8. "Mrs. Baker," *The Townsman*, May 9, 1919.

9. Major George W. Bishop, Commanding Officer, Infantry, Camp Dix, NJ, letter "To whom it may concern," November 30, 1918, Private collection of Eve Loring Tarmey.

10. "The Boston Authors' Club," *New York Times*, January 19, 1901.

11. Mildred Buchanan Flagg, *Notable Boston Authors* (Cambridge, MA: Dreser, Chapman & Grimes, 1965), xiii.

12. *BAC Bulletin*, April 1920.

13. "The Boston Authors' Club," *New York Times*, January 19, 1901.

14. "The Vanquished," *AFS Bulletin, September 1918*; "We disagree with . . ." *AFS Bulletin, November 1918*.

15. Olmsted, Frederick Law, Jr., Personal office files: Correspondence, 1901-1940 in Olmsted Associates Records, 1863-1971, Library of Congress, Washington, D.C.

16. "Frederick Law Olmsted, Jr.," National Park Service profile, History & Culture: People; Online: nps.gov.

17. "Appalachian Club at Seal Harbor," *Bar Harbor Times*, July 2, 1919; Annual Report of the Director of the National Park Service to the Secretary of the Interior (United States: U.S. Government Printing Office, 1919), 247-9.

18. Frederick Sumner Mead, ed., *Harvard in the War* (United States: Harvard Alumni Association, 1921), 237; Secretary's Third Report, Class of 1916 (United States: Harvard University, 1922), 95.

19. Mann, *Emilie Loring*, 13.

Chapter 20 Boston Authors Club

1. *BAC Bulletin*, December 1919.

2. *Notable Boston Authors*, 81-2.

3. Handwritten, Map of Blue Hill by Josephine Preston Peabody, Private collection of Robert K. Slaven, Jr.

4. *Diary and Letters of Josephine Preston Peabody*: Selected and Edited by Christina Hopkinson Baker (Cambridge: The Riverside Press for Houghton Mifflin Co., 1925), 301-2.

5. *BAC Bulletin*, March 1951.

6. Typescript, Sara Ware Bassett, *I Grope My Way*, Sara Ware Bassett Papers, Boston Public Library, 33-4.

7. Flagg, *Notable*, 60.

8. Bassett, *Grope*, 50.

9. Sara Ware Bassett, "Mrs. Christy's Bridge Party," *St. Nicholas Magazine*, 1907.

10. Bassett, *Grope*, 111-2; *BAC Bulletin*, Oct-Dec, 1968. Bassett's account says the question was "What do you know about rope?" but her first book was lumber, and that account is told—in every way the same, but lumber instead of rope—in the *BAC Bulletin*. She published no books about rope.

11. Bassett, *Grope*, 155-7.

12. Cynthia H. Barton, *History's Daughter: The Life of Clara Endicott Sears, Founder of Fruitlands Museums* (Harvard: Fruitlands Museums, 1988).

13. *History's Daughter*, 75-80.

14. *History's Daughter*, 86.

15. Harriet B. Blackburn, "Pioneer Vacation House of Sixty Years Ago Will Welcome City Girls Again This Summer," *Christian Science Monitor*, June 9, 1949.

16. "Sara Ware Bassett," *Princeton Historical Society*, Online, s.v. "Historic Visitors," https://www.princetonmahistory.org/research/people-and-town-organizations/ ("She cut an unusual figure around town, resembling a character in an English detective novel. She dressed as one would think Miss Marple of Agatha Christie fame would have dressed in tweed skirts, a man's shirt and walking shoes. It was always a surprise to see her in Princeton's Post Office and General Store.")

17. Sara Ware Bassett, *Introduction to An American Poilu by Elmer Stetson Harden* (Boston: Little, Brown, 1919).

18. *History's Daughter*, 11.

19. Typescript, *Emilie Loring*, "Try it Out," 1919. Private collection of Eve Loring Tarmey.

20. *History's Daughter*, 32.

21. *BAC Bulletin*, February 1920 and November 1921.

Chapter 21 Identity: 1920–1928

1. Cleveland Amory, *The Proper Bostonians* (Madison, WI: E. P. Dutton, 1957), 16

2. *Proper Bostonians*, 15

3. Charles Henry Pope, *Loring Genealogy*, eds. John Arthur Loring, James Spear

Loring and Katharine Peabody Loring (Cambridge, MA: Murray and Emery, 1917), 93-4.

4. United States Federal Census, Wellesley, Norfolk County, Massachusetts, digital image, s.v. "Victor J. Loring," Ancestry.com.

5. Unpublished Loring family history, Patti Bender, Handwritten.

6. Unpublished Baker family history, Charles Tappan Baker, Handwritten, Private collection of Linda Loring Loveland.

7. Charles Parker Ilsley, *Centennials of Portland, 1675, 1775, 1875* (Somerville, MA: George B. King, 1876), 51-2.

8. Descendants of Nathaniel Shaw, Applicant's Working Sheet, National Society, Daughters of the American Revolution; Approved. DAR National No 306380, Admitted February 1, 1938, Given March 10, 1938. "M. Emily Loring," Johanna Aspinwall Chapter, descent from Corporal Nathaniel Shaw.

9. "Harvard Magazine Holds Elections," *Harvard Magazine*, January 25, 1921.

10. *BAC Bulletin*, May 1921.

11. Robert H. Davis, "Why Are Manuscripts Rejected?" *The Bookman*, May 1916.

12. Contracts, Emilie Loring Collection, Boston University Libraries, Howard Gotlieb Archival Research Center.

13. *BAC Bulletin*, February 1922.

14. *I Grope My Way*, 210

15. Sara Ware Bassett, *Granite and Clay* (New York: A. L. Burt, 1922), 76, 80, 305.

16. *History's Daughter*, page 58.

17. Clara Endicott Sears, *The Romance of Fiddler's Green* (United States: Houghton Mifflin, 1922), 13, 235.

18. Willard E. Hawkins, "Web-Work Plot Structure," *The Student-Writer*, June, 1917.

19. Emilie Loring, "Do You Care?" *The Townsman*, June 10, 1921.

20. *The Trail of Conflict*, inscribed to Emilie Loring by Charles Shoemaker, Private collection of Selden M. Loring, Jr.

21. *The Trail of Conflict* inscribed to BAC, Boston Authors Club Records Collection, Boston Public Library.

22. "Barnstable: The Trail of Conflict," *Barnstable Patriot*, October 9, 1922.

23. "The Dragon Slayer," *Aberdeen Journal*, July 23, 1924.

24. Flyer, "Novels of Romance and Adventure," Emilie Loring Collection, Boston University Libraries, Howard Gotlieb Archival Research Center.

25. Clark's Boston Blue Book for 1924: The Elite Private Address and Club Directory and Ladies' Visiting List (Boston: Sampson & Murdock, Co., 1924), 748.

26. Rachel E. Gale, death certificate, November 9, 1923, certificate 096413, City of Boston Registrar, copy in possession of author.

27. "Died-Gale," *Boston Herald*, November 10, 1923; "Funeral of Author of 'Mr. Bob': Services for Mrs. Rachel Elizabeth Gale Are Held at Second Church," Boston Evening Transcript, November 12, 1923; "Service in Second Church for Mrs. Rachel E. Gale," *Boston Daily Globe*, November 13, 1923.

28. "Table Gossip," *Boston Globe*, January 6, 1924; "Social Calendar," New York Times, February 10, 1924.

29. "Not Much Left but the House," *Boston Post*, March 5, 1920; "In Cross Suits for Damages," *Boston Post*, April 18, 1922; "Lucey Says He Was Turned out of House," *Boston Evening Globe*, April 18, 1922; "Wins Suits Against Miss Clara E. Sears," *Boston Globe*, April 28, 1922.

30. "Literary & Trade Notes," *The Publishers Weekly*, Volume 83, May 10, 1913.

31. Handwritten, Emilie Loring, Emilie Loring Collection, Boston University Libraries, Howard Gotlieb Archival Research Center.

32. "Here Comes the Sun!" *New York Herald-Sun*, June 1, 1924.

33. Robert H. Davis, "Why Are Manuscripts Rejected?" *The Bookman*, May 1916.

34. Emilie Loring, "Avoiding Rhetorical Bypaths in the Novel," *The Editor*, March 15, 1924.

35. Clayton Hamilton, *A Manual of the Art of Fiction* (New York: Doubleday, Page & Co., 1919), 14.

36. Loring, "Rhetorical."

37. Clara Endicott Sears, *Days of Delusion* (United States: Houghton Mifflin, 1924), 203.

38. Loring, "Rhetorical."

39. "The Rum Fleet," *Biddeford Journal*, May 6, 1924.

40. Typescript, Alvin Dohme, "A Brief History of the Kollegewidgwok Yacht Club," 1958. Private collection of Robert K. Slaven, Jr.

41. Barnabee, *Reminiscences*, 309-10.

42. Downeast Dilettante (Brad Emerson), "The Pinafore Sails Down East," November 30, 2010. Online, thedowneastdilettante.blogspot.com.

43. "Wellesley Hills," *Wellesley Townsman*, September 12, 1924.

44. Mann, *Emilie Loring*, 26.

45. Emilie Loring, "Dan Kicks a Goal," *Munsey's Magazine*, December 1924.

46. "Harper's 3 Prizes for Short Stories are Won by Women," *Chicago Daily Tribune*, June 21, 1924.

47. "Thousands Enter 'Harper's' Competition," *Hartford Courant*, March 8, 1925.

48. W. D. Steele Winner First Harper Award, *Washington Post*, March 22, 1925.

49. "J. Jefferson Jones, Publisher, Is Dead," *New York Times*, November 2, 1941, ProQuest Historical Newspapers.

50. "Boston Authors' Club to Honor Its Twenty-Fifth Anniversary," *The Christian Science Monitor*, January 5, 1925; ProQuest Historical Newspapers.

51. Emilie Loring to Clara Endicott Sears, February 8, 1925. ARC

52. "Wellesley Hills Locals: Four Homes Entered at Hills," *Wellesley Townsman*, February 27, 1925.

53. New York, U.S., Wills and Probate Records, 1659-1999, s.v. "Rachel Elizabeth Gale," Ancestry.com.

54. "Best Sellers of the Week," *Boston Daily Globe*, April 25, 1925.

55. "The New Books: A Certain Crossroad," *The Saturday Review of Literature*, April 25, 1925.

56. "A Certain Crossroad," *Saturday Review*.

57. Boston Authors Club Bulletin, May 7, 1925, 1; Boston Authors Club Collection, Boston Public Library.

58. "Quiet Bridal," *Boston Herald*, July 19, 1925.

59. Allen Chamberlain, Beacon Hill: Its Ancient Pastures and Early Mansions (United States: Houghton Mifflin, 1925),

60. Chamberlain, *Beacon Hill*, 180-1.

61. "Real Estate Transactions," *Boston Daily Globe*, August 5, 1925.

62. Jim Vrabel, *When in Boston: A Time Line & Almanac* (Boston: Northeastern University Press, 2004), 154.

63. *History's Daughter*, 111

64. Mildred Buchanan Flagg, *Notable Boston Authors* (Boston: Dresser, Chapman & Grimes, 1965), 16.

65. "Country Neighbors," *Spectator*, June 25, 1910.

66. Amy Loveman, "Review: The Mysteries of Ann by Alice Brown," *The Saturday Review*, April 18, 1925.

67. Baker and Baker, "After Taps," 6.

68. "The Townswoman Makes a Hit," *Wellesley Townsman*, February 12, 1926.

69. "A Delightful Lunatic by Meade Minnigerode. Lord Timothy Dexter of Newburyport, Massachusetts, by John P. Marquand," *The Saturday Review*, October 17, 1925.

70. Martha Bayard, "The Man Who Sold Mittens in the Tropics," *Literary Digest International Book Review*, Volume 4, 1926.

71. Dorothea Lawrance Mann, "The Bookworm," *Sunday Morning Star* (Wilmington, Delaware), January 24, 1926.

72. *BAC Bulletin*, May 1926.

73. Typescript, Sara Ware Bassett, *I Grope My Way*, Sara Ware Bassett Papers, Boston Public Library, 218-22

74. "Will Reproduce Famous Dickens Dinner of 1842," *Boston Daily Globe*, May 5, 1926.

75. Hancock County Records, Book 1703:494, $20,000, three years at 6%, signed July 3, 1926, Bucksport, Maine.

76. Dorothea Lawrance Mann, "Mary Christmas: An Armenian Peddler of the Maine Coast," *Bar Harbor Times*, June 20, 1924.

77. "Lunch in Boston Public Schools," *Boston Daily Globe*, May 1, 1927.

78. "Local Lines," *Boston Daily Globe*, March 8, 1926, 9 May 1926,

79. "Prof Rogers to speak at NE Women's Club," *Boston Daily Globe*, November 5, 1926.

80. John Clair Minot, "An Orchard Story: A New England Tale of Mystery and Adventure," *Boston Herald*, February 19, 1927.

81. Rotogravure Section, *Boston Herald*, April 24, 1927.

82. Angie Brackett to Emilie Loring, March 6, 1927, Emilie Loring Collection, Boston University Libraries, Howard Gotlieb Archival Research Center.

83. Unpublished Loring family history, Patti Bender, Handwritten.

84. "Books and Authors," *Boston Herald*, September 24, 1927.

85. Clara Endicott Sears to Emilie Loring, 1927, ARC

86. Front Page, Special to the *New York Times*, October 29, 1927.

87. Robert Grant to Sara Ware Bassett, Sara Ware Bassett Papers, Boston Public Library

88. Robert Grant to Sara Ware Bassett, Sara Ware Bassett Papers, Boston Public Library.

89. Clara Endicott Sears to Sara Ware Bassett, ARC

90. "Second Prize Play Contest," *New York Times*, November 27, 1927.

91. *BAC Bulletin*, November 1928.

92. Emilie Loring to Clara Endicott Sears, August 24, 1933, ARC.

93. Harvard Class of 1892, Report XI, 1928, p. 12.

94. Harvard Class of 1892, Report XI, 1928, p. 12.

95. Robert Grant to Sara Ware Bassett, May 11, 1928; Sara Ware Bassett Papers, Boston Public Library. He mentions her previous communication.

96. *BAC Bulletin*, June 1929.

97. *BAC Bulletin*, April 1928.

98. Selden M. Loring, Jr., in discussion with the author, May 23, 2007.

99. "Our Public Schools: Sandy Creek High School: Reluctant Romeo," *Sandy Creek News* (Sandy Creek, NY) March 7, 1929.

100. Victor J. Loring, II in conversation with the author.

101. Mann, *Emilie Loring*.

102. *BAC Bulletin*, February 1934.

Chapter 22 Crisis: 1929

1. "Funeral Rites on Saturday for C. T. Baker," *Patriot Ledger* (Quincy, MA), December 17, 1942.

2. "Dam Threat Causes Panic Near Rutland," *New York Times*, November 6, 1927.

3. *Brief Biographies of Some Well Known Authors and Illustrators*, (Philadelphia, Penn, 1929), 63.

4. Emilie Loring, "Lighted Windows," *The Editor*, 27 Dec 1930.

5. "Pen Women Have Many Noted Guests: Boston Branch Gives a 'Celebrity Breakfast,'" *Boston Daily Globe*, April 23, 1929.

6. Robert M. Baker, death certificate, May 6, 1929, No. 13015, New York City Bureau of Records, copy in possession of author. (Age 60, playwright, died at PM, cause fractured skull, lacerated brain, hemorrhagic shock, fell or jumped from residence, the 12th floor to sidewalk below. In the city 1 month, living at hotel; former/usual residence 15 E. 69th St.)

7. "R. M. Baker Estate to Widow," *New York Times*, May 18, 1929.

8. "Theaters, Amusements, Entertainments," *Los Angeles Times*, May 17, 1929.

9. "March Hares," *Ellsworth American*, June 30, 1929.

10. Year's Worst Break Hits Stock Market, *New York Times*, October 4, 1929.

11. *BAC Bulletin*, November 1929.

12. John Dodge, "'Cats and Dogs' Redux," December 18, 2016. Online at www.dodgeretort.com.

13. "Mary C. Sears Estate is Nearly $6,000,000," *Boston Daily Globe*, September 13, 1929.

Chapter 23 Resilience: 1930–34

1. George M. Baker, 23 Cornhill Road, listed in *The American Philatelist*, 1887, 290.

2. Unpublished manuscript, "By Audacity Alone Are High Things Accomplished"/"How Doth the Busy Little Bee," Emilie Loring Collection, Boston University Libraries, Howard Gotlieb Archival Research Center.

3. David L. Goodrich, *The Real Nick and Nora: Frances Goodrich and Albert*

Hacket: Writers of Stage and Screen Classics (Carbondale: Southern Illinois University Press, 2001), 127.

4. "Edward Jewett Brooks: A Loving Tribute to a Husband and Father," *Ellsworth American*, June 11, 1930.

5. "Magistrate McAdoo Dies Suddenly at 76," *New York Times*, June 8, 1930. ("He had expected to pass his vacation at Blue Hill, Me., and had leased a house there for the summer.")

6. "Bluehill," *Ellsworth American*, August 13, 1930

7. Linda Loring Loveland in conversation with the author.

8. Notable American Women, 249. Attributed to Alice Brown: "I have a genius for writing what nobody wants."

9. *BAC Bulletin*, March 1930.

10. "New Novel Has Country Setting," *Falmouth Enterprise*, September 25, 1930.

11. Emilie Loring to Clara Endicott Sears, August 23, 1930, ARC.

12. Emilie Loring to Clara Endicott Sears, September 14, 1930, ARC.

13. Emilie Loring to Clara Endicott Sears, 14 Sept 1930, ARC.

14. Note: Remodeling by later owners removed the chimneys, but the home survived on its promontory above Blue Hill's inner bay and returned, eventually, to Coggans' descendants.

15. Interview with Victor J Loring, II in Westminster, CA, 2006.

16. "Safe Robbers Steal $50 in Four Tries," *Boston Daily Globe*, August 18, 1930.

17. Boston Authors Club, Bulletin, February 1931. Boston Authors Club Records Collection, Boston Public Library.

18. Emilie Loring, "Lighted Windows," *The Editor*, 27 Dec 1930.

19. *Little, Brown and Co., One Hundred and Fifty Years of Publishing, 1837-1987* (Boston: Little, Brown and Company, 1987), 84-5.

20. Bassett, *I Grope My Way*, 222.

21. *BAC Bulletin*, Jan 1933 (Dedication was June 11, 1932.)

22. "Bremen Fliers Get Tributes at Albany," *New York Times*, May 22, 1928.

23. Typescript, Emilie Loring, "That Little Matter of Age," Emilie Loring Collection, Boston University Libraries, Howard Gotlieb Archival Research Center.

24. *BAC Bulletin*, February 1934.

25. *One Hundred and Fifty Years of Publishing, 1837-1987* (Boston: Little, Brown, 1987), 84-85.

26. "Professional Women's Club Presents Play," *Daily Boston Globe*, March 2, 1932.

27. "Miss Sears is Hostess to Boston Pen Women," *Daily Boston Globe*, March 8, 1932.

28. *BAC Bulletin*, December 1922.

29. *BAC Bulletin*, March 1932.

30. John Clair Minot, "Chatter and Comment," *Boston Herald*, July 2, 1932; GenealogyBank.

31. "Fine Romance of the Turf World by Emilie Loring," *Boston Daily Globe*, October 8, 1932.

32. John Clair Minot, "Mrs. Loring's Turf Romance," *Boston Herald*, September 24, 1932.

33. *Bar Harbor Times*, July 27, 1932.

34. Hymns and Tunes with Services for Congregational Worship: Selected from the Hymn and Tune Book and the Service Book (United States: Beacon Press, 1914).

35. *BAC bulletin*, January 1933.

36. Jeanne G. Shain to Emilie Loring, May 20, 1933, Emilie Loring Collection, Boston University Libraries, Howard Gotlieb Archival Research Center.

37. "Hilltops Clear," *Atlanta Constitution*, July 16, 1933.

38. Emilie Loring to Clara Endicott Sears, June 18, 1933, ARC.

39. Emilie Loring to Clara Endicott Sears, October 10, 1933, ARC

40. Emilie Loring to Clara Endicott Sears October 19, 1933, ARC.

41. Emilie Loring to Clara Endicott Sears, November 23, 1933, ARC.

42. Emilie Loring, dedication of *We Ride the Gale!* (Boston: Little, Brown, 1934).

Chapter 24 Make Good: 1934–1939

1. "We Ride the Gale!," *Hopewell Herald* (Hopewell, NJ), April 4, 1934.

2. "Emilie Loring Appeals Again with Romance," *Philadelphia Inquirer*, February 17, 1934.

3. "Realm of Books: Mrs. Loring in Important Spring Romance, 'We Ride the Gale,'" *Boston Herald*, February 16, 1934.

4. *BAC Bulletin*, February 1934.

5. Emilie Loring, "A Writer in the Making," *The Village Booklet*, March 1934.

6. *BAC Bulletin*, May 1934.

7. Emilie Loring to Clara Endicott Sears, undated. ARC.

8. Unattributed clipping, Station WABI, Bangor, Maine, October 25, 1934. Emilie Loring Collection, Boston University Libraries, Howard Gotlieb Archival Research Center.

9. Note: Melville Baker movie credits: *The Swan* (Adolphe Menjou), *High Hat*, *The Circus Kid*, *Fashions in Love* (Adolphe Menjou), *Darkened Rooms*, *One Romantic Night* (Lillian Gish), *His Woman* (Gary Cooper and Claudette

Colbert), *Downstairs* (John Gilbert and Virginia Bruce), *Zoo in Budapest* (Loretta Young and Gene Raymond), *Now and Forever* (Gary Cooper, Carole Lombard, and Shirley Temple), and *Mills of the Gods* (Fay Wray, Victor Jory, and Oscar-nominated May Robson).

10. Bassett, *I Grope My Way*, 94.

11. Dorothea Lawrance Mann, "Emilie Loring Says It's a Great World: Her Latest Novel Takes Her Readers Into the Whirlpool of Washington Social and Political Life," *Boston Evening Transcript*, Book Section, June 22, 1935.

12. Mann, "Great World."

13. Mann, "Great World."

14. Eve Loring Tarmey in conversation with the author.

15. Emilie Loring to Clara Endicott Sears, July 14, 1935, ARC.

16. Ibid.

17. Emilie Loring to Clara Endicott Sears, August 19, 1935, ARC.

18. Transcription, WEEI interview, "Meet the Author" with Charles Lee, Literary Editor of the *Boston Herald*, 4 PM, May 3, 1939. Emilie Loring Collection, Boston University Libraries, Howard Gotlieb Archival Research Center.

19. "Mrs. Larz Anderson Disagrees with 'Mrs. McConnachie,'" *Boston Herald*, June 2, 1935.

20. "Love at First Sight with a Maine Coast Setting," *Boston Daily Globe*, August 1, 1936.

21. Emilie Loring, *Prepared remarks for As Long as I Live*, Emilie Loring Collection, Boston University Libraries, Howard Gotlieb Archival Research Center.

22. Charles Shoemaker to Emilie Loring, November 28, 1936. Emilie Loring Collection, Boston University Libraries, Howard Gotlieb Archival Research Center.

23. Newspaper clipping, "1938 Boston paper," Emilie Loring Collection, Boston University Libraries, Howard Gotlieb Archival Research Center.

24. Elizabeth Cobbs, "Why the Pulitzer Prize Committee Keeps Ignoring Women," *Washington Post*, April 13, 2018.

25. Pulitzer Prize Board Members, https://www.pulitzer.org/board

26. Ron Charles, "Finally, a comic novel gets a Pulitzer Prize. It's about time," Book Section, *Washington Post*, April 17, 2018.

27. "Charming Novel Ends on a High Note of Romance," *Boston Globe*, March 6, 1937.

28. Typescript, Emilie Loring Collection, Boston University Libraries, Howard Gotlieb Archival Research Center.

29. "Hundred Years at Publishing Books," *Baltimore Sun*, March 25, 1937.

30. *The Detroit Free Press*, 8 March 1936, p. 97.

31. "WHBL Schedule," *Sheboygan Press* (Sheboygan, WI), January 25, 1937.

32. "Mighty Magic," *Rock Island Argus*, 26 June 1937.

33. "Pulitzer Prize for Novel Won by 'Gone With Wind," *New York Times*, May 4, 1937.

34. "C. C. Shoemaker, 76, Publisher, Is Dead: Founder of Penn Company of Philadelphia 56 Years Ago; Its Head Ever Since," *New York Times*, May 23, 1937.

35. "Hundred Years at Publishing Books," *Baltimore Sun*, 25, March 1937; Newspapers.com.

36. Contract, Emilie Loring and Little, Brown Publishing Company, August 25, 1937. Emilie Loring Collection, Boston University Libraries, Howard Gotlieb Archival Research Center.

37. William Alcott, "King's Abdication Held World Spotlight in 1936: Edward's Romantic Sacrifice of British Throne for Love of Mrs. Simpson Held by Many to Be Most Spectacular News Story of All Time," *Boston Globe*, January 1, 1937.

38. "Duke Greets Wally in Castle: Embraces her on Doorstep," *Boston Globe*, May 4, 1937.

39. Typescript, Radio interview with Charles Lee, WEEI, "Meet the Author," May 3, 1939. Emilie Loring Collection, Boston University Libraries, Howard Gotlieb Archival Research Center.

40. "Mrs. Charles Gilmore Kerley," *The Living Church*, Volume 105, November 8, 1942.

41. Partial clipping, "Novelist Loring Retains Public Minus Publicity: Her 'Today Is Yours' Sells Without Need for Bally-hoo," *Boston Herald*, 1938. Emilie Loring Collection, Boston University Libraries, Howard Gotlieb Archival Research Center.

42. "The Best-Selling Books: Fiction Non-Fiction," *New York Times*, March 6, 1938.

43. J. Y. Smith, "A. J. Cronin, Writer of Best-Selling Novels, Is Dead at 84, *Washington Post*, January 10, 1981.

44. "D. C. Woman Second in Writing Contest," *Evening Star*, 24, April 1938.

45. "The Screen," *New York Times*, May 13, 1938.

46. "Bogarts Plan Trip to Seattle," *Los Angeles Times*, August 22, 1938.

47. Mayflower Log, February 1940, 27. Collection of the Mayflower Hotel, Washington, D.C.

48. Mayflower Log, March 1937, 9.

Chapter 25 Favorite American Novelist

1. Emilie Loring to Mrs. Elmo, February 27, 1939. Emilie Loring Collection, Boston University Libraries, Howard Gotlieb Archival Research Center.

2. Handbook of labor statistics, U.S. Department of Labor, Bureau of Labor Statistics, Washington: U.S. G. P. O. 1941, pp. 297-311

3. Typescript, Emilie Loring Collection, Boston University Libraries, Howard Gotlieb Archival Research Center.

4. Margaret Ford, "Where Pens, in Golden Silence, Indite Imperishable Memories of Old Boston," *Boston Herald*, March 26, 1939.

5. "Meet Your Favorite Author Over the Radio," *Boston Herald*, section B, March 19, 1939, 5.

6. Partial transcript, "WEEI Meet the Author," review with Charles Lee, Literary Editor of the *Boston Herald*, May 3, 1939. Emilie Loring Collection, Boston University Libraries, Howard Gotlieb Archival Research Center.

7. Typescript, Emilie Loring Collection, Boston University Libraries, Howard Gotlieb Archival Research Center.

8. "Aid Chinese War Orphans: Chinese Jewelry Sale at White's Attracts Crowd," *Daily Boston Globe*, November 2, 1939.

9. "Favorites Played by Philharmonic," *New York Times*, November 11, 1938.

10. John I. Taylor, Jr., "Year's List Shows Belief in Ourselves," *Daily Boston Globe*, December 3, 1939.

11. "Women's Clubs: American Penwomen," *Daily Boston Globe*, December 17, 1939.

12. "Poets to Speak Before Meeting of Penwomen," *Daily Boston Globe*, February 18, 1940.

13. "Beacon Hill Swastika Furled; Police Relax," *Boston Herald*, April 21, 1940.

14. "Leominster Divorcee Has Ex-Spouse Arrested," *Boston Globe*, January 13, 1940; "Baker Case May Drag for Months," *Fitchburg Sentinal*, January 13, 1940; "Arraigned But Police Not Notified," *Fitchburg Sentinel*, February 7, 1940; "Divorce is Granted Mrs. Baker from Former Clinton Publisher; Is Awarded $300 a Month, Home," *Fitchburg Sentinel*, March 22, 1940; "Bigamist, Baker, in Buenos Aires, Transfer Shows," *Fitchburg Sentinel*, May 3, 1940;

15. "French Fall Back to Marne in Final Stand to Save Paris," "Nazis Reach Battleground of First Marne," *Boston Herald*, June 12, 1940.

16. "Poetry Honor Roll," *Boston Herald*, May 14, 1939. Eleven children listed, each from a different town, including Valentine Loring, Lexington.

17. "President Bolstered Hopes of World," *Boston Herald*, June 12, 1940.

18. Agnes Carr, "Romance, Thrills in Latest Loring," *Boston Herald*, June 22, 1940.

19. Olga Owens to Emilie Loring, June 17, 1940. Emilie Loring Collection, Boston University Libraries, Howard Gotlieb Archival Research Center.

20. Olga Owens to Emilie Loring, July 1, 1940. Emilie Loring Collection, Boston University Libraries, Howard Gotlieb Archival Research Center.

21. Typescript, Priscilla Fortesque interview, Emilie Loring Collection, Boston University Libraries, Howard Gotlieb Archival Research Center.

22. Pearl Strachan, "Ask the Children," *Christian Science Monitor*, January 1, 1941.

23. Charles Lee to Emilie Loring, November 1940. Emilie Loring Collection, Boston University Libraries, Howard Gotlieb Archival Research Center.

24. Emilie Loring to Charles Lee, November 26, 1940, Emilie Loring Collection, Boston University Libraries, Howard Gotlieb Archival Research Center.

25. Emilie Loring to Charles Lee, December 4, 1940, Emilie Loring Collection, Boston University Libraries, Howard Gotlieb Archival Research Center.

26. "Schloss' Boner Bounces as Scholars Score 7 in 11," *Philadelphia Record*, December 18, 1940.

27. Emilie Loring to Miss Enid Hager, *Philadelphia Record*; December 25, 1940. Emilie Loring Collection, Boston University Libraries, Howard Gotlieb Archival Research Center.

28. Transcript, WEEI, January 9, 1941, Emilie Loring Collection, Boston University Libraries, Howard Gotlieb Archival Research Center.

29. Natalie Gordon, "Our Gracious Ladies: Emilie Baker Loring," *Boston Traveler*, February 12, 1941.

30. Agnes Carr, "New Loring Novel Has Exciting Plot," *Boston Herald*, March 22, 1941.

31. Typescript, Emilie Loring remarks for Boston Authors Club, April 4, 1941. Emilie Loring Collection, Boston University Libraries, Howard Gotlieb Archival Research Center.

32. Olga Owens, "Beloved Boston Novelist Talks About Work and Play," *Boston Sunday Post*, June 8, 1941.

33. Secretary, Maine State Library to Emilie Loring, April 3, 1941, Emilie Loring Correspondence, Maine Writers Correspondence, Maine State Library Special Collections.

34. Mary Ellen Chase, *A Goodly Heritage* (New York: Henry Holt & Co., 1932), 241.

35. Mary Ellen Chase, "Novels," p. 15.

36. Secretary, Maine State Library to Emilie Loring, Emilie Loring Correspondence, Maine Writers Correspondence, Maine State Library Special Collections.

37. Telephone communication, Maine State Library Special Collections to the author.

38. Advertisement, "Thank you, once again, Mrs. Loring," *New York Times*, November 2, 1941.

39. Handwritten note, Emilie Loring, Emilie Loring Collection, Boston University Libraries, Howard Gotlieb Archival Research Center.

Chapter 26 Fight for the Right: 1941–1945

1. "Correct Air Raid Signals," *Wellesley Townsman*, January 8, 1942.

2. "All Axis Now US Foe," *Boston Herald*, December 10, 1941.

3. Transcript, Franklin D. Roosevelt, Fireside Chat, December 9, 1941. Online, https://millercenter.org/the-presidency/presidential-speeches/december-9-1941-fireside-chat-19-war-japan.

4. "Mental Uplift in Time of War Topic of Authors' Luncheon," *Boston Herald*, January 18, 1942.

5. Moying Li-Marcus, *Beacon Hill: The Life and Times of a Neighborhood* (Boston: Northeastern University Press, 2002), 82.

6. Paul Hume, "Pianists Gold & Fizdale," *Washington Post*, August 10, 1979.

7. Victor J. Loring, II in conversation with the author.

8. "No Rationing is Required Among Boston Book Lovers," *Boston Post*, Book Section, December 6, 1942.

9. Emilie Loring, "Emilie Loring Remembers Her Own White Christmas," *Boston Post*, December 6, 1942.

10. "Funeral Rites on Saturday for C. T. Baker," *Patriot Ledger*, December 17, 1942.

11. Emilie Loring's grandchildren (Victor J. Loring, II; Valentine Loring Titus, Selden Melville Loring, Linda Loring Loveland, Sandra Loring Fischer, Eve Loring Tarmey) in conversation with the author.

12. "Text of OPA Gasoline Order," *Evening Star*, January 6, 1943.

13. Julian Street, Jr., Consultant, Office of the Secretary of the Treasury, to Emilie Loring, December 20, 1945. Emilie Loring Collection, Boston University Libraries, Howard Gotlieb Archival Research Center.

14. Frederic Babcock, "Among the Authors," *Chicago Daily Tribune*, September 12, 1943.

15. Correspondence between Winifred Willard and Emilie Loring, August 27, 1943. Emilie Loring Collection, Boston University Libraries, Howard Gotlieb Archival Research Center.

16. Transcription, Ruth Moss interview, August 1943. Emilie Loring Collection, Boston University Libraries, Howard Gotlieb Archival Research Center.

17. Transcription, Alice Dixon Bond interview, WEEI, April 24, 1943. Emilie Loring Collection, Boston University Libraries, Howard Gotlieb Archival Research Center.

18. Emilie Loring to Miss Ruth Moss, Sept 23, 1943, Emilie Loring Collection, Boston University Libraries, Howard Gotlieb Archival Research Center.

19. "At Midnight Stroke, Samuel Kelsey and Mrs. Visel Were Made One: Sleeping Town Clerk and Parson Were Roused by Persistent Pair," *Boston Daily Globe*, April 13, 1901.

20. *BAC Bulletin*, January 1944.

21. Photo Caption: "Jacket Design for When Hearts Are Light Again," *Boston Herald*, August 25, 1943.

22. Correspondence, Division of University Extension, February 1944, Emilie Loring Collection, Boston University Libraries, Howard Gotlieb Archival Research Center.

23. "Famous Authors Subject in Book Course Tuesday," *Daily Boston Globe*, February 27, 1944; Typescript notes, Emilie Loring, Emilie Loring Collection, Boston University Libraries, Howard Gotlieb Archival Research Center.

24. Typescript, Emilie Loring, prepared remarks for "Reader Response," Emilie Loring Collection, Boston University Libraries, Howard Gotlieb Archival Research Center.

25. Dorothy Hillyer, "Over the Fence," *Boston Globe*, May 17, 1944.

26. "Redheads and Saboteurs," *Boston Herald*, October 16, 1944.

27. Mrs. J. W. Bonner, "The Literary World: Editor Sees Emergence from Gloomy Literature," *Tampa Bay Times*, February 25, 1945.

28. "Film Will Use Tokyo Bombing Shots," *Los Angeles Times*, May 30, 1945.

29. Leonard Lyons, "Broadway Medley," *The Times* (San Mateo, CA), August 22, 1945.

30. Anna L. Waring, "In Heavenly Love Abiding," *Christian Science Hymnal* (Boston: Christian Science Publishing Society, 1932).

31. "Emilie Loring Writes Her 25th Anniversary Novel," *Boston Herald*, November 14, 1945.

32. "Books to Read," *Daily Boston Globe*, November 15, 1945.

33. "Celebrity Breakfast," *Boston Traveler*, November 2, 1945.

Chapter 27 Individual Spirit: 1946–1951

1. Victor J Loring, II in conversation with the author, Westminster, CA, 2006.
2. "John Gould Speaks at Authors' Luncheon," *Boston Daily Globe*, February 8, 1946.
3. "News of Other Women's Activities: New England Woman's Press Association," *Boston Daily Globe*, May 19, 1946.
4. Alvin R. L. Dohme, "The Yacht Club that Blue Hill Built," *Down East*, August 1964.
5. Homer Heller to Victor and Emilie Loring, September 1946, Private collection of Eve Loring Tarmey.
6. Rev. Charles M. Hyde, *A Memoir of the Life of Samuel Austin Hitchcock of Brimfield, Mass.* (Boston: Alfred Mudge & Son, 1874), 4.
7. Unfinished typescript and handwritten manuscript, Emilie Loring, Emilie Loring Collection, Boston University Libraries, Howard Gotlieb Archival Research Center.
8. "Victor J. Loring, Prominent churchman and Lawyer was 88," *Daily Boston Globe*, February 9, 1947.
9. Inscribed copy, *Beckoning Trails*, Private collection of Selden M. Loring, Jr.
10. Hancock County Deed, Book 717 page 21-22, #1947047467, signed April 14, 1947, recorded June 30, 1947.
11. Doris Ricker Marston, "She Has Written 28 Books in Longhand," *Boston Sunday Globe*, January 23, 1949.
12. Advertisement, *Boston Herald*, December 17, 1947.
13. *History's Daughter*, 37.
14. "In Memoriam, Sara Ware Bassett," *BAC Bulletin*, Oct-Dec 1968.
15. "She Fits Gowns, Decides Fates of Cape Cod Folk," *Chicago Tribune*, July 20, 1947.
16. "Emilie Loring's Book Sales Now Nearly at Million Mark," *Boston Herald*, January 30, 1949.
17. Doris Ricker Marston, "She Has Written 28 Books in Longhand," *Boston Sunday Globe*, January 23, 1949.
18. Ibid.
19. Natalie Gordon, "Reception Jan. 25 for Emilie Loring," *Boston Traveler*, January 21, 1949.
20. Ibid.
21. Doris Ricker Marston, "Emilie Loring Gets Inspiration From Maine for Many Stories," *Lewiston Evening Journal*, Magazine section, June 4, 1949.

22. Ibid.

23. Emilie Loring to Mr. Bradford, July 4, 1949, Private collection of Eve Loring Tarmey.

24. Emilie Loring to Linda Loring, January 16, 1949, Private collection of Linda Loring Loveland.

25. Emilie Loring to Linda Loring, July 5, 1949, Private collection of Linda Loring Loveland.

26. Emilie Loring to Bradford, July 4, 1949, Private collection of Eve Loring Tarmey.

27. Emilie Loring to Mr. Bradford, July 23, 1949, Private collection of Eve Loring Tarmey.

28. Emilie Loring, *To Love and to Honor* (Boston: Little, Brown, 1950), front matter.

29. Eve Loring Tarmey in conversation with the author.

30. Sandra Loring Fischer in conversation with the author.

31. Advertisement, *Boston Herald*, November 3, 1950.

32. "Society Events," *Boston Traveler*, January 3, 1951.

33. Emilie Loring (Mrs. Victor J. Loring), death certificate, March 13, 1951, Registered No. 41, Town of Wellesley, Massachusetts, copy in possession of author. (Died March 13, 1951, 12:45 AM, Broncho pneumonia 48 hrs, Lyryngo-tracheo-bronchitis with virus-type infection 72 hrs, rheumotoid arthritis 11 months, cardiac hypertrophy and dilatation 3 yrs; Dr. Conrad Wesselhaft attended November 24, 1947 to March 13, 1951, last saw her March 12, 1951. Occupation, Author. Usual place of abode: Hotel Bellevue, 21 Beacon St., at 67 Longfellow Road, Wellesley Hills, for 9 months. Informant Robert M. Loring, son).

34. Loring grandchildren—Victor, Valentine, Selden, Linda, and Eve—in conversations with the author, 2003-2022.

35. *BAC Bulletin*, April 1951

36. Selden M. Loring, Jr. in conversation with the author.

37. Flagg, *Notable*, 67.

38. Robert M. Loring to Clara Endicott Sears, March 20, 1951. ARC

39. "Emilie Loring '82," Dean Academy newsletter, Dean Academy Records, Franklin, Massachusetts.

40. Emilie Loring's last will and testament, Private collection of Eve Loring Tarmey.

Chapter 28 The Real Emilie Loring

1. "The Unsinkable Emilie Loring," *Christian Science Monitor*, July 3, 1963.
2. Advertisement, "Emilie Loring," *New York Herald Tribune Weekly Book Review*, February 4, 1945.
3. "Club Women Hear Author," *Courier-News* (Bridgewater, NJ), March 2, 1948.
4. "Alice Dixon Bond Tells Ilium Club of Progress in Quality of Literature," *Times Record* (Troy, New York), February 4, 1950.
5. "The Unsinkable Emilie Loring," *Christian Science Monitor*, July 3, 1963.
6. Robert W. Stock, "Underground in Oshkosh," *New York Times*, February 16, 1969.
7. Fan letters, Emilie Loring Collection, Boston University Libraries, Howard Gotlieb Archival Research Center.
8. Dorothy Van Doren, "Easy-to-Read Authors Fill Public Need," *Delaware County Daily Times*, November 1, 1969.

INDEX